HISTORY
of the
27th GEORGIA

VOLUNTEER INFANTRY REGIMENT

CONFEDERATE STATES ARMY

William A. Bowers Jr.

ISBN: 978-0-9846536-9-0
Library of Congress Control Number: 2014900986
Published by Global Authors Publications

Filling the GAP in publishing

Edited by Elizabeth Bowers Hall,
Interior Design by KathleenWalls
Cover Design by William A. Bowers, III
Cover photograph of the 27th Georgia Volunteer Infantry flag
Courtesy of the Capital Flag Collection
Georgia Secretary of State

Printed in USA for Global Authors Publications

HISTORY
of the
27th GEORGIA
VOLUNTEER INFANTRY REGIMENT

CONFEDERATE STATES ARMY

Compiled by:

WILLIAM A. BOWERS, JR.

ACKNOWLEDGEMENT AND THANKS:

The Compilation of a Regimental History is a long and arduous task. The nearly 20 years taken to bring this work to this point is worth all the toil to make this information available to those interested in this "Storied Regiment." There are so many people who have aided my research and given encouragement to me in this quest. There are too many to name them all.

Most of all I need to thank my wife, Deloris for standing by me in thick and thin, always there when I would bog down in research. She and my son, Billy, have been in so many libraries, cemeteries and on so many battlefields with me as I attempted to understand facts surrounding the events, locate where my ancestors had been and their part in the battles.

I also want to thank my son, Billy, for keeping me up to date with my computer.

Thanks to my sister, Elizabeth Bowers Hall, for all her proofreading assistance on this work.

I wish to thank my fellow members in the Appling Grays Camp #918 Sons of Confederate Veterans for helping me get started and encouraging me along the way. Also I would like to thank the members of the of the Sons of Confederate Veteran Camps around Georgia for their help and encouragement and for sharing information with me.

Special thanks to my Aunt Mary Ketus Holland and my Uncle Zachry Grantham Holland who researched the Family Genealogies and sparked my interest in the period which concluded in my becoming a part of the Sons of Confederate Veterans.

My debt is great to these and all the others that have assisted at the State Parks and National Parks I have visited and all of the patient librarians and government officials who have put up with my inquiries.

Special thanks to my eighth grade Georgia History Teacher, Mrs. Carolyn McCall, for peaking my interest in the "War For Southern Independence" and for taking our class to Atlanta to expose us more.

Thanks to my cousin, friend and author, E. Randall Floyd, who shared my beginnings of interest in the 2nd grade as we would draw Confederate Soldiers in battle on scraps of paper "way back then."

Last but not least the descendants of the 27th soldiers who have shared valuable information, photos and data with me.

INTRODUCTION

Although the brave and heroic men that fought for the cause of the Confederate States of America were unequaled in the performance of their duty, there has been altogether too little of their history preserved for posterity. When I became interested in retracing the footsteps of my Confederate ancestors, this fact was painfully obvious. As I searched for information on units such as the Twenty-seventh Regiment, Georgia Volunteer Infantry, only small bits and pieces emerged. A paragraph here and a page there was the extent of their traces that were available. The more research that was performed the more their story began to unfold. At some time I realized that what I needed to do was to compile all the small fragments that I had been able to uncover into a comprehensive history so that those who were to follow in the search would have the history of this valiant and much campaigned regiment readily available. It seemed that wherever the thick of the battle was, you would find the Twenty-seventh Georgia. This regiment was called upon to perform some very difficult missions and their valor is quite evident. There leaders were courageous and without fear, leading their troops in an exemplary fashion.

To my Uncles, Corporal John W. Bowers and Private John Carney of the Rutland Grays (Bibb County), Company B and Sergeant Henry Mann, Jr and Private Peter Kemp of the Appling Grays (Appling County), Company I and also to all my cousins that were in the regiment I dedicate this work. It is to honor their sacrifice and dedication that this history is submitted.

WILLIAM A. BOWERS, JR.

TABLE OF CONTENTS

PHOTOGRAPHS

The Twenty-Seventh Regiment Georgia Volunteer Infantry

A Brief History of a Most Gallant Regiment

The 27th Georgia Regiment was formed September 1, 1861 at Camp Stephens in Griffin, Georgia. It was comprised of the following companies: Company A, the Georgia Drillers, from Marion and Schley Counties, Company B, the Rutland Grays or the Bibb Grays, from Bibb County, Company C, the Jackson Guards, from Crawford County, Company D from Hall County, Company E, the Bethsadia Rifle Guards, from Campbell and Fayette Counties, Company F, the Taylor Guards, from Taylor County, Company G, the County Line Guards, from Pike and Spaulding Counties, Company H, the Zachry Rangers, from Henry County, Company I, the Appling Grays, from Appling County and Company K from Talbot County. September 10 and 11 the Regiment elected Regimental and Company officers. Levi B. Smith was elected Colonel of the regiment. Also elected were Septimus L. Brewer, Lt. Colonel, Charles T. Zachry, Major, Charles F. Redding, Adjutant.

They drilled and trained at the camp of instruction there in Griffin until October 31 when they left via rail to make the trip to Richmond and to join the Army of Northern Virginia. They left several soldiers in Griffin due to "Camp Sickness" which was a variety of contagious diseases that were contracted due to the men coming from regions where settlement was sparse and young people were not exposed to these diseases such as; measles, mumps and stomach ailments. They arrived in Richmond "without arms." They were then sent to Camp Pickney near Manassas, Virginia. In December 1861 the regiment was sent to build a bridge across the Occoquan River. They wintered at Camp Pickney and were in Colonel G.B. Anderson's brigade. He was under the commanded of Major General Kirby Smith who was the commander of the fourth division. General Smith's division was under General P. G. T. Beauregard who commanded the Potomac division. General Joseph E. Johnston was then in command of the Army of Northern Virginia. Anderson's brigade at the time consisted of the 27th and 28th Georgia, the 49th Virginia and the 4th North Carolina. On March 9, 1862 they were ordered to Clark's Mountain. On April 9, 1862 General W.S. Featherstone assumed command of Anderson's brigade and the brigade was moved by rail to Richmond. The next day they were taken by boat to Grover's Landing on the James River and then marched across country to Yorktown. During the siege of Yorktown Captain Hardaway's battery of the Confederate artillery was being harassed by federal sharpshooters

1

located in a pine grove between the Union and Confederate lines. The 27th Georgia and the 13th Alabama, who had become a part of that Regiment, were ordered in front of the works to dislodge the enemy sharpshooters. They quickly put the enemy sharpshooters to flight and returned back into the line. The mission was accomplished without the loss of a single soldier in the 27th Georgia.

April 30, 1862 the brigade was placed in General G.J. Raines division under Major General Daniel Harvey Hill. On May 3 the Confederate Army began to withdraw toward Williamsburg. On the morning of May 5 they again begin to withdraw toward Richmond. They had only covered about 5 miles when they received orders to return to Williamsburg in "double quick time" to assist the troops in Williamsburg, as the battle there had begun. When they arrived the battle was raging, the rain was falling, the roads were in terrible condition and the weather extremely cold. When they arrived in Williamsburg everything that could possibly interfere with the fight was discarded. Knapsacks, haversacks, blankets and everything of the sort were piled up as they went into battle. They were assigned a position to the left of town which they occupied for several hours. They were then marched toward another position that was in a large wheat field. They remained in that wheat field during the night suffering the bitter cold and wet conditions until about 2 o'clock in the morning of May 6 when they formed up and again resumed their march toward Richmond. They arrived at Long Bridge and struck camp. They remained in camp there for almost two weeks. They arrived at Long Bridge and struck camp. They remained in camp there for almost two weeks. The brigade then under the command of General Anderson consisted of: the 13th Alabama, the 6th Georgia, the 23rd Georgia, the 27th Georgia and the 28th Georgia.

On May 31, 1862 General Johnston in an attempt to overwhelm and destroy the Federal Corps, that appeared isolated south of the Chickahominy River, sent his troops forward. The 27th Georgia was located south of the railroad at at Seven Pines, Virginia on the right of Colonel Jenkins South Carolina Sharpshooters. They entered the battle about 2 o'clock in the afternoon and fought into the teeth of the enemy. It was said that they pursued through briars, tangles and swamps driving the enemy before them. As they pressed forward there was a point in time when the 27th Georgia color bearer went down. General Anderson grabbed up the colors and encouraged his men forward. Later in the battle they assisted Colonel Jenkins in driving back a flanking federal force at the end of the day's action. They continued on and took the center of the federal line. General Anderson planted the 27th Georgia colors on the enemy's breastwork. Captain William W. De Lamar of Company H, the Zachary Rangers, was killed in the battle and Captain Osgood A. Lee was killed that afternoon leading the charge of his company, the Appling Grays, Company I. The 27TH Georgia lost 154 killed and wounded that day.

As General McClellan began to mass his troops on the Peninsula,

General Joseph E. Johnston took the opportunity to attack, although outnumbered, so as to drive the advancing federal force backwards toward the James River. On the morning of June 26, 1862 the 27TH Georgia took up a line of march at about 1:30 in the afternoon and halted near the town of Mechanicsville. In General Daniel Harvey Hill's report on the battle of the Seven Days around Richmond, he commented that Colonel Colquitt commanding the brigade did not give his men in hand since three of his regiments did not "draw trigger". He remarked that the 6th and 27th Georgia of the same brigade commanded by Lieutenant Colonel J. M. Newton and Colonel Levi B. Smith behaved most heroically and maintained their ground, although one half their number had been struck down. That afternoon they were engaged again at Cold Harbor. The brigade charged the enemy and gained a very important position on the battlefield. This position was held by the 27th Georgia for some time without any assistance from any of the other regiments of the brigade. Then the 61st Georgia was ordered forward to relieve the 27th, but mistaking them from the enemy fired into the Regiment until Adjutant Gardner could pass from the extreme right of the Regiment to its center and have the colors lifted. By that means they signaled the 61st that they were friends and after they recognized the colors, they ceased firing and quickly came forward to relieve the 27th in that position. They fought their way from Cold Harbor through Gaines Mill, Chickahominy, Savage Station, White Oak Swamp, and ended up on the last day in the center at Malvern Hill. The 27th Georgians were hurled against the enemy who laid down devastating fire of double canister from the artillery positioned in the center of the hill where the attack was. The losses for the 27th were especially severe during that battle. The 27th suffered a loss in the Seven Days of 126 men killed and wounded.

In late August Colquitt's Brigade, which included the 27th Georgia, was ordered to report to General Lee near Fairfax, Virginia. They begin to move into Maryland and arrived at Frederick via Leesburg. September 7, 1862 they marched toward Boonsboro, Maryland across South Mountain. They were ordered back to South Mountain and given the responsibility to hold National Pike at Turner's Gap. Colonel Colquitt placed two of his regiments to the left of the National Pike and three regiments to the right. The 6th was on the extreme right with the 27th in their normal position to the left of the 6th Georgia. They were led to believe by General Jeb Stuart that there were no more than two brigades of federals advancing in their direction. Unknown to General Lee one set of his orders, which had been lost, had been found and turned into the federal headquarters, and was in possession of the commanders of the federal forces. The federals knew exactly what General Lee's plans were and the whole Army of the Potomac was drawing close to the foot of the mountain. As the Regiments of Colquitt's Brigade were in their positions at Turner's Gap they saw more and more campfires being lit all over the valley. They knew that there were more federals than they expected and that they were in for a fight the next day.

The next morning with Colquitt's artillery firing down upon them, the federals were at bay at first but then charged the position. The position, which was a strong one, held as the Georgians poured hot fire into the ranks of the federals as they tried to advance up the slope. Three times that day the Federal Army would come up the mountain and three times Colquitt's Brigade would send them back. Every time that they would repulse the federals, they would raise the rebel yell and at the Mountain House, on the crest of the mountain, the young men of General Hill's and General Longstreet's staff would laugh and clap their hands and exclaimed "Hurrah for Georgia, Georgia is having a free fight". It has been recorded that Colquitt's brigade did not give an inch that day. General Colquitt would be known as "the Rock of South Mountain." Captain Hezekiah Bussey, of Company K, was captured and Captain Elisha Duncan Graham, of Company I, was wounded in the fight. After the battle was over and all of General Lee's supply train had passed through and were in safety, the next day Confederate forces withdrew to a sleepy little town in Maryland named Sharpsburg. Sergeant Benjamin Millikin, of Company I, told the story of how they had found spirits in the basement of an outbuilding and several of them drank more than they should have, including himself.

Around 7 o'clock on the morning of September 17, 1862, the 27th Georgia and the rest of Colquitt's Brigade had been positioned on the left end of a sunken road with the rest of Daniel Harvey Hill's division. The three brigades of Hill's were ordered forward to assist General Hood's Texans at Miller's Cornfield. Ripley's was on the left, Colquitt's in the center and McRae's on the right. Hill's forces were the extreme right of Hood's forces as they advanced. The confederates moved quickly into the cornfield with Colquitt's pressing the issue. In a short time Colquitt had pushed the federals in his front, out of the North end of the cornfield. Ripley's Brigade held back and McRae's Brigade retreated, leaving both flanks of Colquitt's exposed. The brigade was in normal positions with the 6th Georgia in the extreme right, with the 27th to their immediate left. Suddenly Greene's Brigade of Federals emerged from the East Wood and enfiladed Colquitt's right flank from rearward. The 6th caught the worst of it with the 27th getting next worse. The enflade fire took its toll on those two regiments that were on the right. As one of the soldiers said, "The enemy unleashed murderous volley in our flank and then hand-in-hand ensued with bayoneting and clubbing." After receiving fire from left to right and in front, Colquitt was forced to withdraw from the field. Hill's three brigades moved back and eventually ended up in their original position in the sunken road. The sunken road later became known as Bloody Lane because the carnage that ensued there. The 27th and the rest of Colquitt's Brigade spent three hours on the left in the Bloody Lane. They took more and more casualties on top of those experienced in the cornfield. When they were finally ordered to retire from the sunken road, what was left of the 27th was in the fight at Dunker Church when A.P. Hill came up and swept the field late in the afternoon. There were four major engagements in Sharpsburg that day and the 27th Georgia was in the midst of three of the four. All of General Colquitt's field grade officers went down that day, with half of them being killed, including Colonel Levi Smith of the 27th. The other half were wounded which included Lieutenant Colonel Charles Thornton Zachry. When General Lee decided to re-cross the Potomac, the Army of Northern Virginia had been a part of the bloodiest day of American history. In the official report for the battles of South Mountain and Sharpsburg, the 27th Georgia had 149 killed and wounded and another 42 missing in action presumed captured.

Over the next two months the 27th Georgia mostly marched and helped tear up railroads. One report said that they could march an average of 22 miles per day and that many of the men were forced to take rawhide and make sandals because their brogans were worn completely out. On December 11, 1862 Colonel Colquitt was promoted to Brigadier General and Charles Thornton Zachry was promoted to Colonel and was now commanding the 27th Georgia Regiment.

December 13, 1862 when General Ambrose Burnside crossed the Rappahannock River and threw his forces against the well defended Army of Northern Virginia, Colquitt was on the extreme right in order to protect from a flanking movement from the left side of the federal Army. They were lightly engaged and still suffered two privates wounded in the action. After the battle of Fredericksburg the 27th Georgia went into winter quarters near Guinea Station, Virginia. Their duty consisted of picket duty on the Rappahannock River, in case the federal forces tried to cross again and otherwise just to survive the harsh Virginia winter, with the snow and wet conditions. After the battle of Fredericksburg, D.H. Hill's division was placed in the Corps commanded by Lieutenant General Thomas J. "Stonewall" Jackson, Hill's brother-in-law.

As the cold winter of 1863 began to thaw the soldiers begin to drill and prepare for what they knew was the upcoming battle. On April 27, 1863 the 27th Georgia took up a line of march toward Chancellorsville, Virginia. They arrived on April 28 and were engaged with the enemy on the 29th and the 30th of May at Wilderness Church. They became a part of the famous flanking movement of Stonewall Jackson. Colquitt's brigade was the lead element in the march on the Orange Plank Road. They would march for two hours and then rest. At 4 o'clock that afternoon the brigade reached the road that ran through Chancellorsville and General Colquitt received intelligence that a body of the enemy was on his right flank. Possibly remembering the cornfield at Sharpsburg Colquitt sent the 19th Georgia into battle array. They quickly captured the pickets from a Union Calvary unit and resumed their progress forward. On May 2, the 27th Georgia received well-directed fire of shell grape and shrapnel from artillery on the left and in front. Their loss that day was 10 wounded one killed. The total casualties for the action at Chancellorsville was 18 wounded and two killed for the 27th Georgia. Although the Army of Northern Virginia won a decisive victory, their loss was severe. Lieutenant General Thomas Jonathan "Stonewall" Jackson was fired upon by Confederate pickets as he was reconnoitring for the next day. The wound was in his left arm, which he lost several days later. General Robert E. Lee made the statement that "General Jackson has lost his left arm and I have lost my right". "Stonewall" never recovered from the wound and the loss of his arm. He later succumbed to pneumonia. Just as he began to leave this life he said, "Let us cross the river and rest in the shade on the other side". After saying that he passed and the South had lost its most brilliant general, the General that struck fear in the hearts of the federal officers and men when they had to face him.

On May 20, 1863 Colquitt's Brigade which included the 27th Georgia was ordered to proceed by rail to Goldsboro, North Carolina and to report to Major General Daniel Harvey Hill, who was commanding there. They arrived in Kinston, North Carolina and reported to General Hill. Their orders at the time were to join with some local partisan Rangers and pursue deserters from North Carolina Units, which had the most severe rate of desertion in the Confederacy. They also had begun to build a works in Kinston. In July they were ordered back to Richmond and then turned around almost immediately and were sent back to North Carolina. Afterward they were mostly engaged in picket duty at Topsail Sound. On August 10, 1863 they received orders to report to General P. G. T. Beauregard at Charleston, South Carolina. They arrived and set up camp on James Island and on the last of August were ordered to report to Morris Island. On September of the 27th Georgia was placed on the beach in front of Battery Wagner. General Beauregard had made the decision to withdraw from Battery Wagner, stealthily removing the big guns for use in defense of the Charleston Harbor. As the withdrawal began federal troops advanced from their position on Morris Island and the 27th Georgia became the rear guard for the withdrawal. Their total was only 219 effective for this task. There casualties were two killed and seven wounded. The remainder of 1863 consisted of rotating in and out of Fort Sumter in the mouth of Charleston Harbor. While there they endured bombardments by the US ironsides and monitors and by the 6th of November their casualties from duty around Charleston were two killed and 12 wounded.

As 1864 dawned the 27th Georgia continued with their rotations from James Island to Johns Island, Fort Johnson and to Fort Sumter. On February 8, 1864 the 27th Georgia received orders to report to Major General Gilmer at Savannah, Georgia. On February 10 the Regiment was on the marched and Colonel Zachary is relieved from commanding Fort Johnson. Before they could depart James Island they were called to march to Johns Island to assist General Wise in driving back to federal forces that had established a position on that island. February 14, 1864 they boarded the Charleston and Savannah railroad and departed for Savannah. When they arrived in Savannah they changed over to the Atlantic and Gulf Railroad and headed west. They changed trains again at Teabeauville and rode to near present day Valdosta Georgia. On February 16 they disembarked the trains at Valdosta and took up a line of march toward Madison, Florida. They boarded the train in Madison on the Tallahassee and Jacksonville railcars, en route to a small railroad town east of Lake City, Florida named Olustee.

General Finegan, who was in charge, despite out ranking General Colquitt, deferred to Colquitt's experience in battle. They reconnoitered the area and found a place which was a narrow pine barren located between a natural lake named Ocean Pond and a dense swamp on the other side. General Colquitt placed the 19th Georgia, the 23rd Georgia and the 28th Georgia in line with Bonaud's Battalion which included the 32nd Georgia plus Florida units into the fray. He held the 6th Georgia and the 27th Georgia in reserve and ordered them to be on the lookout for any flanking movement by the enemy and block it. Both Florida Cavalry and Clinch's 4th Georgia Cavalry were involved in the reconnoitring and into placing the skirmishers in the correct position so that they might draw the federal forces into the ground of their choosing. There were approximately 5500 federals and 5200 Confederates, which was not the usual odds. For the most part General Colquitt had been used to facing 2 to 1 odds or better. The battle raged back and forth until about four in the afternoon. The Confederates had exhausted most of their ammunition and had to be resupplied but held their line with General Colquitt's brother, Lieutenant Colquitt grabbing up the Georgia flag, placing the staff in his stirrup and riding up and down the line to stir the Georgia troops there. About the time that they were resupplied, General Colquitt sent for the 6th and the 27th to move up, impressing upon them their importance in the outcome of the battle.

Colonel Zachary ordered the 27th to fix bayonet and as they moved up, they unleashed a tremendous volley into the enemy and went forward at the "double quick". They began a rout of the union forces, as they moved so fast through them that they left their dead and wounded on the field. The rest of the Confederate forces followed their lead and after losing about 50 percent of their soldiers, the union troops headed back toward Jacksonville. The 27th Georgia suffered more than 20 killed and at least twice that wounded. On March 4, 1864 Colonel Zachary had the remainder of the union forces bottled up at Cedar Creek, Florida. The 27th Georgia and the 11th South Carolina on Colonel Zachary's orders executed the attack and according to Colonel Zachary's report if Colonel Duncan Clinch and his 4th Georgia Cavalry had swung the gate shut, as was planned the remainder of the union force would've been killed or captured. Nevertheless those that were not killed, wounded or captured, escaped back to Jacksonville never to invade the center of Florida again. After that General Colquitt was called the "Hero of Olustee" and Colonel Zachary was named Blucher (Field Marshall) of the battle of Olustee.

The 27th Georgia remained encamped at Fort Milton, Florida until they received orders to return to South Carolina. They were ordered to move from Fort Milton, Florida via Callahan, Traders Hill, Teabeauville and Savannah on their return to Charleston, South Carolina. By April 25, 1864 they were back encamped on James Island. May 3, 1864 General Colquitt received orders for his brigade to report to Richmond, Virginia and to return to the Army of Northern Virginia.

May 16, 1864 in the second battle of Drewry's Bluff at Fort Darling the 27th was originally placed in the reserve but it was brought into action early in the morning in support of General Ransom's Division and later were called to assist General Hoke in repulsing the federal troops. On May 31st the 27th was ordered to Cold Harbor where they had fought in June 1862. On June 1, 1864 the 27th and the 28th Georgia were rushed in to support Clingman's Brigade. Five companies (B, C, D, G and I) of the 27th were sent to retake the breastworks that Clingman had lost. They rushed right onto the breastworks where the union soldiers were and they fought for some good time with the union soldiers trying to get them to surrender. Of the five companies they suffered 11 killed and 54 wounded. After a hot engagement the five companies had to withdraw back to the other breastworks. They fought there until June 13, 1864 inflicting severe losses on General U. S. Grant's forces, as he continued to send his troops onto the killing field that General Robert E. Lee had set up there. General Grant's war of attrition earned him the name "The Butcher". On June 13 they left Cold Harbor and marched to Malvern Hill, passing the Seven Pines battlefield where they had fought their first large scale engagement. On June 18 the federal Army that was garrisoned at Fort Stedman charged their position on the Petersburg line that was held by the 27th. They repulsed the union forces heavily to the point that they left over 200 lying on the field in front. This place became known as "Colquitt's Salient" and the 27th held this position for six days without relief. On another day they retook the salient which another brigade had lost and held it without reinforcements for four days. In the fights at "Colquitt's Salient" the 27th lost 20 killed 56 wounded, including Lieutenant Colonel James B. Gardner, one of the most valiant soldiers of the Regiment. They defended this position often due to being rotated in and out of the salient until well into July. There was much disagreeable sharpshooting that went on during those times so a soldier had to keep his head down to avoid been taken out by sharpshooter. On the morning of July 30 a great explosion was heard to their right. There was much musketry and the men of the 27th later learned that the Yankees had tunneled up under the breastworks and ignited a large quantity of black powder, blowing a giant crater in the ground. But as the Yankees tried to advance in the crater, it was like shooting fish in a barrel and the Confederates poured hot musketry on them, until they were finally forced to withdraw back to safety.

They remained on the Petersburg line facing an overwhelming number of federal troops until August 17 when they were relieved by Martin's brigade at "Colquitt's Salient". On August 18 the enemy took possession of the Weldon and Petersburg railroad. On August 19 General Colquitt ordered an attack on the flank of the Fifth Federal Corps near City Point, Virginia about 3 pm. This action resulted in the capture of many prisoners, including a general and his staff. Then later that day an overwhelming force of federals flanked them, retaking the general and most of the prisoners with the Union taking some prisoners, from the 27th which also lost a stand of colors.

September 19 they were engaged in the battle of Fort Harrison (Chaffin's Farm) where the position they fought from and defended became known as Fort Colquitt. They held that position until late December, when the last companies of the 27th were ordered to rejoin the rest of their brigade in Goldsboro, North Carolina.

General Colquitt was given orders to take over command of Fort Fisher near Wilmington, North Carolina. Colonel Zachary and the 27th Georgia were escorting him out on January 13, when the commander of Fort Fisher surrendered. They were on a narrow spit of land between the Atlantic Ocean and the Cape Fear River, with federal gunboats on either side. The 27th Georgia again became the rear guard in the withdrawal from Fort Fisher.

They then were stationed on Sugarloaf, North Carolina at Fort Anderson. Fort Anderson stayed under constant attack from monitors and ironsides. The officers knew that after the fall of Fort Fisher, Wilmington would not last long and on February 21, 1865 the battle for Wilmington, North Carolina began. Again the 27th was the rearguard under Colonel Zachary and again the enemy had to pay dearly for the real estate that they got. March 8 the battle moved to Kinston, North Carolina. The 27th engaged the enemy several times, fighting near Great Dover Swamp. The battle raged on with the 27th taking a breastworks and capturing many prisoners.

March 13 they were ordered to Goldsboro along with the rest of Colquitt's Brigade, with Colonel Charles T. Zachary commanding. March 18, 1865 General Joseph E. Johnston organized his troops, which included Hoke's Division and Colquitt's Brigade, engaged General William Tecumseh Sherman and his forces at Bentonville, North Carolina. The 27th Georgia broke the center of Sherman's breastworks but due to lack in reinforcements, they could not take advantage and press the issue further. They suffered several losses on that breastworks. They fought one more time at Sugarloaf, North Carolina on March 30, 1865. General Johnston and General Sherman settled on the Articles of Surrender on April 26, 1865. Surrendering with the 27th were Brigadier General Charles T. Zachary, Lieutenant Colonel Hezekiah Bussy and Major Elisha Duncan Graham, the officers in charge. The 27th Georgia Volunteer Infantry Regiment was a shadow of its former self. The once proud regiment of nearly 1000 men had now been reduced to between 100 to 200 men. Some companies had as few as 12 men left. They had been involved in 44 engagements, in five states and taking a heavy toll on the enemy that challenged them. The 27th suffered an almost 150% causality rate with some soldiers being wounded four or more times during the war.

Those that survived this conflict went back home to be leaders in their communities and to help bring their counties and their states through Reconstruction and to try to bring them back to their former glory. Some like General Colquitt became governor and US Senator Colonel Zachary went on to become a state representative for the Henry County area. These men who were leaders in time of war became leaders in time of peace. They shall not be forgotten.

The 27th Regiment - Georgia Volunteer Infantry Confederate States Army

The following is a historical sketch depicting the events that took place, during the time of the War Between the States, between the years of 1861 and 1865. It will hopefully shed light on all that was encountered by the brave officers and men that gave so much for a cause, so dear to them. This will record their gallant deeds and track the regiment through this trying and tumultuous period of time;

1861

17 May 1861: Georgia Drillers elected the following officers:

Perry C. Carr	Captain
Adam Carson	1st Lieutenant
William E. Dougherty	2nd Lieutenant
Robert Patton	Jr. 2nd Lieutenant

12 June 1861: Rutland Grays elected the following officers:

John W. Stubbs	Captain
John J. Allen	1st Lieutenant
Luther R. Johnson	2nd Lieutenant
Miles G. Stephens	Jr. 2nd Lieutenant

14 June 1861: Zachry Rangers elected the following officers:

Charles T. Zachry	Captain
William W. DeLamar	1st Lieutenant
Robert A. Harkey	2nd Lieutenant
Wade H. Harper	3rd Lieutenant

6 July 1861: Jackson Guards elected the following officers:

Charles J. Dennis	Captain
James W. Murray	1st Lieutenant
William H. Robinson	2nd Lieutenant
William W. Johnson	Jr. 2nd Lieutenant

The Appling Grays elected the following officers:

Osgood A. Lee	Captain
Alfred S. Hall	1st Lieutenant
Lawrence W. Clay	2nd Lieutenant
Zedekiah W. Little	Jr. 2nd Lieutenant

9 August 1861: Bethsaida Rifle Guards elected the following officers:

Jesse M. Spratlin	Captain
William J. Sams	1st Lieutenant
William H. Renfroe	2nd Lieutenant

Josiah H. Elder	Jr. 2nd Lieutenant

10 August 1861: Company organized in Hall County elected the following officers:

Jasper N. Dorsey	Captain
William Kennedy	1st Lieutenant
Richard V. Cobb	2nd Lieutenant
John F. Dorsey	Jr. 2nd Lieutenant

21 August 1861: The County Line Guards elected the following officers:

William Dozier Redding	Captain
Thomas C. Stanley	1st Lieutenant
John C. Beeks	2nd Lieutenant
George B. Buchanan	Jr. 2nd Lieutenant

27 August 1861: The Appling Grays left the "Campground" in Appling County for a camp of instruction at Camp Stephens in Griffin, Georgia.

1 September 1861: Twenty-seventh Regiment, Georgia Infantry organized at Camp Stephens, Griffin, Spaulding County, Georgia

9 September 1861: The Bethsaida Rifle Guards (Co. E) elected the following:

Thomas B. Swanson	2nd Sergeant
Asa L. Dodd	3rd Sergeant
George M. Dodd	4th Sergeant
Thomas C. Russell	1st Corporal
D. T. Jennings	4th Corporal

The Taylor Guards (Co. F) elected the following:

Septimus L. Brewer	Captain
Jordan Wilcher	1st Lieutenant
L. Q. C. McCrary	2nd Lieutenant
John Bunyan Wright	Jr. 2nd Lieutenan
James B. Sorrells	1st. Sergeant
D. Jeptha Newton	2nd Sergeant
William J. Mitchell	3rd Sergeant
Robert C. Bailey	4th Sergeant
David N. Bloodsworth	5th Sergeant
J. W. Seracy	1st Corporal
Allen E. Cody	2nd Corporal
W. G. McGlamery	3rd Corporal
Leroy Tuggle	4th Corporal

The County Line Guards (Co. G) elected the following:

James C. Adams	1st Sergeant
James J. Beckham	2nd Sergeant
Joseph C. Chapman	3rd Sergeant
John B. Copeland	4th Sergeant
Miles R. Hagan	5th Sergeant
Morgan T. Carriker	1st Corporal
Colby J. Cook	2nd Corporal
William J. Hambrick	3rd Corporal

12

James D. Carriker	4th Corporal

The Zachry Rangers (Co. H) elected the following:

William W. Delamar	Captain
Robert A. Harkey	1st Lieutenant
Robert C. Evans	2nd Lieutenant
Wade H. Harper	Jr. 2nd Lieutenant
Iverson B. Bryans	1st Sergeant
Thomas J. Duke	2nd Sergeant
J. Henry Carroll	3rd Sergeant
W. Callaway Nolan	4th Sergeant
John N. Mason	5th Sergeant
Winfield A. Copeland	1st Corporal
Burrell P. Pryor	2nd Corporal
T. Jefferson Kitchens	3rd Corporal

10 September 1861:

The Georgia Drillers (Co. A) elected the following:

G. W. Chapman	1st Sergean
John C. Smith	2nd Sergeant
John C. Calhoun	3rd Sergeant
Rufus A. Dodson	4th Sergeant
Septimus W. Myrick	1st Corporal
Killight Woodall	2nd Corporal
T. W. Mitchell	3rd Corporal
Peter Stewart	4th Corporal

The Rutland Grays (Co. B) elected the following:

John F. Burnett	2nd Lieutenant
James W. Cowart	1st Sergeant
Samuel G. B. Odom	2nd Sergeant
Luther J. Thomas	3rh Sergeant
Redmond V. Forrester	4th Sergeant
Jesse T. Avant	5th Sergeant
Vincent E. Walton	1st Corporal
T. M. Brown	2nd Corporal
John W. Bowers	3rd Corporal
C. B. Bond	4th Corporal

The Jackson Guards (Co. C) elected the following:

James T. Gregory	1st Sergeant
John C. Murchison	2nd Sergeant
T. J. Hancock	3rd Sergeant
W. A. Webb	4th Sergeant
L. C. Futrell	5th Sergeant
James W. Robinson	1st Corporal
John W. Worsham	2nd Corporal
Benjamin F. Kennedy	3rd Corporal
Frederick Hutto	4th Corporal

Company organized in Hall County (Co. D) elected the following:

A. S. Sears	1st Sergeant
Michjah Bagwell	2nd Sergeant
Wiley Rouse	3rd Sergeant
H. B. Smith	4th Sergeant
C. H. Cape	5th Sergeant
M. W. Mabry	2nd Corporal
John K. Moore	4th Corporal

The Appling Grays (Co. I) elected the following:

D. M. Livingston	1st Sergeant
Willis Baxley	2nd Sergeant
A. M. Crosby	3rd Sergeant
William Griffin	4th Sergeant
Benjamin F. Hutto	5th Sergeant
Henry Harrison Becher	1st Corporal
LaFayette H. Johnson	2nd Corporal
James M. McLendon	3rd Corporal
O. F. Carter	4th Corporal

Company organized in Talbot County (Co. K) elected the following officers:

Levi B. Smith	Captain
Hezekiah Bussey	1st Lieutenant
Wilkins J. Raine	2nd Lieutenant
Calvin Calhoun	Jr. 2nd Lieutenant
Garry T. Williamson	1st Sergeant
Josiah B. Parker	2nd Sergeant
David Green	3rd Sergeant
William C. Smith	4th Sergeant
William Calhoun	5th Sergeant
Robert H. Kellum	1st Corporal
R. Marion Smith	2nd Corporal
William H. Drew	4th Corporal

Private William S. Perry of Company A died of Measles

11 September 1861: The 27th Regiment is organized the following officers were elected:

Levi B. Smith	Colonel
Septimus L. Brewer	Lt. Colonel
Charles T. Zachry	Major
Charles F. Redding	Adjutant
Thomas M. Darnell	Surgeon
Thomas H. Butler	Assistant Surgeon
Christopher C. Parker	Sergeant Major
Henry B. Holliday	Assistant Quartermaster
Wade A. Turner	Ordinance Sergeant
Thomas J. Bacon	Assistant Commissary

	Sergeant
George Henry Pattillo	Chaplin
Company F: Jordan Wilcher	Captain
L. Q. C. McCrary	1st Lieutenant
John Bunyan Wright	2nd Lieutenant
Company K:	
Hezekiah Bussey	Captain
Wilkins J. Raines	1st Lieutenant
Calvin Calhoun	2nd Lieutenant

22 October 1861: Private Simeon Reaves of Company G died of disease at Camp Stephens, Georgia.

31 October 1861: The 27th Regiment left Camp Stephens for Richmond, Virginia.

November 1861: The following changes occurred in the Twenty-seventh Regiment:

Lieutenant Colonel Septimus Brewer resigned his commission.

George Henry Pattillo resigned as Chaplain.

1 November 1861: William B. Giddins elected 1st Sergeant - Co. K

2 November 1861: Private Patrick Lynn of Company I died of Typhoid Fever at Manassas, Virginia.

3 November 1861: Private William H. Page of Company C died of pneumonia at Camp Stephens, Griffin, Georgia.

9 November 1861: Private J. T. Jones of Company A died of Typhoid Fever at Griffin, Georgia.

12 November 1861: Private William Martin of Company I died of disease in Raleigh, North Carolina.

13 November 1861: Private Jesse Francis Lancaster of Company B died of disease at Manassas, Virginia.

Private Richard V. Laseter of Company E died of disease at Petersburg, Virginia.

15 November 1861: Colonel Smith's 27th Georgia Regiment sent to Potomac District to be assigned to General Joseph E. Johnston (Special Order 206 -from Jno. Winters, 99 Asst. Adjutant-General.).

Regiment arrived at Manassas Junction, Virginia without arms. The regiment began to build a bridge over the Occoquan River near Manassas.

Private Joseph Perry of Company A died of Pneumonia in Richmond, Virginia.

18 November 1861:

Private James A. Johnson of Company B died of Pneumonia at Richmond, Virginia.

Private William H. Boyd of Company G died of Pneumonia at Manassas, Virginia.

21 November 1861: Private John Hughes of Company I died of Pneumonia at Raleigh, North Carolina

22 November 1861: Private David Jack Hester of Company I died of

Pneumonia at Richmond, Virginia.

23 November 1861: Private Joshua Barker of Company G died of Typhoid Pneumonia in hospital # 18 at Richmond, Virginia.

24 November 1861: Private Robert J. Wheeler of Company G died of Typhoid Pneumonia in Hospital # 18 at Richmond, Virginia.

25 November 1861: Private William E. Clark of Company B died in Hospital # 18 at Richmond, Virginia.

Private Matthew Wood of Company G died of Typhoid Pneumonia in Hospital #18 at Richmond, Virginia.

Private Jacob Rentz of Company I died of Typhoid Fever in Hospital #18 at Richmond, Virginia.

Private Moses Tomberlin of Company I died of disease at Culpepper, Virginia.

26 November 1861: Captain Jesse E. Spratlin of Company E died of disease at Richmond, Virginia.

Private John D. Beckham of Company G died in General Hospital # 18, Richmond, Virginia.

27 November 1861: Private William Milligan King of Company E died of disease at Camp Stephens, Georgia.

Private David J. Tuten of Company I died of disease at Richmond, Virginia.

28 November 1861: Private John W. Simpson of Company B died at Charlottesville, Virginia.

Private Britton A. Brown of Company E died of Pneumonia at Richmond, Virginia.

30 November 1861: Private Moulton A. Peacock of Company F died of Pneumonia at Manassas, Virginia.

Private William H. Lyle of Company H died of Pneumonia at Richmond, Virginia.

December 1861: Private Joseph Jones of Company I died at Raleigh, North Carolina.

3 December 1861: Private Isham Crosby of Company I died of disease at Manassas. Virginia.

4 December 1861: The following changes occurred in the Twenty-seventh Regiment:
Company I: Elisha Duncan Graham elected 2nd Lieutenant
Silas A. Crosby appointed 1st Corporal

6 December 1861: Private William H. H. Head of Company E died of disease at Camp Pickens, Virginia.

10 December 1861: The Following changes occurred in the Twenty-seventh Regiment:
Company B: Redmond V. Forrester elected 2nd Lieutenant
John R. Seymore appointed 4th Sergeant

12 December 1861: Corporal Colby J. Cook of Company G died of

Pneumonia at Camp Pickens, Virginia.

15 December 1861: Regiment completed building a bridge across the Occoquan River and ordered into winter quarters at Camp Pickens near Manassas.

20 December 1861: The following changes occurred in the Twenty-seventh Regiment:

Company E: William H. Rentfro elected Captain

       John T. Abercrombie elected 2nd Lieutenant

21 December 1861: Private William Eason of Company I died at Richmond, Virginia.

24 December 1861: The Following changes occurred in the Twenty-seventh Regiment:

       Charles Thornton elected Lieutenant Colonel

       Henry B. Holliday elected Major

       James B. Gardner appointed Adjutant

26 December 1861: Private G. W. L. Nix of Company I died of disease at Manassas, Virginia.

1862

1 January 1862: Private Benjamin F. Pendley of Company E died of Pneumonia in General Hospital at Mount Jackson, Virginia.

       Sergeant Garry T. Williamson of Company K died of Erysipelas at Camp Pickens, Virginia.

2 January 1862: Lieutenant William H. Robinson of Company C died.

3 January 1862: Private James Joseph Whaley of Company G died of Typhoid Fever in General Hospital #18 at Richmond, Virginia.

6 January 1862:

       Private Robert R. Edison of Company D died of Measles in the Culpepper, Virginia hospital.

       Sergeant William J. Mitchell of Company F died of Pneumonia at Camp Pickens, Virginia.

       Sergeant Edward Proctor of Company K died of Pneumonia at Camp Pickens, Virginia.

       John Hart appointed 3rd Sergeant - Co. F

7 January 1862: Private Edward H. Lynch of Company G died of Typhoid Pneumonia in General Hospital #1 at Danville, Virginia.

8 January 1862: Sergeant Carey Strickland of Company G died of Typhoid Pneumonia at Camp Pickens, Virginia.

10 January 1862: W. S. Baker appointed Chaplain.

12 January: Private Job Allen of Company C died of disease at Camp Pickens, Virginia.

14 January 1862: Centreville, Headquarters of the Army of Northern Virginia,

Gen. Joseph E. Johnston, Commanding
General G. T. Beauregard - Commander, Potomac District
Maj. Gen. Kirby Smith - Commander, 4th Division
Colonel G. B. Anderson - Commander, Troops at Manassas
Colonel Levi. B. Smith - Commander, 27th Georgia Regiment

15 January 1862: Private Marcus Sullivan of Company B died of disease at Richmond, Virginia.

19 January 1862: Private J. A. Walker of Company C died of disease at Camp Pickens, Virginia.

20 January 1862: Thomas A. Grace elected 2nd Lieutenant - Co. C

27 January 1862: The following changes occurred in the Twenty-seventh Regiment:

Company I   Benjamin Milikin appointed 1st Sergeant

Company K William H Fuller appointed 1st Sergeant

Company G Lieutenant Thomas C. Stanley resigned his commission

Private Samuel Robinson of Company B died of disease at Deep Bottom, Virginia hospital.

February 1862:

Lieutenant Andrew J. Fontaine of Company F died.

Private Frank Jones of Company I died at Richmond, Virginia.

5 February 1862: Private Henry Thomas of Company B died of Pneumonia in Moore Hospital at Manassas, Virginia.

8 February 1862: Private Jefferson Cooner of Company I died of Pneumonia at Camp Pickens, Virginia.

9 February 1862: Private Stephen Luther Thomas of Company B died of Pneumonia in Moore Hospital at Manassas, Virginia.

14 February 1862: Sergeant James Wiley Mangham of Company G died of Typhoid Pneumonia at Camp Pickens, Virginia.

20 February 1862: The following changes occurred in the Twenty-seventh Regiment:

Company G   John C. Beeks elected 1st Lieutenant

George B. Buchanan elected 2nd Lieutenant

22 February 1862: Private Henry Willard of Company H died of disease in Moore Hospital at Manassas, Virginia.

24 February 1862: The following changes occurred in the Twenty-seventh Regiment:

Company D Thomas J Carter elected 3rd Corporal

Company K Henry C. Downs elected 3rd Corporal

28 February 1862: Private Robert W. McBride of Company H died of Pneumonia in Moore Hospital at Manassas, Virginia.

March 1862: Private A. R. Hudson of Company F died at Clark Mountain, Virginia.

1 March 1862: John Lewis King elected 5th Sergeant - Co. E

4 March 1862: The following changes occurred in the Twenty-seventh

Regiment:

Company A John C. Calhoun elected 3rd Sergeant

Company D William Bagwell elected 1st Corporal

Company K Raleigh H. Turner elected 3rd Sergeant

7 March 1862: Private James Harper of Company G died of congestion of the brain in Chimborazo Hospital #2 at Richmond, Virginia.

9 March 1862: Regiment ordered to Clark's Mountain to join a Brigade commanded by Col. G. B. Anderson, of North Carolina. Anderson's Brigade was composed of the Fourth North Carolina Troops, Forty-ninth Virginia Infantry, Twenty-seventh Georgia Volunteer Infantry and Twenty-eighth Georgia Volunteer Infantry.

13 March 1862: Private Henry L. Bentley of Company H died of Typhoid Pneumonia in the South Carolina Hospital, Post Jefferson at Charlottesville, Virginia.

15 March 1862: William J. Jones elected Jr. 2nd Lieutenant - Co. K

20 March 1862: Anderson's Brigade arrived at Clark's Mountain.

4 April 1862: Wiley J. Williamson elected 5th Sergeant - Co. A

5 April 1862: Private Henry Stewart of Company A died of Pneumonia in Chimborazo Hospital #1 at Richmond, Virginia.

7 April 1862: Corporal James M. Kimbrew of Company B died in the General Receiving Hospital at Gordonsville, Virginia.

9 April 1861: Brigadier General W. S. Featherstone assumed command of Anderson's Brigade at Clark's Mountain. The regiment moved by rail to Richmond, Virginia.

Private James B. McDonald of Company B died of Pneumonia in the General Hospital at Farmville, Virginia.

10 April 1862 : Featherstone's Brigade ordered, by boat, to Grover's Landing, on the James River, then to march across country to Yorktown, Virginia.

11 April 1862: Private Reuben Roberts of Company B died of Tuberculosis in the General Hospital at Charlottesville, Virginia.

12 April 1862: Private J. E. Wright of Company C died in the General Hospital at Farmville, Virginia.

14 April 1862: *The Siege of Yorktown, Virginia:*

McClellan had his 150,000 man army in position to conquer the peninsula of Virginia. A small force of 10,000 men blocked their way in a fortified position. They had painted logs black (called "Quaker Guns") in order to appear more of a threat that they were. McClellan was impressed with their fortifications and laid siege to Yorktown. This enabled the small Confederate force to be reinforced with Joseph E. Johnston's Army, of which the Twenty-seventh Georgia Regiment was a part.

The First Encounter with the Enemy:

The Twenty-seventh Georgia and the Thirteenth Alabama were ordered in front of the works to assist Captain Hardaway's Battery in dislodging Union sharpshooters from a pine grove between the Confederate and

Union works. This successful mission was accomplished without any of the Twenty-seventh Georgians being killed in action.

16 April 1862: Private Burwell McCullers of Company F died of Diarrhea and Typhoid Fever in Chimborazo Hospital # 4 at Richmond, Virginia.

18 April 1862: Private James W. Hudson of Company C died of disease.

19 April 1862: Private William Haskins, of Company C, killed while on picket duty at Yorktown, Virginia.

20 April 1862: Lieutenant Adam Carson of Company A died.

Private Jacob Crosby of Company I died of Typhoid in Chimborazo Hospital #4 at Richmond, Virginia.

21 April 1862:

Private Seaborn B. Thornton of Company E died of Fever at Yorktown, Virginia.

Private F. P. Layfield of Company F died of Pneumonia in Chimborazo Hospital at Richmond, Virginia.

22 April 1862: Private John J. Dilborn of Company I died at Yorktown, Virginia.

25 April 1862: Corporal Morgan T. Carriker of Company G died of Typhoid Pneumonia in Chimborazo Hospital at Richmond, Virginia.

27 April 1862: Private Kinchen Peacock of Company F died of Typhoid in General Hospital #21 at Richmond, Virginia.

28 April 1862:

John B. Walton elected 3rd Sergeant - Co. B

Private R. Peacock of Company D died at Richmond, Virginia.

29 April 1862: Marcus L. Billingsly elected Jr. 2nd Lieutenant - Co. G

30 April 1862: Organization of the Army of Northern Virginia:

General Joseph E. Johnston, Commanding

Major General Daniel H. Hill - Commander, Left of Position

Brigadier General G. J. Raines - Division Commander

Brigadier General W. S. Featherston - Brigade Commander

Colonel Levi B. Smith - Commander, 27th Georgia Regiment

J. W. Lewis elected sergeant - Co. H

Private Thomas Howell Courson of Company I died of Pneumonia in Chimborazo Hospital #1, Richmond, Virginia.

1 May 1862: Marcus L. Billingsly elected 2nd Lieutenant - Co. G

3 May 1862: The Twenty-seventh Georgia, along with the rest of the army, withdrew from Yorktown, Virginia.

4 May 1862: The Twenty-seventh Georgia passed through Williamsburg, Virginia this day on the retreat from Yorktown.

5 May 1862: *The Battle of Williamsburg, Virginia:*

"............on the morning of the 5th the retreat was resumed. The Twenty-seventh Georgia had marched about five miles, when orders were received for it to return to Williamsburg in *double-quick time*, to assist our troops in the battle of Williamsburg, which was then raging. The rain was falling, the roads were in a terrible condition, and the weather was extremely cold;

the regiment, however, caring nothing for these discomforts, about faced (instead of countermarching) and started at the double-quick. Arriving at Williamsburg, knapsacks, haversacks, blankets and every thing which could interfere with efficiency in battle were thrown off, by our boys, as quickly as possible.

A position was assigned to the Twenty-seventh Georgia beyond and to the left of the town. This position they occupied for several hours, when they were marched to another position in a large wheat field, where they remained during the night, suffering immensely from the cold, fatigue, and the knawing pangs of hunger............" (Heroes and Martyrs of Georgia by James M. Folsom)

Private W. J Simmons, of Company G, wounded and captured.

6 May 1862: ".........About two o'clock on the morning of the 6th, the wheat field was evacuated and the line of march resumed toward the city of Richmond. Upon the arrival of the regiment at Long Bridge, they struck camp and remained for ten of twelve days.........." (Heroes and Martyrs of Georgia by James M. Folsom)

Private Edward Y. Denson of Company E died of Typhoid Fever in the General Hospital at Charlottesville, Virginia.

7 May 1862: Private Gilbert Caudle of Company D died of Measles at Richmond, Virginia.

8 May 1862: The Twenty-seventh Georgia Regiment arrived at Long Grove, Virginia and pitched camp.

Sergeant Josiah D. Eubanks of Company C died in Alabama Hospital at Richmond, Virginia.

Private Colbert McKinley of Company G died at Richmond, Virginia.

Private Elihu C. Nash of Company H died in Moore Hospital at Richmond, Virginia.

9 May 1862: Private H. T. Cook of Company E died of Typhoid in General Hospital, Camp Winder at Richmond, Virginia.

13 May 1862: J. P. S. Nash elected 4th corporal - Company H

Private Thomas Arnett of Company B died at Richmond, Virginia.

Private Elijah Bradley of Company F died at Chickahominy River, Virginia.

14 May 1862: Private J. Fields of Company I died at Richmond, Virginia.

21 May 1862: Army of Northern Virginia:

General Joseph E. Johnston, Commanding

Major General Daniel H. Hill - Division Commander

Brigadier General W. S. Featherston - Brigade Commander

Colonel Levi B. Smith - Commander, 27th Georgia Regiment

Private Charles Williams of Company E died of Typhoid Fever in Chimborazo Hospital #1 at Richmond, Virginia. Private

Thomas J. M. King of Company G died at Richmond, Virginia.
24 May 1862: Private Josiah Belyen of Company K died at Richmond, Virginia.
27 May 1862: Private Enoch M. Herndon of Company E died of Typhoid Fever at Richmond, Virginia.

31 May 1862: *The Battle of Seven Pines (Fair Oaks), Virginia:*

The Battle of Seven Pines, also known as Fair Oaks, took place May 31 - June 1, 1862, in Henrico County, Virginia, just to the east of Richmond. There more than 84,000 men were engaged. On May 31st, CSA Commander Gen. Joseph E. Johnston attempted to overwhelm two Federal corps that appeared isolated south of the Chickahominy River. The Twenty-Seventh Georgia was in Daniel Harvey Hills' Corp and W. S. Featherson's Brigade with Colonel Levi B. Smith commanding. On the right of Colonel Jenkins' South Carolina Sharpshooters and to the South of the Railroad, the Twenty-seventh Georgia entered into the battle about 2 p.m. that afternoon. The Twenty- seventh Georgia assisted Colonel Jenkins in driving back a flanking federal force at the end of the day's action and had advanced far beyond any other Confederate Troops in driving the enemy.

The Confederate assaults succeeded in driving back the Federal IV Corps and inflicting heavy casualties in the Union ranks. Union reinforcements arrived and both sides fed more and more troops into the battle. One of the bloodiest battles of the war, in two days, there were 13, 736 casualties spread over the battlefield of Seven Pines; 5,739 Union and 7,997 Confederate. The most notable result of the battle was that Commander Joseph Johnston, at which time, commanded of the Army of Northern Virginia, was seriously wounded. A day later, the job fell to Gen. Robert E. Lee.

Major General Daniel H. Hill's division was ordered to attack along the Williamsburg Road which was to be the center of the assault on the Federal troops. Major General James Longstreet was to attack on the enemy's right and Major General Benjamin Huger was to attack their left. Due to miscommunication Hill's Division was alone in the attack at 1 p.m. They charged the federals, storming through the swampy, wooded terrain. They waded hip deep bogs and pools of water. They fought their way through briars and dense undergrowth, pushing back the enemy forces. The battle lasted until 6 p.m. The successful attack of General D. H. Hill's division against the enemy forces is considered to be the main part of this battle. Two Georgia regiments were "conspicuous" in the Battle, the Twenty-seventh and the Twenty-eighth.

".......At the battle of Seven Pines, fought on the 31st of May, this regiment participated, going into action at two o'clock in the afternoon, a little to the left of the Williamsburg road. General Featherstone being sick, the command devolved upon Colonel G. B. Anderson, of North Carolina. Colonel Smith, of this regiment, was wounded in the early part of the engagement, but did not quit the field until the brigade was relieved. About four o'clock p. m., Colonel Jenkins, of South Carolina, with his sharpshooters, came to the relief of the Twenty-seventh Georgia, when a charge was ordered and the enemy was completely routed in front of their position. At this juncture the brigade was relieved, excepting the Twenty-seventh Georgia, who were ordered to keep in supporting distance of Colonel Jenkins, who was then in pursuit of the enemy, and render him any assistance which might be necessary. Just before sundown Colonel Jenkins ordered Lieutenant Colonel Zachry (who was then in command of the Twenty-seventh Georgia, Colonel Smith having retired) to form on his (Colonel Jenkins') right as the enemy in heavy force were attempting to flank him in that direction. The regiment moved up at the double-quick, and were forming line, when some little confusion occurred; which lasted, however, but a moment. It was at this time that Adjutant Gardner displayed that coolness and marked bravery which elicited from Colonel Jenkins a personal complement and recommendation for promotion. Colonel Jenkins succeeded, with the aid of the Twenty-seventh Georgia, in baffling the designs of the enemy upon our flank, and drove him one-fourth of a mile from the position, when night put an end to the conflict. The loss of the Twenty-seventh Georgia in this engagement was severe, amounting to one hundred and fifty-four (154) killed and wounded............" (Heroes and Martyrs of Georgia by James M. Folsom)

".......During this engagement Colonel Anderson seized the flag of the Twenty-seventh Georgia Regiment and dashed forward holding it aloft.............

Before their restless sweep the stubborn foe reeled and fled, and the colors which Colonel Anderson bore were planted on their breastwork.

Such men were worthy of being commanded, as they were, by the bravest of the brave, and the cordial thanks and commendation of a division commander, who was not given to laudation of any one, caused the immediate recognition of Colonel Anderson's merits by the President, who, being on the field, at once promoted him, and his well won commission of Brigadier General was forwarded and received by him on the 9th day of July 1862........" Southern Historical Society Papers, Rev. J. William Jones, D. D., Vol. XIV No. 106

Report of Lieut. Col. Charles T. Zachry, Twenty-seventh Georgia Infantry

HDQRS. TWENTY-SEVENTH GEORGIA REGIMENT,
Bivouac below Richmond, Virginia, June 5, 1862.

CAPTAIN: I have the honor to submit the following report of the operations of the Twenty-seventh Georgia Regiment on Saturday, May 31, and Sunday,

June 1:
About 2 p. m. we emerged from the woods through which we had advanced rapidly and with great fatigue to the men, in the open field just in the rear of the Fourth North Carolina State Troops and the Forty-ninth Virginia Regiment, who were both engaging the enemy. We were ordered left into the woods, and our line reached along the abatis of the enemy 75 or 100 yards in width. One captain (O. A. Lee, Company I) and several men had been killed before we arrived at this position. The enemy had concealed himself on the other edge of the abatis, and when we arrived within the easy range opened a tremendous fire of musketry, with some grape and shell. We replied with greater effect upon the enemy, as shown by their dead and wounded, for a brief period, then charged over the abatis, the enemy's sense of danger on seeing our bayonets intrepidly advancing allowing him to take but little advantage of the exposure of our men in crossing such a place. Advancing beyond where the enemy had been and discovering he had flanked us, we fell back across the abatis.

Scarcely was our line well in its position before the enemy, with three fiendish yells, opened from the same place on us a terrific fire, which we returned till re-enforced by Colonel Jenkins' South Carolina regiment; then charged the abatis again. The enemy fled so rapidly we saw him no more until we had passed three of his camps.

In the first charge, or while falling back after it, the gallant Captain Bacon fell mortally wounded. The officer's loss is irreparable. In his regular duties his attentiveness and faithfulness challenged the admiration of every member of the command. His courage, coolness and judgment rendered his services on the battle-field invaluable. Between the first and second charge Colonel Smith was severely wounded, but kept his saddle through the second charge until about 5 p. m., when exhausted by loss of blood, he reluctantly retired. Of the colonel's distinguished gallantry I need not speak; you witnessed it, captain. He bore himself a full man.

After passing the first camp of the enemy I was ordered to follow up Colonel Jenkins' South Carolina regiment and support him if necessary. My adjutant went hastily to the front and reported to Colonel Jenkins our proximity and purpose. The gallant Jenkins replied, "Come on, Georgia; I want you!" We moved up on his right and the two regiments advanced on a dense body of woods. As we arrived in the woods we discovered the enemy advancing in heavy force to recapture, I suppose, two pieces of artillery captured by Colonel Jenkins and now in our rear. Colonel Jenkins' regiment, to get a better position, I imagine, after advancing ten of fifteen paces in the woods, fell back quickly to the edge. My left companies unfortunately mistook the movement for retreat, and soon along the line the cry was "Retreat; the order is retreat!", and the whole line fell back. Just here the enemy opened at 75 yards the heaviest fire I had yet heard, and in spite of every exertion of myself and the adjutant the regiment fell back 70 or 80 yards in the field.

I cannot in words do justice to Adjutant Gardner for the gallant heroism displayed by him in this crisis. Stung to the quick by the behavior of the men, but originating in an honest mistake, he dashed boldly to where our line should be, and under an awful fire at deadly range rode back and forth, waving his sword defiantly at the enemy, by every gesture and motion appealing to the regiment to follow him. His efforts were not in vain; the whole regiment dashed gallantly in on the right of the Carolinians, determined to retrieve themselves, and in fine style drove the enemy from the woods, capturing several prisoners at the edge of the field beyond. We ceased firing a little after 8 p. m. at least one mile in advance of any other troops save Colonel Jenkins' South Carolina regiment. Dark forced us to stop our pursuit.

Before closing this report I desire to mention Sergeant Latham, of Company D, color-bearer, and the color guard for their gallant and intrepid bearing through the entire day. Our colors were pierced twenty times. Men and officers behaved themselves heroically.

Coming out into the field to the house and tents, I had my wounded and killed brought there, and meeting my quartermaster when I rejoined the brigade, about 10 at night, I had the wounded removed to hospital in charge of Dr. Butler, assistant surgeon.

Early Sunday we were in line of battle across the abatis we charged the day before, and remained there under arms the entire day. A major, whose name has escaped my memory, from one of the Mississippi regiments, with 15 of his men, fell in with my command and conducted themselves gallantly during the entire conflict; also Virginians, Carolinians, and Alabamians, who were not able to find their respective commands, fell in with me and fought bravely.

I am, captain, very respectfully, yours, &c,.
C. T. ZACHRY,
Lieutenant-Colonel, Comdg. Twenty-seventh Georgia Regiment.
Capt. GEORGE P. FOOTE, Assistant Adjutant-General.

Official Record of the Union and Confederate Armies
SERIES I - VOLUME XI - PART I

The causality list for this engagement was as follows: Killed: 2 Captains 5 Sergeants and 9 Privates - total 16. Wounded: 1 Colonel, 3 Captains 5 1st Lieutenants, 4 2nd Lieutenants, 6 Sergeants, 10 Corporals, 100 privates - total 129. Missing: 9 Privates.

Killed: Captain Thomas J. Bacon
              Private George W. Williams - Co. C
              Private Thomas Nelson Williams - Co. C
              Private John Shirah - Co. F
              Private Henry McCullers - Co. F
              Private Robert H. Ross - Co. G
              Captain William W. DeLamar - Co. H
              1st Sergeant James G. Turner – Co. H
              Private Samuel G. W. Harkness - Co. H
              Captain Osgood A. Lee - Co. I
              Private Jackson Cooner -Co. I
              Private Franklin Quinn - Co. I
              Private William Smith - Co. I
              Private Jacob T. Thompson - Co. I
              Lieutenant David Green - Co. K
              Private William H. Fuller - Co. K
Wounded: Private Robert D. Flurry - Co. A
              Private Nathan W. Myrick – Co. A
              Private Lewis M. Avant - Co. B
              Private James J. Causey - Co. C
              Private I. I. J. Cutts - Co. C
              Private Green Davis - Co. C
              Private William H. McKinney - Co. C
              Lieutenant Richard V. Cobb - Co. D
              Sergeant Micajah Bagwell - Co. D
              Corporal Lewis Burton - Co. D
              Private James T. Hawks – Co. D
              Private H. M. Langford – Co. D (died of wounds)
              Private H. McKinney – Co. D
              Private Benjamin W. Reed - Co. D
              Private Joseph R. Reed – Co. D
              Private William T. Wood - Co. D
              Lieutenant Josiah H. Elder - Co. E
              Private George D. Carter - Co. E
              Private T. J. Horton - Co. E
              Private James R. Thompson - Co. E
              Lieutenant L. Q. R. McCrary - Co. F
              Private Cornelius B. Fountain - Co. F
              Private Lewis Hill - Co. F
              Private Green Massey - Co. F
              Private James Monroe Parks - Co. F
              Private William Henry Parks – Co. F
              Lieutenant John C. Beeks - Co. G
              Sergeant John B. Copeland - Co. G

Sergeant Miles R. Hagan - Co. G
Corporal James R. Jordan - Co. G
Private J. W. Boyd - Co. G
Private B. J. Foster - Co. G
Private E. J. Fowler - Co. G
Private James H. Horton - Co. G
Private T. J. Howard – Co. G
Private William R. M. Jones - Co. G
Private James S. Lifsey - Co. G
Private John W. Taylor - Co. G
Sergeant Willis Baxley - Co. I
Corporal Henry Harrison Beecher - Co. I
Private William Alfred Becher - Co. I
Private William H. Dilbon - Co. I
Private Nathaniel A. Thomas - Co. I
Lieutenant Wilkins J. Raines - Co. K
Corporal Charles E. Dozier - Co. K
Private James A. Dozier - Co. K

Captured: Private Joseph H. Burns
Private I. I. J. Cutts - Co. C
Private John Dyer - Co. C
Private Julius Hoskins – Co. C
Private D. C. Sawyer – Co. C
Private S. Elberson - Co. D
Private William T. Wood - Co. D
Private W. A. J. Denson - Co. E
Private T. J. Horton - Co. E
Sergeant Miles R. Hagan - Co. G
Private John L. Banks - Co. G
Private Warren Brooks - Co. G
Private T. J. Howard – Co. G
Private George T. Embry – Co. H
Private John T. D. Harris – Co. H
Private S. M. Henry - Co. H
Private Frank W. McClendon - Co. H
Private B. F. Turner – Co. H
Private Thomas Hardy - Co. K
Private Christopher C. Watts of Company G died in Front Royal, Virginia.

1 June 1862: Private Andrew Jackson Peters of Company E died of Dysentery in Chimborazo Hospital#1 at Richmond, Virginia.

3 June 1862: Private Erwin Williams of Company F died in Richmond, Virginia

4 June 1862: Private Thomas C. Smith of Company G died in Richmond, Virginia.

27

5 June 1862: Captain Perry C. Carr of Company A died of disease in Richmond, Virginia.

Private John J. Betsill of Company E died of Typhoid Fever in the General Hospital at Farmville, Virginia.

Private J. H. Dixon of Company E died in Richmond, Virginia.

Private James E. Davis of Company I died in Richmond, Virginia.

6 June 1862: Private J. J. Rudicil of Company E died in Richmond, Virginia.

9 June 1862:

Private Amasa M. Burnett of Company B died in Virginia.

Private James Andrew Cook of Company E died of Typhoid Fever in General Hospital, Camp Winder at Richmond, Virginia.

Sergeant Sidney Boyd of Company G died in Richmond, Virginia.

10 June 1862: The following changes occurred in the Twenty-seventh Regiment:

Company A:William E. Dougherty elected Captain

Robert Patton elected 1st Lieutenant

Eli Stewart elected 2nd Lieutenant

Company B:Andrew J. Wilson appointed 2nd Sergeant

Company I: Elisha Duncan Graham elected Captain

Alexander W. Johnson elected 2nd Lieutenant

Private Martin G. Chandler of Company D died.

Private Andrew C. Howard of Company K died in Richmond, Virginia.

12 June 1862: Corporal John F. Coxwell of Company B died in Virginia.

13 June 1862: Lieutenant William J. Sams of Company E died in Richmond Virginia.

14 June 1862:

Lieutenant John H. Eubanks of Company C. died of Typhoid Fever in General Hospital at Farmville, Virginia.

Private Lovick Washington Weaver of Company C died of Typhoid Fever in General Hospital, Camp Winder at Richmond, Virginia.

Lieutenant William Kennedy of Company D died.

15 June 1862: Captain William W. De Lamar of Company H died. The following changes occurred in the Twenty-seventh Regiment:

Company H: Robert A. Harkey elected Captain

Robert C. Evans elected 1st Lieutenant

Wade H. Harper elected 2nd Lieutenant

George Edward Wise elected Jr. 2nd lieutenant

Private John G. McClure of Company G died of Typhoid Fever in General Hospital #18 at Richmond, Virginia.

18 June 1862: Private Michael C. Hennigar of Company B died of Typhoid Fever in Chimborazo Hospital #4 in Virginia.

19 June 1862: Private John Layfield of Company F died of disease in

28

Richmond, Virginia.

20 June 1862: The following changes occurred in the Twenty-seventh Regiment:

Company E: John T. Abercrombie elected 1st. Lieutenant
William J. Abercrombie elected 2nd Lieutenant

21 June 1862: The following change occurred in the Twenty-seventh Regiment:

Company D:George W. Lathem elected 1st Lieutenant

24 June 1862: Confederate Forces around Richmond, Virginia:

General Joseph E. Johnston, Commanding
Major General Thomas J. Jackson - Corps Commander
Major General Daniel H. Hill - Division Commander
Colonel Alfred H. Colquitt - Brigade Commander
Colonel Levi B. Smith - Commander, 27th Georgia Regiment

25 June 1862: General Robert E. Lee takes command of the Army of Northern Virginia.

Wounded: Private W. J. Deans - Co. C

26 June 1862: *The Seven Days Campaign around Richmond, Virginia:*

Although McClellan had the troops and opportunity to make an attack on the Confederate capitol of Richmond, his caution and reluctance to commit his superior numbers to the task at hand cause him to squander the opportunity. On the other side the audacity of General Robert E. Lee was about to become known to all that observed this the greatest of American Generals in action. The beginnings of this magnificent defense by offense were primed and ready to be fired. Robert E. Lee had assumed command of the Army of Northern Virginia on the 25th of June and was about to embark on a campaign that would cause McClellan to retreat and withdraw from the peninsula of Virginia.

"........On the morning of the 26th of June the regiment took up a line of march at half past one o'clock, and halted near Mechanicsville.............."
(Heroes and Martyrs of Georgia by James M. Folsom)

27 June 1862: Mechanicsville:

General A. P. Hill having engaged at Beaver Dam Creek, near Mechanicsville was unsuccessful in his assault. General Daniel H. Hill's troops were sent forward in support. The entrenched Federals held, but withdrew after dark to another prepared position behind Boatswain Swamp.

General D. H. Hill's report on the Seven days around Richmond stated that on this date 'Colonel Colquitt, commanding brigade in like manner did not keep his brigade in hand, and three of his regiments did not draw trigger. The Sixth and Twenty-seventh Georgia, of this brigade, commanded by those pure, brave, noble Christian soldiers Lieutenant Colonel J. M. Newton and Colonel Levi B. Smith, behaved most heroically, and maintained their

29

ground when half their number had been struck down.

Killed: Private William C. Wadsworth - Co. G

             Private James McGauley – Co I

Wounded: Private Jeremiah J. Burnett - Co. B

             Private William R. Altman - Co. C

             Private William W. Hemphill – Co. D

             Private John T Aiken - Co. G

             Sergeant John N. Mason - Co. H

             Private Franklin Alexander - Co. H

             Private George M. Chafin - Co. H

             Corporal Henry Harrison Becher - Co. I

             Private William Alfred Becher - Co. I

No.305.

Report of Brigadier General Roger A. Pryor,

C.S. Army, commanding Fifth Brigade, of the battle of Gaines' Mill, and Frazier's Farm (Nelson's Farm, or Glendale).

HEADQUARTERS FIFTH BRIGADE, July 29, 1862.

MAJOR: I beg to submit the following report of the operations of the Fifth Brigade in the recent engagement around Richmond:

About 11 o'clock in the night of June 26 I was directed by Major-General Longstreet to relieve the brigade of Colonel Colquitt in its advanced position on the field of the day's fight. Expecting the enemy to renew the combat in the morning I disposed my regiments in such.

Cold Harbor:

"............The regiment was engaged in the battle of Mechanicsville on the morning of the 27th and at Cold Harbor on the evening of the same day. At the battle of Cold Harbor, Gen. Colquitt's Brigade charged the enemy and gained a very important position, which was held by the Twenty-seventh Georgia for some time, without any assistance from the other regiments of the brigade. The Sixty-first Georgia Regiment was ordered forward to relieve the Twenty-seventh, but, mistaking them for the enemy, fired into the regiment, until Adjutant Gardner could pass from the extreme right of the regiment to its centre, and have the colors raised, by that means signifying to them that we were friends. The Sixty-first, recognizing the colors, ceased firing, and coming quickly forward, relieved the Twenty-seventh........." (Heroes and martyrs of Georgia by James M. Folsom)

D. H. Hill's Division marched toward Old Cold Harbor and Boatswain

Swamp. Early in the afternoon the Division encountered the right flank of General Porter's Federal defenses. They held their position until late afternoon. General Lee ordered a concerted charge. About sundown the charge began on the extreme left with D. H. Hill's Division. Hill's troops struggled through a dense swamp emerging on the southern edge striking the enemy and driving them back. The Confederates in Hill's Division then made a flanking charge on the federals routing them. One of Hill's men exclaimed, "They ran like turkeys......". In his report, D. H. Hill claims to have broken the Federal line first.

The causality list for the Twenty-seventh Georgia included:
Gaines Mill: 9 killed, 76 wounded, 1 missing - 86 total
Malvern Hill: 2 killed, 26 wounded, 0 missing - 28 total

Killed: Sergeant Samuel G. B. Odum - Co. B
               Private James W. Perdue - Co. B
               Private E. R. Fortson - Co. E
               Lieutenant John Bunyan Wright - Co. F
               Private John M. Humphries - Co. F
               Private J. B. Lyon - Co. F
               Private John T. D. Harris - Co. H
               Private James M. McGauley - Co. I
Wounded: Private Bailey Armstrong Heard - Co. B
               Sergeant G. W. White – Co. C
               Corporal W. S. McNiece - Co. C
               Private Sanders Bond - Cop. C
               Private Frederick Hutto – Co. C
               Private William H. Hayes - Co. D
               Private Anderson J. Reynolds – Co. D
               Private James Miles Mason - Co. E
               Private Cornelius Fountain Co. F
               Private John T. Akin - Co. G
               Private William A. Moreland –Co. G
               Lieutenant Wade H. Harper - Co. H
               Sergeant John N. Mason - Co. H
               Private Franklin Alexander – Co. H
               Private A. G. Duke - Co. H
               Private L. W. J. Turner - Co. H
               Corporal Henry Harrison Beecher Co. I
               Corporal James M. Mclendon - Co. I
               Private William Alfred Beecher - Co. I
               Private Henry Mann, Jr. Co. I
               Sergeant Raleigh H. Turner - Co. K
               Sergeant Samuel Zachariah Webster - Co. K
               Private George Bolton - Co. K

31

Private Calvin Calhoun - Co. K

Gaines Mill:

Company F: William Posey Edwards elected 2nd Lieutenant
            James F. Boland elected Jr. 2nd Lieutenant

31 June 1862: D. H. Hill's Division pursued the retreating Federal troops. While in pursuit they came under intense artillery fire from the rear guard of the enemy in White Oak Swamp.

White Oak Swamp:

Wounded: Private John C. O' Hern - Co. F

1 July 1862:
Malvern Hill:

Battle lines were drawn on both sides of Willis Church Road. The Twenty-seventh Georgia and the rest of Colquitt's Brigade were hurled against the Union works and came under severe enemy fire, both shellfire and canister.

"......at Malvern Hill we were hurled upon the foe, losing very severely in killed and wounded, Adjutant Gardner being among those who were severely wounded......." (Heroes and Martyrs of Georgia by James M. Folsom)

The causality list for the Twenty-seventh Georgia Regiment for June 26 through July 1, 1862 indicated; 11 killed, 102 wounded, 113 total

Wounded: Captain James B. Gardner- adjutant
            Sergeant Francis M. Barfield - Co. B
            Private Phillip Harrison Schofield - Co. B
            Private Enos M. Causey - Co. C
            Private J. E. Hudson – Co. C.
            Private B. E. Hutto – Co. C
            Private John W. Robinson – Co. C
            Private William A. Webb – Co. C
            Lieutenant George W. Latham - Co. D
            Private Hiram B. Smith – Co. D
            Private W. R. Walker – Co. E
            Private John C. O'Hern - Co. F
            Private John C. Moore - Co. G
            Private John B. Peters – Co. G
            Private Judge H. Donald - Co. H
            Sergeant A. M. Crosby - Co. I
            Private J. C. Cooner - Co. I
            Private James M. Puckett - Co. I
            Sergeant Raleigh H. Turner -Co. K
Captured: Private John B. Peters – Co. G

In the Seven Days Battle around Richmond the Twenty-seventh Georgia

Regiment suffered a loss of 126 killed and wounded.

2 July 1862 Private John Thomas Pound of Company K died of Fever in Chimborazo Hospital #5 at Richmond, Virginia.

3 July 1862: Private George Bolton - Company K. died of wounds.

5 July 1862: Private James Hill of Company E died of Typhoid in General Hospital at Farmville, Virginia.

Private Warren T. Brooks died of wounds at Richmond, Virginia.

6 July 1862: Regiment returns to Richmond, Virginia.

10 July 1862: Company K: A. C. McCrory elected Jr. 2nd Lieutenant

11 July 1862: Private Elisha Aldridge of Company I died of Typhoid Fever in Chimborazo Hospital #1 at Richmond, Virginia.

13 July 1862: Company G: John C. Beeks elected Captain
Marcus L. Billingsley elected 1st Lieutenant

15 July 1862: Private R. Binson of Company A died in Richmond, Virginia.

17 July 1862: Private F. Denson of Company F died in Richmond, Virginia.

20 July 1862:
Company A: W. C. Dodson elected Jr. 2nd lieutenant
Private Jesse A. Carter of Company E died of disease in Richmond, Virginia.

23 July 1862:   Organization of the Army of Northern Virginia:
General Robert E. Lee, Commanding
Major General Thomas J. Jackson
Major General Daniel H. Hill - Division Commander
Colonel Alfred H. Colquitt - Commander, 2nd Brigade
Colonel Levi B. Smith - Commander, 27th Georgia Regiment

25 July 1862:
Company B: John Wesley Forrester elected Jr. 2nd Lieutenant
Private Jacob T. Woodall of Company A died of Typhoid in General Hospital #1 at Danville, Virginia.

26 July 1862: George B. Buchanan appointed Captain and Assistant Quartermaster.

28 July 1862: Private W. J. Anderson of Company G died in Richmond, Virginia.

August 1862: Private James T. Smith of Company C died.

1 August 1862: Private Peter Kemp of Company I died of Typhoid in Chimborazo Hospital #4 at Richmond, Virginia.

11 August 1862: Private Elsbury Hambrick of Company G died in Richmond, Virginia.

13 August 1862: Company G:James M. Slade elected 2nd Lieutenant.

17 August 1862: Private Peter Guice of company E died of Diarrhea and Typhoid Fever in General Hospital at Farmville, Virginia.

Private J. J. Carter of Company G died in Richmond, Virginia.

33

19 August 1862: The Twenty-seventh Georgia moved by railcar from Richmond to Orange Court House.

24 August 1862: John W. Stubbs elected Major

John J. Allen elected Captain Company B

Miles G. Stephens elected 1st. Lieutenant Company B

John Wesley Forrester elected 2nd Lieutenant Company B

27 August 1862: The Twenty-seventh Georgia took up the line of march, to join Generals Lee and Jackson near Fairfax, Virginia.

3 September 1862: The regiment arrived at Fairfax, Virginia.

4 September 1862: The regiment moved to Frederick, Maryland via Leesburg.

7 September 1862: The Twenty-seventh Georgia marched toward Boonsboro via South Mountain.

Private James L. Owen of Company B died of Fever in General Hospital #14 at Richmond, Virginia.

Private J. Kerlin of Company E died in Richmond, Virginia.

9 September 1862:

Private John Coleman of Company E died at Manassas, Virginia.

Private A. G. Duke of Company H died in Richmond, Virginia.

Private R. W. Duke of Company H died in Richmond, Virginia.

12 September 1862: Organization of the Army of Northern Virginia - Maryland Campaign:

General Robert E. Lee, Commanding

Major General James Longstreet - Corps Commander

Major General Daniel H. Hill - Division Commander

Colonel Alfred H. Colquitt - Brigade Commander

Colonel Levi B. Smith - Commander, 27th Georgia

13 September 1862: D. H. Hill and A. H. Colquitt were reconnoitering around Boonesboro, Maryland when Hill received a request for support on the National Pike at Turners Gap. Colquitt marched his Brigade up the National Pike to the Mountain House, a tollhouse on the apex of the gap. Colquitt dispatched his troops on both sides of the pike. The Twenty-seventh was assigned in the center of the right side of the pike, between the Sixth Georgia on the extreme right and the Thirteenth Alabama that was next to the National Pike. (Other sources indicate that the 27th Georgia was on the extreme right past the 6th Georgia and the 13th Alabama who were also on the right of the National Pike.) The Artillery kept the Federal forces at the foot of the mountain until the next day.

14 September 1862: *The Battle of South Mountain - Turners Gap, Maryland:*

Colquitt's Brigade maintained their position in the gap all day long. Then late in the afternoon they were attacked by a detached brigade under the command of Union General John Gibbon. The attack continued for several hours, continuing into the night.

"......The Georgians, who had held their strong position all day with not much more than heavy skirmishing, now repulsed every attempt to drive them. After each success they would raise the rebel yell, and at the Mountain House, the young men of Hill's Staff would laugh and clap their hands and exclaim "Hurrah for Georgia, Georgia is having a free fight......" (Lee's Maverick General, Daniel Harvey Hill -- Hal Bridges)

".....On the morning of the 14th, a position was assigned to the Twenty-seventh by Major General D. H. Hill, to whose division Colquitt's Brigade belonged; which position it held all that day. At night we were withdrawn and marched to Sharpsburg....." (Heroes and Martyrs of Georgia - James M. Folsom)

It has been recorded that Colquitt's Brigade did not give an inch that day and they were facing the bulk of McClellan's Federal Army. The Georgia Historic Marker located by General Alfred Holt Colquitt's grave, in Rose Hill Cemetery - Macon, Georgia, states that he is known as the "Rock of South Mountain."

"Confident in their superior numbers, the enemy's forces advanced to a short distance of our lines, when, raising a shout, they came to a charge. As they came full into view upon the rising ground, 40 paces distant, they were met by a terrific volley of musketry from the stone fence and hillside. This gave sudden check to their advance. They rallied under cover of the uneven ground, and the fight opened in earnest. They made still another effort to advance, but were kept back by the steady fire of our men. The fight continued with fury until after dark"
Colonel Alfred Colquitt
(Inscription at South Mountain State Park Museum)

Wounded:	Captain Elisha Duncan Graham - Co. I
	Private S. J. Jones - Co. E
	Private Francis M. Theulkeld – Co. F
Captured:	Captain Hezekiah Bussey - Co. K
	Sergeant Freeman Walker – Co. K
	Private James M. Pound – Co. K
	Private Lewis Wright - Co. C
	Private William R. Gardner - Co. D
	Sergeant James E. Adams - Co. F
	Private Francis M. Theulkeld – Co. F

In his report on the activities at South Mountain, Robert E. Lee wrote;"..... Several attacks on the center were gallantly repulsed by Colquitt's Brigade........."

15 September 1862: The Twenty-seventh Georgia Regiment is withdrawn to Sharpsburg, then to the north shore of the Potomac opposite Shepherdstown, Virginia.

Private F. M. Kerlin of Company E died of Chronic Diarrhea in General Hospital, Camp Winder at Richmond, Virginia.

35

17 September 1862: *The Battle of Sharpsburg (Antietam), Maryland:*

In the battle near Sharpsburg, the Twenty-seventh was originally positioned on the left end of the sunken roadbed and around seven o'clock a.m. was ordered to move up in support of General Hood's Texans who were engaged early in the morning at Miller's cornfield near Dunkard Church. By eight o'clock they were in the cornfield and moved through it to the northern edge of the cornfield engaged in a hotly contested fight with the federals. Ripley's Brigade on the left was slowed and Garland's Brigade under the command of Colonel D. K. McRae vacated their prescribed position which left the right flank of Colquitt's Brigade exposed. The 6th Georgia was in line on the right with the 27th Georgia second to the right side of Colquitt's Brigade. General Greene's Brigade of Union troops emerged from the east woods and took the position formerly held by Garland's Brigade. They unleashed what was described as a murderous volley and charged into Colquitt's flank. There ensued a short hand to hand fight where the soldiers employed bayonets and swung their muskets as clubs. Finally just before nine o'clock the Georgians were compelled to fall back loosing half of their field officers and men. The loss to the Twenty-seventh Georgia was severe as was the other regiments of Colquitt's Brigade.

They fell back to a position near the Hagerstown Pike and continued the fight until again they were compelled to fall back.

The brigade then took up a position on the far left in an old sunken road (later this road became known as "Bloody Lane"). The Twenty-seventh Regiment was prominent in the three hour defense of this position. This three hour stand may well have been the "Bloodiest" three hours in American history. The Confederate muskets took a terrible toll on the advancing federal troops and one federal soldier upon entering the sunken road after General D. H. Hill had extracted his forces remarked that the Confederate dead were three deep in the lane.

Around one o'clock in the afternoon the remnant of Colquitt's Brigade (the Twenty-seventh Georgia) were active along with Evans Brigade on the Boonsboro Pike and checking the Federal advance there.

BRIGADE HEADQUARTERS
Near Bunker Hill, Va., October 13, 1862

SIR: I give you below an account of the part taken by this brigade in the battle of September 17.

About 7 o'clock in the morning my brigade entered the fight. It was moved to the front and formed on the right of General Ripley's brigade which was engaged. After a few rounds had been discharge, I ordered in advance, and at the same time sent word to the regiments on my left to advance simultaneously. The order was responded to with spirit by my men, and, with a shout, they moved through the cornfield in front, 200 yards wide, and formed on the line of fence. The enemy was near and in full view. In a moment or two his ranks began to break before our fire, and the line soon disappeared under the crest of the hill upon which it had been established. It was soon replaced by another, and the fire opened with renewed vigor.

In the meantime Garland's brigade, which had been ordered to my right, had given way, and the enemy was advancing unchecked. The regiments upon my left having also failed to advance, we were exposed to fire from all sides and nearly surrounded. I sent in haste to the rear for re-enforcements, and communicated to General Hill the exposed condition of my men. With steady supports upon the right we could yet maintain our position. The support was not at hand and could not reach us in time. The enemy closed in upon the right so near that our ranks were scarcely distinguishable. At the same time his line in front advanced. My men stood firm until every field officer but one had fallen, and then made the best of their way out.

In this sharp and unequal conflict I lost many of my best officers and one-half of the men in the ranks. If the brigades upon the right and left had advanced, we should have driven the enemy from the field. He had at one time broken in our front, but we had not the strength to push the advantage.

Colonel (L. B.) Smith, of the Twenty-seventh Georgia; Colonel (W. P.) Barclay, of the Twenty-third Georgia; and Lieutenant-Colonel (J. M.) Newton, commanding the Sixth Georgia, fell at the head of their regiments. Their loss is irreparable. Upon every battlefield they distinguished themselves for coolness and gallantry. Colonel (B. D.) Fry, of the Thirteenth Alabama, and Captain (N. J.) Garrison, commanding Twenty-eighth Georgia, were severely wounded.

Subsequent to the action of the forenoon, portions of my brigade encountered the enemy in two desultory engagements, in which they stood before superior numbers and gave check to their advance. In one of these a small party was placed under the command of Lieutenant-Colonel (W. H.) Betts, and directed to deploy as skirmishers along the crest of a hill upon which the enemy was advancing. They did so with good effect, keeping back a large force by their annoying fire and the apprehension, excited by their boldness, that they were supported by a line in rear.

During the engagements of this day I had the misfortune to loose my acting assistant adjutant-general (Lieutenant R. P. Jordan). He fell while gallantly dashing toward the enemy's line. I have not known a more active, efficient, and fearless officer. Lieutenant Gratton, my aide-de-camp, was conspicuously bold in the midst of danger and untiring in the discharge of his duties. I regret that I cannot here mention the names of all, dead and living, who are entitled to a tribute at my hands.

Respectfully, your obedient servant,
A. H. Colquitt,
Colonel, Commanding Brigade.
Major Ratchford,
Assistant Adjutant-General

Killed:
- Colonel Levi B. Smith
- Corporal H. H. Kendrick – Co. A
- Private John T. Perdue - Co. B
- Private William R. Sonneborn - Co. B
- Private James Dyer -Co. C
- Private Henry Hancock, Sr. - Co. C
- Private Charles M. Hope - Co. D
- Private Cornelius Latimer, Co. D
- Private W. M. Burgess - Co. E
- Private Edward Benjamin Butler - Co. E
- Private James M. Fortson - Co. E
- Corporal William H. Harper - Co. E
- Private Joel M. Hemplay - Co. E
- Private John Murphey - Co. E
- Private William M. Nelson - Co. E
- Lieutenant James F. Boland - Co. F
- Private Elisha Forshe - Co. F
- Private Willis Herricks - Co. F
- Private Christopher C. Shirah Co. F
- Captain John C. Beeks - Co. G
- Private J. B. Creamer - Co. G
- Private James M. Lee Co. G
- Lieutenant James F. Maxley - Co. G
- Private John Taylor - Co. G
- Private Henry H. Miller - Co. H
- Lieutenant Alexander W. Johnson - Co. I
- Sergeant Adolph H. Lessure - Co. I
- Private Francis M. Hester - Co. I
- Private Levi Johnson - Co. I
- Private John D. Huff – Co. K
- Private John Russell – Co. K
- Private Zeph B. Sealey - Co. K

Wounded:
- Lieutenant Colonel Charles T. Zachry
- Private Edward O. Little – Co. A
- Sergeant John R. Seymore - Co. B
- Private William H. Hall - Co. B
- Private Julius G. Skipper – Co. B
- Private William W. Woodward - Co. B

Private Enos M. Causey, Co. C
Private B. Franklin Dreher - Co. C
Private William G. Jordan - Co. C
Private D. C. Sawyer – Co. C
2nd Lieutenant Richard V. Cobb - Co. D
Sergeant H. B. Smith - Co. D
Private James D. Blackstock - Co. D
Private William A. Martin- Co. D
Private S. P. McKinney – Co. D
Private Anderson J. Reynolds – Co. D
Lieutenant James Mancy – Co. E
Private A. Z. Booth - Co. E
Private George D. Carter Co. E
Private John Murphey – Co. E
Private Horsey Peters - Co. E
Private James R. Thompson - Co. E
Private John H. West - Co. E
Private William West - Co. E
Lieutenant William Posey Edwards - Co. F
Sergeant James B. Sorrells – Co. F
Private Allen F. Cody - Co. F
Private W. H. Sheppard – Co. F
Private Slaughter Hill - Co. F
Private N. W. Scott - Co. F
Private Smith Turner – Co. F
Sergeant John B. Copeland - Co. G
Private John B. Creamer - Co. G
Private Leonard O. Harris – Co. G
Private Henry T. Lifsey - Co. G
Private William A. Moreland - Co. G
Private Robert Reeves – Co. G (died of wounds)
Private F. J. Wadsworth – Co. G
Private Aaron F. Henry – Co. H
Private D. H. Herrin – Co. H
Private Willis Herricks – Co. H (died of wounds)
Private Joel M. Hewferty – Co. H (died of wounds)
Private George W. Rape – Co. H
Private Slaughter Hill – Co. H
Private H. C. Turner - Co. H
Private James C. Turner - Co. H
Private George W. Hester - Co. I
Sergeant Benjamin Milikin - Co. I
Private James A. Belyean- Co. K
Private Jesse W. Hobbs - Co. K
Private John Howard - Co. K

Private John A. Michaels – Co. K

Captured: Private Thomas Downing - Co. A

Private William A. J. Teat – Co. A

Private J. J. Williams – Co. A

Private William W. Woodward - Co. B

Private B. Franklin Dreher - Co. C

Lieutenant Richard V. Cobb - Co. D

Sergeant H. B. Smith - Co. D

Private James D. Blackstock - Co. D

Private Minor Bryant - Co. D

Private John W. Clarke - Co. D

Private Abner Hunter – Co. D

Private S. P. McKinney – Co. D

Lieutenant James Mancy – Co. E (Died of Wounds)

Private John Murphey – Co. E (Died of Wounds

Private Horsey Peters - Co. E

Private William J. Williams – Co. E

Lieutenant William Posey Edwards - Co. F

Private Seaborn G. W. Mullins – Co. F

Private N. W. Scott - Co. F

Private Smith Turner – Co. F

Private John B. Creamer - Co. G

Private Robert J. Brooks - Co. G

Private Flemming Brown - Co. G

Private Leonard O. Harris – Co. G

Private Robert Reeves – Co. G

Private Russell Ross – Co. G

Private F. J. Wadsworth – Co. G

Private Aaron F. Henry – Co. H

Private Willis Herricks – Co. H

Private Joel M. Hewferty – Co. H

Private Slaughter Hill – Co. H

Private Litt Lewis - Co. H

Private W. Roe Maddox – Co. H

Private Augustus J. Peek – Co. H

Private George W. Rape – Co. H

Sergeant Benjamin Milikin - Co. I

Private James A. Belyean- Co. K

Private Jesse W. Hobbs - Co. K

Private John A. Michaels – Co. K

Private Ruben M. Smith – Co. K

Missing in Action Private D. F. Gaines - Co. H

Private Litt Lewis – Co. H

The following changes occurred in the Twenty-seventh Regiment:

Charles T. Zachry elected Colonel

John W. Stubbs elected Lt. Colonel
Charles J. Dennis elected Major
Company C: James W. Murray elected Captain
Thomas A. Grace elected 1st Lieutenant
William W. Johnson elected 2nd Lieutenant
Company G: John D. Jones elected Jr. 2nd Lieutenant

The loss in killed and wounded for the Twenty-seventh Georgia Regiment in the battles of South Mountain and Sharpsburg was 149 killed and wounded.

In General D. H. Hill's report concerning the Maryland Campaign he stated that General Hood's men were handsomely supported by Colquitt's Brigade in the "Corn-field". General Hill's report lists the casualties for Colquitt's Brigade as follows: 129 killed, 518 wounded, 184 missing - 831 total. He also states that of ten field officers in the brigade; 4 were killed, 5 badly wounded and 1 stunned by a shell. General Hill also reported that "....The officers in the Twenty-seventh and Twenty-eighth Georgia Regiments report that it is impossible for them to make distinctions where so many acted with distinguished bravery. In the Twenty-seventh every commissioned officer except one was killed or wounded at Sharpsburg, and this sole survivor was unwilling to discriminate among so many brave men........"

19 September 1862: The Twenty-seventh Georgia crossed the Potomac River before day and marched to Martinsburg, Virginia.

21 September 1862: Company G: Marcus L. Billingsley elected Captain

22 September 1862: The Regiment was ordered to Bunker Hill, Virginia.

23 September 1862: The Twenty-seventh Georgia Regiment left Martinsburg, Virginia and marched to Bunker Hill, Virginia.

24 September 1862: The Twenty-seventh Regiment left Martinsburg and assisted in tearing up the railroad between Harpers Ferry and Charlestown (Company E is indicated as destroying a railroad between Winchester and Harpers Ferry), Virginia.

26 September 1862: The Regiment pitched camp between Paris and Upperville, Virginia.

30 September 1862: The following changes occurred in the Twenty-seventh Regiment:
Company C: James W. Robinson elected 2nd Lieutenant
Company F: Robert C. Bailey elected Jr. 2nd Lieutenant
John N. Duke appointed 4th Sergeant
Company G: John D. Jones elected 2nd Lieutenant
Henry T. Lifsey elected Jr. 2nd Lieutenant
Wounded: Private William M. Childs - Company H

2 October 1862: Captured Private Amos Allen Adams - Company F

6 October 1862: Company B: John Wesley Forrester elected 1st Lieutenant

21 October 1862: Private D. M. Murray of Company D died of Measles.
23 October 1862: The Twenty-seventh Georgia left Bunker Hill and marched across the Shenandoah River.
1 November 1862: The Twenty-seventh Regiment camped between Paris and Upperville. They helped destroy a railroad at Staunton, Virginia and another at Strasburg.
Wounded: Private Simon Johnson – Company C
              Private George W. Hesters – Company I
4 November 1862: Private Jeremiah J. Burnett of Company B died in General Hospital at Staunton, Virginia.
8 November 1862: Lieutenant Richard V. Cobb of Company D Paroled in Maryland.
10 November 1862: Captain Hezekiah Bussey of Company K exchanged at Aiken's Landing, Virginia.
15 November 1862: ".......Between the 15th and 20th of November, we were ordered to march, and passing Guinea's Station *via* Orange Court House, arrived at our destination in the vicinity of Port Royal, on the Rappahannock, on the first day of December. The troops on this march made an average of twenty-two miles per day, and large numbers of them were forced the necessity of wearing sandals made of raw hide......" (Heroes and Martyrs of Georgia by James M. Folsom)
22 November 1862: Private J. Apperson of Company G died in Richmond, Virginia.
25 November 1862:
Lieutenant James W. Robinson of Company C died in Mount Jackson, Virginia.
Company C: William M. Ross elected Jr. 2nd Lieutenant
26 November 1862:
          Private James J. Causey of Company C died of Typhoid Fever in Chimborazo Hospital #5 at Richmond, Virginia.
          Private Wilson R. Howington of Company D died in General Hospital #26.
30 November 1862: Private D. C. Sawyer of Company C died of Variola in General Hospital #21 at Richmond, Virginia.
December 1862: Company E: John J. Buffington appointed 1st Sergeant
1 December 1862: The Regiment arrived near Port Royal, Virginia.
3 December 1862: Captain Jordan Wilcher of Company F resigned his commission.
7 December 1862: Private Thomas H. Gregory of Company C died of Pneumonia in General Recovery Hospital at Gordonsville, Virginia.
11 December 1862: Organization of the Army of Northern Virginia:
          General Robert E. Lee, Commanding
     Lieutenant General Thomas J. Jackson - Commander, 2nd Corps
     Major General Daniel H. Hill - Commander, Hill's Division
Brigadier General Alfred H. Colquitt - Commander, Colquitt's (3rd) Brigade

Colonel Charles T. Zachry - Commander, 27th Georgia Regiment
The following change occurred in the Twenty-seventh Georgia Regiment:
Joseph R. Stubbs elected Jr. 2nd Lieutenant - Co. B

13 December 1862: *The Battle of Fredericksburg, Virginia:*
The Army of the Potomac, under the new command of General Ambrose E. Burnside, crossed the Rappahannock River and threw themselves against General Robert E. Lee's well placed Confederates. The Twenty-seventh Georgia was on the extreme right in General D. H. Hill's Division. They were in support of General Early's Division.
Wounded: Private Lindsay Bowin - Co. G
            Private William H. C. Slade - Co. G
            Private W. H. Slade - Co. G

The causality list for the battle of Fredericksburg, Virginia lists the following for the Twenty-seventh Georgia Regiment; 3 wounded - total causalities 3.
15 December 1862: After the Battle of Fredericksburg the Twenty-seventh Georgia went into winter quarters near Guinea's Station, Virginia. The winter was spent performing Picket duty along the Rappahannock River.
            2nd Lieutenant Richard V. Cobb Exchanged at Fortress Monroe, Virginia
17 December 1862: Private Leonard O. Harris of Company G died of Variola in General Hospital at Danville, Virginia.
20 December 1862: Organization of the Army of Northern Virginia:
            General Robert E. Lee, Commander
Lieutenant General Thomas J. Jackson - Commander, 2nd Corps
            Major General Daniel H. Hill - Commander, Hill's Division
Brigadier General Alfred H. Colquitt - Commander, Colquitt's (3rd) Brigade
            Colonel Charles T. Zachry - Commander, 27th Georgia Regiment
Private Zacus W. Hudgins of Company D died in Danville, Virginia.
25 December 1862: Private Lemon M. Causey of Company C died in Richmond, Virginia

1863

6 January 1863: Wallter H. Drane appointed Surgeon - 27th Georgia Regiment
7 January 1863: The following changes occurred in the Twenty-seventh Regiment:
Company F: William Posey Edwards elected Captain
            Robert C. Bailey elected 2nd Lieutenant
10 January1863: The following changes occurred in the Twenty-seventh Regiment:
            Lt. Colonel John W. Stubbs Resigned his commission
            Jasper N. Dorsey elected Lt. Colonel - 27th Georgia

43

Regiment
Company D: George W. Latham elected Captain
    John F. Dorsey elected 2nd Lieutenant
    Titus V. Brazelton elected Jr. 2nd Lieutenant
10 February 1863: Company E   Joseph W. West elected Jr. 2nd Lieutenant
12 February 1863: The following changes occurred in the Twenty-seventh Regiment:
Company C: Thomas A. Grace elected Captain
    William W. Johnson elected 1st Lieutenant
    William M. Ross elected 2nd Lieutenant
    L. C. Futrell elected Jr. 2nd Lieutenant
    Columbus M. Newberry elected Jr. 2nd Lieutenant
23 February 1863: The following changes occurred in the Twenty-seventh Regiment:
Company F: Robert C. Bailey elected 1st Lieutenant
    James Shirah elected 2nd Lieutenant
    Warren F. Waters elected Jr. 2nd Lieutenant
5 March 1863: Company A: William A. J. Teat elected Jr. 2nd Lieutenant
13 March 1863: Sergeant Simon K. Watkins of Company C died in Guinea Station, Virginia.
16 March 1863: The following changes occurred in the Twenty-seventh Regiment:
Company K: Calvin Calhoun elected 1st Lieutenant
    A. C. McCrory elected 2nd Lieutenant
    Freeman Walker elected Jr. 2nd Lieutenant
1 April 1863: Lieutenant Alfred S. Hall, - Company I, died.
6 April 1863: Private F. M. Pate of Company E died of Typhoid Dysentery in Chimborazo Hospital #1 at Richmond, Virginia.
27 April 1863: The Twenty-seventh Georgia Regiment took up a line of march toward Chancellorsville, Virginia.
28 April 1863: The Twenty-seventh Georgia Regiment arrived at Chancellorsville, Virginia.
29 April 1863: The Twenty-seventh Georgia Regiment is engaged this evening at Wilderness Church.
30 April 1863: The Twenty-seventh Georgia is engaged again at Wilderness church.
May 1863: Private Jacob Scofield of Company B died in Rapidan River, Virginia.
Private D. C. Hagan of Company I died in Richmond, Virginia.
1 May 1863: *The Battle of Chancellorsville, Virginia:*
The Twenty-seventh Georgia Regiment is engaged at Wilderness Tavern.

Number 382.

Report of Brigadier General A. H. Colquitt, C. S. Army, Commanding Brigade.

NEAR FREDERICKSBURG, May 15, 1863.

SIR: Herewith I submit a report of the part taken by my brigade in the recent engagement at Chancellorsville and the affairs connected with it.

On the morning of April 29, intelligence being received that a portion of the Federal Army had succeed in crossing the river near Fredericksburg, my brigade was put under arms and marched to Hamilton's Crossing. Under cover of a hill, protected from the enemy's artillery, we lay during the day, and at 3 o'clock next morning took position upon a line of temporary entrenchments in front of the enemy. At intervals during the day a fire of artillery was opened upon us, but without effect.

At dawn on the morning of May 1, we took up the line of march, and, after proceeding 6 or 7 miles above Fredericksburg, came upon a portion of our forces who had been engaging the enemy. Discharges of our forces who had been engaging the enemy. Discharges of artillery and musketry were still heard. The division being formed in line of battle, my position was upon the right. In this order we advanced a few hundred yards, when my command was thrown into some confusion by coming in contact with the troops of General McLaws' command, formed perpendicular to my own line. The line being rectified, we began again to advance, when instructions were received that we should halt and await future orders. The skirmishers, moving in advance, picked up 15 or 20 prisoners. At sundown we were withdrawn to the Plank road and continued the march for 2 or 3 miles, when we bivouacked for the night.

Early the next morning we were again put in motion, my brigade in front and, turning to the left from the Plank road leading from Fredericksburg to Orange Court-House, it was obvious that we were aiming for the flank and rear of the enemy. On reaching the furnace, 1 mile distant from the point of divergence, I detached, by order of General Jackson, a regiment (the Twenty-third Georgia, Colonel [E. F.] Best), with instructions to guard the flank of the column in motion against a surprise and to call, if necessary upon any officer whose command was passing for re-enforcements. For the subsequent action and fate of this regiment, I refer to the accompanying report of Colonel Best.

After a circuitous march of 6 miles, we again reached the Plank road, which we had left. My brigade was placed in ambush along the line of the road, with the expectation that some demonstration would be made by the enemy's cavalry. In the meantime the division filed past, and I closed in upon the rear.

At 4 o'clock we reached the road running through Chancellorsville to -- --. Here we formed line of battle, my brigade upon the right, and uniting with Doles upon the left. In this order we advanced for a few hundred yards, when intelligence was communicated to me by the skirmishers that a body of the enemy was upon my right flank. I ordered a halt, and called back the Sixth Georgia, which had continued to advance. The regiment upon the right (the Nineteenth Georgia) was quickly thrown into position to meet any demonstration upon the flank, and ordered to advance about 100 yards to the summit of a hill. The enemy's force proved to be a small body of cavalry, which galloped away as soon as the regiment advancing toward was discovered, and a picket of infantry, which was captured by my skirmishers. All apprehension in this quarter being allayed, we advanced again to the front, to renew connection with the line that had preceded us. As we emerged from the woods into an open field, I discovered Doles' brigade hotly engaged with the enemy at his works. With a shout, and at a double-quick, we moved to his support, but before we reached musket range the enemy broke in confusion and fled. I halted in the open field, and brought up two of my regiments which had been delayed in crossing a creek and in climbing its steep banks. It was now nearly dark, and too late for further action.

At 10 o'clock I relieved the brigade of General McGowan, watching a road leading to one of the enemy's main positions, and detailed the Sixth Georgia Regiment to support a battery in front. During the night, the alarm being given, my whole command was moved to the support of the battery, and was subjected at intervals to a fierce artillery fire from the enemy.

Early the ensuing morning, I took my position in line of battle on the extreme right, and, in pursuance of orders, was advancing upon the enemy's position, when I received orders to move to the support of General Archer, a guide being furnished to direct me to him. I had proceeded but a short distance when I was ordered to repair in haste to the extreme left of our line, where the enemy threatened to turn our flank. I had scarcely reached the new position when I was again ordered to the right, and thence again to the left.

While our forces were occupied in the assault on Chancellorsville, the enemy sought to assail them in flank, and made desperate efforts to regain possession of the turnpike. It was to defeat this object that my brigade was thrown to the left. Forming line of battle parallel to the road, I advanced in face of a severe fire to a line of breastworks from which the enemy had been driven. Here I found the Third Alabama, of Rodes' brigade, and some

Louisiana and South Carolina regiments stubbornly resisting his advance. They had well nigh exhausted their ammunition. Upon my arrival they withdrew, producing some confusion in rushing through my ranks; it was momentary, however. Advancing beyond the breastworks, we opened a furious and well-directed fire upon the enemy. The contest was sharp and fierce for a few moments. I ordered a charge, which was responded to with a shout and at double-quick. The enemy broke and fled in confusion, throwing away arms, accouterments, and every incumbrance. We continued the pursuit for half a mile, killing and capturing many, and driving the fugitives into their fortifications in rear of Chancellorsville. Coming to a halt, we lay under cover of woods within 400 yards of their works for four or five hours. Some demonstrations being made upon my left, the brigade of General Lane was sent to my support. Previously the Fiftieth Virginia [?], Captain Mathews,* and a detachment of a South Carolina [Alabama] regiment, under Major [A. M.] Gordon, had joined me as re-enforcements. The enemy did not show himself again outside of his works.

At 4 p. m. I was relieved by the division of Major General A. P. Hill, under the command of General Pender. We took position soon after in the trenches about Chancellorsville, where we lay until ordered back to our camp near Grace Church.

Colonels [Charles T.] Zachry, [John T.] Lofton, [Tully] Graybill, and [A. J.] Hutchins led their regiments with spirit and energy.

Captain [G. G.] Grattan, assistant adjutant-general, and Lieutenant [James] Randle, aide-de-camp, were indefatigable in their efforts and conspicuously bold in the discharge of their duties.

Mr. H. H. Colquitt, acting upon my staff, bore himself with spirit and coolness.

Especial credit is due Captain William M. Arnold, Sixth Georgia Regiment, who commanded the battalion of skirmishers. His energy, zeal, and gallantry won my admiration.

A. H. COLQUITT,
Brigadier-General

No. 386

Report of Col. C. T. Zachry, Twenty-seventh Georgia Infantry

CAMP NEAR GUINEY'S STATION, Virginia

May 8, 1863

CAPTAIN: I have the honor to submit the following report of the operations of this regiment from April 29 to May 6, inclusive:

Shortly after 8 a.m. on the 29th, I received orders to march to the field beyond Mr. Dickinson's. In ten minutes I proceeded, in heavy marching order, to the indicated point. Half an hour later, the other regiments of the brigade having arrived, I proceeded with the brigade to the open field to the right of Hamilton's crossing, where we remained in line of battle throughout the day and bivouacked at night. Before day I moved to the front, occupying with the Twenty-eighth Georgia a rifle-pit in front of two batteries, my right reaching the road leading from Guiney's to Hamilton's Crossing. Here I remained till before day on the 1st instant (Friday).

From 5 till 7 p.m. on the 30th, we were under a heavy shelling, which injured no one, but convinced many that they had exaggerated ideas of the danger of shells.

Before day Friday morning (1st), we marched about 6 miles in a westerly direction till we struck the Plank road leading from Orange Court-House to Fredericksburg, resting twice. We took the left end of the Plank Road. Artillery and musketry could now be distinctly heard about 1 mile in front. Proceeding about that distance, we halted, loaded, unslung knapsacks, faced to the right, and advanced in the order of battle about 1 mile, passing two lines of General McLaws' troops. The brigade during this move wheeled to the left.

About 7 p.m. we returned to the Plank Road; marched up it to where the road leading to Spotsylvania Court-House diverges, and bivouacked.

Early on the 2nd (Saturday), we were on the march again. Proceeding half a mile, we turned to the left off the Plank road, and marched around to the west of Chancellorsville; formed a line of battle, facing eastward. This march was a trying one to the men; the day was very warm; many fell out of ranks exhausted, some fainting and having spasms; only a few had eaten anything since the morning before. About 6 o'clock in the evening, the order for an advance was given. We moved forward through thick woods, a portion of the ground swampy and boggy. In the worst of this ground, being crowded by the regiment on my left changing direction several degrees to the right I had to halt and rectify my alignment. The enemy's skirmishers were being driven in by ours, advancing rapidly; a loud shout ran along the whole line. The enemy gave us a well-directed fire of shell, grape and shrapnel. On our left and in front the battle roared fiercely. Emerging from the woods, we hastened at double-quick diagonally across the Plank road to where Doles was driving the enemy. We reached the opposite woods just after dark. My loss was10 wounded and1 killed.

About an hour after dark we were moved down the Plank road 7 of 8 rods into the woods. About 10 o'clock in the night a furious fire of musketry and artillery was opened in our front. The enemy had the range of our position; the shelling was terrific; 2 of my men were wounded.

A few moments afterward all was quiet again, and I was moved across the road under the crest of a small hill; had been there but a short while when the firing was renewed for a few minutes.

Early Sunday (3d) morning, the enemy renewed his furious cannonade. We moved back to the open field and to the extreme right; advanced in the order of battle through dense woods the distance of half a mile; then by a left-flank and file-left movement we came out and moved to the extreme left of the field, a distance of about 1 1/2 miles. After a halt of about ten minutes, we moved back toward the right, till we came upon the road diverging from the Plank road nearly at right angles; moved on this road in the direction of Plank road about the length of the brigade by the left flank; then by the right flank till I came to an abandoned breastwork of the enemy; then by the left flank till I came to the Plank road; broke by files to the right on the Plank road; faced to the left in the order of battle, my line parallel to the road; changed front, forward obliquely, facing the river, and advanced several hundred yards, when I came upon a regiment of Thomas' brigade, A. P. Hill's division, lying down, receiving and returning hot fire. Passing over them I fired two rounds, and calling on Captain (W. M.) Arnold, commanding skirmishing battalion, who was on my right, to support me, I ordered a charge. With a shout my men dashed forward, putting the enemy to flight, pursuing him to the edge of the field, near his fortifications, when I was ordered back.

My loss in this action was 18 wounded and 2 killed.

About 4 p.m. we were relieved by General A. P. Hill, and moved to the rifle- pits on the right of the burned house at Chancellorsville. Next morning we took position at the works on the road leading to United States Ford. While here (Monday and Tuesday) we were twice shelled vigorously for a short time by the enemy. Wednesday we marched back to camp, arriving about 10 p.m.

Lieut. George W. Lathem, commanding Company S, and Lieut. William P. Edwards, commanding Company F, attracted my attention by their coolness and the prompt discharge of their duties upon the field.

I inclose a list of names of enlisted men who were reported to me by company commanders for coolness and gallantry. I append a list of causalities.

I have the honor to be, very respectfully, your obedient servant,

C. T. ZACHRY,
Colonel.

Capt. G. G. GRATTAN
Assistant Adjutant-General.
(Inclosure.)

Names of enlisted men who distinguished themselves in the Twenty-seventh Georgia Regiment in the late battles: Company E, Privates A. L. Dodd, John J. Buffington, G. M. Dodd, A. J. Whitaker, James Laster,

Thomas J. Horton. Company G, Privates James T. Reeves, J. C. Curtice. Company H, Sergts. J. B. Bryans, T. J. Dukes; Corpl. B. P. Pryor; Privates B. F. Norris, G. W. Rape, J. M. Lindsey, John H. Lewis. Company F, Sergt. James Shirah. Company C, Sergts. J. Murchison, W. A. Webb; Corpls. L. C. Fentrell, C. M. Newberry; Privates H. Newberry, M. Merritt, J. Hoskins, J. Worsham, W. G. Clary, Simon Johnson. Company K, Private William Connel.

C. T. ZACHRY,
Colonel   Twenty-seventh   Georgia

Regiment.
2 May 1863:

Killed:	Private Henry McCullers – Co. F
Wounded:	Corporal Peter Stewart - Co. A
	Private Robert D. Cody - Co. A
	Private James T. Self – Co. B
	Private Enos M Causey, Co. C
	Private J. C. Sanders – Co. D
	Private J. J. Chambers - Co. E (died of wounds)
	Private T. J. Horton - Co. E
	Private Robert S. Cameron - Co. K
	Private John Crapps - Co. I
	Private Charles M. Douglas Co. I

Private Beverly Carter of Company D died of Catarrh in Chimborazo Hospital at Richmond, Virginia.

3 May 1863:

Wounded:	Sergeant Rufus A. Dodson - Co. A
	Private John R. Flurry - Co. A
	Lieutenant John Burnett - Co. B
	Corporal l. L. Murray – Co. B
	Corporal Vincent E. Walton – Co. B
	Private David Kite – Co. E
	Private Enoch Barfield - Co. F
	Corporal James R., Jordan – Co. G
	Corporal John S. Sullivan – Co. G
	Sergeant James H. Darnell- Co. H
	Private William Childs - Co. H
	Private J. W. Hearn – Co. H (died of wounds)
	Private Lewis Hill – Co. H
	Private J. M. Lindsey – Co. H
	Private L C. McMullen – Co. H
	Private John Taylor – Co. H
	Private Joseph W. Baxley - Co. I
	Private William Burke - Co. I
	Private L. Johnson – Co. I
	Private William Connell - Co. K

4 May 1863: The Twenty-seventh Georgia Regiment returned to their winter quarters at Guinea's Station, Virginia.

5 May 1863: Organization of the Army of Northern Virginia:

General Robert E. Lee, Commanding

Lieutenant General Thomas J. Jackson - Commander, 2nd Corps

Brigadier General R. E. Rhodes - Co.-Commander, Hill's Division

Brigadier General S. D. Ramseur - Co.-Commander, Hill's Division

Brigadier General Alfred H. Colquitt - Commander, Colquitt's Brigade

Colonel Charles T. Zachry - Commander, 27th Georgia Regiment

The causality list for the Battle of Chancellorsville, Virginia lists the following for the Twenty-seventh Georgia Regiment; 2 killed, 39 wounded; 1 captured, total causalities 42.

Killed:
- Private Eli Mackey – Co. A
- Private John Alexander - Co. B
- Private George Vane - Co. I

Wounded:
- Lieutenant C. W. Smith – Co. A
- Lieutenant Eli Stewart – Co. A
- Lieutenant William A. J. Teat – Co. A
- Private Andrew Jackson Rogers – Co A
- Private S. W. Bryant - Co. A
- Private T. L. Sims – C0. B
- Private G. W. Dullin - Co. F.
- Private Thomas S. Norris – Co. F
- Private D. H. Williams - Co. F
- Private William H. C. Slade - Co. G
- Private John Crapps - Co. I
- Corporal James M. McLendon - Co. I
- Private J. M. Connell - Co. K

Captured:
- Private William J. Williams – Co. A

Lieutenant W. C. Dodson of Company A died.

James B. Gardner elected Major

20 May 1863: Colquitt's Brigade ordered to Proceed by rail to Goldsboro, North Carolina and report for orders to Major General D. H. Hill commanding.

25 May 1863: George T. Embry appointed Chaplain

28 May 1863: The Twenty-seventh Georgia Regiment arrived in Kinston, North Carolina and reported to General D. H. Hills Command.

22 June 1863: Twenty-seventh Regiment engaged in building works at Kinston, North Carolina (Correspondence from Brigadier General A. H. Colquitt to General D. H. Hill).

27 June 1863: The Following changes occurred in the Twenty-seventh Regiment.

Company F:
- James Shirah elected 1st Lieutenant
- Warren F. Waters elected 2nd Lieutenant
- B. A. Freeman elected Jr. 2nd Lieutenant

30 June 1863: Organization of Department of North Carolina:
Major General Daniel H. Hill, Commanding
Brigadier General Alfred H. Colquitt - Commander, Colquitt's Brigade
Colonel Charles T. Zachry - Commander, 27th Georgia Regiment
1 July 1863: Colquitt's Brigade in Goldsboro, North Carolina.
A dispatch form J. A. Seddon, Secretary of War, C. S. A. in Richmond orders to General Colquitt :
"'.....You will move your Brigade by railroad, as soon as practicable, to this city. This order is at General Hill's insistence, he being some miles from the city, in command........."
Company E: Pitt M. McLeroy elected 2nd Corporal.
3 July 1863: The Twenty-seventh Georgia ordered back to Richmond to repel an anticipated raid of the Federals.
4 July 1863:

Weldon, July 4 1863
Hon. James A. Seddon, Secretary of War,

Have halted my Brigade here; gone into camp and will await instructions.

A. H. Colquitt
Brigadier General.

Richmond, Va., July 4, 1863
General Colquitt, Weldon, N. C.:

Come here with your Brigade with all dispatch. We are threatened seriously.

J. A. Seddon
Sec. of War
5 July 1863: Dispatch from D. H. Hill to James A. Seddon: "....I would suggest that Colquitt be placed on the Meadow Bridge..............."
6 July 1863: Raleigh, July 6 1863

Z. B. Vance to James A. Seddon
".......Please send Colquitt's Brigade or part of it to this city immediately. A heavy cavalry force is threatening us, and we have no telegraphic communications north of south..............."
The Twenty-seventh Georgia Regiment arrived in Richmond, Virginia.
10 July 1863: Colquitt ordered to Wilmington, North Carolina to report to General Whiting.
11 July 1863:

Wilmington, July 11, 1863
W. H. C. Whitting to D. H. Hill
".....Hurry Colquitt's Brigade......"
20 July 1863: The following changes occurred in the Twenty-seventh Regiment.
Company A: Robert Patton elected Captain
              Eli Stewart elected 1st Lieutenant
              Joseph Harrison Little elected 2nd Lieutenant
21 July 1863: The Twenty-seventh Georgia Regiment arrived in Wilmington, North Carolina.
22 July 1863: The Twenty-seventh Georgia Regiment is ordered to Topsail Sound.
31 July 1863: Company I: Silas A. Crosby elected 2nd Lieutenant
3 August 1863: Twenty-seventh Georgia Regiment - Major James Gardner commanding
Effective Total - 363   Total Present - 414
10 August 1863: The Twenty-seventh Georgia Regiment is on Pickett duty at Topsail Sound. The Regiment is ordered to report to General Beauregard at Charleston, South Carolina.
13 August 1863: The Twenty-seventh Georgia Regiment arrived in Charleston, South Carolina and marched to James Island.
28 August 1863: The Twenty-seventh Georgia Regiment is ordered to Morris Island.
30 August 1863: The Twenty-seventh Regiment reported to General A. H. Colquitt on Morris Island, South Carolina this night under the command of Major James Gardner with the following strength. 27 Commissioned Officers, 42 Non-Commissioned Officers and 155 Privates for a total of 224.
31 August 1863: Organization of the Department of South Carolina, Georgia and Florida:
General G. T. Beauregard, Commanding
Brigadier General Roswell S. Ripley - Commander, District
Brigadier General W. B. Taliaferro - Commander, 1st Sub-District
Major James Gardner - Commander, 27th Georgia Regiment.
Colonel Alfred Rhett - 4th Sub-Division
Captain Hezekiah Bussey - Commander, Co. B, 27th Georgia (detached)
1 September 1863: The Twenty-seventh Regiment under the command of Major James Gardner is on Morris Island, South Carolina. Effective strength of the regiment (as per General Colquitt's report) was 27 Commissioned Officers, 42 Non-Commissioned Officers, 150 Privates for a total of 219.
Battery Wagoner, Morris Island, South Carolina
Killed: Private Isham Gaines - Co. G
Wounded: Private Alexander - Co. H
2 September 1863: The Twenty-seventh Regiment under the command of Major James Gardner is positioned on the Beach at Morris Island, South

Carolina in front of Battery Wagner. Effective strength 27 Commissioned Officers, 42 Non-Commissioned Officers, 145 Privates for a total of 214.

3 September 1863: Forces on Morris Island, South Carolina include the following:

27th Georgia - 24 commissioned officers, 38 non-commissioned officers and 151 privates on duty

6 September 1863: *Battery Wagner – Morris Island, South Carolina The Withdrawal – The Rear Guard:*

The Twenty-seventh Georgia Regiment covers the retreat of the Confederate forces from Morris Island during the evacuation of Battery Wagner. The Twenty-seventh Georgia lost 2 killed and 4 wounded from July 10, 1863 to September 6, 1863.

Wounded:	Private Adam Hagler – Co A
	Private J. A. Cape - Co. B
	Private Columbus Robinson – Co. C
	Private Robert S. Cameron - Co. K
Captured:	Private Alexander Stewart – Co. A

7 September 1863: Charleston, South Carolina - Major James Gardner is shown commanding the Twenty-seventh Regiment after the evacuation of Morris Island. The Regiment is assigned to Garrison duty at Fort Sumter, South Carolina.

8 September 1863: Fort Sumter, S. C.

Wounded: Private G. W. Amerson - Co. F

10 September 1863: Company D: Wiley Rouse elected 3rd Sergeant

20 September 1863: Organization of the Department of South Carolina, Georgia and Florida:

General G. T. Beauregard, Commanding

Brigadier General Robert S. Ripley - District Commander

Brigadier General William B. Taliferro - Commander, 1st sub District

Major James Gardner - Commander, 27th Georgia Regiment

13 October 1863: Fort Sumter, S. C.

Wounded:	Private R. W. J. Nail - Co. H
	Private William J. St. John - Co. H

23 October 1863: James Island, South Carolina: A private from Company D was apprehended for stealing a watermelon. He was "bucked and gagged' as punishment. Several members of his company participated in freeing him from his bonds. Subsequently they were all brought up on charges and were scheduled for Court Martial (the charges were later dropped).

1 November 1863: Organization of the Department of South Carolina, Georgia and Florida:

General G. T. Beauregard, Commanding

Brigadier General William B. Taliferro - Commander, 7th District

Brigadier General Alfred H. Colquitt - Commander, Western Division

Colonel Charles T. Zachry - Commander, 27th Georgia Regiment

The following changes occurred in the Twenty-seventh Regiment.
Company E: Joseph W. West elected 2nd Lieutenant
                                  William C. Reeves elected Jr. 2nd Lieutenant
                                  Seaborn V. Abercrombie appointed 3rd Sergeant

2 November 1863: Twenty-seventh Georgia Regiment at Fort Sumter, South Carolina.

3 November 1863: Fort Sumter, South Carolina
Wounded: Private E. R. Douglas - Co. I
                                  Private William B. Eastes - Co. E

4 November 1863: Fort Sumter, South Carolina (Morris Island, South Carolina.)
Wounded: Private Columbus Robinson – Co. C
                                  Private John A. Smith - Co. D
                                  Private William B. Estes - Co. E
                                  Private James Chambers - Co. E
                                  Private J. R. Morris - Co. E
                                  Private I. R. Stephens - Co. E
                                  Private B. F. Morris - Co. H

6 November 1863: Fort Sumter, South Carolina; The fort is bombarded by the U. S. Ironsides and 4 Monitors. Causalities for the Twenty-seventh were 2 killed, 12 wounded, - 14 total.

14 November 1863:
Wounded: Private William Ments – Co. H
                                  Private James R. Wilson – Co. K

19 November 1863: Reports indicate that Twenty-seventh Georgia Regiment at Fort Sumter, South Carolina.

25 November 1863: Ford Sumter continued to be bombarded by monitors.
Wounded: Private J. A. Smith – Co. D
                                  Private J. R. Morris- Co. E
                                  Private B. F. Morris- Co. H.

27 November 1863: Records indicate that the Twenty-seventh Georgia Regiment still at Fort Sumter, South Carolina.

1 December 1863: John M. Zachry appointed Commissary Sergeant

9 December 1863: Fort Sumter, South Carolina
Wounded: Private Joseph M. Hemphill - Co. D
                                  Private Abraham Little - Co. D

11 December 1863: Fort Sumter, South Carolina
Wounded: Private S. Hodges – Co. H

12 December 1863: Fort Sumter, South Carolina
Killed: Private J. S. T. Ford - Co. G
Wounded: Private John C. Calhoun - Co. A
                                  Private W. Dunning, Co. A

13 December 1863: Fort Sumter, South Carolina
Killed: Private T. Ford - Co. G

Wounded:	J. Hodge - Co. A.
	W. F. Dannan - Co. A
	J. C. Calhoun - Co. A
	J .Hamphill - Co. C
	W. Dunning - Co. H

16 December 1863: Fort Sumter, South Carolina - Twenty-seventh Regiment lost their blankets in a fire.

18 December 1863: Fort Sumter, South Carolina
Wounded: Sergeant John B. Copeland - Co. G

22 December 1863: Records indicate that the Twenty-seventh Georgia Regiment on duty at Fort Sumter, South Carolina.

31 December 1863: Organization of the Department of South Carolina, Georgia and Florida:
General G. T. Beauregard, Commanding
Brigadier General Johnson Hagood - Commander, 1st Sub District
Colonel Charles T. Zachry - Commander, 27th Georgia Regiment
Twenty-seventh Regiment commanded by Colonel Charles T. Zachry temporarily detached from Colquitt's Brigade and assigned to the 1st Sub-District.

1863: Private S. T. Arnold of Company A died.

8 January 1864: Private Daniel J. Phillips of Company I died in Charleston, South Carolina.

1864

18 January 1864: Private C. M. Douglas of Company I died in Charleston, South Carolina.

23 January 1864: The strength of the Twenty-seventh Georgia Regiment is shown as: 605 men, 10 Companies.

31 January 1864: Organization of the Department of South Carolina, Georgia and Florida:
General G. T. Beauregard - Commanding
Brigadier General William B. Taliferro - Commander, 7th District
Brigadier General Alfred H. Colquitt - Commander, Colquitt's Brigade
Colonel Charles T. Zachry - Commander, 27th Georgia Regiment

8 February 1864: Colquitt's Brigade ordered to report to Major General Gilmer at Savannah, Georgia.

10 February 1864: The Twenty-seventh Georgia Regiment on the march to Rantowles, South Carolina. Colonel Zachry is relieved at Fort Johnson, South Carolina.
Charleston: Colonel Zachry's (27th) regiment, with 3 days provisions will move at 3 in the morning to the support of Gen. Wise on Johns Island.

11 February: Company C Captain Thomas A. Grace resigned his commission.

12 February 1864: The Twenty-seventh Georgia marched for John's Island, arriving just in time to assist General Wise in driving the Federal troops from their position on the Island.

14 February 1864: Colquitt's Brigade sent to Lake City, Florida. The troops were boarded on the Charleston and Savannah railroad to Savannah, Georgia and thence boarding the Atlantic and Gulf railroad for Valdosta, Georgia.

15 February 1864: The Twenty-seventh Georgia Regiment arrived in Valdosta, Georgia.

16 February 1864: The Twenty-seventh Georgia Regiment began a march to Madison, Florida

17 February 1864: The Twenty-seventh Georgia Regiment along with the other regiments of Colquitt's Brigade boarded the Tallahassee and Jackson railcars for the trip to Olustee Station, east of Lake City, Florida.

20 February 1864: *The Battle of Olustee (Ocean Pond), Florida:*
The Federal Troops under Brigadier General Truman Seymour had pushed westward from a position near the present city of Jacksonville, Florida toward the interior of the state with the intention of cutting the rail line from the southern part of Florida into Georgia and to the northern states of the Confederacy. Their aim was to inhibit the supply of goods, mainly beef to the Confederate Army. On this date the division of Federal troops met with a force of Confederate troops under Brigadier General Joseph Finegan, commander of the District of East Florida about two miles east of Olustee Station. General Finegan had been re-enforced with two brigades, one of which was General Alfred H. Colquitt's (including the Twenty-seventh Georgia Regiment). The Federals were drawn into a narrow pine barren along the Florida, Atlantic & Gulf Railroad that was located between a natural lake known as Ocean Pond and a dense swamp. (Reports indicate that scouts from the Twenty-seventh Georgia Regiment had discovered the presence of the Federal troops.) A fierce Battle then ensued. The Twenty-seventh Georgia was held in Reserves until about four o'clock p.m. Colonel Charles T. Zachry led the Twenty-seventh Georgia Regiment into the center of the line. The hardened veterans of the battles in Virginia immediately charged, breaking the enemy in front and contributing greatly to the utter rout of the Federals. The rout was so complete that the Federal division left the dead and wounded in the field.

General Colquitt from this day was to be known as the "Hero of Olustee" and Colonel Zachry was named "Blucher" (Field Marshall) of the Battle of Olustee.

No. 20.

Report of Brig. Gen. Alfred H. Colquitt, C. S. Army, commanding
First Brigade, of engagement at Olustee.
BALDWIN, FLA., *February 26, 1864*
            CAPTAIN; I have the honor to submit the following

account of the engagement of the 20th instant, near Ocean Pond:

Intelligence having been received of the approach of the enemy, I was instructed to take three regiments of my own brigade, with a section of Gamble's artillery, and proceed to the front and assume command of all the forces which had preceded me, consisting of two regiments of cavalry, under command of Colonel Smith; the Sixty-fourth Georgia Regiment, and two companies of the Thirty-second Georgia Regiment. Subsequently other troops were sent forward, and I was directed to call for such re-enforcements as might be needed.

About 2 miles from Olustee Station I found the enemy advancing rapidly and our cavalry retiring before them. I threw forward a party of skirmishers and hastily formed a line of battle under brisk a fire form the enemy's advance. The Nineteenth Georgia was placed on the right and the Twenty-eighth Georgia on the left, with a section of Captain Gamble's artillery in the center. The Sixty-fourth Georgia and the two companies of the Thirty-second Georgia were formed on the left of the Twenty-eighth, and the Sixth Georgia Regiment was sent still farther to the left to prevent a flank movement of the enemy in that direction. Instructions were sent to Colonel Smith, commanding cavalry, to place his regiments on the extreme flanks and to guard against any movement of the enemy from either side.

The line of infantry was then ordered to advance, which was gallantly done, the enemy contesting the ground and giving way slowly. Perceiving the enemy were in strong force, I sent back for re-enforcements and a fresh supply of ammunition. The Sixth Florida Battalion and the Twenty-third Georgia soon arrived for my support. The Sixth Florida Battalion was formed on the right of the Nineteenth Georgia and in such position as to come in on the left flank of the enemy. The Twenty-third Georgia was put on the left of the Sixty-fourth Georgia. Colonel Harrison, coming up with the Thirty-second and First Georgia Regulars, took position on the left, between the Twenty-third and Sixth Georgia Regiments, and was instructed to assume the general direction of the left side of the line.

The section of Gamble's artillery in the center having been disabled by the loss of horses and injury to limber, Captain Wheaton, who had early arrived on the field with the Chatham Artillery and had take position on the right was ordered to the center to relieve Captain Gamble. The battery moved forward and took position under a heavy fire, and continued to advance with the line of infantry until the close of the action. Toward night, when Captain Wheaton's ammunition was almost expended, a section of Guerard's battery, of Harrison's brigade, under Lieutenant Gignilliat, moved up and opened fire on the enemy, furnishing Captain with part of his ammunition.

After our line had advanced about one-quarter of a mile the engagement became general and the ground was stubbornly contested. With two batteries of artillery immediately on our front and a long line of infantry strongly supported, the enemy stood their ground for some time, until the Sixth Florida Battalion, on the right flank, with all the troops in front pressing steadily forward, compelled them to fall back and leave five pieces of artillery in our possession. At this time, our ammunition beginning to fail, I ordered the commanding officers to halt their regiments and hold their respective positions until a fresh supply could be brought from the ordinance wagons, which, after much delay, had arrived upon the field.

Major Bonaud's battalion came upon the field, followed soon after by the Twenty-seventh Georgia Regiment and the First Florida Battalion. These troops were put in position near the center of the line and a little in advance, to hold the enemy in check until the other commands could be supplied with cartridges. As soon as this was accomplished I ordered a general advance, at the same time sending instructions to Colonel Harrison to move the sixth and Thirty-second Georgia Regiments around on the right flank of the enemy. The Twenty-seventh Georgia Regiment, under Colonel Zachry, pushing forward with great vigor upon the center, and the whole line moving as directed, the enemy gave way in confusion. We continued the pursuit for several miles, when night put an end to the conflict. Instructions were given to cavalry to follow close upon the enemy and seize every opportunity to strike a favorable blow.

The results of the engagement in the killed, wounded, and prisoners of the enemy and our own loss will be found in the reports rendered directly to you.

The gallantry and steady courage of officers and men during the last engagement are beyond all praise. For more than four hours they struggled with unflinching firmness against superior numbers until they drove them in confusion and panic to seek safety in flight.

Col. George P. Harrison, who commanded on the left, displayed skill, coolness, and gallantry. The commanding officers of the various regiments did their duty nobly. Colonel Evans, commanding Sixty-fourth Georgia, and Captain Crawford, commanding Twenty-eighth Georgia, both gallant officers, were wounded. Lieutenant Colonel Barrow, of Sixty-fourth Georgia, a brave and gallant officer, received a fatal shot while gallantly attempting to rally his men. Captain Wheaton and the officers and men of his battery are entitled to special commendation for their courage, coolness, and efficiency. Captain Grattan, assistant adjutant-general; Lieutenant Colquitt, aide-de-camp; Major Ely and Lieutenant Estill, of my staff, were active and conspicuous in every part of the field. My thanks are due to Lieutenant Thomson, Second Florida Regiment, and Mr. Sterling Turner, volunteer aids, for their gallant services.

The names of those in the ranks entitled to be particularly mentioned may by furnished in a subsequent report.

Very respectfully, your obedient servant.

A. H. COLQUITT
Brigadier-General

Captain CALL,
Assistant Adjutant-General

Killed:

Private Samuel Hargroves - Co. B
Private William Parker - Co. B
Private G. W. Perdue - Co. B
Private Isaac Poole - Co. B
Sergeant James W. Avera - Co. C
Private Michael Merritt - Co. C
Private Julius T. Sawyer - Co. C
Private Leroy J. Creel - Co. E
Private W. M. Foster - Co. E
Private Josiah Hart - Co. E
Private Wesley Barfield -Co. F
Private W. Green Holland - Co. F
Private Josiah N. Williams - Co. G
Private John Cooner - Co. I
Sergeant James Carlisle - Co. K
Private Michael Carlisle - Co. K

Wounded:

Private William F. Carlisle - Co. B
Captain Robert Patton – Co A.
Lieutenant George E. Wise – Co. H
Private Samuel Hargrove – Co. B
Private Isaac Poole – Co. B (died of wounds)
Privaate Nelson Thomas – Co. B
Private George Walton - Co. B
Sergeant Benjamin F. Kennedy - Co. C
Sergeant John Murchison – Co. C
Sergeant W. A. Webb - Co. C
Sergeant Green C. Whittington - Co. C
Corporal James Martin Wilson - Co. C
Corporal John W. Worsham - Co. C
Private William Averett - Co. C
Private Enos M. Causey - Co. C
Private Obediah E. Daniel - Co. C
Private James G. Fitzpatrick - Co. C
Private A. R. Harrison – Co. C
Private Franklin H. Hartman - Co. C
Private Julius Hoskins – Co. C
Private John W. Smith – Co. C
Private Job J. Webb - Co. C
Private Allen Yawn - Co. C
Corporal Thomas C. Russell - Co. E
Corporal D. T. Jennings - Co. E
Private William R. Cook - Co. E
Private J. C. Creek - Co. E
Private Leroy J. Creel - Co. E
Private W. A. J. Denson - Co. E

Private Josiah Hart – Co. E.
Private Franklin Hartman – Co. E (Died of Wounds)
Private James W. Milam – Co. E
Private William H. Norton – Co. E
Private Thomas L. Todd - Co. E
Private Andrew J. Whitaker - Co. E
Captain William Posey Edwards - Co. F
Lieutenant Benjamin Freeman - Co. F
Lieutenant James Shirah – Co. F
Sergeant John Hart - Co. F
Corporal Wesley Barefield - Co. F.
Private J. M. Duke - Co. F
Private James P. Lawson - Co. F
Private Thomas S. Norris – Co. F
Private Smith Turner - Co. F
Private Robert Marion Whittington - Co. F
Lieutenant Henry T. Lifsey - Co. G
Private Benjamin F. Ganous - Co. G
Private William R. M. Jones - Co. G
Private Thomas Zachry Jones – Co. G
Lieutenant Wade H. Harper - Co. H
Private Elijah W. Harper – Co. H
Private W. T. Harper - Co. H
Private Solomon King - Co. H
Private D. R. Lewis – Co. H
Private Daniel N. Lindsey - Co. H
Private J. M. Lindsey – Co. H.
Private John C McClendon - Co. H
Private J. Robert McCullough - Co. H
Private Augustus J. Peek – Co. H
Private P. F. Stewart – Co. H
Private John Taylor - Co. H
Corporal James M. McLendon - Co. I
Corporal Ohen. F. Carter - Co. I
Private Benjamin Leggett - Co. I
Private Benjamin Franklin Hutto – Co. I
Private A. H. Thomas – Co I
Lieutenant Freeman Walker – Co. K
Private Wesley F. Belyen - Co K
Private Robert S. Cameron - Co. K
Private E. J. Colley - Co. K
Private Thomas Hardy – Co. K

26 February 1864: William T. Dennis elected Sergeant Major
28 February 1864: Lovet W. Baxley appointed 2nd Corporal - Co. I
1 March 1864: *The Battle of Cedar Creek, Florida:*

The Twenty-seventh Georgia along with the Eleventh South Carolina and a force of cavalry were near Cedar Creek reconnoitering when they met a Federal force. The commander, Colonel Charles T. Zachry of the Twenty-seventh Georgia, gave the order to attack. In a short time the Federals were routed and retreated to the east. In subsequent reports it appears that if the Confederate cavalry had executed Colonel Zachry's orders, the entire Federal force would have been taken prisoner instead of being allowed to retreat.

Killed: Private Joseph Moore - Co. D
                       Private Joseph H. Tanner - Co. D
                       Private Francis Marion Hale – Co. H
                       Private F. M. Nail – Co. H

Wounded: Private James S. Brazile - Co. D
                       Private William C. Thomas - Co. D

3 March 1864: The Twenty-seventh Georgia Regiment is camped at Camp Milton, Florida.

8 March 1864:
Wounded: Lieutenant. William A. J. Teat of Co. A

15 March 1864:
Wounded: Private William S. Phelps of Co. A

16 March 1864: Lake City, Florida
                       Private William C. Thomas - Co. D died in Lake City Florida
Killed: Private Francis Marion Hale - Co. H

29 March 1864: James Wilson Clements transferred to the Twenty-seventh Regiment as a Hospital Steward.

1 April 1864: The following changes occurred in the Twenty-seventh Regiment:
                       Lieutenant Colonel Jasper N. Dorsey Resigned
                       James B. Gardner elected Lieutenant Colonel
                       Hezekiah Bussey elected Major

7 April 1864: Fort Sumter, South Carolina
Wounded: Private William H. Hall - Co. B
                       Private Jesse Shinholster - Co. F

16 April 1864: A dispatch form Jno. Otley, Asst. Adjutant General to Brigadier General Taliaferro on this date orders Colquitt's Brigade to Hatch's Point, South Carolina (near Charleston).

18 April 1864: Brigadier General Alfred H. Colquitt ordered to move his brigade from Fort Milton, Florida via Callahan, Trader's Hill, Tebeauville, and Savannah to Charleston and report on arrival there to the general commanding Department of South Carolina, Georgia, and Florida. They marched to Tebeauville and boarded the rail cars on the Atlantic and Gulf railroad for the trip to Savannah.

21 April 1864: The Twenty-seventh Georgia Regiment is ordered to James Island, South Carolina.

25 April 1864: A dispatch from General Beauregard to General Bragg states that "Colquitt's Brigade is on James Island", South Carolina.

30 April 1864: Organization of the Department of South Carolina, Georgia and Florida:

Major General Samuel Jones, Commanding
Major General Patton Anderson - Commander, District of Florida
Brigadier General Alfred H. Colquitt - Commander, Colquitt's Brigade
Colonel Charles T. Zachry - Commander, 27th Georgia Regiment
Richard V. Cobb elected 1st Lieutenant - Company D

1 May 1864: The following changes occurred in the Twenty-seventh Regiment:

Company K	Calvin Calhoun elected Captain
	A. C. McCrory elected 1st Lieutenant
	Freeman Walker elected 2nd Lieutenant

2 May 1864: Jesse B. Pye elected Adjutant

3 May 1864: Colquitt's Brigade ordered to Richmond, Virginia and transferred to the Army of Northern Virginia. The Twenty-seventh Georgia garrisoned at Fort Sumter, South Carolina along with the Sixth and Nineteenth Georgia.

5 May 1864: Colquitt's Brigade transferred to the Army of Northern Virginia.

Organization of Forces in the Richmond and Petersburg Lines:
General Robert E. Lee, Commanding
General G. T. Beauregard - Commander, Department of North Carolina and Southern Virginia
Brigadier General Alfred H. Colquitt - Commander, Colquitt's Brigade
Lieutenant Colonel James Gardner - Commander, 27th Georgia Regiment

10 May 1864: Organization of the Forces in the Richmond and Petersburg Lines:
General G. T. Beauregard, Commanding - Department of N. C. and S. Va.
Brigadier General Alfred H. Colquitt commander - Colquitt's Division
Colonel Charles T. Zachry commander - Colquitt's Brigade
Lt. Colonel James Gardner commander - 27th Georgia Regiment

11 May 1864: The Twenty-seventh Georgia Regiment is on James Island, South Carolina and is ordered to Charleston.

12 May 1864: The Twenty-seventh Georgia left Legare's Point this morning. Colquitt's Brigade arrived at Petersburg, Virginia and were engaged in battle with Federal cavalry.
Private Samuel Hargroves of Company B - Wounded

13 May 1864: The Twenty-seventh Georgia Regiment arrived at Weldon, North Carolina to re-enforce to troops there in anticipation of a raid by Federal forces.

16 May 1864: *The Second Battle of Drewry's Bluff, Virginia (Fort Darling):*

With a force of 39,000 union troops under the command of Major General Benjamin F. Butler seriously threatening both Richmond and Petersburg form a position on the peninsula between the James and

Appomattox rivers, three Confederate divisions were sent to defend the critical position. General Colquitt was in command of a division so the command of Colquitt's Brigade devolved to Colonel Charles T. Zachry. With Colonel Zachry commanding the Brigade Lieutenant- Colonel James Gardner was in command of the Twenty-seventh Georgia.

Initially the Twenty-seventh Regiment was deployed in reserve but was brought into the action at Swift Creek early in the morning in support of General Ransom's Division. Later the brigade was recalled to assist General Hoke in repulsing the Federal Troops. There is no listing for the Causalities for the Twenty-seventh Regiment, but the following is the report for Colquitt's Brigade; 11 men killed - 17 officers wounded, 129 men wounded, 146 wounded - total causalities 157.

(The following is an excerpt from the May 23, 1864 report of Major General Robert Ransom, Jr. on the activities of May 16, 1864 around Drewry's Bluff, Virginia).

"..............I sent to General Beauregard for fresh troops to continue the pressure upon the enemy. Before these fresh troops arrived and before we had gotten ammunition, the enemy made a vigorous and telling assault upon Hoke's left, driving hastily toward the intermediate line to the right of Fort Stevens. At once Colonel Lewis was ordered to throw the only regiment he had in hand at the double-quick to that point, which was handsomely done, and he engaged the enemy long enough to allow Colquitt's Brigade, of the reserve, to arrive, and it was at once thrown to the same point and rapidly attacked and drove back the enemy. Arrangements were at once made to perfect our line, and so soon as it was the order to advance was given. Just at this juncture I received orders from General Beauregard to send Colquitt's brigade to the right, as it was badly needed there. This brigade being now in the front line and engaging the enemy, it could not be detached, and I ordered Barton's to the right in its stead........"

Colquitt's Brigade suffered the following losses; 11 men killed, 17 officers wounded, 129 men wounded - 157 total.

19 May 1864: The Twenty-seventh Georgia Regiment is assigned a position the front lines between the James and Appomattox rivers.

20 May 1864: Special Order No. 9 - Brigadier General Colquitt's Brigade to Relieve Gracie's Brigade.

The Twenty-seventh Georgia Regiment is in a line of battle, in reserve about six miles from Petersburg, Virginia north of the Appomattox River.

21 May 1864: Organization of Hoke's Division:

Major General Robert F. Hoke - Commander, Hoke's Division

Brigadier General Alfred H. Colquitt - Commander, Colquitt's Brigade

Colonel Charles T. Zachry - Commander, Twenty-seventh Georgia

A report of the strength of Colquitt's Brigade indicates that out of 2900 soldiers there were:

122 officers, 1433 men - 1596 total.

The Twenty-seventh Georgia Regiment was moved to the front line in some rifle pits. They remained there all day and night. There was a severe skirmish on the left of their line.

22 May 1864: The Regiment moved to the right of their position and threw up a breast works. In his diary Washington L. Dunn of Company A states that: "We threw up some very good works."

23 May 1864: The Twenty-seventh remained in the line of battle all day. There was a little picket fight on the right.

25 May 1864: " There was some skirmishing all day and at night there was a right smart little fight on our left." (Washington L. Dunn, Company A)

26 May 1864: A dispatch from Jno. Richardson to D. H. Hill states that Colquitt's Brigade occupying a temporary line.

28 May 1864: Private George Roland Thompson of Company H died.

30 May 1864: Just before night the pickets of the Twenty-seventh advanced to find the enemy's position. "We went till we came in sight of their works and then we fell back to our line. Our works are a right smart piece apart. We found out how their line ran and then we fell back." (Washington L. Dunn, Company A)

31 May 1864: The Twenty-seventh Regiment ordered to Cold Harbor. They marched to the halfway station between Richmond and Petersburg and boarded the train for Richmond.

".......We arrived at Richmond about 9 or 10 and then we started toward Mechanicsville. We went through it and went on to Cold Harbor and when we got to Cold Harbor the enemy was driving our Cavalry in and we arrived there just in time to save our position and all the good positions close by. We arrived here about sunset. We formed in line of battle and some of the brigade went to work and threw some breast works up. Our company was on picket. We were not engaged tonight, Hoke's Division formed in line of battle here and Colquitt's Brigade formed in line of battle on some of the same ground they fought on in '62 at the Seven Days fight. We acquired a good position............." (Washington L. Dunn, Company A)

1 June 1864: *The Second Battle at Cold Harbor, Virginia:*

".........All quite till 8 a. m. when a brisk skirmish took place on our left and the left of the brigade was engaged. The enemy charged our men but was repulsed. Then our brigade went to work and threw up a breast works. Co. A is still on Picket on the flank and in the evening the Yankees shelled us severely. The skirmishing of Martin's Brigade ran the enemy's Picket in and their brigade formed on our right, and they went to work and by the next morning they had a very good breast works thrown up, with bayonets and shingles. Their works were six feet across the top. About five or six o'clock this evening the enemy charged Clingman's Brigade and took a portion of their breast works, so there was a gap open that the enemy was flanking of them. Five companies of the 27th were sent to retake them. The 28th was sent to support them; but both the 27th and the 28th rushed right into their works before they knew it and the Yankees ordered them to surrender; but they would not. They fought them for some time. They saw that they could not stay there, so our men came out, but lost a good many men. The regiment suffered severely in the charge. It was a severe charge........." (Washington L. Dunn, Company A)

Five companies of the Twenty-seventh Regiment charged and re-captured a portion of the Confederate line that had been lost by the left of General Clingman's Brigade. The causalities for the five companies were: eleven (11) killed and fifty-four (54) wounded. The following is a partial list of the causalities:

Killed:
Private G. M. Brown - Co. B
Private T. J. Skipper- -Co. B
Sergeant John C. Murchison - Co. C
Private R. N. Clary - Co. C
Sergeant Asa L. Dodd - Co. E
Private John Futch -Co. E
Private Henry F. Norris - Co. E
Lieutenant Henry T. Lifsey - Co. G
Private T. Jefferson Howard - Co. G
Sergeant D. M. Livingston - Co. I

Wounded:
Lieutenant John Wesley Forrester - Co. B
Private Stansbury B. Evans - Co. B
Sergeant James T. Gregory - Co. C
Private Sanders Bond - Co. C
Private John Q. Campbell - Co. C
Private Enos M. Causey - Co. C
Private Obadiah E. Daniel - Co. C
Private Elbert Merritt – Co. C
Private Benjamin F. Newberry – Co. C
Private Robert Jackson Roland Co. C
Private Robert Sanders - Co. C
Private J. J. Webb – Co. C
Lieutenant John T. Abercrombie - Co. E
Sergeant Seaborn V. Abercrombie - Co.
Private George D. Creel - Co. E
Private W. A. J. Denson - Co. E
Private James H. Waller - Co. E
Private William J. Williams – Co. E
Private William Henry Parks – Co. F
Lieutenant William H. Ross – Co. G
Sergeant James R. Jordan - Co. G
Private James J. Beckham - Co. G
Private John M. Burns - Co. G
Private Thomas P. Hagan - Co. G
Private James S. Lifsey - Co. G
Sergeant Iverson B. Bryans - Co. H

Sergeant J. B. Bryans - Co. H
Private William M. Childs - Co. H
Private John Pickney Copeland, Jr. - Co. H
Private J. P. Hilley – Co. H
Private Richard M. Wilson - Co. H
Private Owen F. Carter, Co. I

Captured:
Private Green Lambert - Co. B
Private W. G. Hancock - Co. C
Private Robert Jackson Roland - Co. C

2 June 1864: Cold Harbor, Virginia
"............A portion of our company fell back in the line and went to fortifying the line to fall back to in time of a charge. They worked like it was for life, which it came as near as any that I saw before. There have been several charges on our left and one on our life, and there was one severe one about four miles on our left. I have not heard the result of it, though we've repulsed them here with great slaughter. There was some skirmishing all night. I believe we've held ours on all the line........." (Washington L. Dunn, Company A).

The following changes occurred in the Twenty-seventh Regiment:
Company G: John D. Jones elected 1st Lieutenant
        Joseph C. Chapman elected Jr. 2nd Lieutenant

3 June 1864: Cold Harbor, Virginia:
"............This morning the enemy made a general attack on right and left and in front of us; they did not come closer than our rifle pits. They were repulsed with heavy loss, and on the right we killed all the field officers of one regiment and took one stand of colors; we took a good many prisoners. At night General Martin wanted to take his rifle pits back; so, half after 7 o'clock his brigade fired two volleys and then his pickets charged and some of them took their works, while some failed; so they all had to fall back And, at the same time the enemy charged Colquitt's Brigade. They were repulsed with heavy loss. Then our pickets of our brigade fell back without letting our Company know of it; so our Regiment fired into our Company, but did not hurt any of them........." (Washington L. Dunn, Company A).

Wounded:
Private Seaborn S. Lesueur - Co. G
Private Marion Pickney Harkness - Co. H
Private Elijah W. Harper – Co H
Private M. L. Noland – Co. H
Private G. Frank Stallsworth – Co. H
Corporal William H. Drew - Co. K

4 June 1864: Cold Harbor, Virginia
"............The sharp-shooters are very numerous. The enemy made an attack on our left, but was repulsed with heavy loss. Captain Grattan was wounded and lost his leg........" (Washington L. Dunn, Company A).

Wounded:
Private James F. Cain - Co. B
Private Thomas M. Brown - Co. B

Private T. G. Pate – Co. B (later died of wounds)
Private R. N. Clary - Co. C
Private Wiley G. Clary - Co. C
Private S. E. Cook - Co. E
Private John C. Belyen - Co. K
Private T. B. Higgins – Co. C
Private m. M. Minchew – Co. B

5 June 1864: Cold Harbor, Virginia
Wounded: Private Bradford A. Johnson – Co. F
Private Isaac Hightower – Co. H

6 June 1864: Cold Harbor, Virginia
"...........The sharp-shooters continued all day and in the early evening the enemy made another charge on our left, but they were repulsed, and at night there was another charge on the line. Captain Patten came in from Georgia and brought a recruit with him. M. Gordon came in, that left us at Charleston. There was a flag of truce came in this evening to bury their dead.........." (Washington L. Dunn, Company A).
Wounded: Private Harrison P. Schofield – Co. B
Private Robert M. Warren – Co. B
Private H. Pennington – Co. E (shell)
Private W. Callaway Nolan – Co. H
Private M. L. Nolen – Co. H
Private John M. Burnes - Co. I

7 June 1864: Cold Harbor, Virginia
"...........No engagement today more than sharp-shooters. There was another flag of truce sent in this evening for them to finish their burying their dead, they just threw dirt on their dead as they lay. Colquitt's Brigade was relieved tonight and we went out about one mile to rest........." (Washington L. Dunn, Company A):
9 June 1864: Cold Harbor, Virginia
Killed: Private Charles T. Smith – Co. K
Wounded: Private James H. Waller – Co. E
Private A. Howard Sealy – Co. K

10 June 1864: Cold Harbor, Virginia
The Twenty-seventh Georgia Regiment went back to the front line tonight.
Killed: Private Andrew J. Whitaker - Co. E
13 June 1864: The regiment left Cold Harbor and marched to Malvern Hill, Virginia.
"......This morning when day came, we saw that the enemy had left our front and it was supposed they had gone in off Malvern Hill. We all went over their battle field and picked up some guns and perused their works and about 8 a. m. we started and marched towards Malvern Hill. We marched very hard till night, passing through the Seven Pines battle field, marching near Malvern Hill and then we stopped and stayed for the night. We did not

lose but very few men at Cold Harbor, except the times our men charged the enemy; but the enemy charged our works a great many times and was repulsed very nearly every time, with heavy loss on their side. There was a little fight on or near Malvern Hill today. We drove them back or repulsed them..........." (Washington L. Dunn, Company A).

Sergeant W. Callaway Nolan of Company H died in Richmond, Virginia.

Private J. P. Hilly of Company H died in Richmond, Virginia.

14 June 1864: The regiment left Malvern Hill for Richmond, Virginia.

15 June 1864: At twelve o'clock midnight the regiment marched to Chester Station, on the Richmond and Petersburg railroad, and boarded railcars for Petersburg, Virginia.

"............we arrived in Petersburg about night and we heard and saw that the enemy had whipped what troops we had here and had taken our batteries from No. 1 to No. 9 or 10. We marched on towards the Yankees and we formed in line of battle in one mile of the city. We found no troops or pickets in our front. The men went to work with bayonets and tin cups and two spades and by morning they had a very good breast works. Company A had to go on picket. We had advanced about a quarter mile from our line of battle and there we found the Yankees fixing to deploy their pickets. We fired on them and drove them in and then one of the New Hampshire Regiments advanced on us but we held them in check till morning. We dug some little rifle pits to protect us next morning. We did not get a man hurt tonight. I do not believe they have many troops at those breastworks they took from us..........." (Washington L. Dunn, Company A).

Lieutenant Robert C. Evans of Company H died in Petersburg, Virginia.

16 June 1864: "............Company A is on picket out in front of the 27th and in 200 yards of the Yankee breast works that they took from us. At daybreak the Yanks advanced on the skirmishers of Haygood's brigade. They were repulsed the first time; but they advanced their line of battle and drove our men in and then we had to fall back and they had the advantage of us. As we fell back they played on us with their line of battle and Artillery. One of Company A. was seen shot down and there are six more missing; they are either wounded or prisoners; we do not know which. Captain Patten is amongst the missing.

We fell back to the breast works and took our position in the breast works and we had to keep pickets in the front. I was one that was on picket. I was under as hard a shelling as I ever was, or very near it. I saw a trying time out there on picket. This evening the Yankees made several charges on the right of our line; but they were repulsed with heavy loss. The Yankees took the Richmond Railroad today; but they did not hold it............" (Washington L. Dunn, Company A).

Private James F. Cain of Company B died of amputation of the right arm in Richmond, Virginia.

Wounded: Sergeant John C. Calhoun - Co. A
Captured: Captain Robert Patton, - Co. A.

Private, George T. Murphey - Co. A

Private J. M. Towns – Co.- K

June 1864: *The Siege of Petersburg, Virginia - Colquitt's Salient:*

The Twenty-seventh Regiment ordered to hold an important salient in the line of defense. They again entrenched themselves and waited.

"............There has been very disagreeable sharp-shooting today. There have been several engagements today and they took our breast works on our right. They ran out Wise's Brigade and took their works and Clingman's Brigade retook them. About twelve o'clock in the night our men moved back and established a new line to get a better position............" (Washington L. Dunn, Company A).

The following changes occurred in the Twenty-seventh regiment:

George M. Chafin appointed Ensign

Company H   John M. Zachry elected 1st Lieutenant

18 June 1864: On this evening, the Federal army charged the position of the Regiment in three heavy columns. The Twenty-seventh repulsed them heavily. They were forced to leave their dead, over two hundred in number, in the field of battle. The regiment was to hold "Colquitt's Salient" for the next six days alone and without relief.

".........We went to work as soon as we arrived on our new line. We went to work as there was but little don to it; we worked for life and at day break here they came yelling as they thought that Petersburg they were bound to have. They shelled us very much and they came and charged our brigade with several columns; but they were repulsed with heavy loss. They came up and established their line in 200 yards of our line of battle and their batteries came up right in front of four pieces of ours and planted them, in spite of our boys. The sharp-shooters were very bad all day; we lost a good many by sharp-shooters today........." (Washington L. Dunn, Company A).

Wounded on this date was Lieutenant Colonel James Gardner who died of his wounds in a few days. The causality list for the stand at "Colquitt's Salient" was seventy-six (76) killed and wounded.

Killed: Lieutenant Colonel James B Gardner

Sergeant James T. Gregory - Co. C

Corporal Frederick Hutto - Co. C

Corporal W. S. McNiece - Co. C

Corporal John W. Worsham - Co. C

Private J. Wesley Mitchell - Co. C

Private Andrew J. Whitaker - Co. E

Lieutenant Robert C. Evans - Co. H

Sergeant W. Callaway Nolan - Co. H

Private J. P. Hilly - Co. H

Private William H. Nelson - Co. I

Private William Storey - Co. I

Sergeant William Calhoun - Co. K

Private George H. Matthews - Co. K

Private Charles T. Smith - Co. K

Wounded: Sergeant Jesse T. Avant - Co. B

Private J. A. Cape - Co. B

Private James M. Jordan – Co. B

Private James M. Jordan – Co. B

Lieutenant William M. Ross - Co. C

Private James Henry Newberry – Co. C

Private John N. Wilder – Co. C

Lieutenant John F. Dorsey - Co. D

Private J. M. Whelchel – Co. D

Private Hiram M. Laseter - Co. E

Private Wesley Cape - Company H

Private Wesley Crapps – Co. H (died of wounds)

Private J. A. Nash – Co. H

Private R. J. Nail - Co. H

Private George W. Rape - Co. H

Private Joseph A. Crapps - Co. I

Corporal James M. McLendon - Co. I

Private Benjamin F. Carlisle - Co. K

Private George F. Cole - Co. K

Private Thomas D. Goodwin - Co. K

Private George Y. McDowell - Co. K

Private A. H. Sealey - Co. K

Private E. J. Colley of Company K died of Pneumonia in Ladies General Hospital #3 at Columbia, South Carolina. The report of Union Colonel George H. Sharpe states that; ".....Colquitt's Brigade retired to 1/2 mile this side of Petersburg....."

19 June 1864: Colquitt's Salient--Near Petersburg, Virginia.

"........There has been very disagreeable sharp-shooting all day on both sides but the Yankees have an invading fire on our line and have killed and wounded a good many. Thomas Harrel was wounded in shoulder, the Yankees are busy working; the enemy has a mortar that they shell us with............." (Washington L. Dunn, Company A).

20 June 1864: Colquitt's Salient

Killed: Sergeant William Calhoun - Co. K

Wounded: First Sergeant James C. Adams - Co. G

Corporal John W. Robinson–Co C (died of wounds July 5))

Private W. L. Hutto – Co. C

Private William H. Hayes – Co. D

Private Joseph A. Watson – Co. D

Private T. J. Horton – Co. E

Private S. Lasiter – Co. E

Corporal James R. Jordan – Co. G

Private James C. Adams – Co. G

Private B. F. Herrin – Co. H

Private Jasper William Mason – Co. H (drummer)
Private L. Whit Russell – Co. H (drummer)
Private William H. Nelson – Co. I
Private Henry D. Bedell - Co. K

21 June, 1864: Colquitt's Salient
Wounded: Private Obediah E. Daniel - Co. C.

22 June 1864: Colquitt's Salient
Wounded: Sergeant Thomas A. Harrell – Co. A
23 June 1864: Private Stanberry Evans of Company B died in Richmond, Virginia.
24 June 1864: The Twenty-seventh Georgia relieved at Colquitt's Salient after holding the position for seven days.
".........This morning Haygood's Brigade, or a portion of it, was going to charge the Yankee breast works to see if they had much force. The 27th and 6th Georgia were drawn up to be ready to charge if those other troops succeeded in taking the works, we were going to charge. Haygood's men charged and the Yankees jumped out on the breast works and told them to come along. There were some went on to try the Yankees and they could not take their works so they fell back. They lost a good many men, killed, wounded, and captured. I did not like the thought of going over those breast works. Sergeant G. W. Chapman was shot in the head and killed dead. E. Williams shot himself in the hand............" (Washington L. Dunn, Company A)
The following changes occurred in the Twenty-seventh Regiment:
         William H. Renfroe elected Major
Company E   John J. Buffington elected 2nd Lieutenant
         Robert W. Mason appointed 1st Sergeant
Captured: Private Israel Abraham - Co. B
25 June 1864: Lieutenant Colonel James B. Gardner died of wounds this date.
Private T. G. Pate of Company B died in Division #1 Jackson Hospital at Richmond, Virginia.
27 June 1864: The Twenty-seventh Georgia returns to Colquitt's Salient near Petersburg, Virginia with Colquitt's Brigade.
Killed: Private James R. Wilson – Co. K
Wounded: Sergeant Jeptha D. Newton - Co. F
The following change occurred in the Twenty-seventh Regiment:
Company K   William T. Dennis elected Jr. 2nd Lieutenant
26 June 1864: Private William H. Nelson – Co. I died of wounds in C. S. A. Hospital, Petersburg, Virginia.
30 June 1864: Colquitt's Salient - Near Petersburg, Virginia.
".........The Yankees made an attack on our right late this evening; but they had better sense than to charge our works. We whipped them again on the extreme right of our line and we took a good many prisoners and three

hundred negroes. Colquitt's Brigade was relieved off the front line tonight. We went near the city to rest............" (Washington L. Dunn, Company A). The Twenty-seventh Georgia is relieved at Colquitt's Salient. Colquitt's Brigade is relieved by Martin's Brigade with Colonel Zachry commanding. A report indicates that losses to Colquitt's Brigade on this date were 4 men killed, 3 officers wounded, 24 men wounded - 31 total.

Wounded: Private W. J. Deans - Co. C
                              Private Eli Pierce – Co. E
                              Sergeant D. J. Newton – Co. F

2 July 1864: The Twenty-seventh Georgia Regiment relieved Haygood's Brigade on the Petersburg line.
Private Anthony Lavender of Company F died of Typhoid Fever in Richmond, Virginia.

3 July 1864: Private Asa Gordy of Company G died in Richmond, Virginia.

4 July 1864: The Twenty-seventh Georgia returns to Colquitt's Salient Petersburg, Virginia, with Colquitt's Brigade.

Killed: Private Warren Reeves - Co. G
                              Private James R. Wilson - Co. K
Wounded: Private William T. Donnan - Co. A
                              Private B. F. Avant - Co. B
                              Private William J. Grisham - Co. G
                              Private Cornelius Barber - Co. I
                              Private Henry Mann - Co. I

5 July 1864: Colquitt's Brigade relieved Martin's Brigade at Colquitt's Salient.

6 July 1864: Colquitt's Salient-- Near Petersburg, Virginia.
"..................There has been a good many shells thrown today, and several men have been killed and wounded in our regiment. William Dennan of Company A was wounded in arm and side and had to have it cut off................" (Washington L. Dunn, Company A).
The Twenty-seventh Georgia is relieved at Colquitt's Salient. Colquitt's Brigade is relieved by Martin's Brigade commanded by Colonel Zachry.

8 July 1864: Colquitt's Salient:
Wounded: Private P. S. Strawn – Company E
                              3rd Sergeant John Hart – Company F

9 July 1864: The Twenty-seventh Georgia returns to Colquitt's Salient Petersburg, Virginia with Colquitt's Brigade.
                              James Wilson Clements appointed Assistant Surgeon
Wounded: Corporal Pitt M. McLeroy - Company E
                              Private Henry Mann, Jr. – Company I

10 July 1864: Colquitt's Salient:
Wounded: Lt. Colonel James B. Gardner

11 July 1864: The following changes occurred in the Twenty-seventh Regiment:

Company C   William W. Johnson elected Captain
William G. Ross elected 1st Lieutenant

12 July 1864: Colquitt's Brigade relieved at Colquitt's Salient by Martin's Brigade under Colonel Zachry.

15 July 1864: The Twenty-seventh Georgia returns to Colquitt's Salient with Colquitt's Brigade. The Brigade was assailed at what was known by the Federals as Hare's Hill which was south of City Point Road.
Wounded: W. J. Davis - Company A

18 July 1864: Colquitt's Brigade relieved at Colquitt's Salient by Martin's Brigade under Colonel Zachry.

21 July 1864: The Twenty-seventh Georgia returns to Colquitt's Salient with Colquitt's Brigade.
Private Simeon P. Lawhorne of Company A died of Measles in Division #1 Hospital at Richmond, Virginia.

24 July 1864: Colquitt's Brigade relieved at a Colquitt's Salient by Martin's Brigade under Colonel Zachry.
Wounded: G. W. Denning - Company A
Lt. Colonel James B. Gardner died of wounds on this date.

27 July 1864: The Twenty-seventh Georgia returns to Colquitt's Salient with Colquitt's Brigade.

30 July 1864: *The Battle of the Crater - Petersburg, Virginia:*
"............This morning about day break our men were surprised on our right by a blow up by Grant, he blew up a place from 40 to 60 ft. long and 30 ft. wide and 20 ft. deep, covering up a portion of 4 companies and a Battery. They charged so soon there were some of them covered up in the dirt. Their guns opened all the way on the line and it was kept up very near all the day. The Yankees captured a good position of our line and held it "Till Evening." They were driven out by our men, by several times charging. We captured our line and over one thousand prisoners and 14 stands of Colors and a good many negroes. Their loss is estimated to 3500 and our (loss) to 800 or 1000. It was a very hot day; the weather was very warm and it was warm with shells and balls......" (Washington L. Dunn, Company A).
Colquitt's Brigade relieved at Colquitt's Salient by Martin's Brigade under Colonel Zachry.
In a report of the Eighteenth Corps of the United States Army a deserter informed them that Colonel Charles Zachry of the Twenty-seventh Georgia was now in command of Martin's Brigade.
Wounded: Private Robert H. Kellum – Co. K

1 August 1864: Private W. T. Donnan of Company A died.

2 August 1864: The Twenty-seventh Georgia returns to Colquitt's Salient with Colquitt's Brigade.

5 August 1864: Colquitt's Salient - Near Petersburg, Virginia.
"..........There is some excitement about blowing the Yankees up. Beauregard blew them up in front of Gracie's Brigade and they shot them as they ran

out; but they did not make any charge. I do not know the results of the blow up. It threw dirt very high. James Highsmith was mortally wounded in the head today............." (Washington L. Dunn, Company A).
Colquitt's Brigade relieved at Colquitt's Salient by Martin's Brigade under Colonel Zachry.

Killed: Private J. T. Highsmith – Company A
Wounded: Private Warren Reeves – Company G (died of wounds)

8 August 1864: The Twenty-seventh Georgia returns to Colquitt's Salient with Colquitt's Brigade.
9 August 1864:   Colquitt's Salient - Near Petersburg, Virginia.
"...........We are in our breast works today. Lieutenant Shirah - Company F was killed today. Everything is quiet on the line today........." (Washington L. Dunn, Company A).

Organization of the Army of Northern Virginia:
Robert E. Lee, Commanding
General G. T. Beauregard - Commander, Department of North Carolina and Southern Virginia
Major General Robert F. Hoke - Commander, Hoke's Division
Brigadier General Alfred H. Colquitt - Commander, Colquitt's Brigade
Major Hezekiah Bussey - Commander, 27th Georgia Regiment

10 August 1864: Colquitt's Salient
Wounded: Private James M. Puckett – Company I
11 August 1864: Colquitt's Brigade relieved at Colquitt's Salient by Martin's Brigade under Colonel Zachry.
Lieutenant James Shirah of Company F died.
The following changes occurred in the Twenty-seventh Regiment:
Company F Warren F. Walters elected 1st Lieutenant
Company C B. A. Freeman elected 2nd Lieutenant
13 August 1864: Company H Wade A. Turner elected Jr. 2nd lieutenant
14 August 1864: The Twenty-seventh Georgia returns to Colquitt's Salient with Colquitt's Brigade.
15 August 1864:
Private J. W. Carter of Company E died of Diarrhea and Fever in Jackson Hospital at Richmond, Virginia.
Private R. J. Tate of Company H died in Richmond, Virginia.
17 August 1864: Colquitt's Brigade relieved at Colquitt's Salient by Martin's Brigade under Colonel Zachry.

18 August 1864: *The Battle at Weldon Railroad (Globe Tavern), Virginia:*
"..........On the eighteenth of August, while the Twenty-seventh Georgia was in reserve, the enemy took possession of the Weldon and Petersburg railroad, when the Twenty-seventh was ordered to the point attacked by the enemy, and engaged them on the evening of the same day......." (Heroes and Martyrs of Georgia by James Folsom).
"..............We are out near Petersburg. It rained today and about 1 o'clock

P. M. we received orders that the Yankees were on the Weldon Road, about 4 miles from the city and we received orders to go there and we started something after one and marched down on the road, and, as we formed our line of Battle, the Yankees raised a yell and charged some troops in front of ours; but they were repulsed. Our men drove them back a mile or more. We, Colquitt's Brigade, formed awhile before. The Yankees advanced a time or two but did not come near our line. About 9 o'clock our line fell back; at 10 o'clock our pickets fell back to our breast works and Colquitt's Brigade went near the Iron Bridge. We did not get to rest much tonight. I know they can't get further tonight.........." (Washington L. Dunn, Company A).

Killed: Private Bluford Sapp - Co. I
Wounded: Private William H. Slade - Co. G
                              Corporal Henry C. Downs - Co. K

Lieutenant Wade W. Harper of Company H, resigned his commission.

19 August 1864: Weldon Railroad, Virginia:

General Colquitt ordered an attack on the flank of 5th Corps near City Point, Virginia about 3:p.m.

"...........this regiment formed a portion of a flanking party, who inflicted a heavy loss on the enemy in killed and wounded. Many Prisoners were taken.

The Twenty-seventh Georgia on this occasion, was under the command of Major. H. Bussey. Owing to the natural features of the country, consisting as they did of thickly wooded spots, with a very dense undergrowth, it was impossible to preserve intact the advancing line of battle, large gaps would frequently be made of our lines, through which the enemy would make their way in detached parties, so that friend and foe would become thoroughly intermingled, and of necessity the fighting was very desperate, being sometimes hand to hand. It was an occasion which required great coolness and decision on the part of the commanding officers. The whole regiment was several times in imminent danger of being captured, inspired however, by the unwavering coolness and intrepid valor of their leaders, these war-worn and battle-scarred veterans of many a bloody field would rally with enthusiasm around their tattered battle flag, and drive back with severe loss the advances of their assailants. A heavy rain having fallen a short time before the battle opened, and continuing to fall during its progress, the soil had become miry and slippery; The Twenty-seventh Georgia however, with other regiments of the brigade, making a gallant charge, drove the enemy with great slaughter from his entrenched line. Night put an end to the contest. The loss in killed and wounded in the Twenty-seventh Georgia was thirty and twenty were taken prisoners. To compensate for this loss, besides the number of the enemy killed and wounded, a very large number of prisoners were taken; even the ambulance corps, in addition to attending to the wants of the wounded, captured eighty (80) Prisoners......"(Heroes and Martyrs of Georgia - James

M. Folsom).

"............We started and left here about 12 o'clock and went to our work near the railroad and it rained very heavy, and after the rain was over Colquitt's and Clingman's Brigades went down on the left and A. P. Hill went down on the railroad in front of the enemy. We marched in the rear of the enemy's lines and until our left struck them and then we advanced and charged them for about two miles and drove them one or two lines before us with but little trouble, and we came up to one of their lines of battle that caused us to see a good deal of trouble. They flanked our Brigade on the left and they took a good many of our Brigade and Clingman's Brigade prisoners, but we recaptured them and took 2 or 3 thousand prisoners. We did not do but little fighting and we got badly scattered. I do not think that there were many killed on either side. There is one of Company A missing; we supposed he is killed or captured; one other slightly wounded, and, also Lieutenant Teat shot through the thigh. The Yankees held their position in the front and still hold the road. Colquitt's and Clingman's Brigades went back to Petersburg............" (Washington L. Dunn, Company A).

Heavy losses were inflicted upon the Federals in killed and wounded. Many Federal prisoners were taken. Losses to the Twenty-seventh Georgia were;

Killed:	Lieutenant John F. Burnett - Co. B
	Private J. Anderson Reynolds - Co. D
Wounded:	Lieutenant William A. J. Teat - Co. A
	Corporal Nathaniel Wesley Myrick - Co. A
	Private Robert D. Cody - Co. A
	Private Samuel L. Rook – Co. A
	Sergeant John B. Walton - Co. B
	Corporal Vincent Everett Walton - Co. B
	Sergeant W. A. Webb - Co. C
	Private Joshua Aultman - Co. C
	Private H. T. Altman - Co. C
	Private J. C. Creel - Co. E
	First Sergeant David N. Bloodsworth - Co. F
	Private William B. Rogers – Co. F
	Private Francis M. Threlkeld - Co. F
	Private Thomas Zachry Jones – Co. G
	Private Augustus N. Powell – Co. G
	Private W. F. Blyer - Co. K
	Private Staten Fulford, Sr. - Co. K
Captured:	Corporal Nathaniel Wesley Myrick - Co. A
	Private Samuel L. Rook – Co. A
	Sergeant William F. Cain - Co. B
	Corporal Vincent Everett Walton - Co. B
	Corporal John W. Bowers - Co. B
	Private William F. Cain - Co. B

Private Henry Henniger - Co. B
Private John M. Page - Co. B
Private C. Thompson – Co. B
Private George Walton - Co. B
Sergeant Charles A. Green - Co. C
Sergeant Micajah Bagwell - Co. D
Lieutenant B. A. Freeman - Co. F
Private Thomas S. Norris -Co. F
Private Francis M. Threlkeld - Co. F
Corporal James D. Carriker - Co. G
Private William J. Colquitt - Co. G
Sergeant J. Henry Carroll - Co. H
Private Benjamin F. Norris - Co. H

20 August 1864: Colquitt's Brigade relieved Ransom's Brigade.

22 August 1864: Colquitt's Brigade relieved some troops on the North of the Petersburg line.

25 August 1864: Petersburg Line - Petersburg, Virginia:
"............We are still on the front line. We fought the enemy on the railroad and took one line of works, 2 thousand prisoners and 8 pieces of artillery........" (Washington L. Dunn, Company A).

27 August 1864: Private Wesley Capps - Company H died of wounds in General Hospital, Petersburg, Virginia.
Wounded: Private John Willoughby - Company B (shell)

30 August 1864: Petersburg Line - Petersburg Virginia:
"...................We were relieved this morning and went out to rest. Wiley Williamson (Wilson) wounded on head. I hear of no more important news.............." (Washington L. Dunn, Company A).

31 August 1864:
Sergeant John Hart of Company F died in Jackson Hospital at Richmond, Virginia.
Company F   William B. Rogers appointed 3rd Sergeant

1 September 1864: Organization of the Army of Northern Virginia:
General Robert E. Lee, Commanding
General G. T. Beauregard - Commander, Department of North Carolina and Southern Virginia
Major General Robert F. Hoke - Commander, Hoke's Division
Brigadier General Alfred H. Colquitt - Commander, Colquitt's Brigade
Colonel Charles T. Zachry - Commander, 27th Georgia Regiment

5 September 1864: Sergeant Benjamin F. Hutto of Company I died of Typhoid in Jackson Hospital at Richmond, Virginia.

9 September 1864: Petersburg Line- Petersburg, Virginia:
"................We are on reserve. I hear of no news interesting. Samuel Blythe was wounded in leg.........." (Washington L. Dunn, Company A).

10 September 1864: Colquitt's Brigade (General Colquitt, commanding) and Martin's Brigade (Colonel Zachry, commanding) in the lines at

Petersburg, Virginia.

".....................We stayed on reserve till night and then went to the front. I hear on no news. Today we have been in Service three years............" (Washington L. Dunn, Company A).

Wounded: Private Samuel L. Blythe - Co. A

14 September 1864: The following changes occurred in the Twenty-seventh Regiment;

Company F Allen E. Cody elected 2nd Lieutenant
Company K Josiah Bunkley Parker elected 2nd Lieutenant

15 September 1864: Petersburg Line - Near Petersburg, Virginia: The Twenty-seventh Georgia Regiment marched up on the right on the Weldon Railroad and camped near Battery 45.

16 September 1864: Private John M. Page of Company B died from amputation in Carver U. S. A. General Hospital Washington, D. C.

18 September 1864: The Twenty-seventh Georgia Regiment moved down near the "waters mark" in Petersburg this morning and put up camp.

19 September 1864: Petersburg, Virginia:

".........Our cooking utensils were brought in today for us to cook our own rations. We have been eating cold rations ever since the 20th of May..........." (Washington L. Dunn, Company A).

22 September 1864: Petersburg, Virginia:

Wounded: Private William Henry Parks – Co. F

26 September 1864: Petersburg, Virginia:

"..........We left the front and went to be on general review. General Lee was out on review. He rode up and down the line and then took his stand and we marched in review and it was a very nice review..........." (Washington L. Dunn, Company A).

27 September 1864: Hezekiah Bussey elected Lieutenant Colonel.

28 September 1864: Corporal John S. Sullivan of Company G died in Richmond, Virginia.

29 September 1864: *The Battle of Fort Harrison, Virginia: (Chaffin's Farm)*

General Ord's Federal forces attacked Fort Harrison which protected Confederate bridges, camps and batteries along the James River. These were the Southern Defenses of the Confederate capital of Richmond, Virginia.

Killed: Private Asberry Washington Cook - Co. E
Wounded: Ensign George M. Chaffin
  Private Jesse A. Walton - Co. B

The Twenty-seventh Georgia Regiment left Petersburg for Deep Bottom on the north side of the James River. They marched for two or three miles and then boarded the train. Two or three miles across the river the regiment left the train. They stopped around 2:00 to 3:00 A. M.

30 September 1864: Colquitt's Brigade launched an attack on the Federal forces that were holding Fort Harrison, Virginia.

"………We marched 2 or 3 miles and stopped near the enemy. We started to charge the fort that they had taken from us and we commenced the charge between 2 and 3. Clingman's Brigade made the charge and Colquitt's supported them, but we charged and they did, but we failed to take the fort and had to fall back. Three regiments of Clingman's Brigade went in to the Yankees. It was a very bad charge and on our side, we lost a good many and had to fall back entirely. It was a bad place as I ever was in. I think it impossible to take a fort at night. We fell back and camped till morning………" (Washington L. Dunn, Company A).

Killed: Private E. W. Cook - Co. F
Wounded: Sergeant John R. Seymore - Co. B
                            Private J. M. Campbell - Co. C
                            Private R. W. Amerson - Co. F
                            Private Warren Amerson - Co. F

1 October 1864: Near Fort Harrison, Virginia:
"…………We went and formed another line of battle and built another breast works. We lost some over 200 in our brigade and about 7 or 8 hundred in all…………" (Washington L. Dunn, Company A).
Private William T. Spinks of Company K died in medical College Hospital at Richmond, Virginia.
Wounded: Private J. C. Sanders – Co. D

2 October 1864: near Fort Harrison:
Wounded: Sergeant C. H. Cape – Co. D
                            Corporal J. M. Duke - Co. F

October 3, 1864:
Wounded: Private Joseph R. Reed – Co. D
                            Private J. T. Snipes – Co. C

October 4, 1864:
Wounded: Private J. Cross - Co. I

6 October 1864: The Twenty-seventh Georgia Regiment marched toward Richmond.

8 October 1864:
Wounded: Private Joseph Avery - Co. H
                            Private William M. Childs - Co. H

11 October 1864: Private B. E. Hutto of Company C died of Chronic Diarrhea in Jackson Hospital at Richmond, Virginia.
19 October 1864: Private James H. Horton of Company G died of disease in Jackson Hospital at Richmond, Virginia.
24 October 1864: Fort Harrison:
Wounded: Private James M. Puckett - Co I
27 October 1864: Richmond - Petersburg Line:
"………The Yankees were trying to flank us and we had to stretch our line for several miles………" (Washington L. Dunn, Company A).
28 October 1864: Richmond - Petersburg Line:
"………They charged our line on the left, but were repulsed. They could

not flank our boys. They charged our line a good many times over about Petersburg and were repulsed with heavy loss. At night we went to the right and stopped. I think Grant is satisfied for the winter......" (Washington L. Dunn, Company A).

31 October 1864: Organization of the Army of Northern Virginia:
General Robert E. Lee, Commanding
Lieutenant General James Longstreet - Commander, 1st Corps
Major General Robert F. Hoke - Commander, Hoke's Division
Brigadier General Alfred H. Colquitt - Commander, Colquitt's Brigade
Colonel Charles T. Zachry - Commander, 27th Georgia Regiment

17 November 1864: Sergeant Samuel H. Hodge of Company H captured.

24 November 1864: The following changes occurred in the Twenty-seventh Georgia:
Company H Captain Robert A. Harkey, resigned his commission
John M. Zachry elected Captain

26 November 1864: William Larkin Williams appointed Hospital Steward

30 November 1864: Organization of the Army of Northern Virginia:
Robert E. Lee, Commanding
General Braxton Bragg - Commander, S. Va. and N. C
Lieutenant General Richard H. Anderson - Commander, Anderson's Corps
Major General Robert H. Hoke - Commander, Hoke's Division
Brigadier General Alfred H. Colquitt - Commander, Colquitt's Brigade
Captain Elisha D. Graham - Commander, 27th Georgia Regiment

4 December 1864: Sergeant T. J. Handcock of Company C died in Richmond, Virginia.

22 December 1864: The Twenty-seventh Georgia Regiment marched to Richmond, crossed the James River and boarded the train bound for Danville, Virginia.

23 December 1864: The Twenty-seventh Georgia Regiment arrived in Danville, Virginia about 3:00 P.M. The trip was about 140 miles.

24 December 1864: The Regiment left Danville, Virginia and marched nine miles to the first station, arriving about 3:00 P. M., they camped for the night.

25 December 1864: A letter from Major General Hoke in Greensboro, North Carolina to General Robert E. Lee states; "......Have ordered Colquitt and Clingman to march here where ample provisions are made for their immediate transport....."

"...........Today is Christmas. This is the fourth Christmas for me in this terrible war. We marched to the second station today. It is named Ruffin Station and it is about 6 miles from the other station. All of our Brigade left here on the train today except three Companies and we stayed all night......" (Washington L. Dunn, Company A).

Colquitt's Brigade sent to Fort Anderson, North Carolina by General

Braxton Bragg.

26 December 1864: The remaining three Companies of the Twenty-seventh Georgia Regiment left Ruffin Station this morning and joined the remainder of the Regiment in Greensboro, North Carolina this afternoon.

27 December 1864: The Twenty-seventh Georgia Regiment left Greensboro and moved to Raleigh, North Carolina today.

28 December 1864: The Regiment moved by rail from Raleigh to Goldsboro to Wilmington, North Carolina today.

29 December 1864: The Twenty-seventh Georgia Regiment took a boat to Fort Anderson from Wilmington and was reunited with the remainder of Colquitt's Brigade

30 December 1864: General Braxton Bragg sent a dispatch to General A. H. Colquitt sending Colquitt's Brigade to Wilmington, North Carolina by steamer. The Brigade went back to Wilmington and set up an encampment.

31 December 1864: Organization of the Army of Northern Virginia:
General Robert E. Lee, Commanding
Lieutenant General Richard H. Anderson - Commander, Anderson's Corps
Major General Robert F. Hoke - Commander, Hoke's Division
Brigadier General Alfred H. Colquitt - Commander, Colquitt's Brigade
Captain Elisha D. Graham - Commander 27th Georgia Regiment

1865

1 January 1865: Colquitt's Brigade encamped at Wilmington, North Carolina.

".........Today it is the First of 1865 and the war is still going on; no prospect for peace. I went foraging today and walked about 15 miles and I made out to get my dinner. Our rations we drew today was (sorgum) Chiney Corn Flour. I have no interesting news........" (Washington L. Dunn, Company A).

3 January 1865: Private R. B Hudgins of Company D died of Pneumonia in Raleigh, North Carolina.

12 January 1865: The Twenty-seventh Georgia Regiment marched to Sugar Loaf, North Carolina.

13 January 1865: *Fort Fisher, North Carolina:*
The Twenty-seventh Georgia escorting General Colquitt to Fort Fisher, North Carolina. General Colquitt had been given command of Fort Fisher but the fort was under siege and the Union soldiers blocked the land bridge leading to the fort.

"...........This morning about 2 A. M. we received orders to get ready in a moment to march, which we did, our Division, and we marched down to Sugar Loaf. But before we arrived there the Yankees made an attack on Fort Fisher, but did little damage and there were a good many landed and formed a line from the Sound to the River, cutting Fisher entirely off by land. They made a very hard attack on Fisher just before night, lasting from 2 to 3 hours; but failed to take the Fort.....” (Washington L. Dunn, Company A).

14 January 1865: Fort Fisher falls. The enemy then advanced upon Colquitt’s Brigade, located on the narrow strip of land between the mainland and Fort Fisher. The strip of land was located between the Atlantic Ocean and the Cape Fear River. Federal Gunboats enflading and reverse fire with what is called “every species known to modern warfare” of cannon and rifle. The Twenty-seventh Georgia under Colonel Zachry is the rear guard and inflicts heavy losses on the enemy pursuers.

“............We moved down and fronted the enemy that has Fisher cut off, I thought we were going to charge them; but we did not..........” (Washington L. Dunn, Company A).

15 January 1865: Fort Fisher, North Carolina:

“............Our Regiment went on the front line and our Company on picket. The enemy made a dreadful attack on the Fort. I do not know the result yet. This has been done before A. M. The enemy kept shelling the Fort till about 3 P. M. It seemed they blew every boat they had and ceased firing for a while and our men charged their line with a double picket line and ran their pickets in; but they had to fall back afterwards. Colonel Lofton of the 6th Georgia was killed and several men killed and several men wounded. J. C. Smith of our Company was wounded in shoulder and arm and General Hoke was wounded slightly in the arm while up a tree looking at the charge and at the enemy, and General Colquitt was sent to Fort Fisher by General Bragg to hold at all hazards. The enemy attacked the fort again before night and before General Colquitt could get there General Whiting surrendered the Fort with 2500 men in it. Colquitt arrived there; but made his escape. We fell back off the line about 3 A. M. and moved back about 2 miles to our breast works..........” (Washington L. Dunn, Company A).

16 January 1865: Fort Fisher, North Carolina:

Wounded: Private John C. Smith – Co. A
                                  Private Andrew White – Co. D
                                    Private W. A. Darnell - Co. H
                                    Private Jon T. Ward – Co. E

18 January 1865: The Twenty-seventh Georgia Regiment - Near Fort Fisher, North Carolina.

“............The enemy came up and attacked our pickets; but we held our picket line.....” (Washington L. Dunn, Company A).

Wounded: Private J. M. Blue - Co. K

19 January 1865: The Twenty-seventh Georgia Regiment - Near Fort Fisher, North Carolina.

“..............The enemy came again and attacked our pickets and brought a line of battle in sight. We still held our line; we killed a great many and lost many. It rained today. There was a Yankee boat came up near our works;

but did not fire a gun............" (Washington L. Dunn, Company A).
22 January 1865: Private Emerald M. Rickerson of Company K died of Pneumonia in Goldsboro, North Carolina.
25 January 1865: The following dispatches were made:

Wilmington, January 25, 1865
Maj. Gen. Hoke,
Sugar Loaf:
Send Colquitt's Brigade here immediately, prepared to move by rail.

Braxton Bragg
Sugar Loaf, January 25, 1865
Colonel Anderson,
Official papers received by mail carrier. Colquitt's Brigade left here at 2:30 p.m. No changes in my front to report.

R. F. Hoke
Major General

The Twenty-seventh Georgia Regiment marched to within two miles of Wilmington. They left at about 3:00 P. M. and arrived about 10:00 P. M. Private Dempsey Griffin of Company K died of Pneumonia in Wilson, North Carolina.
28 January 1865: The following dispatch was made:

Wilmington, January 28, 1865
Maj. Gen. Hoke,
Sugar Loaf:
Colquitt's Brigade returning to you this morning. Leave was granted the General.

Archer Anderson
Assist. Adjutant-General

The Twenty seventh Georgia Regiment arrived back at Sugar Loaf about 3:00 P. M.
29 January 1865: Sugar Loaf, North Carolina:
".................We remained in camps all day. William Phelps came in today. I hear that K. Woodall died at Goldsboro on the 13th of this month........" (Washington L. Dunn, Company A).
30 January 1865: Sugar Loaf, North Carolina:
"...........The Yankees came up and attacked our pickets, but did not run them in. They went back just before night............." (Washington L. Dunn, Company A).
31 January 1865: Organization of the Department of North Carolina:
General Braxton Bragg, Commanding
Major General Robert H. Hoke - Commander, Hoke's Division
Colonel Charles T. Zachry - Commander, Colquitt's Brigade

Captain Elisha D. Graham - Commander, 27th Georgia Regiment

February 1865: Charles Thornton Zachry Appointed Brigadier General P. A. C. S.

10 February 1865: Organization of the Department of North Carolina:

General Braxton Bragg, Commanding

Major Robert F. Hoke - Commander, Hoke's Division

Colonel Charles T. Zachry - Commander, Colquitt's Brigade

Captain Elisha D. Graham - Commander, 27th Georgia Regiment

11 February 1865: Sugar Loaf, North Carolina:

".......The Yankees Advanced on our pickets and drove them in and they have thrown up breast works. There were 17 of our regiment left here last night and started home. Captain Calhoun was captured today. Our regiment lost one wounded........" (Washington L. Dunn, Company A).

Wounded: Private William J. Williams – Co. E
Captured: Captain Calvin Calhoun - Co. K
                  Private James P. Vaughn – Co. G

17 February 1865: Sugar Loaf, North Carolina:

".............The Monitor came up and attacked Fort Anderson, but did no injury to the Fort. She went back at night. I hear that the Yankees are shelling Columbia, South Carolina....." (Washington L. Dunn, Company A).

18 February 1865: Sugar Loaf, North Carolina:

".................The one Monitior and about 15 gun boats came up and attacked Fort Anderson and kept up a continuous fire all day and night. Our troops fell back to our line today......" (Washington L. Dunn, Company A).

19 February 1865: Sugar Loaf, North Carolina:

"........About one hour before day break we evacuated Sugar Loaf and fell back near Wilmington. We fell back about 8 miles and made a stand; but had to fall back further on account of being flanked there. I suppose Columbia and Charleston, S. C. are now in the hands of the enemy. I hear that Haygood's Brigade were all captured, though I do not know whether it is so or not......" (Washington L. Dunn, Company A).

20 February 1865: Wilmington, North Carolina:

".......We are in line of battle, building breast works......" (Washington L. Dunn, Company A).

21 February 1865: *The Battle at Wilmington, North Carolina:*

After the fall of Fort Fisher the City of Wilmington was not to stand long. As Federal troops advanced upon the city and captured Fort Anderson, it was decided that the city would have to be evacuated. The Twenty-seventh Georgia under Colonel Zachry again assumed the post of Honor, the rear guard. They gave up ground grudgingly and caused the union troops to pay dearly for the ground taken.

Captured: Private Thomas J. Shipp - Co. A
                  Private George W. Wall - Co. A
                  Sergeant John N. Duke - Co. F
                  Sergeant William W. Matthews - Co. F

Private Cornelius B. Fountain - Co. F

22 February 1865: Wilmington, North Carolina:
The final evacuation of the city occurred in the early hours of this morning.

Captured: Lieutenant John J. Buffington - Co. E
                       Private Bradford Augustus Johnston - Co. C
                       Sergeant William Robinson Kellum Co. K

The Regiment moves to Schofield, North Carolina.

29 February 1865: The Twenty-seventh Georgia Regiment entrenched near Scofield, North Carolina.

March 1865: Henry Mann, Jr. appointed 1st Sergeant - Co. I

2 March 1865: Private J .S. Sesnos of Company E died in Raleigh, North Carolina.

8 March 1865: *The Battle at Kinston, North Carolina:*

General Braxton Bragg had entrenched his forces, consisting of Hoke's Division in order to slow the progress of the Federal Army. They held the advance until this date when Hoke's Division was sent against the left of the enemy with minimal effect. They engaged the enemy several times in bitter fighting over great Dover Swamp.

Captured: Private R. A. Snellgroves - Co. A
                       Private John B. Willis - Co. A
                       Private William M. Childs - Co. H
                       Private P. F. Stewart - Co .H
                       Private Thomas D. Goodwin - Co. K

10 March 1865: Kinston, North Carolina;
Colquitt's Brigade (under Colonel Zachry) and Kirkland's Brigade executed a flank movement against the Union Force and carried the Breastworks, capturing most of the troops as prisoners and their artillery pieces.
The report of Colonel John S. Jones of the174th Ohio Volunteer Infantry states;(Wise's Forks, N. C., March 3 1865)
".....About 11:00 a.m. a furious and determined assault was made on our front by the enemy......lasting until 12:30 p.m.........made by Hoke's Division......center was General Colquitt's Brigade."

Killed: Private William W. Stembridge - Co. C
Wounded: Private G. W. Tumlin – Co. D.
Captured: Private Joseph D. Gray - Co. C

13 March 1865: The Twenty-seventh Georgia Regiment ordered from Kinston, North Carolina to Goldsboro, North Carolina along with Colquitt's Brigade (Colonel Charles T. Zachry, Commanding) -dispatch from John B. Sale, Assistant Adjutant General and from General Braxton Bragg.

11 March 1865: Dover Swamp, North Carolina: The Twenty-seventh Georgia Regiment retreated toward Goldsboro, North Carolina.

16 March 1865: Federal troops under General Slocum briefly were engaged with Confederate forces at Averasborough, North Carolina.

17 March 1865: Colquitt's Brigade, present for duty: 114 officers, 1052

men - 1118 total effective - 1300 aggregate present (out of 2595 total present and absent).

18 March 1865: *The Battle of Bentonville, North Carolina:*

General Joseph E. Johnston decided to attack General Slocum's Federals at Bentonville, North Carolina because they were separated from the rest of General Sherman's army. The Twenty-seventh Georgia under the command of Colonel Charles T. Zachry broke through the Federal lines in this final battle but due to a lack of support were unable to take advantage and suffered severe losses on the works of the enemy.

Killed:	Sergeant James B. Sorrells - Co. F
	Private J. M. Rucker - Co. G
	Private Elijah Alexander - Co. H
Wounded:	Lieutenant Joseph Harrison Little - Co. A
	Sergeant H. B. Smith - Co. D
	Private John D. Dodd - Co. E
	Private James S. Lifsey - Co. G
	Private Eli A. Biggers - Co. H
	Private Solomon King - Co. H
Captured:	Corporal R. Marion Smith - Co. K

Elisha Duncan Graham appointed Major
Willis Baxley elected Captain of Company I

19 March 1865:

Killed:	Private J. R. Mason - Co. D
	Corporal D. T. Jennings - Co. E
	Private J. O. Cook - Co. E
	Private Joseph A. Crapps - Co. I
Wounded:	Major, William H. Rentfroe, Field Staff (died of wounds)
	Adjutant Jesse B. Pye Field Staff
	Lieutenant Richard V. Cobb - Co. D
	Lieutenant John D. Jones - Co. G
	Private William R. M. Jones - Co. G
	Corporal Elli A. Biggers - Co. H
	Corporal J. P. S. Nash - Co. H
	Private R. J. Nail - Co. H
	Private William H. Burk - Co. I
Captured:	Private Isaac M. Abercrombie - Co. E
	Private J. Marion Abercrombie - Co. E
	Private William Kelley - Co. F
	Sergeant James R. Jordan - Co. G
	Private Joseph Avery - Co. H
	Private David King - Co. H
	Lieutenant Silas A. Crosby - Co. I
	Private John Crapps - Co. I
	Private Benjamin Leggett - Co. I
	Lieutenant A. C. McCrory - Co. K

20 March 1865:
Captured: Private Andrew Ellis - Co. D
21 March 1865:
Wounded: Corporal Septimus Weathersby Myrick - Co. A
                                Private W. J. Clemons - Co. D
                                Private Smith Turner - Co. F
                                Private Benjamin F. Carlisle - Co. K
Captured: Private Andrew White - Co. D
22 March 1865:
Captured: Private Alexander Green Hamilton - Co. D
                                Private William J. Parker - Co. D

25 March 1865: Colquitt's Brigade; 771 effective present, 986 total present - 1093 aggregate

30 March 1865: *Sugar Loaf, North Carolina:*
Wounded: W. J. Clemons - Co. D
                                William Jackson Williams - Co. E
Captured: Corporal Henry Harrison Becher - Co. I
                                Corporal O. F. Carter - Co. I

31 March 1865: Organization of the Confederate Forces in North Carolina:
            General Joseph E. Johnston, Commanding
     Lieutenant General William J. Hardee - Commander, Hardee's Corps
       Major General Robert F. Hoke - Commander, Hoke's Division
   Brigadier General Alfred H. Colquitt - Commander, Colquitt's Brigade
 Lieutenant Colonel Hezekiah Bussey - Commander, 27th Georgia Regiment
Colquitt's Brigade - 885 men present

6 April 1865: Private Thomas R. Sealey of Company G died in Raleigh, North Carolina.

9 April 1865: Organization of Confederate Forces in North Carolina:
            General Joseph E. Johnston, Commanding
     Lieutenant General William J. Hardee - Commander, Hardee's Corps
       Major General Robert F. Hoke - Commander, Hoke's Division
   Brigadier General Alfred H. Colquitt - Commander, Colquitt's Brigade
 Lieutenant Colonel Hezekiah Bussey - Commander, 27th Georgia Regiment
Major William H. Rentfroe died of wounds in hospital at Smithfield, North Carolina

26 April 1865: *Surrender - Greensboro, North Carolina:*
On This day General Joseph E. Johnston signed the final papers surrendering the remainder of the army of the Confederate States of America. Surrendering with him was the Twenty-seventh Regiment, Georgia Volunteer Infantry. They were as follows:
            Brigadier General Charles T. Zachry
                    Lieutenant Colonel Hezekiah Bussey
                    Major Elisha Duncan Graham
                    Walter H. Drane, Surgeon
                    James Wilson Clements, Assistant Surgeon

William Larkin Williams, Hospital Steward
Sergeant Wade A. Turner
Sergeant Raleigh H. Turner

Company A:

Captain Robert Patton
Sergeant John C. Calhoun
Sergeant Thomas A. Harrell
Corporal Peter Stewart
William Joseph Davis
Richard Goodroe
H. H. Kendrick
A. McKinney
Stephen Murray
James R. Shipp
L. W. Wall
Jordan F. Willis

Lieutenant Eli Stewart
Sergeant Rufus A. Dodson
Corporal Daniel Kilcrease
Privates;James F. Braselton
Robert D. Flurry
J .J. Hunley
William E. Kendrick
Mike Murphy
William S. Phelps
W. F. Taylor
William J. Williams

Company B:

Lieutenant John Wesley Forrester
Sergeant James J. Cowart
Sergeant John B. Walton
Joel Robert Forrester
Joseph F. Peavy
Joel T. Taylor
Robert M. Warren

Sergeant John R. Seymore
Privates:John Dyer
J. K. Jackson
T. LaFayett Syms
Jesse A. Walton

Company C:

Captain William W. Johnson
Lieutenant William M. Ross
Sergeant W. H. Green
Corporal James Martin Wilson
William Russell Aultman
B. F. Dreher
Thomas C. Green
Franklin H. Hartman
John C. Kennedy
David J. Ross
J. T. Snipes
Richard Yarbrough

Lieutenant L. C. Futrell
Sergeant Benjamin F. Kennedy
Sergeant G. W. White
Privates:Joshua Aultman
William Averett
P. W. Glynn
J. M. Hammock
Jackson E. Johnson
James William Molen
J. W. Smith
Rufus White
L. H. Zachry

Company D:

Captain George W. Lathem
Sergeant C. H. Cape
Corporal Thomas J. Carter

Lieutenant John F. Dorsey
Sergeant H. J. Cooper
Corporal John K. Moore

Privates: Amos M. Brooks   Lewis F. Burton
Henry H. Cooper   Green K. C. Evans
J. O. Farmer   S. D. Farmer
H. W. T. Gaines   Jackson Gaines
John L. Gaines   James D. Howington
W. B. Hubbard   S. W. Kizer
James S. Lathem   Robert H. Lowery
J. J. Martin   Joshua McKinney
Scott Moore   Benjamin W. Reed
Joseph R. Reed   J .A. Reed
J. W. Reed   M. M. Reed
Albinus Smith   John A. Smith
S. T. Watson

Company E:
Lieutenant William C. Reeves   Sergeant George M Dodd
Corporal Pitt M. McLeroy   Corporal Thomas L. Todd
Privates:Henry Abercrombie   William A. Betsill
George D. Carter   Joel J. Chambers
Shem E. Cook   William R. Cook
J .F. Creel   William S. Ewing
Leonard Fuller   Joseph Grizzard
T. W. Horton   S. T. Jones
Benjamin S. Kite   David Kite
George W. Kite   James Laseter
Joel Laseter   Robert W. Mason
J. William H. Norton   E. R. Pyle
Ephraim Rountree   P. S. Strawn
James H. Waller

Company F:
Lieutenant Allen E. Cody   Lieutenant Warren F. Walters
Sergeant David N. Bloodsworth Sergeant T. L. Jinks
Sergeant William B. Rogers   Sergeant W. T. Streetman
Privates:John Q. Adams   G. W. Amerson
Warren Amerson   Thomas Bynum
J. T. Handcock   D. H. Herring
W. H. Layfield   J. M. McGlamery
E. B. Rogers   W. F. Shepherd
Jesse Shinholster

Company G:
Captain Marcus L. Billingsley Lieutenant James M. Slade
Lieutenant Joseph C. Chapman Sergeant James J. Beckman
Corporal John T. Akin   Privates:John L, Banks

J. W. Boyd
A. Flemming Brown, Jr.
E. J. Fowler
W. M. Hinsley
George Kinney
James S. Lifsey
William H. C. Slade
Theophilus Williams

A. Flemming Brown
William Thomas Chapman
Thomas P. Hagan
Thomas Zachry Jones
Benjamin Hawkins Lifsey
Augustus N. Powell
James M. Sullivan

Company H:

Captain John M. Zachry
Sergeant Winfield A. Copeland
Eli A. Biggers
Daniel R. Lewis
J. T. Lewis
John C. McClendon
R. W. J. Nail
Q. L. Nash
G. Frank Stallworth
B. F. Turner
L. W. J. Turner
Michael Wallace

Lieutenant Wade A. Turner
Privates:Franklin Alexander
James T. Fields
J. H. Lewis
Daniel N. Lindsey
B. W. Nail
John Adam Nash
William J. St. John
J. W. Taylor
J. H. Turner

Company I:

Captain Willis Baxley
Sergeant Henry Mann, Jr.
Sergeant William Griffin
Corporal James M. McLendon
Privates:Cornelius Barber
William Lumpkin Becher
Cohen Carter
William B. Dobson
George W. Hester
A. D. Leslie
Andrew H. Thomas

Sergeant Thomas Fletcher Barnett
Sergeant A. M. Crosby
Corporal La Fayette H. Johnson
Corporal Joseph W. Baxley
William Alfred Becher
William O. Bryant
William H. Dilborn
James E. Harper
William H. Hughes
Reuben Reaves
Nathaniel A. Thomas

Company K:

Lieutenant Josiah Bunkley Parker
Sergeant Robert H. Kellum
Sergeant William J. Thompson
Corporal Wesley F. Belyen
Henry D. Bedell
John C. Belyen
John F. Bias
General Jackson Bruce

Sergeant William B. Giddings
Sergeant William C. Smith
Corporal Henry C. Downs
Privates:Lewis Alsabrook
Berry B. Belyen
Richard Belyen
John F. Bins
George F. Cole

John F. Downs

William T. Hall

Royal McClung

Rober H. Milling

James Jason Tigner

Thomas Daniel Hall

James M. Johnson

Robert A. McDowell

N. A. Thompson

Colonel Charles Thornton Zachry

HON. CHARLES THORNTON ZACHRY
(HENRY COUNTY)

Contributed by Hon. Henry Jackson

The stern, brave and chivalric man, the subject of this sketch, was born near Covington, Georgia, in the county of Newton at what is known as the "Old Zachry Homestead." This property has never passed from the ownership of the family since its settlement by his parents, James B. and Olive Zachry. They moved from Putnam County where his father's ancestors settled after their arrival from the eastern shore of Maryland, and his mother from the vicinity of Alexandria, Virginia. There are still on the eastern shore of Maryland some of the Zachry family, while around Orange Court House in Fairfax county, Virginia, a few of the good and virtuous relatives of the Christian mother of Colonel Zachry may yet be found.

In his boyhood years schools and colleges were very rare, hence, like most men of that day, he had not the advantages of a University education. This fact made him zealous in behalf of the education of his children, and he has given them almost every advantage which money could command.

His devotion to active business in his success in its pursuit, have kept him out of politics, and, for the most part, out of public service.

When the late War Between the States came on, he was a member of the Whig party, and opposed to secession, but when the call for volunteers was made, he was one of the first who responded, "ready." Here Colonel Zachry began a course where success rewarded bravery. A braver officer never drew his sword in behalf of constitutional liberty. His war record began by his election as Captain of a company of Henry county volunteers, named in honor of the commanding officer, the *"Zachry Rangers."* The flag of this company was subsequently taken by General Sherman, and is on exhibition at the Army and Navy Museum in Washington City.

The "Zachry Rangers" were first ordered by Governor Brown to rendezvous at Camp Stephens, near Griffin. On the organization of a regiment, Captain Zachry was unanimously elected Major. This regiment afterwards became the famous Twenty-Seventh Georgia, and Major Zachry was promoted to the rank of Lieutenant-Colonel, while absent in an effort to see his wife whose death occurred before he could reach his home. This election, evidenced the high esteem and confidence entertained for him by the men of his command.

After the evacuation of Manassas, the Twenty-Seventh Georgia Regiment was transferred to Yorktown with Johnston's army, and rendered valuable aid in resisting the march of McClelland to Richmond. It remained with General Anderson until after the battle of Seven Pines, when it became a part of Colquitt's Brigade. At the Battle of Seven Pines Colonel Smith became disabled, and the command devolved upon Lieutenant-Colonel Zachry, who led it to the battle of Sharpsburg.

In the sanguinary seven days' fight around Richmond, the command of Lieutenant-Colonel Zachry greatly distinguished itself as one of the best in the service. This was due as well to the valor of his men, as to the masterly leadership of its commanding officer.

At the battle of Sharpsburg Lieutenant-Colonel Zachry was wounded twice, one of the balls he still carries in his person. For several days his life was dispared of and his family telegraphed as to the disposition of the remains. But, after an illness of several weeks, he recovered. When he was immediately promoted to the rank of Colonel, and was in command of his regiment when the Federals made their first attack from the north branch of the Rappahannock River, at Fredericksburg. Too much cannot be said of Colonel Zachry's bravery and skill on that occasion. It seems that in no emergency was the Twenty-Seventh found lacking --none to which it was not equal.

At the second battle of Cold Harbor, Generals Hoke and Wilcox lost their lines, but they were successfully retaken by Colonel Zachry at the head of five companies. The efficiency of this command was largely due its commanding officer who was every inch a soldier.

At the battle of Olustee, Florida, Colonel Zachry's command greatly distinguished itself--acting the most part in achieving that brilliant victory. Near the close of that eventful day, when the tide of battle seemed to turn, alternately, from one side to the other of the contending hosts, General Colquitt sent one of his staff officers to show the Twenty-Seventh Georgia into position in the line of battle and to remind Colonel Zachry that everything depended on his command. The reply of Colonel Zachry showed that he was of the stuff of which a soldier is made. As he rode at the head of his regiment with the fire of battle in his eye, he said: "Major, tell the General that I will do my best--not only he but the enemy shall know it when we are in line." This was no vain boast for, soon the enemy were in full retreat, leaving their dead and wounded in the field.

Colonel Zachry was not only brave and fearless himself, but he inspired his command with courage. Cowardice either in the officer or in the ranks, he unsparingly punished. The discipline he exercised was a marked characteristic of his military qualities.

In the summer of 1864, he was ordered to report to General Alfred H. Colquitt, as Adjutant-General of the brigade, to supply the place of Captain George Grattan, who had been seriously wounded a short time previously. I found the command in the trenches before Petersburg, on that portion of line which was afterwards known as "Colquitt's Salient." Soon after my arrival I heard of "Old Zach." Whenever allusion was made to any severe fighting, in which the brigade had engaged previous to my connection with it, what "Old Zach" had done would be stated in the most glowing terns. Regarding General Colquitt, now the distinguished Governor of the State, as the head of the brigade, "Old Zach" was certainly his right arm. Upon inquiry as to who this gallant soldier was, and what had become of him, I was informed that he was Charles T. Zachry, of the Twenty-Seventh Georgia Regiment, and then on duty in command of Martin's North Carolina Brigade; that he was rarely with his own regiment because when the head of a brigade was removed by the casualties of war, "Old Zach was very apt to be assigned to the command of it. The first time that I ever saw him was when Colquitt's Brigade was ordered to report to Mahone to make the attack of the 19th of August, on the Fifth (Warren's) Corps, then entrenched along the line of the Weldon Railroad. To my surprise he was by no means old; though known by the soubriquet of "Old Zach." He was in the very prime of life, and the soldier was to be seen in every inch of him, from the crown of his head to the soles of his feet. He had the cool, gray eye that is always accompanied by the most determined courage, and his wiry, iron- gray moustache involuntarily re-called the immortal "Old Guard" of Napoleon. Whilst I then had but a moment's conversation with him, I fully realized that I was in the presence of one of those men who's home is the battle-field, and who's name would become historic if the war but lasted long enough. Colonel Zachry returned to his brigade and I saw no more of him until January, 1865 when he took command of Colquitt's Brigade, the latter having gone to Georgia on leave of absence. This position he occupied until a few days before the surrender, when General Colquitt returned.

Hoke's Division, in which the brigade was, had been detached from the Army of Northern Virginia , and ordered to report to General Bragg at Wilmington, to assist in the defense of Fort Fisher, then threatened by the expedition under General Terry. Though sent all the way from Richmond, thus weakening that immortal band which headed by the beloved Lee, was defending the Capital of the Southern Confederacy, Bragg allowed Fort Fisher to be carried by assault in the very presence of this magnificent division, without firing a gun. Soon after the fort fell, the enemy of course advanced upon us and it was just at this juncture that Colonel Zachry took command. Never was more arduous service done by soldiers--stationed on a narrow strip of land, with the ocean on one side and the Cape Fear river on the other, both swarming with Federal gunboats and monitors, they were subjected for days to a direct enfilading and reverse fire of every species known to modern warfare, mortars, eleven-inch guns, parrotts, and last, but far from least, the rifle played upon them incessantly, and could you have seen "Old Zach" under these circumstances, you would have supposed him happier and much more at home than in his present seat in the House of Representatives. I am quite confident that he would rather face an eleven-inch shell than rise up at his desk and say: "Mr. Speaker." Wilmington was evacuated and "Old Zach", as usual , had the post of honor, the command of the rear guard. Slowly and stubbornly he fell back, and many of the enemy were made to bite the dust when they pressed him too closely.

Hoke's Division moved to the neighborhood of Kinston, where it was joined by some of Johnston's army then falling back before Sherman. It was discovered by those in command that a division of the enemy was disconnected from the rest of the Federal army in that section, and a flank movement was projected by which to take it in rear and capture it if possible. This flank movement was executed by Zachry's Georgia and Kirtland's North Carolina brigades, and a most brilliant success it was. When these two brigades were in the immediate vicinity of the rear of the enemy, a deserter informed them of their danger, just as they were endeavoring to extricate themselves the attack was made. Most of them were taken prisoners, together with what artillery they had. The successful execution of this movement required coolness and quickness, and "Old Zach" was fully equal to the emergency. Stonewall Jackson could not have handled his troops more beautifully. The battle commenced when his brigade was moved by the flank, and the rapidity and precision with which he brought them into line under a severe fire, was beautiful to behold.

For the next week the fighting was almost daily and wherever the most bullets could be found, there would be seen the gallant Colonel.

The next general engagement in which he participated was the battle of Bentonville. Here Hoke's Division was united with the main body of Johnston's army. It had been said that Lee's soldiers had never met the same class of troops as composed the army of Sherman, or they would not have been so universally victorious. Longstreet's Division had met them at Chickamauga and the result is known. Now, a second division of Lee's was to face them, and I believe that command would have died to a man before it would have given an inch. Early in the morning blankets were piled, guns inspected, and everything prepared for a desperate engagement. The skirmishers were informed that it was expected of them to drive back Sherman's line without assistance from the main body of the command. "Old Zach" was everywhere, happy at the thought of a brilliant victory, and inspiring courage and hope wherever he went. On came Sherman, but Zachry's skirmishers soon stopped his line and wonderful to say, they were never driven in. For two hours that little band of devoted veterans, emulating their brethren upon the glorious fields of Virginia and Maryland, drove back line after line, and never for a moment, fell back on the main body. Soon the command to advance was given, and Hoke's division went through the enemy in front of it, and over their works, capturing their artillery, with the same ease that Stonewall Jackson was accustomed to march on Banks. Being unsupported on the right, it was compelled to halt, and this fearful delay subsequently cost Zachry half his brigade, for by the time the line was perfected and the forward movement resumed, the enemy had erected heavy earthworks in front and protected themselves by abattis which no human being could penetrate under fire. Yet right into the abattis went Colonel Zachry with his devoted followers, but all to no purpose. This handful of men could not carry the position, though one half of them were left on the field in the attempt. The position we occupied was held until Sherman had sent a corps to take us in rear, but a rapid change in front saved us, and soon we were, in turn, entrenching. Never did a line of breastworks arise more rapidly from the ground, and not a moment too soon, for here came the enemy upon like an avalanche. But Lee's soldiers were not to be run over, and they retired probably more rapidly than they advanced.

Here was enacted a scene which never can pass from my memory, for it united the highest dramatic effect, even though in the midst of the terrible tragedy being enacted, with comedy. Our line was so thin that the men were often more than a yard apart. The North Carolina Junior Reserves were with us, composed of boys fifteen and sixteen years of age, and gallantly did these little fellows bleed and die for their country. Even now I can see a small, pale faced boy of fifteen, with his rifle clasped in one hand, and the other arm torn off by a shell, lying down in the trench praying to God that he might see his mother before he died. The enemy were not one hundred yards from us, and as successive bodies of fresh troops came up they would assault our line endeavoring to carry it by storm. If a hat was lifted above the works, in a minute a ball would be through it. As the firing would grow more severe on the right, the men and boys would close down in that direction; if the attack was on the left, a corresponding movement would be made in that direction. But above artillery, musketry and cheering, would be herd the ringing voice of "Old Zach:" "Now, boys, *sachez* to the right." "Now, boys, *sachez* to the left." He was carrying on a dancing class in the midst of one of the most terrific battles in history!

Georgia sent many a gallant son to Virginia, but none did more to illustrate her in his place than Charles T. Zachry, of Henry. And I do not hesitate to say, the larger the command given him, in my humble opinion, the greater would have been the success achieved. A better regimental or brigade commander never drew a sword or set a horse, and when the surrender was made no more stainless blade was returned to the scabbard. I am informed that his appointment to Brigadier General was ordered when the "Stars and Bars" were furled forever.

As I see the quiet and unassuming member from Henry moving about in the House of Representatives, I can hardly realize that he is now the battle-scarred veteran, and once the brilliant cavalier beside whom I was so proud to ride upon many a hard fought field.
Georgians should honor him everywhere!

Georgia'sGeneral Assembly 1880-1881, James P. Harrison & Company, Atlanta,1881

General Alfred Holt Colquitt – Colquitt's Brigade

GENERAL ALFRED HOLT COLQUITT

1824-1894

William A. Bowers, Jr., 1995

*B*orn in Monroe, Walton County, Georgia April 20, 1824 the son of Senator Walter Terry Colquitt and Nancy H. Lane. He was married first to Dorothy Tarver and after her death in 1855 he married Sarah Tarver, The Widow of Fred Tarver. His first wife had received from her father a plantation in Baker County. Alfred, having graduated from the College of New Jersey (Princeton) in 1844, studied Law in Milledgeville (then the Capitol of Georgia) and was admitted to the bar in Columbus, Ga. in 1846.

When the Mexican war broke out in 1847 he postponed entering a Law practice and volunteered for service in defense of his country. He served as a staff officer with the rank of Major for two years. When the war ended he began his law practice and was elected to the Twenty-third Congress in 1852 at the age of twenty-eight. Colquitt served one term, declining the nomination for a second term. He remained active in politics serving in the state legislature in 1859 and in 1860 he campaigned for the election of and served as a Presidential elector on the ticket of John C. Breckinridge. After the election of Lincoln he was a member of the secession convention for Georgia.

After Georgia seceded from the Union he became a company Captain and took up arms to protect his state. Upon the organization of the Sixth Georgia Regiment in May 1861, he was elected Colonel and was in command of the regiment when it was ordered to Richmond and then Manassas, Virginia in the concentration of Confederate troops. Although the Sixth Georgia Regiment did not participate in the battle of First Manassas, they were engaged on the Peninsula in the spring of 1862. Colonel Colquitt and the Sixth Georgia saw action in the battle of Seven Pines and upon the reorganization under General D. H. Hill he replaced General W. S Featherston in command of a brigade which included the Sixth, Twenty-third, Twenty-seventh and Twenty-eighth Georgia Regiments and the Thirteenth Alabama Regiment. This brigade became known as Colquitt's Brigade and remained essentially the same for the duration of the war with the exception of the substitution of the Nineteenth Georgia for the Thirteenth Alabama in early 1863.

In the Seven Days Battle around Richmond Colquitt's Brigade was prominent in the action and Colonel Colquitt's leadership had attracted the attention of General Daniel H. Hill. This coupled with the success of the brigade in holding Turner's Gap on the National Pike where it crossed over South Mountain, where the brigade essentially held off McClelland's Army of the Potomac for a day which bought valuable time for General Lee's Army of Northern Virginia, secured a promotion to Brigadier General in early September. His promotion was effective as of September 2, 1862. After the Battle of South Mountain General Colquitt was known as the "Rock of South Mountain". It was stated that the brigade "gave not one inch that day".

On September 17, 1862 at seven o'clock Colquitt's Brigade was sent up to the "Cornfield to support the right of General Hood's Texans along with two more Brigades of General D. H. Hill's Division. Colquitt's Brigade had begun to advance on the enemy but the regiments on both sides did not advance leaving Colquitt and his men vulnerably. The took fire from the front and both sides and were engaged in hand to hand combat with Green's Federal brigade which had attacked from the east woods. After half of his command and all of his field officers had gone down the brigade withdrew to the sunken road later known as "Bloody Lane" and held this position for more than three hours of the fiercest fighting in the history of American warfare.

General Colquitt commanded his rebuilt brigade at the battle of Fredericksburg, although they were not positioned where the heaviest action was occurring. General D. H. Hill was reassigned to North Carolina and the Division was commanded by General Robert Rhodes and was a part of Jackson's Corps at Chancellorsville. They were a part of Jackson's flanking movement on May second, a battle in which General Colquitt's hesitation, when he had reason to believe that a large force of the enemy was on his right, caused him to come under criticism. After this battle the brigade was down from 2900 to around 1700 and was transferred to General D. H. Hill in North Carolina for two brigades that were at full strength. This was in June of 1863, just prior to the Pennsylvania campaign and Gettysburg.

Colquitt and his Brigade were involved in the defense of the Carolinas, spending most of their time in the defense of Charleston. The Federal troops under General Seymour were near the mouth of the St. Johns River and the Confederate commanders in Florida were certain that they would attempt to cut the railroad near Lake City. The call for help went out and Colquitt's Brigade was sent along with some Florida infantry, the 4th Georgia Cavalry and the Chatham Artillery. Colquitt's Brigade, veterans from the Army of Northern Virginia, were the most experienced troops available and were expected to provide the leadership in repelling the enemy troops.

General Finegan placed General Colquitt in charge of the small army consisting of about 5200 troops including infantry, cavalry and artillery. He moved the force east of Lake City, Florida near to Olustee Station along the railroad and took position between a swamp and a natural lake named Ocean Pond. He deployed skirmishers and waited to draw the enemy into the narrow strip of dry land. The conclusion was an utter rout, with the enemy in flight back to the east and leaving their causalities behind. General Colquitt was considered the "Hero of Olustee" for his leadership in that victory. After that battle and a small engagement at Cedar Creek Colquitt and his brigade were ordered back to the Charleston area.

As General Lee began to concentrate troops in the Richmond/ Petersburg area General Colquitt and his troops were returned to Virginia. In May of 1864 General Colquitt was placed in command of "Colquitt's Division" and was in command of the division in the Second Battle of Drewry's Bluff and Cold Harbor. Later Colquitt's command held an important salient near Petersburg resulting in it being named "Colquitt's Salient". Later he commanded troops at Weldon Railroad (Globe Tavern) and Fort Harrison before the Brigade being transferred back to North Carolina to take command of Fort Fisher. Before he could take command the fort fell to the enemy and General Colquitt commanded troops in the defense of Wilmington, North Carolina.

Colquitt's Brigade surrendered at Greensboro on the 26th of April 1865 and was promoted to the rank of Major General as the Confederate Army was in it's waning days. General Colquitt returned home and resumed his practice of law and the planting of his crops. He was unable to stay out of politics and became, along with John B. Gordon and Governor Joseph Brown, became a part of the "GEORGIA TRIUMVIRATE", a most powerful political force. He was elected for two terms as Governor of Georgia and was later a United States Senator until his death. The Constitution of 1877 was written during his term of office as Governor. Alfred Colquitt was also a licensed Methodist preacher and was active in both the activities of the Methodist Church and the "Temperance Movement." Alfred Holt Colquitt, who is buried in Rose Hill Cemetery, was much honored for his outstanding leadership both on the field of battle and in his life of public service to his fellow Georgians. He gave over forty years of his life to the great state of Georgia and Georgians everywhere can be proud of his accomplishments.

Corporal John Wesley Bowers
Company B, Rutland Grays
Bibb County

Samuel W. Albertson
Company D – Hall County

Harrison Kennedy
Company D – Hall County

Henry Washington Tanner Gaines
Company D – Hall County

James H. Kiser
Company D – Hall County

James S. Lathem
Company D – Hall County

**Jim Leckie, Captain
Company D – Hall County**

Jim Little
Company D – Hall County

Old Jim Little
Company D – Hall County

**John K. Moore
Company D, Hall County**

"Bacon" Joe Reed
Company D, Hall County

Lie'n Joe Reed

Company D – Hall County

Private William Tapley Streetman
Company F – Taylor Guards
Taylor County

**G. M. Chaffiln
Company H, Zachry Rangers
Henry County**

**Francis Marion Hale
Co H – Zachry Rangers
Henry County**

Patrick Henry Hale
Company H – Zachry Rangers
Hall County

James Hambree Nash
Company H – Zachry Rangers
Hall County

Major Elisha Duncan Graham
(Former Captain Company I – Appling Grays)
Appling County

Henry Harrison Beacher
Company I, Appling Grays
Appling County

Joseph Crapps
Company I – Appling Grays
Appling County

**Sergeant Benjamin Milikin,
Company I, Appling Grays
Appling County**

Veterans identified in the picture are:
front row left to right: #2 Robert Clinton Young Co. A
11th GA #5 Lie'n Joe Reed Co. D 27th GA
middle row left to right: #3 Bacon Joe Reed Co. D 27th
GA #5 Allen J Gunter Co. F 43rd GA
#7 Jim Little Co. D 27th GA

Confederate Veterans Participated in the
Celebration.
The flag bearer, Mr. Will Hamilton; to his right
Mr. Sam P. Green; the two in gray uniforms are
Judge A. G. Harris and Mr. W. H. Bryant (Uncle
Billy). On the right with sword and Medal of
Honor is Mr. J. C. Daniel and the last on the end
is Mr. Wade Allan Manson Turner.

Henry County UCV

CONFEDERATE VETERANS IDENTIFIED—All of the above Confederate veterans were identified by R. S. Wolfe and H. G. (Cap) Branch. The picture was taken at the site of the old Spring Branch Baptist Church in 1908. Several readers recognized some of them. They are, front row, left to right, Ben B. Milikin, Henry V. Beecher, John Gardner, Mathew (Luck) Johnson, Absalon Stone, Duncan Campbell, Tom Knight, Daniel W. Long, Jacob White and Lovett Baxley; back row, Jim Hall, Berry White, W Lumpkin Beecher, Joe Baxley, W. Alfred Beecher, Nat A. Thomas, Clem Byrd, Noah Altman W. D. Simmons, Mitchell Stone, E. T. Kennedy and Thomas H. Willoughby.

UCV Reunion, Spring Branch Church– Appling Couinty

**Nail Brothers
Henry County**

**Zachry Brothers
Henry County**

General A. H. Colquitt

MOTES,   ATLANTA, GA.

Colonel Charles Thornton Zachry

ROSTER OF THE FIELD, STAFF AND BAND
27TH REGIMENT GEORGIA VOLUNTEER INFANTRY
ARMY OF TENNESSEE C. S. A.

Name	Highest Rank Attained	Remarks
Levi B. Smith	Colonel	
Charles T. Zachry	Colonel	
Septimus L. Brewer	Lt. Col.	
John W. Stubbs	Lt. Col.	
Jasper N. Dorsey	Lt. Col.	
James B. Gardner	Lt. Col.	
Hezekiah Bussey	Lt .Col.	
William P. Edwards	Lt. Col.	
Henry B. Holliday	Major	Also Assistant Quartermaster
Charles J. Dennis	Major	
William H. Renfroe	Major	
Elisha Duncan Graham	Major	
George B. Buchannan	Captain	Also Assistant Quartermaster
Charles F. Redding	Adjutant	
Jesse B. Pye	Adjutant	2 May 1864
George Henry Pattillo	Chaplain	Resigned November 1861
W. S. Baker	Chaplain	
George T. Embry	Chaplain	Resigned October 31, 1864
Christopher C. Parker	Sgt. Major	
J. W. Lewis	Sgt. Major	
William T. Dennis	Sgt. Major	26 Februray 1864
J. G. Russell	Sgt.	Quartermaster
Wade A. Turner	Sgt.	Ordinance
Thomas M. Darnall	Surgeon	Resigned 1 June 1862
Walter H. Drane	Surgeon	
Thomas H. Butler	Asst. Surgeon	Resigned 18 June 1862
James Wilson Clements	Asst. Surgeon	
Zedekiah W. Little	Asst. Surgeon	
J. J. Crawford	Hosp. Stew.	
William Larkin Williams	Hosp. Stew.	
John M. Zachry	Comm. Sgt.	
Raleigh H. Turner	Comm. Sgt.	
Thomas J. Bacon	Asst. Com. Sgt.	Killed Seven Pines Va.
George M. Chaffin	Ensign	
Russell L. Whitt	Musician	
J. William L. Mason	Musician	

COMPANY COMMANDERS

Co. "A" Georgia Drillers
(Marion and Schley counties)

Capt. Perry C. Car
Capt. William E. Dougherty
Capt. Robert Patton

Co. "B" Rutland Grays
(Bibb Grays)
(Bibb County)

Capt. John W. Stubbs
Capt. John J. Allen
Capt. John Wesley Forrester
Capt. Seaborn W. Thornton

Co. "C" Jackson Guards
(Crawford County)

Capt. Charles J. Dennis
Capt. James W. Murray
Capt. Thomas A. Grace
Capt. William W. Johnson

Co. "D"
(Hall County)

Capt. Jasper N. Dorsey
Capt. George W. Latham

Co. "E" Betahsida Rifle Guards
(Campbell and Fayette counties)

Capt. Jesse M. Spratlin
Capt. William H. Renfroe
Capt. Abercrombie

Co. "F" Taylor Guards
(Taylor County)

Capt. Septimus L. Brewer
Capt. Jordan Wilcher
Capt. William Posey Edwards

Co. "G" County Line Guards
(Pike and Spalding counties)

Capt. William Dozier Redding
Capt. John C. Beeks
Capt. George B. Buchanan
Capt. Marcus L. Billingsly

Co. "H" Zachry Rangers
(Henry County)

Capt. Charles T. Zachry
Capt. Wm. W. DeLamar
Capt. Robert A. Harkey
Capt. John M. Zachry

Co "I" Appling Grays
(Appling County)

Capt. Osgood A. Lee
Capt. Elisha Duncan Graham
Capt. Willis Baxley

Co. "K"
(Talbot County)

Capt. Levi B. Smith
Capt. Hezekiah Bussey
Capt. Calvin Calhoun

COMPANY A - MARION AND SCHLEY COUNTIES, GEORGIA
GEORGIA DRILLERS

William Alexander
S. T. Arnold
R. Binston
Samuel L. Blythe
James F. Braselton (Brazelton)
S. W. Bryant
John C. Calhoun
Perry C. Carr
Adam Carson
G. W. Chapman
R. D. Cody
William Joseph Davis
G. W. Denning
W. C. Dodson
Rufas A. Dodson
W. T. Donnan
William E. Dougherty
Washington L. Dunn
John R. Flurry
Robert D. Flurry
Richard B. Goodroe
Thomas A. Harrell
E. J. Highsmith
J. T. Highsmith
Samuel D. Highsmith

J. B Hobbs
David B. Holt
J. J. Hunley
J. T. Jones (or T. J.)
James M . Jordan
H.H.Kendrick
William E. Kendrick
Daniel Kilcrease
Simeon P. Lawhorne
Edward O. Little
Joseph Harrison Little
Andrew J. McElmurray
S. F. McGahee
A. McKinney
Daniel McSwain
T. W. Mitchell
George T. Murphy
Mike Murphy
Stephen Murray
Nathaniel Wesley Myrick
Septimus Weathersby Myrick
Robert Patton
Joseph Perry
William S. Perry
William S. Phelps

A.J.Rogers(Rodgers)
M.R.Rogers(Rodgers)
James R. Shipp
Thomas J. Shipp
Columbus W. Smith
John C. Smith
R. A. Snellgroves
Eli Stewart
Henry Stewart
Peter Stewart
W. T. Stone
W. F. Taylor
William A. J. Teat(Teate)
Wiley B. Tidd
William J. Tidd
George W. Wall
L. W. Wall
E. T. Williams
J. J. Williams
William J. Williams
Wiley J Williamson
John B. Willis
Jordan F. Willis
Jacob T. Woodall
Killight Woodall

133

COMPANY B - BIBB COUNTY, GEORGIA
RUTLAND GRAYS OF BIBB GRAYS

John Alexander
John J. Allen
J. P. Arnett
Thomas Arnett
B. F. Avant
Jesse T. Avant
Josiah L. Avant
Lewis M. Avant
B. F. Barfield
Thomas Marion Barfield
C. B. Bond
John W. Bowers
G. M. Brown
John T.(L.) Brown
T. M. Brown
Henry B. Bulloch(Bullock)
James Bulloch(Bullock)
Amasa M. Burnett
Jeremiah J. Burnett
John F. Burnett
James F. Cain
William F. Cain
J. A. Cape
William F. Carlisle
James M. Carney (Kearney)
John A.Carney (Kearney)
William E. Clark
James W. Cowart
John F. Coxwell
Thomas J. Crow
John Dyer
Stanberry Evans
Joel Robert Forrester
John Wesley Forrester
Redmond V. Forrester
C. H. Fuller
James R. Galman
Thomas Hall

William H. Hall
Samuel Hargroves
Bailey Armstrong Hear
Henry Henniger(Heniger)
Michael C. Henniger(Heniger)
Isaac Hightower
James Jackson
J. K. Jackson
James A. Johnson
Luther R. Johnson
William D. Jones
J. Jordan
James M. Kimbrew
Green Lambert
Jesse Francis Lancaster
Thomas C. Lancaster
Cullen Mathews
Samuel Mathews
James B. McDonald
Maltimore M. Minchew
Jack Mise(Mize)
Leseur L. Murray
James L. Owen
Samuel G. B. Odom
John M. Page
William Parker
T. G. Pate
Joseph S. Peavy
G. W. Perdue
James W. Perdue
John T. Perdue
F. M. Pledger
Isaac Pool
Patrick Reeves
Joab Roach
Reuben Roberts
Samuel Robinson (Robertson)
William Ryder

Phillip Harrison Schofield
Jacob Schofield
John Scott
James T. Self
John R. Seymore
William C. Simmons
John W. Simpson
T. J. Skipper
William F. Sonneborn
William R. Sonneborn
Miles G. Stephens(Stevens)
John W. Stubbs
Joseph R. Stubbs
Thomas Stubbs
Marcus Sullivan
T. LaFayette Syms
H. Willis Tankersley
Joel T. Taylor
William Tharpe
Henry Thomas
Luther J. Thomas
Stephen Luther Thomas
Seaborn W. Thornton
W. J. Totton
B. Frank Wainwright
George Walton
Jesse A. Walton
John B. Walton
Vincent Everett Walton
Robert M. Warren
Isham (Isom) Wheeler
William Wheeler
Henry Whittington
John (Jonathan) Willoughby
William Willoughby
Andrew J. Wilson
David Wilson
Thomas A. Wimbish
William P. Wood
William W. Woodward

COMPANY C - CRAWFORD COUNTY, GEORGIA
JACKSON GUARDS

Job Allen	Thomas H. Gregory	Columbus M. Newberry
Daniel H. Arnold	J. M. Hammock	J. Henry Newberry
Joshua Aultman	J. Hamphill	William H. Page
William Russell Aultman	Henry Hancock, Jr	Walter Parks
James W. Avera	Henry Hancock, Sr,	A. J. Robinson (Roberson)
Sikes Avera	Jackson Hancock	James W. Robinson (Roberson)
Archibald Averett	James C. Hancock	William H. Robinson (Roberson)
William Averett	John H. Hancock	Robert Jackson Roland(Rowland)
Sanders Bond	T. J. Hancock	David J. Ross
Thomas Bridges	W. G. Hancock	William M. Ross
J. Q. Campbell	Henry Haney	Robert Sanders
J. J. Cates	William D. Harp	D. C. Sawyer
Enos M. Causey	Franklin H. Hartman	John Sawyer
James J. Causey	Julius Haskins (Hoskins)	Julius T. Sawyer
Lemon M. Causey	William Haskins (Hoskins)	G. (J) W. Sheppard
L. D. Causey	James A. Holloman	James T. Smith
J. M. Chance	James W. Hudson	J. W. Smith
R. N.(M.) Clary	Joseph Hudson	T. Y. Smith
Wiley G. Clary	B. E. Hutto	J. T. Snipes
G.(J.) A. Culverhouse	Frederick Hutto	Wm. W.Stembridge(Steinbridge)
Obediah E. Daniel	Reuben Hutto	Simon K. Wadkins
Andrew J. Davis	Darnell Johnson	J. A. Walker
Green Davis	Jackson E. Johnson	Lovick Washington Weaver
W. J. Deans	Simon Johnson	Job J. Webb
Charles J. Dennis	William W. Johnson	W. A. Webb
C. T. Dennis	Bradford Augustus Johnston	G.W.White
B. F. Dreher	William G. Jordan	Henry Clay White
Wince Dreher	Benjamin F. Kennedy	Rufus White
James Dyer(Dyes)	John C. Kennedy	Green C. Whittington
John Dyer (Dyes)	Green Long	John N. Wilder
John H. Eubanks	C. H. Marshall	George W. Williams
Josiah D. Eubanks	W. H. McKinney	Thomas Nelson Williams
James G. Fitzpatrick	Leroy B. McMichael	William Williams
L. C. Futrell	W. S .McNiece (McNiese)	James Martin Wilson
P. W. Glynn	Elbert Merritt	John W. Worsham
Thomas A. Grace	Michael Merritt	J. E. Wright
Frank Gray	Riley Merritt	Lewis Wright
Joseph D. Gray	J .Wesley Mitchell	Richard Yarbrough
J M. Gray	James William Molen	Allen Yaughn (Yawn)
Charles A. Green	John C. Murchison	Fredrick Yaughn (Yawn)
Thomas C. Green	James W. Murray	L. H. Zachry
W. H. Green	B. F. Newberry	James T. Gregory

135

COMPANY D - HALL COUNTY, GEORGIA

Samuel W. Albertson	Henry Hall	Scott Moore
R. O. Allen	James Hall	J. M. Morrison
Micajah Bagwell	Alexander Green Hamilton	D. M. Murray
William Bagwell	William H. Hayes	Wade Parker
William Batchelor	James J. Head	William J. Parker
Absalom M. Bell	Joseph M. Hemphill	R. Peacock
James D. Blackstock	Charles M. Hope	Harvey S. Presley (Pressley)
Titus V. Brazelton	J. T. Hope	Benjamin W. Reed
James S. Brazile	James D. Howington	Joseph R. Reed
Amos M. Brooks	M .B. Howington	J. A. Reed
James W. Brooks	Wilson R. Howington	J. W. Reed
J. L. Brooks	W. B. Hubbard	M. M. Reed
Hardy Bryant	R. B. Hudgins	Anderson J. Reynolds
William M. Burd	Zacus W. Hudgins	Elijah N. Ritchie
Lewis F. Burton	Abner Hunter	J. W. Rouse
C. H. Cape	Thomas H. Jenkins	Wiley Rouse
Beverly Carter	Harrison Kennedy	J. C. Sanders
Thomas J. Carter	Henry C. Kennedy	A. S. Sears
William J. Carter	William Kennedy	D. C. Sexton
Gilbert Caudle (Caudell)	J. H. Kizer	Albinus Smith
Martin G. Chandler	S.W. Kizer	H. B. Smith
Sterling Chandler	George W. Lathem	John A. Smith
John W. Clark	James S. Lathem	Joseph H. Tanner
W. J. Clemons(Clements)	James Leckie	William C. Thomas
Richard V. Cobb	Abraham Little	H. H. Thurmond
Henry H. Cooper	J. M. Little	G. W. Tumlin
H .J. Cooper	W. H. Little	W. M. Vermillion
Anderson Glenn Dorsey	T. Y. Lovett	M .G. Wade
Jasper N. Dorsey	H .A. Lowery	J. B. Warren
John F. Dorsey	Robert H.(S.) Lowery	Joseph A. Watson
Robert R. Edison	David A. Mabry	S. T. Watson
Andrew Ellis	M. W. Mabry	J. M. Whelchel
Madison J. Ellis	J. J. Martin	Andrew White
Green K. C. Evans	William A. Martin	D. T. Williams
J. O. Farmer	J. R. Mason	John Witzel (Wetzel)
S. D. Farmer	Joshua McKinney	William T. Wood
F. H. Gaines	S. P. Mc Kinney	H. W. T. Gaines
Freling Huyser Moore	Jackson Gains	John K. Moore
John L. Gains	Joseph Moore	

COMPANY E - CAMPBELL AND FAYETTE COUNTIES, GEORGIA
BETHSAIDA RIFLE GUARDS

Henry Abercrombie
John T. Abercrombie
J. (I.) Marion Abercrombie
Seaborn V. Abercrombie
William J. Abercrombie
John J. Betsill
William A. Betsill
A.Z. Booth
Augustus Bray
Britton A. Brown
William Brown
John J. Buffington
W. M. Burgess
Edward Benjamin Butler
George D. Carter
Jesse A. Carter
J. W. Carter
James Chambers
Joel J. Chambers
Joseph A. Chambers
J. C. Chambers
John Coleman
Parker R. Coleman
Asberry Washington Cook
E. W. Cook
H. T. Cook
James Andrew Cook
J. O. Cook
Shem E. Cook
William R. Cook
W. C. Costley(Castley)
George D. Creel
James C. Creel
J. F. Creel
Leroy J. Creel
James M. Darnell
Elijah Davis
J. C. Davis
Marion Davis
Edward Y. Denson
John Denson
W. A. J. Denson
J. H. Dixon

John D. Dodd
J. Thompson Dodd
James Eason
Josiah H. Elder
W. B. Estes
R. D. Ewing
William S. Ewing
E. R. Fortson
James N. Fortson
W. M. Foster
Leonard Fuller
John Futch
E. M. Graves
Benjamin W. Griggs
Joseph Grizzard
Peter Guice
William H. Harper
Josiah Hart
William H. H. Head
Edward T. Hemplay
Joel M. Hemplay
Enoch M. Herndon
Richard Herndon
James (John) Hill
James F. Hindman
C. A. Hobson
William T. Hollis
T. J. Horton
T. W. Horton
W. L. Horton
D. T. Jennings
Lloyd Jones
S. J. Jones
S. T. Jones
F. M. Kerlin
J .Kerlin
Charles Edward Kimberly
John Lewis King
Lewis W. King
Thomas H. King
William Milligan King
Benjamin S. Kite
David Kite

Renfroe Kite
Hiram M. Laseter (Lassiter)
James Laseter (Lassiter)
Joel Laseter (Lassiter)
J. A Laseter (Lassiter)
Richard V. Laseter (Lassiter)
Israel E. Lindler
Jerry E. Lindler
James Miles Mason
Robert W. Mason
Joseph McKee
Pitt M. McLeroy
James W. Milam
William J. Mitchell
John Murphey (Murphy)
William M. Nelson
Henry F. Norris
J. R. Norris
J. William H. Norton
L. Norton
J. J. Parker
F. M. Pate
Benjamin F. Penly (Pendly)
Andrew Jackson Peters
Horsey Peters
Eli Pierce
E. R. Pyle
John H. Reeves
William C. Reeves
William H. Rentfroe
Graves Roberts
L. E. Roberts
Ephraim Roundtree
J. J. Rudicil (Rudisil)
Thomas C. Russell
William J. Sams
J. S. Sesnos
A. J. Smith
W. Morgan Smith
Jesse M. Spratlin
I. R. Stephens
P. S. (W.) Strawn
Thomas B. Swanson

137

Asa L. Dodd
George M .Dodd

George W. Kite
Josiah Kite

Ephraim Thompson
James R. Thompson

Muster Roll of Company E, 27th Regiment
(continued)

Thomas Thompson
Seaborn B. Thornton
Thomas L. Todd
William B. Turner
Henry Walker
James H. Waller
W. R. Waller

Ephraim West
Isom(Isham) West
John H. West
Joseph West
Joseph W. West
Lloyd West
William West

Willis West
Andrew J. Whitaker
James BoykinWhitaker
Charles Williams
WilliamJacksonWilliams
John T. Word

COMPANY F - TAYLOR COUNTY, GEORGIA
TAYLOR GUARDS

Amos Allen Adams
James E. Adams
Garrett Altman (Alman)
G. W. Amerson
Warren Amerson
James M. Askew
Robert C. Bailey
A. P. Barfield
Enoch J. Barfield
Warren Barfield
Wesley Barfield
David N. Bloodworth
James F. Boland
Elijah Bradley
Septimus L. Brewer
Robert Brown
Cullen Bryant
Thomas J. Bynum
B. F. Cochran
William Cochran
Allen E. Cody
E. W. Cook
John F. Coxwell
M. T. Davis
F. Denson (Dunson)
John N. Duke
J. M. Duke
William Posey Edwards
Elisha Forshe (Ferchee)
Andrew J. Fontaine(Fountain)
Cornelius B. Fountain
Jesse Fowler
B. A. Freeman
J. T(F) Hancock
John Hart
D. H. Herring
T. G. Herricks

Willis Herricks
D. Hill
Joseph W. Hill
Lewis Hill
Slaughter Hill
W. Green Holland
A. R. Hudson
John Hudson
John M. Humphries
H. N. L. Ingram
T. L. Jinks
Wesley Jones
William Kelly (Kelley)
Anthony Lavender
D. B. M. Lawson
James P. Lawson
Julius Lawson
F. P. Layfield
John Layfield
W. H. Layfield
J. B. Lyon (Lyons)
J. W. Lyon (Lyons)
Green Massey
William M. Massey
William W. Matthews
L. Q. C. McCrary
Burwell McCullers
Henry McCullers
George McGinty
Richard H. McGinty
J. M. McGlamry
W.G.McGlamry(McGlamey)
T. M. McInvale
W. H. McInvale
William J. Mitchell
William H. Moore
D. Jeptha Newton

Thomas S. Norris
John C. O'Hern
James Monroe Parks
William Henry Parks
Kinchen Peacock
Moulton A. Peacock
G. W. Pullin
E. B. Rogers
William B. Rogers
N .W. Scott
J. W. Searcy
Daniel Sells
W. F. Shepherd
Jesse Shinholster
Charles Shirah
Christopher C. Shirah
James Shirah
John Shirah
James B. Sorrells
W. T. Streetman
H. T. Thompson
Francis M. Threlkeld(Threlkeld)
Leroy Tuggle
Grigsby Tune
Smith Turner
Warren F. Walters
William Walter
Elijah Watson
Robert MarionWhittington
Jordan Wilcher
D. H. Williams
Erwin(Irwin) Williams
Wiley Wilson
Jerry Windham
William A. Windham
John Bunyan Wright

COMPANY G - PIKE AND SPALDING COUNTIES, GEORGIA
COUNTY LINE GUARDS

James C. Adams
John T. Akin
W. J. Anderson
J. Apperson
John L. Banks
Joshua Barker
Hiram Beckham
James J. Beckham
John D. Beckham
Simeon G. Beckham
John C. Beeks
Marcus L. Billingsley
Lindsay Bowin
J. W. Boyd
Sidney Boyd
William H. Boyd
Andrew J. Brooks
Robert J. Brooks
A. Flemming Brown, Jr.
George B. Buchanan
John M. Burns
James D. Carriker
Morgan T. Carriker
J. J. Carter
Joseph C. Chapman
William Thomas Chapman
Daniel M. Childs
William J. Colquitt
Colby J. Cook
Thomas J. Cook
John B. Copeland
J. J. Crawford
J. B. Creamer
John C. Curtis (Curtice)
Thomas Dewberry
Osburn Ellis
William Ezell
T. Ford
B. J. Foster
E. J. Fowler

G. W. Fowler
Benjamin F. Ganous
Isham S. Ganous
Asa Gordy
William J. Grisham
Miles R. Hagan (Hagins)
Thomas P. Hagan (Hagins)
James N. Hall
Elsbury Hambrick
William J. Hambrick
James Harper
Leonard O. Harris
W. M. Hinsley (Hinesly)
James H. Horton
T. Jefferson Howard
John D.Jones
Thomas Zachry Jones
William R. M. Jones
James R. Jordan
Thomas J. M. King
George Kinney
James M. Lee
J. D. Lee
Seaborn S. Lesueur
Benjamin Hawkins Lifsey
Henry T. Lifsey
James S. Lifsey
John Lifsey
Edward H. (A) Lynch
Wiley James Mangham
James F. Maxey
John (James) C. McClure
Colbert McKinley
John W. McKinley
W. H. Means
John C. Moore
William A. Moreland
Christopher C. Parker
Walter Parks

John B. Peters
Augustus N.(M) Powell
John F. Rainey
Simeon Reaves
Willian Dozier Redding
James B. Reeves
Warren Reeves
Columbus A. Reid (Reed)
Robert H. Ross
Russell Ross
James B. Rucker
J. M. Rucker
R. Thomas Sealey (Seeley)
W. J. Simmons
James M. Slade
William H. Slade
William H. C. Slade
Thomas C. Smith
Thomas C. Stanley
David R. Steger
William B. Stewart
Carey Srtickland
James M. Sullivan
John S. Sullivan
John Sweat (Sweete)
John Taylor
John W. Taylor
Elba H. Threlkeld
J. H. Vaughn
Frederick J. Wadsworth
William C. Wadsworth
Christopher C. Watts
James Joseph Whaley
Robert J. Wheeler
James Wilder
Josiah N. Williams
Theophilus Williams
William Jasper Williamson
Matthew Wood

COMPANY H - HENRY COUNTY, GEORGIA
"ZACHRY RANGERS"

Elijah Alexander
F. Alexander
Uriah Alexander
Joseph Avery
Henry L. Bentley
Eli A. Biggers
Iverson B. Bryans
Wesley Capps (Capes)
W. B .Capps (Capes)
J. Henry Carroll
George M. Chaffin
William M. (A) Childs
John Pinkney Copeland, Jr.
Windfield A. Copeland
James H. Darnell
Thomas J. Dearing
William W. DeLamar
W. F. Dickson
Charles Driver
A. G. Duke
R. W. Duke
Scott Duke
Sherod Duke
Thomas J. Duke
W. Dunning
Jacob Dyes
Judge Eddleman
George T. Embry
Robert C. Evans
Franklin B. Ferguson
James T. Fields
James Floyd
David Gaines
W. J. Gunn
Francis Marion Hale(Hail)
Patrick Henry Hale
Robert A. Harkey
Marion Pinkney Harkness
Samuel G. W. Harkness
Elijah W. Harper
James W. Harper
Wade H. Harper
William Wallace Harper
W. T. Harper

John T. D. Harris
Benjamin G. (Tobe) Hearn
J. W. Hearn
H.(A) F. Henry
S. M. Henry
B. F. Herron
J. P. Hilley
J. W. Hilley
Samuel H. Hodge(Hodges)
S. Hodge(Hodges)
David King
Lemon King
Solomon King
T. Jefferson Kitchens
Daniel R. Lewis
J. H. Lewis
J. T. Lewis
J .W. Lewis
Litt Lewis
Sandford Lewis
S. P. Lewis
Daniel N. Lindsey
J. M. Lindsey
William H. Lyle
Roe Maddox
John N. Mason
J. William L. Mason
Isaac McBride
Robert W. McBride
Frank W. McClendon
John C. McClendon
J. Robert McCullough
W. Perry McCullough
L. O. (C) McMullin
Henry H. Miller
B. W. Nail
R. J. Nail
R. W. J. Nail
Thomas Nail
Elihu C. Nash
James Hambree Nash
John Adam Nash
J. P. S. Nash
Q. L. Nash

W. Callaway Nolan
Benjamin F. Norris
Matthew Orr
Aug. J. W. Peek
A. F. Phillips
Madison Phillips
Burrell P. Pryor
George W. Rape
Samuel Rix
John Robinson
William Robinson
William Rolan
James Russell
L. Whit Russell
Thomas L. Russell
William J. St. John
G. Frank Stallworth
P. F. Stewart
R. J. Tate
JohnTaylor
J. W. Taylor
George Roland Thompson
B. F. Turner
H. C. Turner
James C. Turner
J. H. Turner
L. W. J. Turner
Wade A. Turn
William G. Turner
Michael Wallace
Frank Welch
John W. Welch
H. Lee Whitaker
Henry Willard
James W. Willard
John L. Willard
Marvin Willard
Joseph N. Wilson
Richard M. Wilson
William B. Wilson
George Edward Wise
John M. Zachry
Charles Thornton Zachry
Andrew Harris

141

COMPANY I - APPLING COUNTY, GEORGIA
"APPLING GRAYS"

Elisha Aldridge
W. T. Argo
Cornelius Barber
Thomas Fletcher Barnett
Joseph W. Baxley
Lovet W. Baxley
Willis Baxley
Henry Harrison Becher
William Alfred Becher
William Lumpkin Becher
Mark Brannon
William O. Bryant
William H. Burk
Cohen Carter
O. F. Carter
Lawrence W. Clay
Jackson Cooner
Jefferson Cooner
John Cooner
Thomas Howell Courson
John Crapps
Joseph A. Crapps
A. M. Crosby
Isham Crosby
Jacob Crosby
Silas A. Crosby
William Custer (Kutler)
James E. Davis
John J. Dilbon
William H. Dilbon
William B. Dobson
A. C. Douglas

C. M. Douglas
William Eason
J. Fields
Mathew Fiveash
Elisha Duncan Graham
William Wallace Graham
William Griffin
D. C. Hagan (Hagin)
Alfred S. Hall
James E. Harper
David Hester(s)
David Jack Hester(s)
Francis M. Hester
George W. Hester
John Hughes
William H. Hughes
Benjamin F. Hutto
Alexander W. Johnson
LaFayette H. Johnson
Levi Johnson
Samuel M. Johnson
Frank Jones
Joseph Jones
Peter Kemp
William Kutler
Osgood A. Lee
Benjamin Leggett
A. D. Leslie (Laslie)
Adolph S. Lessure
Zedekiah W. Little
D. M. Livingston

Daniel E. Lynn
Patrick Lynn
William Lynn
Henry Mann, Jr.
William Martin
James McGauley (McGalley)
James M. McLendon
Benjamin Milikin
William H. Nelson
G. W. L. Nix
P. F. O'Conner
Daniel J. Phillips
Henry Prescott
John A. Prescott
James M. Puckett
Franklin Quinn
Reuben Reaves
Jacob Rentz
Bluford (Buford) Sapp
William Smith
William Story
Andrew H. Thomas
Nathaniel A. Thomas
Jacob T. Thompson
Moses Tomberlin
William Tomberlin
David J Tuten
George Vane

COMPANY K - TALBOT COUNTY, GEORGIA

Lewis Alsabrook
Abner W. Bedell
Henry D. Bedell
Berry Belyen
Freeman Belyen
John A. Belyen
John C. Belyen
Josiah Belyen
Richard Belyen
Wesley F. Belyen
John F. Bins
James Whit Bonner
General Jackson Bruce
Hezekiah Bussey
John F. Byers
Calvin Calhoun
Samuel John Calhoun
William Calhoun
Robert S. Cameron
Benjamin F. Carlisle
James Carlisle
Michael(Mekaga) Carlisle
George F. Cole
E. J. Colley
John F. Connell
William Connell
William Cooper
Solomon R. DeLoach
William T. Dennis
James P. Dent
Henry C. Downs
John F. Downs
Charles E. Dozier
R. H. Murphy

Short Dozier
James Drew
William H. Drew
Samuel H. Ellison
Staten Fulford, Sr.
William H. Fuller
William B. Giddings
Thomas D. Goodwin
David Green
Dempsey Griffin
Thomas Daniel Hall
William T. Hall
Thomas Hardy
Jesse W. Hobbs
Andrew C. Howard
James Ingram
Thomas J. (T) Jarrell
James M. Johnson
William M. Johnson
William J. Jones
Robert H. Kellum
William Robinson Kellum
.... Lampkin
Freeman Mathews
George H. Mathews
Royal McClung
A. C. McCrory
George Y. McDowell
Robert A. McDowell
Telemachus P. McDowell
Robert H. Milling
Joseph M. Murphy
Michael Murphy

Daniel R. Owen
Josiah Bunkley Parker
John Thomas Pound
Joseph Gilbert Pound
Mathew J. Pound
Edward Proctor
Jesse B. Pye
Wilkins J. Raines
Richard Radcliff, Jr.
Richard Radcliff, Sr
Emerald M. Rickerson
A. H. Sealy
Zeph B. Sealy
John K. Sibley
Charles T. Smith
Levi B. Smith
R. Marion Smith
William C. Smith
Benjamin F. Spinks
William T. Spinks
N. A. Thompson
William J. Thompson
James Jason Tigner
O. V. Tommie
Raleigh H. Turner
Freeman Walker
Samuel Zachariah Webster
Robert White
J. T. Williams
Garry T. Williamson
Andrew Willis (Wallis)
James R. Wilson
James A. Dozier

HEROES AND MARTYRS OF GEORGIA

GEORGIA'S RECORD OF THE REVOLUTION OF 1861

BY JAMES M. FOLSOM

MACON, GA.
BURKE, BOYKIN & COMPANY
1864

TWENTY-SEVENTH REGIMENT GEORGIA VOLUNTEERS

STATISTICAL RECORD

Number of men originally enlisted	684
Number of recruits and conscripts	467
Total strength of regiment	1151

LOSSES

Number of men killed in action	104
Number of men died of wounds, disease & c	268
Loss by death	372
Number of men discharged, &c	174
Total loss of regiment	546

CHANGES IN FIELD OFFICERS.

The original field officers were: Levi B. Smith of Talbotton, Colonel; S. L. Brewer, of Taylor County, Lieutenant Colonel; Charles T. Zachry, of Henry County, Major. Lieutenant Colonel Brewer resigned in December, 1861, and Major Zachry was elected Lieutenant Colonel, and Captain H. B. Halliday elected Major. Major Halliday resigned in August 1862, and senior Captain John W. Stubbs was appointed major. Colonel L. B. Smith was killed at Sharpsburg on the 17th of September, 1862, and Lieutenant Colonel Zachry was appointed Colonel to fill the vacancy. Major Stubbs was appointed Lieutenant Colonel, and senior Captain Charles J. Dennis was appointed Major. Major Dennis resigned in December, 1862, and Captain Jasper N. Dorsey appointed Major. Lieutenant Colonel Stubbs resigned in December, 1862, and Major Dorsey was appointed Lieutenant Colonel. First lieutenant and Adjutant James Gardner, promoted to Major for distinguished gallantry in action. Lieutenant Colonel Dorsey was dismissed the service in May, 1864, by sentence of General Court Martial, and Major Gardner appointed Lieutenant Colonel. Captain H. Bussey Major. Lieutenant Colonel Gardner was killed on the 18th of June 1864, and Major Bussey was appointed Lieutenant Colonel.

(Captain William H. Renfroe appointed Major. Major Renfroe was killed in the Battle of Bentonville March 18, 1865 and Captain Elisha Duncan Graham was appointed Major. At their surrender, April 26, 1865, the officers were: Colonel, Charles T. Zachry; Lieutenant Colonel, Hezikiah Bussey; Major, Elisha Duncan Graham)

The Twenty-seventh Regiment of Georgia Volunteer Infantry was organized at Camp Stephens, near Griffin, Georgia, and was mustered into the service of the Confederate States on the 9th and 10th days of September, 1861.

On the 31st of October it was ordered to Richmond, Virginia, and thence to Manassas, where it arrived about the 15th of November, without arms. The first service it rendered was in the building of a bridge across the Occoquan River, which was completed about the 15th of December, when the regiment was ordered into winter quarters at Camp Pickens, near Manassas. At this point the regiment performed garrison duty until the 9th day of March 1862, when they were ordered to Clark's Mountain. Colonel G. B. Anderson, of north Carolina, was commanding the brigade, composed of the Fourth North Carolina Troops, the Forty-ninth Virginia Infantry, and the Twenty-seventh and Twenty-eighth Georgia Volunteer Regiments. The brigade arrived at Clark's Mountain on the 20th of March, 1862. On the

9th of April, Brigadier General W. S. Featherstone was assigned to and assumed command of the brigade. While encamped at Clark's Mountain the weather was very inclement, and the troops suffered exceedingly.

On the evening of the 9th of April, the regiment marched to the railroad to take the cars for Richmond, through snow and sleet from four to six inches in depth. Upon the arrival of the regiment in the city, they were ordered to take boat for Grover's Landing on the James River, (this was on the 10th of April) and from thence were marched across the country to Yorktown. On the 14th day of April the Twenty-seventh Georgia Regiment, with the Thirteenth Alabama Regiment, was ordered in front of the works to assist Captain Hardaway's Battery in dislodging some sharpshooters, who were annoying us to a considerable extent, from a pine grove between our works and those of the enemy. The orders being successfully carried out, the sharpshooters having been dislodged, the regiment returned to camp jubilant over their first engagement with the enemy, without the loss of a single life. On the evening of May 3rd, the regiment commenced its retreat with the whole army from Yorktown; it passed through Williamsburg on the 4th, and on the morning of the 5th the retreat was resumed. The Twenty-seventh Georgia had marched about five miles, when orders were received for it to return to Williamsburg in double-quick time, to assist our troops in the battle of Williamsburg, which was then raging. The rain was falling, the roads were in a terrible condition, and the weather was extremely cold; the regiment, however, caring nothing for these discomforts, about faced, (instead of countermarching) and started at the double-quick. Arriving at Williamsburg, knapsacks, haversacks, blankets and everything which could interfere with their efficiency in battle were thrown off, by our boys, as quickly as possible.

A position was assigned to the Twenty-seventh Georgia beyond and to the left of the town. This position they occupied for several hours, when they were marched to another position in a large wheat field, where they remained during the night, suffering immensely from cold, fatique, and the knawing pangs of hunger.

About two o'clock on the morning of the 6th, the wheat field was evacuated and the line of march resumed toward the city of Richmond. Upon the arrival of the regiment at Long Bridge, they struck camp and remained there for ten or twelve days, and then moved to the vicinity of Richmond.

At the Battle of Seven Pines, fought on the 31st of May, this regiment participated, going into action at two o'clock in the afternoon, a little to the left of the Williamsburg road. General Featherstone being sick, the command of the brigade devolved upon Colonel G. B. Anderson, of North Carolina. Colonel Smith, of this regiment, was wounded in the early part of this engagement, but did not quit the field until the brigade was relieved. About four o'clock, P. M., Colonel Jenkins of South Carolina, with his sharpshooters, came to the relief of the Twenty-seventh Georgia, when a charge was ordered and the enemy were completely routed in front of their position. At this juncture the brigade was relieved, excepting the Twenty-seventh Georgia, who were ordered to keep in supporting distance of Colonel Jenkins, who was then in pursuit of the enemy, and before sundown Colonel Jenkins ordered Lieutenant Colonel Zachry (who was then in command of the Twenty-seventh Georgia, Colonel Smith having retired) to form on his (Colonel Jenkins') right, as the enemy in heavy force were attempting to flank him in that direction. The regiment moved up at the double quick, and were forming line, when some little confusion occurred; which lasted, however, but a moment. It was at this time that Adjutant Gardner displayed that coolness and marked bravery which elicited from Colonel Jenkins a personal compliment and recommendation for promotion. Colonel Jenkins succeeded, with the aid of the Twenty-seventh Georgia, in baffling the designs of the enemy upon our flank, and drove him one-fourth of a mile from their position, when night put an end to the conflict. The loss of the Twenty-seventh Georgia in this engagement was severe, amounting to one hundred and fifty-four (154) killed and wounded.

After the battle of Seven Pines a brigade was formed, consisting of the Sixth, Twenty-third, Twenty-seventh and Twenty-eighth Georgia Regiments and the Thirteenth Alabama Regiment, General Featherstone commanding. In A few days, however, General Featherstone was assigned to duty elsewhere, and the command of the brigade devolved upon Colonel A. H. Colquitt, commanding the Sixth Georgia Regiment.

On the morning of the26th of June the regiment took up the line of march at half past one o'clock, and halted near Mechanicsville. The regiment was engaged in the battle of Mechanicsville on the morning of the 27th, and at Cold Harbor on the evening of the same day. At the battle of Cold Harbor, Gen. Colquitt's Brigade charged the enemy and gained a very important position, which was held by the Twenty-seventh Georgia for some time, without any assistance from the other regiments of the brigade. The Sixty-first Georgia Regiment was ordered forward to relieve the Twenty-seventh, but, mistaking them for the enemy, fired into the regiment, until Adjutant Gardner could pass from the extreme right of the regiment to its centre, and have the colors raised, by that means signifying to them that we were friends. The Sixty-first, recognizing the colors, ceased firing, and coming quickly forward, relieved the Twenty-seventh.

This regiment next engaged the enemy at White Oak Swamp, on the evening of the 31st of June; and again on the evening of the 1st of July, at Malvern Hill, we were hurled upon the foe, losing very severely in killed and wounded, Adjutant Gardner being among those who were severely wounded.

About the 6th of July the regiment returned to the vicinity of Richmond, having suffered a loss of one hundred and twenty-six men, killed and wounded, in the series of engagements, known as the battles around Richmond.

From the 10th of July until the 17th of August, the Twenty-seventh Georgia marched several times from the vicinity of Richmond to Malvern Hill and back, when the movements of the enemy would indicate an advance from that point.

On the 19th of August the regiment took the cars at Richmond, and proceeded to Orange Court House, where it remained until the 27th of August, when it took up the line of march, and joined Generals Lee and Jackson near Fairfax, Virginia, two days after the second battle of Manassas, where it rested twenty-four hours, and then proceeded, *via* Leesburg to Frederick, Maryland. After resting three days at Frederick, it marched *via* South Mountain and Boonesboro, to within six miles of Hagerstown, Maryland; when orders were received to return at once to South Mountain pass, which was performed on the night of the 12th of September. On the morning of the 14th, a position was assigned to the Twenty-seventh by Major General D. H. Hill, to whose division Colquitt's Brigade belonged; which position it held all that day. At night we were withdrawn and marched to Sharpsburg, from thence to the north bank of the Potomac, opposite Shepherdstown, Virginia, where we arrived about eleven o'clock on the morning of the 15th. On the morning of the 16th, the brigade was marched back to Sharpsburg, and assigned to different positions during the day. On the morning of the 17th, the Twenty-seventh Georgia Regiment went into the fight early in the morning, and fought long and well. Among the many fatal casualties in the Twenty-seventh, was Colonel Smith, as gallant and generous a heart as ever beat, and whose loss will be long deplored by his surviving comrades. Lieutenant Colonel Zachry was severely wounded in this engagement.

The loss of the Twenty-seventh Georgia in the battles of South Mountain and Sharpsburg amounted to one hundred and forty-nine (149) men killed and wounded.

Leaving Sharpsburg on the morning of the 19th, the regiment crossed the Potomac River before day, and marched to Martinsburg, where it rested two or three days, and then proceeded to Bunker Hill. We left Bunker Hill about the 23rd of October and assisted in tearing up the railroad, leading from Harper's Ferry to Charlestown, on or about the night of the 24th of September. Here again the troops suffered incredibly from the excessive cold, the men being generally poorly clad, and in many instances barefooted, their sufferings were very severe. After destroying the above mentioned railroad, the regiment marched across the Shenandoah River, and camped between Paris and Upperville, about the 1st of November. Leaving Paris it marched to Front Royal, thence to Strasburg, where another railroad was destroyed.

Between the 15th and 20th of November, we were ordered to march, and passing Guinea's Station *via* Orange Court house, arrived at our destination in the vicinity of Port Royal, on the Rappahannock, on the

1st day of December. The troops on this march made an average of twenty-two miles per day, and large numbers of them were forced to the necessity of wearing sandals, made of raw hide.

On the 13th of December, the Twenty-seventh participated in the battle of Fredericksburg. After the battle of Fredericksburg, we went into winter quarters near Guinea's Station, and performed picket duty on the Rappahannock. On the 27th day of April, 1863, we took up the line of march for Chancellorsville, where we were engaged on the evening of the29th, and again on the 30th at Wilderness Church, and again on the 1st day of May at Wilderness Tavern. Losing in the three engagements fifty-seven (57) men

killed and wounded. On the 4th day of May we returned to our old winter quarters, near Guinea's Station.

About the 19th of May the Twenty-seventh Georgia was ordered to report without delay to Major General D. H. Hill, commanding the Department of North Carolina and Southern Virginia. The regiment arrived at Kinston, North Carolina, about the 28th of May and remained there until the 3rd of July, when it was ordered back to Richmond to repel an anticipated raid of the enemy; arriving in Richmond on the 6th only to remain a few days, as it received orders to report at Wilmington, North Carolina, to General Whiting commanding that post. Upon the arrival of the regiment at Wilmington, it was immediately ordered to Topsail Sound, on the coast. Here the regiment remained until the 10th of August, when it was ordered to report to General Beauregard at Charleston, South Carolina, where it arrived on the 13th and marched to James Island. About the 28th of August we were ordered to Morris Island, where we remained until its evacuation, this regiment covering the retreat of the troops from the Island.

From September, 1863, until February, 1864, the Twenty-seventh remained on James Island doing picket duty there, and performing garrison duty at Fort Sumter. On the morning of the 12th of February the regiment marched for John's Island where it arrived to assist General Wise in driving the enemy from their position on that Island.

On the 14th of February the Twenty-seventh, with the other regiments of Colquitt's Brigade, were ordered to Florida, and taking the cars on the Charleston and Savannah railroad it proceeded to Savannah, thence by the Atlantic and Gulf railroad to Valdosta, Georgia, where it arrived on the 15. From Valdosta the regiment marched to Madison, Florida, and thence by railroad to Olustee Station, on Tallahassee and Jackson railroad. During the early part of the day the battle of Ocean Pond, the Twenty-seventh Georgia Regiment was held in reserve; but about four o'clock, P. M., it was ordered into the engagement and immediately charging the enemy, contributed greatly to the utter rout and demoralization of the enemy. Colonel Zachry on this memorable occasion was termed the *"Blucher"* of the day. The loss of the Twenty-seventh Georgia in the battle of Ocean Pond was very severe for the time it was engaged, amounting to eighty-seven (87) in killed and wounded. After the battle the enemy were pursued to Baldwin, Florida.

On the 1st day of March the Eleventh South Carolina, Twenty-seventh Georgia, and a force of cavalry, all under the command of Colonel Zachry, were ordered on a reconnoitering expedition. Near Cedar Creek they met with a force of the enemy, supposed to have been sent out for a similar purpose. After a short engagement the enemy were completely routed; and but for the failure of the cavalry to execute Colonel Zachry's orders, the entire party would have been captured. After the battles of Ocean Pond and Cedar Creek, the Twenty-seventh Georgia remained in camp at Camp Milton, eight miles south of Baldwin, Florida, until the 19th of April, when it marched for Tebeauville, on the Atlantic and Gulf railroad. Arriving at that point they took cars, and proceeded by way of Savannah to Charleston, South Carolina. Upon arriving there it was ordered to James Island, where the regiment remained until May 11th, when it returned to Charleston, thence by railroad to Petersburg, Virginia, stopping, however, a few days at Weldon, North Carolina, in anticipation of a raid on that place. Arriving at Petersburg on the 19th, the Twenty-seventh was assigned a position on the front lines between the James and Appomattox Rivers, where it remained until the 31st, when it was ordered to Cold Harbor. At the battle of Cold Harbor, on the first of June, five companies of this regiment charged and re-captured that portion of our lines lost by the left of General Clingman's Brigade. These five companies lost in the engagement, eleven (11) killed and fifty-four (54) wounded. The regiment remained on the front at Cold Harbor until the 13th of June, when it marched to Malvern Hill, leaving which place on the 14th, it marched to the vicinity of Richmond, where it remained until twelve o'clock P. M., on the15th, when the march was resumed to Chester Station, on the Richmond and Petersburg railroad, where it took the cars for Petersburg, where it arrived a little after dark, the same day.

The enemy having gained our works by assault before dark, the Twenty-seventh Georgia was assigned a position, and entrenched themselves during the night. On the night of the 17th of June the entire line was changed, and the Twenty-seventh Georgia was ordered to hold a very important salient, where they again entrenched themselves, as soon as it was possible so to do.

On the evening of the 18th of June, the enemy in three heavy columns, charged the position of this regiment. They were handsomely repulsed, with severe loss, over two hundred of their dead being left on the field. This salient was held by the Twenty-seventh Georgia regiment, without relief until the 24th of June, with a loss of seventy-six (76) men killed and wounded. Among the wounded on the 18th was the gallant Lieutenant Colonel Gardner, who was mortally wounded, and died a few days thereafter. He was promoted to the position he held for distinguished gallantry, and his name and noble deeds will live forever embalmed in the hearts of his surviving comrades.

From the 24th of June until the 18th of August, this regiment was on the front, on -half of their time, alternating every three days, with a portion of General Martin's Brigade. On the 18th of August, while the Twenty-seventh Georgia was in reserve, the enemy advanced and took possession of the Weldon and Petersburg railroad, when the Twenty-seventh was ordered to the point attacked by the enemy, and engaged them on the evening of the same day. On the 19th this regiment formed a portion of a flanking party, who inflicted a heavy loss of the enemy in killed and wounded. Many prisoners were taken.

The Twenty-seventh Georgia on this occasion, was under the command of Major H. Bussey. Owing to the natural features of the country, consisting as they did of thickly wooded spots, with very dense undergrowth, it was impossible to preserve intact the advancing line of battle, large gaps would frequently be made in our lines, through which the enemy would make their way in detached parties, so that friend and foe would become thoroughly intermingled, and of necessity the fighting was very desperate, being sometimes almost hand to hand. It was an occasion which required great coolness and decision on the part of the commanding officers. The whole regiment was several times in imminent danger of being captured, inspired however, by the unwavering coolness and intrepid valor of their leaders, these war-worn and battle-scarred veterans of many a bloody field would rally with enthusiasm around their tattered battle flag, and drive back with severe loss the advances of their assailants. A heavy rain having fallen a short time before the battle opened, and continuing to fall during its progress, the soil had become miry and slippery; The Twenty-seventh Georgia however, with other regiments of the brigade, making a gallant charge, drove the enemy with great slaughter from his entrenched line.

Night put an end to the contest. The loss in killed and wounded in the Twenty-seventh Georgia was thirty and twenty were taken prisoners. To compensate for the loss, besides the number of the enemy killed and wounded, a very large number of prisoners was taken; even the ambulance corps, in addition to attending to the wants of the wounded, captured eighty (80) prisoners.

At the present time, August 30th, 1864, the Twenty-seventh Georgia occupies an important position upon the defensive lines, around the city of Petersburg, Virginia.

Recapitulation of losses in the different battles in which the Twenty-seventh Georgia has been engaged:

Seven Pines	killed and wounded	149
Battles around Richmond	" " "	125
Sharpsburg and South Mountain	" " "	154
Chancellorsville	" " "	57

Ocean Pond	"	"	"	87
Cold Harbor	"	"	"	65
Salient at Petersburg	"	"	"	76
on Weldon Railroad	"	"	"	30
total casualties				744
loss in killed(as from statistical record)				104
Loss in wounded				640

The losses in the regiment have certainly been severe. By adding to the real losses of the regiment, amounting to five hundred and forty-six men, the number wounded six-hundred and forty, we find that the losses of this regiment, like those of the Third, Sixth and other Georgia regiments, *exceeds the total number of men enlisted and recruited.* This explained by the fact that the only wounded men *lost* to the regiment, are those who have been discharged. Many of the men have also been wounded more than once.

TWENTY-SEVENTH GEORGIA REGIMENT

(Completed June 1995)

On the 29th of September General Ord's Federal troops struck against Fort Harrison near Chaffin's farm, capturing the fort. The Twenty-seventh Georgia along with the other regiments of Colquitt's Brigade launched an attack on the fort, but were unable to re-capture the works. December 25th Major General Hoke ordered The Twenty-seventh Georgia to Greensboro, North Carolina along with the other regiments of the brigade, they were ordered to Fort Anderson by General Braxton Bragg and on the 30th they were sent to Wilmington, North Carolina by steamer. General Colquitt was given the command of Fort Fisher and January 13, 1865 the regiment was involved in escorting him to take over his new command. The fort was under siege and fell before General Colquitt and his troops could traverse the narrow strip of land leading to the fort. They were caught in enflading fire from the gunboats and the Federals on the land. The Twenty-seventh Georgia under Colonel Zachry were placed as the rear guard and inflicted heavy losses to the enemy as they grudgingly relinquished the ground. February 21st the regiment was engaged at the battle of Wilmington, North Carolina, again on the 22nd the Twenty-seventh Georgia was assigned the post of honor, the rear guard, and again the enemy was made to pay dearly by Colonel Zachry's seasoned veterans.

March 8, 1865 General Hoke's Division was ordered to slow the advance of General Sherman's army. They met in Kinston, North Carolina and the battle of Kinston ensued. On the 10th around eleven o'clock, A. M., the Twenty-seventh Georgia Regiment , the other regiments in Colquitt's Brigade and the regiments of Kirkland's Brigade executed a flanking movement against the Federals at Kinston and carried the breast works capturing most of the troops as prisoners along with their artillery pieces.

The regiment was ordered to Goldsboro, North Carolina on the 13th of March and were engaged at Averasboro and on the 18th were engaged in the battle of Bentonville. Colonel Zachry's Twenty-seventh Georgia broke through the enemy lines but due to lack of support were unable to take advantage and suffered severe loss on the enemy's works in killed and wounded, including Major W. H. Renfroe.

April 26, 1865 the war worn veterans of the Twenty-seventh Georgia Regiment furled their banners and stacked arms as the remnant of the mighty army of the Confederate States surrendered with General Joseph E. Johnston at Greensboro, North Carolina.

Completed By: William A. Bowers, Jr.

GEORGIA DRILLERS

COMPANY A

The following is taken from the Confederate Veteran, XXI (1913), 583

TWENTY-SEVENTH GEORGIA REGIMENT
By Sam Blythe

I left home for the war on September 1, 1861, and went into bivouac with the other boys at Camp Stevens, Ga. There we were organized as the 27th Georgia, in which I served in Company A. The regiment went from Camp Stevens to Manassas, where we spent the winter. In the spring of 1862 we went to Yorktown and in about two months to Richmond. We left there between suns; but the enemy found it out, pursued us and overtook us at Williamsburg. There was some sharp skirmishing , and afterwards it was necessary for us to stand in line of battle all night. It was bitter cold and we were allowed no fire. Next morning some of the boys were so numb that they could hardly get one foot before the other.

We met the Yankees next at Seven Pines, where we had a severe introduction. We got the best of them, but fell back that night and left them the battle field, which is the reason the Federals claim the victory. We need not have fallen back; but Lee, with Jackson, was planning the Seven Day's fight around Richmond. We routed them at every fight except Malvern Hill; and if they had not gained the heights on and gotten under the shelter of the gunboats, we would likely have killed them all or they would have drowned in the river, for they had running in their heads. After this our company was made into a company of skirmishers of sharpshooters.

Veterans often tell about the tight places they got into during the war and the brave things they did; but I don't think I ever did but one plucky thing, and that was accidental. It was like this; in one of Stonewall's flank movements we got in the enemy's rear. We got into their cooking forces; and having nothing but cooks to contend with, we ran them away, and then the chance to fill our haversacks with cooked rations was too good to waste shooting Yankees. I sampled my captured haversack and, lo, found fried steak and soda crackers! I held to the grub, but with a sharp eye out for the Yanks.

We were now ordered to do some charging and counter charging; but I was too busy eating to get the orders right, and I ended by running through a pine thicket right into a line of bluecoats. I darted back, and when I herd someone coming double-quick I dropped my gun meaning to surrender. But when he got near me I saw that he had no gun, so I picked up mine and thus got the drop on him. I walked up to him at a charge bayonet,

154

gun cocked, and he smiled all over his face and said: "You got me." He then said, "Let's get out of this," and started toward the blue line I had just discovered, saying we were in range of a battery in the other direction. I turned him about and ordered a bee line toward the setting sun. But before we had gone far his words came true about the battery. We were right in line of it, and the grapeshot and canister fell like hail. The Yank went faster and faster, and I had to run to keep up with my prisoner. Pretty soon we came up against a squad of Yankee soldiers, but they were all prisoners. I turned my special prize over to the officer in charge, who ordered me to cross the road and lie down with the other men, and he added; "Look out for No, 1." It was good advice, though not needed at the particular time. It reminded me of what my best girl said to me the morning I left for the war. When I gave her my hand to say good-by, she looked me in the eye, saying: "Sam, take care of No. 1." I did and still do that.

It is very fortunate that a diary belonging to Washington L. Dunn of Company A. is available in the United Daughters of the Confederacy's bound volumes. It is however unfortunate that it is his third diary and the first two did not survive to better tell the story of this company.

There is also preserved in the United Daughters of the Confederacy's bound volumes a group of letters to and from James Matthew Jordan that give insight to the innermost thoughts and emotions that were shared by the private soldier in the protracted war for the independence of the Confederate states.

APPLING GRAYS
COMPANY I

(The following is from "Footprints in Appling County" by Ruth T. Barron)

The Appling Grays, a company of volunteers, was formed at Holmesville, Georgia in 1860 with Osgood A. Lee as captain, Dr. J. H. Latimer, 1st lieutenant, L. Clary, 2nd lieutenant, and Dr. Zedekiah W. Little as Jr. 2nd lieutenant. The company left for a camp of instruction at Griffin, Georgia in August 1861 and there it was organized into the 27th Georgia Regiment. (Benjamin Milikin's Personal Account of His War Experiences)

At Camp Stephens near Griffin, Georgia on August 27, 1861, Captain Osgood A. Lee of Company I, 27th Regiment of the Georgia Volunteers requisitioned a coffee mill and seven coffee pots for his men. In the requisition he had a note stating that" the listed articles are necessary for the use of the men under my command." The major portion of the articles was as follows:

7 camp kettles	1 spring balance
7 fry pans	2 wall tents
7 mess kits	15 common tents
14 knives and forks	75 blankets
14 tin plates	3 axes and helves
7 spoons	3 hatchets
1 sifter	2 spades
7 ovens	75 tin cups
2 pick axes and helves	

(Jesup Sentinel, op. cit.)
Nearly a hundred men were killed out of this company of 127 men who had volunteered from Appling County.

(The following is from a family history of the Graham family of Appling County --This family includes Captain Elisha Duncan Graham)
"..........Elisha Duncan Graham , son of John Graham , was a farmer and merchant in Holmesville, Georgia. He served in the Confederate Army as a Captain of the "Appling Grays", a company composed of volunteers, which was organized as soon as war was declared. There was an old camp meeting ground known as the "Camp Ground" about three miles south of the present city of Graham, and it was there that the "Appling Grays' practiced their drills, etc.., preparatory to going to the front. This company was composed of the foremost young men of the county. However, after

they reached Richmond they were placed in different regiments and thus the "Appling Grays" lost their identity. (compilers note: no evidence has been found to substantiate this statement. All indications are that Company I, the "Appling Grays" were still together after Bentonville and at the surrender at Greensboro, North Carolina) So eager were they to get to the front that they could not wait to be furnished uniforms from the Government; so while the men were drilling and going through the maneuvers of war at the "Old Camp Ground" the women of the surrounding territory also met and made uniforms for them. A tailor was secured to come and cut out the uniforms; but it was the wives, sisters and sweethearts who did the sewing. Probably many a sigh and heartache from these noble women accompanied the needles they so deftly plied. Of this company only a few came back.............."

Captain Benjamin Miliken dictated the following account of the hardships and suffering endured by him during the war to his granddaughter, Dorothy Milikin Smith Davis:

"...........I was seventeen when I joined a Company of Volunteers at Holmesville, Appling County, Georgia in 1861. O. A. Lee was elected captain; Dr. J. H. Latimer, first lieutenant; L. Clary, second lieutenant; and Dr. Z. E. Little, 3rd lieutenant. The company was named the Appling Grays. We left for a camp of instruction at Griffin, Georgia on 27 August, 1861 and left there for Richmond, Virginia in October of that year. The company was organized in the 27th Georgia Regiment at Griffin and was one of the original companies of Colquitt's Brigade and remained in said Brigade until the end of the war.

I was appointed a sergeant in said company and served around Manassas, and then went to Yorktown in the defense of that city until it was evacuated. In the spring of 1862 I was in the retreat from Yorktown and was in the Battle of Williamsburg. I was in the Battle of Seven Pines (The Yankees call it Fair Oaks), and on the 31st day of May and the 1st day of June, 1862 was in camp with the Command but sick during the Seven Days Battle around Richmond. Then I was on the march from Richmond to Maryland in August and September, 1862 and waded the Rappahannock, Rapidan, and Potomac Rivers with my regiment and brigade to get into Maryland and then went to Boonesboro and got on South Mountain on September 14, 1862 and was in that battle.

I was in the Battle of Sharpsburg September 17th, 1862(Yankees called this the Battle of Antietam) and was severely wounded early in the morning when I was shot down. I called on one of my comrades, Blue Sapp, to drag me behind a tree. He laid down his gun, took me from behind under the arms and dragged me behind an oak tree, picked up his gun and ran on after the Command which was advancing. I was not down very long before some 15 or 20 Yankee soldiers passed over me in double ranks passed over me. From that time on during the day and all night I was under fire. Our men were back and to, but I was still inside the Yankee lines, a Prisoner. I was not taken up until I had been lying on the battlefield for more than 24 hours. I was hauled off in an ambulance and was carried to a yard where I lay for about two days. Then I was put in a stable where I stayed for ten or twelve days and maggots got into the wound. After remaining in the stable as above stated, I was taken with the other wounded who were with me to an old church, Dunkard, in the village of Sharpsburg. Here I stayed a week or two, lying on straw mattresses on the floor until I was paroled and sent in an ambulance to Baltimore, Fort McHenry, and on to Aikens Landing on the James River to Richmond. I was placed in a hospital there until November 11, 1862 and was given a 40 day furlough to go home.........."

The following is an alphabetical listing of the soldiers of the 27th Georgia Volunteer Infantry Regiment extracted from the data contained in the National Archives.

ABERCROMBIE, HENRY: Company E, private. September 9, 1861 enlisted as a private in Co. E, 27th Regiment, Georgia Infantry at Camp Stephens, Griffin, Spalding County, Georgia. April 26, 1865 surrendered, Greensboro North Carolina.

ABERCROMBIE, ISAAC M.: Company E, private. September 9, 1861 enlisted as a private in Co. E, 27th Regiment, Georgia Infantry at Camp Stephens, Griffin, Spalding County, Georgia. June 1863 received clothing. December 1863 received pay. January 1864 and February 1864 present. February 1864 received pay. March 1864 and April 1864 appears on roll present. March 19 1865 captured, Bentonville, North Carolina. March 30, 1865 arrived at New Bern, North Carolina. June 22, 1865 took oath of allegiance to the United States Government and was released from Point Lookout, Maryland. He is described as residing in Fayette County, Georgia and having dark complexion, light brown hair, blue eyes and was 5 foot 10 1/4 inches in height.

ABERCROMBIE, J. D.: Company E, lieutenant. He was elected sergeant and later was elected 1st lieutenant.

ABERCROMBIE, J. H.: Company E, private. June 4, 1862 admitted to General Hospital No.1 at Danville, Virginia with Typhoid Fever. June 9, 1862 died in General Hospital No.1 at Danville, Virginia of Cholera Morbus (Cholera). June 9, 1862 effects: 1 overcoat, 1blanket and 1 pair of shoes.

ABERCROMBIE, J. MARION: Company E, private. September 9, 1861 enlisted as a private in Co. E, 27th Regiment, Georgia Infantry at Griffin, Spalding County, Georgia. March 19 1865 captured at Bentonville, North Carolina. June 22, 1865 released at Point Lookout, Maryland.

ABERCROMBIE, JOHN J.: Company E, sergeant. He enlisted as a private in Co. E, 27th Regiment, Georgia Infantry. January 1862 appears on roll of Company E as sergeant.

ABERCROMBIE, JOHN T.: Company E, lieutenant. September 9, 1861 enlisted as a private in Co. E, 27th Regiment, Georgia Infantry at Griffin, Spalding County, Georgia. December 20, 1861 elected 2nd lieutenant Co. E, 27th Georgia. January - February 1862 roll shows him present at Camp Pickens near Manassas, Virginia. March 1, 1862 received pay from December 1861 to March 1862 of $221.33. May 21, 1862 received pay of $160.00. June 30, 1862 received pay of $166.33. July 1862 received pay of $90.00. September 3, 1862 received pay of $90.00. September 4, 1862 admitted to General Hospital at Camp Winder at Richmond, Virginia

159

with Febris Typhoid (Typhoid Fever).   September 30, 1862 received pay consisting of $90.00.   October 16, 1862 Report shows he was released from Winder Division No.2 Hospital at Richmond, Virginia to return to duty. December 1862 roll shows him present at Guinea Station.   June 20 1862 elected 1st lieutenant Co. E, 27th Georgia.   September 8, 1863 received pay of $90.00.   September 30, 1863 requested stationary near Wilmington, North Carolina consisting of paper, quills and envelopes and appears on roll.   October 1, 1863 issued stationary.   January 31, 1864 received pay. January - February 1864 roll shows him present.   March - April 1964 Roll shows him present.   April 5, 1864 he was on roll of "Men of Gallantry" by Major James Gardner of the 27th Regiment, Georgia Infantry.   June 1, 1864 wounded in the right arm necessitating amputation at above the elbow at Cold Harbor, Virginia.   June 3, 1864 admitted to Jackson Hospital at Richmond, Virginia - amputation of right arm.   June 15, 1864 received pay at Jackson Hospital at Richmond, Virginia.   November 1864 roll shows him present.   August 14, 1864 Gen. A. H. Colquitt's report shows him wounded sent to Richmond, Virginia.   September 12, 1864 applies to appear before Examining board for retirement at Richmond, Virginia. October 3, 1864 admitted to General Hospital No.4 at Richmond, Virginia due to old wound.   October 6, 1864 recommended for retirement by Medical Director's Office, General Hospital No.4, at Richmond, Virginia due to amputation of right arm in the middle 3rd.   October 8, 1864 report at Dove Hill Farm, Virginia shows him present.   October 18, 1864 furloughed from General Hospital No.4 at Richmond, Virginia.   October 30, 1864 roll shows him in Fayetteville, Georgia "has certificate medical examination board for retirement".   December 3, 1864 roll shows him absent wounded. 1864 discharged due to disability.   December 31, 1864 roll shows him absent wounded.   He died in Carroll County, Georgia on August 1, 1919.

ABERCROMBIE, SEABORN V.: Company E, corporal.   September 25, 1861 enlisted as a private in Co. K, 30th Regiment, Georgia Infantry at Fairburn, Georgia.   November 1, 1863 transferred and appointed 3rd corporal Co. E, 27th Georgia.   December 1863 received pay.   January - February 1864 roll shows him present.   March - April 1864 roll shows him present.   May 12, 1864 Pettigrew General Hospital No.13 at Raleigh, North Carolina returned to duty.   June 1, 1864 wounded at Cold Harbor, Virginia.   June 3, 1864 admitted to General Hospital No.9 at Richmond, Virginia.   June 6, 1864 sent to Jackson Hospital at Richmond, Virginia wounded in the right breast.   June 30, 1864 he was on the roll at Jackson Division No.2 Hospital at Richmond, Virginia.   July 14, 1864 furloughed for 30 days from Jackson Hospital at Richmond, Virginia.   October 28, 1864 Fayetteville, Georgia, certificate of Medical Examining Board for retirement.

ABERCROMBIE, WILLIAM J.: Company E, lieutenant.   He enlisted as a private in Co. E, 27th Regiment, Georgia Infantry.   November 18, 1861 assigned as nurse to Georgia Hospital at Chimborazo Hospital

No.4 at Richmond, Virginia. December 1861 roll shows him at Hospital in Richmond, Virginia. January 1862 roll shows him at Hospital in Richmond, Virginia. February 1862 roll shows him on sick leave for 30 days beginning February 19, 1862. May 10, 1862 through May 13, 1862 he was in Chimborazo Hospital No. 2 at Richmond, Virginia with dysentery. June 20, 1862 elected 2nd lieutenant in Co. E, 27th Regiment, Georgia Infantry. June 11, 1862 received pay of $84.03. July 14, 1862 received pay of $50.00. July 30, 1862 received pay of $80.00. August 1862 received pay consisting of $80.00. September 13, 1862 received pay of $80.00. October 1862 received pay of $80.00. He was wounded in left ankle date and place not given. December 1862 roll shows him absent sick and he received pay of $80.00. February 1863 received pay of $80.00. March 19, 1863 resigned on account of wounds at Richmond, Virginia. September 12, 1863 received pay of $60.00 for apprehending two deserters. July 8, 1864 appointed sub enrolling officer for Fayette County, Georgia.

ABRAHAM, ISRAEL: Company B, private. He enlisted in Co. B, 27th Regiment, Georgia Infantry. June 24, 1864 captured at Petersburg, Virginia. October 11, 1864 paroled at Elmira Prison, New York. October 25, 1864 transferred from Elmira Prison, New York to Baltimore, Maryland and then to Point Lookout Maryland as invalid Prisoner. October 29, 1864 received, paroled and exchanged at Venus Point, Savannah River, Georgia and released.

ADAMS, AMOS ALLEN: Company F, private. September 9, 1861 enlisted as a private in Co. F, 27th Regiment, Georgia Infantry at Camp Stephens, Griffin, Spalding County, Georgia. December 23, 1861 admitted to General Hospital No.1 at Danville, Virginia with Rheumatism. December 24, 1861 admitted to C. S. A. General Hospital at Charlottesville, Virginia with Catarrh and Rheumatism. December 31, 1861 received pay. September 1861 - December 1861 roll shows he was at hospital in Charlottesville, Virginia, admitted on December 24, 1861 and returned to duty on January 17, 1862, complaint Catarrh. February 12, 1862 sent to hospital at Warrenton, Virginia. March 1, 1862 sent to Charlottesville, Virginia. March 2, 1862 admitted to C. S. A. General Hospital at Charlottesville, Virginia with deafness. March 1, 1862 - March 12, 1862 in General Hospitals at Warrenton, Virginia. March 28, 1862 furloughed from C. S. A. General Hospital at Charlottesville, Virginia with certificate of disability for discharge. September 15, 1862 captured at Boonsboro, Maryland. October 2, 1862 sent for exchange from Fort Delaware, Delaware to Aiken's Landing, Virginia. November 10, 1862 exchanged at Aiken's Landing, Virginia. August 25, 1863 received clothing. December 31, 1863 paid. April 11, 1864 called for trial in the Department of South Carolina, Georgia and Florida. May 12, 1864 roll indicates that he deserted from Camp Milton, Florida on March 27, 1864. He was born in Georgia in 1839.

ADAMS, A. L.: Company H, private. He enlisted in Co. H, 27th Regiment, Georgia Infantry. August 11, 1864 admitted to Jackson Hospital at Richmond, Virginia with Febris Remitting (Malaria). August 26, 1864 furloughed for 30 days from Jackson Hospital at Richmond, Virginia. He was from Bear Creek, Georgia.

ADAMS, JAMES C.: Company G, sergeant. September 9, 1861 enlisted and appointed 1st sergeant in Co. G, 27th Regiment, Georgia Infantry at Camp Stephens, Griffin, Spalding County, Georgia. November 6, 1861 admitted to General Hospital at Petersburg, Virginia with dysentery. November 18, 1861 returned to duty. October 18, 1862 received at Wayside Hospital, of General Hospital at Richmond, Virginia and transferred to Chimborazo Hospital at Richmond Virginia. October 18, 1862 admitted to Chimborazo Hospital No.5 with Chronic Rheumatism. November 1, 1862 received pay. November 30, 1862 transferred to Huguenot Springs, Virginia Hospital. December 31 1862 roll for Hospital at Huguenot Springs, Virginia shows him present and shows he was attached to the hospital on December 1, 1862. October 30, 1863 and November 24, 1863 received clothing. December 31, 1863 received pay. January - February and March - April 1864 rolls show him present. March - April 1864 roll shows him present. June 20, 1864 wounded at Petersburg, Virginia. June 20, 1864 admitted to General Hospital at Petersburg, Virginia with Vulnus Sclopeticum (Gunshot Wound). June 22, 1864 admitted to Jackson Hospital at Richmond, Virginia with Vulnus Sclopeticum (Gunshot Wound) in the right leg (mini ball). June 28, 1864 furloughed for 40 days from Jackson Hospital, at Richmond, Virginia. June 30, 1864 hospital muster roll for 2nd Division Jackson Hospital at Richmond, Virginia shows him present. July 28, 1864 furloughed for 90 days from Jackson Hospital at Richmond, Virginia.

ADAMS, JAMES E.: Company F, sergeant. September 9, 1861 enlisted as a private in Co. F, 27th Regiment, Georgia Infantry at Camp Stephens, Griffin, Spalding County, Georgia. January and February 1862 roll shows he was on fatigue duty at Post headquarters. 1862 appointed sergeant Company F, 27th Regiment, Georgia Infantry. September 15, 1862 captured at Turners Gap, South Mountain near Boonsboro Maryland. October 2, 1862 sent for exchange from Fort Delaware, Delaware to Aiken's Landing, Virginia. November 10, 1862 exchanged at Aiken's Landing, Virginia. August 1863 received clothing. December 31, 1863 received pay. May 2, 1864 roll dated this date for January and February and March - April 1864 indicates that he deserted from Camp Milton, Florida on March 27, 1864. He was born in Macon County, Georgia in 1837.

ADAMS, JOHN Q.: Company F, private. He enlisted as a private in Co. F, 27th Regiment, Georgia Infantry. May 19, 1865 surrendered at Augusta, Georgia and paroled.

AIKEN, JOHN T.: Company G, private. September 9, 1861 enlisted as a private in Co. G, 27th Regiment, Georgia Infantry at Camp Stephens,

Griffin, Spalding County, Georgia. March 7, 1862 admitted to Chimborazo Hospital No. 1 at Richmond, Virginia listed as convalescent. March 25, 1862 returned to duty. June 27, 1862 wounded in thigh and heel at Cold Harbor, Virginia. January 26, 1863 issued clothing. December 31, 1863 received pay. June 16, 1863 issued clothing. January - February 1864 roll shows him present. February 29, 1864 received pay. March -April 1864 roll shows him present. July 1864 issued clothing. September 20, 1864 issued clothing. October 30, 1864 issued clothing. 1865 appointed 4th sergeant of Company G, 27th Regiment, Georgia Infantry. April 26, 1865 surrendered, Greensboro, North Carolina. May 1, 1865 paroled at Greensboro, North Carolina.

ALASBROOK, LEWIS: Company K, private. September 10, 1861 enlisted as a private in Co. K, 27th Regiment, Georgia Infantry at Camp Stephens, Griffin, Spalding County, Georgia. April 26, 1865 surrendered, Greensboro, North Carolina. He was born in Georgia. He died June 17, 1922.

ALBERTSON, SAMUEL W.: Company D, private. September 10, 1861 enlisted as a private in Co. D, 27th Regiment, Georgia Infantry at Camp Stephens, Griffin, Spalding County, Georgia. April, May and June of 1863 issued clothing and again in the 4th quarter of 1863. July 12, 1863 appears on a register of C. S. A. General Military Hospital, No. 4 at Wilmington, North Carolina with Diarrhoea (Post Office is Gainesville, Georgia). July 20, 1863 returned to duty. February 29, 1864 received pay. March -April 1864 roll shows him present. July 1864 issued clothing. February 22, 1865 appears on "Roll of Prisoners of War who voluntarily surrendered themselves and took the Oath of Allegiance and who were allowed to return to their homes" at Wilmington, North Carolina. He was born in Georgia February 16, 1848 (He is shown as having dark complexion, black hair, blue eyes and was 5 foot 10 inches tall and was a resident of Hall County, Georgia). May 25, 1865 subscribed to oath of allegiance to the United States Government.

ALDRICH, ALBERT S.: Company B, private. September 20, 1861 enlisted as a private in Company B, 27th Regiment, Georgia Infantry at Camp Stephens, Griffin, Spalding County, Georgia. September to December 1861 roll shows him sick in Georgia since October 31, 1861. January and February 1862 roll shows he was left sick in Georgia October 31, 1861. May 12, 1862 died. November 6, 1862 death benefit claim was filed by his mother, Jane S. Aldridge. January 14, 1863 Death benefit claim was paid $185.43 (#2628).

ALDRIDGE, ELISHA: Company I, private. April 15, 1861 enlisted as a private in Company I, 27th Regiment, Georgia Infantry. July 11, 1862 died of Typhoid Fever in Chimborazo Hospital No.1, at Richmond, Virginia. Most likely buried in Oakwood Cemetery at Richmond Virginia.

ALEXANDER, B. T.: Company H private. He enlisted as a private in Co. A, 27th Regiment, Georgia Infantry. September 1, 1863 wounded (slightly) at Fort Sumter, South Carolina. February 20, 1864 wounded (slightly) at Olustee, Florida.

ALEXANDER, BENJAMIN F.: Company A, private. September 10, 1861 enlisted as a private in Co. A, 27th Regiment, Georgia Infantry at Camp Stephens, Griffin, Spalding County, Georgia. Received pay and clothing December 31, 1862. January 22, 1862 sent to Moore Hospital at Virginia with Pneumonia. February 11, 1862 died of Pneumonia in Moore Hospital, Virginia. December 27, 1862 death benefit claim was filed by William Alexander, his father. September 26, 1863 death benefit claim paid $65.00 (# 9128). He was a resident of Buena Vista, Marion County, Georgia.

ALEXANDER, E. M. A.: Company H, private. He enlisted as a private in Co. H, 27th Regiment, Georgia Infantry. June 5, 1864 appears on register of Receiving and Wayside Hospital of General Hospital No. 9, Richmond, Virginia and was transferred to Jackson Hospital, Richmond, Virginia on that date.

ALEXANDER, ELIJAH: Company H, private. September 9, 1861 enlisted as a private in Co. H, 27th Regiment, Georgia Infantry at Camp Stephens, Griffin, Spalding County, Georgia. October 31, 1861 roll shows he was left in Griffin, Georgia sick. December 1861, January 1862 and February 1862 rolls show he was left sick at Griffin, Georgia October 31, 1861. April 25, 1862 received pay for period from September 9, 1861 to February 28, 1862. September 1, 1862 he appears on register of General Hospital No. 13, at Richmond, Virginia with General Debility. September 8, 1862 returned to duty. August 23, 1862 appears on a register for General Hospital No. 13 at Richmond Virginia with croup. August 30, 1862 transferred to Mayo Island (indicates his Post Office as McDonald, Henry County, Georgia). January – February and March - April 1864 rolls show him present. March 18, 1865 killed at Bentonville, North Carolina.

ALEXANDER, FRANKLIN: Company H, private. March 1, 1862 enlisted as a private in Co. H, 27th Regiment, Georgia Infantry at McDonald, Georgia. May 18, 1862 admitted to General Hospital No. 18, Richmond, Virginia with Diarrhoea. June 16, 1862 returned to duty. June 29, 1862 wounded at Cold Harbor, Virginia. June 29, 1862 admitted to General Hospital No. 18, Richmond, Virginia with a Vulnus Sclopeticum (Gunshot Wound). June 30, 1862 transferred to Camp Winder, Virginia. July 7, 1862 received pay. January, February and March - April 1864 rolls show him present. July 1864 issued clothing. April 26, 1865, surrendered at Greensboro, North Carolina. May 1, 1865 paroled at Greensboro, North Carolina.

ALEXANDER, JOHN: Company B, private. October 28, 1863 enlisted as a private in Co. B, 27th Regiment, Georgia Infantry in Decatur, Georgia. October, November and December 1863 issued clothing. December 31, 1863 received pay. January and February 1864 roll shows him present.

May 6, 1864 wounded at Wilderness, Virginia. May 7, 1864 died of wounds received in action.

ALEXANDER, N.: Company H, private. He enlisted as a private in Co. H, 27th Regiment, Georgia Infantry.

ALEXANDER, URIAH I.: Company H, private. September 9, 1861 enlisted as a private in Co. H, 27th Regiment, Georgia Infantry at Camp Stephens, Griffin, Spalding County, Georgia. October 31, 1861 left in Griffin, Georgia sick. December 31, 1861 shows he was left in Griffin, Georgia sick. January and February 1862 roll shows he was left in Griffin, Georgia sick on October 31, 1861. April 25, 1862 received pay from September 1861 to February 1862. 1862 detailed as a pioneer. July 7, 1862 received pay. December 1862 roll shows he was detailed as a pioneer. January and February 1863 rolls show him present. April and May 1863 records show he was detailed on extra duty at Fredericksburg as a pioneer from April 1, 1863 to June 1, 1863. June 1863 records show he was detailed as a pioneer at Kinston, North Carolina from June 1, 1863 to July 1, 1863. July 1, 1863 detailed as a pioneer at Topsail Sound, North Carolina from July 1, 1863 to August 1, 1863. August 1863 to January 1864 records show he was detailed as a pioneer at James Island, South Carolina. March - April 1864 roll shows him present on detailed on extra daily duty as a pioneer. May 14, 1864 and September 20, 1864 issued clothing. April 5, 1865 admitted to Pettigrew General Hospital No. 13, Raleigh, North Carolina. April 6, 1865 issued clothing. April 14, 1865 died in Pettigrew General Hospital, at Raleigh, North Carolina.

ALEXANDER, W.: Company H, private. He enlisted as a private in Co. H, 27th Regiment, Georgia Infantry. February 1863 he was in Winder Division 3, Hospital at Richmond, Virginia. February 12, 1863 returned to duty.

ALEXANDER, W. P.: Company H, private. He enlisted as a private in Co. H, 27th Regiment, Georgia Infantry.

ALEXANDER, WILLIAM W.: Company A, private. September 10, 1861 enlisted as a private in Co A, 27th Regiment, Georgia Infantry at Camp Stephens, Griffin, Spalding County, Georgia. March 30 1862 admitted to Chimborazo Hospital No. 5, Richmond, Virginia with Debility. May 7, 1862 in Chimborazo Hospital No. 5 at Richmond, Virginia and was transferred this date to Farmville, Virginia hospital. July 2, 1862 admitted to C. S. A. General Hospital at Danville, Virginia with Erysipelas. August 20, 1862 returned to duty. October 31, 1862 received pay in hospital. June 12, 1862 received pay from September 10, 1861 to May 31, 1862 ($95.70). November 6, 1862 received from W. M. Pinkard, surgeon in charge of Palmyra Hospital 1 pair of pants @ $6.12. November 12, 1862 received pay from June 1862 to October 1862 ($50.00). November 31, 1862 to November 29, 1863 absent without leave. December 1862 regimental return indicates he was sent off sick. January - February and March - April 1864 rolls show him present. March 17, 1864 appears on register of General Hospital No. 1, Oglethorpe Barracks at Savannah, Georgia. July 1864 issued clothing. September 10, 1864 discharged disability, Petersburg, Virginia. He was born in Jones County, Georgia in 1804. Disability records shows he was fifty-seven years old, five foot ten inches high, fair complexion, blue eyes, dark hair, and was a farmer before the war.

ALLEN, JOB: Company C, private. September 10, 1861 enlisted as a private in Co. C, 27th Regiment, Georgia Infantry at Camp Stephens, Griffin, Spalding County, Georgia. January 21, 1862 died of disease at Camp Pickens near Manassas, Virginia.

ALLEN, JOHN: Company C, private. He enlisted as a private in Co. C, 27th Regiment, Georgia Infantry. January 12, 1862 died at Camp Pickens near Manassas, Virginia.

ALLEN, JOHN J.: Company B, captain. September 10, 1861 enlisted in Co. B, 27th Regiment, Georgia Infantry as 1st lieutenant at Camp Stephens, Griffin, Spalding County, Georgia. December 1861, January - February 1862 rolls show him present at Camp Pickens near Manassas, Virginia. March 1, 1862 received pay for December 21, 1861 to February 28, 1862 ($180.00). June 23, 1862 received pay for period from April 30, 1862 to May 31, 1862 ($90.00). July 8, 1862 received pay for period from May 31, 1862 to June 30, 1862 ($90.00). June 12, 1862 elected 1st lieutenant Company B, 27th Georgia Infantry. August 24, 1862 elected captain Company B, 27th Georgia Infantry. September 12, 1862 received pay for period from July 31, 1862 to August 31, 1862 ($90.00). December 1862 roll shows him present at Guinea Station, Virginia. December 18, 1862 received pay for period from August 27, 1862 to October 31, 1862 ($195.00). September 30, 1863 he is shown on Roster of General A. H. Colquitt's Brigade. January, February, March and April 1864 rolls do not state whether present or absent. April 11, 1864 requisitioned stationary for Company B at Camp Milton, Florida. March - April 1864 roll shows him present. August 23, 1864 received pay from April 30 1864 to June 30, 1864 ($260.00). November 1864 roll shows him present.

ALLEN, ROBERT O.: Company D, private. September 23, 1861 enlisted as a private in Co. D, 27th Regiment, Georgia Infantry at Camp Stephens, Griffin, Spalding County, Georgia. April, May and June 1863 issued clothing. October, November and December 1863 issued clothing. February 29, 1864 received pay. March - April 1864 rolls show him present. September 20, 1864 issued clothing. July 1864 issued clothing.

ALSABROOKS, LEWIS: Company K, private. September 10, 1861 enlisted as a private in Co. K, 27th Regiment, Georgia Infantry at Camp Stephens, Griffin, Spalding County, Georgia. June 6, 1862 admitted to General Hospital at Farmville, Virginia with Debility. July 26, 1862 returned to duty. September 16, 1862 received pay. December 30, 1862 returned to duty from Winder Division No. 1 Hospital at Richmond, Virginia. On Furlough from June 10, 1863, July 1, 1863, October 22, 1863, October

29, 1863 and December 18, 1863 issued clothing. March - April 1864 roll shows him present. May 30, 1864 issued clothing. July 1864 issued clothing. May 1, 1865 paroled at Greensboro, North Carolina.

ALTMAN, A.: Company C, private. He enlisted in Co. C, 27th Regiment, Georgia Infantry. March 7, 1862 admitted to Chimborazo Hospital No. 5 at Richmond, Virginia with Chronic nephritis. March 23, 1862 returned to duty.

ALTMAN (AULTMAN), (ALMAN), GARRETT: Company F, private. September 9, 1861 enlisted as a private in Co. F, 27th Regiment, Georgia Infantry at Camp Stephens, Griffin, Spalding County, Georgia. December 1861 roll indicates that he was left in Georgia sick on October 31, 1861. January 1862 roll indicates he was left in Georgia sick on October 31, 1861. March 31, 1862 admitted to Chimborazo Hospital No. 2 at Richmond, Virginia with Diarrhoea. June 27, 1862 transferred to Camp Winder at Richmond, Virginia. September 11, 1862 discharged, over age and disability (hemorrhoids, Debility and over age). Discharge papers indicate that he was born in South Carolina, was 5' 11" high with light complexion, blue eyes and sandy hair and was a farmer before enlisting.

ALTMAN, H. T.: Company C, private. He enlisted in Co. C, 27th Regiment, Georgia Infantry. August 19, 1864 wounded at Weldon Railroad, Virginia. August 21, 1864 admitted to Jackson Hospital, Richmond, Virginia with Vulnus Sclopeticum (Gunshot Wound) to the hip (mini ball). August 25, 1864 furloughed for 30 days from Jackson Hospital, Richmond, Virginia.

ALTMAN, JOSHUA: Company C, private. He enlisted in Co. C, 27th Regiment, Georgia infantry.

ALTMAN (AULTMAN), WILLIAM RUSSELL: Company C, private. September 10, 1861 enlisted as a private in Co. C, 27th Regiment, Georgia Infantry at Camp Stephens, Griffin, Spalding County, Georgia. January 17, 1862 admitted to Moore Hospital at General Hospital, No. 1 at Danville, Virginia with Fever. He was transferred to Front Royal, Virginia. January 22, 1862 he was in hospital at Front Royal, Virginia. June 27, 1862 wounded in the Seven Days Battle around Richmond (Cold Harbor). June 28 1862 admitted to General Hospital at Camp Winder at Richmond, Virginia with wound in neck. July 10, 1862 returned to duty. August 22, 1862 received pay ($22.00). June 30, 1863 received pay. June 16, 1863, June 20, 1863 and September 30, 1863 issued clothing. January and February 1864 rolls show him present. January 21, 1864 admitted to Ocmulgee Hospital at Macon, Georgia. February 9, 1864 returned to duty. February 29, 1864 received pay. March - April 1864 rolls show him present. July 1864 issued clothing. September 20, 1864 issued clothing. May 1, 1865 paroled at Greensboro, North Carolina.

AMERSON, G. W.: Company F, private. September 20, 1861 enlisted as a private in Co. F, 27th Regiment, Georgia Infantry at Camp Stephens, Griffin, Spalding County, Georgia. December roll for September through December 1861 shows he was left in Griffin, Georgia sick on October 31,

1861. January 1862 roll shows him left in Griffin Georgia sick October 31, 1861. September 8, 1862 received pay for period from April 30, 1862 to August 31, 1862 ($69.00). November 6, 1862 received of W. M. Pinkard, surgeon in charge of Palmyra Hospital 1 pair pants of $6.12 and 1 coat of $5.00. January 31, 1863 the return for December 1862 shows that he was sick since January 1, 1863. January 9, 1863 admitted to General Hospital No. 9 at Richmond, Virginia. January 20, 1863 transferred to and admitted to Chimborazo Hospital No. 2 with Pneumonia. March 13, 1863 transferred to Danville, Virginia. March 14, 1863 admitted to C. S. A. General Hospital at Danville, Virginia with Debilitas. May 21, 1863 issued clothing. July and August 1863 issued clothing. September 8, 1863 wounded, Ft. Sumter, South Carolina. October 31, 1863 received pay. May 2, 1864 roll dated this date for January - February 1864 shows him present. February 29, 1864 received pay. March - April 1864 roll shows him present. July 4, 1864 issued clothing. September 20, 1864 issued clothing. October 11, 1864 admitted to Receiving and Wayside Hospital or General Hospital No. 9 at Richmond and transferred the next day to Jackson Hospital, Richmond, Virginia. October 12, 1864 admitted to Jackson Hospital at Richmond, Virginia with abscess right thigh. October 19, 1864 issued clothing at Jackson Hospital at Richmond, Virginia. April 26, 1865 surrendered, Greensboro, North Carolina. May 1, 1865 paroled at Greensboro, North Carolina.

AMERSON, J. W.: Company F, private. He enlisted as a private in Co. F, 27th Regiment, Georgia Infantry. October 12, 1864 admitted to Jackson Hospital, Richmond Virginia. November 1, 1864 returned to duty.

AMERSON, R. W.: Company F, private. September 24, 1862 received bounty pay. September 30, 1864 wounded at Fort Harrison, Virginia in left foot by a shell. September 30, 1864 admitted to Jackson Hospital at Richmond, Virginia. November 12, 1864 returned to duty.

AMERSON, WARREN: Company F, private. September 9, 1861 enlisted as a private in Co. F, 27th Regiment, Georgia Infantry at Camp Stephens, Griffin, Spalding County, Georgia. December 1862 roll shows him in Georgia. July and August 1863 issued clothing. December 31, 1863 received pay. February 29, 1864 received pay. May 2, 1864 rolls for January and February 1864 show him present. March - April 1864 roll shows him present. September 30, 1864 wounded in left foot by shell at Fort Harrison, Virginia. September 30, 1864 he was admitted to Jackson Hospital, Richmond, Virginia Vulnus Sclopeticum (Gunshot Wound) to the left foot (shell). November 12, 1964 returned to duty. April 26, 1865 surrendered, Greensboro, North Carolina. May 1, 1865 paroled at Greensboro, North Carolina.

AMISON, W.: Company F, private. He enlisted as a private in Co. F, 27th Regiment, Georgia Infantry.

ANDERSON, R. W.: Company F, private. He enlisted as a private in Co. F, 27th Regiment, Georgia Infantry.

ANDERSON, REUBEN L.: Company G, private. March 18, 1862 enlisted in Company G, 27th Regiment, Georgia Infantry at Culpepper, Virginia. February 28, 1862 to November 1, 1862 he was at Medical College Hospital at Atlanta, Georgia. December 1862 roll shows him absent without leave. February 21, 1863 received pay. June 20, 1863 received pay for period from November 1, 1862 to April 30, 1863 ($66.00).

ANDERSON, W. A.: Company A, private. September 10, 1861 enlisted as a private in Co. A, 27th Regiment, Georgia Infantry. December 24, 1861 he died.

ANDERSON W. J.: Company G, private. September 10, 1861 enlisted as a private in Co. G, 27th Regiment, Georgia Infantry at Camp Stephens, Griffin, Spalding County, Georgia. July 28, 1862 died at Richmond, Virginia. He was buried in Hollywood Cemetery at Richmond, Virginia.

APPERSON, J.: Company G, private. September 9, 1861 enlisted as a private in Co. G, 27th Regiment, Georgia Infantry at Camp Stephens, Griffin, Spalding County, Georgia. November 22, 1862 died at Richmond, Virginia. He was buried in Hollywood Cemetery at Richmond, Virginia.

ARGO, W. T.: Company I, private. November 1864 enlisted as a private in Co. I, 27th Regiment, Georgia Infantry.

ARNETT, J. P.: Company B, private. September 10, 1861 enlisted as a private in Co. B, 27th Regiment, Georgia Infantry at Camp Stephens, Griffin, Spalding County, Georgia.

ARNETT, THOMAS: Company B, private. September 10, 1861 enlisted as a private in Co. B, 27th Georgia Infantry at Camp Stephens, Griffin, Spalding County, Georgia. May 13, 1862 died, Richmond, Virginia. September 3, 1862 death benefit claim was filed by his widow, Bethany Arnett. January 6, 1863 death benefit claim paid for $123.76 (#2482).

ARNOLD, DANIEL H.: Company C, private. September 10, 1861 enlisted as a private in Co. C, 27th Regiment, Georgia Infantry at Camp Stephens, Griffin, Spalding County, Georgia. November 26, 1861 through December 14, 1861 he was in Richmond, Virginia hospital. April 1, 1863 he died.

ARNOLD, S.T.: Company A, private. 1862 enlisted as a private in Co. A, 27th Regiment, Georgia Infantry. He died in 1863.

ASKHEW, JAMES M.: Company F, private. August 1, 1862 enlisted as a private in Co. F, 27th Regiment, Georgia Infantry in Randolph County, Georgia. December 1862 roll shows him sick in Richmond, Virginia. January 30, 1863 admitted to Hospital No. 3, Lynchburg, Virginia with Bronchitis. April 21, 1863 roll shows he was still in hospital No. 3, at Lynchburg Virginia. July 15, 1863 issued clothing. May 2, 1864 for January – February and March - April 1864 rolls show him on sick furlough since August 15, 1863 - April 30, 1864. May 18, 1864 pension records show he was discharged on surgeon's certificate of disability. He was born in Chattahoochee County, Georgia July 1, 1840.

ATKINS, B. L.: Company C, private. He enlisted as a private in Co. C,

27th Regiment, Georgia Infantry. June 26, 1862 he was placed on a 30 day furlough.

ATKINSON, T. J.: Company A, private. He enlisted as a private in Co. A, 27th Regiment, Georgia Infantry. December 1861, January and February 1962 rolls shows he was left in Georgia sick on October 31, 1861. December 1862 roll shows he was absent without leave since November 1, 1862

AULTMAN, JOSHUA: Company C, private. September 10, 1861 enlisted as a private in Co. C, 27th Regiment, Georgia Infantry at Camp Stephens, Griffin, Spalding County, Georgia. July 26, 1862 returned to duty from Chimborazo Hospital No. 5, Richmond, Virginia. April 19, and June 16, 1863 issued clothing. June 30, 1863 and September 30, 1863 issued clothing. December 31, 1863 received pay. January – February and March - April 1864 rolls show him present. July 1864 issued clothing. August 20, 1864 admitted to Receiving and Wayside Hospital or General Hospital No. 9 at Richmond Virginia. August 20, 1864 transferred to and admitted to Jackson Hospital at Richmond, Virginia. August 25, 1864 furloughed for 30 days from Jackson Hospital, Richmond, Virginia. April 26, 1865 surrendered, Greensboro, North Carolina. May 1, 1865 paroled at Greensboro, North Carolina. His Post Office was Fort Valley, Georgia.

ALTMAN (AULTMAN), WILLIAM J.: Company F, private. September 9, 1861 enlisted as a private in Co. F, 27th Regiment, Georgia Infantry at Camp Stephens, Griffin, Spalding County, Georgia. November 8, 1861 died of Pneumonia at Camp Stephens, Griffin, Spalding County, Georgia (Surgeons report of death from Manassas Station, Virginia). March 19, 1862 death benefit claim was filed by his widow, Caroline Aultman of Taylor, County, Georgia (they were married May 12, 1859). January 30, 1864 death benefit claim was paid $97.00 (#12640).

AVANT, B. F.: Company B, private. March 4, 1862 enlisted as a private in Co. B, 27th Georgia Infantry at Macon, Bibb County, Georgia. September 30, 1862 received pay. April 30, 1863 received pay. July 1863 and November 2, 1863 received pay. October 3, 1863 to December 3, 1863 received pay for rations while on detached duty. December 11, 1863 received pay. January 1, 1864 received pay ($22.00). January 22, 1864 - February 22, 1864 received extra duty pay. January - February 1864 roll shows he was absent with leave to return March 26, 1864. March - April 1864 roll shows he was absent without leave since March 26, 1864. February 22, 1864 - May 22, 1864 received extra duty pay of $112.50. June 30 1864 sick to this date in 1st Division Jackson Hospital at Richmond, Virginia. July 4, 1864 wounded in the left arm, necessitating amputation above the elbow, at Petersburg, Virginia. July 7, 1864 admitted to Jackson Hospital at Richmond, Virginia. July 18, 1864 furloughed for 30 days from Jackson Hospital at Richmond, Virginia. September 30, 1864 received pay at Macon, Georgia. January 30, 1865 appears on roll at Floyd House and Ocmulgee Hospitals at Macon, Georgia (shows his disease as Vulnus

Sclopeticum (Gunshot Wound) to left forearm - amputated at upper portion of lower 3rd).

AVANT, J. D.: Company B, sergeant. He enlisted as a private in Co. B, 27th Regiment, Georgia Infantry. He was elected sergeant of Company B, 27th Regiment, Georgia Infantry. December 1861 roll shows he was in hospital at Richmond, Virginia (admitted on November 16, 1861).

AVANT, JESSE T.: Company B, sergeant. September 10, 1861 elected 5th sergeant of Co. B, 27th Regiment, Georgia Infantry at Camp Stephens, Griffin, Spalding County, Georgia. December 1961 roll shows that on November 15, 1861 in hospital at Richmond, Virginia. January 1862 roll shows he was detailed from Richmond, Virginia to Georgia on January 18, 1862. August 22, 1863 received pay at James Island, South Carolina. October, November and December 1863 issued clothing. December 31, 1863 received pay. January 1864 - February 1864 roll and March 1864 - April 1864 rolls show him present. June 18, 1864 admitted to General Hospital, Petersburg, Virginia wounded in the hip (shoulder). June 20, 1864 transferred to hospital in Farmville, Virginia. June 21, 1864 admitted to General Hospital at Petersburg, Virginia. July 2, 1864 appears on roll of soldiers remaining in General Hospital at Petersburg, Virginia. July 19, 1864 received pay ($68.00). January 15, 1865 furloughed from General Hospital at Petersburg, Virginia for 60 days.

AVANT, JOSIAH L.: Company B, sergeant. September 10, 1861 enlisted as a private in Co. B, 27th Regiment, Georgia Infantry at Camp Stephens, Griffin, Spalding County, Georgia. December 16, 1861 discharged due to disability at Richmond, Virginia and received pay.

AVANT, L. M. (M. L.): Company B, private. April 12, 1862 enlisted as a private in Co. B, 27th Regiment, Georgia Infantry in Macon, Bibb County, Georgia. June 28, 1862 admitted to General Hospital No. 17, Richmond, Virginia. June 30, 1862 transferred to Camp Winder Hospital, Richmond, Virginia. August 1, 1862 received pay. October 27, 1862 received pay ($88.50). November 1, 1862 received pay. December 1862 roll shows he was absent sick in hospital since December 13, 1862. December 15, 1862 admitted to General Hospital No. 17, Richmond, Virginia. December 16, 1862 roll of General Hospital No. 17 for October 31, 1862 shows him present. January 5, 1863 roll of General Hospital No. 17, Richmond, Virginia for November and December 1862 shows him present. January 1863 he was in Winder Hospital at Richmond, Virginia. January 8, 1863 returned to duty from Winder Hospital at Richmond, Virginia. January 26, 1863 admitted to General Hospital at Farmville Virginia with Vulnus Sclopeticum (Gunshot Wound) in left hand and furloughed for 90 days. January 15, 1863 transferred to General Hospital at Farmville, Virginia. January 24 (27), 1863 furloughed for 90 days to report to regiment from General Hospital at Farmville, Virginia. March 5, 1863 received pay. April 27, 1863 furloughed for 60 days. July 6, 1863 received pay ($66.00). June 27, 1863 furloughed for 90 days. October 9, 1863 received pay ($33.00).

December 1, 1863 received pay ($92.25).

AVANT, LEWIS M.: Company B, private. September 10, 1861 enlisted as a private in Co. B, 27th Regiment, Georgia Infantry at Camp Stephens, Griffin, Spalding County, Georgia.   May 31, 1862 wounded in the hand permanently disabled, and in head at Seven Pines, Virginia.   January 16, 1863 discharged due to disability.   March 5, 1863 received pay ($72.00). He was born in Georgia April 9, 1838.

AVERA, G. W.: Company C, private. He enlisted as a private in Co. C, 27th Regiment, Georgia Infantry.   June 5, 1862 transferred from Chimborazo Hospital No. 5, Richmond Virginia to Lynchburg, Virginia Hospital.

AVERA, J. W.: Company C, private.   He enlisted as a private in Co. C, 27th Regiment, Georgia Infantry.   February 29, 1864 furloughed for 35 days disease Vulnus Sclopeticum (Gunshot Wound) left leg.

AVERA, JAMES W.: Company C, sergeant. September 10, 1861 enlisted as a private in Co. C, 27th Regiment, Georgia Infantry at Camp Stephens, Griffin, Spalding County, Georgia.   He was appointed sergeant in Co. C, 27th Regiment, Georgia Infantry.   February 20, 1864 killed at Olustee, Florida.

AVERA, SIKES: Company C, private. June 15, 1862 enlisted as a private in Co. C, 27th Regiment, Georgia Infantry.

AVERETT (AVERITT), A.: Company C, private.   March 16, 1862 enlisted as a private in Co. C, 27th Regiment, Georgia Infantry at Macon, Bibb County, Georgia.   May 14, 1862 admitted to Chimborazo Hospital No. 4 at Richmond, Virginia with Debility.   December 1862 roll shows him absent on sick furlough.

AVERETT (AVERITT), A. V.: Company C, private.   March 16, 1862 enlisted as a private in Co. C, 27th Regiment, Georgia Infantry at Macon, Bibb County, Georgia.   May 1, 1862 received pay.   September 7, 1862 attached to hospital at Huguenot Springs, Virginia. October 1, 1862 roll for August 1862 shows him present at hospital at Huguenot Springs, Virginia.

AVERETT (AVERITT), ARCHIBALE: Company C, private. June 15, 1862 enlisted as a private in Co. C, 27th Regiment, Georgia Infantry. 1862 he was on sick furlough. 1862 he died.

AVERETT (AVERITT), J. M.: Company C, private. He enlisted as a private in Co. C, 27th Regiment, Georgia Infantry. June 3, 1864 received pay at Macon, Georgia ($73.75).

AVERETT (AVERITT), WILLIAM: Company C, private. March 15, 1862 enlisted as a private in Co. C, 27th Regiment, Georgia Infantry. June 2, 1862 admitted to General Hospital Camp Winder, Richmond Virginia with Febris Typhoidis (Typhoid Fever).   June 12, 1862 returned to duty. December 16, 1862 returned to duty from Winder Division No. 1 Hospital at Richmond, Virginia.   January - February 1864 roll shows him wounded in action at Olustee, Florida.   February 20, 1864 wounded at Olustee, Florida. March - April 1864 roll shows him absent wounded since February 20, 1864. April 26, 1865 surrendered, Greensboro, North Carolina. May

1, 1865 paroled at Greensboro, North Carolina.

AVERY (AVERA), G. W.: Company C, private. He enlisted as a private in Co. C, 27th Regiment, Georgia Infantry. June 16, 1862 admitted to General Hospital, Farmville, Virginia with Debility. September 11, 1862 account at C. S. A. General Hospital at Farmville, Virginia $7.75 for clothing furnished. October 20, 1862 received pay of $65.63 minus $7.75 (for clothing advance) net $57.88. November 12, 1862 admitted to C. S. A. General Hospital at Danville, Virginia with Varicose Veins of the left leg and thigh producing ulcers. November 17, 1862 discharged from service at General Hospital at Farmville, Virginia due to Varicose Veins of leg. (His discharge states that he is from Crawford County, Georgia and is 20 years of age, 6 feet high, fair complexion, dark eyes and dark hair - occupation before enlistment was a farmer).

AVERY, J. M.: Company C, private. He enlisted as a private in Co. C, 27th Regiment, Georgia Infantry.

AVERY (AVARY), JOSEPH: Company H, private. March 20, 1864 enlisted as a private in Co. H, 27th Regiment, Georgia Infantry at Macon, Bibb County, Georgia. April 30, 1864 roll, last on file, shows him present. October 8, 1864 wounded near Richmond, Virginia. October 8, 1864 admitted to the Receiving and Wayside Hospital or General Hospital No. 9 at Richmond, Virginia with wound in left hand. October 8, 1864 transferred to and admitted to Jackson Hospital, Richmond, Virginia with wound in left hand (min B). October 19, 1864 received clothing at Jackson Hospital at Richmond, Virginia. October 23, 1864 returned to duty. March 19, 1865 captured at Bentonville, North Carolina. April 3, 1865 arrived at New Bern, North Carolina. June 24, 1865 died at Point Lookout, Maryland. He is buried in the prisoner of war graveyard at Point Lookout, Maryland.

AVERY, W. S.: Company C, private. He enlisted as a private in Co. C, 27th Regiment, Georgia Infantry. April 11, 1862 admitted to Seminary Hospital, Williamsburg, Virginia with Rubeola. April 17, 1862 died of Rubeola and Pneumonia at Seminary Hospital, Williamsburg, Virginia (effects were 1 pair of shoes, 1 hat, 1 cap, 4 socks, 1 cotton shirt, one over shirt, 2 pairs of suspenders, 2 coats, 1 vest, 4 pairs of pants, bag with Contents, 1 comfort, 1 haversack, 1 knapsack, 1 knife, post money, and 15 cents in money).

AVETT, A. V.: Company C, private. September 10, 1861 enlisted as a private in Co. C, 27th Regiment, Georgia Infantry at Camp Stephens, Griffin, Spalding County, Georgia.

AVETT, WILLIAM: Company C, private. March 20, 1862 enlisted as a private in Co. C, 27th Regiment, Georgia Infantry at Crawford County, Georgia. September 1, 1862 received pay. December 10, 1862 on roll for Camp Winder General Hospital at Richmond, Virginia.

AVREA, J. W.: Company C, private. He enlisted as a private in Co. C, 27th Regiment, Georgia Infantry. April 11, 1862 admitted to Seminary Hospital, Williamsburg, Virginia with Fibrous Typhoidis (Typhoid Fever).

April 16, 1862 sent to General Hospital. April 19, 1862 admitted to Chimborazo Hospital No. 5 at Richmond, Virginia with Diarrhoea. June 5, 1862 transferred to Lynchburg, Virginia Hospital. August 13, 1862 returned to duty. September 20, 1862 paroled, Keedysville, Maryland. May 9, 1863 admitted to C. S. A. General Hospital at Charlottesville, Virginia with Debilitas. May 10, 1863 transferred to General Hospital at Lynchburg, Virginia. September 30, 1863 issued clothing.

AVREA, JAMES W.: Company C, private. September 10, 1861 enlisted as a private in Co. C, 27th Regiment, Georgia Infantry at Camp Stephens, Griffin, Spalding County, Georgia. April 17, 1862 admitted to Chimborazo Hospital No. 5 at Richmond, Virginia with Catarrh. June 28, 1862 transferred to C. S. A. General Hospital at Danville, Virginia. June 29, 1862 admitted to C. S. A. General Hospital at Danville, Virginia with Chronic Rheumatism. December 31, 1863 received pay. February 20, 1864 killed in action at Olustee, Florida.

AVRETT, WILLIAM: Company C, private. March 15, 1862 enlisted as a private in Co. C, 27th Regiment, Georgia Infantry at Knoxville, Georgia. May 1, 1862 received pay. December 16, 1862, April 19, June 16 and June 26, 1863 issued clothing. September 7, 1862 attached to the Hospital at Huguenot Springs, Virginia. June 30 - September 30, 1863 issued clothing. October 1, 1862 he is shown present on roll for Hospital at Huguenot Springs, Virginia. December 31, 1863 received pay. February 20, 1864 wounded seriously at Olustee, Florida. January - February 1864 shown as absent due to wounds received at Olustee, Florida. February 29, 1864 received pay. March - April 1864 roll shows him absent due to wounds received at Olustee, Florida. September 20, 1864 issued clothing. May 1, 1865 paroled at Greensboro, North Carolina.

BACHELOR, WILLIAM: Company D, private. August 1862 enlisted as a private in Co. D, 27th Regiment, Georgia Infantry. December 1862 roll shows him in hospital from August of 1862. 1862 died of Measles.

BACON, J. J.: Company I, sergeant. He enlisted as a private in Co. I, 27th Regiment, Georgia Infantry. He was elected sergeant in Co. I, 27th Regiment, Georgia Infantry. October 6, 1864 admitted to Receiving and Wayside Hospital or General Hospital No. 9 at Richmond Virginia. October 7, 1864 transferred to Jackson Hospital, Richmond, Virginia.

BACON, THOMAS J.: Field Staff, Assistant Commissary Sergeant. September 10, 1861 appointed Asst. Commissary Sergeant, 27th Regiment, Georgia Infantry. December 21, 1861 received pay ($396.00). December 1861 roll shows him present at Camp Pickens near Manassas, Virginia. January 1862 roll shows him present at Camp Pickens near Manassas, Virginia. February 1962 roll indicates he was still at Camp Pickens near Manassas, Virginia. April 2, 1862 signed Request No. 73, request for supplies for 27th Georgia. May 31, 1862 killed at Seven Pines, Virginia.

BAGWELL, MICAJAH: Company D, sergeant. September 23, 1861 elected 2nd sergeant, in Co. D, 27th Regiment, Georgia Infantry at Camp

Stephens, Griffin, Spalding County, Georgia. December 1861, January and February 1862 rolls show he was left sick in Georgia on October 31, 1861. May 31, 1862 wounded at Seven Pines, Virginia. June 1, 1862 admitted to General Hospital 21, Richmond, Virginia with Vulnus Sclopeticum (Gunshot Wound). June 7, 1862 received pay ($131.83). April, May and June 1863 issued clothing. December 31, 1863 received pay. March - April 1864 roll shows him present. December 1863 issued clothing. July 1864 issued clothing. August 19, 1864 captured, Weldon Railroad, Virginia. August 21, 1864 forwarded to Provost Marshal, Army of the Potomac. August 24, 1864 received at Point Lookout, Maryland from City Point, Virginia. March 14, 1865 paroled at Point Lookout, Maryland and transferred to Aiken's Landing, James River, Virginia for exchange. He was born in Hall County, Georgia June 1, 1832.

BAWELL, WILLIAM: Company D, corporal. March 4, 1862 enlisted as a private in Co. D, 27th Regiment, Georgia Infantry at Gainesville, Hall County, Georgia. May 14, 1862 admitted to Chimborazo Hospital No. 1, Richmond, Virginia with Continuing (Typhus) Fever. He was 1st corporal Co. D, 27th Regiment, Georgia Infantry. April, May and June 1863 issued clothing. December 1863 issued clothing. December 31, 1863 received pay. March - April 1864 roll shows him present. July 1864 issued clothing. September 5, 1864 received pay at Athens, Georgia ($65.00). September 20, 1864 issued clothing.

BAILEY, ROBERT C.: Company F, lieutenant. September 9, 1861 elected 4th sergeant in Co. F, 27th Regiment, Georgia Infantry at Camp Stephens, Griffin, Spalding County, Georgia. June 16, 1862 furloughed from General Hospital No. 8 (St. Charles Hospital) at Richmond, Virginia. June 21, 1862 received pay ($85.00). August 23, 1862 returned to duty from General Hospital No. 8 (St. Charles Hospital) at Richmond, Virginia. September 30, 1862 elected Jr. 2nd lieutenant in Co. F, 27th Regiment, Georgia Infantry. October 9, 1862 received pay ($143.56). December 1862 roll shows him present near Guinea Station, Virginia as Brevet 2nd lieutenant. January 7, 1863 he was elected 2nd lieutenant in Co. F, 27th Regiment, Georgia Infantry. February 23, 1863 elected 1st lieutenant in Co. F, 27th Regiment, Georgia Infantry. June 8, 1863 camped near Kinston, North Carolina. June 27, 1863 resigned commission on surgeon's certificate.

BAKER, W. S.: Field Staff, Chaplin. January 10, 1862 appointed Chaplin 27th Georgia Infantry. November 26, 1862 declined and returned commissions.

BALLICH, H.: Company B, private. He enlisted as a private in Co. B, 27th Regiment, Georgia Infantry. January 25, 1862 admitted to Moore Hospital at General Hospital No. 1, Danville, Virginia with Fever. He transferred to Warrenton, Virginia.

BALLOO, RICHARD: Company K, private. He enlisted as a private in Co. K, 27th Regiment, Georgia Infantry.

BALLOO, W. T.: Company K, private. He enlisted as a private in Co. K., 27th Regiment, Georgia Infantry. April 24, 1862 admitted to Chimborazo Hospital No. 5, Richmond, Virginia.

BALYEW, E. A.: Company B, private. He enlisted as a private in Co. B, 27th Regiment, Georgia Infantry. May 27, 1862 transferred from Chimborazo Hospital No. 5 to Lynchburg, Virginia.

BALYEW, J. A.: Company K, private. He enlisted as a private in Co. K, 27th Regiment, Georgia Infantry.

BANKS, JOHN L.: Company G, private. September 9, 1861 enlisted as a private in Co. G, 27th Regiment, Georgia Infantry at Camp Stephens, Griffin, Spalding County, Georgia. November 9, 1861 admitted to General Hospital No. 18 (formerly Greaner's Hospital) at Richmond, Virginia (Post Office shown as Zebulon, Pike County, Georgia). December 1, 1861 roll shows him in Hospital at Richmond, Virginia. January 27, 1862 returned to duty from General Hospital No. 18 at Richmond, Virginia (shows he went home with Joshua Barker's corpse). May 31, 1862 captured at Seven Pines, Virginia. June 5, 1862 sent from Fort Delaware, Delaware to Fort Monroe, Virginia (describes him as 18 years of age, 6 foot 1 inch high, dark hair, hazel eyes with fair complexion). He is shown on roll of prisoners captured at Fair Oaks, Virginia (Seven Pines) on the Steamer Coatzacoalcos. June 9, 1862 arrived at Aiken's Landing, Virginia. August 5, 1862 exchanged at Aiken's Landing, Virginia. August 15, 1862 received pay ($156.70). August 26, 1862 admitted to General Hospital Camp Winder at Richmond, Virginia with fib Typhoid. October 2, 1862 received pay ($83.00) in Richmond, Virginia. October 3, 1862 roll for 2nd Division General Hospital Camp Winder at Richmond, Virginia shows he was furloughed for 30 days on October 1, 1862. He received pay of $10. 00 for time while on furlough. April 12, 1863 issued clothing. June 16, 1863 issued clothing. June 26, 1863 issued clothing. August 31, 1863 received pay. October 1, 1863 received pay ($22.00). October 30, 1863 issued clothing. January - February 1864 roll shows him present (Absent Without Leave from December 24, 1863 to February, 1, 1864). February 29, 1864 received pay. March - April 1864 roll shows him present. July 1864 issued clothing. September 20, 1864 issued clothing. April 26, 1865 surrendered Greensboro, North Carolina. May 1, 1865 paroled at Greensboro, North Carolina.

BANNER, JAMES WHIT: Company K, private. March 4, 1862 enlisted as a private in Co. K, 27th Regiment, Georgia Infantry. An undated roll shows him as 27 years old. May 24, 1862 received pay ($45.90) at Richmond, Virginia.

BANTON, N. P: Company A, private. He enlisted as a private in Co. A, 27th Regiment, Georgia Infantry.

BARBER, CORNELIUS: Company I, private. September 10, 1861 enlisted as a private in Co. I, 27th Regiment, Georgia Infantry at Camp Stephens, Griffin, Spalding County, Georgia. June 16 and June 27, 1863 issued clothing. December 31, 1863 received pay. January - February 1864 roll shows him present. February 29, 1864 received pay. March - April 1864 roll shows him present. May 30, 1864 issued clothing. June 30, 1864 roll for Jackson Hospital at Richmond, Virginia shows him present. July 1864 issued clothing. July 1864 wounded in right thigh at Colquitt's Salient on the Petersburg Line. July 13, 1864 admitted to Jackson Hospital at Richmond, Virginia with a Vulnus Sclopeticum (Gunshot Wound) in the right thigh (mini ball). July 22, 1864 returned to duty and furloughed for 40 days from Jackson Hospital at Richmond, Virginia. April 26, 1865 surrendered, Greensboro, North Carolina. May 1, 1865 paroled at Greensboro, North Carolina.

BARFIELD (BAREFIELD), A. P.: Company F, private. September 9, 1861 enlisted as a private in Co. F, 27th Regiment, Georgia Infantry at Camp Stephens, Griffin, Spalding County, Georgia. December 1862 roll shows he was absent sick since May 3, 1862.

BARFIELD (BAREFIELD), BENJAMIN F.: Company B, private. September 10, 1861 enlisted as a private in Co. B, 27th Regiment, Georgia Infantry at Camp Stephens, Griffin, Spalding County, Georgia. May 19, 1862 admitted to General Hospital Camp Winder at Richmond, Virginia with Diarrhoea. May 28, 1862 admitted to C. S. A. General Hospital at Danville, Virginia with Rubeola. September 30, 1862 appears on roll for C. S. A. General Hospital at Danville, Virginia with Rheumatism. October 22, 1862 returned to duty. February 20, 1863 returned to duty. October, November and December 1863 issued clothing. December 31, 1863 received pay. January-February 1864 roll shows him present. February 29, 1864 received pay. March-April 1864 roll shows him present. May 30, 1864 issued clothing. July 1864 issued clothing.

BARFIELD (BAREFIELD), CLARK B.: Company F, private. He enlisted as a private in Co. F, 27th Regiment, Georgia Infantry. December 1861, January 1862 and February 1862 rolls show him left in Georgia sick on October 31, 1861. May 4, 1862 died in Alabama Hospital, Richmond, Virginia. August 12, 1863 death benefit claim was filed by Jesse Barfield, his father. He was a resident of Butler, Taylor County, Georgia. He was born in Macon County, Georgia, July 4, 1838. He was unmarried.

BARFIELD (BAREFIELD), ENOCH J.: Company F, private. September 20, 1861 enlisted as a private in Co. F, 27th Regiment, Georgia Infantry at Camp Stephens, Griffin, Spalding County, Georgia. December 1861 and January 1962 rolls show he was left sick in Georgia October 31, 1861. May 1, 1862 received pay. October 31, 1862 roll (dated November 21, 1862) shows him present. November 17, 1862 admitted to Winder Division No. 4 Hospital at Richmond, Virginia. December 16, 1862 returned to duty. May 3, 1863 wounded at Chancellorsville, Virginia. May 9, 1863 list of causalities from Chancellorsville, Virginia includes him at camp near Guiney's Station, Virginia. July and August 1863 issued clothing. September 18, 1863 deserted from camp James Island, South Carolina.

January - February 1964 and March - April 1864 rolls show he deserted from James Island, South Carolina on September 18, 1863.

BARFIELD (BAREFIELD), FRANCIS M.: Company B, sergeant. September 10, 1861 enlisted as a private in Co. B, 27th Regiment, Georgia Infantry at Camp Stephens, Griffin, Spalding County, Georgia. February 1862 roll shows him on recruiting service from February 13, for 30 days. July 1862 wounded in the Seven Days Battle around Richmond, Virginia. July 2, 1862 admitted to C. S. A General Hospital at Danville, Virginia with a Vulnus Sclopeticum (Gunshot Wound). December 28, 1862 returned to duty. November and December 1863 issued clothing. December 31, 1863 received pay. January - February 1864 and March - April 1864 rolls show him at home discharging duties as tax collector of Bibb County, Georgia.

BARFIELD (BAREFIELD), THOMAS MARION: Company B, private. September 10, 1861 enlisted as a private in Co. B, 27th Regiment, Georgia Infantry at Camp Stephens, Griffin, Spalding County, Georgia. March - April 1864 roll shows him "at home discharging duties of Tax Receiver of Bibb, County, Georgia". October 27, 1864 asked for discharge. He was a resident of Georgia since 1840. Note: Thomas Marion and Francis M. may be the same person.

BARFIELD (BAREFIELD), W. P.: Company F, private. He enlisted as a private in Co. F, 27th Regiment, Georgia Infantry. March 7, 1862 admitted to Chimborazo Hospital No. 5 at Richmond, Virginia with Gonorrhea. August 5, 1862 received pay ($133.53). September 1862 wounded in head in Maryland campaign. September18, 1862 admitted to Chimborazo Hospital No. 5 at Richmond, Virginia with wound to head. November 25, 1862 returned to duty. November 26, 1862 admitted to Institute Hospital at Richmond, Virginia with Diarrhoea. November 26, 1862 appears on roll for General Hospital No. 4 at Richmond, Virginia with Diarrhoea. January 7, 1863 he died. He was born in 1841. Records show he was a farmer prior to the war. February 27, 1864 death benefit claim was filed by his mother, Mrs. Penelope Barfield of Taylor County, Georgia stating that he had no wife, child or father living at the time. April 30 1864 death benefit claim was paid.

BAREFIELD (BARFIELD), WARREN: Company F, private. September 9, 1861 enlisted as a private in Co. F, 27th Regiment, Georgia Infantry at Camp Stephens, Griffin, Spalding County, Georgia. April 23, 1862 he was admitted to Chimborazo Hospital No. 5 at Richmond, Virginia with Bronchitis. May 25, 1862 returned to duty. May 3, 1862 he was admitted to Chimborazo Hospital No. 5 at Richmond, Virginia with Diarrhoea. June 21, 1862 returned to duty. July 1, 1862 received pay. November 15, 1862 admitted to General Hospital, Camp Winder at Richmond, Virginia. November 21, 1862 roll shows him present at General Hospital, Camp Winder at Richmond, Virginia. December 1862 roll shows he was absent sick since November. October 14, 1863 through April 30, 1864 he was on sick furlough since October 14, 1863. He was born in Macon County,

Georgia in 1833.

BARFIELD (BAREFIELD), WESLEY: Company F, corporal. September 9, 1861 enlisted as a private in Co. F, 27th Regiment, Georgia Infantry at Camp Stephens, Griffin, Spalding County, Georgia. December 1861 and January 1862 rolls show he was left sick in Georgia on October 31, 1861. April 23, 1862 he was admitted to Chimborazo Hospital No. 5 at Richmond, Virginia with Bronchitis. May 25, 1862 returned to duty. May 3 1862 he was admitted to Chimborazo Hospital No. 5 at Richmond, Virginia with Diarrhoea. June 21, 1862 returned to duty. July 7, 1862 received pay ($156.33). July 23, 1862 admitted to C. S. A. General Hospital at Danville, Virginia with Diarrhoea. November 1, 1862 he received pay. July 15, 1863 issued clothing. December 31, 1863 received pay. February 20, 1864 seriously wounded at Olustee, Florida. May 2, 1864 report indicated he was killed in action at Olustee, Florida on February 20, 1864.

BARFIELD (BAREFIELD), WILLIAM O.: Company F, private. September 9, 1861 enlisted as a private in Co. F, 27th Regiment, Georgia Infantry at Camp Stephens, Griffin, Spalding County, Georgia. December 1861 and January 1862 rolls show he was left in Georgia sick October 31, 1861.

BARKER, JOSHUA: Company G, private. September 9, 1861 enlisted as a private in Co. G, 27th Regiment, Georgia Infantry at Camp Stephens, Griffin, Spalding County, Georgia. November 11, 1861 admitted to General Hospital No. 18 at Richmond, Virginia with Typhoid Fever and Pneumonia. November 23, 1861 died in Richmond, Virginia. February 17, 1862 death benefit claim was filed by mother.

BARNES (BURNES), J. M.: Company G, private. He enlisted as a private in Co. G, 27th Regiment, Georgia Infantry.

BARNETT, THOMAS FLETCHER (F. F.) (T. F.): Company I, lieutenant. 1861 enlisted as a private in Co. I, 27th Regiment, Georgia Infantry. 1861 appointed 5th sergeant of Co. I, 27th Regiment, Georgia Infantry. December 10, 1861 discharged due to disability (physical inability), Camp Pickens near Manassas, Virginia. March 4, 1862 appointed 2nd sergeant of Co F, 11th Battalion, Georgia Infantry. May 12, 1862 transferred to Co. F, 47th Regiment, Georgia Infantry. August 5, 1862 appointed 1st sergeant of Co. F, 47th Regiment, Georgia Infantry. October 26, 1862 elected Jr. 2nd lieutenant of Co. F, 47th Regiment, Georgia Infantry. March 30, 1864 elected 2nd lieutenant of Co. F, 47th Regiment, Georgia Infantry. April 26, 1865 pension records show he surrendered at Greensboro, North Carolina. He was born in Madison, Florida in 1845.

BATTLE, M. L.: Company A, private. He enlisted as a private in Company A, 27th Regiment, Georgia Infantry. December 1861 and February 1862 rolls show he was left sick in Georgia October 31, 1861. March 30, 1862 admitted to Chimborazo Hospital No. 2, Richmond, Virginia with Bronchitis. April 29, 1862 returned to duty. May 17, 1862 admitted to Chimborazo Hospital No. 2 at Richmond, Virginia with parotitis. June

12, 1862 received pay ($113.00). December 1862 roll shows he deserted. March 1, 1863 in General Hospital No. 9 at Richmond, Virginia. March 2, 1863 admitted to General Hospital No. 9 at Richmond, Virginia with Chronic Bronchitis and Chronic Nepritis. March 3, 1863 admitted to Receiving and Wayside Hospital or General Hospital No. 9 at Richmond, Virginia and transferred to General Hospital No. 1 at Richmond, Virginia. He was discharged April 7, 1863 according to Medical Director's Office, Richmond, Virginia.

BAXLEY, JOSEPH W.: Company I, corporal. September 10, 1861 enlisted as a private in Co. I, 27th Regiment, Georgia Infantry at Camp Stephens, Griffin, Spalding County, Georgia. December 1861 roll shows he was left in Georgia sick on October 31, 1861. January 1862 roll shows he was on furlough. February 1862 roll shows him absent sick. March 30, 1862 admitted to Chimborazo Hospital No. 1 at Richmond, Virginia with dysentery. April 19, 1862 returned to duty. May 3, 1863 wounded at Chancellorsville, Virginia. He was appointed corporal of Co. I, 27th Regiment, Georgia Infantry. June 16 and 23, 1863 issued clothing. December 31, 1863 received pay. January - February 1864 roll shows him present. February 29, 1864 received pay. March - April 1864 roll shows him present. July and September 20, 1864 issued clothing. April 26, 1865, surrendered at Greensboro, North Carolina. May 1, 1865 paroled at Greensboro, North Carolina. He died March 16, 1913 in Appling County, Georgia. He is buried at Baxley Cemetery in Appling County, Georgia.

BAXLEY, LOVETT W.: Company I, corporal. September 10, 1861 enlisted as a private in Co. I, 27th Regiment, Georgia Infantry at Camp Stephens, Griffin, Spalding County, Georgia. December 20, 1861 admitted to Moore Hospital at General Hospital, No. 1 at Danville, Virginia with Catarrh and sent to Orange Court House, Virginia Hospital. January 13, 1862 C. S. A. General Hospital at Farmville, Virginia register shows he was returned to O. A. Lee at Manassas, Virginia on January 13, 1862. March 9, 1862 admitted to Chimborazo Hospital No. 4 at Richmond, Virginia with Diarrhoea. December 18, 1862 admitted to General Hospital at Orange Court House, Virginia with Fever. December 1862 roll shows him in hospital at Farmville, Virginia. January 13, 1863 returned to duty. June 16 and 27, 1863 issued clothing. December 31, 1863 received pay. February 1864 appointed corporal of Co. I, 27th Regiment, Georgia Infantry. February 29, 1864 received pay. January - February 1864 roll shows him present. March - April 1864 roll shows him absent since April 26, 1864. March - April 1864 roll shows him present. March 1864 pension records show he left command on sick furlough for 90 days. He was unable to return. He was born in Georgia in 1838. He died June 29, 1916 in Appling County, Georgia. He is buried at Baxley Graveyard Cemetery in Appling County, Georgia

BAXLEY, WILLIS: Company I, captain. September 10, 1861 elected 2nd sergeant of Co. I, 27th Regiment, Georgia Infantry at Camp Stephens,

Griffin, Spalding County, Georgia. December 1861 roll shows him sick in hospital. March 7, 1862 admitted to Chimborazo Hospital, No. 3 at Richmond, Virginia. March 16, 1862 record of Chimborazo Hospital, No. 5 at Richmond, Virginia shows he was at Mrs. Bowman's of Franklin Street (nr. old M.) on March 15, 1862 and returned this date. May 4, 1862 returned to duty and transferred to Camp Winder. May 16, 1862 admitted to Chimborazo Hospital, No. 3 at Richmond, Virginia with Typhoid Fever. May 16, 1862 furloughed for 30 days from Chimborazo Hospital, No. 3 at Richmond, Virginia. May 31, 1862 wounded at Seven Pines, Virginia. June 22, 1862 returned to duty. July 18, 1862 to August 18, 1862 furloughed and received $7.50 for rations during that period at Guinea Station, Virginia. June 16 and 27, 1863 issued clothing. December 31, 1863 received pay. January - February 1864 roll shows him present. February 29, 1864 received pay. March - April 1864 roll shows him present. September 20, 1864 issued clothing. He was elected captain of Company I, 27 Regiment, Georgia Infantry. April 26, 1865 pension records show he surrendered, Greensboro, North Carolina. He is buried at Ten Mile Creek Baptist Church Cemetery in Appling County, Georgia

BEAR, JOHN: Company K, private. He enlisted as a private in Co. K, 27th Regiment, Georgia Infantry. December 1862 roll shows him on extra duty as a teamster.

BEECHER (BECHER) (BEACHER), HENRY HARRISON: Company I, corporal. September 10, 1861 elected 1st corporal of Co. I, 27th Regiment, Georgia Infantry at Camp Stephens, Griffin, Spalding County, Georgia. May 31, 1862 wounded at Seven Pines, Virginia. June 27, 1862 wounded at Cold Harbor, Virginia. June 16 and 27, 1863 issued clothing. July 5, 1862 received pay ($7.50) for rations while furloughed from June 5, 1862 to July 5, 1862. October 12 and 29, 1863, November 24, 1863 and December 18, 1863 issued clothing. December 31, 1863 received pay. June 18, 1864 issued clothing in Jackson Hospital at Richmond, Virginia. January - February 1864 roll shows him present. February 29, 1864 received pay. March - April 1864 roll shows him present. April 30, 1864 (dated June 21, 1864) roll of soldiers sick in 1st Division Jackson Hospital, Richmond, Virginia shows him present (admitted June 11, 1864). June 10, 1864 admitted to Receiving and Wayside Hospital or General Hospital No. 9 at Richmond, Virginia and transferred to Jackson Hospital at Richmond, Virginia on June 11, 1864. July 13, 1864 furloughed from Jackson Hospital, Richmond, Virginia for 30 days. September 20, 1864 issued clothing. March 30, 1865 pension records show he was captured at Sugar Loaf, North Carolina. He was in Military prison at Wilmington, North Carolina until the close of the war. He was born in Appling County, Georgia June 30, 1842.

BEECHER (BECHER) (BEACHER), L. W.: Company I, private. September 10, 1861 enlisted as a private in Co. I, 27th Regiment, Georgia Infantry at Camp Stephens, Griffin, Spalding County, Georgia.

BEECHER (BECHER) (BEACHER), WILLIAM ALFRED: Company I, private. September 10, 1861 enlisted as a private in Co. I, 27th Regiment, Georgia Infantry at Camp Stephens, Griffin, Spalding County, Georgia. April 10, 1862 admitted to Chimborazo Hospital, No. 5, Richmond, Virginia with Bronchitis. May 4, 1862 appears on a roll of Chimborazo Hospital, No. 5, Richmond Virginia with note; transferred to Camp Winder at Richmond, Virginia on May 4, 1862. May 31, 1862 wounded at Seven Pines, Virginia. June 27, 1862 wounded at Cold Harbor. June 30, 1862 admitted to Chimborazo Hospital No. 3 at Richmond, Virginia with Vulnus Sclopeticum (Gunshot Wound) in side. July 1, 1862 transferred to Lynchburg, Virginia. July 2, 1862 admitted to C. S. A. General Hospital at Danville, Virginia with Vulnus Sclopeticum (Gunshot Wound). July 6, 1862 returned to duty. July 13, 1862 admitted to Chimborazo Hospital No. 5 at Richmond, Virginia with Debility. July 17, 1862 returned to duty from Chimborazo Hospital No. 5 at Richmond, Virginia. August 22, 1862 received pay ($44.00). December 31, 1863 received pay. January 2, 1864 - January 31, 1864 received pay for extra duty as an oarsman at Fort Jackson for that time period. January - February 1864 roll shows him present. February 29, 1864 received pay. March - April 1864 roll shows him present. June 24, 1864 appears on roll of 1st Division Jackson Hospital at Richmond, Virginia for April 30, 1864. June 20, 1864 admitted to Jackson Hospital at Richmond, Virginia wounded in the heel by a shell. July 11, 1864 issued clothing at 1st Division Jackson Hospital at Richmond, Virginia. July 15, 1864 furloughed for 30 days from 1st Division Jackson Hospital at Richmond, Virginia. September 30, 1864 admitted to Receiving and Wayside Hospital or General Hospital No. 9 at Richmond, Virginia. October 1, 1864 transferred to Jackson Hospital at Richmond, Virginia. October 1, 1864 admitted to Jackson Hospital at Richmond, Virginia with Vulnus Sclopeticum (Gunshot Wound) to left hand. October 17, 1864 issued clothing at Jackson Hospital, Richmond, Virginia. October 19, 1864 returned to duty. April 26, 1865 surrendered, Greensboro, North Carolina. He was born in Appling County, Georgia January 31, 1840. He is buried at Ten Mile Baptist Church Cemetery in Appling County, Georgia.

BEECHER (BECHER) (BEACHER), WILLIAM LUMPKIN: Company I, private. March 4, 1862 enlisted as a private in Co. F, 11th Battalion, Georgia Infantry. May 12, 1862 transferred to Co. F, 47th Regiment, Georgia Infantry. August 1, 1862 transferred to Co. A, 1st Battalion, Georgia Sharpshooters. September 1862 he was sick at Springfield, Georgia. There is no later record in this company. September 10, 1863 enlisted as a private in Co. I, 27th Regiment, Georgia Infantry at Holmesville, Appling County, Georgia. December 31, 1863 received pay. January - February 1864 roll shows him present. February 29, 1864 received pay. March - April 1864 rolls show him present. July 1864 issued clothing. August 20, 1864 admitted Jackson Hospital, Richmond, Virginia with Vulnus Sclopeticum (Gunshot Wound) to thigh. August 29,

1864 issued clothing at Jackson Hospital, Richmond, Virginia. August 31, 1864 furloughed for 30 days from Jackson Hospital, Richmond, Virginia and passport issued for Fort Gaines, Georgia. April 26, 1865 surrendered, Greensboro, North Carolina. May 1, 1865 paroled at Greensboro, North Carolina. He is buried at Ten Mile Baptist Church Cemetery in Appling County, Georgia.

BECK, M. J.: Company E, private. He enlisted as a private in Co. E, 27th Regiment, Georgia Infantry. June 15, 1864 returned to duty from Jackson Hospital, Richmond, Virginia.

BECKHAM, HIRAM: Company G, private. September 9, 1861 enlisted as a private in Co. G, 27th Regiment, Georgia Infantry at Camp Stephens, Griffin, Spalding County, Georgia. November 8, 1861 admitted to General Hospital No. 18, at Richmond, Virginia. December 26, 1861 discharged due to disability at Richmond, Virginia. He was born January 29, 1832. His post office is listed as Flat Shoals, Meriwether County, Georgia

BECKHAM, JAMES J.: Company G, sergeant. September 9, 1861 enlisted as a private in Co. G, 27th Regiment, Georgia Infantry at Camp Stephens, Griffin, Spalding County, Georgia. September 9, 1861 elected 2nd sergeant in Co. G, 27th Regiment, Georgia Infantry. He was appointed 1st sergeant. December 1861 roll shows him in hospital at Richmond, Virginia. January 1862 roll shows he was left in Georgia sick October 31, 1861. October 30, 1863, November 24, 1863 and December 16, 1863 issued clothing. December 31, 1863 received pay. January - February 1864 roll shows him present. February 20, 1864 wounded at Olustee, Florida. February 29, 1864 received pay. March - April 1864 roll shows him present. September 1984 issued clothing for the 3rd quarter of 1864. October 7, 1864 admitted to Jackson Hospital, Richmond, Virginia with Febris Remt (malaria). October 14, 1864 returned to duty. April 26, 1865 surrendered, Greensboro, North Carolina. May 1, 1865 paroled at Greensboro, North Carolina.

BECKHAM, JOHN D.: Company G, private. September 9, 1861 enlisted as a private in Co. G, 27th Regiment, Georgia Infantry at Camp Stephens, Griffin, Spalding County, Georgia. November 1, 1861 he is shown on report at Manassas, Virginia as being sick with Pneumonia. November 14, 1861 admitted to General Hospital No.18, at Richmond, Virginia with Diarrhoea. November 26, 1861 died in General Hospital No. 18, Richmond, Virginia (cause of death listed as Nervous Prostration). February 5, 1862 death benefit claim was filed by Sarah A. Beckham, his widow. March 20 1862 received death benefit of $53.60 (#220).

BECKHAM, SIMEON G.: Company G, private. September 9, 1861 enlisted as a private in Co. G, 27th Regiment, Georgia Infantry at Camp Stephens, Griffin, Spalding County, Georgia. October 31, 1861 left in Griffin, Georgia sick. December 1861 roll shows he was left in Griffin, Georgia sick on October 31, 1861. November 13, 1863 admitted to hospital in Richmond, Virginia. November 29, 1861 admitted to General

Hospital No.18, at Richmond, Virginia. December 19, 1861 discharged and received pay. January - February 1862 roll shows him in hospital in Richmond, Virginia. May 5, 1862 enlisted as a private in Co. H, 53rd Regiment, Georgia Infantry. December 1863 appointed 4th sergeant of Co. H, 53rd Regiment, Georgia Infantry. April 9, 1865 surrendered at Appomattox, Virginia. His Post Office is shown as Zebulon, Pike County, Georgia.

BEEKS, JOHN C.: Company G, captain. He enlisted as a 2nd lieutenant in Co. G, 27th Regiment, Georgia Infantry at Camp Stephens, Griffin, Spalding County, Georgia. August 21, 1861 elected 2nd lieutenant in Co. G, 27th Regiment, Georgia Infantry. December 1861 roll shows him present at Camp Pickens near Manassas, Virginia. December 20, 1861 received pay ($173.33). January 1862 roll shows him present at Camp Pickens near Manassas, Virginia. February 1862 roll shows him present at Camp Pickens near Manassas, Virginia. February 20, 1862 promoted to 1st lieutenant in Co. G, 27th Regiment, Georgia Infantry. July 13, 1862 promoted to captain in Co. G, 27th Regiment, Georgia Infantry. September 17, 1862 wounded and captured at Sharpsburg, Maryland. September 21, 1862 died of wounds at Mrs. Hoffman House Hospital. (He is buried in Confederate Cemetery at Hagerstown, Maryland.

BEASLEY (BEESLEY), JOHN: Company E, private. He enlisted as a private in Co. E, 27th Regiment, Georgia Infantry. May 23, 1865 surrendered at Augusta, Georgia. May 23, 1865 paroled at Augusta, Georgia.

BEDELL, ABNER W.: Company K, private. March 4, 1862 enlisted as a private in Co. K, 27th Regiment, Georgia Infantry at Talbotton, Georgia. June 1863 issued clothing for 2nd quarter of 1863. December 31, 1863 received pay. March - April 1864 roll shows him present. September 2, 1864 issued clothing. September 12, 1864 deserted, received by Provost Marshal General, Washington D. C., a Confederate Deserter, with the following remarks relative to him. "Released on oath of allegiance to the United States Government and furnished transportation to Arkansas". September 1864 described by Union Army as deserter 27 years of age, born in Western Georgia, 5 feet7 inches tall, blue eyes, dark hair, dark complexion and was sent to Indiana.

BEDELL (BEDSELL), HENRY D.: Company K, private. September 10, 1861 enlisted as a private in Co. K, 27th Regiment, Georgia Infantry at Camp Stephens, Griffin, Spalding County, Georgia. February 1862 roll shows he was detailed as a courier at Post Headquarters. February 4, 1863 - March 6, 1863 on furlough and received $10.00 for rations for that period. June 1863 issued clothing for 2nd quarter of 1863. October 29, 1863, November 24, 1863 and December 18, 1863 issued clothing. December 31, 1863 received pay. March - April 1864 rolls show him present. June 20, 1864 admitted to Jackson Hospital, Richmond, Virginia with Vulnus Sclopeticum (Gunshot Wound) in right arm at Colquitt's Salient, Petersburg,

Virginia. June 30, 1864 he is shown on roll of Jackson Hospital at Richmond, Virginia. July 14, 1864 issued clothing and furloughed for 60 days at Jackson Hospital at Richmond, Virginia. October 3, 1864 issued clothing. April 26, 1865 surrendered, Greensboro, North Carolina. May 1, 1865 paroled at Greensboro, North Carolina.

BEDSIL (BEBSILL) (BIDSEL), JOHN J.: Company E, private. He enlisted as a private in Co. E, 27th Regiment, Georgia Infantry. June 5, 1862 died in C. S. A. Hospital, Farmville, Virginia.

BELL, A. H.: Company K, private. He enlisted as a private in Co. K, 27th Regiment, Georgia Infantry. October 8, 1864 admitted to Jackson Hospital, Richmond, Virginia. November 10, 1864 he was furloughed.

BELL, ABSALOM M.: Company D, private. March 4, 1862 enlisted as a private in Co. D, 27th Regiment, Georgia Infantry in Gainesville, Hall County, Georgia. March 25, 1862 received $50.00 bounty for enlisting. May 4, 1862 admitted to Chimborazo Hospital No. 3, Richmond, Virginia with Rubeola and Typhoid Fever. June 18, 1862 died of Typhoid Fever in Chimborazo Hospital No. 3, Richmond, Virginia. Most likely buried in Oakwood Cemetery at Richmond Virginia. June 11, 1863 death benefit claim was filed on behalf of Amanda E. Bell of Gainesville, Hall County, Georgia.

BELL, C. R.: Company K, private. He enlisted as a private in Co. K, 27th Regiment, Georgia Infantry.

BELL, ELI R.: Company K, private. March 24, 1862 enlisted as a private in Co. K, 27th Regiment, Georgia Infantry (at age 23). April 9, 1862 admitted to Chimborazo Hospital No. 1, Richmond, Virginia with Pneumonia. April 22, 1862 died of Pneumonia at Chimborazo Hospital, No. 1, Richmond, Virginia. Most likely buried in Oakwood Cemetery at Richmond Virginia.

BELL, WILLIAM (WELLBORN) R.: Company D, private. He enlisted as a private in Co. D, 27th Regiment, Georgia Infantry. December 17, 1861 admitted to Moore Hospital at General Hospital No. 1, Danville, Virginia with Pneumonia and was transferred to General Hospital, Richmond, Virginia. December 1861 roll shows he was in the hospital at Richmond, Virginia. January 11, 1862 died of disease in Richmond, Virginia Hospital. May 29, 1862 death benefit claim was filed on behalf of Nancy Bell, mother.

BELYEN (BELYEW), BERRY B.: Company K, private. September 10, 1861 enlisted as a private in Co. K, 27th Regiment, Georgia Infantry at Camp Stephens, Griffin, Spalding County, Georgia. January 1862 roll shows him detailed as regimental teamster. February 1862 roll shows him as teamster in regimental Quartermasters Department. November 29, 1862 records show he was returned to duty from General Hospital No. 17. Richmond, Virginia. March 17, 1863 received pay ($10.00) for rations from February 2, 1863 to March 4, 1863. October 22 and 29, 1863, November 24, 1863 and December 18, 1863 issued clothing. December 31, 1863 received pay. March - April 1864 rolls show him present. September 24, 1864 issued clothing. April 26, 1865 surrendered, Greensboro, North Carolina. May 1, 1865 paroled at Greensboro, North Carolina.

BELYEN, FREEMAN: Company K, private. September 10, 1861 enlisted as a private in Co. K, 27th Regiment, Georgia Infantry at Camp Stephens, Griffin, Spalding County, Georgia. December 1862 sent to Yorktown, Virginia hospital. October 22, and 29, 1863, November 24, 1863 issued clothing. July 1864 issued clothing.

BELYEAN, JAMES A.: Company K, private. March 24, 1862 enlisted as a private in Co. K, 27th Regiment, Georgia Infantry (at age 19). April 24, 1864 admitted to Chimborazo Hospital No. 5, Richmond, Virginia with Bronchitis. June 7, 1862 returned to duty from C. S. A. General Hospital, Farmville, Virginia. September 30, 1862 paroled by Provost Marshall, Army of the Potomac. November 29, 1862 admitted to C. S. A. General Hospital, Charlottesville, Virginia with a Vulnus Sclopeticum (Gunshot Wound) and transferred to General Hospital at Lynchburg, Virginia. October 22 and 29, 1863 and November 24 1863 issued clothing. July 1864 issued clothing. March 11, 1865 issued clothing at Pettigrew General Hospital No. 13, Raleigh, North Carolina.

BELYEN, JOHN: Company K, private. September 10, 1861 enlisted as a private in Co. K, 27th Regiment, Georgia Infantry at Camp Stephens, Griffin, Spalding County, Georgia. December 1862 sent to hospital from Sharpsburg, Maryland.

BELYEN, JOHN A.: Company K, private. March 4, 1862 enlisted as a private in Co. K, 27th Regiment, Georgia Infantry at Talbotton, Georgia. August 3, 1863 received pay ($52.47) from January 13, 1863 to June 22, 1863. December 31, 1863 received pay. March - April 1964 rolls show him present.

BELYEN, JOHN C.: Company K, private. June 10, 1863 enlisted in Co. K, 27th Regiment, Georgia Infantry at Talbotton, Georgia. August 8, 1863 received pay for rations ($13.60) for time from June 10, 1863 to July 9, 1863. October 22 and 29, 1863 and December 18, 1863 issued clothing. December 31, 1863 received pay. January 5, 1864 received pay ($22.00) for service from November 1, 1863 to December 31, 1863. January 5, 1864 received pay ($22.00). March - April 1864 roll shows him present. June 3, 1864 wounded in right hand at Cold Harbor, Virginia and admitted to Receiving and Wayside Hospital No. 9 at Richmond, Virginia. June 4, 1864 admitted to C. S. A. General Hospital at Danville, Virginia with Vulnus Sclopeticum (Gunshot Wound) in right hand (shows he was age 40 and was a farmer). June 7(8), 1864 furloughed. September 20, 1864 issued clothing. April 26, 1865 surrendered, Greensboro, North Carolina. May 1, 1865 paroled at Greensboro, North Carolina.

BELYEN (BELYEAN), JOSIAH: Company K, private. March 10, 1862 enlisted as a private in Co. K, 27th Regiment, Georgia Infantry (age 17). May 24, 1862 died at Richmond, Virginia. He is buried in Hollywood

Cemetery at Richmond, Virginia. December 15, 1863 death benefit claim was filed by Thomas Belleyen, his father.

BELYEN (BELYEAN), RICHARD: Company K, private. March 4, 1862 (February 26, 1862) enlisted as a private in Co. K, 27th Regiment, Georgia Infantry at Talbotton, Georgia (age 23). April 24, 1862 admitted to Chimborazo Hospital No. 3, Richmond, Virginia. May 1, 1862 received pay. June 26, 1862 transferred to Lynchburg, Virginia Hospital. October 31, 1862 roll shows him present. November 19, 1862 admitted to General Hospital No. 17, Richmond, Virginia. June 1863 issued clothing for 2nd quarter of 1863. September 30 1863 received pay ($22.00) for time from July 1, 1863 to August 31, 1863. September 29, 1863 to November 29, 1863 on furlough and received $19.60 for rations for that period. December 31, 1863 received pay. March - April 1864 roll shows him present. July 1864 issued clothing. September 24, 1864 issued clothing. April 26, 1865 surrendered, Greensboro, North Carolina. May 1, 1865 paroled at Greensboro, North Carolina.

BELYEN (BELYEAN), WESLEY F.: Company K, corporal. March 4, 1862 (February 24, 1864) enlisted as a private in Co. K, 27th Regiment, Georgia Infantry (age 23) at Talbotton, Georgia. April 24, 1862 admitted to Chimborazo Hospital No. 3 at Richmond, Virginia. June 26, 1862 transferred to Lynchburg, Virginia hospital. August 1, 1862 attached as nurse at General Hospital at Liberty, Virginia. August 31, 1862 received pay (plus 60 days extra duty as nurse a $.25 per day ($15.00). September - October 1862 roll for General Hospital at Liberty, Virginia indicates he was employed as a nurse. Paid for 60 days extra duty as nurse a $.25 per day ($15.00). November - December roll for General Hospital at Liberty, Virginia indicates he was employed as a nurse. Paid for 60 days extra duty as nurse a $.25 per day ($15.00) December 31, 1863 received pay. January - February, 1863 roll for General Hospital at Liberty, Virginia shows he was employed as a nurse, Paid for 60 days extra duty as nurse a $.25 per day ($15.00). February 28, 1863 received pay. March - April roll of General Hospital at Liberty, Virginia shows he was employed as a nurse until March 18, 1863 (18 days extra duty as nurse from March 1, 1863 to March 18, 1863). February 20, 1864 slightly wounded at Olustee, Florida. March - April 1864 roll shows him absent and that on April 25, 1864 he was in Charleston, South Carolina Hospital. September 20, 1864 issued clothing. He was appointed corporal in Co. K., 27th Regiment, Georgia Infantry. April 26, 1865 surrendered, Greensboro, North Carolina. May 1, 1865 paroled at Greensboro, North Carolina.

BENSON (BENSTONE) (BENSTON), ROBERT: Company A, private. February 26, 1862 enlisted in Co. A, 27th Regiment, Georgia, Infantry, in Marion County, Georgia. May 2, 1862 admitted to General Hospital at Camp Winder at Richmond, Virginia with Febris Typhoid. July 4, 1862 died at C. S. A. General Hospital at Farmville, Virginia of Febris Typhoid. November 20, 1862 roll shows he was paid a bounty of $50.00

for enlistment.   December 27, 1862 death benefit claim was filed by Sarah Benson, wife.   September 18, 1863 death benefit claim was paid $83.30 (#8966).

BENTLEY, HENRY L. (D.): Company H, corporal.   September 9, 1861 enlisted as a private in Co. H, 27th Regiment, Georgia Infantry at Camp Stephens, Griffin, Spalding County, Georgia.   October 31, 1861 received pay. He was appointed corporal in Co. H, 27th Regiment, Georgia Infantry. December 21, 1861 admitted to Moore Hospital at General Hospital No. 1, Danville, Virginia with tonsillitis and was sent to Richmond, Virginia Hospital.   December 31, 1861 received pay and clothing was issued. January 1862 roll shows he was in hospital at Mt. Jackson, Virginia admitted on January 25, 1862.   March 13, 1862 died of Typhoid Pneumonia in South Carolina Hospital at Post Jefferson, Charlottesville, Virginia.   September 23, 1862 death benefit claim was filed by Emily F. Bentley, wife (they were married April 1, 1856).

BENTON, N. P.: Company A, private. He enlisted in Co. A, 27th Regiment, Georgia, Infantry, October 31, 1861 left sick in Georgia.   December 1861 and January 1862 rolls show he was left sick in Georgia October 31, 1861.   May 17, 1862 admitted to Chimborazo Hospital No. 2 at Richmond, Virginia with Debility.   May 17, 1862 transferred to Lynchburg, Farmville, Virginia.   June 1863 issued clothing.   July 8, 1863 admitted to Chimborazo Hospital No. 2 at Richmond, Virginia with Debility.   July 7, 1863 admitted to Receiving and Wayside Hospital or General Hospital No. 9 at Richmond, Virginia.   July 8, 1863 transferred to Chimborazo Hospital No. 2 at Richmond, Virginia.   July 22, 1863 furloughed for 35 days from Chimborazo Hospital No. 2 at Richmond, Virginia.   November 14, 1863 wounded (scalp, slightly) at Fort Sumter, Charleston, South Carolina.

BETSILL, JOHN J.: Company E, private.   September 9, 1861 enlisted as a private in Co. E, 27th Regiment, Georgia Infantry at Camp Stephens, Griffin, Spalding County, Georgia.   June 2, 1862 admitted to General Hospital, Camp Winder at Richmond, Virginia with Typhoid Fever.   June (4) 5, 1862 died of Typhoid Fever in C. S. A. General Hospital at Farmville, Virginia.   August 14, 1862 death benefit claim was filed by William H. Rentfrow attorney.

BETSILL (BEDCIL), M. A. L.: Company E, private.   He enlisted as a private in Co. E, 27th Regiment, Georgia Infantry.

BETSILL (BETSEL), WILLIAM A.: Company E, private.   September 9, 1861 enlisted   as a private in Co. E, 27th Regiment, Georgia Infantry at Camp Stephens, Griffin, Spalding County, Georgia.   October 31, 1861 left sick in Georgia.   December 1961 roll shows he was left sick in Georgia. January and February 1862 rolls show him sick in Georgia.   June 6, 1862 admitted to General Hospital Camp Winder at Richmond, Virginia with Diarrhoea. June 9, 1862 returned to duty.   July 1, 1862 admitted to General Hospital Camp Winder at Richmond, Virginia with Diarrhoea.   November 19, 1862 admitted to General Hospital No. 17 at Richmond, Virginia.

November 29, 1862 returned to duty. December 19, 1862 admitted to Winder Division 1 Hospital at Richmond, Virginia. January 7, 1863 shown on Winder Division 1 Hospital records as having deserted. December 31, 1863 received pay. April, May and June 1864 issued clothing. September 20, 1864 issued clothing for the 3rd quarter January - February 1864 roll shows him present. February 29, 1864 received pay. March - April 1864 roll, last on record, shows him present. June 14, 1864 admitted to Jackson Hospital for Chronic Diarrhoea. June 18, 1864 he is shown on roll of Jackson Hospital at Richmond, Virginia as being issued clothing. June 20, 1864 returned to duty. June 20, 1864 received pay ($22) for service from January 1, 1864 to February 29, 1864. April 26, 1865 surrendered Greensboro, North Carolina. May 1, 1865 paroled at Greensboro, North Carolina. He was born in Fayette County, Georgia March 5, 1846.

BETSILL (BEDCIL), WILLIAM M.: Company E, private. He enlisted as a private in Co. E, 27th Regiment, Georgia Infantry.

BINS (BIAS), JOHN F.: Company K, private. September 10, 1861 enlisted as a private in Co. K, 27th Regiment, Georgia Infantry at Camp Stephens, Griffin, Spalding County, Georgia, February 1862 roll shows February 20, 1862 sent to Moore Hospital, Virginia. April 11, 1862 admitted to Chimborazo Hospital No 5 at Richmond, Virginia with Debility. June 13 1862 returned to duty from Chimborazo Hospital No. 5 at Richmond, Virginia. May 16, 1863 - May 31, 1863 detailed as an ambulance driver. August 16, 1863 - December 31, 1863 detailed as ambulance driver, Quartermasters Department at James Island, South Carolina. December 31, 1863 received pay. June 1863 issued clothing. He was detailed as a teamster in the Quartermasters Department at James Island, South Carolina. October 22, October 29 and November 24, 1863 issued clothing. January 1864 detailed as an ambulance driver in the Quartermasters Department at James Island, South Carolina and received $.25 extra pay. February 1, 1864 - June 9, 1864 detailed as a teamster at Petersburg, Virginia and received $.25 in extra pay. March - April 1864 roll shows him present. May 1864 detailed as teamster. May 30, 1864 issued clothing. July 1864 issued clothing. September 20, 1864 issued clothing. April 26, 1865 surrendered at Greensboro, North Carolina. May 1, 1865 paroled at Greensboro, North Carolina.

BIGGERS, ELI A.: Company H, corporal. September 9, 1861 enlisted as a private in Co. H, 27th Regiment, Georgia Infantry at Camp Stephens, Griffin, Spalding County, Georgia. July 9, 1862 received pay ($91.00). August 1862 roll shows him present. October 4, 1862 admitted to General Hospital at Richmond, Virginia. December 1862 roll shows him absent without leave. January 9, 1863 was paid for 35 days of commutation of rations at Atlanta, Georgia. December 31, 1863 received pay. January - February 1864 roll shows him present. March - April 1864 roll shows him present. May 13, 1864 issued clothing. July 1864 issued clothing. September 20, 1864 issued clothing. March 19, 1865 wounded in the leg, necessitating amputation, at Bentonville, North Carolina. April 26, 1865 surrendered, Greensboro, North Carolina as corporal (was a patient at Way Hospital No. 2 at Greensboro, North Carolina at the time). May 1, 1865 paroled at Greensboro, North Carolina. He was born March 22, 1841.

BILLINGSLEY, MARCUS L.: Company G, captain. September 9, 1861 enlisted as a private in Co. G, 27th Regiment, Georgia Infantry at Camp Stephens, Griffin, Spalding County, Georgia. November 14, 1861 admitted to General Hospital No. 18 at Richmond, Virginia. December 1, 1861 roll shows he was in the Hospital at Richmond, Virginia at the rank of sergeant. January 27, 1862 returned to duty and detailed to take home the corpse of J. Barker. April 29, 1862 elected Jr. 2nd lieutenant in Co. G, 27th Regiment, Georgia Infantry. May 1, 1862 elected 2nd lieutenant in Co. G, 27th Regiment, Georgia Infantry. June 12, 1862 received pay ($85.00). July 13, 1862 elected 1st lieutenant in Co. G, 27th Regiment, Georgia Infantry. August 30, 1862 received pay ($80.00). September 17, 1862 promoted to captain. September 21, 1862 elected captain Co. G, 27th Regiment, Georgia Infantry. October 13, 1862 received pay ($98.00). December 1862 shows him present at Guinea Station, Virginia. April and June 1863 issued clothing. September 30, 1863 roll shows him present. February, March - April 1864 roll indicate him only. May 1864 he was in Pettigrew General Hospital No. 13 at Raleigh, North Carolina. August 14, 1864 roll at Petersburg, Virginia indicates he was in the hospital since August 9, 1864. May 27, 1864 returned to duty. June 13, 1864 admitted to Jackson Hospital Richmond, Virginia with Febris Infection. June 20, 1864 returned to duty. August 20, 1864 received pay ($260.00). April 26, 1865 surrendered, Greensboro, North Carolina. May 1, 1865 paroled at Greensboro, North Carolina. His Post Office was listed as Zebulon, Pike County, Georgia.

BINS, JOHN F.: Company K, private. September 10, 1861 enlisted as a private in Co. K, 27th Regiment, Georgia Infantry at Camp Stephens, Griffin, Spalding County, Georgia. April 26, 1865 surrendered, Greensboro, North Carolina.

BINSON, R.: Company A, private. September 10, 1861 enlisted as a private in Co. A, 27th Regiment, Georgia Infantry at Camp Stephens, Griffin, Spalding County, Georgia. July 7, 1862 died at Richmond, Virginia. He is buried in Hollywood Cemetery at Richmond, Virginia.

BIRD (BURD) (BYRD), A. H.: Company D, private. May 13 1862 admitted to Chimborazo Hospital No. 3, Richmond, Virginia with Parotitis. May 16, 1862 transferred to Camp Winder at Richmond, Virginia. December 10, 1862 died in General Hospital No. 2, Lynchburg, Virginia of Typhoid Fever.

BIRD (BURD) (BYRD), WILLIAM: Company D, private. He enlisted as a private in Co. D, 27th Regiment, Georgia Infantry.

BLACKSTOCK, JAMES D.: Company D, private. September 10, 1861 enlisted as a private in Co. D, 27th Regiment, Georgia Infantry at Camp

Stephens, Griffin, Spalding County, Georgia. June 29, 1862 wounded at Cold Harbor, Virginia. June 29, 1862 admitted to General Hospital No. 18 at Richmond Virginia with a bullet wound. June 30, 1862 transferred to Camp Winder at Richmond, Virginia. September 17, 1862 wounded and captured at Sharpsburg, Maryland. October 1, 1862 admitted to Summit House General Hospital at West Philadelphia, Pennsylvania with fractured left arm. December 5, 1862 returned to duty. December 5, 1862 paroled at Fort Delaware, Delaware and sent to Fortress Monroe, Virginia for exchange. December 18, 1862 received at City Point, Virginia. December 19, 1862 admitted to General Hospital at Petersburg, Virginia with Vulnus Sclopeticum (Gunshot Wound) left arm. December 27, 1862 furloughed for 60 days. July 3, 1863 to September 6, 1863 detailed as sub enrolling officer of Hall County, Georgia. September 7, 1863 received pay and expenses ($38.75). December 1863 issued clothing. December 19, 1863 received pay ($245.53). December 14, 1863 discharged due to disability due to damage by Vulnus Sclopeticum (Gunshot Wound) to left arm and received pay ($194.50). He was born in Hall County, Georgia November 8, 1841. He is described on discharge document dated October 1863 as being 22 years of age and 6 feet tall, fair complexion, blue eyes and light hair. His occupation was a farmer.

BLOODSWORTH, DAVID N.: Company F, 1st sergeant. September 9, 1861 elected 5th sergeant in Co. F, 27th Regiment, Georgia Infantry at Camp Stephens, Griffin, Spalding County, Georgia. January 20, 1862 admitted to Moore Hospital at General Hospital No. 1 at Danville, Virginia with deafness. January 21, 1862 admitted to General Hospital at Orange Court House, Virginia with an ear Infection. January 24, 1862 returned to duty. July 5, 1862 admitted to Chimborazo Hospital No. 4 at Richmond, Virginia with acute Diarrhoea and transferred to Farmville, Virginia. July 11, 1862 admitted to General Hospital at Farmville, Virginia with Rheumatism. September 11, 1862 issued clothing and charged $5.50 and $3.50. September 12, 1862 returned to duty. August 1863 issued clothing. October 29, 1863 received pay. December 31, 1863 received pay. January - February, 1864 roll shows him present. March - April 1864 roll shows him present. June 1864 issued clothing. He was appointed 1st sergeant in Co. F, 27th Regiment, Georgia Infantry. August 19, 1864 wounded at Weldon Railroad near Petersburg, Virginia. August 22, 1864 admitted to Jackson Hospital at Richmond, Virginia with Vulnus Sclopeticum (Gunshot Wound) left leg. September 5, 1864 received pay ($155.13). September 6, 1864 furloughed for 30 days. April 26, 1865 surrendered, Greensboro, North Carolina. May 1, 1865 paroled at Greensboro, North Carolina. His home was Butler, Georgia.

BLUE, J. M.: Company K, private. He enlisted as a private in Co. K, 27th Regiment, Georgia Infantry. January 18, 1865 admitted to Pettigrew General Hospital No. 13, Raleigh, North Carolina with Vulnus Sclopeticum (Gunshot Wound) right thigh (flesh) March 13, 1865 he was transferred to

E. Ch. Hospital. He was a resident of Tolbert County, Georgia, Post Office Keaton, Georgia.

BLUE, W. T.: Company K, private. He enlisted as a private in Co. K, 27th Regiment, Georgia Infantry. December 22, 1864 admitted to Jackson Hospital at Richmond, Virginia with Febris Infection. January 5, 1865 returned to duty.

BLUNT, G. W.: Company K, private. He enlisted as a private in Co. K, 27th Regiment, Georgia Infantry. July 4, 1864 admitted to Stuart Hospital at Richmond, Virginia with Chronic Diarrhoea. July 16, 1864 died in Stuart Hospital at Richmond, Virginia. (His clothing was valued at $8.00)

BLYER, W. F.: Company K, private. He enlisted as a private in Co. K, 27th Regiment, Georgia Infantry. August 19, 1864 wounded at Weldon Railroad, Virginia. December 22, 1864 admitted to Receiving and Wayside Hospital or General Hospital No. 9, Richmond, Virginia. December 23, 1864 transferred to Jackson Hospital at Richmond, Virginia.

BLYTHE, SAMUEL L.: Company A, private. September 10, 1861 enlisted as a private in Co. A, 27th Regiment, Georgia Infantry at Camp Stephens, Griffin, Spalding County, Georgia. November 9, 1861 admitted to General Hospital No. 18, Richmond, Virginia. September 1, 1862 admitted to General Hospital No. 13 at Richmond, Virginia with Dyspepsia. September 20, 1862 received pay ($60.00). October 21, 1862 admitted to Winder Division 4 Hospital at Richmond, Virginia. December 4, 1862 returned to duty. June 1863 issued clothing. July, August and September 1863 issued clothing. October 31, 1863 received pay. January - February 1864 roll shows him present. February 29, 1864 received pay. March - April 1864 roll shows him present. July 1864 issued clothing. September 10, 1864 wounded at Petersburg, Virginia. September 10, 1864 admitted to Jackson Hospital at Richmond, Virginia with Vulnus Sclopeticum (Gunshot Wound) left thigh. October 13, 1864 furloughed for 30 days. April 6, 1865 transferred to General Hospital at Macon, Georgia. April 20-21, 1865 captured by the 1st Brigade, 2nd U. S. Cavalry and paroled at Macon, Georgia. His Post Office listed as Buena Vista, Marion County, Georgia

BOLAND (BORLAND), JAMES F.: Company F, lieutenant. September 9, 1861 enlisted as a private in Co. F, 27th Regiment, Georgia Infantry at Camp Stephens, Griffin, Spalding County, Georgia. He was elected 1st sergeant in Co. F, 27th Regiment, Georgia Infantry. December 10, 1861 sent to hospital in Richmond, Virginia. December 1861 and January 1862 rolls show him in hospital at Richmond, Virginia. February 1, 1862 elected 2nd lieutenant in Co. F, 27th Regiment, Georgia Infantry. June 27, 1862 elected Jr. 2nd lieutenant in Co. F, 27th Regiment, Georgia Infantry. September 17, 1862 killed at Sharpsburg, Maryland. He was a resident of Butler, Taylor County, Georgia.

BOLCH, J.: Company D, private. October 14, 1862 admitted to General Hospital No. 21 at Richmond, Virginia. November 18, 1862 returned to duty.

BOLTON, GEORGE: Company K, private. September 10, 1861 enlisted as a private in Co. K, 27th Regiment, Georgia at Camp Stephens, Griffin, Spalding County, Georgia. June 27, 1862 wounded at Cold Harbor, Virginia. July 3, 1862 died of wounds. 20 years of age, hazel eyes, light hair and light complexion, five feet nine inches tall, born in Talbot County Georgia and was a farmer. April 1863 death benefit claim was filed. November 23, 1863 Death benefit was paid $142.10 (#11204).

BOND, CHARLES B.: Company B, corporal. September 10, 1861 enlisted and elected 4th corporal in Co. B, 27th Regiment, Georgia Infantry at Camp Stephens, Griffin, Spalding County, Georgia. December 21, 1861 admitted to Moore Hospital at General Hospital, No. 1 at Danville, Virginia and sent to the General Hospital at Richmond, Virginia with parotitis. December 1861 roll shows him in the hospital at Richmond, Virginia. January 11, 1862 sent to Moore Hospital at General Hospital No. 1 at Danville, Virginia with Fever. January 1862 roll shows he was sent to hospital. February 1862 roll shows he was on sick leave for 30 days from February 5, 1862. April 10, 1862 admitted to Chimborazo Hospital No. 3 at Richmond, Virginia (sent there from Georgia Hospital and returned there). August 31, 1862 received pay. September, October, November and December 1862 rolls show he was attached to the 4th Division Camp Winder Hospital, Richmond, Virginia as a cook beginning May 24, 1862. December 1862 roll shows he was detailed to the Confederate States Armory, Macon, Georgia. July 1863 roll shows he was at the C. S. A. Arsenal at Macon, Georgia and was paid $2.50 per day for 28 days. August 1863 he was at the C. S. Arsenal and was paid as a carpenter for 25 1/4 days at $2.50 per day. September 1863 roll shows he worked for the C. S. Arsenal at Macon, Georgia 25 3/4 days at $2.75 per day. October 1863 roll shows he worked for the C. S. Arsenal at Macon, Georgia for 29 days at $2.75 per day. November 1863 roll shows he was at C. S. Arsenal at Macon, Georgia and was paid $2.75 per day for 20 days. December 31, 1863 roll shows he was paid at the C. S. Arsenal at Macon, Georgia at a rate of $2.75 per day for 28 days work. January, February, March and April 1864 rolls show him absent detailed at the Confederate States Armory in Macon, Georgia by order of General Beauregard. January 1864 roll shows he worked for the C. S. Arsenal at Macon, Georgia for 28 days at $3.00 per day. February 1864 roll shows he was at the C. S. Arsenal at Macon, Georgia and worked 29 days for $3.00 per day. March 1864 roll shows he was at the C. S. Arsenal at Macon, Georgia and worked 29 days for $3.00 per day. April 30, 1864 on detail duty in Confederate States Armory at Macon, Georgia. May 1864 return from the Confederate States Arsenal at Macon, Georgia shows he worked 29 days at $3.00 per day for a total of $87.00. June 1864 return for Confederate States Arsenal Macon, Georgia shows he worked for 28 1/2 days at $3.00 per diem for $84.75. July 1864 return for the Confederate States Arsenal at Macon, Georgia shows he earned $175.00.

February 1865 return from the Confederate States Arsenal at Macon, Georgia shows him working as a carpenter (he worked 24 days that month at a rate of $5.50 per day for a total of $132.00). March 1865 the return of the Confederate States Arsenal at Macon Georgia shows he worked as a carpenter for 18 days at $5.50 per day for a total of $99.00.

BOND (BARNES), SANDERS): Company C, private. September 10, 1861 enlisted as a private in Co. C, 27th Regiment, Georgia Infantry at Camp Stephens, Griffin, Spalding County, Georgia. December 1861 and January 1862 rolls show he was left sick in Georgia October 31, 1861. May 7, 1862 admitted with Debility and attached as a nurse to 2nd Division, General Hospital, Camp Winder at Richmond, Virginia. May 16, 1862 detailed as nurse by Secretary of War at General Hospital, Camp Winder at Richmond, Virginia. August 15, 1862 furloughed for 30 days. November - December 1862 roll for 2nd Division, General Hospital, Camp Winder at Richmond, Virginia shows him there as nurse since May 7, 1862 and present. November 1, 1862 received pay. December 1862 roll shows him absent on sick furlough. January 1, 1863 received pay. January - February 1863 roll shows him present at 2nd Division, General Hospital, Camp Winder at Richmond, Virginia. June 30, 1863 received pay. July - August 1863 roll for 2nd Division, General Hospital, Camp Winder at Richmond, Virginia shows him present as a nurse detailed by the Secretary of War on a Surgeon's Certificate. September 1, 1863 received pay. October 14, 1863 admitted to General Hospital, Camp Winder at Richmond, Virginia with Pneumonia. October 30, 1863 roll shows him present at 2nd Division, General Hospital, Camp Winder at Richmond, Virginia. January 8, 1864 returned to duty. January, February, March and April 1864 rolls show him present. June 1, 1864 wounded in the right arm and permanently disabled at Cold Harbor, Virginia. October 19, 1864 admitted to Floyd House and Ocmulgee Hospitals, Macon, Georgia with Vulnus Sclopeticum (Gunshot Wound) to right arm involving elbow with permanent damage recommended for retirement in Invalid Corps. He was born in 1834 in Crawford County, Georgia. Post Office was Knoxville, Georgia. February 1865 described as 40 years of age, five feet nine inches high, fair complexion, grey eyes and light hair. His occupation was a farmer.

BONNER, JAMES WHIT: Company K, private. September 10, 1861 enlisted as a private in Co. K, 27th Regiment, Georgia Infantry at Camp Stephens, Griffin, Spalding County, Georgia. April 30, 1864, received pay. He was born in Upson County, Georgia April 8, 1833.

BONNER, W. H.: Company E, private. He enlisted as a private in Co. E, 27th Regiment, Georgia Infantry. January 14, 1865 admitted to Way Hospital at Meridian, Mississippi with a wound.

BOOTH, A. Z.: Company E, private. September 9, 1861 enlisted as a private in Co. E, 27th Regiment, Georgia Infantry at Camp Stephens, Griffin, Spalding County, Georgia. November 14, 1861 admitted to

General Hospital No. 18, Richmond, Virginia. November 18, 1861 returned to duty. April 10, 1862 admitted to Chimborazo Hospital No. 5 at Richmond, Virginia with Debility. May 15, 1862 admitted to Chimborazo Hospital No. 2 at Richmond, Virginia with Diarrhoea. May 18, 1862 returned to duty. June 2, 1862 admitted to General Hospital Camp Winder, Richmond, Virginia with Febris Int. (Malaria). June 8, 1862 returned to duty. June 30, 1862 received pay. August 1862 roll shows him present (A. Z. Boothe). September 17, 1862 wounded, Sharpsburg, Maryland. October 4, 1862 admitted to Receiving and Wayside Hospital or General Hospital No. 9 at Richmond, Virginia and transferred to General Hospital No. 21 at Richmond, Virginia. October 5, 1862 admitted to General Hospital No. 21 at Richmond, Virginia with Vulnus Sclopeticum (Gunshot Wound). October 10, 1862 furloughed for 30 days. May 3, 1863 admitted to Receiving and Wayside Hospital or General Hospital No. 9 at Richmond, Virginia and was transferred to Chimborazo Division Hospital at Richmond, Virginia. May 2, 1863 admitted to Chimborazo Hospital No. 2 at Richmond, Virginia with bone Infection in left hand. May 12 1863 returned to duty. He died in service at Charleston, South Carolina. His description was 21 years of age, dark eyes, dark hair, fair complexion and five feet nine inches high. He was from Fayette County, Georgia and was a farmer. He was born in 1842.

BOWD, T.: Company C, private. He enlisted as a private in Co. C, 27th Regiment, Georgia Infantry. June 20, 1864 admitted to Receiving and Wayside Hospital or General Hospital No. 9 at Richmond, Virginia. June 22, 1864 sent to Petersburg, Virginia.

BOWERS, JOHN WESLEY: Company B, corporal. September 10, 1861 enlisted and elected 3rd corporal in Co. B, 27th Regiment, Georgia Infantry at Camp Stephens, Griffin, Spalding County, Georgia. March 30, 1862 admitted to General Hospital No. 18 at Richmond, Virginia with Chronic Diarrhoea. April 22, 1862 returned to duty. August 27, 1862 received pay ($47.00). August 31, 1862 roll shows him getting payment. October 27, 1862 received pay ($72.00). May 19, 1863 received $8.75 pay for commutation of rations for furlough for 30 days beginning August 29, 1862. October, November and December 1863 issued clothing. December 31, 1863 received pay. January, February, March and April 1864 rolls show him present. July 1864 issued clothing. August 19, 1864 captured, Weldon Railroad, Virginia. August 24, 1864 received at Point Lookout, Maryland from City Point, Virginia. October 30, 1864 exchanged at Point Lookout, Maryland. November 15, 1864 received at Venus Point, Savannah River, Georgia. He was born in Bibb County, Georgia in 1832. He moved to Cleburne, Texas after the war. He died in 1910 in El Dorado, Jackson County, Oklahoma. He is buried in Antioch Cemetery, Jackson County, Oklahoma.

BOWIN, LINDSEY: Company G, private. He enlisted as a private in Co. G, 27th Regiment, Georgia Infantry. December 13, 1862 wounded in the arm, necessitating amputation at Fredericksburg, Virginia.

BOYD (BOYED), J. W.: Company G, private. May 19, 1862 enlisted as a private in Co. G, 27th Regiment, Georgia Infantry in Richmond, Virginia. May 31, 1862 wounded at Seven Pines, Virginia. June 2, 1862 received pay ($29.40). October 17, 1862 received pay ($83.00). December 1862 roll shows him absent without leave. November 24, 1863 issued clothing. December 31, 1863 received pay. January - February 1864 roll shows him present. February 1 - February 14, 1864 detailed as a teamster and received pay. February 29, 1864 received pay. March - April 1864 roll shows him present. July 1864 issued clothing. September 20, 1864 issued clothing. April 26, 1865 surrendered, Greensboro, North Carolina. May 1, 1865 paroled at Greensboro, North Carolina.

BOYD (BOYED) (BOYER), SIDNEY A.: Company G, sergeant. September 9, 1861 enlisted as a private in Co. G, 27th Regiment, Georgia Infantry at Camp Stephens, Griffin, Spalding County, Georgia. He was appointed 5th sergeant in Co. G, 27th Regiment, Georgia Infantry. November 6, 1861 admitted to General Hospital at Petersburg, Virginia with Rubeola. December 17, 1861 returned to duty. June 9, 1862 died at Richmond, Virginia. October 4, 1862 death benefit claim was filed by Nathan Boyed (father).

BOYD, W. C.: Company D, private. May 14, 1862 admitted to Chimborazo Hospital No. 2, Richmond, Virginia with Continua Fever. May 18, 1862 died of Fever in Richmond, Virginia.

BOYD, WILLIAM H.: Company G, sergeant. September 9, 1861 enlisted as a private in Co. G, 27th Regiment, Georgia Infantry at Camp Stephens, Griffin, Spalding County, Georgia. October 18, 1861 died of disease at Camp Stephens, Griffin, Spalding County, Georgia. December 1861 roll indicates that he died in Georgia on October 18, 1861 of disease. November 1861 roll from Manassas, Virginia indicates that on November 18, 1861 died of Pneumonia. January 29, 1862 death benefit claim was filed by Nathan Boyd, his father. February 25, 1862 death benefit was paid $47.00 (#30).

BRADLEY, ELIJAH: Company F, private. September 9, 1861 enlisted as a private in Co. F, 27th Regiment, Georgia Infantry at Camp Stephens, Griffin, Spalding County, Georgia. December 1861 received pay and was issued clothing. May 13, 1862 died at Chickahominy River, Virginia. June 16, 1863 death benefit claim was filed by Cornelius Bradley, his father. September 23, 1863 death benefit claim was paid $123.76 (#9130).

BRADY, ABNER W.: Company K, private. He enlisted as a private in Co. K, 27th Regiment, Georgia Infantry.

BRAKEFIELD, JESSE W.: Company D, private. He enlisted as a private in Co. D, 27th Regiment, Georgia Infantry.

BRANNON, MARK: Company I, private. September 10, 1861 enlisted as a private in Co. I, 27th Regiment, Georgia Infantry at Camp Stephens, Griffin, Spalding County, Georgia. July 10, 1862 received pay and clothing allowance ($91.00).   May 13, 1863 (age 15) deserted and was captured at U. S. Ford.   May 30, 1863 took oath of allegiance to the United States Government at Philadelphia, Pennsylvania.   Record shows he was from England and had been in the country five years and was never naturalized and was farming in Appling County, Georgia

BRAYSMITH, N. E.: Company D, private. He enlisted as a private in Co. D, 27th Regiment, Georgia Infantry.   April 25, 1863 admitted to General Hospital No. 1 at Savannah, Georgia.   April 25, 1863 died in Savannah of "Moribus".

BRAY, AUGUSTUS: Company E, private. March 4, 1862 enlisted as a private in Co. E, 27th Regiment, Georgia Infantry at Fayetteville, Georgia. April 6, 1862 admitted to General Hospital at Orange Court House, Virginia.   June 2, 1862 admitted to General Hospital No. 13 at Richmond, Virginia.   June 3, 1862 transferred to 2nd Georgia Hospital.   June 6, 1862 admitted to General Hospital at Farmville, Virginia with Debility. August 11, 1862 listed on report at General Hospital at Farmville, Virginia as having hypertrophy of the heart.   August 16 (17) (27), 1862 discharged due to disability from General Hospital at Farmville, Virginia.   September 1, 1862 received pay ($87.36).   August 27, 1862 discharge papers describe him as 26 years of age, five foot nine inches high, fair complexion, blue eyes and sandy hair. His occupation was listed as a jeweler. His Post Office listed as Liberty Hill, Pike County, Georgia.

BRAZELTON (BRASELTON), JAMES F.: Company A, private. 1864 enlisted as a private in Co. A, 27th Regiment, Georgia Infantry.   April 26, 1865 surrendered, Greensboro, North Carolina.

BRAZELTON, TITUS V.: Company D, lieutenant.   September 10, 1861 enlisted as a private in Co. D, 27th Regiment, Georgia Infantry at Camp Stephens, Griffin, Spalding County, Georgia.   He was elected sergeant of Co. D, 27th Regiment, Georgia Infantry.   March 1, 1862 - letter of recommendation to the Secretary of War for him to become the Quartermaster of the 27th Regiment.   May 18, 1862 admitted to Chimborazo Hospital No. 2 at Richmond, Virginia with dysentery.   August 1862 he is shown on pay report as being 1st sergeant, Co. D, 27th Regiment, Georgia Infantry. August 9, 1862 received pay ($105.00).   January 10, 1863 elected 2nd lieutenant Co. D, 27th Regiment, Georgia Infantry. April 14, 1863 appears on a roster of officers in the provisional Confederate Army.   March - April 1864 roll shows him present.   September 30, 1863 appears on roster of officers of General A. H. Colquitt's Brigade.   August 1864 received pay ($100.00).   August 27, 1864 received pay ($180.0).   November 1864 appears on Roster of Company D, 27th Regiment, Georgia infantry.

BRAZILE, JAMES S.: Company D, private.   September 2, 1863 enlisted as a private in Co. D, 27th Regiment, Georgia Infantry at Charleston, South Carolina.   December 1863 issued clothing.   March 1, 1864 wounded in left side of head and permanently disabled at Fort Sumter, South Carolina. March - April 1864 roll shows him absent sick.   August 3, 1864 admitted to Jackson Hospital at Richmond, Virginia with dysentery. August 11, 1864 furloughed for 30 days from Jackson Hospital at Richmond, Virginia. He was born in Georgia March 27, 1845.

BREWER, SEPTIMUS L.: Field Staff, lieutenant colonel. September 9, 1861 elected captain of Company F, 27th Georgia Infantry at Camp Stephens, Griffin, Spalding County, Georgia. September 11, 1861 elected lieutenant colonel, 27th Georgia Infantry. November 1861 resigned his commission. February 10, 1862 received back pay ($130.00).

BRIDGES, THOMAS: Company C, private. September 1, 1862 enlisted as a private in Co. C, 27th Regiment, Georgia Infantry in Calhoun, Georgia. July 25, 1862 furloughed for 30 days. December 1862 roll shows him absent on sick furlough. June 30, 1863 and September 30, 1863 issued clothing. December 31, 1863 received pay. January - February 1864 roll shows him present. February 29, 1864 received pay. March - April 1864 roll shows him present. September 20, 1864 issued clothing. He died in service.

BRINTLY, H. S.: Company H, private. January 25, 1862 admitted to Moore Hospital at General Hospital No. 1 at Danville, Virginia with Fever and sent to General Hospital at Mt. Jackson, Virginia.

BROOKS, ANDREW J.: Company G, sergeant. September 9, 1861 enlisted as a private in Co. G, 27th Regiment, Georgia Infantry at Camp Stephens, Griffin, Spalding County, Georgia. He was appointed sergeant in Co. G, 27th Regiment, Georgia Infantry. January 22, 1862 admitted to the hospital. January and February 1862 rolls show he was in the hospital. April 1, 1862 died. August 29, 1862 death benefit claim was filed on behalf of his widow Mariah A. Brooks. January 12, 1863 death benefit was paid $151.56 (#2563). He was a resident of Pike County, Georgia.

BROOKS, AMOS M.: Company D, private. March 4, 1862 enlisted as a private in Co. D, 27th Regiment, Georgia Infantry at Gainesville, Hall County, Georgia. March 30, 1862 admitted to General Hospital No. 18 at Richmond, Virginia with Pneumonia. April 16, 1862 transferred. December 1862 roll indicates he was in the hospital. April and May 1863 roll indicates he was detailed on special duty as a pioneer at Fredericksburg, Virginia. June 1863 detailed on special duty as a pioneer at Kinston, North Carolina. April, May and June of 1863 issued clothing. July 1863 detailed on special duty as a pioneer at Topsail, North Carolina. August and September 1863 detailed on special duty as a pioneer at James Island, South Carolina. October, November and December 1863 detailed on special duty as a pioneer at James Island, South Carolina. December 1863 issued clothing. March 25, 1864 roll indicates he was paid bounty ($50.00). February 29, 1864 received pay. March - April 30, 1864 roll shows him present. July 1864 issued clothing. September 1864 issued clothing. April 26, 1865 pension records show he surrendered Greensboro, North Carolina. His Post Office is shown as Sugar Hill, Hall County, Georgia.

BROOKS, J. L.: Company D, private. September 23, 1862 enlisted as a private in Co. D, 27th Regiment, Georgia Infantry in Gordon County, Georgia. October 27, 1862 admitted to General Hospital Camp Winder at Richmond, Virginia. October 31, 1862 roll for General Hospital Camp Winder, Richmond, Virginia shows him present. December 7, 1862 furloughed for 20 days from General Hospital Camp Winder at Richmond, Virginia. December 31, 1863 roll from First Georgia Hospital at Charleston, South Carolina. October 31, 1863 received pay and shows him present. December 1863 issued clothing. March 15, 1864 - April 30, 1864 absent without leave.

BROOKS, JAMES W.: Company D, private. February 22, 1862 enlisted as a private in Co. D, 27th Regiment, Georgia Infantry at Hopewell, Georgia. March 25, 1862 paid bounty ($50.00). September 11, 1862 died in General Hospital at Huguenot Springs, Virginia of Chronic Diarrhoea.

BROOKS, ROBERT J.: Company G, private. September 9, 1861 enlisted as a private in Co. G, 27th Regiment, Georgia Infantry at Camp Stephens, Griffin, Spalding County, Georgia. November 14, 1861 admitted to General Hospital No. 18 at Richmond, Virginia. December 13, 1861 returned to duty. January 16 1862 admitted to Moore Hospital at General Hospital, No. 1 at Danville, Virginia with dysentery and was sent to Front Royal, Virginia. January 1862 roll shows him in hospital. February 13, 1862 furloughed for 30 days. February 1862 roll shows him on furlough. May 28, 1862 admitted to C. S. A. General Hospital, Danville, Virginia with Rubeola. August 2, 1862 returned to duty. September 1862 captured either (at South Mountain or Sharpsburg, Maryland). September 20, 1862 paroled near Keedysville, Maryland. His Post Office listed as Flat Shoals, Meriwether County, Georgia.

BROOKS, WARREN T.: Company G, private. May 19, 1862 enlisted in Co. G, 27th Regiment, Georgia Infantry. May 31, 1862 wounded at Seven Pines, Virginia. July 5, 1862 died of wounds in hospital at Richmond, Virginia. September 20, 1862 death benefit claim was filed by his father, James Brooks. January 12, 1863 death benefit was paid $92.23 (#2564). He was a resident of Pike County, Georgia.

BROWN, A. F. (FLEMMING): Company G, private. September 9, 1861 enlisted as a private in Co. G, 27th Regiment, Georgia Infantry at Camp Stephens, Griffin, Spalding County, Georgia. November 1861 was sick at Manassas Station, Virginia with Pneumonia. November 29, 1861 died of Pneumonia.

BROWN, BRITTON A.: Company E, private. September 9, 1861 enlisted as a private in Co. E, 27th Regiment, Georgia Infantry at Camp Stephens, Griffin, Spalding County, Georgia. November 13, 1861 admitted to General Hospital No. 18 at Richmond, Virginia. November 22 (28), 1861 died of Pneumonia at Richmond, Virginia. December 1861 roll shows he died on November 28, 1861 of disease. October 9, 1862 death benefit claim was filed.

BROWN, A. FLEMMING: Company G, private. September 9, 1861 enlisted as a private in Co. G, 27th Regiment, Georgia Infantry at Camp Stephens, Griffin, Spalding County, Georgia. January 25, 1862 admitted to Moore Hospital at General Hospital, No. 1 at Danville, Virginia with Diarrhoea and sent to Mount Jackson, Virginia. March 16, 1862 admitted to Chimborazo Hospital No. 1 at Richmond, Virginia as a convalescent. June 15, 1862 returned to duty. September 1862 captured (at South Mountain or Sharpsburg, Maryland). October 1, 1862 he appears on list of paroled or exchanged prisoners of war who were paid. October 12, 1862 admitted to General Hospital at Camp Winder at Richmond, Virginia with Diarrhoea. October 13 1862 admitted to Winder Division No 3, Hospital at Richmond, Virginia. October (17) 18, 1862 returned to duty. October 21, 1862 furloughed for 30 days. February 23, 1863 received pay at Richmond, Virginia. January - February 1864 and March - April 1864 rolls show he was absent without leave from May 12, 1863. April 26, 1865, surrendered at Greensboro, North Carolina. May 1, 1865 paroled at Greensboro, North Carolina.

BROWN, A. FLEMMING, JR.: Company G, private. September 9, 1861 enlisted as a private in Co. G, 27th Regiment, Georgia Infantry at Camp Stephens, Griffin, Spalding County, Georgia. 1864 wounded at Petersburg, Virginia. April 26, 1865 surrendered at Greensboro, North Carolina.

BROWN, G. M.: Company B, private. October 24, 1863 enlisted as a private in Co. B, 27th Regiment, Georgia Infantry at Decatur, Georgia. December 31, 1861 received pay. January, October, November and December 1863 issued clothing. February 1864 and March - April 1864 rolls show him present. June 1, 1864 killed at Cold Harbor, Virginia.

BROWN, JAMES: Company A, private. March 3, 1862 enlisted as a private in Company A, 27th Regiment, Georgia Infantry. April 30, 1862 received pay. July 1862 died. November 20, 1862 received pay (bounty - $50.00). December 27, 1862 death benefit claim was filed by Elizabeth Brown, his widow.

BROWN, ROBERT: Company F, private. March 11, 1864 enlisted in Company F, 27th Regiment, Georgia Infantry at Macon, Georgia. January - February and March - April 1864 rolls show him present. June 9, 1864 admitted to Chimborazo Hospital No. 3, Richmond, Virginia with Debilitas. June 17, 1864 returned to duty. July 1864 issued clothing. September 20, 1864 issued clothing. March – April 1864 roll shows him present.

BROWN, THOMAS M. (F. M.): Company B, corporal. September 21, 1861 enlisted in Co. B, 27th Regiment, Georgia at Camp Stephens, Griffin, Spalding County, Georgia and elected 2nd corporal. March 8, 1862 admitted to Chimborazo Hospital No. 4 at Richmond, Virginia with Pneumonia. March 30, 1862 returned to duty. October 27, 1862 received pay ($72.00). March 8, 1862 admitted to Chimborazo Hospital No. 4 at Richmond, Virginia with Pneumonia. March 30, 1862 returned to duty. August 27, 1862 received pay (($47.00). September 20, 1864 issued clothing. October, November and December 1863 issued clothing. October 27, 1862 received pay ($79.00). December 31, 1863 received pay. January - February 1864 roll shows him present. March – April 1864 roll shows him present and he is also shown in the 1st Division Jackson Hospital at Richmond, Virginia. June 4, 1864 wounded at Cold Harbor, Virginia. June 4, 1864 admitted to Wayside Hospital and Receiving Hospital No. 9 at Richmond, Virginia and sent to Camp Winder Hospital. June 4, 1864 admitted to Jackson Hospital at Richmond, Virginia with a Vulnus Sclopeticum (Gunshot Wound) in the right arm. June 16, 1864 furloughed from Jackson Hospital, Richmond, Virginia for 30 days. July 1864 issued clothing. September 20, 1864 issued clothing.

BROWN, WILLIAM: Company E, private. April 25, 1864 enlisted as a private in Co. E, 27th Regiment, Georgia Infantry at Savannah, Chatham County, Georgia. March – April 1864 roll shows him present.

BRUCE, GENERAL JACKSON: Company K, private. September 10, 1861 enlisted as a private in Co. K, 27th Regiment, Georgia Infantry at Camp Stephens, Griffin, Spalding County, Georgia. October 31, 1861 left in Georgia sick. December 1861 roll shows he was left in Georgia sick. January and February 1862 rolls show he was left in Georgia sick. May 1, 1862 received pay. July 1, 1862 received pay. September 26, 1862 admitted to General Hospital No. 20, Richmond, Virginia. August 31, 1862 roll for General Hospital No. 20, Richmond, Virginia shows him present. October 22, 1862 furloughed. August - December 1862 roll shows he was sent home after the battle of Sharpsburg, Maryland. October 29, 1863 and November 24, 1863 issued clothing. December 31, 1863 received pay. April 14, 1864 transferred as a private in Co. I, 46th Regiment, Georgia Infantry. March – April 1864 roll shows he transferred to the 46th Regiment Georgia Infantry on April 14, 1864. July 22, 1864 wounded at Atlanta, Georgia. April 26, 1865, surrendered at Greensboro, North Carolina.

BRYANS, IVERSON B.: Company H, 1st. sergeant. September 9, 1861 elected 1st sergeant of Co. H, 27th Regiment, Georgia Infantry at Camp Stephens, Griffin, Spalding County, Georgia. July 4, 1862 furloughed for 30 days. March 14, 1863 received $10.00 in commutation of rations. January - February 1864 roll shows him present. March - April 1864 roll shows him present. June 1, 1864 wounded in arm, necessitating amputation, at Cold Harbor, Virginia. June 2, 1864 amputated right arm at Jackson Hospital at Richmond, Virginia. June 21, 1864 admitted to Receiving and Wayside Hospital or General Hospital No. 9, Richmond, Virginia. June 22, 1864 sent to Jackson Hospital at Richmond, Virginia. July 14, 1864 furloughed for 30 days. He was born in Georgia, October 7 1836. He died in 1913.

BRYANS, J. B.: Company H, 1st sergeant. September 9, 1861 enlisted as a private in Co. H, 27th Regiment, Georgia Infantry at Camp Stephens, Griffin, Spalding County, Georgia. July 4, 1862 furloughed for 30 days. December 31, 1863 received pay ($40.00). March 14, 1863 received commutation for meals while on furlough ($10.00). December 5, 1863 received pay $40.00. January - February and March - April 1864 rolls show him present. April 30 hospital Muster Roll for 2nd Division Jackson Hospital, Richmond, Virginia shows him present. June 1, 1864 wounded at Cold Harbor, Virginia in right arm. June 2, 1864 admitted to for amputation of right arm. July 13, 1864 furloughed for 30 days from Jackson Hospital at Richmond, Virginia. June 21, 1864 admitted to Receiving and Wayside Hospital or General Hospital No. 9 at Richmond, Virginia. June 22, 1864 transferred to Jackson Hospital at Richmond, Virginia.

BRYANT, CULLEN: Company F, private. 1861 enlisted as a private in Co. F, 27th Regiment, Georgia Infantry. January 20, 1862 admitted to Moore Hospital, No. 1 at Danville, Virginia with Lumbago also shown that he was sent to Orange Court House. January 21, 1862 admitted to General Hospital, Orange Court House, Virginia with Lumbago. January 1862 roll shows him in Moore Hospital. February 6, 1862 returned to duty. February 6, 1862 appears on roster of C. S. A. General Hospital at Farmville, Virginia. March 7, 1862 admitted To Chimborazo Hospital No. 4, Richmond, Virginia with Rheumatism. April 9, 1862 returned to duty. December 1862 roll shows him present. January 19, 1863 discharged due to disability, at Guinea Station, Virginia after 18 months service. January 21, 1863 received pay ($79.85 - 8.25 total $ 71.60). He was born in North Carolina in 1799.

BRYANT, HARDY: Company D, private. October 16, 1861 enlisted as a private in Co. D, 27th Regiment, Georgia Infantry at Camp Stephens, Griffin, Spalding County, Georgia. November 26, 1861 admitted to Chimborazo Hospital No. 1, Richmond, Virginia (note: Deserted from the Hospital without the knowledge of the surgeon). December 31, 1863 received pay. December 1863 issued clothing. April 24, 1864 he deserted.

BRYANT, J.: Company G, private. June 1862 appears on a report of sick and wounded at Chimborazo Hospital No.3, Richmond, Virginia with Typhoid Fever. June 9, 1862 died of Typhoid Fever in Richmond, Virginia. He is most likely buried in Oakwood Cemetery at Richmond Virginia.

BRYANT, JOHN: Company D, private. November 3, 1861 died of Pneumonia at Camp Stephens, Griffin, Spalding County, Georgia.

BRYANT, MINOR B.: Company D, private. September 15, 1861 enlisted as a private in Company D, 27th Regiment, Georgia Infantry at Camp Stephens, Griffin, Spalding County, Georgia. December 1861 roll indicates he is in the hospital in Richmond, Virginia. April 6, 1862 he is shown on roll at General Hospital at Orange Court House, Virginia with Diarrhoea. September 17, 1862 captured at Sharpsburg, Maryland. September 25, 1862 (October 3, 1862) paroled. October 17, 1862 appears on roll of prisoners of war at Fort McHenry, Maryland sent to Fort Monroe, Virginia for exchange. October 24, 1862 admitted to Chimborazo Hospital No. 4 at Richmond, Virginia with Chronic Diarrhoea. December 1, 1862 transferred to Palmyra Hospital, Virginia. November 1, 1862 received pay. December 1862 roll shows he was captured at Sharpsburg, Maryland. December 20, 1862 admitted to Palmyra Hospital with Variola. December 31, 1862 appears on hospital muster roll from the hospital at Palmyra, Virginia. January 1, 1863 received pay. January - February 1863 appears on hospital muster roll from the hospital at Palmyra, Virginia. April 21, 1863 he is still at Palmyra Hospital. April 21, 1863 died of Variola at Palmyra, Virginia (his effects consist of $80.00).

BRYANT, ROBERT: Company A, private. He enlisted as a private in Co. A, 27th Regiment, Georgia Infantry. He died prior to February, 1863. March 9, 1863 death benefit claim was filed on behalf of his mother Nancy Ethridge.

BRYANT (BRIANT) STEPHEN W.: Company A, private. February 26, 1862 enlisted as a private in Co. A, 27th Regiment, Georgia Infantry in Schley County, Georgia. April 25, 1862 admitted to Chimborazo Hospital No. 1 at Richmond, Virginia with Rubeola. May 2, 1862 admitted to Chimborazo Hospital No. 1 at Richmond, Virginia with Debility. July 1, 1862 transferred to Danville, Virginia. July 2, 1862 admitted to C. S. A. General Hospital at Danville, Virginia with Diarrhoea. August 22, 1862 furloughed for 60 days. December 30, 1862 received pay ($90.20). February 28, 1863 received pay. March - April 1863 appears on roll of sick and wounded at General Hospital No. 1 at Richmond, Virginia. May 6, 1863 wounded through both thighs at Wilderness (Chancellorsville), Virginia. May 9, 1863 list from Camp Guiney's Virginia indicates he was severely wounded on May 5, 1863 at or about Chancellorsville, Virginia. June 30 1863 received pay in hospital. July 7, 1863 furloughed for 60 days from General Hospital No. 1 at Richmond, Virginia (his residence is shown as Poindexter, Georgia). July 9, 1863 received pay ($22.00). January - February 1864 rolls show him absent wounded since May 5, 1863. March - April 1864 rolls show he was absent without leave since January 1864.

BRYANT, SANFORD: Company D, private. November 20, 1862 received pay in Richmond, Virginia ($50.00). December 1862 roll shows him in the hospital. April 24, 1863 admitted to Chimborazo Hospital No. 3, Richmond, Virginia. May 9, 1862 died in Chimborazo Hospital No. 3, Richmond, Virginia. June 10, 1862 sent for burial (Oakwood Cemetery at Richmond, Virginia).

BRYANT, WILLIAM O.: Company I, private. March 23, 1864 enlisted as a private in Co. I, 27th Regiment, Georgia Infantry at Decatur, Georgia. March - April 1864 roll shows him present. July 1864 issued clothing. April 26, 1865, pension records show he surrendered at Greensboro, North Carolina.

BUCHANAN, GEORGE B.: Field Staff, captain. August 21, 1861 enlisted and elected Jr. 2nd lieutenant of Co. G, 27th Georgia Infantry at Camp Stephens, Griffin, Spalding County, Georgia. December 11, 1861 joined his company from Camp Stephens, Griffin, Georgia. December 1861 roll shows him present. January 9, 1862 granted sick leave. January

10, 1862 placed on sick leave for 30 days. January 11, 1862 received pay ($160.00). January and February 1862 rolls show him absent sick for 30 days from Camp Pickens near Virginia. February 20, 1862 elected 2nd lieutenant for Co. G, 27th Georgia Infantry. May 1, 1862(July 26, 1862) elected captain. March 8, 1862 received pay ($160.00). June 3, 1862 received pay ($160.00). July 29, 1862 received pay ($340.00). August 1, 1862 received pay ($140.00). September 24, 1862 received pay ($140.00). November 1, 1862 received pay ($160.00). December 16, 1862 received pay ($420.00). December 1862 roll shows him present at Guinea Station, Virginia as AQM of the 27th Regiment. September 30, 1862 appears on a roster of officers in General A. H. Colquitt's Brigade. September 21, 1863 detailed Assistant Quartermaster of the 27th Regiment. April 30, 1864 appears on the Field and Staff Muster Roll at James Island, South Carolina as A Q M of the 27th Regiment. September 20, 1864 relieved of duty with this regiment and reassigned to assistant to Brigade Quartermaster of Colquitt's Brigade, where he was serving March 5, 1865. November 1864 roll shows him present.

BUFFINGTON, JOHN J.: Company E, lieutenant. May 27, 1861 enlisted as a private in Co. E, 27th Regiment, Georgia Infantry at Fayetteville, Georgia. December 1862 appointed 1st sergeant of Co. E, 27th Regiment, Georgia Infantry. September 14, 1863 elected 2nd lieutenant Co. E, 27th Regiment, Georgia Infantry. December 31, 1863 received pay. January - February 1864 and March - April rolls show him present. June 1, 1864 wounded at Cold Harbor, Virginia. June 20, 1864 admitted to Receiving and Wayside Hospital or General Hospital No. 9 at Richmond, Virginia and sent to Petersburg. June 2, 1864 appears on register at Receiving and Wayside Hospital or General Hospital No. 9 at Richmond, Virginia and was sent to Petersburg, Virginia on June 22, 1864. June 24, 1864 elected 2nd lieutenant Co. E, 27th Regiment, Georgia Infantry. November 1864 appears on roster for the 27th Georgia. March 1865 captured near Wilmington, North Carolina. May 1865 released at Fortress Monroe, Virginia. He was born in Georgia 1843.

BULLOCH, HARRY: Company B, private. September 10, 1861 enlisted as a private in Co. B, 27th Regiment, Georgia Infantry at Camp Stephens, Griffin, Spalding County, Georgia. January 25, 1862 sent to Moore Hospital, Virginia. January 1862 roll shows him at Moore Hospital, Virginia sick. February 1862 roll shows him absent sent to Moore Hospital, Virginia on January 25, 1862. December 1862 roll shows him absent sick since August 20, 1862.

BULLOCH (BULLOCK), HENRY B.: Company B, private. September 10, 1861 enlisted as a private in Co. B, 27th Regiment, Georgia Infantry at Camp Stephens, Griffin, Spalding County, Georgia. December 28, 1861 admitted to C. S. A. Hospital at Charlottesville, Virginia from Culpepper Court House, Virginia with Contusion. January 2, 1862 returned to duty. January 28, 1862 admitted to C. S. A. Hospital at Charlottesville,

Virginia with Bronchitis. April 14, 1862 returned to duty. August 28, 1862 admitted to General Hospital No. 21 at Richmond, Virginia. August 30, 1862 transferred to Mayo's Island. August 31, 1862 received pay. September 1, 1862 admitted to General Hospital No. 21 at Richmond, Virginia with Dysentery Conv. September 6, 1862 received pay ($ 60.00). September 7, 1862 transferred to Huguenot Springs, Virginia Hospital. October 23, 1862 attached to the Hospital at Huguenot Springs, Virginia. November 1, 1862 and December 31, 1862 appears on Hospital muster rolls for the Hospital at Huguenot Springs, Virginia. He was wounded in the eye, left shoulder and right arm, date and place not given. January 1, 1863 received pay ($11.40). January 28, 1863 discharged due to disability, at General Hospital, Huguenot Springs, Virginia due to Hepatization of the Lung. January 31, 1863 received pay ($11.40). He was born in Barnwell, South Carolina in 1821. January 28, 1863 he is shown on discharge papers as being 34 years of age, six foot one inch in height, light complexion, grey eyes, dark hair and occupation was farmer.

BULLOCH (BULLOCK), JAMES: Company B, private. September 10, 1861 enlisted as a private in Co. B, 27th Regiment, Georgia Infantry at Camp Stephens, Griffin, Spalding County, Georgia. November 18, 1861 admitted to C. S. A. General Hospital at Charlottesville, Virginia with Measles and Mumps. December 26, 1861 returned to duty. January 22, 1862 admitted to Moore Hospital at General Hospital No. 1 at Danville, Virginia with Hernia. January 30, 1862 discharged due to disability on account of Double Hernia, at Camp Pickens near Manassas, Virginia and died at Moore Hospital from Manassas Junction, Virginia of Fever the same day. October 27, 1862 death benefit claim was filed by his father, Josiah Bulloch. September 18, 1863 death claim was paid $126.33 (#8964).

BULLOCH, R. H.: Company K, private. January 21, 1862 admitted to Moore Hospital at General Hospital No. 1 at Danville, Virginia also states he was sent to Charlottesville, Virginia. January 22, 1862 admitted to C. S. A. General Hospital at Charlottesville, Virginia with Catarrh. January 24, 1862 sent to General Hospital at Richmond, Virginia. January 1862 roll show him in hospital. February 1862 roll show him absent without leave since February 13, 1862. December 1862 roll shows he deserted in February 1862 at Manassas Junction, Virginia.

BYRD, WILLIAM M.: Company D, private. February 24, 1862 enlisted as a private in Co. D, 27th Regiment, Georgia Infantry at Gainesville, Hall County, Georgia. March 25, 1862 received bounty pay ($50.00) and appears last on roll of recruits dated this date. May 4, 1862 admitted to Chimborazo Hospital No. 5 at Richmond Virginia with Typhoid Fever. May 20, 1862 died in Chimborazo Hospital No. 5 at Richmond, Virginia of Typhoid Fever. He is most likely buried in Oakwood Cemetery at Richmond Virginia.

May 18, 1863 death benefit claim was filed by his widow, Rhoda A. Byrd.

BURGESS, A. J.: Company A, private. He enlisted as a private in Co. A, 27th Regiment, Georgia Infantry. December 1862 his name appears on roll as absent sick since January 24, 1863.

BURGESS, W. M.: Company E, private. September 9, 1861 enlisted as a private in Co. E, 27th Regiment, Georgia Infantry at Camp Stephens, Griffin, Spalding County, Georgia. August 1862 received pay ($91.00) at Richmond, Virginia. September 17, 1862 killed at Sharpsburg, Maryland.

BURK, WILLIAM, H.: Company I, private. September 10, 1861 enlisted as a private in Co. I, 27th Regiment, Georgia Infantry at Camp Stephens, Griffin, Spalding County, Georgia. May 3, 1863 wounded at Chancellorsville, Virginia. May 9, 1863 on list at camp near Guiney's, Virginia as on list of causalities at Chancellorsville, Virginia. May 16, 1863 appears on a register of C. S. A. Hospital at Petersburg, Virginia Containing a record of clothing and accoutrements states delivered June 12, 1863 and "Duty". June 16th and 27th, 1863 issued clothing. December 31, 1863 received pay. January - February 1864 roll shows him present. April 19, 1863 issued clothing. February 29, 1864 received pay. March - April 1864 roll shows him present. July 1864 issued clothing. September 20, 1864 issued clothing. March 19, 1865 pension records show he was wounded at Bentonville, North Carolina, and was at home on furlough at the close of the war.

BURNES, JOHN M.: Company I, private. He enlisted as a private in Co. I, 27th Regiment, Georgia Infantry. June 6, 1864 wounded, Cold Harbor, Virginia.

BURNETT, AMASA M.: Company B, private. September 10, 1861 enlisted as a private in Co. B, 27th Regiment, Georgia Infantry at Camp Stephens, Griffin, Spalding County, Georgia. February 1862 roll shows him on extra duty as a provost Marshall Guard at Headquarters Post. March 16 1862 admitted to Chimborazo Hospital No. 3 at Richmond, Virginia. March 23, 1862 returned to duty. June 9, 1862 died in Virginia. May 6, 1863 death benefit claim was filed by Susan M. Burnett, his mother.

BURNETT, JEREMIAH J.: Company B, private. March 4, 1862 enlisted as a private in Co. B, 27th Regiment, Georgia Infantry. June 10, 1862 received pay ($58.00). June 27, 1862 wounded at Gaines Mill, Virginia. June 28, 1862 admitted to General Hospital No. 18 at Richmond, Virginia with Vulnus Sclopeticum (Gunshot Wound). June 30, 1862 transferred to Camp Winder at Richmond, Virginia. October 31, 1862 he is absent sick. November 4, 1862 died of Chronic Diarrhoea in General Hospital at Staunton, Virginia and is buried in Thornrose Cemetery at Staunton, Virginia. Inventory of his effects at the time of death were: $8.25 in cash, 1 pair drawers, 1 vest, 2 jackets, 1 gum coat, 1 pair pants, 1 hat, 1 pair shoes, 1 canteen and 1 knapsack. May 6, 1863 death benefit claim was filed by Mary Ann Burnett, widow.

BURNETT, JOHN F.: Company B, lieutenant. September 10, 1861 enlisted as a private in Co. B, 27th Regiment, Georgia Infantry at Camp Stephens, Griffin, Spalding County, Georgia. He was elected sergeant of Company B, 27th Regiment, Georgia Infantry. September 9, 1862 received pay ($80.00). September 30, 1862 elected 2nd lieutenant Co. B, 27th Regiment, Georgia Infantry. October 6, 1862 promoted to 2nd lieutenant. October 17, 1862 received pay ($70.00). December 1862 roll shows him present at Guinea Station, Virginia. May 3, 1863 wounded at Chancellorsville, Virginia. May 9, 1863 he appears on list at Camp near Guiney's, Virginia of causalities at Chancellorsville, Virginia. September 30, 1863 appears on a roster of officers of General A. H. Colquitt's Brigade. January 5, 1864 granted a 25 day leave of absence based on surgeons certificate of disability. January - February and March - April 1864 appears on rolls. August 19, 1864 killed, Weldon Railroad, Virginia.

BURNS, JOHN M.: Company G, private. February 10, 1864 enlisted as a private in Co. G, 27th Regiment, Georgia Infantry at Decatur, Georgia. March - April 1864 roll shows him present. June 1, 1864 wounded at Cold Harbor, Virginia. June 18, 1864 admitted to General Hospital at Petersburg, Virginia with Vulnus Sclopeticum (Gunshot Wound) to thigh. June 29, 1864 transferred to Richmond, Virginia hospital. June 30, 1864 admitted to Jackson Hospital at Richmond, Virginia, wounded in both hips. July 13, 1864 furloughed for Jackson Hospital, Richmond, Virginia for 50 days. Pension records show, he was at home on disabled furlough at the close of the war. He was born in Georgia December 12, 1823.

BURNS, JOSEPH H.: private. He enlisted as a private in the 27th Regiment, Georgia Infantry. May 31, 1862 captured at Seven Pines, Virginia. June 9, 1862 delivered from Fort Monroe. August 5, 1862 exchanged at Aiken's landing, Virginia.

BURTON, LEWIS F.: Company D, corporal. February 23, 1862 enlisted as a private in Co. D, 27th Regiment, Georgia Infantry at Sugar Hill, Hall County, Georgia. March 25, 1862 paid bounty at Atlanta, Georgia. June 5, 1862 received pay ($48.83). May 31, 1862 wounded at Seven Pines, Virginia. June 7, 1862 in C. S. A. General Military Hospital, No. 4 at Wilmington, North Carolina roll shows he was furloughed and was at home. April, May and June 1863 issued clothing. December 1863 issued clothing. March - April 1864 roll shows him present. July 1864 issued clothing. April 26, 1865 surrendered Greensboro, North Carolina. May 1, 1865 paroled at Greensboro, North Carolina. He was born in Hall County, Georgia in 1840. His Post Office was listed as Sugar Hill, Hall County, Georgia.

BUSH, J. M. (N.): private. He enlisted as a private in the 27th Regiment, Georgia Infantry. May 18, 1865 paroled at Albany, Georgia.

BUSSEY, HEZEKIAH: Field Staff, lieutenant colonel. September 10, 1861 elected 1st lieutenant Co. K, 27th Georgia Infantry at Camp Stephens, Griffin, Spalding County, Georgia. September 11, 1861 elected captain of Co. K, 27th Georgia Infantry. December 1, 1861 roll at Camp

Pickens near Manassas, Virginia shows him present. February 1862 roll at Camp Pickens near Manassas, Virginia shows him present. March 1, 1862 received pay ($260.0). June 7, 1862 received pay ($180.00). July 1862 roll at Camp Pickens near Manassas, Virginia shows him present. July 4, 1862 received pay ($180.00). September 1, 1862 received pay ($130.00). September 13, 1862 captured Turner's Gap, South Mountain, Maryland. October 2, 1862 sent from Fort Delaware, Delaware to Aiken's Landing, Virginia for exchange. October 6, 1862 received with other prisoners at Aiken's Landing, Virginia for exchange. November 10, 1862 exchanged at Aiken's Landing, Virginia. October 1862 received pay ($130.00). December 1862 roll at camp near Guinea Station, Virginia shows him present. June 2, 1863 received pay ($180.00). September 30, 1863 appears on Roster of Officers of Gen. A. H. Colquitt's Brigade. March -April 1864 shown on roll as captain of Co. K, 27th Regiment, Georgia Infantry. April 1, 1864 elected major 27th Regiment, Georgia Infantry. April 30, 1864 commissioned major of the 27th Regiment, Georgia Infantry at James Island, South Carolina. September 26, 1864 furloughed. September 27, 1864 (June 25, 1864) elected lieutenant colonel, 27th Regiment, Georgia Infantry. August 14, 1864 appears on report at Petersburg, Virginia. August 23, 1864 received pay ($130.00). August 20, 1864 received pay (4300.00). August 26, 1864 sick leave, by General Beauregard. September 23, 1864 admitted to General Hospital No 4 at Richmond, Virginia with Febris Remit. September 26 1864 report from the examining board of General Hospital No. 4 at Richmond, Virginia finds he has general Debility and intermittent Fever and should be furloughed to Talbotton, Georgia. September 30, 1864 furloughed. October 28, 1864 report from Laurel Hill, Virginia indicates he is on sick furlough in Talbotton, Georgia approved by General Lee. December 31, 1864 report of Hoke's Division at Camp Whiting, near Wilmington, North Carolina shows him on sick leave. April 26, 1865 surrendered, Greensboro, North Carolina. May, 1, 1865 paroled at Greensboro, North Carolina. He was born in Talbotton, Talbot County, Georgia April 18, 1840.

BUTLER, EDWARD BENJAMIN: Company E, private. September 9, 1861 enlisted as a private in Co. E, 27th Regiment, Georgia Infantry at Camp Stephens, Griffin, Spalding County, Georgia. April 6, 1862 admitted to General Hospital at Orange Court House, Virginia with Fever. September 17, 1862 killed at Sharpsburg, Maryland. December 1862 roll shows he was missing in action at Sharpsburg, Maryland. February 27, 1863 death benefit claim was filed by James Butler, father.

BUTLER, THOMAS H.: Field Staff, Assistant Surgeon. September 2, 1861 appointed Assistant Surgeon 27th Regiment, Georgia Infantry. December 19, 1861 received pay ($198.88). December 1861 roll at Camp Pickens near Manassas, Virginia shows him present. January 1862 roll at Camp Pickens near Manassas, Virginia shows him absent without leave since January 21, 1861. January 25, 1862 admitted to Moore Hospital at General Hospital, No. 1, Danville, Virginia with Pneumonia (sent to Richmond). February 1862 roll s at Camp Pickens near Manassas, Virginia does not state his presence. May 17, 1862 received pay ($220.00). June 19, 1862 resigned as Asst. Surgeon. July 9, 1862 received pay ($124.64).

BYERS, JOHN F.: Company K, private. September 10, 1861 enlisted as a private in Co. K, 27th Regiment, Georgia Infantry at Camp Stephens, Griffin, Spalding County, Georgia. 1862 admitted to Chimborazo Hospital No.5, at Richmond, Virginia. June 13, 1862 returned to duty.

BYNUM, THOMAS J.: Company F, private. September 9, 1861 enlisted as a private in Co. F, 27th Regiment, Georgia Infantry at Camp Stephens, Griffin, Spalding County, Georgia. September 1861 to December 1861 shows him in "Hospital, Culpepper, Virginia". December 20, 1861 admitted to Moore Hospital, General Hospital No.1 at Danville, Virginia with Pneumonia. April 10 1862 admitted to Chimborazo Hospital No. 5 at Richmond, Virginia with Dysentery. May 9, 1862 transferred to Lynchburg, Virginia. He was wounded in foot date and place not given. February 7, 1863 discharged due to disability, July 9, 1863 received pay ($57.90). August 6, 1863 appointed sergeant of Co. D, 28th Battalion, Georgia Siege Artillery. April 26, 1865 surrendered at Greensboro, North Carolina. He was born in Jefferson County, Georgia May 10, 1835.

CADY (CODY), A. E.: Company F, lieutenant. He enlisted as a private in Co. F, 27th Regiment, Georgia Infantry.

CADY (CODY), N. E.: Company I, private. March 30, 1862 admitted to Chimborazo Hospital No. 2 at Richmond, Virginia with Rheumatism. April 29, 1862 returned to duty.

CAIN, J. L.: Company B, private. He enlisted as a private in Co. B, 27th Regiment, Georgia Infantry. June 3(4), 1864 transferred from Wayside and Receiving Hospital or General Hospital No, 18 at Richmond, Virginia to Danville, Virginia.

CAIN (KANE), JAMES F.: Company B, private. April 12, 1862 enlisted as a private in Co. B, 27th Regiment, Georgia Infantry in Macon, Bibb County, Georgia. March - April 1864 roll shows him present. May 28, 1864 admitted to Wayside and Receiving Hospital or General Hospital No. 18 at Richmond, Virginia wounded in the right arm. June 4, 1864 "wounded in battle near Cold Harbor, Virginia by a minie ball in shoulder and arm. Ball entered left arm outer side, left side upper 3rd passing through arm fracturing bone. Ball then entered side two inches below axilla passing backwards and outwards (Speculas of bone resected same day of admission). June 10, 1864 arm amputated circular operation. June 16th died". June 4, 1864 admitted to Wayside and Receiving Hospital or General Hospital No, 18 at Richmond, Virginia. June 1864 appears on a roll of Receiving and Wayside Hospital or General Hospital No. 9 at Richmond, Virginia with a Vulnus Sclopeticum (Gunshot Wound). June 16, 1864 died as a result of amputation of the right arm in Richmond, Virginia hospital.

CAIN, WILLIAM F.: Company B, sergeant. November 15, 1861 admitted to hospital in Richmond, Virginia.   December 1861 roll shows him in hospital in Richmond, Virginia.   December 23, 1861 discharged due to disability, Richmond, Virginia.   April 11, 1864 enlisted as a private in Co. B, 27th Regiment, Georgia Infantry in Macon, Bibb County, Georgia. March - April 1864 roll shows him present.   May 30, 1864 issued clothing. July 1864 issued clothing.   August 19, 1864 captured at Weldon Railroad, Virginia.   August 24, 1864 arrived at City Point, Maryland.   December 24, 1864 received payment ($63.45) March 17, 1865 paroled at Point Lookout, Maryland and exchanged.   March 19, 1865 received at Boulware and Cox's Wharves, James River, Virginia.

CALHOUN, CALVIN: Company K, captain.   September 10, 1861 elected Jr. 2nd lieutenant of Co. K, 27th Regiment, Georgia Infantry at Camp Stephens, Griffin, Spalding County, Georgia.   September 11, 1861 elected 2nd lieutenant of Co. K, 27th Regiment, Georgia Infantry.   December 1861 and January and February 1862 rolls show him present at Camp Pickens near Manassas, Virginia.   March 1, 1862 received pay ($160.00).   June 29, 1864 wounded at Cold Harbor, Virginia.   June 29, 1862 admitted to General Hospital, Howard's Grove at Richmond, Virginia with a Vulnus Sclopeticum (Gunshot Wound) in the thigh (flesh).   June 30, 1862 sent to Mr. Smith, Grace St. Church Hill.   June 1862 received pay ($160.00). July 4, 1862 received pay ($80.00).   July 4, 1862 furloughed until August 4, 1862.   October 5, 1862 received pay ($160.0).   September 24, 1862 received pay ($80.0).   December 1862 received pay ($250.00).   December 1862 roll shows him present near Guinea Station, Virginia.   March 16, 1863 elected 1st lieutenant of Co. K, 27th Regiment, Georgia Infantry. September 30, 1863 appears on roster of Officers of Gen. A. H. Colquitt's Brigade.   He is listed in the personal papers of Major James Gardner as "Men for Gallantry" (date not known).   November 21, 1863 approved for leave.   March - April 1864 appears on roll as present.   May 1, 1864 elected captain of Co. K, 27th Regiment, Georgia Infantry.   August 19, 1864 received pay ($180.00).   February 11 (16), 1865 he was captured near Fort Fisher, North Carolina.   February 28, 1865 arrived at Fort Anderson.   February 28, 1865 transferred to Washington, D. C.   March 1, 1865 committed to Old Capital Prison at Washington, D. C. (shows him captured at Sugar Loaf, North Carolina, on February 11, 1865).   March 24, 1865 sent to Fort Delaware, Delaware.   March 25, 1865 received at Fort Delaware, Delaware.   June 17, 1865 released at Fort Delaware, Delaware. He is shown on release as being from Talbot, County, Georgia.   He is shown with ruddy complexion, mixed hair and grey eyes five foot ten inches high.

CALHOUN, JOHN C.: Company A, 3rd sergeant.   March 4, 1862 elected 3rd sergeant. Co. A, 27th Regiment, Georgia Infantry in Marion County, Georgia.   August 20, 1862 received pay ($47.00).   October 18, 1862 received pay ($22.00).   November 20, 1862 received bounty ($50.00) at Richmond, Virginia.   March 1863 received ($16.17) in commutation for rations while sick from August 22, 1862 to October 9, 1862. June, July, August and September 1863 issued clothing. December 12, 1863 wounded at Fort Sumter, South Carolina. December 31, 1863 received pay. January - February and March - April 1864 rolls show him present. June 16, 1864 wounded at Colquitt's Salient near Petersburg, Virginia. June 16, 1864 admitted to Confederate States Hospital at Petersburg, Virginia. June 19, 1864 admitted to Wayside and Receiving Hospital or General Hospital No. 18 at Richmond, Virginia. June 20 (18), 1864 transferred to Chimborazo Hospital, Richmond, Virginia. June 21, 1864 admitted to Chimborazo Hospital No. 6 at Richmond, Virginia. June 30, 1864 admitted to Chimborazo Hospital No. 4 at Richmond, Virginia with Debility. July 1, 1864 admitted to Chimborazo Hospital, No. 2 at Richmond, Virginia with Intermittent Fever (Malaria). August 25, 1864 issued clothing at Chimborazo Hospital, Richmond, Virginia. August 29, 1864 received pay ($39.13). August 29, 1864 returned to duty. September 30, 1864 issued clothing. April 26, 1865 surrendered at Greensboro, North Carolina. May 1, 1865 paroled at Greensboro, North Carolina.

CALHOUN, SAMUEL JOHN: Company K, private. July 2, 1862 enlisted as a private in Co. K, 27th Regiment, Georgia Infantry in Marion County, Georgia. July 5, 1862 admitted to Chimborazo Hospital No. 4 at Richmond, Virginia with Intermittent Fever (Malaria). November 4, 1862 received pay ($150.16). December 1862 he was placed on furlough. October 29, 1863 and November 24, 1863 issued clothing. December 31, 1863 received pay. March - April 1864 roll shows him present. May 30, 1864 issued clothing. July 1864 issued clothing. September 20, 1864 issued clothing.

CALHOUN, WILLIAM: Company E, private. May 23, 1865 paroled at Augusta, Georgia.

CALHOUN, WILLIAM: Company K, 5th sergeant. September 10, 1861 elected 5th sergeant of Co. K, 27th Regiment, Georgia Infantry at Camp Stephens, Griffin, Spalding County, Georgia. January 1, 1862 received pay. January 16, 1862 sent to hospital at Orange Court House, Virginia. January 17, 1862 admitted to General Hospital at Orange Court House, Virginia with Jaundice. January and February 1862 rolls show him in Hospital at Orange Court House, Virginia. March 20, 1862 sent to General Hospital at Farmville, Virginia. May 1, 1862 sent to hospital. July 7, 1862 received pay ($ 76.00). July 16, 1862 admitted to Moore Hospital at General Hospital No. 1 at Danville, Virginia with Jaundice. September - October 1862 roll for General Hospital at Liberty, Virginia shows him present. December 1862 roll shows him in hospital since May 1, 1862. March 12 1863 paid for commutation of rations ($10.00) while on furlough from July 1862 to August 1862. June 1863 issued clothing. October 12, 22 and 29, 1863 and November 1863 issued clothing. December 31, 1863 received pay. March - April 1864 roll shows him present. June 19, 1864 killed at Colquitt's Salient, Petersburg, Virginia.

CALLAHAN (CALLAHEN), JOSEPH: Company E, private.   He enlisted as a private in Co. E, 27th Regiment, Georgia Infantry. January 17, 1865 deserted at Savannah.   February 10, 1865 appears on roll of deserters at Hilton Head, South Carolina.   His residence is shown as Savannah. Description 25 years of age, brown eyes, brown hair, dark complexion, five feet six inches high.

CALLMAN, JAMES R.: Company B, private. He enlisted as a private in Co. B, 27th Regiment, Georgia Infantry.   December 1862 roll shows him absent sick since November 1, 1862.

CALLOWAY, G. (V.) W.: Company B, private.   September 10, 1861 enlisted in Co. B, 27th Regiment, Georgia Infantry at Camp Stephens, Griffin, Spalding County, Georgia.   January 11, 1862 admitted to Moore Hospital at General Hospital, No. 1, Danville, Virginia with Fever (sent to Richmond, Virginia).   January 1862 roll shows him in the hospital in Richmond since January 11, 1862. March 30, 1862 admitted to Chimborazo Hospital No. 4, Richmond, Virginia with Diarrhoea.   (May 30, 1862) June 4, 1862 discharged.   June 4, 1862 discharge papers state that he was discharged by surgeon's certificate of disability (for physical Debility and mental imbecility). He was born in Monroe County, Georgia and is 24 years of age. It states that he was six feet high with florid complexion, blue eyes, sandy hair and by occupation ws a farmer.   June 5, 1862 received pay ($81.11).

CAMPBELL, J. M.: Company B. private.   He enlisted as a private in Co. B, 27th Regiment, Georgia Infantry.

CAMPBELL, J. M.: Company C. private.   He enlisted as a private in Co. C, 27th Regiment, Georgia Infantry.   October 1, 1864 wounded at Fort Harrison, Richmond, Virginia.   October 3, 1864 admitted to Jackson Hospital at Richmond, Virginia with a Vulnus Sclopeticum (Gunshot Wound) to the head.   October 6, 1864 furloughed for 30 days.

CAMPBELL, JOHN A. N.: Company B. private.   September 28, 1861 enlisted as a private in Co. B, 27th Regiment, Georgia Infantry at Camp Stephens, Griffin, Spalding County, Georgia.   November 6, 1861 admitted to General Hospital at Petersburg, Virginia with Rubeola.   December 1861 received pay.   December 17, 1861 returned to duty.   May 28, 1862 appears on roster of C. S. A. General Hospital at Danville, Virginia with Parotitis. August 20, 1862 died in General Hospital No. 1 at Danville, Virginia of Chronic Diarrhoea. Effects were 2 pair pants, 1 shirt, 1pr drawers, coat, 1 pair socks, 1 cap, 1 pair shoes and 1 purse.   He is described as 23 years of age, hazel eyes, light hair, sallow complexion, 5 feet 8 inches high, born in Bibb County, Georgia and by occupation was a farmer.   October 27, 1862 death benefit claim was filed by Walter Campbell, father.

CAMPBELL, JOHN Q.: Company C, private.   March 10 (15), 1862 enlisted as a private in Co. C, 27th Regiment, Georgia Infantry at Knoxville, Crawford County, Georgia.   May 14, 1862 admitted to Chimborazo Hospital No. 4 at Richmond, Virginia with Intermittent Fever (Malaria).

October 31, 1863 received pay. December 31, 1863 received pay. January - February 1864 roll shows him present. March - April 1864 roll shows him present. June 2, 1864 wounded at Cold Harbor, Virginia. June 2, 1864 admitted to Jackson Hospital at Richmond, Virginia with a Vulnus Sclopeticum (Gunshot Wound) in the left arm. September 2, 1864 received pay ($22.00).

CAMERON, ROBERT S.: Company K, private. September 10, 1861 enlisted as a private in Co. K, 27th Regiment, Georgia Infantry at Camp Stephens, Griffin, Spalding County, Georgia. October 31, 1861 left in Georgia sick. December 1861, January and February 1862 rolls show he was left in Georgia sick. August 2, 1862 admitted to General Hospital No. 13 at Richmond, Virginia with diabetes. August 14, 1862 furloughed for 30 days (sick). February 28, 1863 received pay. March - April 1863 roll for General Hospital No. 1 at Richmond, Virginia shows him present. May 2, 1863 wounded in thigh by a shell at Chancellorsville, Virginia. May 2, 1863 admitted to General Hospital No. 1 at Richmond, Virginia. June 13, 1863 furloughed for 30 days (sick). September 6, 1863 wounded in the leg at Battery Wagoner, Morris Island, South Carolina. October 28, 1863 issued clothing. December 31, 1863 received pay. February 20, 1864 wounded at Olustee, Florida. March - April 1864 roll shows him present. September 20, 1864 issued clothing. March 11, 1865 admitted to C. S. A. General Hospital, No. 3 at Greensboro, North Carolina (Transferred from Kinston, North Carolina. His home was Talbotton (Pleasant Hill), Georgia.

CANDELL, GILBERT: Company D, private. March 4, 1862 enlisted as a private in Co. D, 27th Regiment, Georgia Infantry at Gainesville, Hall County, Georgia. March 25, 1862 paid bounty ($50.00).

CANIVOL (CANNIVEL), J.: Company C, private. He enlisted as a private in Co. C, 27th Regiment, Georgia Infantry. June 2, 1864 appear on roll of Receiving and Wayside Hospital or General Hospital at Richmond, Virginia. June 21, 1864 admitted to Receiving and Wayside Hospital or General Hospital No. 9 at Richmond, Virginia. June 22, 1864 transferred to Jackson Hospital at Richmond, Virginia.

CANNON, PETER: Company I, private. He enlisted as a private in Co. I, 27th Regiment, Georgia Infantry. July 31, 1863 received at Camp Douglas, Illinois. February 6, 1863 died at Camp Douglas, Illinois as a prisoner of war.

CAPE, C. H.: Company D, 5th sergeant. September 10, 1861 elected 5th sergeant in Co. D, 27th Regiment, Georgia Infantry at Camp Stephens, Griffin, Spalding County, Georgia. September 5, 1862 admitted to General Hospital Camp Winder at Richmond, Virginia with Febris Typhoid. September 29, 1862 returned to duty. September 30, 1862 returned to duty from Camp Winder Hospital Division 2 at Richmond, Virginia. April, May and June 1863 issued clothing. December 1863 issued clothing. February 29, 1864 received pay. March - April 1864 roll shows him present. May

213

30, 1864, July 1864 and September 20, 1864 issued clothing. October 2, 1864 wounded at Fort Harrison near Richmond, Virginia. October 2, 1864 admitted to Receiving and Wayside Hospital or General Hospital No. 9 at Richmond, Virginia. October 3, 1864 transferred to Jackson Hospital at Richmond, Virginia. October 4, 1864 admitted to Jackson Hospital at Richmond, Virginia with Vulnus Sclopeticum (Gunshot Wound) to left foot. November 11, 1864 issued clothing at Jackson Hospital at Richmond, Virginia. November 12, 1864 returned to duty. April 26, 1865 surrendered, Greensboro, North Carolina. May 9, 1865 paroled at Greensboro, North Carolina. He was born in Hall County, Georgia October 11, 1842.

CAPE, HIRAM F.: Company D. private. August 26, 1861 enlisted in Co D, 27th Regiment, Georgia infantry at Gainesville, Hall County, Georgia. August 5, 1862 died at Goldsboro, North Carolina. November 17, 1863 death benefit claim was filed by his father, Hiram Cape.

CAPE, J. A.: Company B, private. September 19, 1862 enlisted as a private in Company B, 27th Regiment, Georgia infantry at Calhoun, Georgia. October 31, 1862 roll from 2nd Division, General Hospital Camp Winder at Richmond, Virginia shows him present. November 1, 1862 received pay. December 7 (8), 1862 admitted to General Hospital at Camp Winder at Richmond, Virginia with Debilitas. December 31, 1862 appears on roll of 2nd Division, General Hospital Camp Winder at Richmond, Virginia. March 13, 1863 returned to duty. March 14, 1863 admitted to General Hospital Camp Winder at Richmond, Virginia. September 6, 1863 killed in the evacuation of Battery Wagoner, Morris Island, South Carolina.

CAPPS, J. A.: Company I, private. He enlisted as a private in Co. I, 27th Regiment, Georgia Infantry. June 18, 1864 wounded at Colquitt's Salient, Petersburg, Virginia. June 18, 1864 admitted to General Hospital at Petersburg, Virginia with a Vulnus Sclopeticum (Gunshot Wound) to the breast. June 24, 1864 transferred to Richmond, Virginia.

CAPPS (CAPES), WESLEY: Company H, private. September 9, 1861 enlisted as a private in Co. H, 27th Regiment, Georgia Infantry at Camp Stephens, Griffin, Spalding County, Georgia. January 14, 1862 admitted to Moore Hospital at General Hospital No. 1 at Danville, Virginia with Pneumonia. January 14, 1862 sent to hospital in Richmond, Virginia. January and February 1862 rolls show him in the hospital in Richmond, Virginia. December 1862 roll shows him absent without leave. December 31, 1863 received pay. January - February 1864 roll shows him present. March - April 1864 roll shows him present. May 18, 1862 admitted to General Hospital No. 18 at Richmond, Virginia with Diarrhoea. June 6, 1864 returned to duty from Pettigrew General Hospital No. 13 at Raleigh, North Carolina. 1864 wounded in Virginia (most likely at Colquitt's Salient, Petersburg, Virginia on June 17, 1864). June 18, 1864 admitted to General Hospital at Petersburg, Virginia with a Vulnus Sclopeticum (Gunshot Wound) to the right thigh. July 2, 1864 appears on list of men remaining in General Hospital. August 27, 1864 died of wounds in right thigh at Petersburg, Virginia.

CAPPS (CAPES), W. B.: Company H, private. November 25 (23), 1862 enlisted as a private in Co. H, 27th Regiment, Georgia Infantry at James Island, South Carolina. March 12, 1863 received commutation of rations for furlough from October 4, 1862 to November 3, 1862 ($10.00). December 31, 1863 received pay. January - February 1864 roll shows him present. February 29, 1864 received pay. March -April 1864 roll shows him present. July 1864 issued clothing. September 20, 1864 issued clothing.

CARIKER (CARRIKER), G. D.: Company G, corporal. He enlisted as a private in Co. G, 27th Regiment, Georgia Infantry. He was elected corporal in Co. G, 27th Regiment, Georgia Infantry.

CARIKER (CARRIKER), H. J.: Company G, private. He enlisted as a private in Co. G, 27th Regiment, Georgia Infantry. September 20, 1864 issued clothing.

CARIKER (CARRIKER), JAMES D.: Company G, corporal. September 9, 1861 elected 4th corporal in Co. G, 27th Regiment, Georgia Infantry at Camp Stephens, Griffin, Spalding County, Georgia. October 31, 1861 left in Georgia sick. December 1861 roll shows him in Richmond, Virginia in the hospital (most likely in Georgia in the hospital). January 1862 roll shows he was left in Georgia sick. July 2, 1862 admitted to C. S. A. General Hospital at Danville, Virginia with Fever. August 20, 1862 returned to duty. October 1, 1862 admitted to Receiving and Wayside Hospital or General Hospital No. 9 at Richmond, Virginia and sent to Howard's Grove Hospital at Richmond, Virginia. He received $6.60 in commutation of rations for time between October 29, 1863 and November 18, 1863 while on furlough. October 30, 1863 issued clothing. December 16, 1863 issued clothing. December 31, 1863 received pay. January - February and March - April 1864 rolls show him present. July 1864 issued clothing. August 19, 1864 captured at Weldon Railroad, Virginia. August 24, 1864 arrived at City Point, Maryland as prisoner of war. March 14, 1865 paroled at Point Lookout, Maryland and transferred to Aiken's landing, Virginia for exchange. March 16, 1865 received at Boulware and Cox's Wharves, James River, Virginia.

CARIKER (CARRIKER), MORGAN T.: Company G, corporal. September 9, 1861 elected 1st corporal in Co. G, 27th Regiment, Georgia Infantry at Camp Stephens, Griffin, Spalding County, Georgia. November 13, 1861 admitted to General Hospital No. 18, Richmond, Virginia. December 1861 and January 1862 rolls show him in hospital in Richmond, Virginia. January 4, 1862 furloughed sick for 30 days from General hospital No. 18, Richmond, Virginia. March 31, 1862 admitted to Chimborazo Hospital No. 2 at Richmond, Virginia with Debility. April 25 (19), 1862 died of Typhoid Fever and Pneumonia, in Chimborazo Hospital No. 2 at Richmond, Virginia. He is most likely buried in Oakwood Cemetery at Richmond Virginia. November 17, 1862 death benefit claim was filed for

215

by his widow, Mary E. Cariker. September 24, 1863 death benefit claim paid $197.50 (#8986). He was a resident of Pike County, Georgia

CARLISLE, BENJAMIN F.: Company K, private. March 4, 1862 enlisted as a private in Co. K, 46th Regiment, Georgia Infantry in Talbotton, Georgia. April 1, 1864 transferred as a private to Co. K, 27th Regiment, Georgia Infantry. March - April 1864 roll shows he was absent on furlough. June 17, 1864 wounded in the left shoulder at Colquitt's Salient, Petersburg, Virginia. June 17, 1864 admitted to General Hospital at Petersburg, Virginia with Vulnus Sclopeticum (Gunshot Wound). June 20, 1864 transferred to C. S. A. General Hospital at Farmville, Virginia. July 5, 1864 furloughed for 40 days. March 19 (21), 1865 wounded in the left elbow at Bentonville, North Carolina. March 21, 1865 admitted to General Hospital No.13 at Raleigh, North Carolina. 1865 left arm amputated below the elbow. March 24, 1865 issued clothing at Pettigrew General Hospital No. 13 at Raleigh, North Carolina. April 7, 1865 furloughed for 60 days. He was born in Georgia November 27, 1842. He was a resident of Talbot County, Georgia. His Post Office is shown as Columbus, Georgia.

CARLISLE, JAMES: Company K, sergeant. September 10, 1861 enlisted as a private in Co. K, 27th Regiment, Georgia Infantry at Camp Stephens, Griffin, Spalding County, Georgia. He was appointed corporal. November 17, 1861 admitted to Chimborazo, Hospital No. 1 at Richmond, Virginia. May 1, 1862 transferred to Huguenot Springs, Virginia Hospital and returned to duty. July 7, 1862 received pay ($75.06). October 19, 1862 attached to the Hospital at Huguenot Springs, Virginia. October 28 (29), 1862 admitted to Chimborazo Hospital No.1 at Richmond, Virginia with dysentery. November 1, 1862 received pay. November 30, 1862 transferred to Huguenot Springs, Virginia Hospital. December 31, 1862 roll for the Hospital at Huguenot Springs, Virginia shows him present. June 1863 issued clothing. August 5, 1863 received $15.00 for commutation of rations for sick furlough from March 25th 1863 to May 11, 1863 (45 days). October 22, 29, November 21, 24 and December 18, 1863 issued clothing. December 31, 1863 received pay. He was appointed sergeant in Co. K, 27th Regiment, Georgia Infantry. February 20, 1864 killed at Olustee, Florida. March - April 1864 roll shows he was killed at Olustee, Florida.

CARLISLE, MICHAEL: Company K, private. July 2, 1863 enlisted as a private in Co. K, 27th Regiment, Georgia Infantry at Macon, Bibb County, Georgia. October 12, 1863 issued clothing. December 31, 1863 received pay. February 20, 1864 killed at Olustee, Florida. March - April 1864 roll shows he was killed at Olustee, Florida.

CARLISLE, WILLIAM F.: Company B, private. October 28, 1863 enlisted as a private in Co. B, 27th Regiment, Georgia Infantry in Decatur, Georgia. December 31, 1863 received pay. January - February 1864 roll shows him present. February 20, 1864 wounded in right arm, necessitating amputation above the elbow at Olustee, Florida. March - April 1864 roll shows him absent due to wound. He was absent, wounded at the close of the war.

CARNEY (KEARNEY), JAMES M.: Company B, private. August 4, 1863 enlisted as a private in Co. B, 27th Regiment, Georgia Infantry in Macon, Bibb County, Georgia. September 30, 1863 received pay. October 1, 1863 received pay ($20.90). December 2, 1863 was absent sick beginning this date. January 19, 1864 admitted to Floyd House and Ocmulgee Hospitals at Macon, Georgia. January - February 1864 roll shows him absent sick. March - April 1864 roll shows him present. April 8, 1864 to April 24, 1864 was absent without leave. May 30, 1864 issued clothing. July 15, 1864 admitted to Jackson, Hospital at Richmond, Virginia with Rubeola. July 1864 issued clothing. August 11, 1864 furloughed sick for 30 days from Jackson Hospital, Richmond, Virginia. October 31, 1864 received pay. December 15, 1864 issued clothing. December 1864 detailed with Co. E, 1st Regiment Troops and Defense at Camp Wright near Macon, Georgia. December 30, 1864 roll shows him present.

CARNEY (KEARNEY), JOHN A.: Company B, private. March 1, 1863 enlisted as a private in Co. B, 27th Regiment, Georgia Infantry at Macon, Bibb County, Georgia. October, November and December 1863 issued clothing. December 31, 1863 received pay. January - February 1864 roll shows him present. July 1864 issued clothing. July 24, 1864 admitted to Jackson, Hospital at Richmond, Virginia with Rubeola. August 11, 1864 furloughed sick for 30 days. October 31, 1864 received pay. 1864 detailed with Co. E, 1st Regiment Troops and Defense at Camp Wright near Macon, Georgia. December 15, 1864 issued clothes at Camp Wright near Macon, Georgia. December 30, 1864 roll shows him present. He is buried at Sardis Primitive Baptist Church Cemetery, Bibb County, Georgia. Born in 1829 in South Carolina

CARR, HENRY A.: Company A, sergeant. He enlisted as a private in Co. A, 27th Regiment, Georgia Infantry. December 8, 1861 admitted to Chimborazo Hospital No. 4 at Richmond, Virginia with Fever and Pneumonia. February 1, 1862 returned to duty. February 1862 roll shows him on extra duty as a courier for headquarters post. May 17, 1862 admitted to Chimborazo Hospital No. 2 at Richmond, Virginia with Rheumatism. May 29, 1862 returned to duty. June 18, 1862 received pay ($ 77.27). August 2, 1862 received pay ($36.00). December 1862 appears on roll. March 19, 1863 received $10.00 for commutation of rations while on furlough from February 4, 1863 to March 6, 1863. July, August and September 1863 issued clothing. September 5, 1863 received pay ($34.00). November 22, 1863 at James Island, South Carolina, he made a request for transfer to the 2nd Regiment, Florida Cavalry (as a citizen of Florida who was born in Florida and now resides there).

CARR, J. A.: Company A, private. He enlisted as a private in Co. A, 27th Regiment, Georgia Infantry. November 30, 1861 entered hospital at Richmond, Virginia. December 1861 roll shows him in hospital at Richmond, Virginia.

CARR, PERRY C.: Company A, captain. May 17, 1861 was elected captain of Co. A, 27th Regiment Georgia Infantry. September 10, 1861 became captain of Company A, 27th Regiment Georgia Infantry at Camp Stephens, Griffin, Spalding County, Georgia. December 8, 1861 admitted to Chimborazo Hospital No. 4, Richmond, Virginia with Intermittent Fever (Malaria). December 18, 1861 returned to duty. December 18, 1861 furloughed sick to January 8, 1862 by Medical Director. December 1861 roll shows him present at Camp Pickens near Manassas, Virginia. January 7, 1862 admitted to Moore Hospital at General Hospital No. 1 at Danville, Virginia with Jaundice (sent to 9th Ward). January 8, 1862 went into hospital at Richmond, Virginia. January 1862 roll shows him absent in hospital in Richmond, Virginia. February 1862 roll shows him present at Camp Pickens near Manassas, Virginia. March 3, 1862 received pay ($260.00). June 5, 1862 he died of disease at Richmond, Virginia. March 9, 1863 death benefit claim was filed by Henry A. Carr, attorney. He was a resident of Schley County, Georgia

CARR, W. D.: Company H, private. August 31, 1864 captured near Jonesboro, Georgia. September 19-22, 1864 exchanged at Rough and Ready, Georgia.

CARRITHERS, J. J.: Company G, private. He enlisted as a private in Co. G, 27th Regiment, Georgia Infantry. August 13, 1864 admitted to Jackson Hospital at Richmond, Virginia with Rubeola. August 15, 1864 died in Jackson Hospital at Richmond, Virginia. His effects were 1 coat, 1 blanket and 1 cap.

CARROL, J. HENRY: Company H, sergeant. September 9, 1861 elected 3rd sergeant Co. H, 27th Regiment Georgia Infantry at Camp Stephens, Griffin, Spalding County, Georgia. September 17, 1862 captured at Sharpsburg, Maryland. October 2, 1862 sent from Fort Delaware, Delaware to Aiken's Landing, Virginia for exchange. November 10, 1862 exchanged at Aiken's Landing, Virginia. December 31, 1863 received pay. January - February 1864 roll shows him present. March - April 1864 roll shows him present. July 1864 issued clothing. August 19, 1864 captured, Weldon Railroad, Virginia. August 24, 1864 arrived at City Point, Maryland. February 18, 1865 paroled at Point Lookout, Maryland. February 20 (21), 1865 received at Boulware and Cox's Wharves, James River, Virginia. He was born in Pike County, Georgia December 19, 1842. He died at Confederate Soldier's Home, at Atlanta, Georgia September 13, 1924. He is buried at Oxford, Georgia.

CARSON, ADAM: Company A, lieutenant. June 29, 1861 enlisted in Company A, 27th Regiment, Georgia Infantry at Camp Stephens, Griffin, Spalding County, Georgia. June 29, 1861 promoted, elected 1st lieutenant Co. A, 27th Regiment Georgia Infantry. December 20, 1861 received pay ($ 180.00). December 1861, January 1862 and February 1862 rolls show him present at Camp Pickens near Manassas, Virginia. February 10, 1862 received pay ($180.00). March 6, 1862 received pay ($ 180.00). April

6, 1862 admitted to General Hospital at Orange Court House, Virginia. April 13 (April 20), 1862 died at C. S. A. General Hospital at Farmville, Virginia.

CARTER, BEVERLY: Company D, private. 1863 enlisted as a private in Co. D, 27th Regiment, Georgia Infantry. December 23, 1861 admitted to Moore Hospital at General Hospital No. 1 at Danville, Virginia with Fever and was sent to Charlottesville, Virginia. April 8, 1863 admitted to Receiving and Wayside Hospital or General Hospital No. 9 at Richmond, Virginia. April 8, 1863 admitted to Chimborazo Hospital at Richmond, Virginia with Catarrh. May 2, 1863 died Chimborazo Hospital at Richmond, Virginia. He is most likely buried in Oakwood Cemetery at Richmond Virginia.

CARTER, COHEN: Company I, private. September 10, 1861 enlisted as a private in Co. I, 27th Regiment, Georgia Infantry at Camp Stephens, Griffin, Spalding County, Georgia. June 16 and 27, 1863 issued clothing. December 31, 1863 received pay. January - February 1864 roll shows him present. February 29, 1864 received pay. March - April 1864 roll shows him present. July 1864 issued clothing. September 20, 1864 issued clothing. April 26, 1865 surrendered, Greensboro, North Carolina. May 1, 1865 paroled at Greensboro, North Carolina. He was born in Georgia May 10, 1842.

CARTER, GEORGE D.: Company E, private. September 9, 1861 enlisted as a private in Co. E, 27th Regiment, Georgia Infantry at Camp Stephens, Griffin, Spalding County, Georgia. October 31, 1861 left in Georgia sick. December 1861, January 1862 and February 1862 rolls show him sick in Georgia. May 31, 1862 wounded in right side at Seven Pines, Virginia. September 17, 1862 wounded through right lung at Sharpsburg, Maryland. August 31, 1862 appears on roll from General Hospital No. 21 at Richmond, Virginia. October 4, 1862 admitted to Receiving and Wayside Hospital or General Hospital No. 9 at Richmond Virginia and sent to General Hospital 21 or 22 at Richmond, Virginia. October 5, 1862 admitted to General Hospital No. 21 at Richmond, Virginia with Vulnus Sclopeticum (Gunshot Wound). October 10, 1862 furloughed for 60 days from General Hospital No. 21 at Richmond, Virginia (is shown as being 26 years of age). February 10, 1863 admitted to General Hospital No. 16 at Richmond, Virginia. March 4, 1863 received pay ($170.16). March 6, 1863 admitted to C. S. A. General Hospital at Danville, Virginia with Debilitas. March 7, 1863 admitted to C. S. A. General Hospital at Danville, Virginia with Vulnus Sclopeticum (Gunshot Wound). May 5, 1863 transferred and detailed for hospital service at Richmond, Virginia. July 8, 1863 admitted to C. S. A. General Hospital at Danville, Virginia with Vulnus Sclopeticum (Gunshot Wound). August 3, 1863 issued clothing at 3rd Division, General Hospital No. 1 at Danville, Virginia. December 31, 1863 received pay. January - February 1864 roll shows him present. February 29, 1864 received pay. March - April 1864 shows him absent on detached duty in Florida. April 13, 1864 placed on detached duty in

Florida guarding commissaries September 1864 issued clothing. April 26, 1865 surrendered, Greensboro, North Carolina May 1, 1865 paroled at Greensboro, North Carolina. Resident of Georgia since October 20, 1836.

CARTER, J.: Company A, private. He enlisted as a private in Co. A, 27th Regiment, Georgia Infantry. March 5, 1863 died at Chimborazo Hospital at Richmond, Virginia.

CARTER, J. F.: Company I, private. December 1862 roll shows him detailed as guard at Guinea Station, Virginia.

CARTER, J. J.: Company G, private. September 10, 1861 enlisted as a private in Co. G, 27th Regiment, Georgia Infantry. April 17, 1862 died at Richmond, Virginia. He is buried in Hollywood Cemetery at Richmond, Virginia.

CARTER, JESSE: Company E, private. September 9, 1861 enlisted as a private in Co. E, 27th Regiment, Georgia Infantry at Camp Stephens, Griffin, Spalding County, Georgia. November 6, 1861 admitted to General Hospital at Petersburg, Virginia with Rubeola. November 27, 1861 returned to duty. April 16, 1862 admitted to Chimborazo Hospital No. 3 at Richmond, Virginia and is shown as being discharged date not shown. May 19, 1862 (May 23, 1862) records indicate he was discharged. June 1862 report from Chimborazo Hospital No. 3 at Richmond, Virginia shows he was discharged from service by a surgeons Certificate for Chronic Rheumatism and Senility on June 12, 1862. July 20, 1862 died of disease in Richmond, Virginia Hospital. He is described on certificate as fifty-four years of age, five foot eight inches high, dark complexion, blue eyes, gray hair born in Charles District, South Carolina and occupation was a farmer before enlistment.

CARTER, JESSE A.: Company E, private. September 9, 1861 enlisted as a private in Co. E, 27th Regiment, Georgia Infantry at Camp Stephens, Griffin, Spalding County, Georgia. July 20, 1862 died of disease in Richmond, Virginia Hospital. May 19, 1863 death benefit claim was filed by Jesse Carter, father. Death benefit claim paid $94.80 (#935). Description: 25 years of age, blue eyes, light hair, fair complexion, 5 feet 1 inch high. Born in Fayette County, Georgia and by occupation was a farmer.

CARTER, JOHN WESLEY: Company E, private. March 1, 1862 enlisted as a private in Co. E, 27th Regiment, Georgia Infantry in Fairburn, Georgia. July 23, 1862 appears on register of C. S. A. General Hospital at Danville, Virginia with Dyspepsia. December 1862 roll shows he is at Danville, Virginia sick and has been there since January 1862. January 15, 1863 issued clothing at 3rd Division General Hospital at Danville, Virginia. May 8, 1863 assigned to temporary duty at General Hospital No. 12 at Richmond, Virginia. Also states that subsistence and quarters will be furnished at the hospital until further orders. May 27, 1863 received pay in General Hospital No. 12 at Richmond, Virginia ($5.00). May 29,

1863 appears on roll of C. S. A. General Hospital at Danville, Virginia as being returned to duty on June 5, 1863. June 4, 1863 issued clothing at 3rd Division General Hospital, Danville, Virginia. December 31, 1863 received pay. January - February 1864 roll shows him present. April 26, 1864 sent to Charleston, South Carolina hospital. March - April 1864 roll shows he was sent to Charleston Hospital. 3rd quarter 1864 issued clothing. August 9, 1864 admitted to Jackson Hospital at Richmond, Virginia with Diarrhoea and Fever. August 15, 1864 died in Jackson Hospital at Richmond, Virginia. Effects at time of death were: 1 blanket, 1 pair shoes, 1 jacket, 1 shirt, 2pr. drawers, 1 cap. He is buried in Hollywood Cemetery at Richmond, Virginia.

CARTER OHEN F.: Company I, corporal. September 10, 1861 elected 4th corporal of Co. I, 27th Regiment, Georgia Infantry at Camp Stephens, Griffin, Spalding County, Georgia. June 16 and June 27, 1863 issued clothing. December 31, 1863 received pay. July 1, 1864 wounded at Malvern Hill, Virginia. July 4, 1864, admitted to Chimborazo Hospital No. 1 at Richmond, Virginia with Vulnus Sclopeticum (Gunshot Wound) in the shoulder. February 20, 1864 wounded at Olustee, Florida. January 1864 - February 1864 roll shows him absent wounded. February 29, 1864 received pay. March - April 1864 roll shows him absent wounded. May 30, 1864 issued clothing. May 31, 1864 wounded in the right leg at the second battle of Cold Harbor. May 31, 1864 admitted to Receiving and Wayside Hospital or Hospital No. 9 at Richmond, Virginia. May 31, 1864 transferred to Jackson Hospital at Richmond, Virginia with a Vulnus Sclopeticum (Gunshot Wound) in the right leg. June 6, 1864 returned to duty. July 1864 issued clothing. September 20, 1864 issued clothing. March 30, 1865 pension records show he was captured at Sugar Loaf, North Carolina.

CARTER, THOMAS J.: Company D, corporal. February 24, 1862 enlisted as a private in Co. D, 27th Regiment, Georgia Infantry in Gainesville, Hall County, Georgia. March 25, 1862 received a $50.00 bounty in Atlanta, Georgia. July 4, 1862 received pay ($66.00). May 9, 1863 issued clothing at General Hospital No. 1 at Lynchburg, Virginia. He was appointed 3rd corporal. April, May and June 1863 issued clothing. December 1863 issued clothing. February 29, 1864 received pay. March - April 1864 roll shows him present. July 1864 issued clothing. September 20, 1864 issued clothing. He was appointed 2nd corporal of Co. D, 27th Regiment, Georgia Infantry. April 26, 1865 surrendered, Greensboro, North Carolina. May 1, 1865 paroled at Greensboro, North Carolina.

CARTER, WILLIAM (WALTER) T.: Company K, private. November 1864 enlisted as a private in Co. K, 27th Regiment, Georgia Infantry at the age of 19 years. May 17, 1862 admitted to Chimborazo Hospital No. 2 at Richmond, Virginia with Catarrh. May 22, 1862 returned to duty. June 18, 1862 died at Winder Hospital, Richmond, Virginia His effects were $6.50. April 14, 1863 death benefit claim was filed by his widow Martha

E. Carter.

CARTER, WILLIAM J.: Company D, private. February 24, 1862 enlisted as a private in Co. D, 27th Regiment, Georgia Infantry in Gainesville, Hall County, Georgia. March 25, 1862 received pay ($50.00 bounty). July 4, 1862 received pay ($66.00). December 31, 1862 he was absent without leave.

CASTLEY (COSTLEY), W. C.: Company E, private. February 17, 1864 enlisted as a private in Co. E, 27th Regiment, Georgia Infantry. January - February 1864 roll shows him absent. March - April 1864 roll shows him present. August 3, 1864 admitted to Jackson Hospital, Richmond, Virginia with Febris Remit (Malaria). August 11, 1864 furloughed for 30 days. August 30, 1864 furloughed for 30 days.

CATES, J. J. (T.): Company C, private. September 10, 1861 enlisted as a private in Co. C, 27th Regiment, Georgia Infantry.

CAUDLE (CAUDELL), GILBERT: Company D, private. March 4, 1862 enlisted as a private in Co. D, 27th Regiment, Georgia Infantry. May 7, 1862 died of Measles at Richmond, Virginia. He is buried in Richmond, Virginia in Hollywood Cemetery.

CAUSEY, D. L.: Company C, private. He enlisted as a private in Co. C, 27th Regiment, Georgia Infantry. April 10, 1862 admitted to Chimborazo Hospital No. 2 at Richmond, Virginia with Diarrhoea. May 4, 1862 returned to duty. May 7, 1862 transferred to and admitted to General Hospital at Farmville, Virginia with Hepatitis.

CAUSEY, ENOS M.: Company C, private. September 10, 1861 enlisted as a private in Co. C, 27th Regiment, Georgia Infantry at Camp Stephens, Griffin, Spalding County, Georgia. December 2, 1862 admitted to Chimborazo Hospital No. 4 at Richmond, Virginia. May 1, 1862 roll show him present as a patient at Chimborazo Hospital at Richmond, Virginia. July 1, 1862 wounded, Malvern Hill, Virginia. September 17, 1862 wounded at Sharpsburg, Maryland. September 28, 1862 admitted to Chimborazo Hospital No. 5 at Richmond, Virginia with a Vulnus Sclopeticum (Gunshot Wound) to shoulder. November 25, 1862 returned to duty. November 26, 1862 admitted to General Hospital No. 4 at Richmond, Virginia with Rheumatism at age 20 years. November 26, 1862 transferred to Institute Hospital at Richmond, Virginia. December 2, 1863 transferred to Chimborazo Hospital No. 4 at Richmond, Virginia with Syphilis. December 22, 1863 returned to duty. May 2, 1863 wounded at Chancellorsville, Virginia. May 9, 1863 appears on a list of wounded at Chancellorsville, Virginia. September 30, 1863 issued clothing. December 31, 1863 received pay. February 20, 1864 wounded, Olustee, Florida. January - February 1864 roll shows him absent wounded at Olustee. March - April 1864 roll shows him present. June 1, 1864 wounded, Cold Harbor, Virginia. June 30, 1864 roll for 2nd Division, Jackson Hospital at Richmond, Virginia shows him present. July 14, 1864 wounded at Colquitt's Salient, Petersburg, Virginia. July 1864 issued clothing. July

14, 1864 admitted to Jackson Hospital at Richmond, Virginia with a Vulnus Sclopeticum (Gunshot Wound) to the head. July 30, 1864 issued clothing at Jackson Hospital at Richmond, Virginia. July 31, 1864 furloughed for 30 days. September 10, 1864 received pay $37.50. September 12, 1864 operated on at Ocmulgee Hospital at Macon, Georgia for fracture of left parietal bone. His address was Knoxville, Georgia

CAUSEY, JAMES J.: Company C, private. September 10, 1861 enlisted as a private in Co. C, 27th Regiment, Georgia Infantry. May 31, 1862 wounded, Seven Pines, Virginia. July 4, 1862 admitted to Chimborazo Hospital No. 5 at Richmond, Virginia with Diarrhoea. July 10, 1862 received pay ($66.00). October 6, 1862 received pay ($69.00). October 27 1862 died of Typhoid Fever in Chimborazo Hospital No.5 at Richmond, Virginia. October 28, 1862 he was buried at Oakwood Cemetery in Richmond, Virgiinia. July 16, 1864 death benefit claim was filed by Ellefaro (Elefero) E. Causey, widow. He was a resident on Knoxville, Crawford County, Georgia.

CAUSEY, LEMON M.: Company C, private. 1861 enlisted as a private in Co. C, 27th Regiment, Georgia Infantry. January 1862 roll shows he was bricklaying at headquarters post on December 16, 1861 and was employed as a mechanic from January 1, 1862 to January 25, 1862 at Camp Pickens near Manassas, Virginia. March 31, 1862 admitted to Chimborazo Hospital No. 2 at Richmond, Virginia with Diarrhoea. April 30, 1862 received pay and issued clothing. May 4, 1862 returned to duty. June 19, 1862 received pay ($60.00). July 22, 1862 admitted to Chimborazo Hospital No. 5 at Richmond, Virginia with Debility. October 2, 1862 received pay ($ 69.00). November 21, 1862 admitted to General Hospital No. 21 at Richmond, Virginia and transferred to the small pox hospital. December 15 (17), 1862 admitted to General Hospital at Howard's Grove at Richmond, Virginia. December 17 (25), 1862 died in the General Hospital at Howard's Grove at Richmond, Virginia of Variola. He was 27 years of age at his death. His effects at death were $205.00. January 16, 1863 death benefit claim was filed by Selina M. Causey, widow. January 16, 1863 document shows effects were given to Selina M. Causey (his wife). He is described as born in Knoxville, Georgia, 52 years of age, 5 feet 3 inches high, dark complexion, dark eyes, dark hair and by occupation was a farmer.

CAUSEY, L. D.: Company C, private. September 10 (21), 1861 enlisted as a private in Co. C, 27th Regiment, Georgia Infantry at Camp Stephens, Griffin, Spalding County, Georgia. December 1861 roll shows he was left sick in Georgia October 31, 1861. _June 12 (16) 1862 discharged due to disability. Described on his discharge papers as age 52, 5 foot 3 inches high, light complexion, gray eyes and dark hair and shows he was a farmer.

CAUSEY, W. D.: Company C, private. March 15, 1862 enlisted as a private in Co. C, 27th Regiment, Georgia Infantry at Knoxville, Crawford

County, Georgia. April 24, 1862 admitted to Chimborazo Hospital No. 5 at Richmond, Virginia with Measles. July 15, 1862 returned to duty from Chimborazo Hospital No.5 at Richmond, Virginia. June 26, 1863 issued clothing. September 30, 1863 issued clothing. December 31, 1863 received pay. January - February 1864 roll shows him present. March - April 1864 roll shows him present.

CELING, R. N.: Company K, private. He enlisted as a private in Co. K, 27th Regiment, Georgia Infantry. October 5, 1864 admitted to Receiving and Wayside Hospital or General Hospital No. 9 at Richmond, Virginia. October 6, 1864 transferred to Jackson Hospital, Richmond, Virginia.

CHAFFIN, GEORGE M.: Field Staff, ensign and lieutenant. September 9, 1861 enlisted as a private in Co. H, 27th Regiment Georgia Infantry at Camp Stephens, Griffin, Spalding County, Georgia. June 26, 1862 wounded in the right side at Mechanicsville, Virginia. July 2, 1862 admitted to C. S. A. General Hospital at Danville, Virginia with a Vulnus Sclopeticum (Gunshot Wound). August 13, 1862 returned to duty. November 18, 1862 received pay ($94.00). December 31, 1863 received pay. January - February 1864 roll shows him present. February 29, 1864 received pay. March - April 1864 roll show him present. April 1864 listed as the Regimental Color Bearer. September 29, 1864 wounded, Fort Harrison near Richmond, Virginia. June 17, 1864 appointed Ensign, 27th Regiment Georgia Infantry. August 27, 1864 received pay ($129.00). October 3, 1864 admitted to Receiving and Wayside Hospital or General Hospital No. 9 at Richmond Virginia and was transferred to Jackson Hospital at Richmond, Virginia on October 4, 1864. October 1, 1864 admitted to Jackson, Hospital at Richmond, Virginia with a Vulnus Sclopeticum (Gunshot Wound) to right ankle (severing the Achilles tendon). October 15, 1864 furloughed for 30 days. October 30, 1864 roll shows him wounded on furlough from Dove Hill Farm, Virginia. On October 10, 1864 to McDonough, Henry County, Georgia. December 31, 1864 report shows him on sick leave. January 21, 1865 admitted to Hood Hospital at Cuthbert, Georgia after being re-furloughed from Richmond, Virginia, his wound unhealed (Achilles Tendon severed with ulcer). February 25, 1865 in Hood Hospital, Cuthbert, Georgia with wound unhealed and was furloughed for 60 days sick. Born in Georgia March 16, 1841

CHAMBERS, J. C.: Company E, private. August 28, 1861 enlisted as a private in Co. E, 27th Regiment, Georgia Infantry. April 1, 1862 discharged, result of Measles. 1863 pension records show he reenlisted. January 1864 transferred to Co. K, 30th Regiment, Georgia Infantry. February 1865 sent home on account of illness. He was unable to return. He was born in 1836.

CHAMBERS, J. J.: Company E, private. He enlisted as a private in Co. E, 27th Regiment, Georgia Infantry. May 2, 1863 wounded mortally at Chancellorsville, Virginia. He died of wounds by May 9, 1863.

CHAMBERS, JAMES: Company E, private. He enlisted as a private in

Co. E, 27th Regiment, Georgia Infantry. November 3, 1863 wounded at Fort Sumter, Charleston, South Carolina.

CHAMBERS, JOEL J.: Company E, private. September 9, 1861 enlisted as a private in Co. E, 27th Regiment, Georgia Infantry. April 26, 1865 surrendered, Greensboro, North Carolina.

CHAMBERS, JOSEPH A.: Company E, private. September 9, 1861 enlisted as a private in Co. E, 27th Regiment, Georgia Infantry. January 25, 1862 discharged on account of Tuberculosis. Discharge papers show he was born in Texas and was 21 years of age, 5 feet 5 1/2 inches high, light complexion, blue eyes, light hair and by occupation was a farmer. Transferred to Co. K, 30th Georgia Regiment.

CHANCE, B. M.: Company C, private. He enlisted as a private in Co. C, 27th Regiment, Georgia Infantry. February 1862 roll shows him as Provost Marshall's Guard at Headquarters Post.

CHANCE, J. M.: Company C, private. September 10, 1861 enlisted as a private in Co. C, 27th Regiment, Georgia Infantry. May 3, 1862 admitted to Chimborazo Hospital No.5 at Richmond, Virginia with Fever. May 12, 1862 sent to Camp Winder at Richmond, Virginia.

CHANDLER, C. M.: Company D, private. He enlisted as a private in Co. D, 27th Regiment, Georgia Infantry. April 28, 1865 paroled at General Hospital No. 12 at Greensboro, North Carolina.

CHANDLER MARTIN G.: Company D, corporal. February 28, 1862 enlisted as a private in Co. D, 27th Regiment, Georgia Infantry at Chestnut Mountain, Hall County, Georgia. March 25, 1862 received pay at Atlanta, Georgia ($50.00). June 10, 1862 he died in Camp Winder Hospital at Richmond, Virginia. August 29, 1862 death benefit claim was filed by his widow, Sarah E. Chandler of Hall County, Georgia. September 20, 1863 death benefit claim paid $194.60 (#2790).

CHANDLER, STERLING: Company D, private. March 3, 1862 enlisted as a private in Co. D, 27th Regiment, Georgia Infantry at Chestnut Mountain, Hall County, Georgia. March 25, 1862 received pay in Atlanta, Georgia ($50.00). October 1862 - December 1862 returns show he was sent to hospital. November 7, 1862 died in General Hospital.

CHANDLER, WALKER V.: Company D, private. September 10, 1861 enlisted as a private in Co. D, 27th Regiment, Georgia Infantry at Camp Stephens, Griffin, Spalding County, Georgia. December 1861 roll shows him in hospital in Richmond, Virginia. January - February 1862 rolls show him in hospital in Richmond, Virginia. May 1, 1862 died in Richmond, Virginia. July 10, 1862 death benefit claim was filed by Wilson Chandler his father. December 4, 1862 death benefit claim paid $185.06 (#2067).

CHANDLER, WILLIAM: Company D, private. September 10, 1861 enlisted as a private in Co. D, 27th Regiment, Georgia Infantry at Camp Stephens, Griffin, Spalding County, Georgia. December 1861, January 1862 and February 1862 rolls show he was left sick in Georgia October 31, 1861. April 10, 1862 admitted to Chimborazo Hospital No. 1 at Richmond,

Virginia with Hemorrhoids. June 10, 1862 transferred to Winder Hospital at Richmond, Virginia. June 11, 1862 admitted to Chimborazo Hospital No. 1 at Richmond, Virginia with Enlargement of the Heart. June 17, 1862 received pay ($120.70). July 4, 1862 died in Chimborazo Hospital No. 1 at Richmond, Virginia of Enlarged Heart. July 5, 1862 buried in Oakwood Cemetery at Richmond, Virginia. August 28, 1862 (December 16, 1862) death benefit claim was filed by his widow, Margaret Chandler in Hall County, Georgia.

CHAPMAN, G. W.: Company A, 1st sergeant. September 10, 1861 elected 1st sergeant in Co. A, 27th Regiment Georgia Infantry at Camp Stephens, Griffin, Spalding County, Georgia. June 9 1862 received pay ($55.00). December 1862 roll shows him furloughed in October due to wounds. December 12, 1862 to January 22, 1863 on furlough and received commutation for rations for 40 days. June 16, 1863 issued clothing. July, August and September 1863 issued clothing. December 31, 1863 received pay. January - February 1864 rolls show him present. March - April 1864 roll shows him present.

CHAPMAN, HENRY E.: Company K, private. March 4, 1862 enlisted as a private in Co. K, 27th Regiment, Georgia Infantry in Georgia at age 36 years. June 1863 issued clothing. October 29, 1863 and November 8, 1863 issued clothing. November 1, 1863 transferred to Co. B, 32nd Regiment, Georgia Infantry.

CHAPMAN, JOSEPH C.: Company G, lieutenant. September 9, 1861 elected 3rd sergeant in Co. G, 27th Regiment, Georgia Infantry at Camp Stephens, Griffin, Spalding County, Georgia. February 4, 1863 to March 6, 1863 on 30 day furlough and paid ($10.00) commutation for rations. June 16, and June 26 1863 issued clothing. October 30, 1863 issued clothing. November 24, 1863 issued clothing. December 31, 1863 received pay. January - February 1864 rolls show him present. February 29, 1864 received pay. March - April 1864 rolls show him present. June 2, 1864 elected Jr. 2nd lieutenant Co. G, 27th Regiment, Georgia Infantry. July 1864 issued clothing. September 14, 1864 elected 2nd lieutenant Co. G, 27th Regiment, Georgia Infantry. November 1864 roster shows him present and indicates his election to 2nd lieutenant. April 26, 1865 surrendered, Greensboro, North Carolina. May 1, 1865 paroled at Greensboro, North Carolina.

CHAPMAN, WILLIAM THOMAS: Company G, private. March 4, 1862 enlisted as a private in Co. H, 44th Regiment, Georgia Infantry. May 1862 wounded in foot while drilling at Goldsboro, North Carolina. May 22, 1862 discharged at Camp McIntosh near Goldsboro, North Carolina, on account of Varicose Veins in legs. August 4, 1863 enlisted as a private in Co. G, 27th Regiment, Georgia Infantry in Zebulon, Pike County, Georgia. August 1863 detailed as wagon master at James Island, South Carolina. October 30, 1863 he was shown on roll as being detailed as wagon master and issued clothing. December 31, 1863 received pay as wagon master at James Island, South Carolina from September1, 1863 to December 31, 1863 ($.25 per day). December 31, 1863 received pay. January 1, 1864 - January 31, 1864 he was employed on extra duty at Fort Johnson as wagon master. February received extra pay as wagon master ($.25 per day). January - February 1864 roll shows him absent sick from February 20, 1864. February 20, 1864 - April 30, 1864 he was absent, sick. February 29, 1864 received pay. March - April 1864 rolls show him absent sick from February 20, 1864. May 1864 issued clothing. May 1, 1864 to May 31, 1864 he was on extra duty as wagon master. February 1, 1864 to August 31, 1864 was on extra duty as teamster and wagon master ($25 per day) paid at Petersburg, Virginia September 20, 1864. September 20, 1864 issued clothing. April 26, 1865 surrendered, Greensboro, North Carolina. May 1, 1865 paroled at Greensboro, North Carolina. He was born in Georgia December 6, 1830.

CHIDLDS, DANIEL M.: Company G, private. September 9, 1861 enlisted as a private in Co. G, 27th Regiment, Georgia Infantry at Camp Stephens, Griffin, Spalding County, Georgia. December 31, 1861 received pay. March 30, 1862 admitted to Chimborazo hospital No. 4 at Richmond, Virginia with Diarrhoea. April 13, 1862 admitted to Chimborazo Hospital No, 1 at Richmond, Virginia with Icterus (Jaundice). April 15, 1862 returned to duty. August 31, 1862 received pay and roll for Hospital at Huguenot Springs, Virginia shows him present. September 7, 1862 attached to the Hospital at Huguenot Springs, Virginia. October 14, 1862 roll for hospital at Huguenot Springs, Virginia shows him present. October 14, 1862 discharged due to disability. He is described on his discharge certificate a being born in Upson County, Georgia, 21 years of age, 5 foot 6 inches high, dark complexion, brown eyes, brown hair and was a farmer. October 16, 1862 received pay. He enlisted as a private in Co. C, 1st Battalion, Georgia Reserve Cavalry (Blount's). He was born in Upson County, Georgia March 1837.

CHILDS, WILLIAM M.: Company H, private, September 9, 1861 enlisted as a private in Co. H, 27th Regiment, Georgia Infantry at Camp Stephens, Griffin, Spalding County, Georgia. December 1861, January 1862 and February 1862 rolls show he was left in Georgia sick on October 31, 1861. April 25, 1862 received pay ($88.06). May 7, 1862 admitted to General Hospital Camp Winder at Richmond, Virginia with Icterus (Jaundice). June 8, 1862 returned to duty. June 30, 1862 received pay. July 4, 1862 admitted to General Hospital Camp Winder at Richmond, Virginia with Typhoid Fever (also states that he deserted on July 12, 1862). February 28, 1862 to August 31, 1862 he is shown on roll for General Hospital No. 12 at Richmond, Virginia. September 30, 1862 wounded through leg and arm (age 17 - farmer). October 1, 1862 admitted to Receiving and Wayside Hospital or General Hospital No. 9 at Richmond, Virginia. October 1, 1862 admitted to 4th Division, General Hospital Camp Winder at Richmond, Virginia. October 7, 1862 returned to duty from Winder Division 4 Hospital at Richmond, Virginia. October 10, 1862 admitted to General Hospital No. 12 at Richmond, Virginia, vaccinated and was transferred to Camp Winder at Richmond, Virginia. October 24, 1862 admitted to Winder Division 3 Hospital at Richmond, Virginia. October 25, 1862 furloughed for 15 days. October 30, 1862 furloughed for 30 days. February 28, 1863 received pay. May 1, 1863 roll for General Hospital No. 19, Richmond, Virginia shows him present. May 3, 1863 wounded in the right knee just above the tibia at Chancellorsville, Virginia. June 1, 1863 received pay ($11.00). June 6, 1863 furloughed for 30 day from General Hospital No. 19 at Richmond, Virginia. June 8, 1863 received pay ($11.00). December 31, 1863 received pay. January - February 1864 rolls show him present. February 29, 1864 received pay. March - April 1864 rolls show him present. June 2, 1864 wounded in the shoulder at Cold Harbor, Virginia. June 3, 1864 he was admitted to and transferred from Receiving and Wayside Hospital or General Hospital No. 9 at Richmond, Virginia to Jackson Hospital at Richmond, Virginia. June 4, 1864 admitted to C. S. A. General Hospital at Danville, Virginia with a Vulnus Sclopeticum (Gunshot Wound) to the shoulder (shown as 19 years old - farmer). June 17, 1864 transferred and furloughed. June 23, 1864 returned to duty from Pettigrew General Hospital No. 13 at Raleigh, North Carolina. October 8, 1864 wounded near Fort Harrison near Richmond, Virginia in the right hand. October 17, 1864 returned to duty. October 8, 1864 admitted to Jackson Hospital at Richmond, Virginia with a Vulnus Sclopeticum (Gunshot Wound) to the right hand. He was wounded in left eye, knee joint and hip date and place not given. March 8, 1865 captured near Kinston, North Carolina. March 16, 1865 arrived in New Bern, North Carolina as a POW. June 26, 1865 released at Point Lookout, Maryland where he took the Oath of Allegiance to the United States. Release documents show he lived in Henry County, Georgia and had light complexion, dark brown hair, dark gray eyes and was 5 foot 10 1/4 inches high. He was born in Henry County, Georgia April 28, 1844. He died at Confederate Soldier's home, at Atlanta, Georgia January 23, 1923. He is buried at Locust Grove, Georgia.

CLARK (CLARKE), CASWELL: Company D, private. September 10, 1861 enlisted as a private in Co. D, 27th Regiment, Georgia Infantry at Camp Stephens, Griffin, Spalding County, Georgia. December 1861 roll shows him in hospital in Richmond, Virginia. December 31, 1861 received pay and issued clothing. March 8, 1862 admitted to Chimborazo Hospital No. 4 at Richmond, Virginia with Typhoid Fever. March 20, 1862 died of Typhoid Fever in Chimborazo Hospital No. 4 at Richmond, Virginia. He is most likely buried in Oakwood Cemetery at Richmond Virginia. December 13, 1862 death benefit claim was filed by his widow, Talitha Clark.

CLARK (CLARKE), JOHN W.: Company D, private. August 4, 1862 enlisted as a private in Co. D, 27th Regiment, Georgia Infantry at Richmond, Virginia. September 17, 1862 captured at Sharpsburg, Maryland. September 27, 1862 he appears on list to be paroled by the Provost Marshall of the

Army of the Potomac. October 1, 1862 admitted to Summit House U. S. A. General Hospital, West Philadelphia, Pennsylvania with Debility. November 24, 1862 returned to duty (POW). December 15, 1862 sent from Fort Delaware, Delaware to Fortress Monroe, Virginia, and was paroled. March 1, 1863 received pay. March 16, 1863 admitted to Chimborazo Hospital No. 2 at Richmond, Virginia with Erysipelas. March 17, 1863 transferred to Chimborazo Hospital Division No. 2 at Richmond, Virginia. April 1, 1863 returned to duty. April 8, 1863 admitted to General Hospital No. 7 at Richmond, Virginia. April 8, 1863 admitted to Receiving and Wayside Hospital or General Hospital No. 9 at Richmond, Virginia with Pneumonia. April 19, 1863 transferred to Henningsen Hospital at Richmond, Virginia. March - April 1863 shown on roll for Henningsen Hospital at Richmond, Virginia. April, May, June and December 1863 issued clothing. December 31, 1863 received pay March - April 1864 roll shows that on April 24, 1864 he deserted.

CLARK (CLARKE), WILLIAM: Company B, private. June 12, 1861 enlisted as a private in Co. B, 27th Regiment, Georgia Infantry. November 11, 1861 admitted to General Hospital No.18 at Richmond, Virginia with Typhoid Fever. November 25 (or December 3), 1861 died in General Hospital 18 at Richmond Virginia. December 1861 roll shows him in the hospital at Richmond, Virginia. January 1862 roll shows that he died in Richmond, Virginia of disease on November 25, 1861.

CLARY ROBERT M.: Company C, private. April 1, 1864 enlisted as a private in Co. C, 27th Regiment, Georgia Infantry at Charleston, South Carolina. March - April 1864 roll shows him present. June 4, 1864 wounded, Cold Harbor, Virginia. June 4, 1864 admitted to the Receiving and Wayside Hospital or General Hospital No. 9 at Richmond, Virginia. June 5, 1864 admitted to Jackson Hospital at Richmond, Virginia with mini ball wound in right leg. July 23, 1864 died from wounds at Jackson Hospital at Richmond, Virginia. July 25, 1864 effects at Jackson Hospital at Richmond, Virginia were: 1 coat, 1 hat, 1pair socks, 1 pair pants, 1 vest - total value $20.00. He is buried in Hollywood Cemetery, Richmond, Virginia.

CLARY, WILEY G.: Company C, private. September 1, 1862 enlisted as a private in Co. C, 27th Regiment, Georgia Infantry at Calhoun, Georgia. December 1862 roll shows him absent sick since January 12, 1863. June 16, June 26, June 30 and September 30, 1863 issued clothing. December 31, 1863 received pay. January - February 1864 roll shows him present. March - April 30, 1864 roll shows him present. June 4, 1862 wounded in the left leg at Cold Harbor, Virginia. June 4, 1864 admitted to Chimborazo Hospital No. 3 at Richmond, Virginia with a Vulnus Sclopeticum (Gunshot Wound) to the left leg. July 18, 1864 furloughed for 40 days due to injury.

CLAY, LAWRENCE W.: Company I, lieutenant. July 6, 1861 elected 2nd lieutenant of the Appling Grays. September 10, 1861 joined Co. I, 27th Regiment, Georgia Infantry as 2nd lieutenant at Camp Stephens,

Griffin, Spalding County, Georgia. November 29, 1861 (December 2, 1861) resigned his commission. July 23, 1864 died at Jackson Hospital at Richmond, Virginia.

CLEMENTS, J. C.: Field Staff, Hospital Steward. He enlisted as a private in the 27th Regiment, Georgia Infantry. December 31, 1863 to April 30 1864 Field and Staff Muster roll shows him detached as a Hospital Steward for the 23rd Georgia.

CLEMENTS, JAMES WILSON: Field Staff, Assistant Surgeon. August 31, 1861 appointed 1st corporal of Co. H, 23rd Regiment, Georgia Infantry. 1861 he was a Hospital Steward. March 29, 1864 transferred to the 27th Georgia Infantry as Hospital Steward. July 9, 1864 appointed Assistant Surgeon 27th Georgia Infantry. April 26, 1865 surrendered, Greensboro, North Carolina.

CLEMONS, W. J.: Company D, private. December 22, 1863 enlisted as a private in Co. D, 27th Regiment, Georgia Infantry in Charleston, South Carolina. 1865 wounded. February 29, 1864 received pay. March - April 1864 roll shows him present. May 30, 1864, July 1864 and September 20, 1864 issued clothing. March 21, 1865 wounded in left arm at Bentonville, North Carolina. March 1865 admitted to C. S. A. General Hospital No. 3 at Greensboro, North Carolina. March 29, 1865 admitted to C. S. A. General Hospital No.11 at Charlotte, North Carolina with wound in left arm. April 11, 1865 furloughed.

COBB, RICHARD V.: Company D, lieutenant. August 10, 1861 elected 2nd lieutenant in the Militia Company from Hall County. September 10, 1861 became 2nd lieutenant of Co D, 27th Regiment, Georgia Infantry at Camp Stephens, Griffin, Spalding County, Georgia. December 1861 roll shows him present at Camp Pickens near Manassas, Virginia. December 31, 1861 admitted to Moore Hospital at General Hospital, No. 1 at Danville, Virginia with Fever and was sent to Richmond, Virginia. January 1862 roll shows him absent at Richmond hospital since January 1, 1862. February 1862 roll shows he rejoined his company on February 28 from hospital. March 4, 1862 received pay ($320.00). May 31, 1862 wounded in the right leg at Seven Pines, Virginia. June 4, 1862 received pay ($240.00). August 2, 1862 received pay ($160.00). September 17, 1862 captured at Sharpsburg, Maryland. His name appears on a list of wounded Confederate officers in Hospital near Sharpsburg, Maryland. November 8, 1862 paroled in Maryland and exchanged in Aikens, Virginia. October 1, 1862 admitted to Summit House U. S. A. General Hospital at West Philadelphia, Pennsylvania with a Vulnus Sclopeticum (Gunshot Wound) and compound fracture of the right arm. December 5, 1862 returned to duty. December 6, 1862 his name appears on a list of "Rebel Prisoners' sent from provost Barracks, Philadelphia, Pennsylvania to Fort Delaware, Delaware by order of Brig. General Montgomery, commanding in Philadelphia, Pennsylvania. December 15, 1862 paroled and sent from Fort Delaware, Delaware to Fortress Monroe, Virginia for exchange.

December 19, 1862 admitted to General Hospital at Petersburg, Virginia with a Vulnus Sclopeticum (Gunshot Wound) in the right arm. December 20, 1862 admitted to General Hospital at Petersburg, Virginia. December 24, 1862 furloughed for 40 days (paroled prisoner). December 27, 1862 list shows him in the General Hospital at Petersburg, Virginia as having been furloughed. January 10, 1863 elected 1st. lieutenant Co. D, 27th Regiment, Georgia Infantry. March 12, 1863 letter sent from Alexander Stephens, Quartermaster General, offering him the Quartermaster position in Athens, Georgia at the Arsenal. September 30, 1863 appears on roster of officers in Brig. General A. H. Colquitt's Brigade. March - April 30, 1864 roll shows him present. August 22, 1864 received pay ($180.00). November 1864 roll shows him present. March 19, 1865 wounded in the left arm, Bentonville, North Carolina. He was born in Georgia August 8, 1837.

COCHRAL, F.: Company K, private. He enlisted as a private in Co. K, 27th Regiment, Georgia Infantry. March 7, 1862 admitted to Chimborazo Hospital No. 4 at Richmond, Virginia with Mumps. April 9, 1862 returned to duty.

COCHRAN, BENJAMIN F.: Company F, private. September 9, 1861 enlisted as a private in Co. F, 27th Regiment, Georgia Infantry at Camp Stephens, Griffin, Spalding County, Georgia. December 29, 1861 admitted to Moore Hospital at General Hospital, No. 1 at Danville, Virginia with Continua Fever. December 1861 roll shows him in Culpepper, Virginia hospital. January 8, 1862 was in Moore Hospital at Danville, Virginia. January 1862 roll shows him in Moore Hospital since January 8, 1862. July 11, 1862 died in First Georgia Hospital at Richmond, Virginia. He was born in Talbot County, Georgia. January 13, 1863 death benefit claim was filed by Benjamin Cochran, his father. Death benefit claim paid $145.03 (#7463). Death benefit claim description born in Talbot County, Georgia, 22 years of age, blue eyes, dark hair, fair complexion, 6 feet 1 inch high and was a farmer.**COCHRAN, GEORGE T.:** Company E, private. December 1861 roll shows he was in hospital in Richmond, Virginia. January 10, 1862 furloughed for 30 days. January 1862 roll shows him on furlough from Department Henrico for 30 days. January 11, 1862 received pay ($63.56). January 1862 received commutation for rations while on furlough ($6.60). February 1862 roll shows him absent without leave. Records show he was transferred to Co. C, 33rd Georgia.

COCHRAN, WILLIAM: Company F, private. September 9, 1861 enlisted as a private in Co. F, 27th Regiment, Georgia Infantry at Camp Stephens, Griffin, Spalding County, Georgia. 1862 died at Manassas, Virginia. January 13, 1863 death benefit claim was filed by Elizabeth Cochran, his widow.

COCHRAN, WILLIAM: Company F, private. May 17, 1863 enlisted as a private in Co. F, 27th Regiment, Georgia Infantry in Butler Georgia. May 22, 1863 he died at Camp near Richmond, Virginia. A death benefit claim was filed   An affidavit filed by Benjamin Cochran, father.   He was a resident of Talbot County.   Description: 25 years of age, blue eyes, black hair, fair complexion 6 feet 4 inches high, born in Talbot County, Georgia and by occupation was a farmer.

CADY (CODUY) (CODEY), ALLEN E.:   Company F, lieutenant. September 9, 1861 elected 2nd corporal in Co. F, 27th Regiment, Georgia Infantry at Camp Stephens, Griffin, Spalding County, Georgia.   December 1861 and January 1862 rolls show he was left in Georgia sick on October 31, 1861.   May 18, 1862 admitted to Chimborazo Hospital No. 2 at Richmond, Virginia with Continuing Fever (Malaria).   September 17, 1862 wounded at Sharpsburg, Maryland.   October 4, 1862 admitted to Receiving and Wayside Hospital or General Hospital No. 9 at Richmond, Virginia and was transferred to General Hospital No. 4 at Richmond, Virginia.   October 4, 1862 register shows him in General Hospital No. 4 at Richmond, Virginia with a Vulnus Sclopeticum (Gunshot Wound) received September 17, 1862, also shows he was a farmer and was 22 years old.   December 1862 roll shows he was wounded September 17, 1862.   October 4, 1862 admitted to General Hospital No. 14 at Richmond, Virginia.   October 8, 1862 admitted to institute Hospital at Richmond, Virginia with a Vulnus Sclopeticum (Gunshot Wound).   October 9, 1862 furloughed to Butler. July and August 1863 issued clothing.   December 31, 1863 received pay.   January - February 1864 roll shows him present and that he was a 2nd corporal.   February 29, 1864 received pay.   March - April 1864 roll shows him present.   July 1864 issued clothing.   September 14, 1864 elected 2nd lieutenant in Co. F, 27th Regiment, Georgia Infantry.   April 26, 1865 surrendered, Greensboro, North Carolina.   May 1, 1865 paroled at Greensboro, North Carolina.

CODY, ROBERT D.: Company A, sergeant.   February 28, 1862 enlisted as a private in Co. A, 27th Regiment, Georgia Infantry in Schley County, Georgia.   November 20, 1862 received pay (bounty) at Richmond, Virginia ($50.00).   December 1862 roll shows him absent from wounds.   May 2, 1863 wounded in the right thigh at Chancellorsville, Virginia.   May 6, 1863 admitted to Receiving and Wayside Hospital or General Hospital No. 9 at Richmond, Virginia and transferred to and admitted to Chimborazo Hospital No. 4 at Richmond, Virginia with a Vulnus Sclopeticum (Gunshot Wound) to the right thigh.   May 9, 1863 transferred to Lynchburg, Virginia hospital.   May 25, 1863 issued clothing at General Hospital No. 1 at Lynchburg, Virginia.   July 24, 1863 paid commutation for rations for 40 days (from July 1, 1862 to August 10, 1862) ($10.00).   June, July, August and September 1863 issued clothing.   December 31, 1863 received pay.   January - February 1864 roll shows him present.   February 29, 1864 received pay.   March - April 1864 roll shows him present.   May 30, 1864 and July 1864 issued clothing.   August 19, 1864 wounded in the left foot by a mini ball at Weldon Railroad, Virginia.   August 20, 1864 admitted to Jackson Hospital at Richmond, Virginia.   September 5, 1864 report of

Jackson Hospital at Richmond, Virginia shows him furloughed this date for 30 days. September 5, 1864 received pay ($85.13) and furloughed for 30 days. September 10, 1864 register of Jackson Hospital at Richmond, Virginia shows him furloughed at Butler, Georgia. He was appointed sergeant Co. A, 27th Regiment, Georgia Infantry. September 10, 1864 he was in Jackson Hospital at Richmond, Virginia.

COLE, GEORGE F.: Company K, private. February 4, 1864 enlisted as a private in Co. K, 27th Regiment, Georgia Infantry Macon, Bibb County, Georgia. March - April 1864 roll shows him present. June 19 or 20, 1864 wounded at Colquitt's Salient, Petersburg, Virginia. June 20, 1864 admitted to Receiving and Wayside Hospital or General Hospital No. 9 at Richmond, Virginia. June 21, 1864 transferred and admitted to Jackson Hospital at Richmond, Virginia with Vulnus Sclopeticum (Gunshot Wound) (mini ball) to the head. June 30, 1864 roll of 1st Division, Jackson Hospital at Richmond, Virginia shows him present. July 23, 1864 issued clothing at Jackson Hospital, Richmond, Virginia. July 24, 1864 furloughed for 30 days. September 24, 1864 issued clothing. April 26, 1865 surrendered, Greensboro, North Carolina. May 9, 1865 paroled at Greensboro, North Carolina.

COLEMAN, JOSEPH K.: Company E, private. September 30, 1861 enlisted in Co. E, 27th Regiment, Georgia Infantry at Camp Stephens, Griffin, Spalding County, Georgia. January 2, 1862 admitted to Moore Hospital at General Hospital No. 1 at Danville, Virginia with Dysentery and was sent to Richmond, Virginia. January 6, 1862 discharged due to disability and received pay ($25.12). January 1862 roll shows him discharged January 6, 1862 in Richmond due to disability.

COLEMAN, JOHN: Company E, private. September 9, 1861 enlisted as a private in Co. E, 27th Regiment, Georgia Infantry at Camp Stephens, Griffin, Spalding County, Georgia. September 9, 1862 died at Manassas, Virginia.

COLEMAN, PARKER R.: Company E, private. September 9, 1861 enlisted as a private in Co. E, 27th Regiment, Georgia Infantry at Camp Stephens, Griffin, Spalding County, Georgia. January and February 1862 rolls show he was left sick in Georgia October 31, 1861. December 1862 roll shows he was on wagon detail. April, May and June 1863 issued clothing. June 30, 1863 received pay. August 13, 1863 deserted while en route to Charleston, South Carolina.

COLEMAN, W. W.: Company B, private. He enlisted as a private in Co. B, 27th Regiment, Georgia Infantry. July 27, 1864 captured in Atlanta, Georgia (August 31, 1864 captured near Jonesboro, Georgia). September 19 and 22, 1864 exchanged at Rough and Ready, Georgia.

COLLEDGE, WILY: Company H, sergeant. He enlisted as a private in Co. H, 27th Regiment, Georgia Infantry. November 1, 1864 he appears on roll at Louisville, Kentucky of Prisoners of War who arrived at the Military Prison at Louisville, Kentucky during the six days ending October 31,

1864. Records indicate he was from Nashville, Tennessee.

COLLEY (CALLY) (COLLY), E. J.: Company K, private. February 11, 1864 enlisted as a private in Co. K, 27th Regiment, Georgia Infantry in Macon, Bibb County, Georgia. February 20, 1864 wounded at Olustee, Florida. March - April 1864 roll shows him present. June 2, 1864 transferred to Petersburg from Receiving and Wayside Hospital or General Hospital No. 9 at Richmond, Virginia. June 11, 1864 appears on roll of Pettigrew General Hospital No. 13 at Raleigh, North Carolina as being transferred to Columbia, South Carolina. June 18, 1864 died of Pneumonia in Ladies' General Hospital No.3 at Columbia, South Carolina. His effects were $6.50.

COLQUITT, WILLIAM J.: Company G, private. February 10, 1864 enlisted as a private in Co. G, 27th Regiment, Georgia Infantry at Decatur, Georgia. March - April 1864 roll shows him present. August 19, 1864 wounded in the left shoulder at Weldon Railroad, Virginia. August 21, 1864 admitted to Jackson Hospital at Richmond, Virginia with a Vulnus Sclopeticum (Gunshot Wound) to the left shoulder. August 31, 1864 issued clothing at Jackson Hospital, Richmond, Virginia. September 1, 1864 received pay ($56.44) at Richmond, Virginia and furloughed for 30 days to Jackson County, Georgia.

COMMANDER, BENJAMIN F.: Company C, private. He enlisted as a private in Co. C, 27th Regiment, Georgia Infantry. November 30, 1861 he was discharged due to disability at Camp Pickens near Manassas, Virginia. December 1, 1861 received pay.

CONIEL, THOMAS: Company H, private. September 20, 1861 enlisted as a private in Co. H, 27th Regiment, Georgia Infantry at Camp Stephens, Griffin, Spalding County, Georgia. January 15, 1862 died in the Hospital at Richmond, Virginia. April 13, 1863 death benefit claim was filed by Amanda Coniel, his widow of Meriwether County, Georgia

CONNELL, J. M.: Company K, private. He enlisted as a private in Co. K, 27th Regiment, Georgia Infantry. May 5, 1863 wounded at Chancellorsville, Virginia and was discharged disability.

CONNELL, JOHN H.: Company K, private. September 10, 1861 enlisted as a private in Co. K, 27th Regiment, Georgia Infantry at Camp Stephens, Griffin, Spalding County, Georgia. February 24, 1862 furloughed for 30 days on account of sickness. February 1862 roll shows him on sick leave. August 2, 1862 discharged due to disability. August 16, 1862 received pay ($44.00).

CONNELL, ROBERT P.: Company K, private. September 21, 1861 enlisted as a private in Co. K, 27th Regiment, Georgia Infantry at Camp Stephens, Griffin, Spalding County, Georgia. December 1861, January 1862 and February 1862 rolls show he was left sick in Georgia October 31, 1861. April 3, 1863 received pay ($69.66) and was discharged at Guinea Station, Virginia. He is described on his discharge as being born in Talbot County, Georgia, 35 years of age, 5 foot 6 inches high, light complexion, blue eyes, auburn hair and was a farmer. He was a resident of Talbot County, Georgia

CONNELL, THOMAS J.: Company K, private. He enlisted as a private in Co. K, 27th Regiment, Georgia Infantry. November 6, 1861 admitted to General Hospital at Petersburg, Virginia with Rubeola. December 10, 1861 returned to duty. January 17, 1862 died of Pneumonia at Camp Pickens near Manassas, Virginia. January 1862 roll indicates he died at Camp Pickens near Manassas, Virginia.

CONNELL (CONNEL), W. H. M.: Company F, private. He enlisted as a private in Co. F, 27th Regiment, Georgia Infantry. May 1, 1865 paroled at Greensboro, North Carolina.

CONNELL, WILLIAM: Company K, private. May 4, 1862 enlisted as a private in Co. K, 27th Regiment, Georgia Infantry at Talbotton, Talbot County, Georgia. May 3, 1863 pension records show he lost sight of right eye and arm was permanently disabled, at Chancellorsville, Virginia. June 30, 1863 received pay and was issued clothing. March - April 1864 roll shows him absent without leave since December 20, 1863. He was in Columbus, Georgia Hospital at the close of the war. He was born in Talbot County, Georgia.

COOK, ASBERRY (BERRY) WASHINGTON: Company E, private. September 9, 1861 enlisted as a private in Co. E, 27th Regiment, Georgia Infantry at Camp Stephens, Griffin, Spalding County, Georgia. September 29, 1864 killed at Fort Harrison near Richmond, Virginia.

COOK, COLBY J.: Company G, corporal. September 9, 1861 elected 2nd corporal in Co. G, 27th Regiment, Georgia Infantry at Camp Stephens, Griffin, Spalding County, Georgia. November 9, 1861 admitted to General Hospital No. 18 at Richmond, Virginia. November 14, 1861 returned to duty. December 11, 1861 died of Pneumonia at Camp Pickens near Manassas, Virginia. February 26, 1862 death benefit claim was filed by Lucretia Cook, widow. March 18, 1863 death benefit claim was paid $115.30 (#4092). He was a resident of Zebulon, Pike County, Georgia.

COOK, E. W.: Company E, private. August 1, 1863 enlisted as a private in Co. E, 27th Regiment, Georgia Infantry at Fairburn, Campbell County, Georgia. December 31, 1863 received pay. January, February, March and April 30, 1864 rolls show him present. February 29, 1864 received pay. September 20, 1864 issued clothing. September 30, 1864 killed at Fort Harrison near Richmond, Virginia.

COOK, HARBAND T.: Company E, private. September 9, 1861 enlisted as a private in Co. E, 27th Regiment, Georgia Infantry at Camp Stephens, Griffin, Spalding County, Georgia. May 7, 1862 admitted to General Hospital at Camp Winder at Richmond, Virginia with Typhoid Fever. May 9, 1862 died at Camp Winder at Richmond, Virginia. He is buried in Hollywood Cemetery at Richmond, Virginia. August 16, 1862 death benefit claim was filed by Sarah M. Cook, widow. March 23, 1863 death benefit paid $122.30 (#4168). He had a minor child. Described as being

22 years old, blue eyes, dark hair, fair complexion 5 foot 6 inches high born in Fayette County, Georgia and was a farmer.

COOK, ANDREW JAMES: Company E, private. September 9, 1861 enlisted as a private in Co. E, 27th Regiment, Georgia Infantry at Camp Stephens, Griffin, Spalding County, Georgia. June 2, 1862 admitted to General Hospital at Camp Winder at Richmond, Virginia with Typhoid Fever. June 9, 1862 died in General Hospital at Camp Winder, Richmond, Virginia. He is buried in Hollywood Cemetery at Richmond, Virginia. August 10, 1862 death benefit claim was filed by James B. Cook, father. August 11, 1862 death benefit claim was paid $83.30 (#956). He was born in Fayette County, Georgia. Description on death record is 20 years old, blue eyes, dark hair, dark complexion, 5 foot 7 inches high, born in Fayette County, Georgia and by occupation was a farmer.

COOK, JAMES O.: Company E, private. September 9, 1861 enlisted as a private in Co. E, 27th Regiment, Georgia Infantry at Camp Stephens, Griffin, Spalding County, Georgia. September 29, 1862 he is shown on morning report of General Hospital No, 22 at Richmond, Virginia. October 1, 1862 received pay ($94.00). October 8, 1862 transferred from General Hospital No. 22 at Richmond, Virginia to Camp Winder Hospital at Richmond, Virginia. October 10, 1862 furloughed for 20 days from Camp Winder Division 4, Hospital at Richmond, Virginia. October 14, 1862 received pay (bounty $50.00). April, May and June 1863 issued clothing. December 31, 1863 received pay. January - February 1864 roll shows him present. February 29, 1864 received pay. March - April 1864 roll shows him present. September 1864 issued clothing. March 19, 1865 killed at Bentonville, North Carolina.

COOK, SHEM E.: Company E, private. July 1, 1863 enlisted as a private in Co. E, 27th Regiment, Georgia Infantry at Fairburn, Campbell County, Georgia. December 31, 1863 received pay. January - February 1864 roll shows him present. February 29, 1864 received pay. March - April 1864 roll shows him present. June 4, 1864 wounded at Cold Harbor, Virginia and admitted to Receiving and Wayside Hospital or General Hospital No. 9 at Richmond , Virginia with a Vulnus Sclopeticum (Gunshot Wound) by a mini ball in the right hand and was transferred to Jackson Hospital at Richmond, Virginia this date. June 29, 1864 returned to duty. September 20, 1864 issued clothing. April 26, 1865 surrendered, Greensboro, North Carolina. May 1, 1865 paroled at Greensboro, North Carolina.

COOK, THOMAS J.: Company G, private. September 9, 1861 enlisted as a private in Co. G, 27th Regiment, Georgia Infantry at Camp Stephens, Griffin, Spalding County, Georgia. November 13, 1861 admitted to General Hospital No. 18 at Richmond, Virginia. December 19, 1861 discharged. His Post Office is listed as Zebulon, Pike County, Georgia.

COOK, WILLIAM R.: Company E, private. September 9, 1861 enlisted as a private in Co. E, 27th Regiment, Georgia Infantry at Camp Stephens, Griffin, Spalding County, Georgia. August 29, 1862 admitted to General

Hospital, Camp Winder at Richmond, Virginia with Rheumatism Acute. September 6, 1862 received pay ($113.00). September 30, 1862 returned to duty from 2nd Division, General Hospital Camp Winder at Richmond, Virginia. April, May and June 1863 issued clothing. December 31, 1863 received pay. February 20, 1864 wounded at Olustee, Florida. January - February 1864 and March - April 1864 rolls show him present. June 30, 1864 Roll of 1st Division, Jackson Hospital at Richmond, Virginia shows him present. July 21, 1864 admitted to Jackson Hospital at Richmond, Virginia with Chronic Diarrhoea. July 28, 1864 furloughed for 30 days. September 1864 issued clothing. April 26, 1865 surrendered, Greensboro, North Carolina. May 1, 1865 paroled at Greensboro, North Carolina. He was born in Fayette County, Georgia June 28, 1838.

COONER, JACKSON: Company I, private. August 25, 1861 enlisted in the Appling Grays at Holmesville, Georgia. September 9, 1861 enlisted as a private in Co. I, 27th Regiment, Georgia Infantry at Camp Stephens, Griffin, Spalding County, Georgia. November 12, 1861 admitted to General Hospital No. 18, Richmond, Virginia. December 13, 1861 returned to duty. December 31, 1861 received pay. May 31, 1862 killed at Seven Pines, Virginia. July 11, 1863 (January 16, 1863) death benefit claim was filed by James Cooner, his father. October 5, 1863 death benefit claim paid $130.00 (#9024).

COONER (CONNER), JEFFERSON: Company I, private. He enlisted as a private in Co. I, 27th Regiment, Georgia Infantry. February 8, 1862 died of Pneumonia at Camp Pickens near Manassas, Virginia.

COONER, JOHN C.: Company I, private. September 10, 1861 enlisted as a private in Co. I, 27th Regiment, Georgia Infantry at Camp Stephens, Griffin, Spalding County, Georgia. July 1, 1862 wounded at Malvern Hill (Seven Days around Richmond), Virginia. July 4, 1862 admitted to Chimborazo Hospital, No. 1 at Richmond, Virginia with a Vulnus Sclopeticum (Gunshot Wound). July 7, 1862 received pay ($91.00). December 31, 1863 received pay. February 20, 1864 killed at Olustee, Florida. January - February 1864 roll shows he was killed at Olustee, Florida.

COOPER, H. J.: Company D, sergeant. September 10, 1861 enlisted as a private in Co. D, 27th Regiment, Georgia Infantry at Camp Stephens, Griffin, Spalding County, Georgia. April, May and June 1863 issued clothing. December 1863 issued clothing. March - April 1864 roll shows him present. May 30, 1864 issued clothing. July 1864 issued clothing. September 20, 1864 issued clothing. April 26, 1865 surrendered Greensboro, North Carolina. May 1, 1865 paroled at Greensboro, North Carolina.

COOPER, HENRY H.: Company D, sergeant. February 23, 1863 enlisted as a private in Co. D, 27th Regiment, Georgia Infantry in Hall County, Georgia. December 1863 issued clothing. February 29, 1864 received pay. March - April 1864 roll shows him present. May 30, 1864 issued clothing. July 1864 issued clothing. He was appointed 4th sergeant Co. D, 27th Regiment, Georgia Infantry. April 26, 1865 surrendered, Greensboro, North Carolina. May 1, 1865 paroled at Greensboro, North Carolina.

COOPER, J. B.: Company I, private. He enlisted as a private in Co. I, 27th Regiment, Georgia Infantry. September 2, 1864 appears on register of Floyd House and Ocmulgee, Hospitals at Macon, Georgia with Typhoid Fever and Debility. His Post Office is shown as Valdosta, Alabama.

COOPER, WILLIAM: Company K, private. September 10, 1861 enlisted as a private in Co. K, 27th Regiment, Georgia Infantry at Camp Stephens, Griffin, Spalding County, Georgia. January 16, 1862 admitted to Moore Hospital, at General Hospital No. 1 at Danville, Virginia. January 16, 1862 sent to General Hospital at Orange Court House, Virginia. January 17, 1862 admitted to General Hospital, Orange Court House, Virginia with Pneumonia. January 1862 and February 1862 show him in hospital at Orange Court House, Virginia. March 15, 1862 returned to duty. October 8, 1862 died while at home on sick furlough. October 28, 1862 death benefit claim was filed by Julia E. Cooper, widow. September 18, 1863 death claim paid $157.93 (#8968). His home was Talbot County, Georgia

COPELAND, J. F.: Company G, private. He enlisted as a private in Co. G, 27th Regiment, Georgia Infantry. September 24, 1864 admitted to Jackson Hospital, Richmond, Virginia with Diarrhoea and Fever. October 1, 1864 died of Typhoid Fever at Division 1, Jackson Hospital at Richmond, Virginia (also states he was a paroled prisoner).

COPELAND, JOHN B.: Company G, 4th sergeant. September 9, 1861 elected 4th sergeant in Co. G, 27th Regiment, Georgia Infantry at Camp Stephens, Griffin, Spalding County, Georgia. November 8, 1861 admitted to General Hospital No. 18 at Richmond, Virginia (His Post Office shown as Flat Shoals, Meriwether County, Georgia). December 13, 1861 returned to duty. May 31, 1862 wounded in left arm at Seven Pines, Virginia. September 17, 1862 wounded in leg at Sharpsburg, Maryland. June 26, 1863 issued clothing. October 30, 1863, November 24, 1863 and December 16, 1863 issued clothing. December 18, 1863 hip crushed at Fort Sumter, South Carolina. December 31, 1863 received pay. January - February 1864 roll shows him absent sick in hospital since February 14, 1864. March - April 1864 roll shows him present. June 30, 1864 appears on Roll of General Hospital No. 1 at Summerville, South Carolina as present. September 20, 1864 issued clothing. April 17, 1865 received at 2nd Georgia Hospital, Augusta, Georgia. He was born September 15, 1836. (Records of Hollywood Cemetery at Richmond, Virginia show he died October 1, 1864 and is buried there.)

COPELAND, JOHN PICKNEY, JR.: Company H, private. September 9, 1861 enlisted as a private in Co. H, 27th Regiment, Georgia Infantry at Camp Stephens, Griffin, Spalding County, Georgia. November 15, 1861 admitted to General Hospital No. 18 at Richmond, Virginia. November 25, 1861 returned to duty. June 11, 1862 received pay ($80.00). April

17, 1863 admitted to Gordonsville Hospital with Pneumonia. April 27, 1863 admitted to C. S. A. General Hospital at Charlottesville, Virginia with Debilitas. May 10, 1863 transferred to General Hospital, Lynchburg, Virginia. December 31, 1863 received pay. January 9, 1864 - January 31, 1864 he was on duty at Fort Johnson as a teamster. February 7, 1864 received pay as a teamster (at $.25 per day extra). January - February 1864 roll shows him present. February 29, 1864 received pay. March - April 1864 roll shows him present. June 1, 1864 wounded in right arm, necessitating amputation below the elbow, at Cold Harbor, Virginia. June 2, 1864 transferred to Petersburg from Receiving and Wayside Hospital or General Hospital No. 9 at Richmond, Virginia. June 20, 1864 admitted to Receiving and Wayside Hospital or General Hospital No. 9 at Richmond, Virginia. June 22, 1864 transferred to Petersburg. September 16, 1864 appears on a register of Floyd House Hospital at Macon, Georgia with note "Vulnus Sclopeticum (Gunshot Wound) right forearm, amputated lower 3rd, he has applied for retirement". His Post Office is listed as Jackson Springs, Georgia. September 20, 1864 issued clothing. October 15, 1864 issued clothing.

COPELAND, JOHN PICKNEY, SR.: Company H, private. He enlisted in Co. H, 27th Regiment, Georgia Infantry at Macon Georgia. March - April 1864 roll shows him present and yet to be paid.

COPELAND, W. A. (WILLIAM) (WINFIELD): Company H, sergeant. September 9, 1861 elected 1st corporal of Co. H, 27th Regiment, Georgia Infantry at Camp Stephens, Griffin, Spalding County, Georgia, November 15, 1861 admitted to General Hospital No. 18 at Richmond, Virginia. November 25, 1861 returned to duty. January 14, 1862 admitted to Moore Hospital, at General Hospital, No. 1 at Danville, Virginia with Pneumonia and was sent to Richmond, Virginia to the hospital there. January 1862 roll shows he was left in the hospital at Richmond, Virginia. He was appointed corporal of Co. H, 27th Regiment, Georgia Infantry. June 28, 1862 admitted to General Hospital, Howard's Grove at Richmond, Virginia. November 25, 1863 received pay at James Island, South Carolina ($6.65). December 31, 1863 received pay. January - February 1864 roll shows him present. February 29, 1864 received pay. March - April 1864 roll show him present. July 1864 issued clothing. September 20, 1864 issued clothing. Appointed sergeant of Co. H., 27th Regiment, Georgia Infantry. April 26, 1865, surrendered at Greensboro, North Carolina. May 1, 1865 paroled at Greensboro, North Carolina. He was born in Newton County, Georgia July 1, 1842. He died at the Confederate Soldier's Home at Atlanta, Georgia February 11, 1832. He is buried in Winder, Georgia.

CORDIFF, G. P.: Company D, private. He enlisted as a private in Co. D, 27th Regiment, Georgia Infantry. December 1862 roll shows him in the hospital since May.

COURSON, THOMAS HOWELL: Company I, private. He enlisted as a private in Co. I, 27th Regiment, Georgia Infantry. May 30, 1862 admitted to

Chimborazo Hospital No.1, at Richmond, Virginia, with Pneumonia. May 15, 1862 died of Pneumonia in Chimborazo Hospital No.1 at Richmond, Virginia. He is most likely buried in Oakwood Cemetery at Richmond Virginia.

COWART, JAMES J.: Company B, sergeant. September 10, 1861 elected 1st. sergeant Co B, 27th Regiment, Georgia Infantry at Camp Stephens, Griffin, Spalding County, Georgia. May 19, 1863 received $10.00 as commutation for rations for 30 days furlough from February 14, 1863 to March 16, 1863. October, November and December 1863 issued clothing. December 17, 1863 received $6.60 as commutation for rations while on furlough for 20 days from October 30, 1863 to November 18, 1863. December 31, 1863 received pay. January - February 1864 roll shows him present. February 29, 1864 received pay. March - April 1864 roll shows him present. May 13, 1864 admitted to C. S. A. General Military Hospital, No. 4 at Wilmington, North Carolina with Malaria. May 22, 1864 transferred to Goldsboro, North Carolina. May 23, 1864 discharged from Goldsboro Hospital No. 3 at Goldsboro, North Carolina, returned to duty and ordered to report at or near Petersburg, Virginia. July 1864 issued clothing. April 26, 1865 surrendered, Greensboro, North Carolina. May 1, 1865 paroled at Greensboro, North Carolina. His Post Office is shown as Macon, Georgia.

COXWELL, JOHN F.: Company B. corporal. September 10, 1861 enlisted as a private in Co. B, 27th Regiment, Georgia Infantry at Camp Stephens, Griffin, Spalding County, Georgia. June, 12 1862 he died, in Virginia. June 24, 1862 death benefit claim was filed by Mary Coxwell, his mother, a resident of Macon County, Georgia. July 30, 1863 death benefit claim paid $24.60. (Appears also on rolls of Co. F.)

CRAPPS (CRAFT), JOHN: Company I, private. September 10, 1861 enlisted as a private in Co. I, 27th Regiment, Georgia Infantry at Camp Stephens, Griffin, Spalding County, Georgia. December 1861 and January 1862 rolls show him in the hospital at Richmond, Virginia. February 1862 roll shows him on sick furlough for 30 days from February 17, 1862. February 25, 1862 received pay ($40.33). April 30, 1862 received pay. November 1, 1862 roll from General Hospital No. 18 at Richmond, Virginia shows him present. November 19, 1862 admitted to General Hospital No. 16 at Richmond, Virginia. December 5, 1862 admitted to Winder Division No.1 Hospital at Richmond, Virginia. December 30, 1862 returned to duty. May 2, 1863 wounded at Chancellorsville, Virginia. December 31, 1863 received pay. January - February, 1864 roll shows him present. February 29, 1864 received pay. March - April 1864 roll shows him present. May 5, 1864 wounded in left foot at Wilderness, Virginia. July 1864 issued clothing. September 20, 1864 issued clothing. October 4(5), 1864 admitted to Jackson Hospital at Richmond, Virginia with Diarrhoea and Fever. October 14, 1864 returned to duty. March 19, 1865 captured at Bentonville, North Carolina. April 9, 1865 arrived at Point Lookout,

Maryland from New Bern, North Carolina as a prisoner of War. June 26, 1865 released at Point Lookout, Maryland. Release Records show he was a resident of Appling County, Georgia had light complexion, dark hair, hazel eyes, was 5 foot 8 1/2 inches high. He died December 27, 1863 and is buried at Zoar Cemetery in Appling County, Georgia

CRAPPS, JOSEPH A.: Company I, private. September 10, 1861 enlisted as a private in Co. I, 27th Regiment, Georgia Infantry at Camp Stephens, Griffin, Spalding County, Georgia. December 1861 received pay ($65.70). December 1861 and January 1862 rolls show him in hospital at Richmond, Virginia. February 1862 roll shows him absent sick. February 24, 1862 furloughed and received pay ($40.00). July 8, 1862 admitted to Chimborazo Hospital No. 1 at Richmond, Virginia with Debility. December 1862 roll shows him sick in hospital. February 10, 1863 admitted to C. S. A. General Hospital at Charlottesville, Virginia with Pneumonia. February 24, 1863 returned to duty. June 16 and June 27, 1863 issued clothing. September 26, 1863 received pay ($44.00). December 31, 1863 received pay. January - February 1864 roll shows him present. February 29, 1864 received pay. March - April 1864 roll shows him present. June 18, 1864 wounded in the breast at Colquitt's Salient near Petersburg, Virginia. June 18, 1864 admitted to General Hospital at Petersburg, Virginia with a Vulnus Sclopeticum (Gunshot Wound) to the breast. June 24, 1864 admitted to Receiving and Wayside Hospital or General Hospital No. 9, Richmond, Virginia. June 25, 1864 sent to Winder Hospital, Richmond, Virginia. June 30, 1864 he was in General Hospital Camp Winder at Richmond, Virginia. July 21, 1864 issued clothing. March 19, 1865 killed at Bentonville, North Carolina. He is buried at Bentonville Battlefield in an unmarked grave.

CRAPPS, SILAS A.: Company I, lieutenant He enlisted as a private in Co. I, 27th Regiment, Georgia Infantry. April 30, 1863 elected Jr. 2nd lieutenant Co. I, 27th Georgia Infantry.

CRAPPS, WESLEY: Company H, private. He enlisted as a private in Co. H, 27th Regiment, Georgia Infantry. June 18, 1864 wounded at Colquitt's Salient near Petersburg, Virginia (died)

CRAWFORD, JAMES J.: Field Staff, Hospital Steward. September 9, 1861 enlisted as a private in Co. G, 27th Georgia Infantry at Camp Stephens, Griffin, Spalding County, Georgia. September (5), 1861 promoted to Commissary Sergeant at Camp Stephens, Griffin, Spalding County, Georgia. December 1861 roll shows he was promoted to Commissary Sergeant. February 1862 roll shows he was taken up on muster roll by instruction of inspector. February 1862 roll shows he was on duty at Regimental Commissary Department. December 4, 1862 received pay ($22.00). March 12, 1863 received pay ($71.00). May 11, 1863 received $15.25 extra pay for working in the commissary department from March 1, 1863 to April 31, 1863. August 1, 1863 he was commissary sergeant in the subsistence department by order of Colonel Zachry. January - February 1864 and March - April 1864 rolls show him absent sick on furlough from

December 15, 1863. October 30, 1863 appears on list at James Island, South Carolina as commissary sergeant. June 18, 1864 detail extended. June 28, 1864 appears on list of the Medical Examining Board, Dalton Georgia with the following notation "hepatitis Chronic eleven months standing'. September 9, 1864 appointed Hospital Steward 27th Georgia Infantry.

CREAMER, JOHN B.: Company G, private. September 9, 1861 enlisted as a private in Co. G, 27th Regiment, Georgia Infantry at Camp Stephens, Griffin, Spalding County, Georgia. December 1861 roll shows he was in the hospital at Lynchburg, Virginia. January 1862 roll shows he was in the hospital at Richmond, Virginia from December 7, 1861. September 17, 1862 wounded and captured at Sharpsburg, Maryland. September 27, 1862 and October 3, 1862 appears on a roll of "Parole of Prisoners of War". October 17 (27), 1862 died of wounds at U. S. A. General Hospital No.1 at Frederick, Maryland. He is buried in Mount Olive Cemetery, grave No.120, Frederick, Maryland. April 3, 1863 death benefit claim was filed.

CREEL, GEORGE D.: Company E, private. July 1, 1863 enlisted as a private in Co. E, 27th Regiment, Georgia Infantry at Fairburn, Campbell County, Georgia. December 31, 1863 received pay. January - February 1864 and March - April 1864 rolls show him present. May 30, 1864 issued clothing. June 1, 1864 wounded in right hand, necessitating amputation above the wrist at Cold Harbor, Virginia. June 2, 1864 admitted to Receiving and Wayside Hospital or General Hospital No. 9 at Richmond, Virginia and sent to Petersburg, Virginia. June 20, 1864 admitted to Receiving and Wayside Hospital or General Hospital No. 9 at Richmond, Virginia. June 22, 1864 transferred to Petersburg, Virginia. June 30, 1864 admitted to Jackson Hospital at Richmond, Virginia with amputated right hand. August 28, 1864 furloughed from Jackson Hospital at Richmond, Virginia for 60 days. December 28, 1864 admitted to Floyd House Hospitals at Macon, Georgia with amputation of right forearm, middle third. January 3, 1865 furloughed.

CREEL, JAMES (JOSEPH) C.: Company E, private. July 1, 1863 enlisted as a private in Co. E, 27th Regiment, Georgia Infantry at Fairburn, Campbell County, Georgia. December 31, 1863 received pay. February 20, 1864 wounded at Olustee, Florida. January - February, 1864 roll shows him absent sick at Lake City, Florida since February 21, 1864. February 21, 1864 - April 30, 1864 detailed as nurse at Lake City, Florida Hospital. March - April 1864 roll shows him detailed as a nurse in hospital at Lake City, Florida since February 21, 1864. August 19, 1864 wounded in the left thigh at Weldon Railroad, Virginia. August 20, 1864 admitted to Jackson Hospital at Richmond, Virginia with a Vulnus Sclopeticum (Gunshot Wound) to the left thigh. September 1864 issued clothing. October 9, 1864 furloughed for 30 days at Richmond, Virginia to Jonesboro, Campbell County, Georgia.

CREEL, JAMES F.: Company E, private. September 9, 1861 enlisted as a private in Co. E, 27th Regiment, Georgia Infantry at Camp Stephens, Griffin, Spalding County, Georgia. February 1862 roll shows him as Provost Marshals Guard at Post Headquarters. April and May 1863 he was on special detail as a pioneer at Fredericksburg, Virginia. June 3, 1863 he was on special detail as a pioneer at Kinston, North Carolina. July 1863, he was on special detail as a pioneer at Topsail Sound, North Carolina. August, September and October 1863 he was on special detail as a pioneer at James Island, South Carolina. November and December 1863 he was on special detail as a pioneer at James Island, South Carolina. December 31, 18963 received pay. January - February 1864 roll shows him present. February 29, 1864 received pay. March - April 1864 roll shows him present. May 30, 1864 issued clothing. September 1864 issued clothing April 26, 1865 surrendered, Greensboro, North Carolina. May 1, 1865 paroled at Greensboro, North Carolina. He was born in Fayette County, Georgia in 1842.

CREEL, LEROY J.: Company E, private. September 9, 1861 enlisted as a private in Co. E, 27th Regiment, Georgia Infantry at Camp Stephens, Griffin, Spalding County, Georgia. December 7, 1861 discharged on account of disability (Anemia) at Camp Pickens near Manassas, Virginia. Description on discharge certificate show he was born in Fayette County, Georgia was 21 years of age, 5 feet 10 1/2 inches high, light complexion, gray eyes, black hair and was a farmer. May 5, 1862 reenlisted as a private in Co. E, 27th Regiment, Georgia Infantry at Fairburn, Campbell County, Georgia. July 7, 1862 admitted to General Hospital, Camp Winder at Richmond, Virginia with Dyspepsia. September 6, 1862 received pay ($22.00). September 29, 1862 returned to duty. September 30, 1862 admitted to Winder Hospital No. 2 at Richmond, Virginia. September 30, 1862 returned to duty. April, May and June 1863 issued clothing. December 31, 1863 received pay. February 20, 1864 wounded, Olustee, Florida. January - February 1864 roll shows he was wounded in action at Olustee, Florida. March 20, 1864 died of wounds at Tallahassee, Florida. March - April 1864 roll shows he died of wounds received at Olustee, Florida.

CROSBY, A. M.: Company I, sergeant. September 10, 1861 elected 3rd sergeant of Co. I, 27th Regiment, Georgia Infantry. November 15, 1861 admitted to General Hospital No. 18, Richmond, Virginia. December 27, 1861 returned to duty. December 1861 roll shows him in hospital at Richmond, Virginia. July 1, 1862 wounded at Malvern Hill, Virginia. August 6, 1862 received pay ($143.00). June 26 and June 27, 1863 issued clothing. October 11, 1862 furloughed from 5th Division, General Hospital Camp Winder at Richmond, Virginia for 30 days. December 31, 1863 received pay. January - February 1864 roll shows him present. February 29, 1864 received pay. March - April 1864 roll shows him present. February 21, 1865 admitted (transferred from Wilmington,

243

North Carolina) to C. S. A. General Hospital No. 3 at Greensboro, North Carolina for Catarrhs. February 23, 1865 sent to other hospital. April 26, 1865, surrendered at Greensboro, North Carolina. May 2, 1865 paroled at Greensboro, North Carolina. He is listed in the personal papers of Major James Gardner as "Men for Gallantry". His Post Office is shown as Holmesville, Georgia. he died march 15, 1908 and is buried in Pleasant Grove Cemetery in Appling County, Georgia

CROSBY, ISHAM: Company I, private. September 10, 1861 enlisted as a private in Co. I, 27th Regiment, Georgia Infantry at Camp Stephens, Griffin, Spalding County, Georgia. December 3, 1861 died of disease at Manassas, Virginia. December 1861 roll indicates he died December 3, 1861 at Manassas, Virginia. December 15, 1862 death benefit claim was filed by Maryan Crosby, mother. He is buried in Memorial Church Cemetery in Appling County, Georgia.

CROSBY, JACOB: Company I, private. September 10, 1861 enlisted as a private in Co. I, 27th Regiment, Georgia Infantry at Camp Stephens, Griffin, Spalding County, Georgia. November 15, 1861 admitted to General Hospital No. 18 at Richmond, Virginia. December 27, 1861 returned to duty. December 1861 roll shows he was in hospital in Richmond, Virginia. March 14, 1862 admitted to Chimborazo Hospital No. 4 at Richmond, Virginia with Typhoid Fever. April 20, 1862 died of Typhoid Fever in Chimborazo Hospital No.1 at Richmond, Virginia. He is most likely buried in Oakwood Cemetery at Richmond Virginia. December 9, 1862 death benefit claim was filed by Stephen Crosby, his father. Jacob was born and raised in Appling County, Georgia.

CROSBY, SILAS A.: Company I, lieutenant. September 10, 1861 enlisted as a private in Co. I, 27th Regiment, Georgia Infantry at Camp Stephens, Griffin, Spalding County, Georgia. December 26, 1861 admitted to Moore Hospital at General Hospital, No. 1, Danville, Virginia with Pneumonia and was sent to Culpeper, Virginia. December 1861 appointed 1st corporal in Co. I, 27th Regiment, Georgia Infantry. December 1861 roll shows him in hospital at Richmond, Virginia. 1861 appointed sergeant in Co. I, 27th Regiment, Georgia Infantry. February 7, 1863 furloughed for 30 days. March 1863 received $10.00 commutation of rations while on furlough. July 31, 1863 elected Jr. 2nd lieutenant in Co. I, 27th Regiment, Georgia Infantry. July 31, 1863 Elected 2nd lieutenant in Co. I, 27th Regiment, Georgia Infantry. April 3, 1863 appears on roll of officers of Gen. A. H. Colquitt's Brigade. January - February and March - April 1864 rolls show him present. March 19, 1865 captured at Bentonville, North Carolina. April 3, 1865 name appears on list of prisoners arriving at New Bern, North Carolina and transferred to Washington, D. C. April 9, 1865 committed to the Old Capitol prison at Washington, D. C. April 9, 1865 sent to Johnson's Island, Ohio. June 18, 1865 released at Johnson's Island, Ohio. Description at time of release was age 20, dark complexion, dark hair, dark eyes, 5 foot 10 inches high. He died December 2, 1911 and is buried in Crosby Chapel Church Cemetery in Appling County, Georgia.

CROSBY, T. A.: Company G, private. He enlisted as a private in Co. G, 27th Regiment, Georgia Infantry. May 14, 1862 admitted to Chimborazo Hospital No. 4, Richmond, Virginia with Diarrhoea.

CROSS, J.: Company I, private. He enlisted as a private in Co. I, 27th Regiment, Georgia Infantry. October 4, 1864 admitted to Receiving and Wayside Hospital or General Hospital No. 9 at Richmond, Virginia. October 6, 1864 transferred to Jackson Hospital at Richmond, Virginia.

CROW, THOMAS J.: Company B, private. February 16, 1864 enlisted as a private in Co. B, 27th Regiment, Georgia Infantry at Decatur, Georgia. January - February and March - April 1864 rolls show he owes for 1 cartridge box, 1 cap box, 1 waist belt, 1 shoulder strap, 1 scabbard and 40 rounds of ammunition lost neglectfully. July 25, 1864 admitted to Jackson Hospital at Richmond, Virginia, with Dysentery. July 1864 issued clothing. August 28, 1864 furloughed for 30 days, destination Greenville, Alabama.

CULVERHOUSE, GEORGE, A. (J. A.): Company C, private. September 10, 1861 enlisted as a private in Co. C, 27th Regiment, Georgia Infantry at Camp Stephens, Griffin, Spalding County, Georgia. September 11, 1862 discharged from service due to Rheumatism from General Hospital No. 19 at Richmond, Virginia. September 1862 received pay ($119.00). Description on discharge certificate shows him 35 years of age, 5 feet 11 inches high, light complexion, brown eyes, light hair and was a farmer.

CUNNINGHAM, DAVID: Company F, private. He enlisted as a private in Co. F, 27th Regiment, Georgia Infantry. November 5, 1861 died of disease at Camp Stephens, Griffin, Spalding County, Georgia. November 1861 roll seems to indicate he died at Camp Pickens near Manassas, Virginia of Pneumonia. December 1861 roll indicates he died in Georgia.

CURTIS (CURTICE), JOHN C.: Company G, private. September 9, 1861 enlisted as a private in Co. G, 27th Regiment, Georgia Infantry at Camp Stephens, Griffin, Spalding County, Georgia. December 1861, January and February 1862 rolls indicate he was left sick in Georgia. November 1862 Hospital muster roll for Medical College Hospital at Atlanta, Georgia shows him present. December 1862 roll shows him absent without leave. He was appointed sergeant Co. G, 27th Regiment, Georgia Infantry. June 26, 1863 issued clothing. October and November 1863 issued clothing. December 31, 1863 received pay. January - February, and March - April 1864 roll shows him present.

CUSTER (KUTLER), WILLIAM: Company I, private. 1861 enlisted as a private in Co. I, 27th Regiment, Georgia Infantry. He was captured date and place not given. He died at Camp Douglas, Illinois.

CUTTS, I. I. J.: Company C, private. He enlisted as a private in Co. C, 27th Regiment, Georgia Infantry. May 31, 1862 wounded and captured at Seven Pines, Virginia. June 4, 1862 admitted to Mill Creek U. S. A. General Hospital near Fort Monroe, Virginia. July 29, 1862 died of wounds at Mill

Creek U. S. A. General Hospital, near Fort Monroe, Virginia.

DANAN, W. F.: Company A, private. He enlisted as a private in Co. A, 27th Regiment, Georgia Infantry. December 11, 1863 wounded at Fort Sumter, Charleston, South Carolina.

DANIEL, JASON: Company K, private. September 9, 1861 enlisted as a private in Co. K, 27th Regiment, Georgia Infantry at Camp Stephens, Griffin, Spalding County, Georgia. December 21, 1861 died White Sulphur Springs, Virginia. March 7, 1862 death benefit claim was filed by Ezekiel Daniel, father. He was a resident of Terrell County, Georgia.

DANIEL, OBEDIAH E. (S): Company C, private. September 1, 1862 enlisted with as a private in Calhoun, Georgia. September 10, 1862 enlisted as a private in Co. C, 27th Regiment, Georgia Infantry at Camp Stephens, Griffin, Spalding County, Georgia. June 16, June 26, June 30, and September 30, 1863 issued clothing. December 31, 1863 received pay. January - February 1864 roll shows him present. February 20, 1864 wounded at Olustee, Florida. February 29, 1864 received pay. March - April 1864 roll shows him present. June 1, 1864 wounded in left arm and hip by mini ball date at Cold Harbor, Virginia. June 2, 1864 admitted to Receiving and Wayside Hospital or General Hospital No. 9 at Richmond, Virginia. June 2, 1864 transferred to and admitted to Jackson Hospital at Richmond, Virginia. June 21, 1864 admitted to Receiving and Wayside Hospital or General Hospital No. 9 at Richmond, Virginia. June 22, 1864 transferred to Jackson Hospital at Richmond, Virginia. July 1, 1864 issued clothing at Jackson Hospital at Richmond, Virginia. July 2, 1864 returned to duty. July 1864 and September 20, 1864 issued clothing. He was born in Upson County, Georgia January 1, 1831.

DARNELL, JAMES H.: Company H, sergeant. September 9, 1861 enlisted as a private in Co. H, 27th Regiment, Georgia Infantry at Camp Stephens, Griffin, Spalding County, Georgia. December 1861 roll shows him left sick in Griffin, Georgia October 31, 1861. April 25, 1862 received pay ($88.06). May 2, 1863 wounded at Chancellorsville, Virginia. December 31, 1863 received pay. January - February 1864 roll shows him present. March - April 1864 roll shows him absent sick with leave. May 25, 1865 surrendered at Thomasville, Georgia. May 25, 1865 paroled at Thomasville, Georgia.

DARNELL, JAMES M.: Company H, private. September 9, 1861 enlisted as a private in Co. H, 27th Regiment, Georgia Infantry at Camp Stephens, Griffin, Spalding County, Georgia. He was appointed sergeant in Co. H, 27th Regiment, Georgia Infantry. March - April 1864 roll shows him absent sick. May 25, 1865 paroled at Thomasville, Georgia. He was born in Morgan County, Georgia June 15, 1838.

DARNELL, JAMES M.: Company E, private. September 9, 1861 enlisted as a private in Co. E, 27th Regiment, Georgia Infantry at Camp Stephens, Griffin, Spalding County, Georgia. November 22, 1861 received pay and discharged. November - December 1861 roll shows him discharged in Richmond, Virginia and as having Hemophthis (Spitting of Blood). November 22, 1861 received pay. December 7, 1861 discharged due to disability, at Richmond, Virginia.

DARNELL, THOMAS M.: Field Staff, Surgeon. September 10, 1861 appointed Surgeon 27th Regiment, Georgia Infantry at Camp Stephens, Griffin, Spalding County, Georgia. November 1861 his name appears on a list of the names of medical officers for the Army of Northern Virginia. December 20, 1861 received pay ($291.60). December 1861, January 1862 and February 1862 rolls show him present at Camp Pinckney, Manassas, Virginia. May 19, 1862 received pay ($324.00). June 19, 1862 resigned as Surgeon on account of old age (63 years old). July 9, 1862 received pay ($345.50).

DARNELL, WILLIAM A.: Company H, private. September 9, 1861 enlisted as a private in Co. H, 27th Regiment, Georgia Infantry at Camp Stephens, Griffin, Spalding County, Georgia. December 24, 1861 admitted to Moore Hospital at General Hospital, No. 1 at Danville, Virginia with Catarrh Fever and was sent to Richmond, Virginia. December 1861 and January 1862 rolls show him in hospital in Richmond, Virginia since December 24, 1861. December 1862 roll shows him absent with leave. January 12, 1863 received pay ($72.00). November 6, 1863 received $19.80 at James Island, South Carolina. December 31, 1863 received pay. January - February 1864 roll shows him present. February 29, 1864 received pay. March - April 1864 roll shows him present. July 1864 issued clothing. January 16, 1865 wounded at Fort Fisher, North Carolina. January 16, 1865 admitted to C. S. A. General Hospital, No. 4 at Wilmington, North Carolina with a Vulnus Sclopeticum (Gunshot Wound) to the left hand and left groin and was sent to General Hospital No. 3, Goldsboro, North Carolina. January 17, 1865 transferred from Wilmington and admitted to C. S. A. General Hospital No. 3, Goldsboro, North Carolina and sent to Pettigrew General Hospital No. 13 at Raleigh, North Carolina with Vulnus Sclopeticum (Gunshot Wound) to the back. January 30, 1865 issued clothing at Pettigrew General Hospital No. 13 at Raleigh, North Carolina. February 9, 1865 furloughed for 60 days. He was a resident of Henry County, Georgia. His Post Office was listed as McDonough, Georgia.

DAVIS, ANDREW J.: Company C, private. March 1862 enlisted as a private in Co. C, 27th Regiment, Georgia Infantry. May 1, 1862 died (before December 1, 1862 died in Griffin, Georgia). February 6, 1863 death benefit claim was filed by Sarah Davis, widow.

DAVIS, CORNELIUS R.: Company H, private. He enlisted as a private in Co. H, 27th Regiment, Georgia Infantry May 18, 1862 admitted General Hospital No. 18, Richmond, Virginia with Measles. July 27, 1862 died in a General Hospital No. 18 at Richmond, Virginia of Typhoid Fever. September 20, 1862 death benefit claim was filed by John M. F. Davis, father.

DAVIS, DARLING A.: Company A, private. February 27, 1862 enlisted as a private in Co. A, 27th Regiment, Georgia Infantry in Schley County, Georgia and was paid a $50.00 bounty. April 21, 1862 died in General Receiving Hospital at Gordonsville, Virginia of Typhoid Fever with $2.00 in his possession. October 29, 1863 death benefit claim was filed by Eliza A. Davis, widow, of Schley County, Georgia.

DAVIS, ELIJAH: Company E, private. September 9, 1861 enlisted as a private in Co. E, 27th Regiment, Georgia Infantry at Camp Stephens, Griffin, Spalding County, Georgia.

DAVIS, J. C.: Company E, private. September 9, 1861 enlisted as a private in Co. E, 27th Regiment, Georgia Infantry at Camp Stephens, Griffin, Spalding County, Georgia.

DAVIS, JOHN A.: Company D, private. January 28, 1865 admitted to C. S. A. General Military Hospital, No. 4 at Wilmington, North Carolina with Rubeola. February 8, 1865 returned to duty. May 1, 1865 paroled at Greensboro, North Carolina. His Post Office is shown as Gainesville, Georgia.

DAVIS, GREEN: Company C, private. September 10, 1861 enlisted as a private in Co. C, 27th Regiment, Georgia Infantry at Camp Stephens, Griffin, Spalding County, Georgia. May 31, 1862 wounded, Seven Pines, Virginia.

DAVIS, JAMES E.: Company I, private. September 10, 1861 enlisted as a private in Co. I, 27th Regiment, Georgia Infantry. December 31, 1861 was in Manassas, Virginia Hospital. April 3, 1862 admitted to General Hospital at Orange Court House, Virginia with Catarrh. (June 5, 1862) April 17, 1862 died at General Receiving Hospital at Gordonsville, Virginia (Richmond, Virginia). He is buried in Hollywood Cemetery at Richmond, Virginia.

DAVIS, M. T.: Company F, private. August 1863 enlisted as a private in Co. F, 27th Regiment, Georgia Infantry. November 1863 died.

DAVIS, MARION: Company E, private. September 9, 1861 enlisted as a private in Co. E, 27th Regiment, Georgia Infantry at Camp Stephens, Griffin, Spalding County, Georgia.

DAVIS, T. S.: Company I, private. May 1, 1865 paroled at Goldsboro, North Carolina (note: came in for parole and was a resident of Wilson County, North Carolina).

DAVIS, WADE: Company D, private. January 182 roll shows he was a regimental teamster from December 23, 1861.

DAVIS, WILLIAM JOSEPH: Company A, private. September 10, 1861 enlisted as a private in Co. A, 27th Regiment, Georgia Infantry at Camp Stephens, Griffin, Spalding County, Georgia. May 14, 1863 admitted to C. S. A. General Hospital at Danville, Virginia with Debilitas. June 15, 1863 issued clothing at 3rd Division, General Hospital, No. 1 at Danville, Virginia. June 16, 1863 returned to duty. October 31, 1863 received pay. January - February 1864 roll shows him present. February 29, 1864 received pay. March 5, 1864 issued clothing at Camp Milton, Florida. March - April 1864 roll shows him present. July 16, 1864 wounded in the right cheek with a mini ball at Colquitt's Salient, Petersburg, Virginia. July 16, 1864 admitted to Jackson Hospital at Richmond, Virginia with a Vulnus Sclopeticum (Gunshot Wound). August 23, 1864 returned to duty. August 23, 1864 received pay ($22.00). April 26, 1865 surrendered, Greensboro, North Carolina. May 1, 1865 paroled at Greensboro, North Carolina.

DEANS (DEAN), W. J. (J. W.): Company C, private. September 10, 1861 enlisted as a private in Co. C, 27th Regiment, Georgia Infantry at Camp Stephens, Griffin, Spalding County, Georgia. June 25, 1862 wounded in the right side near Mechanicville, Virginia. June 25, 1862 admitted to General Hospital at Petersburg, Virginia with a Vulnus Sclopeticum (Gunshot Wound) to the right side. August 11, 1862 returned to duty. May 3, 1863 wounded severely at Chancellorsville, Virginia. May 16, 1863 issued clothing and accoutrements at Confederate States Hospital, Petersburg, Virginia. June 12, 1863 returned to duty. June 30, 1863 and September 30, 1863 issued clothing. December 31, 1863 received pay. January - February and March - April 1864 rolls show him present. June 30, 1864 wounded at Colquitt's Salient, Petersburg, Virginia. June 14, 1864 admitted to Confederate States Hospital at Petersburg, Virginia. June 16, 1864 returned to duty. June 30, 1864 admitted to Jackson Hospital at Richmond, Virginia with a Vulnus Sclopeticum (Gunshot Wound) to the left hip by a mini ball. July 1864 issued clothing. July 10, 1864 returned to duty.

DEARING, THOMAS J.: Company H, private. September 9, 1861 enlisted as a private in Co. H, 27th Regiment, Georgia Infantry at Camp Stephens, Griffin, Spalding County, Georgia. July 7, 1862 received pay ($91.00). September 26, 1862 admitted to General Hospital No. 17 at Richmond, Virginia and transferred to ward E, 1st Division General Hospital Camp Winder at Richmond, Virginia. October 4, 1862 returned to duty from 1st Division, General Hospital, Camp Winder at Richmond, Virginia. October 31, 1862 received pay. November 13, 1862 received pay ($123.50) at Staunton, Virginia. December 31, 1862 roll for General Hospital at Staunton, Virginia shows him present as a guard. May 2, 1863 admitted to Receiving and Wayside Hospital or General Hospital No. 9 at Richmond, Virginia and transferred to Chimborazo Hospital No. 2 at Richmond, Virginia. May 2, 1863 admitted to Chimborazo Hospital No. 2 at Richmond, Virginia with Lumbago. June 11, 1863 returned to duty. December 31, 1863 received pay. January - February 1864 roll shows him present. February 29, 1864 received pay. March - April 1864 shows him present. July 1864 issued clothing.

DECKER, B. F.: Company E, private. December 21, 1862 admitted to General Hospital at Howard's Grove at Richmond, Virginia with Variola. March 31, 1863 returned to duty.

DE LAMAR, WILLIAM W.: Company H, captain. September 9, 1861 elected captain of Co. H, 27th Regiment, Georgia Infantry at Camp Stephens, Griffin, Spalding County, Georgia. December 18, 1861 received pay ($261.66). December 1861, January 1862 and February 1862 rolls show him present at Camp Pickens near Manassas, Virginia. February 8, 1862 received pay ($260.00). March 1, 1862 received pay ($260.00). May 2, 1862 received pay ($260.00). May 31, 1862 killed at Seven Pines, Virginia.

DE LAMAR (DE LEMAR), JAMES: Company H, private. He enlisted as a private in Co. H, 27th Regiment, Georgia Infantry. November 12, 1862 discharged from service at C. S. A. General Hospital at Danville, Virginia for medical reasons.

DELOACH, SOLOMON R.: Company K, private. September 10, 1861 enlisted as a private in Co. K, 27th Regiment, Georgia Infantry at Camp Stephens, Griffin, Spalding County, Georgia. December 1861 roll shows he was left in Georgia sick October 31, 1861. November 22, 1862 received pay ($155.00). February 25, 1863 transferred as a private to Co. C, 3rd Regiment, Georgia Cavalry. He was appointed 5th sergeant of Co. C, 3rd Regiment, Georgia Cavalry. 1864 wounded. December 31, 1864 in Dandridge, Tennessee Hospital, wounded.

DENNING, GEORGE W.: Company A, private. September 10, 1861 enlisted as a private in Co. A, 27th Regiment, Georgia Infantry at Camp Stephens, Griffin, Spalding County, Georgia. December 1861 roll shows him in hospital in Richmond, Virginia since November 25, 1861. January 1862 roll shows he was left in Georgia sick October 31, 1861. September 25, 1862 admitted to C. S. A. General Hospital at Danville, Virginia with Debilitas. October 10, 1862 returned to duty. October 18, 1862 admitted to Receiving and Wayside Hospital or General Hospital No. 9 at Richmond Virginia and was transferred to Camp Winder. October 18(19), 1862 admitted to Division 2, Hospital Camp Winder at Richmond, Virginia with Debilitas. October 31, 1862 returned to duty. December 1862 roll shows he deserted August 25, 1862. November 5, 1862 admitted to Chimborazo Hospital No. 5 at Richmond, Virginia with Chronic Diarrhoea. December 23, 1862 returned to duty. March 4, 1863 admitted to Chimborazo Hospital No. 2, Richmond, Virginia. March 11, 1863 admitted to Receiving and Wayside Hospital or General Hospital No. 9 at Richmond, Virginia and was transferred to Chimborazo Hospital No. 2, Richmond, Virginia. March 11, 1863 admitted to Chimborazo Hospital No. 2 at Richmond, Virginia with Debility. April 15, 1863 returned to duty. April 30, 1863 received pay at hospital. June 1863 issued clothing. December 1863 issued clothing. January - February 1864 roll shows him in confinement at Charleston, South Caroling jail since November 1863. March - April 1864 roll shows him present. July 1864 issued clothing. September 30, 1864 issued clothing. March 19, 1865 admitted to C. S. A. General Hospital, No. 3 at Greensboro, North Carolina and that he was transferred from Raleigh,

North Carolina.

DENNIS, C. T.: Company C, private. February 25, 1864 enlisted as a private in Co. C, 27th Regiment, Georgia Infantry in Macon, Georgia. January - February 1864 and March - April 1864 rolls show him present.

DENNIS, CHARLES J.: Field Staff, major. July 6, 1861 elected captain of the Jackson Guards of Crawford County. September 10, 1861 became captain of Co. C, 27th Georgia Infantry at Camp Stephens, Griffin, Spalding County, Georgia. November 27, 1861 furloughed for 60 days. December 1861 and January 1861 rolls indicate he was on furlough for 60 days. January 31, 1862 rejoined his company. February 13, 1862 placed on recruiting service for 30 days. February 26, 1862 received pay ($60.66). February 1862 roll indicates he was on recruiting service. March 1, 1862 received pay ($130.00). July 12, 1862 received pay ($260.00). August 2, 1862 received pay ($130.00). September 17, 1862 elected major of the 27th Georgia Infantry. October 4, 1862 received pay ($134.66). December 1862 roll indicates he resigned January 3, 1863. January 2, 1863 resigned his commission.

DENNIS, WILLIAM T.: Company K, lieutenant. May 20, 1862 enlisted as a private in Co. K, 27th Georgia Infantry at Richmond, Virginia. August 24, 1862 received $24.60 for commutation of rations for period from June through August 1862. September 1, 1862 received pay for extra duty $10.25. December 1862 roll shows him on extra duty as commissary sergeant. June 1863 issued clothing. October 29 and November 24, 1863 issued clothing. December 31, 1863 received pay. February 26, 1864 received pay. February 26, 1864 appointed sergeant major 27th Georgia Infantry. April 2, 1864 received 20 days furlough by Special Order No. 233 from Camp Milton, Florida to his home in Talbotton, Georgia. He is described on Special order as being 20 years of age, 5 feet high, blue eyes, light hair, fair complexion and by occupation was a merchant. March - April 1864 roll shows him present. September 1, 1864 issued clothing. September 14, 1864 elected 2nd lieutenant of Co. K, 27th Georgia Infantry. He was paroled in Columbus, Georgia in 1865.

DENSON, EDMUND (EDWARD) Y.: Company E, private. August 27, 1861 enlisted in the Bethesda Rifle Guards in Griffin, Spalding County, Georgia. September 9, 1861 enlisted as a private in Co. E, 27th Regiment, Georgia Infantry at Camp Stephens, Griffin, Spalding County, Georgia. December 31, 1861 received pay. April 6, 1862 admitted to General Hospital at Orange Courthouse, Virginia with Debility. April 16, 1862 admitted to C. S. A. General Hospital at Charlottesville, Virginia with Typhoid Fever. May 6, 1862 died of Typhoid Fever at C. S .A. General Hospital at Charlottesville, Virginia (his effects were $5.00). He is buried in the Confederate Cemetery at Charlottesville, Virginia. September 19, 1862 (January 13, 1863) death benefit claim was filed by Martha Ann Denison, his widow. October 13, 1862 death benefit claim was paid $70.46 (#1518). (January 13, 1863 death benefit claim was filed by Martha Denson, his widow. March 17, 1863 death benefit claim was paid $50.00 (#4068). He was a resident of Fayette County, Georgia. Description from his Regiment shows him 22 years of age, blue eyes, black hair, fail complexion, 5 foot 11 1/2 inches tall He was born in Coweta County, Georgia and was a farmer.

DENSON (DUNSON), F.: Company F, private. September 10, 1861 enlisted as a private in Co. F, 27th Regiment, Georgia Infantry at Camp Stephens, Griffin, Spalding County, Georgia. July 17, 1862 died at Richmond, Virginia. He is buried in Hollywood Cemetery at Richmond, Virginia.

DENSON, J. H.: Company E, private. He enlisted as a private in Co. E, 27th Regiment, Georgia Infantry. July 1, 1862 admitted to General Hospital Camp Winder at Richmond, Virginia with Typhoid Fever. July 15, 1862 died of Typhoid Fever at C. S. A. General Hospital, Farmville, Virginia.

DENSON, JOHN: Company E, private. September 9, 1861 enlisted as a private in Co. E, 27th Regiment, Georgia Infantry at Camp Stephens, Griffin, Spalding County, Georgia. 1863 discharged.

DENSON, W. A. J. (W. H. A.): Company E, private. September 9, 1861 enlisted as a private in Co. E, 27th Regiment, Georgia Infantry at Camp Stephens, Griffin, Spalding County, Georgia. May 31, 1862 captured at Seven Pines, Virginia. June 14 1862 name appears on a list of captured prisoners at Fort Monroe, Virginia. Description shows he was born in Georgia, 29 years old, 5 feet 9 inches high, dark brown hair, hazel eyes and fair complexion. August 5, 1862 on list of Prisoners sent from Fort Delaware, Delaware and exchanged at Aikens Landing, Virginia. August 8, 1862 received pay ($91.00). September 9, 1862 received pay ($47.00). September 29, 1862 admitted to General Hospital Camp Winder at Richmond, Virginia with Typhoid Fever. September 29, 1862 returned to duty. September 30, 1862 admitted to 2nd Division, General Hospital Camp Winder at Richmond, Virginia. September 30, 1862 returned to duty. April, May and June 1864 issued clothing. September 20, 1864 issued clothing. October 31, 1863 received pay. February 20, 1864 wounded at Olustee, Florida. January - February 1864 roll shows him absent wounded in action at Olustee, Florida February 20, 1864. February 29, 1864 received pay. March - April 1864 roll shows him present. June 1, 1864 wounded in the breast at Cold Harbor, Virginia. June 2, 1864 admitted to Receiving and Wayside Hospital or General Hospital No. 9 at Richmond, Virginia. June 6, 1864 received pay ($44.00). June 22, 1864 transferred to Jackson Hospital at Richmond, Virginia. June 23, 1864 issued clothing at Jackson Hospital, Richmond, Virginia and returned to duty.

DENT, JAMES P.: Company K, corporal. September 10, 1861 enlisted as a private in Co. K, 27th Regiment, Georgia Infantry at Camp Stephens, Griffin, Spalding County, Georgia. He was appointed corporal. November 16, 1861 admitted to General Hospital, Petersburg, Virginia with Rubeola. December 15, 1861 returned to duty. December 30 received pay. February

12, 1862 discharged due to disability, at Camp Pickens near Manassas, Virginia due to Paralysis Agitans. His discharge certificate on this date shows he was born in Richland, South Carolina, 34 years of age, 6 feet 1 inch high, dark complexion, blue eyes, dark hair and by occupation was a farmer. February 14, 1862 received pay ($18.86). April 28, 1862 enlisted as a private in Co. C, 3rd Regiment, Georgia Cavalry. January 28, 1863 discharged due to disability.

DEWBERRY, THOMAS: Company G, private. September 9, 1861 enlisted as a private in Co. G, 27th Regiment, Georgia Infantry at Camp Stephens, Griffin, Spalding County, Georgia. January 16, 1862 admitted to Moore Hospital, General Hospital No.1, at Danville, Virginia, with Dyspepsia. He was sent to Front Royal, Virginia.

DEWBERRY, WILLIAM T.: Company G, private. September 9, 1861 enlisted as a private in Co. G, 27th Regiment, Georgia Infantry at Camp Stephens, Griffin, Spalding County, Georgia. November 13, 1861 admitted to General Hospital No. 18 at Richmond Virginia. His Post Office is shown as Zebulon, Pike County, Georgia. December 13, 1861 returned to duty. June 30, 1862 admitted to General Hospital No. 18 at Richmond, Virginia with Dysentery. July 31, 1862 returned to duty to Lynchburg, Virginia. October 2, 1862 discharged. October 6, 1862 received pay.

DICKINS, K.: Company B, private. He enlisted as a private in Co. B, 27th Regiment, Georgia Infantry. May 18, 1865 surrendered at Augusta, Georgia and paroled there that date.

DICKSON, WILLIAM F.: Company H, private. September 9, 1861 enlisted as a private in Co. H, 27th Regiment, Georgia Infantry at Camp Stephens, Griffin, Spalding County, Georgia. January 17, 1862 admitted to Moore Hospital at General Hospital, No. 1 at Danville, Virginia with disability then transferred and admitted to hospital at Front Royal, Virginia. January 1862 roll shows him in hospital at Front Royal, Virginia. July 10, 1862 received pay ($91.00). December 31, 1863 received pay. January - February 1864 roll shows him present. March - April 1864 roll shows him present. May 29, 1864 admitted Episcopal Church Hospital at Williamsburg, Virginia with Typhoid Fever. June 3, 1864 died in South Carolina Hospital at Petersburg, Virginia of Typhoid Fever.

DIGGINS, E.: Company K, private. He enlisted as a private in Co. K, 27th Regiment, Georgia Infantry. 1863 died in service leaving $5.00 in effects.

DILBON, JOHN J.: Company I, private. September 10, 1861 enlisted as a private in Co. I, 27th Regiment, Georgia Infantry at Camp Stephens, Griffin, Spalding County, Georgia. November 12, 1861 admitted to General Hospital No. 18 at Richmond, Virginia. December 1861 roll shows him in Richmond, Virginia hospital. January 13, 1862 returned to duty. April 22, 1862 died at Yorktown, Virginia. He is buried in Hollywood Cemetery at Richmond, Virginia. June 23, 1863 death benefit paid $181.76 (#11068). December 15, 1862 death benefit claim was filed by Pricilla Dilbon, mother.

November 19, 1863 death benefit paid $181.76 (#11068R).

DILBON, WILLIAM H.: Company I, private. September 10, 1861 enlisted as a private in Co. I, 27th Regiment, Georgia Infantry at Camp Stephens, Griffin, Spalding County, Georgia. December 20, 1861 admitted to Moore Hospital at General Hospital, No. 1 at Danville, Virginia with Fever. January 1862 roll shows him in Moore Hospital at Manassas (should be Danville), Virginia. May 31, 1862 wounded through the right hip at Seven Pines, Virginia July 7, 1862 received pay ($87.33). June 16 and June 27, 1863 issued clothing. December 31, 1863 received pay. January - February 1864 roll shows him present. February 29, 1864 received pay. March - April 1864 roll shows him present. September 20, 1864 issued clothing. April 26, 1865, surrendered at Greensboro, North Carolina. May 1, 1865 paroled at Greensboro, North Carolina. He was born in Appling County, Georgia April 5, 1842.

DILLARD, WILLIAM S.: Company A, private. November 28, 1862 died of Typhoid Fever at Manassas, Virginia. November 1861 report shows he died November 16, 1861. January 8, 1863 death benefit claim was filed. He was a resident of Schley County, Georgia.

DIXON, J. H.: Company E, private, September 10, 1861 enlisted as a private in Co. E, 27th Regiment, Georgia Infantry at Camp Stephens, Griffin, Spalding County, Georgia. June 5, 1862 died in Richmond, Virginia. He is buried in Hollywood Cemetery at Richmond, Virginia.

DOBSON (DOPSON) (DAPSAN), WILLIAM B.: Company I, private. September 10, 1861 enlisted as a private in Co. C, 27th Regiment, Georgia Infantry at Camp Stephens, Griffin, Spalding County, Georgia. December 18, 1861 admitted to General Hospital at Orange Court House, Virginia with Fever. December 20, 1861 admitted to Moore Hospital at General Hospital, No. 1 at Danville, Virginia and was sent to Orange Court House, Virginia. January 13, 1862 returned to duty to Captain O. A. Lee at Manassas, Virginia. January 25, 1862 admitted to Moore Hospital at General Hospital, No. 1 at Danville, Virginia with Fever and was sent to Warrenton, Virginia. January 27, 1862 admitted to General Hospital at Orange Court House, Virginia with Congestion of the Liver. January 1862 roll shows him in the hospital at Culpepper, Virginia. February 1862 roll shows him on 20 day furlough from February 20 (24), 1962. March 3, 1862 admitted to C. S. A. General Hospital at Farmville, Virginia with Congestion of the Liver (note states that he is on furlough which expires March 25, 1863). He was furloughed March 29, 1862. July 11, 1862 received pay ($36.00). May 19, 1863 received commutation of wages ($7.50) for furlough February 28, 1863 to March 26, 1863. July 11, 1862 paid ($6.00). May 11, June 16 and June 27, 1863 issued clothing. December 31, 1863 received pay. January - February 1864 roll shows him present. February 29, 1864 received pay. March - April 1864 roll shows him present. March 5, 1864 issued clothing at Camp Milton, Florida. June 7, 1864 issued clothing. July 1864 issued clothing. September 20, 1864 issued clothing. April 26, 1865 surrendered at Greensboro, North Carolina. May 1, 1865 paroled at Greensboro, North Carolina. He was born in South Carolina.

DODD, ASA L.: Company E, sergeant. September 9, 1861 elected 3rd sergeant, Co. E, 27th Regiment, Georgia Infantry at Camp Stephens, Griffin, Spalding County, Georgia. December 1861 roll shows he was in the hospital in Richmond, Virginia. January 1862 roll shows him on 30 day furlough from the Department of Henrico, Virginia beginning January 10, 1861. January 10 1862 received pay ($51.83). February 1862 roll show him absent without leave. April 6, 1862 admitted to General Hospital at Orange Courthouse, Virginia with Catarrh. May 7, 1862 admitted to General Hospital Camp Winder at Richmond, Virginia with Diarrhoea. May 16, 1862 Special Order No. 85 has him to report to Camp Winder Hospital for duty as a Nurse. October 10, 1862 received pay ($75.00). October 12, 1862 appears on a list of soldiers employed as nurses for General Hospital Camp Winder at Richmond, Virginia. October 1862 received pay for commutation of rations ($6.60). April, May and June 1863 issued clothing. December 31, 1863 received pay. January - February 1864 roll shows him present. March - April 1864 roll shows him present. June 1, 1864 killed, Cold Harbor, Virginia. He is listed in the personal papers of Major James Gardner as "Men for Gallantry."

DODD, GEORGE M.: Company E, sergeant. September 9, 1861 elected 4th sergeant in Co. E, 27th Regiment, Georgia Infantry at Camp Stephens, Griffin, Spalding County, Georgia. December 1861, January and February 1862 rolls show he was left in Georgia sick October 31, 1861. April 6, 1862 admitted to General Hospital at Orange Court House, Virginia with Catarrh. July 1, 1862 admitted to General Hospital Camp Winder at Richmond, Virginia with Typhoid Fever. July 26, 1862 transferred to Huguenot Springs, Virginia hospital. January 2, 1863 received pay at Richmond, Virginia ($144.75). December 31, 1863 received pay. January - February 1864 roll shows him present. February 29, 1864 received pay. March - April 1864 roll shows him present. September 20, 1864 issued clothing. April 26, 1865 surrendered, Greensboro, North Carolina. May 1, 1865 paroled at Greensboro, North Carolina.

DODD, JOHN D.: Company E, private. February 1, 1864 enlisted as a private in Co. E, 27th Regiment, Georgia Infantry at Fairburn, Campbell County, Georgia. January - February 1864 roll shows him present. February 29, 1864 received pay. March - April 1864 roll shows him present. May 21, 1864 returned to duty from Pettigrew General Hospital No. 13 at Raleigh, North Carolina. July 1864 pension records show he was sent to hospital at Camp Winder at Richmond, Virginia with Diarrhoea. August 16, 1864 admitted to Receiving and Wayside Hospital or General Hospital No. 9 at Richmond Virginia and was transferred to Jackson Hospital at Richmond, Virginia on August 17, 1864. August 17, 1864 admitted to Jackson Hospital at Richmond, Virginia with Chronic Diarrhoea. August 25, 1864 furloughed for 30 days to Jonesboro, Georgia. August 1864 to February

1865 was sent home on sick furlough. March 1865 rejoined command at Charlotte, North Carolina. March 18, 1865 wounded at Bentonville, North Carolina. He was in Greensboro, North Carolina hospital at the close of the war. He was born in Georgia February 13, 1846.

DODD, J. THOMPSON: Company E, private. September 9, 1861 enlisted as a private in Co. E, 27th Regiment, Georgia Infantry at Camp Stephens, Griffin, Spalding County, Georgia. December 11, 1861 discharge papers describe him as follows: born in Fayette County, Georgia, 35 years old, 5 feet 7 inches high, dark complexion, dark eyes, dark hair, occupation was a physician. December 12, 1861 discharged due to disability at Camp Pickens near Manassas, Virginia.

DODSON, JAMES: Company A, private. February 24, 1862 enlisted as a private in Co. A, 27th Regiment, Georgia Infantry in Marion County, Georgia. October 10, 1862 he was on 30 day furlough. November 20, 1862 received bounty pay ($50.00) at Richmond, Virginia. December 1861 roll shows him absent on furlough. September 30, 1862 admitted to 3rd Division, General Hospital Camp Winder at Richmond, Virginia. October 9, 1862 received pay ($69.00) in Richmond, Virginia. October 10, 1862 returned to duty. October 31, 1862 admitted to General Hospital No. 19 at Richmond, Virginia. November 1, 1862 furloughed for 50 days. November 6, 1862 furloughed. June 25, 1863 discharged. July 24, 1863 received $16.63 for commutations for 50 day furlough in Georgia. August 3, 1864 received final pay.

DODSON, RUFUS A.: Company A, sergeant. September 10, 1861 elected 4th sergeant, Co. A, 27th Regiment, Georgia Infantry at Camp Stephens, Griffin, Spalding County, Georgia. February 4, 1863 to March 6, 1863 furloughed to Georgia. March 18, 1863 received $10.00 for commutation of rations while on furlough. May 3, 1863 wounded at Chancellorsville, Virginia in the thigh, face and hand. May 9, 1863 admitted to General Hospital at Howard's Grove at Richmond, Virginia with Vulnus Sclopeticum (Gunshot Wound)s to the thigh, hand and scalp. July 2, 1863 returned to duty. July, August and September 1863 issued clothing. December 31, 1863 received pay. January - February 1864 roll shows him present. February 29, 1864 received pay. March - April 1864 roll shows him present. July 1864 issued clothing. September 30, 1864 issued clothing. April 26, 1865 surrendered at Greensboro, North Carolina. May 1, 1865 paroled at Greensboro, North Carolina.

DODSON, W. C.: Company A, private. September 10, 1861 enlisted as a private in Co. A, 27th Regiment, Georgia Infantry at Camp Stephens, Griffin, Spalding County, Georgia. July 20, 1862 he was elected Jr. 2nd lieutenant of Co. A, 27th Regiment, Georgia Infantry. He died May 5, 1863.

DODSON, WILLIAM C.: Company A, lieutenant. He enlisted as a private in Co. A, 27th Regiment, Georgia Infantry. May 15, 1862 admitted to Chimborazo Hospital No. 2 at Richmond, Virginia with Continua Fever

(Malaria). June 7, 1862 returned to duty. July 20, 1862 elected 2nd lieutenant Co. A, 27th Regiment, Georgia Infantry. October 9, 1862 received pay ($57.00). December 1862 roll at camp near Guinea Station, Virginia shows him present. January 5, 1863 received pay ($320.00). March 5, 1863 died. December 30, 1863 death benefit claim was filed.

DOLAN, PATRICK: Company B, private. He enlisted as a private in Co. B, 27th Regiment, Georgia Infantry. September 7, 1862 received at Aiken's Landing, Virginia as a prisoner. September 21, 1862 exchanged at Fort Monroe, Virginia.

DONALD, JUDGE H.: Company H, private. June 28, 1862 admitted to General Hospital at Howard's Grove, Richmond, Virginia slightly lame. July 1, 1862 wounded in the hip at Malvern Hill, near Richmond, Virginia. July 4, 1862 admitted to General Hospital, Camp Winder at Richmond, Virginia with a Vulnus Sclopeticum (Gunshot Wound) to the hip. July 12, 1862 deserted from General Hospital, Camp Winder at Richmond, Virginia.

DONALDSON, ELI: Company K, private, September 10, 1861 enlisted as a private in Company K, 27th Regiment, Georgia Infantry at Griffin, Spalding County, Georgia. January 16, 1862 admitted to Moore Hospital at General Hospital, No. 1 at Danville, Virginia with Diarrhoea and was sent to Orange Court House, Virginia. January 17, 1862 admitted to General Hospital at Orange Court House, Virginia with Rheumatism. January 1862 and February 1862 rolls show him in the hospital at Orange Court House, Virginia. March 15, 1862 returned to duty. June 21, 1862 died in the hospital in Richmond, Virginia. August 24, 1863 death benefit claim was filed by Irene Donaldson, mother. He was a resident of Talbotton, Talbot County, Georgia.

DONNAN (DONAN), JOHN C.: Company A, private. He enlisted as a private in Co. A, 27th Regiment, Georgia Infantry. February 1862 shows him on extra duty as a Provost Marshal guard at the Headquarters Post. April 23, 1862 died of Pneumonia at South Carolina Hospital, Post Jefferson at Charlottesville, Virginia. November 12, 1862 death benefit claim was filed.

DONNAN, WILLIAM T.: Company A, private. September 10, 1861 enlisted as a private in Co. A, 27th Regiment, Georgia Infantry at Camp Stephens, Griffin, Spalding County, Georgia. December 1861, January 1862 and February 1862 rolls show he was left sick in Georgia October 31, 1861. October 13, 1862 paid furlough bounty for furlough from July 1, 1862 to August 31, 1862 in Richmond, Virginia. December 1862 roll (dated January 31, 1863) shows him absent on sick furlough since January 24, 1863. January 24, 1863 to February 24, 1863 on sick furlough to Georgia (received $1.00 commutation for rations). June, July, August and September 1863 issued clothing. October 31, 1863 received pay. January - February 1864 roll shows him present. March - April 1864 roll shows him present. July 4, 1864 wounded in the left shoulder at Colquitt's

257

Salient, Petersburg, Virginia. July 8, 1864 admitted to Jackson Hospital at Richmond, Virginia with a Vulnus Slopeticum (Gunshot Wound) in the left shoulder by a mini ball. August 1, 1864 died in Jackson Hospital at Richmond, Virginia. August 1, 1864 cemetery records show he died and was buried in Hollywood Cemetery at Richmond, Virginia. Also appears as Dennon and Dowman.

DORSEY, ANDERSON GLENN: Company D, private. July 3, 1861 enlisted as a private in Co. A, 11th Regiment, Georgia Infantry at Atlanta, Georgia. December 18, 1861 appointed 3rd sergeant in Co. A, 11th Regiment, Georgia Infantry. August 30, 1862 wounded at 2nd Manassas, Virginia. October 1, 1863 transferred to Co. D, 27th Regiment, Georgia Infantry. December 1863 issued clothing. February 29, 1864 received pay. March - April 1864 roll shows him present. July 1864 and September 20, 1864 issued clothing. December 8, 1864 discharged from the 27th Regiment. August 18, 1864 elected 2nd lieutenant Co. I, 11th Regiment, Georgia Cavalry. February 2, 1865 appears on roster this date.

DORSEY, ELIAS D.: Company C, private. March 10, 1862 enlisted as private in Co. C, 27th Regiment, Georgia Infantry. May 7, 1862 admitted to General Hospital, Camp Winder at Richmond, Virginia with Typhoid Fever. May 10, 1862 died of Typhoid Fever at C. S. A. General Hospital at Farmville, Virginia. July 19, 1862 death benefit claim was filed by Sarah Dorsey, widow of Crawford County, Georgia. November 4, 1862 death benefit paid $47.73 (#1772).

DORSEY, JASPER N.: Field Staff, lieutenant colonel. August 10, 1861 elected captain of Co. D, 27th Regiment, Georgia Infantry. December 1861, January 1862 and February 1862 rolls show him present at Camp Pickens near Manassas, Virginia. March 3, 1862 received pay ($260.00). March 31, 1862 received pay ($130.00). July 1862 received pay ($520.00). October 2, 1862 received pay ($260.00). December 1862 roll shows him present at camp near Guinea Station, Virginia and that he was the Brigade Inspector General. January 10, 1863 elected lieutenant colonel, 27th Regiment, Georgia Infantry. September 30 1863 roll of officers of Gen A. H. Colquitt's Brigade shows him present. January 31, 1864 received pay. February 5, 1864 dismissed by court martial (cashiered) for drunkenness. April 1, 1864 resigned. May 2, 1864 enlisted in Co. B, 30th Battalion, Georgia Cavalry. June 16, 1864 elected captain of Co I, 11th Regiment, Georgia Cavalry. December 4, 1864 captured at Waynesboro. December 1864 exchanged. December 29, 1864 signed a special requisition for clothing at Springfield, Georgia. Captured by 3rd U. S. Cavalry Division and sent to Provost Marshal, Savannah, Georgia. He died at Gainesville, Georgia December 5, 1883 and is buried there.

DORSEY, JOHN F.: Company D, lieutenant. August 10, 1861 elected Jr. 2nd lieutenant of Hall County Militia Unit. September 10 appointed Jr. 2nd lieutenant, of Co. D, 27th Regiment, Georgia Infantry. December 11, 1861 received pay ($268.66). December 12, 1861 admitted to hospital in

Culpepper, Virginia. December 1861 roll shows him absent in hospital at Culpepper Court House, Virginia. January 1862 roll shows he rejoined his company in January at Camp Pickens near Manassas, Virginia. February 8, 1862 received pay ($325.33). February 1862 roll shows him present in Camp Pickens near Manassas, Virginia and that he rejoined his company on February 28, 1862 from hospital. March 1, 1862 received pay ($160.00). May 6, 1862 admitted to C. S. A. General Hospital at Danville, Virginia with Debility. May 11, 1862 appears on report of sick and wounded in General Hospital at Danville, Virginia. May 18, 1862 returned to duty. June 6, 1862 received pay ($80.00). July 1, 1862 received pay ($80.00). November 15, 1862 furloughed from hospital in Richmond for 30 days. December 1862 roll shows him absent in the hospital since November 1862. January 10, 1863 elected 2nd lieutenant Co. D, 27th Regiment, Georgia Infantry. January 28, 1863 received pay ($160.00). March - April 1864 roll shows him present. June 18, 1864 wounded in the shoulder at Colquitt's Salient, Petersburg, Virginia. June 23, 1864 transferred from General Hospital, Petersburg, Virginia to Augusta, Georgia. June 29, 1864 records from General Hospital, Petersburg, Virginia show he was transferred to Richmond, Virginia. July 1, 1864 admitted to General Hospital No. 4 at Richmond, Virginia with a Vulnus Sclopeticum (Gunshot Wound) in the left shoulder and was furloughed on July 12, 1864. August 14, 1864 Report of Officers of Gen. A. H. Colquitt's Brigade shows he was sent wounded to Richmond on June 18, 1864. August 19, 1864 received pay ($80.00). April 26, 1865 surrendered, Greensboro, North Carolina. May 1, 1865 paroled at Greensboro, North Carolina.

DOUGHERTY (DAUGHERTY), WILLIAM E.: Company A, captain. May 17, 1861 elected 2nd lieutenant of the Georgia Drillers. September 10, 1861 appointed 2nd lieutenant Co. A, 27th Regiment, Georgia Infantry at Camp Stephens, Griffin, Spalding County, Georgia. December 1861 and January 1862 rolls show him present at Camp Pickens near Manassas, Virginia. February 1861 roll shows him absent on recruiting service for 30 days since February 13, 1862. May 10, 1862 received pay ($240.00). June 10, 1862 elected captain Co. A, 27th Regiment, Georgia Infantry. June 30, 1862 received pay ($80.00). July 4, 1862 received pay ($101.66). October 5, 1862 received pay ($130.00). November 11, 1862 admitted to General Hospital No. 16 at Richmond, Virginia. November 23, 1862 furloughed for 30 days from General Hospital No. 16, Richmond, Virginia. December 1862 roll shows him present near Guinea Station, Virginia. December 21, 1862 received pay ($157.33). July 20 (30), 1863 resigned due to disability at Topsail Sound, North Carolina.

DOUGLAS (DOUGLASS), AMOS C.: Company I, private. September 10, 1861 enlisted as a private in Co. I, 27th Regiment, Georgia Infantry at Camp Stephens, Griffin, Spalding County, Georgia. December 1861 roll shows he was left sick in Georgia October 31, 1861. January 1862 roll shows he was on furlough. February 1862 roll show he was absent sick.

July 8, 1862 received pay ($106.33). September 25, 1862 received pay ($122.00). September 25, 1862 to October 25, 1862 on furlough. He was paid $10.00 commutations for the time on furlough. June 16 and June 27, 1863 issued clothing. December 31, 1863 received pay. January - February 1864 roll shows him present. February 29, 1864 received pay. March - April 1864 roll shows him present.

DOUGLAS (DOUGLASS), CHARLES M. Company I, private. September 10, 1861 enlisted as a private in Co. I, 27th Regiment, Georgia Infantry at Camp Stephens, Griffin, Spalding County, Georgia. January and February 1862 rolls show him on extra duty as fatigue at headquarters post. April 25, 1862 admitted to Chimborazo Hospital No. 4 at Richmond, Virginia with Remittent Fever (Malaria). May 27, 1862 sent to Lynchburg, Virginia hospital. May 28, 1862 admitted to General Hospital at Farmville, Virginia with Pneumonia. September 13, 1862 furnished with clothing allowance of $6.00 at C. S. A. General Hospital at Farmville, Virginia. September 17, 1862 sent to General Hospital at Savannah, Georgia. May 2, 1863 wounded at Chancellorsville, Virginia. May 14, 1863 admitted to C. S. A. General Hospital at Danville, Virginia with a Vulnus Sclopeticum (Gunshot Wound). June 4, 1863 issued clothing at 3rd Division General Hospital, No. 1 at Danville, Virginia. June 5, 1863 returned to duty. June 16 and June 27, 1863 issued clothing. October 31, 1863 received pay. December 31, 1863 roll for 1st Georgia Hospital, Charleston, South Carolina shows him present. January 18(27), 1864 died in 1st Georgia Hospital at Charleston, South Carolina. January - February 1864 roll shows he died of disease in hospital in Charleston, South Carolina, January 18, 1864. May 25, 1864 death benefit claim was filed by Delphia Douglas, widow.

DOUGLAS (DOUGLASS), E. R.: Company I, private. He enlisted in Company I, 27th Regiment, Georgia Infantry. November 3, 1863 wounded in the thigh at Fort Sumter, Charleston, South Carolina.

DOWMAN, W. T.: Company A, private. He enlisted in Company A, 27th Regiment, Georgia Infantry.

DOWNING, THOMAS: Company A, private. February 22, 1862 enlisted in Company A, 27th Regiment, Georgia Infantry at Schley County, Georgia. July 10, 1862 received pay ($71.56). September 17, 1862 captured at Sharpsburg, Maryland. September 21, 1862 paroled near Sharpsburg, Maryland. November 20, 1862 paid bounty $50.00 in Richmond, Virginia.

DOWNS, HENRY C.: Company K, corporal. He enlisted as a private in Co. K, 27th Regiment, Georgia Infantry. February 24, 1862 elected 3rd corporal of Co. K, 27th Regiment, Georgia Infantry at Talbotton, Talbot County, Georgia. June 1863 issued clothing. October 22, October 29 and November 24, 1863 issued clothing. March - April 1864 roll shows him absent sent to the Hospital at Charleston, South Carolina. July 1864 issued clothing. September 20, 1864 issued clothing. September 24, 1864 received pay ($26.00). August 18, 1864 wounded through the hips at

Weldon Railroad, Virginia. April 26, 1865 surrendered, Greensboro. May 1, 1865 paroled at Greensboro, North Carolina. He was born in Georgia June 19, 1844. He was 18 years of age at the outset of the war.

DOWNS, JOHN F.: Company K, private. September 10, 1861 enlisted as a private in Co. K, 27th Regiment, Georgia Infantry at Camp Stephens, Griffin, Spalding County, Georgia. January 10, 1864 enlisted as a private in Co. K, 27th Regiment, Georgia Infantry at James Island, South Carolina. March - April 1864 roll shows him present. July 1864 issued clothing. September 20, 1864 issued clothing. April 26, 1865 surrendered, Greensboro, North Carolina. May 1, 1865 paroled at Greensboro, North Carolina.

DOZIER, CHARLES E.: Company K, corporal. September 10, 1861 enlisted as a private in Co. K, 27th Regiment, Georgia Infantry at Camp Stephens, Griffin, Spalding County, Georgia. He was appointed corporal in Co. K, 27th Regiment, Georgia Infantry. May 31, 1862 wounded at Seven Pines, Virginia. June 17, 1862 received pay ($65.00). December 1862 roll shows him absent wounded since May 31, 1862. June 30, 1863 received pay. March - April 1864 roll shows him absent wounded at Seven Pines May 31, 1862. February 1862 roll for Post of Columbus, Georgia (indicated he arrived February 28, 1865).

DOZIER, JAMES A.: Company K, private. September 10, 1861 enlisted as a private in Co. K, 27th Regiment, Georgia Infantry at Camp Stephens, Griffin, Spalding County, Georgia. May 31, 1862 wounded, right thigh bone shattered, resulting in permanent disability, at Seven Pines, Virginia. August 21, 1862 received pay ($91.00). December 1862 roll shows him absent since May 31st. August 31, 1863 received pay in Georgia. March - April 1864 roll shows him absent furloughed to April 30, 1864. November 9, 1864 recommendation for retirement by Medical Examining Board at Augusta, Georgia, on account of wounds at the battle of Seven Pines, Virginia. Described on the Certificate of Disability for Retiring Invalid soldiers he was 26(24) years of age, 5 feet 10(11) inches high, dark complexion, dark eyed, dark hair and by occupation was a teacher. He was born in Columbia County, Georgia March 20, 1840.

DOZIER, SHORT: Company K, private. September 10, 1861 enlisted as a private in Co. K, 27th Regiment, Georgia Infantry at Camp Stephens, Griffin, Spalding County, Georgia.

DRAHER (DREHER), B. F.: Company C, private. He enlisted as a private in Co. C, 27th Regiment, Georgia Infantry.

DRANE, W. H.: Field Staff, Surgeon. March 4, 1862 enlisted as a private in Co. E, 45th Regiment, Georgia Infantry. December 1862 roll shows him present as surgeon at camp near Guinea Station, Virginia. January 6, 1863 appointed Surgeon 27th Regiment, Georgia Infantry. September 30 1863 roll of officers in Gen. A. H. Colquitt's Brigade shows him present. December 31, 1863 to April 30, 1864 roll of Field and Staff at James Island, South Carolina shows him present. October 28, 1864 inspection report of

261

Gen A. H. Colquitt's Brigade at Laurel Hill, Virginia shows him on sick furlough at Howard Station approved by Beauregard.   October 30, 1864 report of Hoke's Division at Dove Hill Farm, Virginia indicates he was on sick furlough from September 13, 1864.   October 17, 1864 admitted to Ocmulgee Hospital, Macon, Georgia with Chronic Hepatitis.   April 26, 1865 surrendered, Greensboro, North Carolina.   May 1, 1865 paroled at Greensboro, North Carolina.   He was a resident of Taylor County, Georgia.

DREHER (DHREAR) (DOHER) (DREHER) (DREER) (DRESHER), B. FRANKLIN.: Company C, private.   September 10, 1861 enlisted as a private in Co. C, 27th Regiment, Georgia Infantry at Camp Stephens, Griffin, Spalding County, Georgia.   December 1861, January 1862 and February 1862 rolls show he was left sick in Georgia October 31, 1861. May 1, 1862 received pay.   May 15, 1862 admitted to General Hospital No. 18 at Richmond, Virginia with Typhoid Fever.   June 10, 1862 transferred to Lynchburg, Virginia hospital.   September 17, 1862 wounded in the head and captured at Sharpsburg, Maryland.   September 30, 1862 paroled by the Provost Marshall of the Army of the Potomac.   October 31, 1862 on roll at General Hospital No. 20 at Richmond, Virginia as present and due $50.00 bounty.   November 1862 received pay.   November 21, 1862 admitted to General Hospital No. 20 at Richmond, Virginia.   December 2, 1862 returned to duty.   December 12, 1862 admitted to Chimborazo Hospital No. 2 at Richmond, Virginia with a Vulnus Sclopeticum (Gunshot Wound) to the head and developed Variola (Small Pox).   He was age 16 at the time and occupation was shown as a tinner.   December 21, 1862 transferred to and admitted to General Hospital, Howard's Grove at Richmond, Virginia with Variola (Small Pox).   December 1862 roll shows he was absent on sick furlough.   March 31, 1863 returned to duty from small pox hospital in Richmond, Virginia.   June 26, June 30 and September 30, 1863 issued clothing.   December 31, 1863 received pay.   January - February 1864 roll shows him absent on sick leave since October 1863.   March - April 1864 roll shows him present.   July 1864 issued clothing.   September 20, 1864 issued clothing.   April 26, 1865 surrendered at Greensboro, North Carolina.   May 1, 1865 paroled at Greensboro, North Carolina.

DRESHER, WINCE: Company C, private.   June 15, 1862 enlisted as a private in Co. C, 27th Regiment, Georgia Infantry.

DREW, JAMES: Company K, private.   September 10, 1861 enlisted as a private in Co. K, 27th Regiment, Georgia Infantry at Camp Stephens, Griffin, Spalding County, Georgia.

DREW, WILLIAM H.: Company K, corporal.   September 10, 1861 elected 4th corporal of Co. K, 27th Regiment, Georgia Infantry at Camp Stephens, Griffin, Spalding County, Georgia.   December 1861, January 1862 and February 1862 rolls show he was left sick in Georgia October 31, 1861.   May 17, 1862 admitted to Chimborazo Hospital No. 2 at Richmond, Virginia with Intermittent Fever and Diarrhoea.   May 22, 1862 transferred to Lynchburg, Virginia Hospital. October 7, 1862 furloughed for 25 days from General Hospital No. 5 (5th Div., General Hospital) Camp Winder at Richmond, Virginia. June, October 22, October 29 and November 24, 1863 issued clothing. October 8, 1862 received pay ($140.69). December 31, 1863 received pay. March - April 1864 roll shows him present. June 3, 1864 wounded in right hand and shoulder at Cold Harbor, Virginia. June 5, 1864 admitted to Receiving and Wayside Hospital or General Hospital No. 9 at Richmond, Virginia and transferred to Jackson Hospital at Richmond, Virginia. June 5, 1864 admitted to Jackson Hospital at Richmond, Virginia with a Vulnus Sclopeticum (Gunshot Wound) by mini ball to right shoulder. August 7, 1864 furloughed for 50 days from Jackson Hospital at Richmond, Virginia. April 8, 1865 Medical Examining Board at Macon, Georgia recommended an extension to his furlough for 30 more days. He was born in Georgia July 5, 1841.

DRIVER, CHARLES: Company H, private. April 8, 1863 enlisted as a private in Co. H, 27th Regiment, Georgia Infantry at Griffin, Georgia. December 31, 1863 received pay. January - February 1864 roll shows him present. February 29, 1864 received pay. March - April 1864 roll shows him present. May 31, 1864, July 1864 and September 20, 1864 issued clothing. January 7, 1865 admitted to C. S. A. General Hospital at Wilmington, North Carolina with Pneumonia. January 15, 1865 transferred to General Hospital No.3 at Goldsboro, North Carolina. January 16, 1865 shown as sent to Pettigrew General Hospital No 13 at Raleigh, North Carolina. February 12, 1865 issued clothing and returned to duty. His Post Office is shown as McDonald (McDonough), Georgia. He was born in Henry County, Georgia March 28, 1839.

DUGGINS, H. J.: Company B, private. He enlisted as a private in Co. B, 27th Regiment, Georgia Infantry.

DUKE (DUKES), A. G.: Company H, private. September 9, 1861 enlisted as a private in Co. H, 27th Regiment, Georgia Infantry at Camp Stephens, Griffin, Spalding County, Georgia. January 1862 roll shows that January 27, 1862 he was at hospital in Front Royal, Virginia. January 27, 1862 admitted to Moore Hospital, General Hospital at Danville, Virginia with Fever (sent to Front Royal, Virginia). June 27, 1862 wounded at Cold Harbor, Virginia. June 29, 1862 admitted to General Hospital No. 18 at Richmond, Virginia with a Vulnus Sclopeticum (Gunshot Wound). June 29 1862 transferred to General Hospital No.18 at Richmond, Virginia. June 30, 1862 transferred to Camp Winder at Richmond, Virginia. July 8, 1862 received pay at Richmond, Virginia ($91.00). September 9, 1862 died of Typhoid Fever at General Hospital Camp Winder at Richmond, Virginia. He is buried in Hollywood Cemetery at Richmond, Virginia.

DUKE, J. M.: Company F, private. August 7, 1861 enlisted as a private in the Taylor Guards at Randolph County, Georgia. September 9, 1861 enlisted as a private in Co. F, 27th Regiment, Georgia Infantry at Camp Stephens, Griffin, Spalding County, Georgia. November 1862 was in Chimborazo Hospital No, 1 at Richmond, Virginia with Diarrhoea. November 13, 1862 furloughed for 35 days from Chimborazo Hospital No. 1 at Richmond, Virginia. December 1862 roll shows him on sick furlough in Georgia. August 25, 1863 issued clothing. July 7, 1863 admitted to Receiving and Wayside Hospital or General Hospital No.9 at Richmond, Virginia. July 8, 1863 transferred to and admitted to Chimborazo Hospital No. 2 at Richmond, Virginia with Debility. July 22, 1863 returned to duty. December 31, 1863 received pay. February 20, 1864 wounded at Olustee, Florida. January - February 1864 roll shows him absent wounded on furlough since February 20, 1864. March -April 1864 roll shows him on wounded furlough. September 20, 1864 issued clothing. October 3, 1864 admitted to Jackson Hospital at Richmond, Virginia with a Vulnus Sclopeticum (Gunshot Wound) (mini ball) to the left arm (right hand). November 11, 1864 issued clothing at Jackson Hospital at Richmond, Virginia. November 13, 1864 returned to duty.

DUKE, JOHN A.: Company F, private. He enlisted as a private in Co. F, 27th Regiment, Georgia Infantry. January 1, 1862 became Regimental Teamster. January 1862 roll shows him as a regimental teamster.

DUKE, JOHN N.: Company F, sergeant. September 9, 1861 enlisted as a private in Co. F, 27th Regiment, Georgia Infantry at Camp Stephens, Griffin, Spalding County, Georgia. September 20, 1862 paroled near Keedysville, Maryland. September 30, 1862 appointed 4th sergeant, Co. F, 27th Regiment, Georgia Infantry. November 5, 1862 admitted to Chimborazo Hospital No. 1 at Richmond, Virginia. August 25, 1863 issued clothing. December 31, 1863 received pay. January - February 1864 roll shows him present. March - April 1864 roll shows him present. June 20, 1864 admitted to Confederate States Hospital at Petersburg, Virginia. June 29, 1864 furloughed. October 3, 1864 admitted to Jackson Hospital at Richmond, Virginia. October 4, 1864 transferred to Jackson Hospital at Richmond, Virginia. February 21, 1865 captured at the battle of Wilmington, North Carolina. March 10 1865 appears on roll of prisoners at Military Prison, Camp Hamilton, Virginia. June 26, 1865 released at Point Lookout, Maryland. He was born in Marion County, Georgia November 4, 1838. He is shown on release documents as a resident of Taylor County, Georgia, fair complexion, light hair, dark gray eyes and 5 foot 10 1/2 inches high.

DUKE, R. W.: Company H, private. September 9, 1861 enlisted as a private in Co. H, 27th Regiment, Georgia Infantry at Camp Stephens, Griffin, Spalding County, Georgia. September 9, 1862 died at Richmond, Virginia. He is buried in Hollywood Cemetery at Richmond, Virginia. He was born in 1838

DUKE, SCOTT: Company H, private. He enlisted as a private in Co. H, 27th Regiment, Georgia Infantry. February 21, 1865 admitted with Rheumatism to C. S. A. General Hospital, No. 3, Greensboro, North Carolina. His Post Office is shown as Snapping Shoals. February 22,

264

1865 returned to duty.

DUKE, SHERROD: Company H, private. He enlisted as a private in Co. H, 27th Regiment, Georgia Infantry.

DUKE (DUKES) THOMAS J.: Company H, sergeant. September 9, 1861 elected 2nd sergeant of Co. H, 27th Regiment, Georgia Infantry at Camp Stephens, Griffin, Spalding County, Georgia. January 1862 and February 1862 rolls show him as acting commissary sergeant at Post Headquarters same on December 18, 1861. July 11, 1862 admitted to C. S. A. General Hospital at Farmville, Virginia with Debilitas. July 21, 1862 returned to duty from C. S. A. General Hospital at Farmville, Virginia. October 27, 1863 to November 17, 1863 was on detached duty. November 25, 1863 received $6.60 for commutation of rations while on detached duty. December 31, 1863 received pay. January - February 1864 roll shows him present. March - April 1864 roll shows him present.

DUKE, THOMAS M.: Company F, corporal. November 9, 1861 admitted to General Hospital No. 18 at Richmond, Virginia. November 25, 1861 returned to duty. May 22, 1862 received pay in Richmond, Virginia ($69.00). June 25, 1862 admitted to Episcopal Church Hospital at Williamsburg, Virginia with Rheumatism. July 1862 roll for South Carolina Hospital at Petersburg, Virginia shows that he died there of Typhoid Fever July 30, 1862.

DULLIN, G. W.: Company F, private. He enlisted as a private in Co. F, 27th Regiment, Georgia Infantry. May 6, 1863 wounded at Chancellorsville, Virginia.

DUNN, H.: Company A, private. He enlisted as a private in Co. A, 27th Regiment, Georgia Infantry. March 30, 1862 admitted to General Hospital No. 21 at Richmond, Virginia with Rheumatism.

DUNN, WASHINGTON l.: Company A, private. September 10, 1861 enlisted as a private in Co. A, 27th Regiment, Georgia Infantry at Camp Stephens, Griffin, Spalding County, Georgia. December 1861 and January 1862 rolls show he was left sick in Georgia October 31, 1861. May 1, 1862 received pay. August 31, 1862 roll shows his name on roll. He was wounded in the right leg. October 6, 1862 admitted to Chimborazo Hospital No. 4 at Richmond, Virginia with Ennorids and placed on furlough from October 9, 1862 to November 14, 1862. October 14, 1862 admitted to Receiving and Wayside Hospital of General Hospital No, 9 at Richmond, Virginia and transferred to General Hospital No. 20 at Richmond, Virginia. October 21, 1862 returned to duty. December 12, 1862 to January 21, 1863 was on furlough and received $13.20 as commutation of rations on April 24, 1863. December 1862 roll shows him absent sick since September 17, 1862. June 1863 issued clothing. December 31, 1863 received pay. January - February 1864 roll shows him present. February 29, 1864 received pay. March - April 1864 roll shows him present. September 30, 1864 clothing was issued to him. March 1865 transferred to Co. B, 46th Regiment, Georgia Infantry. He surrendered in Greensboro, North

Carolina. He was born in Marion County, Georgia. December 29, 1840 died in Atlanta, Georgia February 8, 1926.

DUNNING, W: Company A, private. He enlisted as a private in Co. A, 27th Regiment, Georgia Infantry. December 11, 1863 wounded at Fort Sumter, Charleston, South Carolina.

DURHAM, SAMUEL S.: Company D, private. October 16, 1861 enlisted as a private in Co. C, 27th Regiment, Georgia Infantry at Camp Stephens, Griffin, Spalding County, Georgia. March 31, 1862 admitted to Chimborazo Hospital No. 2 at Richmond, Virginia with Debility. April 30, 1862 received pay and clothing. May 7, 1862 transferred to and admitted to General Hospital at Farmville, Virginia with Diarrhoea. May 23, 1862 returned to duty on the peninsula. August 28, 1862 died in the 14th Georgia Hospital in Richmond (Scottsville?), Virginia. November 27, 1862 death benefit claim was filed by Elizabeth C. Durham, widow age 31 of Hall County, Georgia.

DUSHAND, JAMES: private. He enlisted as a private in the 27th Regiment, Georgia Infantry. November 25, 1864 deserted, took oath of allegiance and was sent to Philadelphia, Pennsylvania.

DWIGHT, SERENO H. (THOMAS J): Company F, private. November 9, 1861 admitted to General Hospital No. 18 at Richmond, Virginia with a note that he was discharged from service December 11, 1861. December 1861 roll shows he was in the hospital in Richmond, Virginia since November 15, 1861. December 11, 1861 discharged from service and paid. January 1862 roll shows him in the hospital in Richmond, Virginia since November 15, 1861. February 1862 roll shows him left in Richmond, Virginia sick on November 28, 1861.

DYER (DYES), JAMES: Company C, private. September 10, 1861 enlisted as a private in Co. C, 27th Regiment, Georgia Infantry at Camp Stephens, Griffin, Spalding County, Georgia. January 1862 and February 1862 rolls show him detailed as fatigue at Headquarters Post. August 14, 1862 received pay ($66.00 as pay from December 31, 1861 to July1, 1862). September 17, 1862 killed at Sharpsburg, Maryland.

DYER (DYES), JOHN: Company C, private. September 10, 1861 enlisted as a private in Co. C, 27th Regiment, Georgia Infantry at Camp Stephens, Griffin, Spalding County, Georgia. January 24, 1862 admitted to Moore Hospital at General Hospital, No. 1, Danville, Virginia with Fever and sent to Front Royal, Virginia. January 1862 roll shows him in the hospital at Front Royal, Virginia since January 22, 1862. May 16, 1862 detailed to Camp Winder Hospital at Richmond, Virginia as ward master. June 1, 1862 captured, Seven Pines, Virginia. June 5, 1862 sent to Fort Delaware, Delaware from Fort Monroe, Virginia(description shows he was born in Georgia, age 41, 5 feet 7 inches high, black hair, grey eyes, and dark complexion). August 5, 1862 exchanged at Aiken's Landing, James River, Virginia. August 21, 1862 received pay ($47.00) at Richmond, Virginia. November 1, 1862 received pay. November - December

266

roll of the 2nd Division, General Hospital Camp Winder at Richmond, Virginia shows him employed as a nurse with two month extra pay due him. December 1862 roll shows him absent on sick furlough. February 28, 1863 roll from General Hospital Camp Winder at Richmond, Virginia shows him detailed as a nurse and that he deserted February 7, 1863. April 19, 1863, June 16, 1863, June 26, 1863, June 30, 1863 and September 30, 1863 issued clothing. April 30, 1864 received pay. January - February 1864 roll shows him absent in arrest in confinement since February 26, 1864. March - April 1864 roll shows he was absent in arrest. July 6, 1864 admitted to Confederate States Hospital at Petersburg, Virginia. July 8, 1864 transferred to Pettigrew Hospital. July 1864 issued clothing. 1864 died in Virginia.

DYER, JOHN: Company B, private. April 20, 1864 enlisted as a private in Co. B, 27th Regiment, Georgia Infantry at Macon, Georgia. March - April 1864 roll shows him absent with leave until May 1, 1864. August 9, 1864 admitted to Receiving and Wayside Hospital or General Hospital No. 9 at Richmond, Virginia. August 10, 1864 transferred to and admitted to Jackson Hospital at Richmond, Virginia with Diarrhoea and Fever. September 1, 1864 furloughed for 30 days. September 1, 1864 received $44.00 in pay. September 3, 1864 sent to Macon, Georgia from Jackson Hospital at Richmond, Virginia. April 26, 1865 surrendered, Greensboro, North Carolina. May 1, 1865 paroled at Greensboro, North Carolina.

DYER (DYES), JACOB: Company H, private. H enlisted as a private in Co. H, 27th Regiment, Georgia Infantry.

EASON, JAMES. Company E, private. September 9, 1861 enlisted as a private in Co. E, 27th Regiment, Georgia Infantry at Camp Stephens, Griffin, Spalding County, Georgia. February 1862 roll shows him absent sick. March 8, 1862 admitted to Chimborazo Hospital No.2 at Richmond, Virginia with Debility. March 22, 1862 returned to duty. May 1, 1862 received pay. October 31, 1862 roll for sick and wounded in General Hospital No. 17 at Richmond, Virginia shows him present. November 19, 1862 admitted to General Hospital No. 17 at Richmond, Virginia. November 29, 1862 returned to duty. December 1, 1862 to January 25, 1863 employed on extra duty at Sparta, Virginia as a shoemaker. April, May and June 1863 issued clothing. November 1863 pension records indicate that he was injured in the back, right hip and left ankle while destroying a railroad between Winchester, Virginia and Harper's Ferry, Virginia. December 31, 1863 received pay. January - February 1864 roll shows him present. March - April 1864 roll shows him present. May 30, 1864 issued clothing. He was born in Georgia January 11, 1830.

EASON, WILLIAM: Company I, private. September 10, 1861 enlisted as a private in Co. I, 27th Regiment, Georgia Infantry at Camp Stephens, Griffin, Spalding County, Georgia. November 15, 1861 admitted to General Hospital No. 18 at Richmond, Virginia with Typhoid Fever. December 21, 1861 died in General Hospital No.18 at Richmond, Virginia. December

1861 roll shows he died November 21, 1861 at Richmond, Virginia. March 25, 1864 death benefit claim was filed.

EASTES, WILLIAM B.: Company E, private. He enlisted as a private in Co. E, 27th Regiment, Georgia Infantry. November 3, 1863 wounded at Fort Sumter, Charleston, South Carolina.

EDDLEMAN (EDLESMANS), E. S.: Company H, private. He enlisted as a private in Co. H, 27th Regiment, Georgia Infantry at Decatur, Georgia. January 30, 1864 received pay. March - April 1864 roll shows him present. July 1864 issued clothing. August 26, 1864 received pay ($41.06) at Petersburg, Virginia.

EDDLEMAN, JUDGE: Company H, private. He enlisted as a private in Co. H, 27th Regiment, Georgia Infantry.

EDISON, ROBERT R.: Company D, private. September 10, 1861 enlisted as a private in Co. D, 27th Regiment, Georgia Infantry at Camp Stephens, Griffin, Spalding County, Georgia. January 6, 1862 he died.

EDWARDS, MICAJAH T.: Company F, private. May 14, 1862 enlisted as a private in Co. F, 27th Regiment, Georgia Infantry at Charles City County, Virginia. August 1, 1862 discharged disability (Chronic Hepatitis - General Debility) near Richmond, Virginia. Certificate of discharge describes him; born in Jones County, Georgia, 27 years old, 6 feet tall, dark complexion, black eyes, dark hair and by profession was a farmer. August 2, 1862 received pay ($28.23).

EDWARDS, WILLIAM POSEY: Field Staff, lieutenant colonel. September 9, 1861 enlisted as a private in Co. F, 27th Regiment, Georgia Infantry at Camp Stephens, Griffin, Spalding County, Georgia. March 30, 1862 admitted to Chimborazo Hospital No. 4, Richmond, Virginia with Bronchitis. April 9, 1862 returned to duty. May 17, 1862 received pay ($80.00). June 27, 1862 elected 2nd lieutenant Co. F 27th Regiment, Georgia Infantry. September 17, 1862 wounded in the right jaw and neck and captured at Sharpsburg, Maryland. October 5, 1862 was at Frederick, Maryland as a prisoner. October 11, 1862 sent from Baltimore, Maryland to Fortress Monroe, Virginia to be passed through the Federal lines. October 12, 1862 delivered to Aiken's Landing, Virginia for exchange. October 13, 1862 exchanged (on list of Confederate Lieutenants exchanged for Federal Lieutenants). December 1862 roll shows him absent since September 17, 1862. January 7, 1863 elected captain of Co. F, 27th Regiment, Georgia Infantry. March 1863 received pay ($80.00). January 1, 1864 name appears on the register of Floyd House and Ocmulgee Hospitals at Macon Georgia with a furlough extension of 30 days. February 20, 1864 wounded, Olustee, Florida. January - February 1864 roll shows him absent wounded since February 20, 1864. March - April 1864 roll shows him absent wounded and commended for marked gallantry and attention to duty at the battle of Olustee, Florida. August 15, 1864 shown on report of Colquitt's Brigade at Petersburg, Virginia as absent wounded and sent to Macon, Georgia. October 30, 1864 he is shown on report of Colquitt's

Brigade at Laurel Hill, Virginia and on Hoke's Division, Dove Hill Farm, Virginia as being in Butler, Georgia on approval of General Beauregard. November 26, 1864 report of Colquitt's Brigade at Laurel Hill, Virginia and Hoke's Division at Dove Hill Farm, Virginia shows him absent by Conscript Bureau at his residence, Macon, Georgia. December 31, 1864 shown on report of Colquitt's Brigade at Camp Whiting, North Carolina and Hoke's Division, Wilmington, North Carolina as absent wounded. He was elected lieutenant colonel. He was a resident of Georgia since January 1852.

EIDISON, ROBERT R.: Company D, private. September 10, 1861 enlisted as a private in Co. D, 27th Regiment, Georgia Infantry at Camp Stephens, Griffin, Spalding County, Georgia. November 6, 1861 admitted to General Hospital at Petersburg, Virginia with Rubeola. November 14, 1861 returned to duty. December 29, 1861 admitted to Moore Hospital at General Hospital No.1 at Danville, Virginia with Fever (sent to hospital at Culpeper, Virginia). December 1861 roll shows he was in the hospital at Culpeper, Virginia. January 6, 1862 died of Measles in hospital at Culpepper, Virginia. January 1862 roll shows he died of disease at Culpepper, Virginia on January 6, 1862. August 29, 1863 death benefit claim was filed by Nancy Eidison, his widow. December 1, 1862 death benefit claim was paid $117.91 (#2050).

ELBERSON, S.: Company D, private. He enlisted as a private in Co. D, 27th Regiment, Georgia Infantry. September 17, 1862 captured at Sharpsburg, Maryland. October 2, 1862 sent for exchange from Fort Delaware, Delaware to Aikens Landing, Virginia. November 10, 1862 exchanged at Aikens Landing, Virginia.

ELDER, JOSIAH H.: Company E, lieutenant. August 9, 1861 elected Jr. 2nd lieutenant the Bethsaida Rifle Guards. September 10, 1861 appointed Jr. 2nd lieutenant of Co. E, 27th Regiment, Georgia Infantry at Camp Stephens, Griffin, Spalding County, Georgia. December 18, 1861 received pay ($173.84). December 1861, January 1862 and February 1862 rolls show him present at Camp Pickens near Manassas, Virginia. March 1, 1862 received pay ($160.00). July 16, 1862 received pay ($160.00). September 17, 1862 wounded in the left ankle at Sharpsburg, Maryland. October 3, 1862 admitted Receiving and Wayside Hospital or General Hospital No. 9 at Richmond, Virginia and transferred to and admitted to Chimborazo Hospital No. 4 at Richmond, Virginia with a Fractured Ankle. October 6, 1862 admitted to Chimborazo Hospital No. 4 at Richmond, Virginia. October 16, 1862 admitted to General Hospital No. 14 at Richmond, Virginia. December 15, 1862 received pay ($240.00). December 1862 roll shows him present at camp near Guinea Station, Virginia. February 10, 1863 resigned his commission with surgeon's certificate of disability. He was a resident of Fayette County, Georgia.

ELLIOTT, ERASMUS: Company D, private. He enlisted as a private in Co. D, 27th Regiment, Georgia Infantry. December 17, 1861 died of

Meningitis at General Hospital, Culpepper, Virginia. December 17, 1861 he died of disease at Camp Pickens near Manassas, Virginia. December 1861 roll shows he died December 17, 1861.

ELLIOTT, J. T.: Company H, private. He enlisted as a private in Co. H, 27th Regiment, Georgia Infantry. May 1861 paroled as a patient at General Hospital No. 11 at Charlotte, North Carolina.

ELLIS, ANDREW: Company D, private. September 10, 1861 enlisted as a private in Co. D, 27th Regiment, Georgia Infantry at Camp Stephens, Griffin, Spalding County, Georgia. July 2, 1862 received pay ($66.00) at Richmond, Virginia. October 9, 1862 received pay ($97.00) at Richmond, Virginia. April, May, June and December 1863 issued clothing. February 29, 1864 received pay. March - April 1864 roll shows him present. July and September 1864 issued clothing. March 20, 1865 captured at Bentonville, North Carolina. April 20, 1865 received at Harts Island, New York from New Bern, North Carolina. June 15, 1865 released at Hart's Island, New York Harbor. Born in Georgia, parole papers show he was a resident of Hall County, Georgia, fair complexion, dark hair, hazel eyes, 5 foot 11 1/2 inches tall.

ELLIS, MADISON J.: Company D, private. September 10, 1861 enlisted as a private in Co. D, 27th Regiment, Georgia Infantry at Camp Stephens, Griffin, Spalding County, Georgia. June 5, 1862 received pay ($69.00) at Richmond, Virginia. April, May, June and December 1863 issued clothing. December 31, 1863 received pay. March - April 1864 roll shows him present. July 1864 issued clothing. August 19, 1864 captured at Weldon Railroad, Virginia, August 24, 1864 arrived at City point as a prisoner. February 18, 1865 paroled at Point Lookout, Maryland. February 20, 1865 received at Cox's Wharf, James River, Virginia for exchange. He was home with Chronic Diarrhoea at the close of the war. He had been a resident of Georgia since 1848.

ELLIS, OSBURN: Company G, private. September 16, 1863 enlisted as a private in Co. G, 27th Regiment, Georgia Infantry at Macon, Georgia. October 30, 1863 issued clothing. November 24, 1863 issued clothing. December 31, 1863 received pay. January - February 1864 roll shows him present. February 29, 1864 received pay. March - April 1864 roll shows him present. September 20, 1864 issued clothing.

ELLIS, WILLIAM C.: Company D, private. September 10, 1861 enlisted as a private in Co. D, 27th Regiment, Georgia Infantry at Camp Stephens, Griffin, Spalding County, Georgia. December 1861 roll shows he was left sick in Georgia October 31, 1861. January (December) 15 (13), 1861 (conflicting information in service record) died of Pulmonary Apoplexy at Camp Pickens near Manassas, Virginia. May 29, 1862 death benefit claim was filed by Dorcas Ellis, widow.

ELLISON, SAMUEL H.: Company K, private. September 10, 1861 enlisted as a private in Co. K, 27th Regiment, Georgia Infantry at Camp Stephens, Griffin, Spalding County, Georgia. January 1862 and February

1862 rolls show he was detailed as Regimental Postman. April 15, 1862 admitted to Chimborazo Hospital No. 5 at Richmond, Virginia with Intermittent Fever (Malaria). May 1, 1862 returned to duty. December 1862 roll shows he was furloughed for 80 days beginning July 1862. October 29, 1863 and November 24, 1863 issued clothing. December 31, 1863 received pay. March - April 1864 roll shows him present. July 1864 issued clothing. August 9, 1864 admitted to Jackson Hospital at Richmond, Virginia with Acute Colitis (another record states Solis Ictus (Sun Stroke). August 22, 1864 issued clothing. September 5, 1864 was furloughed for 30 days from Jackson Hospital, Richmond, Virginia. September 5, 1864 received pay ($71.13). September 10, 1864 sent from Jackson Hospital at Richmond, Virginia to Columbus, Georgia.

ELLSITON, JAMES R.: Company F, private. 1861 enlisted as a private in Co. F, 27th Regiment, Georgia Infantry at Camp Stephens, Griffin, Spalding County, Georgia. December 1861, January 1862 and February 1862 rolls show he was left sick in Georgia October 31, 1861.

ELROD (ELBOD), JASPER: Company D, private. He enlisted as a private in Co. D, 27th Regiment, Georgia Infantry.

EMBRY (EMBLY), GEORGE T. (E. T.): Field and Staff, Chaplin. September 9, 1861 enlisted as a private in Company H, 27th Georgia Infantry at Camp Stephens, Griffin, Spalding County, Georgia. May 31, 1862 captured Seven Pines, Virginia. June 5, 1862 sent to Fort Delaware, Delaware from Fort Monroe, Virginia. August 5, 1862 exchanged at Aiken's Landing, Virginia. Described on Prisoner record; born in Georgia, 29 years of age, 5 feet 11 inches high, dark brown hair, black eyes, dark complexion. August 7, 1862 admitted to Chimborazo Hospital No. 2 at Richmond, Virginia with Debility. December 1862 roll shows him detailed as Provost Guard and Division headquarters. May 25, 1863 appointed Chaplin 27th Georgia Infantry at James Island, Charleston, South Carolina. September 30, 1863 roll of Colquitt's Brigade officers shows him present. April 30, 1864 roll shows him present. October 31, 1864 resigned to accept a pastoral charge in Georgia. November 8, 1864 received pay ($160.0). His home is stated as McDonough, Henry County, Georgia.

ERNEST, ANDREW A.: Company D, private. August 26, 1861 enlisted as a private in the Hall County Company. September 10, 1861 enlisted as a private in Co. D, 27th Regiment, Georgia Infantry at Camp Stephens, Griffin, Spalding County, Georgia. October 28, 1861 died of disease at Camp Stephens, Griffin, Spalding County, Georgia. December 1861 roll shows he died at Camp Stephens, Georgia of disease on October 28, 1861. June 10, 1863 death benefit claim was filed by Stephen S. Earnest, his father. He was a resident of Hall County, Georgia.

ESTES, STEPHEN J.: Company E, private. He enlisted as a private in Co. E, 27th Regiment, Georgia Infantry. May 1, 1865 paroled at Greensboro, North Carolina.

ESTES, W. B.: Company E, private. July 1, 1863 enlisted as a private in Co. E, 27th Regiment, Georgia Infantry at Fairburn, Campbell County, Georgia. December 31, 1863 received pay. January - February 1864 roll shows him absent sick at Valdosta, Georgia since February 16, 1864. February 29, 1864 received pay. March - April 1864 roll shows him present. June 20, 1864 admitted to Receiving and Wayside Hospital or General Hospital No. 9 at Richmond, Virginia and appears on a register there June 22, 1864. July 5, 1864 and August 1864 issued clothing.

EUBANKS, JOHN H.: Company C, lieutenant. September 10, 1861 enlisted as a private in Co. C, 27th Regiment, Georgia Infantry at Camp Stephens, Griffin, Spalding County, Georgia. He was appointed corporal Co. C, 27th Regiment, Georgia Infantry. He was appointed sergeant Co. C, 27th Regiment, Georgia Infantry. He was elected lieutenant Co. C, 27th Regiment, Georgia Infantry. June 2, 1862 admitted to General Hospital Camp Winder at Richmond, Virginia with Typhoid Fever. June 14, 1862 died of Typhoid Fever, in C. S. A. General Hospital at Farmville, Virginia. August 12, 1862 death benefit claim was filed by James D. Eubanks, his father. November 5, 1862 claim paid for $281.93 (#1768). He was a resident of Crawford County, Georgia.

EUBANKS, JOSIAH D.: Company C, sergeant. September 10, 1861 enlisted as a private in Co. C, 27th Regiment, Georgia Infantry at Camp Stephens, Griffin, Spalding County, Georgia. He was appointed corporal Co. C, 27th Regiment, Georgia Infantry. He was appointed sergeant Co. C, 27th Regiment. May 8, 1862 died in Alabama Hospital at Richmond, Virginia. August 12, 1862 death benefit claim was filed by James D. Eubanks, his father. November 5, 1862 claim paid $147.53 (#1768). He was a resident of Crawford County, Georgia.

EVANS, GREEN K. C.: Company D, private. September 23, 1861 enlisted as a private in Co. D, 27th Regiment, Georgia Infantry at Camp Stephens, Griffin, Spalding County, Georgia. July 3, 1862 received pay ($66.00) at Richmond, Virginia. April 1, 1863 received pay for commutation of rations. April, May June and December 1863 issued clothing. February 29, 1864 received pay. March - April 1864 roll shows him present. July 1864 issued clothing. April 26, 1865 surrendered Greensboro, North Carolina. He was born in Lumpkin County, Georgia July 4, 1833. May 1, 1865 paroled at Greensboro, North Carolina.

EVANS, ROBERT C.: Company H, lieutenant. September 9, 1861 elected 2nd lieutenant of Co. H, 27th Regiment, Georgia Infantry at Camp Stephens, Griffin, Spalding County, Georgia. December 24, 1861 admitted to Moore Hospital at General Hospital, Danville, Virginia with Pneumonia and was sent to Richmond, Virginia. December 1861 roll shows him absent on furlough from December 24, 1861 to January 24, 1862. January 1862 roll shows him present at Camp Pickens near Manassas, Virginia. February 1862 roll shows him present and on extra duty from February 21, 1862 as Fatigue at Post Headquarters. June 15, 1862 elected 1st lieutenant Co. H, 27th Regiment, Georgia Infantry. March 1, 1862 received pay

($160.00). April 3, 1862 received pay ($80.00). April 25, 1862 received pay ($80.00). June 18, 1862 received pay ($80.00). July 1, 1862 received pay ($80.00). August 16, 1862 received pay ($90.00). September 27, 1862 received pay ($180.00) at Richmond, Virginia. December 1862 roll shows him present at camp near Guinea Station, Virginia. January 1863 received pay ($90.00). October 8, 1863 granted leave from James Island, South Carolina on Surgeons certificate of disability. September 30, 1863 roster of officers of Colquitt's Brigade shows him present. January - February 1864 roll shows him absent sick in hospital at Tallahassee, Florida. April 8, 1864 placed on leave of absence. March - April 1864 roll shows him absent with leave sick. June 15(18), 1864 died at Petersburg, Virginia.

EVANS, STANSBURY B.: Company B, private. February 18, 1864 enlisted as a private in Co. B, 27th Regiment, Georgia Infantry at Decatur, Georgia. January - February 1864 and March - April 1864 rolls show him present. June 1, 1864 wounded in the left shoulder at Cold Harbor, Virginia. June 2, 1864 admitted to Receiving and Wayside Hospital or General Hospital No. 9 at Richmond, Virginia with a Vulnus Sclopeticum (Gunshot Wound) to the left shoulder transferred to and admitted to Jackson Hospital at Richmond, Virginia. June 20, 1864 admitted to Receiving and Wayside Hospital or General Hospital No. 9, Richmond, Virginia June 22, 1862 transferred to and admitted to Jackson Hospital, Richmond, Virginia. June 23, 1864 died, in Division 3, Jackson Hospital at Richmond, Virginia of Chronic Diarrhoea and Hemorrhoids. He is buried in Hollywood Cemetery at Richmond, Virginia.

EVERETT, A.: Company C, private. He enlisted as a private in Co. C, 27th Regiment, Georgia Infantry. October 15, 1862 admitted to Division 5 Hospital Camp Winder Richmond, Virginia. January 4, 1863 transferred from Division 5 Hospital Camp Winder at Richmond, Virginia and admitted to Hospital, Howard's Grove at Richmond, Virginia. January 13, 1863 died of Variola at General Hospital, Howard's Grove at Richmond, Virginia. Effects were $15.25.

EWING, R. D.: Company E, private. September 9, 1861 enlisted as a private in Co. E, 27th Regiment, Georgia Infantry at Camp Stephens, Griffin, Spalding County, Georgia.

EWING, WILLIAM S.: Company E, private. September 9, 1861 enlisted as a private in Co. E, 27th Regiment, Georgia Infantry at Camp Stephens, Griffin, Spalding County, Georgia. July 23, 1862 appears on the register of C. S. A. General Hospital, Danville, Virginia with Typhoid Fever. July 30, 1862 returned to duty. April, May and June 1863 issued clothing. He received commutation of rations $5.94 for period August 6, 1863 to August 24, 1863. December 31, 1863 received pay. January - February 1864 roll shows him present. February 29, 1864 received pay. March - April 1864 roll shows him present. June 29, 1864 admitted to Receiving and Wayside Hospital or General Hospital No. 9 at Richmond, Virginia and was transferred to Jackson Hospital, Richmond, Virginia. June 30, 1864 admitted to Jackson Hospital at Richmond, Virginia with Acute Diarrhoea. July 9, 1864 issued clothing at Jackson Hospital at Richmond, Virginia. July 10, 1864 returned to duty. September 20, 1864 issued clothing. April 26, 1865 surrendered, Greensboro, North Carolina. May 1, 1865 paroled at Greensboro, North Carolina.

EZELL, WILLIAM: Company G, private. September 9, 1861 enlisted as a private in Co. G, 27th Regiment, Georgia Infantry at Camp Stephens, Griffin, Spalding County, Georgia. November 6, 1861 died of Pneumonia at Camp Stephens, Griffin, Spalding County, Georgia. December 1861 roll shows he died November 6, 1861 at Camp Stephens, Georgia of disease. January 28, 1862 death benefit claim was filed by Rachael L. Ezell, his widow. February 14, 1862 death benefit claim was paid $46.63 (#220).

FARMER, J. O.: Company D, private. September 10, 1861 enlisted as a private in Co. D, 27th Regiment, Georgia Infantry at Camp Stephens, Griffin, Spalding County, Georgia. December 20, 1862 received pay ($163.00). December 1862 roll shows him present and detailed as a teamster. April, May, June and December 1863 issued clothing. November 24, 1863 to November 30, 1864 detailed as a teamster at James Island, South Carolina. February 18, 1864 to February 29, 1864 detailed on extra duty as a teamster. February 29, 1864 received pay. March - April 1864 roll, last on file, shows him present and detailed as a teamster. May 1, 1864 to May 31, 1864 detailed on extra duty as a teamster. July 1864 and September 20, 1864 issued clothing. September 20, 1864 received extra pay at Petersburg, Virginia of $.25 per day from February 18, 1864 to June 9, 1864 for extra detail as a teamster. April 26, 1865 pension records show he surrendered, Greensboro, North Carolina. He was born in Pickens County, Georgia February 2, 1834.

FARMER, S. D.: Company D, private. September 23, 1862 enlisted as a private in Co. D, 27th Regiment, Georgia Infantry in Virginia. April, May, June and December 1863 issued clothing. February 29, 1864 received pay. March - April 1864 roll shows him present. July 25, 1864 admitted to Jackson Hospital, Richmond, Virginia with Acute Diarrhoea. July 30, 1864 issued clothing. August 10, 1864 returned to duty. September 20, 1864 issued clothing. April 26, 1865 surrendered, Greensboro, North Carolina. May 1, 1865 paroled at Greensboro, North Carolina. He was born February 6, 1840.

FERGUSON, BENJAMIN FRANKLIN: Company H, private. September 9, 1861 enlisted as a private in Co. H, 27th Regiment, Georgia Infantry at Camp Stephens, Griffin, Spalding County, Georgia. January 27, 1862 admitted to Moore Hospital at General Hospital, No. 1, Danville, Virginia with Fever and was sent to the Hospital at Front Royal, Virginia. January 1862 roll shows he was admitted to hospital at Front Royal, Virginia January 27, 1862. March 14, 1862 admitted to Chimborazo Hospital No. 4 at Richmond, Virginia with Rheumatism. April 24, 1864 returned to duty. June 30, 1862 roll of General Hospital No. 13 at Richmond, Virginia shows him there, states his Post Office as Sandy Ridge, Henry County, Georgia, also was furloughed in September 1862. October 26, 1862 returned to duty. November 5, 1862 received pay ($94.00) at Atlanta, Georgia. December 1862 roll shows him absent without leave. December 31, 1863 received pay. January - February 1864 roll shows him present. February 29, 1864 received pay. March - April 1864 roll shows him present on extra duty as a teamster. May1, 1864 to May 31, 1864 detailed as a teamster. July 1864 issued clothing. September 20, 1864 received extra pay 0f $.25 per day for duty as a teamster from March 1, 1864 to June 9, 1864. April 3, 1865 captured at Petersburg, Virginia. April 7, 1865 received at Hart's Island, New York Harbor. June 15, 1865 released at Hart's Island, New York Harbor. He is shown as a resident of Henry County, Georgia, fair complexion, black hair, black eyes and 5 foot 10 inches high.

FEUTRELL, SAMUEL C.: Company C, lieutenant. September 10, 1861 enlisted as a private in Co. C, 27th Regiment, Georgia Infantry at Camp Stephens, Griffin, Spalding County, Georgia. June 30, 1863 issued clothing. July 24, 1863 received $10.00 for commutation of rations for 30 days from January 17, 1863 to February 17, 1863 furlough. September 30, 1863 issued clothing. December 31, 1863 received pay. January - February 1864 roll shows him present. February 29, 1864 received pay. March - April 1864 roll shows him present. May 30, 1864 and July 1864 issued clothing. September 14, 1864 elected as 2nd lieutenant Co. C, 27th Regiment, Georgia Infantry. May 1, 1865 paroled at Greensboro, North Carolina.

FIELDS, JAMES: Company I, private. September 10, 1861 enlisted as a private in Co. I, 27th Regiment, Georgia Infantry at Camp Stephens, Griffin, Spalding County, Georgia. May 14, 1862 died at Richmond, Virginia. He is buried in Hollywood Cemetery at Richmond, Virginia.

FIELDS, JAMES T.: Company H, private. March 20, 1864 enlisted as a private in Co. H, 27th Regiment, Georgia Infantry in Macon, Georgia. March - April 1864 roll shows him present. July 1864 and September 20, 1864 issued clothing. April 26, 1865 surrendered Greensboro, North Carolina. May 1, 1865 paroled at Greensboro, North Carolina.

FITZPATRICK, JAMES G.: Company C, private. September 10, 1861 enlisted as a private in Co. C, 27th Regiment, Georgia Infantry at Camp Stephens, Griffin, Spalding County, Georgia. April 10, 1862 admitted to Chimborazo Hospital No. 5 at Richmond, Virginia with Malaria. May 9, 1862 appears on the register of Chimborazo Hospital No. 5 at Richmond, Virginia with note. He was transferred to Lynchburg, Virginia. June 30 - September 30, 1863 issued clothing. December 31, 1863 received pay. February 20, 1864 wounded at Olustee, Florida. January - February 1864 and March - April 1864 rolls show him absent wounded at Olustee Florida. His is shown as 25 years of age. May 20 1864 shown on roster of Floyd House Hospital at Macon Georgia with note: resection of radius and just recovering from Febrinter. His Post Office is shown as Knoxville, Georgia

275

and placed on 60 day furlough.   July 18, 1864 shown on roster of Floyd House Hospital at Macon Georgia with note: Vulnus Sclopeticum (Gunshot Wound) causing resection of middle third radius.   He was a resident of Crawford County, Georgia.   September 21, 1864 shown on roster of Floyd House Hospital at Macon Georgia with note: Vulnus Sclopeticum (Gunshot Wound) right forearm fracturing radius which was resected about 2 inches. He applied for retirement.

FIVEASH, MATTHEW: Company I, private.   September 17, 1863 enlisted as a private in Co. I, 27th Regiment, Georgia Infantry at Macon, Georgia.   December 31, 1863 received pay.   January - February 1864 roll shows him present.   February 29, 1864 received pay.   March 29, 1864 through April 30, 1864 he was absent, sick.   March - April 1864 roll show him absent sick since March 29, 1864.   July 1864 issued clothing. January 6, 1865 admitted to C. S. A. General Military Hospital, No. 4, Wilmington, North Carolina with Pneumonia.   January 15, 1865 he is on a list at General Hospital No. 4 at Wilmington, North Carolina as transferred to General Hospital No. 3 at Goldsboro, North Carolina with convulsions from Pneumonia.   January 17, 1865 admitted to Pettigrew General Hospital No. 13 at Raleigh, North Carolina with Pneumonia.   March 19, 1865 transferred to Georgia Hospital No. 12 at Charlotte, North Carolina.

FLOURNOY, H.: Company D, private.   He enlisted as a private in Co. D, 27th Regiment, Georgia Infantry.   August 18(23), 1864 sent from Jackson Hospital at Richmond, Virginia to Athens, Georgia.

FLOURNOY, W. H.: Company A, private.   He enlisted as a private in Co. A, 27th Regiment, Georgia Infantry.   May 16, 1862 died in South Carolina Hospital, Post Jefferson, Charlottesville, Virginia of Pneumonia (his effects were; 1 watch).

FLOYD, DANIEL: Company K, private.   He enlisted as a private in Co. K, 27th Regiment, Georgia Infantry.   July 3, 1864 captured at Marietta, Georgia.   July 14, 1864 received at Military Prison, Louisville, Kentucky. July 16, 1864 sent to Camp Douglas Prison.

FLOYD, JAMES D.: Company D, private.   September 10, 1861 enlisted as a private in Co. D, 27th Regiment, Georgia Infantry at Camp Stephens, Griffin, Spalding County, Georgia.   November 1, 1861 died of Typhoid Fever at Camp Stephens, Griffin, Spalding County, Georgia.   December 1861 roll shows his death on November 1, 1861.   July 10, 1862 death benefit claim was filed by Malinda Floyd, his widow.

FLOYD, JAMES G.: Company H, private. August13, 1862 enlisted as a private in Co. H, 27th Regiment, Georgia Infantry at Richmond, Virginia. December 19, 1862 admitted to C. S. A. General Hospital at Danville, Virginia. January 15, 1863 and February 10, 1863 issued clothing. February 13, 1863 returned to duty.   June 10, 1863 admitted to Chimborazo Hospital No. 2 at Richmond, Virginia with Debility.   December 12, 1862 admitted to Chimborazo Hospital No. 2 at Richmond, Virginia with Pneumonia.   July 9, 1863 admitted to Receiving and Wayside Hospital or General Hospital

No. 9 at Richmond, Virginia. December 1862 roll shows him absent without leave. July 10, 1863 transferred to Chimborazo Hospital No. 2 at Richmond, Virginia. July 22, 1863 returned to duty. November 18, 1863 received pay ($22.00). December 31, 1863 received pay. January - February 1864 shows him present. January 31, 1864 record shows he transferred to Co. E, 22nd Battery, Georgia Heavy Artillery.

FLURRY, J. H.: Company A, private. He enlisted as a private in Co. A, 27th Regiment, Georgia Infantry November 17, 1862 admitted to Division 3, Camp Winder Richmond, Virginia. December 8, 1862 died of Variola in General Hospital, Camp Winder at Richmond, Virginia.

FLURRY, JOHN M.: Company A, private. February 27, 1862 enlisted as a private in Co. A, 27th Regiment, Georgia Infantry in Schley County, Georgia. November 20, 1862 received bounty pay $50.00 at Richmond, Virginia. December 4, 1862 admitted to Chimborazo Hospital No. 5 at Richmond with Chronic Rheumatism. December 19, 1862 transferred to and admitted to C. S. A. General Hospital at Danville, Virginia with Rheumatism. January 17, 1863 returned to duty. May 2, 1863 wounded in left arm at Chancellorsville, Virginia. May 6, 1863 admitted to Receiving and Wayside Hospital or General Hospital No. 9 at Richmond, Virginia and transferred to and admitted to Chimborazo Hospital No. 4 at Richmond, Virginia. May 9, 1863 admitted to Chimborazo Hospital No. 2 at Richmond, Virginia with a Vulnus Sclopeticum (Gunshot Wound) in the left arm (mini ball). May 30, July, August, September 1863 issued clothing. December 31, 1863 received pay. January - February 1864, roll shows him present. February 29, 1864 received pay. March - April 1864 roll shows him present. He was born October 13, 1823.

FLURRY, ROBERT D.: Company A, private. February 27, 1862 enlisted as a private in Co. A, 27th Regiment, Georgia Infantry in Schley County, Georgia. May 31, 1862 wounded in hip, Seven Pines, Virginia. November 20, 1862 received bounty pay $50.00 at Richmond, Virginia. December 30, 1862 received pay ($90.20) at Richmond, Virginia. July, August, September 1863 issued clothing. September 28, 1863 received pay ($22.00). December 31, 1863 received pay. January - February 1864, roll shows him present. February 29, 1864 received pay. March - April 1864 roll shows him present. July 1864 issued clothing. April 26, 1865 surrendered, Greensboro, North Carolina. May 1, 1865 paroled at Greensboro, North Carolina.

FLURRY, THOMAS H.: Company A, private. September 10, 1861 enlisted as a private in Co. A, 27th Regiment, Georgia Infantry at Camp Stephens, Griffin, Spalding County, Georgia. December 18, 1861 admitted to Moore hospital at General Hospital, No. 1, Danville, Virginia with Pneumonia and was transferred to and admitted to General Hospital, Orange Court House, Virginia with Fever. January 9, 1862 returned to duty at Manassas, Virginia. June 1, 1862 received pay. August 18, 1862 admitted to General Hospital No. 13 at Richmond, Virginia with Diarrhoea (Post Office shown as Poindexter, Georgia). August 30, 1862 returned to duty. October 31, 1862 name appears on muster roll of 3rd Division, General Hospital Camp Winder at Richmond, Virginia.

FLURRY, WILLIAM H.: Company A, private. March 3, 1862 enlisted as a private in Co. A, 27th Regiment, Georgia Infantry in Schley County, Georgia. November 20, 1862 received bounty pay $50.00 at Richmond, Virginia. December 27, 1862 death benefit claim was filed by his father, Edward Flurry.

FORBS, J. H.: Company C. private. He enlisted as a private in Co. C, 27th Regiment, Georgia Infantry. August 7, 1862 admitted to Chimborazo Hospital No. 5 at Richmond, Virginia with Bronchitis. November 2, 1862 transferred to Danville, Virginia.

FORD, J. S. T.: Company G, private. He enlisted as a private in Co. G, 27th Regiment, Georgia Infantry June 16, 1863 to July 16, 1863 on furlough for 30 days and was paid $9.90 for commutation of rations. October 30, 1863 and November 24, 1863 issued clothing. December 11, 1863 killed at Fort Sumter, Charleston, South Carolina.

FORRESTER, JOEL ROBERT: Company B, private. April 15, 1864 enlisted as a private in Co. B, 27th Regiment, Georgia Infantry at Camp Milton, Florida. March - April 1864 roll shows him present. July 1864 issued clothing. April 26, 1865 surrendered, Greensboro, North Carolina. May 1, 1865 paroled at Greensboro, North Carolina.

FORRESTER, JOHN WESLEY: Company B, lieutenant. September 10, 1861 enlisted as a private in Co. B, 27th Regiment, Georgia Infantry at Camp Stephens, Griffin, Spalding County, Georgia. He was elected 3rd sergeant of Co. B, 27th Regiment, Georgia Infantry. January 9, 1862 sent to the hospital in Richmond, Virginia. January 1862 and February 1862 rolls show he was sent to the hospital in Richmond, Virginia on January 9, 1862. July 2, 1862 admitted to C. S. A. General Hospital at Danville, Virginia. July 16, 1862 returned to duty. July 25, 1862 elected Jr. 2nd lieutenant Co. B, 27th Regiment, Georgia Infantry. August 24, 1862 elected 2nd lieutenant Co. B, 27th Regiment, Georgia Infantry. October 1, 1862 received pay ($77.33). October 6, 1862 elected 1st lieutenant Co. B, 27th Regiment, Georgia Infantry. October 31, 1862 admitted to General Hospital No. 14 at Richmond, Virginia. November 15, 1862 furloughed for 30 days from Richmond, Virginia. December 1862 roll shows him present at camp near Guinea Station, Virginia and was acting adjutant. January 12, 1863 received pay ($180.00). July 30, 1863 received pay ($66.75). September 30, 1863 name appears on a roll of officers of Colquitt's Brigade. November 23, 1863 reported to Fort Sumter, Charleston, South Carolina. November 25, 1863 granted leave. January - February 1864 and March - April 1864 name shown on rolls. April 5, 1864 for the Battle of Olustee, Florida - Shown on list of men of gallantry on Major Gardner's list and shown on General Colquitt's report as having displayed marked gallantry and attention to their respective duties in the battle of February 20, 1864 at

Olustee, Florida. June 1, 1864 appears on list of officers of Hoke's Division at Dove Hill Farm, Virginia. June 1, 1864 wounded, in the right side at Cold Harbor. June 2, 1864 admitted to Jackson Hospital at Richmond, Virginia with a Vulnus Sclopeticum (Gunshot Wound) by a mini ball in the right side. June 2, 1864 admitted to Jackson Hospital at Richmond, Virginia. July 30, 1864 received pay ($180.0). July 31, 1864 furloughed for 40 days from Jackson Hospital, Richmond, Virginia. August 14, 1864 report of Colquitt's Brigade of Hoke's Division shows him wounded on furlough at Richmond, Virginia. October 28, 1864 reports of Colquitt's Brigade at Laurel Hill, Virginia and Hoke's Division at Dove Hill Farm, Virginia show him on sick furlough at Albany, Georgia approved by the examining board. December 31, 1864 reports of Colquitt's Brigade at Camp Whiting, North Carolina and Hoke's Division near Wilmington, North Carolina show him absent wounded. March 9, 1865 transferred from Kinston, North Carolina to and admitted to C. S. A. General Hospital, No. 3 at Greensboro, North Carolina. April 26, 1865 surrendered, Greensboro, North Carolina. May 1, 1865 paroled at Greensboro, North Carolina.

FORRESTER, REDMOND (RICHMOND) V.: Company B, lieutenant. September 10, 1861 elected 4th sergeant, Co. B, 27th Regiment, Georgia Infantry at Camp Stephens, Griffin, Spalding County, Georgia. December 10, 1861 elected 2nd lieutenant Co. B, 27th Regiment, Georgia Infantry at Camp Pickens near Manassas, Virginia. December 1861 and January 1862 rolls show him present at Camp Pickens near Manassas, Virginia. February 1862 roll shows him absent on recruiting service for 30 days beginning February 13, 1862. March 1862 received pay ($80.00). May 8, 1864 resigned due to disability.

FORSHE (FORSHEE) ELISHA: Company F private. September 9, 1861 enlisted as a private in Co. F, 27th Regiment, Georgia Infantry at Camp Stephens, Griffin, Spalding County, Georgia. January 1862 and February 1862 rolls show him on fatigue duty at Headquarters Post since January 1, 1862. September 17, 1862 killed at Sharpsburg, Maryland. February 27, 1864 death benefit claim was filed by Abigail Forshe, his widow. Home was Taylor County, Georgia.

FORTER, J. BURREL: Company G, private. May 19, 1862 enlisted as a private in Co. G, 27th Regiment, Georgia Infantry at Richmond, Virginia. June 1862 received pay ($29.40) at Richmond, Virginia. December 1862 roll shows him absent without leave. February 28, 1863 received pay ($146.00). December 31, 1863 received pay. January - February 1864 and March - April 1864 rolls show him absent on detached service as Assistant Enrolling Officer at Pike County, Georgia since March 25, 1863. July 1864 issued clothing. July 23, 1864 he is shown retired on the invalid corps register.

FORTSON (FORTSEN), E. R.: Company E, private. September 9, 1861 enlisted as a private in Co. E, 27th Regiment, Georgia Infantry at Camp Stephens, Griffin, Spalding County, Georgia. November 13, 1861 admitted to General Hospital No. 18 at Richmond, Virginia. December 4, 1861 returned to duty. June 27, 1862 wounded at Cold Harbor, Virginia. August 26, 1862 died of wounds at Belmont and Grove Hospitals at Lovingston, Virginia. February 8, 1864 death benefit claim was filed by E. R. Fortson, administrator of the estate of B. H. Fortson his late father.

FORTSON (FORTSEN) JAMES N.: Company E, private. September 9, 1861 enlisted as a private in Co. E, 27th Regiment, Georgia Infantry at Camp Stephens, Griffin, Spalding County, Georgia. December 1862 roll shows he was missing in action at Sharpsburg, September 17, 1862. September 17, 1862 killed at Sharpsburg, Maryland. February 8, 1864 death benefit claim was filed by E. R. Fortson, administrator of the estate of B. H. Fortson his late father.

FOSTER, B. J.: Company G, private. May 19, 1862 enlisted as a private in Co. G, 27th Regiment, Georgia Infantry. May 31, 1862 wounded at Seven Pines, Virginia. March 25, 1863 - April 30, 1864 he was on detached duty as Enrolling Officer in Pike County, Georgia. He was born in Georgia January 8, 1841.

FOSTER, W. M.: Company E, private. February 1, 1864 enlisted as a private in Co. E, 27th Regiment, Georgia Infantry at Charleston, South Carolina. February 20, 1864 wounded, Olustee, Florida. January - February 1864 roll shows him absent wounded at Olustee, Florida. March 20, 1864 died of wounds. March - April 1864 shows he died March 20, 1864 of wounds received at Olustee, Florida.

FOUNTAIN (FONTAINE), ANDREW JACKSON: Company F, lieutenant. September 10, 1861 elected Jr. 2nd lieutenant in Co. F, 27th Regiment, Georgia Infantry as Camp Stephens, Griffin, Spalding County, Georgia. December 10, 1861 received pay ($138.66). December 1861 and January 1862 rolls show him present at Camp Pickens near Manassas, Virginia. February 1862 roll shows him absent on recruiting services for 30 days beginning February 13, 1862. February (March) 1862 died. Rebecca Fountain, widow filed death claim. He was a resident of Taylor County, Georgia.

FOUNTAIN (FONTAINE), CORNELIUS B.: Company F, private. September 9, 1861 enlisted as a private in Co. F, 27th Regiment, Georgia Infantry at Camp Stephens, Griffin, Spalding County, Georgia. January 20, 1862 admitted to Moore Hospital at General Hospital No. 1 at Danville, Virginia with Asthma and was sent to Orange Court House, Virginia Hospital. January 21, 1862 admitted to General Hospital at Orange Court House, Virginia with Asthma. January 1862 roll shows him in Moore Hospital since January 20, 1862. February 10, 1862 shown on roll at C. S. A. General Hospital at Farmville, Virginia and returned to duty. February 1862 roll shows he was sent to Moore Hospital, Virginia on February 18, 1862. March 7, 1862 admitted to Chimborazo Hospital No. 2 at Richmond, Virginia with Bronchitis. April 29, 1862 returned to duty. May 21, 1862 pension records show he was wounded in the stomach at Seven

Pines, Virginia.   June 26, 1862 wounded, right forefinger shot off at Cold Harbor, Virginia.   September 2, 1862 received pay ($113.00) at Richmond, Virginia.   December 31, 1863 received pay. January - February 1864 roll shows him present.   February 29, 1864 received pay.   March - April 1864 roll shows him present.   May 7, 1864, July 1864 and September 20, 1864 issued clothing.   1864 wounded in the head at Petersburg, Virginia.   April 6, 1865 captured while on picket duty near Wilmington, North Carolina. His date of release was not given.   He was born in Wilkinson County, Georgia, January 1, 1843.

FOWLER, E. J.: Company G, corporal.   March 19, 1862 enlisted as a private in Co. G, 27th Regiment, Georgia Infantry at Richmond, Virginia. May 31, 1862 wounded at Seven Pines, Virginia.   May 4, 1863 received pay ($22.00).   May 7, 1863 received $7.50 for commutation of rations. October 30, 1863 and November 24, 1863 issued clothing.   December 31, 1863 received pay.   January - February 1864 roll shows him present. February 29, 1864 received pay.   March - April 1864 roll shows him present.   July 1864 and September 20, 1864 issued clothing.   April 26, 1865 surrendered, Greensboro, North Carolina.   May 1, 1865 paroled at Greensboro, North Carolina.   He was born in Monroe County, Georgia in 1830.

FOWLER, G. W.: Company G, private. May 19, 1862 enlisted as a private in Co. G, 27th Regiment, Georgia Infantry at Richmond, Virginia.   April 13, 1863 issued clothing. January - February 1864 and March - April 1864 rolls show him absent without leave from May 12, 1863.   May 12, 1863- April 30, 1864 he was absent without leave.

FOWLER, JESSE: Company F, private.   September 9, 1861 enlisted as a private in Co. F, 27th Regiment, Georgia Infantry at Camp Stephens, Griffin, Spalding County, Georgia.   December 1861 received pay. January 15, 1862 admitted to Moore Hospital at General Hospital, No. 1 at Danville, Virginia and sent to Mount Jackson.   March 30, 1862 admitted to Chimborazo Hospital, No. 2 at Richmond, Virginia with Rheumatism and Diarrhoea.   June 9(11), 1862 discharged due to disability due to Rheumatism and Diarrhoea at Richmond, Virginia. June 12, 1862 received pay ($83.15).   Description on the Certificate of Disability was that he ws born in Pitt County, North Carolina, was 54 years of age, 5 foot 6 inches high, fair complexion, blue eyes, dark hair and was by occupation a farmer. Discharged at Butler, Georgia and $25.00 was due him for clothing.

FREEMAN, BENJAMIN A.: Company F, lieutenant.   September 9, 1861 enlisted as a private in Co. F, 27th Regiment, Georgia Infantry at Camp Stephens, Griffin, Spalding County, Georgia.   January 1862 roll shows him in Moore Hospital since January 20, 1862.   January 20, 1862 admitted to Moore Hospital at General Hospital, No. 1 at Danville, Virginia with Diarrhoea and was sent to Orange Court House, Virginia. January 21, 1862 admitted to General Hospital at Orange Court House, Virginia with Diarrhoea.   February 5, 1862 returned to duty.   April 30,

1862 received pay. September 1, 1862 name appears on roll of General Hospital No. 21, Richmond, Virginia. September 27, 1862 admitted to General Hospital No. 21 at Richmond, Virginia with a Vulnus Sclopeticum (Gunshot Wound) (possibly from Sharpsburg, Maryland on September 17, 1862). September 28, 1862 he was on roll of General Hospital No. 21 at Richmond, Virginia. October 16, 1862 furloughed for 40 days (23 years of age). June 27, 1863 elected Jr. 2nd lieutenant in Co. F, 27th Regiment, Georgia Infantry. July 24, 1863 received $15.00 commutation of rations while on furlough. August 5, 1863 issued clothing. December 24, 1863 leave granted. February 20, 1864 wounded at Olustee, Florida. January - February 1864 and March - April 1864 rolls show him absent sick since April 18, 1864. March 19, 1864 received pay ($160.00). May 2, 1864 at Floyd House Hospital at Macon, Georgia with Intermittent Fever and still not recovered from wound to the thigh received at Olustee, Florida (note: the wound has healed but the use of the leg is somewhat impaired) 45 days leave is suggested. August 11, 1864 elected 2nd lieutenant in Co. F, 27th Regiment, Georgia Infantry. August 19, 1864 captured at Weldon Railroad near Petersburg, Virginia. August 22, 1864 committed to the Old Capitol Prison, Washington, D. C. August 27, 1864 sent to Fort Delaware, Delaware. June 17, 1865 released at Fort Delaware, Delaware. Parole papers show he was a resident of Taylor County, Georgia, light completion, light hair, blue eyes, 6 foot 1/2 inches high.

FRITCH, JOHN: Company E, private. January 1862 roll shows him on furlough for 60 days from January 24, 1862. February 1862 roll shows him on furlough for 60 days from January 26, 1862. May 13, 1862 admitted to General Hospital Camp Winder, Richmond, Virginia with Diarrhoea and was discharged to convalest. June 27, 1862 died near Richmond. August 16, 1862 death benefit claim was filed by his widow, Rhoda Fritch. August 5, 1863 death benefit claim paid $139.90 (#7408).

FULFORD, STATEN SR.: Company K, private. August 10, 1861 enlisted on the Talbot County company as a private in Talbotton, Talbot County, Georgia. September 10, 1861 enlisted as a private in Co. K, 27th Regiment, Georgia Infantry at Camp Stephens, Griffin, Spalding County, Georgia. August 22 and August 24, 1863 issued clothing. December 31, 1863 received pay. March - April 1864 roll shows him present. August 19, 1864 wounded in the left arm at Weldon Railroad, Virginia. August 21, 1864 admitted to Jackson Hospital at Richmond, Virginia with a Vulnus Sclopeticum (Gunshot Wound) to the left arm and groin. October 2, 1864 furloughed for 40 days. December 13, 1864 received pay at Columbus, Georgia ($71.13). March 30, 1865 returned to duty from hospital. He was born in North Carolina April 22, 1821. He died in 1902.

FULLER, C. H.: Company B, private. October 1, 1863 enlisted as a private in Co. B, 27th Regiment, Georgia Infantry. May 16, 1864 pension records show he left his command with Typhoid Pneumonia and was at Columbus, Georgia at the close of the war. He was born in Harris County,

Georgia October 1847.

FULLER (FULLAR), LEONARD: Company E, private. August 1, 1863 enlisted as a private in Co. E, 27th Regiment, Georgia Infantry at Fairburn, Campbell County, Georgia. December 31, 1863 received pay. January - February 1864 roll shows him present. February 29, 1864 received pay. March – April 1864 roll shows him present. August 1864 issued clothing. April 26, 1865 surrendered, Greensboro, North Carolina. May 1, 1865 paroled at Greensboro, North Carolina. He was born in Morgan County, Georgia January 14, 1825.

FULLER, WILLIAM H.: Company K, private. September 10, 1861 enlisted as a private in Co. K, 27th Regiment, Georgia Infantry at Camp Stephens, Griffin Spalding County, Georgia. January 1862 appointed 1st sergeant in Co. K, 27th Regiment, Georgia Infantry. May 31, 1862 killed at Seven Pines, Virginia.

FULTON, DAVID J.: Company I, private. September 10, 1861 enlisted as a private in Co. I, 27th Regiment, Georgia Infantry. November 1861 report from Manassas, Virginia shows he died of Pneumonia November 27, 1861.

FUTCH (FUCH), JOHN: Company E, private. September 9, 1861 enlisted as a private in Co. E, 27th Regiment, Georgia Infantry at Camp Stephens, Griffin, Spalding County, Georgia. January 24, 1862 furloughed for 60 days. January 1862 roll shows him on furlough for 60 days from January 24, 1862. May 13, 1862 admitted to General Hospital at Camp Winder at Richmond, Virginia. June 27, 1862 killed at Cold Harbor, Virginia.

FUTRELL, SAMUEL (L) C.: Company C, lieutenant. September 10, 1861 elected 5th sergeant in Co. C, 27th Regiment, Georgia Infantry at Camp Stephens, Griffin, Spalding County, Georgia. February 12, 1863 elected Jr. 2nd lieutenant in Co. C, 27th Regiment, Georgia Infantry. He was wounded date and place not given. April 26, 1865 surrendered, Greensboro, North Carolina.

GAIN, J. F.: Company B, private. He enlisted as a private in Co. B, 27th Regiment, Georgia infantry. He died circa June 18, 1864.

GAINER, W. R.: Company D, private. He enlisted as a private in Co. D, 27th Regiment, Georgia Infantry.

GAINES, DAVID F. (T.): Company H, private. September 9, 1861 enlisted as a private in Co. H, 27th Regiment, Georgia infantry at Camp Stephens, Griffin, Spalding County, Georgia. December 1861 roll shows he was left sick in Georgia October 31, 1861. April 25, 1862 received pay ($88.06). December 1862 roll shows him as missing in action at Sharpsburg, Maryland September 17, 1862.

GAINES, F. H.: Company D, private. August 29, 1862 enlisted as a private in Co. D, 27th Regiment, Georgia Infantry in Gordon County, Georgia. April, May, June and December 1863 issued clothing. December 31, 1863 received pay. March - April 1864 roll shows him present. Record shows he was held for mutiny at one time.

283

GAINES, G. W.: Company D, private.   He enlisted as a private in Co. D, 27th Regiment, Georgia Infantry.   May 1, 1865 paroled at Greensboro, North Carolina.

GAINES, H. W. T.: Company D, private.   September 1864 enlisted as a private in Co. D, 27th Regiment, Georgia Infantry.   April 26, 1865 surrendered, Greensboro, North Carolina.

GAINES, ISHAM: Company G, sergeant.   He enlisted as a private in Co. G, 27th Regiment, Georgia Infantry.   August 31, 1863 killed at Battery Wagoner, Morris Island, South Carolina.   October 4, 1863 list at Charleston of casualties from July 10 to September 6, 1863 indicate he was killed between August 30 and September 1, 1863.

GAINES, JACKSON: Company D, private. September 23, 1861 enlisted as a private in Co. D, 27th Regiment, Georgia Infantry.   June 5, 1862 received pay ($69.00).   February 29, 1863 received pay.   March - April 1864 roll shows him present.   July, September and December 1864 issued clothing.   April 26, 1865 surrendered, Greensboro, North Carolina.

GAINES, JOHN L.: Company D, private.   February 23, 1862 enlisted as a private in Co. D, 27th Regiment, Georgia Infantry at Hopewell, Hall County, Georgia.   March 25, 1862 paid bounty of $50.00 at Atlanta, Georgia. June 14, 1862 received pay ($33.00) at Richmond, Virginia.   April, May, June and December 1863 issued clothing.   February 29, 1864 received pay.   March - April 1864 roll shows him present.   May 30, 1864 and September 1864 issued clothing.   April 26, 1865 surrendered, Greensboro, North Carolina. May 1, 1865 paroled at Greensboro, North Carolina.   He was born in Georgia in 1842.

GAINES (GAINUS), L. J.: Company G, private.   He enlisted as a private in Co. G, 27th Regiment, Georgia Infantry.   December 1861 roll shows him in Griffin, Georgia.   November 9, 1861 admitted to General Hospital No. 18 at Richmond, Virginia.   Post Office is shown as Zebulon, Pike County, Georgia.   January 29, 1862 returned to duty.

GAINEY, JOHN C.: private. He enlisted as a private in the 27th Regiment, Georgia Infantry.   May 10, 1865 surrendered at Tallahassee, Florida.   May 19, 1865 paroled at Thomasville, Georgia.   He is described as 5 foot 8 inches high, dark hair, grey eyes, light complexion.

GALMAN, JAMES R.: Company B, private.   September 20, 1861 enlisted as a private in Co. B, 27th Regiment, Georgia Infantry.   March 30, 1862 admitted to General Hospital No. 21, Richmond, Virginia with Dysentery.   May 20, 1862 returned to duty.   August 28, 1862 admitted to General Hospital 21at Richmond, Virginia with Debility.   August 30, 1862 transferred to Mayo's Island.   September 1, 1862 admitted to General Hospital No. 21 at Richmond, Virginia with Debility.   September 6, 1862 received pay ($62.50) at Richmond, Virginia.   September 7, 1862 transferred to Huguenot Hospital.   October 1862 sent to the hospital. November 17, 1862 admitted to Division 3, General Hospital Camp Winder at Richmond, Virginia.   November 21, 1862 admitted to General Hospital

No.21 at Richmond, Virginia. November 30 1862 died of Variola at age 29 in General Hospital No.21 at Richmond, Virginia.

GANLY, R. C.: Company F, private. He enlisted as a private in Co. F, 27th Regiment, Georgia Infantry. April 25, 1863 admitted to General Hospital No. 1 at Savannah, Georgia with (Erysipelas) Skin Infection. April 29, 1863 died in General Hospital No. 1 at Savannah, Georgia.

GANN, ALLEN: Company C, private. He enlisted as a private in Co. C, 27th Regiment, Georgia Infantry. December 1862 roll shows him absent. October 7, 1862 admitted to Receiving and Wayside Hospital or General Hospital No. 9 at Richmond, Virginia and was transferred to General Hospital No. 10 at Richmond, Virginia.

GANOUS, BENJAMIN F.: Company G, private. September 9, 1861 enlisted as a private in Co. G, 27th Regiment, Georgia Infantry at Camp Stephens, Griffin, Spalding County, Georgia. November 11, 1861 admitted to General Hospital No. 18 at Richmond, Virginia. Post Office is shown as Zebulon, Pike County, Georgia. December 16, 1861 returned to duty. June 16 and June 26, 1863 issued clothing. October 30 and November 8, 1863 issued clothing. December 31, 1863 received pay. January - February 1864 roll shows him present. February 20, 1864 wounded at Olustee, Florida. February 29, 1864 received pay. March - April 1864 roll shows him present. May 31, 1864, July and September 20, 1864 issued clothing.

GANOUS, ISHAM A.: Company G, private. 1861 enlisted as a private in Co. G, 27th Regiment, Georgia Infantry.

GANUB, Z.: Company G, private. He enlisted as a private in Co. G, 27th Regiment, Georgia Infantry. May 18, 1865 surrendered at Augusta, Georgia. May 18, 1865 paroled at Augusta, Georgia.

GARDNER, JAMES B.: Field Staff, lieutenant colonel. April 26, 1861 appointed 4th sergeant of Co. A, 4th Regiment, Georgia Infantry. November 16, 1861 discharged. Description in discharge, he was born in Talbot County, Georgia, age 21 years, 5 feet 11 inches high, pale complexion, grey eyes, dark hair and by profession a lawyer. November 20, 1861 received pay ($44.76). December 24, 1861 appointed Adjutant of the 27th Georgia Infantry. December 1861 and January 1862 rolls show him as Adjutant and present at Camp Pickens near Manassas, Virginia. February 1862 roll his name is shown on roll. March 4, 1862 received pay ($200.00). May 22, 1862 received pay ($200.00). July 1, 1862 wounded in the stomach at Malvern Hill, Virginia. July 10, 1862 received pay ($200.00). August 4, 1862 received pay ($100.00). August 7, 1862 furloughed to Talbotton, Georgia for 50 days. October 27, 1862 certified for furlough due to disability. November 20, 1862 furloughed for 90 days. December 1862 roll shows him absent of furlough. March 23, 1863 received pay ($100.00). May 2, 1863 elected major 27th Regiment, Georgia Infantry. September 30, 1863 he is shown on roster of officers of Colquitt's Brigade. December 18, 1863 he was on leave of absence of 30 days approved by the board of medical examiners at Columbus, Georgia due to Asthma. December 31, 1863 - April 30, 1864 roll shows him present. April (May) 1, 1864 elected lieutenant colonel 27th Regiment, Georgia Infantry at James Island, South Carolina. June 10, 1864 wounded at Colquitt's Salient, Petersburg, Virginia. June 25, 1864 he died of wounds.

GARDNER, WILLIAM R.: Company D, private. He enlisted as a private in Co. D, 27th Regiment, Georgia Infantry. November 6, 1861 admitted to General Hospital at Petersburg, Virginia with Fever. November 15, 1861 returned to duty. December 21, 1861 admitted to Moore Hospital at General Hospital, No. 1 at Danville, Virginia with Pneumonia and was sent to the hospital at Richmond, Virginia. December 1861, January 1862 and February 1862 rolls show him in the hospital at Richmond, Virginia. September 15, 1862 captured at South Mountain, Maryland. October 2, 1862 sent for exchange from Fort Delaware, Delaware to Aiken's Landing, Virginia. November 10, 1862 exchanged at Aiken's Landing, Virginia.

GARRISON, T. R.: Company D, private. He enlisted as a private in Co. D, 27th Regiment, Georgia Infantry. December 28, 1861 admitted to Moore Hospital at General Hospital, No. 1 at Danville, Virginia with Continua Fever (Malaria) and was sent to the General hospital.

GATES, J. J.: Company C, private. He enlisted as a private in Co. C, 27th Regiment, Georgia Infantry. December 1862 roll shows him absent sick since May 31, 1862.

GEARILL, THOMAS T.: Company F, private. September 20, 1861 enlisted as a private in Co. F, 27th Regiment, Georgia Infantry at Camp Stephens, Griffin, Spalding County, Georgia. October 31, 1861 received pay. December 1861 roll shows him sick in hospital at Culpeper, Virginia. January 1862 roll shows he was discharged from Camp Pickens near Manassas, Virginia due to Disability (Double Hernia). February 10, 1862 received pay ($34.70). Discharge certificate shows, he was born in Talbot County, Georgia, 17 years of age, 5 feet 11 inches high, fair complexion, blue eyes, dark hair and was by occupation a farmer.

GIDDINS, WILLIAM B.: Company K, sergeant. November 1, 1861 enlisted and elected 1st sergeant of Co. K, 27th Regiment, Georgia Infantry at Camp Stephens, Griffin, Spalding County, Georgia. May 1863, October 22 and 29, November 21 and 24, 1863 issued clothing. December 31, 1863 received pay. March - April 1864 roll shows him present. July 1864 issued clothing. April 26, 1865 surrendered, Greensboro, North Carolina. May 1, 1865 paroled at Greensboro, North Carolina.

GILES, C. A.: Company C, sergeant. He enlisted as a private in Co. C, 27th Regiment, Georgia Infantry. December 1862 he is shown on roll as guard at Guinea Station, Virginia since December 14, 1862.

GILLMAN, J. R.: Company B, private. He enlisted as a private in Co. B, 27th Regiment, Georgia Infantry. November 30, 1862 died at General Hospital No. 21 at Richmond, Virginia of Small Pox and left no money or clothing.

286

GILMORE, WILLIAM: Company A, private. He enlisted as a private in Co. A, 27th Regiment, Georgia Infantry. January 1862 roll shows he was discharged due to Disability (fistula in ano) from Camp Pickens near Manassas, Virginia.

GLORY, R. N.: Company C, private. He enlisted as a private in Co. C, 27th Regiment, Georgia Infantry. June 3, 1864 transferred from Receiving and Wayside Hospital or General Hospital No. 9 at Richmond, Virginia to Jackson Hospital at Richmond, Virginia (possibly wounded at Cold Harbor, Virginia on June 1, 1864).

GLYNN, P. W.: Company C, private. September 10, 1861 enlisted as a private in Co. C, 27th Regiment, Georgia Infantry at Camp Stephens, Griffin, Spalding County, Georgia. May 3, 1862 admitted to Chimborazo Hospital No. 5 at Richmond, Virginia with Debility. June 5, 1862 in Chimborazo Hospital No. 5 at Richmond, Virginia and was transferred to Lynchburg, Virginia. June 6 (15), 1862 admitted to General Hospital at Farmville, Virginia with Rheumatism. September 6, 1862 received pay ($88.00). September 11, 1862 issued clothing at General Hospital at Farmville, Virginia. November 17, 1862 returned to duty. June 26, 1863 issued clothing. October 31, 1863 received pay. January - February 1864 roll shows him present. February 29, 1864 received pay. March - April 1864 roll shows him present. July 1864 issued clothing. April 26, 1865 surrendered, Greensboro, North Carolina. May 1, 1861 paroled at Greensboro, North Carolina.

GONG, W.: Company C, private. He enlisted as a private in Co. C, 27th Regiment, Georgia Infantry. March 30, 1862 admitted to General Hospital No. 21, Richmond, Virginia with Debility.

GOODROE, RICHARD B.: Company A, private. July 9 1862 enlisted as a private in Co. A, 27th Regiment, Georgia Infantry at Camp Randolph, Georgia. April 1 - July 1, 1863 employed on extra duty as a pioneer at Fredericksburg, Virginia. June, July, August and September 1863 issued clothing. June 1 to July 1, 1863 employed on extra duty as a pioneer at Kinston, North Carolina. July 1, 1863 to August 1, 1863 employed on extra duty as a pioneer at Topsail Sound, North Carolina. August 7, 1863 admitted to C. S. A. General Military Hospital at Wilmington, North Carolina with Morbis Cutis and was returned to duty on August 8, 1863. (Post Office listed as Buena Vista, Georgia). August 1 to October 1, 1863 to January 1, 1864 employed on extra duty as a pioneer at James Island, South Carolina. November 2, 1863 received $9.90 additional pay for pioneer duty. December 31, 1863 received pay. January - February 1864 roll shows him absent with leave since April 27, 1864. February 29, 1864 received pay. March - April 1864 roll shows him present. July 1864 issued clothing. September 30, 1864 issued clothing. December 22, 1864 admitted to Receiving and Wayside Hospital or General Hospital No. 9 at Richmond, Virginia to Jackson Hospital at Richmond. December 22, 1864 admitted to Jackson Hospital at Richmond, Virginia with Pneumonia.

January 5, 1865 returned to duty. April 26, 1865 surrendered, Greensboro, North Carolina. May 1, 1865 paroled at Greensboro, North Carolina.

GOODWIN, THOMAS D.: Company K, private. May 26, 1863 enlisted as a private in Co. A, 27th Battalion, Georgia Infantry at Columbus, Georgia (non-conscripts). December 31, 1863 received pay. March 15, 1864 transferred as a private to Co. K, 27th Regiment, Georgia Infantry. March - April 1864 roll shows him present. May 30, 1864 issued clothing. June 18, 1864 admitted to General Hospital, Petersburg, Virginia with a Vulnus Sclopeticum (Gunshot Wound) to the head and was transferred to Kittrels, North Carolina. July 1864 wounded, collar bone and three ribs broken at Petersburg, Virginia. September 20, 1864 issued clothing. March 8, 1865 captured near Kinston, North Carolina. March 16, 1865 transferred to Point Lookout, Maryland from New Bern, North Carolina. June 27, 1865 released at Point Lookout, Maryland. Described as; dark complexion, brown hair, blue eyes 6 feet and 1/2 inches high. He was born in Talbot County, Georgia October 22, 1845.

GORDY, ASA (C.): Company G, private. May 16, 1863 enlisted as a private in Co. G, 27th Regiment, Georgia Infantry at Guinea Station, Virginia. June 16 and 26, 1863 issued clothing. October 30, 1863 issued clothing. December 31, 1863 received pay. January - February 1864 and March - April 1864 rolls show him present. June 3, 1864 transferred from Receiving and Wayside Hospital or General Hospital No. 9 at Richmond, Virginia to Jackson Hospital at Richmond, Virginia. July 3, 1864 died at Jackson Hospital at Richmond, Virginia. He is buried in Hollywood Cemetery at Richmond, Virginia.

GORDON, JAMES: Company A, private. September 28, 1863 enlisted in Co. A, 27th Regiment, Georgia Infantry. June 16, 1864 captured at Petersburg, Virginia. September 30, 1864 appears on roll at Elmira Prison, Elmira, New York.

GRACE, THOMAS A.: Company C, captain. September 10, 1861 enlisted as a private in Co. C, 27th Regiment at Camp Stephens, Griffin, Spalding County, Georgia. January 20, 1862 elected 2nd lieutenant Co. C, 27th Regiment, Georgia Infantry (promoted February 3, 1862 at Camp Pickens near Manassas, Virginia). February 1862 roll shows him present at Camp Pickens near Manassas, Virginia. March 3, 1862 received pay ($66.66). March 16, 1862 admitted to Chimborazo Hospital No. 3 at Richmond Virginia with Rheumatismus. March 20, 1862 returned to duty. May 19, 1862 received pay at Manassas, Virginia ($160.0). July 1, 1862 received pay ($160.00). August 20, 1862 received pay ($80.00). September 17, 1862 elected 1st lieutenant Co. C, 27th Regiment, Georgia Infantry. October 4, 1862 received pay (82.66). January 31, 1863 roll at Regal Station near Guinea Station, Virginia shows him absent sick since January 12, 1863. February 12, 1863 elected captain Co. C, 27th Regiment, Georgia Infantry. September 30, 1863 roster of Officers of General A. H. Colquitt's Brigade shows him present. January - February 1864 and

March - April 1864 rolls show him present. June 1, 1864 received pay ($390.00). June 9, 1864 shown on report near Gaines Mill, Virginia. July 11, 1864 resigned as captain Co. C, 27th Regiment, Georgia Infantry due to bad health. August 19, 1864 received pay ($130.00). He was born in Crawford County, Georgia in 1835.

GRAHAM, ELISHA DUNCAN: Company I, major. September 10, 1861 enlisted as a private in Co. I, 27th Regiment, Georgia Infantry at Camp Stephens, Griffin, Spalding County, Georgia. December 4, 1861 elected 2nd lieutenant Co. I, 27th Regiment, Georgia Infantry (promoted June 10, 1862). December 1861, January 1862 and February 1862 rolls show him present at Camp Pickens near Manassas, Virginia. February 18, 1862 received pay ($128.00). March 7, 1862 admitted to Chimborazo Hospital No. 3 with Debility. March 1, 1862 furloughed for 30 days. April 30, 1862 returned to duty. June 2, 1862 received pay ($10.00). June 10, 1862 elected captain of Co. I, 27th Regiment, Georgia Infantry. July 10, 1862 received pay ($130.00). September 14, 1862 wounded, Turner's Gap on South Mountain, Maryland. December 1862 roll shows him present at Guinea Station, Virginia. September 30, 1863 appears on roster of Officers of Gen. A. H. Colquitt's Brigade. December 10, 1863 letter shows him as Judge Advocate. January - February 1864 and March - April 1864 rolls show him present. March 25, 1864 stationed at Fort Johnson, South Carolina. April 31, 1864 received pay ($260.00). October 28, 1864 and November 26, 1864 appears on Inspection report for Colquitt's Brigade, Hoke's Division at Laurel Hill, Virginia. December 31, 1864 appears on inspection report of Colquitt's Brigade, Hoke's Division at Camp Whiting, North Carolina. 1865 elected major in 27th Regiment, Georgia Infantry. April 26, 1865 surrendered, Greensboro, North Carolina. May 1, 1865 paroled at Greensboro, North Carolina. He was born October 1, 1863 in Appling County, Georgia. He died May 7, 1889 in Appling County, Georgia. He is buried in the Graham Family Cemetery near Holmesville, Appling County, Georgia.

GRANT, R. J.: Company G, private. He enlisted as a private in Co. G, 27th Regiment, Georgia Infantry.

GRASS, S. F.: private. He enlisted as a private in the 27th Regiment, Georgia Infantry.

GRAVES, E. M.: Company E, private. March 1, 1862 enlisted as a private in Co. E, 27th Regiment, Georgia Infantry at Fairburn, Georgia. July 6, 1862 admitted to General Hospital at Farmville, Virginia with Typhoid Fever. August 14, 1862 returned to duty. August 16, 1862 received pay ($69.00). December 31, 1863 received pay. January - February 1864 roll shows him present. March - April, 1864 roll shows him present. June 29, 1864 admitted to Receiving and Wayside Hospital or General Hospital No. 9 at Richmond, Virginia and transferred on the 30th. June 30, 1864 admitted to Jackson Hospital at Richmond, Virginia with Diarrhoea. July 8, 1864 transferred from Jackson Hospital at Richmond, Virginia to

Huguenot Springs Hospital.

GRAY, F. M.: Company G, private. He enlisted as a private in Co. G, 27th Regiment, Georgia Infantry. September 23, 1862 died of Rubeola at General Hospital, Warrenton, Virginia.

GRAY, FRANK: Company C, private. June 15, 1863 enlisted as a private in Co. C, 27th Regiment, Georgia Infantry. He died in service.

GRAY, JAMES M.: Company G, private. September 10, 1861 enlisted as a private in Co. G, 27th Regiment, Georgia Infantry at Camp Stephens, Griffin, Spalding County, Georgia. April 24, 1862 admitted to Chimborazo Hospital No. 5 at Richmond, Virginia with Bronchitis. May 12, 1862 transferred to Camp Winder Hospital at Richmond, Virginia. September 29, 1862 appears on list of prisoners taken and paroled at Warrenton, Virginia. November 12, 1862 received pay ($69.00). June 26, 1863 issued clothing. October 7, 1863 received pay ($22.00). December 31, 1863 received pay. January - February 1864 roll shows him present. February 27, 1864 received pay. March - April 1864 roll shows him present. July 1864 issued clothing. September 20, 1864 issued clothing.

GRAY, J. M.: Company C, private. September 10, 1861 enlisted as a private in Co. C, 27th Regiment, Georgia Infantry at Camp Stephens, Griffin, Spalding County, Georgia. 1862 captured. March - April 1864 roll shows him present.

GRAY, JOSEPH D.: Company C, private. April 7, 1864 enlisted as a private in Co. C, 27th Regiment, Georgia Infantry at Macon, Georgia. March - April 1864 roll shows him present. June 10, 1864 issued clothing at General Hospital No. 7 at Raleigh, North Carolina. June 28, 1864 returned to duty from Pettigrew General Hospital No. 13, Raleigh, North Carolina. September 20, 1864 issued clothing. March 10, 1865 captured near Kinston, North Carolina. March 16, 1865 transferred to New Bern, North Carolina as a prisoner. June 17, 1865 released at Point Lookout, Maryland. He was born in Georgia. He was a resident of Crawford County, Georgia. His release papers show him as being fair complexion, brown hair, blue eyes and 5 foot 7 inches tall.

GREEN (GREENE), CHARLES A.: Company C, private. September 10, 1861 enlisted as a private in Co. C, 27th Regiment, Georgia Infantry at Camp Stephens, Griffin, Spalding County, Georgia. December 24, 1861 admitted to Moore Hospital at General Hospital, No. 1 at Danville, Virginia with Rheumatism and was transferred to Hospital in Richmond, Virginia. January 1862 roll shows him absent in Hospital in Richmond, Virginia since December 24, 1861. February 1862 roll shows him on sick furlough since December 24, 1861. June 6, 1862 received pay ($66.00). September 20, 1862 paroled near Keedysville, Maryland. He was appointed sergeant Co. C, 27th Regiment, Georgia Infantry. May 3, 1863 wounded slightly at Chancellorsville, Virginia. May 1863 issued clothing at 1st. Division General Hospital, Camp Winder at Richmond, Virginia. June 26, 1863 issued clothing. June 30 and September 30 1863 issued clothing.

December 29, 1863 detailed as a carpenter at Charleston, South Carolina. December 31, 1863 received pay. January 1, 1864 he was on detached duty at Fort Sumter, South Carolina. February 25, 1864 record shows him detailed as a carpenter in Charleston, South Carolina. January - February 1864 roll and March - April 1864 roll show him on detached duty since January 1, 1864 at Fort Sumter, Charleston, South Carolina. March 1, 1864 to April 30, 1864 detailed as a carpenter at Fort Sumter, Charleston, South Carolina. May 18, 1864 relieved from detail as carpenter. June 2, 1864 wounded at Cold Harbor, Virginia. June 2, 1864 appears on register of Receiving and Wayside Hospital or General Hospital No. 9 at Richmond, Virginia. June 2, 1864 admitted to Jackson Hospital at Richmond, Virginia with Vulnus Sclopeticum (Gunshot Wounds) to the right Hand and to the left arm. June 21, 1864 admitted to Receiving and Wayside Hospital or General Hospital No. 9 at Richmond, Virginia. June 22, 1864 transferred to Jackson Hospital, Richmond, Virginia. July 13, 1864 report of Jackson Hospital at Richmond, Virginia shows he was returned to duty July 13, 1864. August 19, 1864 captured at Weldon Railroad near Petersburg, Virginia. September 15, 1864 issued clothing. October 18, 1864 took oath of allegiance to the United States Government at Point Lookout, Maryland. October 18, 1864 released and enlisted in the United States Service.

GREEN, DAVID: Company K, sergeant. September 10, 1861 elected 3rd sergeant of Co. K, 27th Regiment, Georgia Infantry. May 31, 1862 killed at Seven Pines, Virginia. He was due back pay of $67.00. He was born in Talbot County, Georgia.

GREEN, THOMAS C.: Company C, private. September 10, 1861 enlisted as a private in Co. C, 27th Regiment, Georgia Infantry at Camp Stephens, Griffin, Spalding County, Georgia. April 30, 1862 received pay. August 31, 1862 roll of General Hospital No. 1, Richmond, Virginia shows him present. June 26, 1863 and September 30, 1863 issued clothing. January – February 1864 and March - April 1964 muster rolls show him present. July 1864 issued clothing. April 26, 1865 surrendered Greensboro, North Carolina. May 1, 1865 paroled at Greensboro, North Carolina.

GREEN, W. H.: Company C, sergeant. September 10, 1861 enlisted as a private in Co. C, 27th Regiment, Georgia Infantry. March 10, 1862 admitted to Chimborazo Hospital No. 5 at Richmond, Virginia with Debility. August 29, 1862 admitted to General Hospital, Camp Winder at Richmond, Virginia with Febris Typhoid. October 29, 1862 furloughed from Winder Division 2 Hospital at Richmond, Virginia for 30 days. June 16, 1863 and September 30, 1863 issued clothing. December 31, 1863 received pay. January - February 1864 and March – April 1864 rolls show him present. July 1864 and September 20, 1864 issued clothing. He was appointed sergeant Co. C, 27th Regiment, Georgia Infantry. April 26, 1865 surrendered Greensboro, North Carolina. May 1, 1865 paroled at Greensboro, North Carolina.

GREGORY, J. E.: Company C, private. September 10, 1861 enlisted as a private in Co. C, 27th Regiment, Georgia Infantry. June 20, 1864 admitted to Receiving and Wayside Hospital of General Hospital No. 9 at Richmond, Virginia and was transferred to Petersburg June 22, 1864.

GREGORY, JAMES T.: Company C, sergeant. September 10, 1861 enlisted as a private in Co. C, 27th Regiment, Georgia Infantry. September 10, 1861 elected 1st sergeant in Co. C, 27th Regiment, Georgia Infantry at Camp Stephens, Griffin, Spalding County, Georgia. Roll dated January 31, 1863 shows him absent sick since January 12, 1863. June 20, 1863 and September 30, 1863 issued clothing. December 3, 1863 received $6.00 for rations from August 8, 1863 to August 28, 1863 while on furlough. December 31, 1863 received pay. January – February 1864 and March-April 1964 rolls show him present. June 1, 1864 wounded at Cold Harbor, Virginia. June 3, 1864 admitted to Jackson Hospital at Richmond, Virginia with a Vulnus Sclopeticum (Gunshot Wound) and Fractured Tibia where his left leg was amputated. June 28, 1864 died of wounds in Jackson Hospital at Richmond, Virginia. He is buried in Hollywood Cemetery at Richmond, Virginia. An inventory of his possessions were a jacket and 1 pair shoes ($8) 1 hat ($3) total value $11.

GREGORY, THOMAS H.: Company C, private. June 15, 1862 enlisted as a private in Co. C, 27th Regiment, Georgia Infantry. May 7, 1862 admitted to General Hospital at Camp Winder, Richmond, Virginia with Diarrhoea. May 14, 1862 returned to duty. May 19, 1862 admitted to Chimborazo Hospital No. 5 at Richmond, Virginia with Fever. May 29, 1862 returned to duty. June 29, 1862 admitted to Chimborazo Hospital No. 5 at Richmond, Virginia with Debility. July 3, 1862 admitted to General Hospital at Camp Winder at Richmond, Virginia with Chronic Diarrhoea. December 7, 1862 died of Pneumonia in General Receiving Hospital at Gordonsville, Virginia.

GRIFFIN, DEMPSEY: Company K, private. February 13, 1864 enlisted as a private in Co. K, 27th Regiment, Georgia Infantry in Macon, Georgia. March – April 1864 roll shows him furloughed from the Hospital in Lake City, Florida on April 5, 1864 for 60 days. September 20, 1864 issued clothing. January 25, 1865 died of Pneumonia at General Hospital No.2 at Wilson, North Carolina.

GRIFFIN, JAMES E.: Company G, private. He enlisted as a private in Co. G, 27th Regiment, Georgia Infantry.

GRIFFIN, M. E.: Company E, private. January 18, 1865 transferred from Wilmington to C. S. A. General Hospital No. 3 at Greensboro, North Carolina with Pneumonia. January 21, 1865 transferred to another hospital. He was from Cat Creek, Georgia.

GRIFFIN, WILLIAM: Company I, sergeant. September 10, 1861 elected 4th sergeant of Co. I, 27th Regiment, Georgia Infantry at Camp Stephens, Griffin, Spalding County, Georgia. June 12, 1862 received pay ($69.00). July 18, 1863 received $5 for rations while on furlough June 13, 1862 to July 3, 1862. September 20, 1863 received pay ($34). December 31, 1863 received pay. January – February 1864 roll shows him present. February 29, 1864 received pay. March – April 1864 roll shows him present. October 2, 1864 admitted to Receiving and Wayside Hospital or General Hospital No. 9 at Richmond, Virginia. October 3, 1864 transferred to Jackson Hospital at Richmond at Virginia with Rheumatism. November 28, 1864 returned to duty. April 26, 1865 pension records show he surrendered at Greensboro, North Carolina. He was born in South Carolina in 1818.

GRIGGS, BENJAMIN W.: Company E, private. March 1, 1862 enlisted as a private in Co. E, 27th Regiment, Georgia Infantry at Fairburn, Georgia. August 31, 1862 received pay and clothing allotment ($89.90). August 23, 1862 admitted to General Hospital Camp Winder at Richmond, Virginia with Chronic Diarrhoea. October 29, 1862 placed on 30 day furlough from Winder Division 2 Hospital at Richmond, Virginia. December 1862 roll shows him absent without leave. May 4, 1863 received pay ($22.00). April 2, 1863 issued clothing. July 11, 1863 received pay ($22.00). July 24, 1863 issued clothing. November 1863 detailed nurse in Atlanta, Georgia Hospital. February 29, 1864 received pay. March 16, 1864 received $87.63 for clothing. March - April 1864 roll shows him as being present at Empire Hotel Hospital at Atlanta, Georgia. April 20, 1865 captured at Macon, Georgia.

GRISHAM (GRESHAM), WILLIAM J. J.: Company G, private. September 9, 1861 enlisted as a private in Co. G, 27th Regiment, Georgia Infantry. January and February 1862 rolls show him on duty at headquarters post since January 6. September 28, 1862 admitted to General Hospital No. 8 (St. Charles Hospital) at Richmond, Virginia with Rheumatism (shown as 19 years old). October 25, 1862 returned to duty. June 26, 1863, November 24, 1863 and December 16, 1863 issued clothing. December 31, 1863 received pay. January - February 1864 roll shows him present. March - April 1864 roll shows him present. October 30, 1864 issued clothing. June 1864 wounded at Petersburg, Virginia. June 20, 1864 admitted to C. S. A. General Hospital at Farmville, Virginia with a Vulnus Sclopeticum (Gunshot Wound) in the Popliteal Space. June 27, 1864 furloughed for 60 days. He was in C. S. A. General Hospital at Farmville, Virginia at the close of the war. He was born in Georgia in 1843.

GRIZZARD, JOSEPH: Company E, private. September 9, 1861 enlisted as a private in Co. E, 27th Regiment, Georgia Infantry in Griffin, Georgia. December 1862 roll shows him detailed as a teamster. April, May and June 1863 issued clothing. May 3, 1863 admitted to Receiving and Wayside Hospital or General Hospital No. 9 at Richmond, Virginia and transferred and admitted to Chimborazo Hospital No. 2 at Richmond, Virginia with Debility. May 12, 1863 returned to duty. August 20, 1863 received pay as a teamster ($.25 a day) December 31, 1863 received pay. January – February 1864 roll shows him present. February 29, 1864 received pay. March - April 1864 roll shows him present. September 20, 1864 issued clothing. April 26, 1865 surrendered, Greensboro, North Carolina. May

1, 1865 paroled in Greensboro, North Carolina. He was born in Warren County, Georgia January 22, 1834.

GUICE, PETER: Company E, private. September 9, 1861 enlisted as a private in Co. E, 27th Regiment, Georgia Infantry. March 7, 1862 admitted to General Hospital at Camp Winder, Richmond, Virginia. May 16, 1862 detailed as a nurse at General Hospital Camp Winder at Richmond, Virginia. August 17, 1862 died of Diarrhoea and Typhoid Fever, in C. S. A. General Hospital at Farmville, Virginia. He is buried in Hollywood Cemetery at Richmond, Virginia. November 3, 1862 death benefit claim was filed by Olivia Guice, his widow.

GUNN, WILLIAM J.: Company H, private. September 9, 1861 enlisted as a private in Co. H, 27th Regiment, Georgia Infantry. November 9, 1861 admitted to General Hospital No. 18 (formerly Greaner's Hospital) at Richmond, Virginia. December 9, 1861 discharged due to disability at Richmond, Virginia. November 15, 1862 enlisted as a private in Co. H, 46th Regiment, Georgia Infantry. April 26, 1865, surrendered at Greensboro, North Carolina. He was born in Pike County, Georgia April 1843.

GUNTER (GUINTER), S. G.: Company D, private. He enlisted as a private in Co. D, 27th Regiment, Georgia Infantry. April 26, 1865 surrendered, Greensboro, North Carolina. May 1, 1865 paroled in Greensboro, North Carolina.

GUNTER (GUINTER), SANFORD: Company D, private. He enlisted as a private in Co. D, 27th Regiment, Georgia Infantry. February 12, 1865 admitted to C. S. A. General Hospital No. 4 at Wilmington, North Carolina with Rubeola. February 18, 1865 returned to duty. Post Office shown as Gainesville, North Carolina should be Georgia.

GUTHRIDGE, JAMES W.: Company D, private. He enlisted as a private in Co. D, 27th Regiment, Georgia Infantry. September 6, 1862 admitted to C. S. A. General Hospital at Danville, Virginia. December 16, 1862 furloughed.

HADGER, I: private. He enlisted as a private in the 27th Regiment, Georgia Infantry. May 10, 1865 surrendered at Tallahassee, Florida. May 16, 1865 paroled at Thomasville, Georgia.

HADON, REUBEN: Company C, private. He enlisted as a private in Co. C, 27th Regiment, Georgia Infantry. December 23, 1862 admitted to C. S. A. General Hospital at Charlottesville, Virginia with Debility. December 24, 1862 returned to duty.

HAGAN (HAGINS), D. C.: Company I, private. September 10, 1861 enlisted as a private in Co. I, 27th Regiment, Georgia Infantry. November 15, 1861 admitted to General Hospital No. 18 (formerly Greaner's Hospital) at Richmond, Virginia. November 18, 1861 returned to duty. May 1863 died at Richmond, Virginia.

HAGAN (HAGINS), MILES R.: Company G, sergeant. September 9, 1861 elected 5th sergeant in Co. G, 27th Regiment, Georgia Infantry at Camp Stephens, Griffin, Spalding County, Georgia. November 6,

1861 admitted to General Hospital at Petersburg, Virginia with Rubeola. December 17, 1861 returned to duty. May 31, 1862 wounded and captured at Seven Pines, Virginia. June 5, 1862 sent to Fort Delaware, Delaware from Fort Monroe, Virginia. He is described as; born in Georgia, 24 years old, 5 foot 9 inches high, dark hair, brown eyes and dark complexion. August 2, 1862, paroled and sent up the James River for exchange. August 15, 1862 received pay and clothing allowance of $ 91.00. February 4, 1863 furloughed for 30 days and paid $10.00 for commutation of rations. June 26, 1863, October 30, 1863 and November 24, 1863 issued clothing. December 31, 1863 received pay. January – February 1864 roll shows him present. February 20, 1864 wounded at Olustee, Florida. February 29, 1864 received pay. March - April 1864 roll shows him present. September 20, 1864 issued clothing. April 28, 1865 admitted to General Hospital No.11 at Charlotte, North Carolina with Feb. Inter. April 29, 1865 transferred to another hospital.

HAGAN (HAGINS), THOMAS P.: Company G, private. May 19, 1862 enlisted as a private in Co. G, 27th Regiment, Georgia Infantry at Richmond, Virginia. August 31, 1862 roll of hospital, Huguenot Springs, Virginia indicates he was attached to the hospital September 7, 1862. April 15, 1863 furloughed for 30 days. July 25, 1863 received $10.00 for commutation of rations. April 19, 1863, October 30, 1863 and November 24, 1863 issued clothing. December 31, 1863 received pay. January – February 1864 roll shows him present. March - April 1864 roll shows him present. June 1, 1864 wounded at Cold Harbor, Virginia. June 22, 1864 admitted to Receiving and Wayside Hospital or General Hospital No. 9 at Richmond, Virginia. June 23, 1864 transferred to Jackson Hospital at Richmond, Virginia. April 26, 1865 surrendered, Greensboro, North Carolina. May 1, 1865 paroled in Greensboro, North Carolina.

HAGLER, ADAM: Company A, private. He enlisted as a private in Co. A, 27th Regiment, Georgia Infantry. June 1863 issued clothing. September 6, 1863 wounded in the hip in the withdrawal from Battery Wagner, Charleston, South Carolina.

HAGLER, ANDREW J.: Company A, private. September 28, 1862 enlisted as a private in Co. A, 27th Regiment, Georgia Infantry. October 28, 1862 admitted to Winder Division No. 2 Hospital at Richmond, Virginia. January 22, 1863 died. May 13, 1863 death benefit claim was filed by his widow Pricilla Hagler of Buena Vista, Marion County, Georgia.

HAGLER GARRISON: Company A, private. September 18, 1862 enlisted as a private in Co. A, 27th Regiment, Georgia Infantry. January 30, 1863 died. May 25, 1863 death benefit claim was filed by his widow Emily E. Hagler of Buena Vista, Marion County, Georgia.

HALE (HAIL), FRANCIS MARION: Company H, private. December 9, 1862 enlisted as a private in Co. H, 27th Regiment, Georgia Infantry in Decatur, Georgia. December 1862 roll shows him present. December 31, 1863 received pay. January – February 1864 roll shows him present. March

1, 1864 killed at Cedar Creek, Florida. (March 16, 1864 died at Lake City, Florida.) He is buried at Captain Mooney Cemetery, Jacksonville, Florida. He was born in 1824.

HALE (HAIL), PATRICK HENRY: Company H, private. January11, 1864 enlisted as a private in Co. H, 27th Regiment, Georgia Infantry. January – February 1864 roll shows him present. March - April 1864 roll shows him present. May 31, 1864 issued clothing. October 1864 deserted. October 10, 1864 received by the Provost Marshal at Washington, D. C., a Confederate deserter. October 10, 1864 took oath of allegiance to the United States Government and furnished transportation to Philadelphia, Pennsylvania. He was born January 2, 1845 and died August 16, 1934. He is buried at Liberty Hill Baptist Church Cemetery in Henry County, Georgia.

HALE, W. A.: Company D, private. He enlisted as a private in Co. D, 27th Regiment, Georgia Infantry. April 26, 1865 surrendered at Greensboro, North Carolina. May 1, 1865 paroled in Greensboro, North Carolina.

HALL, ALFRED S.: Company I, lieutenant. July 6, 1861 elected 1st lieutenant of the Appling Grays. September 10, 1861 elected 1st lieutenant of Co. I, 27th Regiment, Georgia Infantry. December 18, 1861 received pay ($192.00). December 1861 roll shows him present at Camp Pickens near Manassas, Virginia. January 1862 roll shows him detailed as an officer in the Provost Marshalls Guard at the General Headquarters at Camp Pickens near Manassas, Virginia. January 4, 1862 received pay ($90.00). February 1862 roll shows him absent on recruiting service for 30 days beginning February 16, 1862. February 3 1862 received pay ($90.00). April 3, 1862 received pay ($100.00) for bounty and expense for recruiting. May 21, 1862 received pay ($90.00). June 2, 1862 received pay ($90.00). July 7, 1862 received pay ($90.00). October 5, 1862 received pay ($90.00). December 1862 roll shows him present at New Guinea Station, Virginia. April 1, 1863 died. He is buried in Philadelphia Methodist Church Cemetery, Jeff Davis County, Georgia

HALL, HENRY: Company D, private. February 23, 1862 enlisted as a private in Co. D, 27th Regiment, Georgia Infantry. March 3, 1865 captured, Cheraw, South Carolina. June 13, 1865 released at Point Lookout Maryland March – April 1864 roll shows him absent, sick. May 18, 1865 paroled at Augusta, Georgia.

HALL, JAMES: Company D, private. February 23, 1862 enlisted as a private in Co. D, 27th Regiment, Georgia Infantry. April, May and June 1863 issued clothing. Fourth quarter 1863 issued clothing. February 29, 1864 received pay. March – April 1864 roll shows him absent sick. July 1864 issued clothing. May 18, 1865 paroled at Augusta, Georgia.

HALL, JAMES N.: Company G, private. September 9, 1861 enlisted as a private in Co. G, 27th Regiment, Georgia Infantry. October 31, 1861 received pay. December 1861 roll of General Hospital No. 18 (Formerly Greaner's Hospital) at Richmond, Virginia, shows him present. January

1862 and February 1862 rolls show him in hospital at Richmond, Virginia since January 9, 1862. January 9, 1862 admitted to Moore Hospital at General Hospital, No. 1 at Danville, Virginia with Rheumatism and sent to General Hospital at Richmond, Virginia. January 9, 1862 admitted to General Hospital No. 18 at Richmond, Virginia with Chronic Rheumatism. January 21, 1862 furloughed for 30 days and received $6.00 in a money voucher for commutation of rations. July 31, 1862 discharged, "unfit for duties of soldier on account of Rheumatism". Description was 29 years of age, 5 feet 10 inches high, dark complexion, blue eyes, dark hair and was a farmer before enlistment. He was a resident of Zebulon, Pike County, Georgia.

HALL, M. J.: Company H, private. He enlisted as a private in Co. H, 27th Regiment, Georgia Infantry. December 1862 roll shows him as a sutler.

HALL, THOMAS: Company B, private. January 30, 1864 enlisted as a private in Co. B, 27th Regiment, Georgia Infantry at Macon, Georgia. January – February 1864 roll shows him present and due a $50.00 bounty. March - April 1864 roll shows him present.

HALL THOMAS DANIEL: Company K, private. January 13, 1863 enlisted as a private in Co. K, 27th Regiment, Georgia Infantry at Wilmington, North Carolina. December 31, 1863 received pay. March - April 1864 roll shows him present.

September 24, 1864 issued clothing. January 5, 1865 admitted to General Hospital No. 4, Wilmington, North Carolina with Catarrh. January 15, 1865 transferred from General Hospital No. 4, Wilmington, North Carolina to General Hospital No. 3 at Goldsboro, North Carolina convalescing from Pneumonia admitted to C. S. A. General Hospital No. 3 at Greensboro, North Carolina with Pneumonia. January 15, 1865 admitted to Pettigrew General Hospital No. 13 at Raleigh, North Carolina with Debilitas. January 31, 1865 returned to duty. April 26, 1865 surrendered, Greensboro, North Carolina. May 1, 1865 paroled in Greensboro, North Carolina. Was a resident of Talbotton, Talbot County, Georgia.

HALL, WILLIAM H.: Company B, private. March 4, 1862 enlisted as a private in Co. B, 27th Regiment, Georgia Infantry. October 4, 1862 admitted to Chimborazo Hospital No. 3, Richmond, Virginia. May 28, 1862 admitted to C. S. A. General Hospital at Danville, Virginia with Acute Rheumatism. July 9, 1862 returned to duty. July 13, 1862 admitted to C. S. A. General Hospital at Danville, Virginia with Debilitas and returned to duty that same day. October 3, 1862 admitted to Receiving and Wayside Hospital or General Hospital No. 9 at Richmond, Virginia and sent to Georgia Hospital No. 4. October 4, 1862 admitted to Chimborazo Hospital No. 3 at Richmond, Virginia with a Vulnus Sclopeticum (Gunshot Wound) in the neck. October 17, 1862 furloughed for 60 days and received pay ($58.00). October 17, 1862 furloughed from Chimborazo Hospital No. 3 at Richmond, Virginia. December 1862 roll shows him furlough expired, reporting to Co. Weems absent without leave. September 17, 1862 wounded at Sharpsburg, Maryland. May 2, 1863 wounded at Chancellorsville, Virginia. May 9, 1863 he was in camp at Guineas Station, Virginia. May 9, 1863 admitted to Receiving and Wayside Hospital or General Hospital No. 9 at Richmond, Virginia and transferred to Camp Winder Hospital at Richmond, Virginia. April 7, 1863 wounded in eye, resulting in loss of sight, at Fort Sumter, South Carolina. October, November and December 1863 issued clothing. December 31, 1863 received pay. January – February 1864 roll shows him present. March - April 1864 roll shows him present. August 15, 1864 admitted to Floyd House and Ocmulgee Hospitals at Macon, Georgia with Pneumonia, Conjunctivitis and General Disability. April 20, 1865 captured at Macon Georgia. April 30, 1865 paroled at Macon, Georgia. He was born in Bibb County, Georgia in 1838. He lived in Fort Valley, Georgia.

HALL, WILLIAM T.: Company K, private. September 10, 1861 enlisted as a private in Co. K, 27th Regiment, Georgia Infantry at Macon, Georgia. October 29, 1863 issued clothing. December 31, 1863 received pay. March - April 1864 roll shows him present. July 9, 1864 admitted to Jackson Hospital at Richmond, Virginia with Chronic Diarrhoea. August 12, 1864 furloughed for 30 days destination Columbus, Georgia. April 26, 1865 surrendered, Greensboro, North Carolina. May 1, 1865 paroled in Greensboro, North Carolina. He lived in Talbotton, Talbot County, Georgia.

HAMBRICK, ELSBURY: Company G, private. September 9, 1861 enlisted as a private in Co. G, 27th Regiment, Georgia Infantry. April 10, 1862 admitted to Chimborazo Hospital No.5 at Richmond, Virginia with Bronchitis. May 25, 1862 returned to duty. August 11, 1862 died near Richmond, Virginia. September 20, 1862 death benefit claim was filed by his widow, Martha Hambrick. January 12, 1863 death benefit claim was paid $137.03 (#2565).

HAMBRICK, WILLIAM J.: Company G, corporal. September 9, 1861 elected 3rd corporal in Co. G, 27th Regiment, Georgia Infantry at Camp Stephens, Griffin, Spalding County, Georgia. November 6, 1861 admitted to General Hospital at Petersburg, Virginia with Rubeola. November 18, 1861 returned to duty. September 28, 1862 admitted to General Hospital No. 8 (St. Charles Hospital) at Richmond, Virginia with Rheumatism. October 30, 1862 granted 30 day furlough from General Hospital No. 8 (St. Charles Hospital) at Richmond, Virginia by the Medical Director's Office, Richmond, Virginia. January 1863 roll indicates he was sent to the hospital in Richmond, Virginia on January 22, 1863. February 17, 1863 granted a 30 day furlough in Richmond, Virginia. January 1863 roll shows him on furlough. May 3, 1863 wounded slightly at Chancellorsville, Virginia. May 9, 1863 was in camp at Guiney's Station, Virginia. March 17, 1863 received $10.00 for commutation of rations while on furlough. April 13, 1863 issued clothing. May 8, 1863 admitted to Receiving and Wayside Hospital of General Hospital No. 9 at Richmond, Virginia and transferred to

Camp Winder Hospital at Richmond, Virginia. June 26, 1863, October 30, 1863 and November 24, 1863 issued clothing. October 30, 1862 received pay ($72.00). December 31, 1863 received pay. January – February 1864 roll shows him present. March - April 1864 roll shows him present. July 1, 1864 admitted to Jackson Hospital at Richmond, Virginia with Chronic Diarrhoea. June 30, 1864 admitted to Receiving and Wayside Hospital or General Hospital No. 9 at Richmond, Virginia and transferred to Jackson Hospital July 1, 1864. July 1, 1864 admitted to Jackson Hospital at Richmond, Virginia with Chronic Diarrhoea. July 17, 1864 returned to duty. September 20, 1864 issued clothing.

HAMILTON, ALEXANDER GREEN: Company D, private. August 1, 1863 enlisted as a private in Co. D, 27th Regiment, Georgia Infantry in Hall County, Georgia. January 30, 1864 received pay ($44.00). February 29, 1864 received pay. March – April 1864 roll shows him absent sick. July 1864 and September 20, 1864 issued clothing. March 22, 1865 captured at Bentonville, North Carolina. April 10, 1865 received at Hart's Island, New York Harbor from New Bern, North Carolina. June 15, 1865 released at Hart's Island, New York Harbor. He was born in Yorkville, South Carolina on June 16, 1839. He is described as light complexion, dark hair, brown eyes and was 5 feet 10 1/2 inches high. He lived in Hall County, Georgia. He died at LaGrange, Georgia November 1923.

HAMMOCK, JAMES M.: Company C, private. September 10, 1861 enlisted as a private in Co. C, 27th Regiment, Georgia Infantry in Griffin, Pike County, Georgia. December 1861 and February 1862 rolls show he was left sick in Georgia October 31, 1861. December 1862 roll shows him on furlough and that the time had expired. June 26, 1863 and September 30, 1863 issued clothing. September 26, 1863 received pay ($58.00). December 31, 1863 received pay. January - February 1864 roll shows him present. February 29, 1864 received pay. March - April 1864 roll shows him present. July 1864 issued clothing. He was wounded, two fingers amputated, date and place not given. April 26, 1865 surrendered Greensboro, North Carolina. May 1, 1865 paroled in Greensboro, North Carolina.

HAMMOCK, JOHN: Company K, private. He enlisted as a private in Co. K, 27th Regiment, Georgia Infantry. December 1861 roll shows he was left sick in Georgia October 31, 1861. February 1862 roll shows he was sent to post Hospital on February 20, 1862. March 7, 1862 admitted to Chimborazo Hospital No. 2 at Richmond, Virginia with Debility. May 18, 1862 admitted to Chimborazo Hospital No. 2 at Richmond, Virginia with Chronic Diarrhoea. August 7, 1862 transferred to Lynchburg, Virginia. August 20, 1862 transferred from Lynchburg and admitted to C. S. A. General Hospital at Danville, Virginia with Debility. October 8, 1862 discharged disability due to **Phthisis Pulmonalis. October 15, 1862 discharged but was unable to leave the hospital, subsequently he died there.** December 1862 roll states he was absent in the hospital since May 1, 1862.

HANCOCK, HENRY H. , Jr.: Company C, private. February 22, 1864 enlisted as a private in Co. C, 27th Regiment, Georgia Infantry in Macon, Georgia. January - February 1864 roll shows him present. February 29, 1864 received pay. March – April 1864 roll shows him present. July, 1864 and September 20, 1864 issued clothing. March 4, 1865 admitted to C. S. A. General Hospital No. 3 at Greensboro, North Carolina with Myopia and was sent to another hospital.

HANCOCK HENRY H., SR.: Company C, sergeant. September 10, 1861 enlisted as a private in Co. C, 27th Regiment, Georgia Infantry. He became ordinance sergeant. September 17, 1862 killed at Sharpsburg, Maryland. He lived in Crawford County, Georgia. He left 2 minor children but no wife. July 14, 1863 death benefit claim was filed. Death Benefit left to Morgan Hancock administrator of estate by will.

HANCOCK, J. T. (J. F.): Company F, private. September 9, 1861 enlisted as a private in Co. F, 27th Regiment, Georgia Infantry at Camp Stephens, Griffin, Georgia. September 29, 1862 received pay ($129.00). December 1862 roll dated January 31, 1863 shows him absent sick since January 12, 1863. August 1863 issued clothing. December 31, 1863 received pay. January – February 1864 roll shows him present. March - April 1864 roll shows him present. May 31, 1864, July 1864 and September 20, 1864 issued clothing. April 26, 1865 surrendered, Greensboro, North Carolina.

HANCOCK, JACKSON: Company C, private. September 10, 1861 enlisted as a private in Co. C, 27th Regiment, Georgia Infantry. July 4, 1862 admitted to Chimborazo Hospital No. 5 at Richmond, Virginia with Typhoid Fever.

HANCOCK, JAMES C.: Company C, private. February 22, 1864 enlisted as a private in Co. C, 27th Regiment, Georgia Infantry. May 7, 1862 admitted to Winder Division No. 2 Hospital at Richmond, Virginia with Rubeola. May 16, 1862 returned to duty. June 30, 1862 admitted to Winder Division No. 2 Hospital at Richmond, Virginia with Vulnus Sclopeticum (Gunshot Wound) to foot. July 10, 1862 furloughed for 20 days. July 12, 1862 admitted to C. S. A. General Hospital No. 4 at Wilmington, North Carolina with a Vulnus Sclopeticum (Gunshot Wound). .August 31, 1862 paid at Richmond, Virginia and furloughed. October 12 1862 admitted to General Hospital Camp Winder at Richmond, Virginia with Debilitas. October 13, 1862 admitted to Winder Division No. 2 Hospital at Richmond, Virginia. October 20, 1862 paid for furlough. December (3) 4, 1862 returned to duty. 1864 died at Guinea Station, Virginia. Lived in Knoxville, Crawford County, Georgia

HANCOCK, JOHN H.: Company C, sergeant. September 21, 1863 enlisted as a private in Co. C, 27th Regiment, Georgia Infantry at Macon, Georgia. He was appointed sergeant Co. C, 27th Regiment, Georgia Infantry. December 31, 1863 received pay. January – February 1864 roll shows him present. February 29, 1864 received pay. March- April 1864 roll shows him present. September 20, 1864 issued clothing. March 4, 1865 admitted to C. S. A General Hospital No.3 at Greensboro, North Carolina with Myopia and sent to another hospital. April 6, 1865 discharged on account of Congenital Myopia. Described as 25 years old, 5 foot 11 inches high, dark complexion, grey eyes, dark hair and when he enlisted he was a farmer. He was a resident of Crawford County, Georgia.

HANCOCK, LEWIS H.: Company C, private. He enlisted as a private in Co. C, 27th Regiment, Georgia Infantry. January 1862 roll shows he was left sick in Georgia October 31, 1861.

HANCOCK, THOMAS JACKSON: Company C, sergeant. September 10, 1861 elected 3rd sergeant in Co. C, 27th Regiment, Georgia Infantry. December 1862 roll shows him detailed as Provost Guard at General Headquarters. January 16, 1862 admitted to Moore Hospital at General Hospital No. 1 at Danville, Virginia with Pneumonia and was sent to General Hospital at Front Royal, Virginia. June 26, 1863 and September 30, 1863 issued clothing. December 31, 1863 received pay. January – February 1864 roll shows him present. February 29, 1864 received pay. March - April 1864 roll shows him present. July 1864 and September 20, 1864 issued clothing. December 1, 1864 admitted to Receiving and Wayside Hospital or General Hospital No. 9 at Richmond, Virginia. December 1, 1864 admitted to Jackson Hospital at Richmond, Virginia with Pneumonia. December 3, 1864 died in Richmond, Virginia. He is buried in Hollywood Cemetery at Richmond, Virginia.

HANCOCK, WILLIAM G.: Company C, private. March 15, 1862 enlisted as a private in Co. C, 27th Regiment, Georgia Infantry. May 7, 1862 admitted to General Hospital Camp Winder at Richmond, Virginia with Rubeola. June 29, 1862 admitted to Chimborazo Hospital No. 3 at Richmond, Virginia with Diarrhoea. July 2, 1862 admitted to C. S. A. General Hospital at Danville, Virginia with Rheumatism. July 29, 1862 transferred to Lynchburg, Virginia. October 17, 1862 furloughed for 40 days from C. S. A. General Hospital at Danville, Virginia. June 26, 1863 and September 30, 1863 issued clothing. December 31, 1863 received pay. January – February 1864 roll shows him present. March - April 1864 roll shows him present. May 30, 1864 issued clothing. June 1, 1864 captured, (Gaines Mill) Cold Harbor, Virginia. June 11, 1864 arrived at Point Lookout, Maryland from White House, Virginia. June 12, 1864 transferred to Elmira Prison, Elmira, New York. July 17, 1864 arrived at Elmira Prison, New York. July 7, 1865 released at Elmira Prison, New York. Address is shown as Fort Valley, Georgia. Description is florid complexion, dark hair, blue eyes, and was 5 foot 11 inches high. He was born in Crawford County, Georgia March 7, 1841.

HANEY, HENRY: Company, C, private. June 15, 1862 enlisted as a private in Co. C, 27th Regiment, Georgia Infantry.

HARBIN, W. J.: Company E, private. He enlisted as a private in Co. E, 27th Regiment, Georgia Infantry. December 31, 1861 admitted to Moore Hospital at General Hospital No. 1 at Danville, Virginia with Fever and was sent to Charlottesville, Virginia.

HARDY, THOMAS: Company K, private. July 2, 1862 enlisted in Co. K, 27th Regiment, Georgia Infantry at Calhoun, Georgia. May 31, 1862 captured at Seven Pines, Virginia. August 29, 1862 admitted to General Hospital Camp Winder at Richmond, Virginia with Diarrhoea. October 11, 1862 received pay ($46.63). October 11, 1862 furloughed for 20 days from 2nd Division General Hospital Camp Winder at Richmond, Virginia. December 1862 roll shows him on furlough time and date unknown. April 8, 1863 received $35.00 for commutation of rations while on furlough from October 11, 1862 until January 26, 1863. October 29, 1863 issued clothing. December 31, 1863 received pay. February 20, 1864 wounded at Olustee, Florida. March - April 1864 roll shows him present. June 1, 1864 captured at Malvern Hill, Virginia. June 11, 1864 arrived at Point Lookout, Maryland from White House, Virginia. June 12, 1864 transferred to Elmira Prison, Elmira, New York. July 17, 1864 received at Elmira Prison, Elmira, New York. March 21, 1865 died of Pneumonia at Elmira Prison, Elmira, New York. He had $ .20 U. S. money in his possession. He is buried in grave No.1633 at Woodlawn Cemetery at Elmira Prison, Elmira, New York Cemetery.

HARGROVES, SAMUEL: Company B, private. March 4, 1862 enlisted as a private in Co. B, 27th Regiment, Georgia Infantry at Macon, Georgia. May 12, 1862 wounded at Spotsylvania, Virginia. July 5, 1862 admitted to Chimborazo Hospital No. 4, Richmond, Virginia with acute Pneumonia. July 29, 1862 transferred to Danville, Virginia. October, November and December 1863 issued clothing. December 31, 1863 received pay. January - February 1864 roll shows him present. February 20, 1864 pension records show he was wounded in the hip at Olustee, Florida. March – April 1864 roll shows he died May 12, 1864 of wounds received at Olustee, Florida. May 12, 1864 died from wounds. He had $70.55 with him.

HARKEY, ROBERT A.: Company H, captain. September 9, 1861 elected 1st lieutenant of Co. H, 27th Regiment, Georgia Infantry at Griffin, Georgia. December 1861 and January 1862 rolls show him present at Camp Pickens near Manassas, Virginia. February 1862 roll shows him absent on recruiting service for 30 days from February 13, 1862. March 30, 1862 received reimbursement for recruiting duty ($115.00). April 22, 1862 received pay ($90.00). April 25, 1862 received pay ($90.00). June 2, 1862 received pay ($90.00). June 15, 1862 elected captain Co. H, 27th Regiment, Georgia Infantry. July 9, 1862 received pay ($90.00). September 30, 1862 received pay ($190.00). December 6, 1862 received pay ($390.00). December 1862 roll shows him present at Guinea Station, Virginia. September 30, 1863 appears on roster of officers in Colquitt's Brigade. January - February 1864 roll shows him present. August 18, 1864 admitted to General Hospital No. 4 at Richmond, Virginia with a gunshot Vulnus Sclopeticum (Gunshot Wound) through the left forearm (flesh). August 18, 1864 furloughed to Atlanta for 40 days. August 20,

1864 received pay ($260.00) November 24, 1864 resigned his commission. It appears that the Company, Regiment or Brigade did not know his whereabouts while in the hospital or on furlough. They had him listed as absent without leave.

HARKNESS, MARION PICKNEY: Company H, private. September 9, 1861 enlisted as a private in Co. H, 27th Regiment, Georgia Infantry at Griffin, Georgia. July 10, 1862 received pay ($91.00). December 31, 1863 received pay. January 1, 1864 received pay. January – February 1864 roll shows him present. March - April 1864 roll shows him present. April 30, 1864 roll of 1st Division, General Hospital Camp Winder at Richmond, Virginia list him. June 2, 1864 appears on register of Receiving and Wayside Hospital or General Hospital No. 9 at Richmond, Virginia. June 3, 1864 wounded in left arm at Cold Harbor, Virginia. June 20, 1864 admitted to Receiving and Wayside Hospital or General Hospital No. 9 at Richmond, Virginia. June 22, 1864 transferred to Jackson Hospital at Richmond, Virginia. August 9, 1864 issued clothing at General Hospital Camp Winder at Richmond, Virginia. November 7, 1864 admitted to Ocmulgee Hospital at Macon, Georgia with Vulnus Sclopeticum (Gunshot Wound) to left elbow joint. November 9, 1864 appears on register of Floyd House and Ocmulgee Hospitals at Macon, Georgia with a Vulnus Sclopeticum (Gunshot Wound) to the left elbow resulting in Ankylosis and still discharging. He was living in McDonough, Henry County, Georgia. He was born in Henry County, Georgia February 12, 1841.

HARKNESS, SAMUEL G. W.: Company H, private. June 1, 1864 wounded at Cold Harbor, Virginia. January 17, 1862 admitted to Moore Hospital at General Hospital No. 1 at Danville, Virginia with Fistula. 1862 sent to General Hospital at Front Royal, Virginia. March 14, 1862 admitted to Chimborazo Hospital No. 2, Richmond, Virginia with Typhoid Fever. May 31, 1862 killed at Seven Pines, Virginia. August 5, 1862 death benefit claim was filed by his mother, Mary A. Harkness.

HARP, WILLIAM D.: Company C, sergeant. September 10, 1861 enlisted as a private in Co. C, 27th Regiment, Georgia Infantry. He was appointed 1st sergeant Co. C, 27th Regiment, Georgia Infantry. October 31, 1861 left sick in Georgia.

HARPER, ELIJAH W.: Company H, private. September 9, 1861 enlisted as a private in Co. H, 27th Regiment, Georgia Infantry at Griffin, Georgia. November 15, 1861 shown on roll of General Hospital No. 13 (formerly Greaner's Hospital) at Richmond, Virginia. December 1861, January 8, 1862 assigned as courier at post headquarters through February 1862. January 1862 and February 1862 rolls show he was left in Georgia sick October 31, 1861. June 4, 1862 received pay ($69.00). August 29, 1862 admitted to General Hospital Camp Winder at Richmond, Virginia with Teteris. December 31, 1863 received pay. January – February 1864 roll shows him present. February 20, 1864 slightly wounded at Olustee, Florida. March - April 1864 roll shows him present. June 3, 1864 wounded in the face by a mini ball at Cold Harbor, Virginia. June 3, 1862 admitted to Receiving and Wayside Hospital or General Hospital No. 9 at Richmond, Virginia. June 3, 1864 transferred from Receiving and Wayside Hospital or General Hospital No. 9 at Richmond Virginia to Jackson Hospital at Richmond, Virginia. June 7, 1862 admitted to Jackson Hospital at Richmond, Virginia with a Vulnus Sclopeticum (Gunshot Wound) to the face. July 13, 1864 furloughed from Jackson Hospital at Richmond, Virginia for 40 days.

HARPER, HIRAM WALLACE: Company H, private. October 13, 1861 enlisted as a private in Co. F, 3rd Regiment, Georgia State Troops. December 23, 1861 discharged. He enlisted as a private in Co. H, 27th Regiment, Georgia Infantry. February 22, 1865 admitted to C. S. A. General Hospital No.3 at Greensboro, North Carolina with Measles. February 23, 1865 sent to another hospital.

HARPER, JAMES: Company G, private. September 9, 1861 enlisted as a private in Co. G, 27th Regiment, Georgia Infantry. October 31, 1861 received pay. December 31, 1861 appears on the Roll of General Hospital No. 18 (formerly Greaner's Hospital) at Richmond, Virginia. January 9, 1862 admitted to Moore Hospital at General Hospital, No. 1 at Danville Virginia with Rheumatism and was sent to Richmond, Virginia. January 10, 1862 admitted to General Hospital No. 13 (formerly Greaner's Hospital) at Richmond Virginia with Chronic Rheumatism. January 22, 1862 returned to duty. March 7, 1862 admitted to Chimborazo Hospital No.2 at Richmond, Virginia. March 7 1862 admitted to and died in Chimborazo Hospital No.5 at Richmond, Virginia of Congestion of Brain (note indicates he arrived at the hospital dead). March 7, 1862 he was buried Oakwood Cemetery, Richmond, Virginia. He was from Pike County, Zebulon, Georgia

HARPER, JAMES E.: Company I, sergeant major. February 3, 1864 enlisted in Decatur, Georgia as a private in Co. I, 27th Regiment, Georgia Infantry. January - February 1864 roll shows him present . February 23, 1864 issued clothing. February 29, 1864 received pay. March - April 1864 roll shows him present. May 30, 1864, July 1864 and September 30, 1864 issued clothing. April 26, 1865 surrendered, Greensboro, North Carolina. May 1, 1864 paroled at Greensboro, North Carolina (listed as sergeant major).

HARPER, JAMES W.: Company H, private. May 13, 1862 enlisted at Chickahominy (Richmond), Virginia as a private in Co. H, 27th Regiment, Georgia Infantry. July 26, 1862 received clothing allowance ($25.00). October 4, 1862 received pay ($89.96). December 31, 1863 received pay. January - February 1864 roll shows him present. March – April 1864 roll shows him present. June 30 1864 received pay. August 26, 1864 received pay at Petersburg, Virginia ($66.00). July 1864 and September 20, 1864 issued clothing. He was born in Butts County, Georgia November 13, 1837 and died June 22, 1922.

HARPER, R. T.: Company H, private. May 5, 1864 enlisted in Macon, Bibb County, Georgia. July 1864 issued clothing. August 7, 1864

discharged with certificate of the Medical Examiners Board. August 19, 1864 received pay ($63.90). He was born in Henry County, Georgia in 1835. He was listed as 5 foot 7 ½ inches high, fair complexion, blue eyes, light hair. He was a merchant by occupation.

HARPER, W. T.: Company H, private. January 18, 1864 enlisted in Carrolton, Georgia as a private in Co. H, 27th Regiment, Georgia Infantry. February 20, 1864 wounded seriously in the left foot and shoulder at Olustee, Florida. January - February 1864 roll shows him absent wounded and was in Lake City, Florida. March –April 1864 roll shows him on wounded furlough from wound received at Olustee, Florida. Pension records show he was never able to return. He was born in Georgia.

HARPER, W. W.: Company H, private. He enlisted as a private in Co. H, 27th Regiment, Georgia Infantry. February 22, 1865 transferred from North East Hospital and admitted to C. S. A. General Hospital, No. 3, Greensboro, North Carolina with Rubeola. February 23, 1865 transferred to another Hospital. He was from Carrolton, Georgia.

HARPER, WADE H.: Company H, lieutenant. September 9, 1861 enlisted as a private in Co. K, 27th Regiment, Georgia Infantry in Griffin, Georgia. September 9, 1861 elected Jr. 2nd lieutenant of Co. H, 27th Regiment, Georgia Infantry. June 15, 1862 elected 2nd lieutenant of Co. H, 27th Regiment, Georgia Infantry. December 30, 1861, January 1862 and February 1862 rolls show him present at Camp Pickens near Manassas, Virginia. March 1862 received pay ($160.00). April 25, 1862 received pay ($160.00). June 15, 1862 promoted to 2nd lieutenant of Company H, 27th Georgia Infantry. June 30, 1862 wounded in left hand, artery severed, at Malvern Hill, Virginia. July 5, 1862 received pay ($160.00). September 27, 1862 paroled by the Army of the Potomac. November 28, 1862 furloughed by the Medical Director's Office at Richmond, Virginia. December 2, 1862 he is shown on 60 day furlough by the Medical Director's Office at Richmond, Virginia. December 1862 roll shows him absent with leave. September 30, 1863 he is shown on rosters of the officers of General A. H. Colquitt's Brigade. February 20, 1864 wounded seriously through the left knee at Olustee, Florida. January – February 1864 and March - April, 1864 rolls show him absent with leave from wounds received at Olustee, Florida. August 14, 1864 report of Colquitt's Brigade at Petersburg, Virginia shows him absent at hospital. August 18, 1864 resigned his commission. August 19, 1864 received pay ($160.00). August 22, 1864 received pay ($368.00). He is mentioned for gallantry in the personal papers of Major James Gardner of the 27th Georgia.

HARPER, WILLIAM H.: Company E, corporal. September 9, 1861 enlisted as a private in Co. E, 27th Regiment, Georgia Infantry. He was appointed corporal Co. E, 27th Regiment, Georgia Infantry. September 17, 1862 killed at Sharpsburg, Maryland. He was born in Pike County, Georgia. April 25, 1863 death benefit claim was filed by his father, John T. Harper. February 6, 1864 death benefit paid $134.36 (#12708).

HARRELL, THOMAS A.: Company A, sergeant. September 8, 1862 enlisted as a private in Co. A, 27th Regiment, Georgia Infantry at Randolph County, Georgia. November 4, 1862 admitted to Winder Division 4 Hospital at Richmond, Virginia. December 16, 1862 admitted to C. S. A. General Hospital at Danville, Virginia with confusion. May 20, 1862 returned to duty. January 15, 1863 issued clothing at 8th Division General Hospital at Danville, Virginia. June, July, August and September 1863 issued clothing. December 14 through December 31, 1863 detailed as a carpenter at Fort Sumter. December 31, 1863 received pay in Charleston, South Carolina. January 1, 1864 – through May 8, 1864 he was on detached duty as a carpenter at Fort Sumter, South Carolina. January – February and March – April 1864 rolls show him absent on detached duty at Fort Sumter. May 8, 1864 relieved of extra duty as a carpenter and paid for 56 days at $2.00 per day. June 18, 1864 wounded in the battle of the retaking of Colquitt's Salient by the 27th Georgia Regiment. June 20, 1864 admitted to General Hospital at Petersburg, Virginia with a Vulnus Sclopeticum (Gunshot Wound). June 22, 1864 transferred to Richmond, Virginia. June 22, 1864 admitted to Receiving and Wayside Hospital or General Hospital No. 9 at Richmond, Virginia and transferred to Jackson Hospital. June 23, 1864 admitted to Jackson Hospital at Richmond, Virginia with a Vulnus Sclopeticum (Gunshot Wound) to the left shoulder (mini ball). July 8, 1864 transferred to Huguenot Springs. September 1, 1864 received pay $22.00. September 1 and September 30, 1864 issued clothing. He was appointed 3rd sergeant. April 26, 1865 surrendered, Greensboro, North Carolina. May 1, 1865 paroled at Goldsboro, North Carolina.

HARRIS, ANDREW: Company H, private. He enlisted as a private in Co. H, 27th Regiment, Georgia Infantry.

HARRIS, JOHN T. D.: Company H, private. September 9, 1861 enlisted as a private in Co. H, 27th Regiment, Georgia Infantry. June 1, 1862 wounded and captured at the battle of Seven Pines, Virginia. June 4, 1862 wounded right thigh (left leg amputated) in Virginia (near Richmond). June 8, 1862 died of Vulnus Sclopeticum (Gunshot Wound)s in U. S. A. General Hospital at Mile Creek, near Fort Monroe, Virginia. January 27, 1863 death benefit claim was filed by his father, Hezekiah H. Harris.

HARRIS, LOENARD O.: Company G, private. September 9, 1861 enlisted as a private in Co. G, 27th Regiment, Georgia Infantry. (He was captured at either South Mountain, Maryland on September 14, 1862 or Sharpsburg, Maryland September 17, 1862) September 30, 1862 paroled by the Army of the Potomac. October 18, 1862 admitted Receiving and Wayside Hospital or General Hospital No. 9 at Richmond, Virginia and transferred to General Hospital No. 22, Richmond, Virginia. December 11, 1862 admitted to General Hospital Camp Winder at Richmond, Virginia with Pneumonia. December 16, 1862 admitted to C. S. A. General Hospital at Danville, Virginia with Rheumatism. December 17, 1862 admitted to C. S .A. General Hospital at Danville, Virginia. December 1862 roll shows him absent sick. December 12, 1862 admitted to Winder Division 2 Hospital at Richmond, Virginia. December 29, 1862 died of Variola in C. S .A. General Hospital at Danville, Virginia. He had $62.45 in his possession at the time of death.

HARRIS, WILLIAM C.: Company D, private. He enlisted as a private in Co. D, 27th Regiment, Georgia Infantry. December 1861 roll shows he was left sick in Georgia (October 31, 1861).

HARRISON, A. R.: Company C, private. He enlisted as a private in Co. C, 27th Regiment, Georgia Infantry. June 25, 1862 died of Pneumonia at General Hospital No. 2, Lynchburg, Virginia. He was buried June 25, 1862 (most likely at the City Cemetery in the Confederate Section).

HART, JOHN: Company F, sergeant. September 9, 1861 enlisted as a private in Co. F, 27th Regiment, Georgia Infantry at Camp Stephens, Georgia. January 6, 1862 appointed 3rd sergeant in Co. F, 27th Regiment, Georgia Infantry. July 5, 1862 admitted to Chimborazo Hospital No.4 at Richmond, Virginia with Congestive Fever (Malaria). July 22, 1862 sent to Hospital at Danville, Virginia. July 23 1862 admitted to C.S. A. General Hospital at Danville, Virginia with Typhoid Fever. August 6, 1862 returned to duty. September 20, 1862 received pay ($94.00). July – August 1863 issued clothing. December 31, 1863 received pay at Charleston, South Carolina. February 20, 1864 wounded at Olustee, Florida. January – February and March – April 1864 rolls show him absent on wounded furlough since February 20, 1864. July 8, 1864 admitted to Jackson Hospital at Richmond, Virginia with a wound to his right thigh from a shell which was received at Colquitt's Salient near Petersburg, Virginia. August 31, 1864 died in Jackson Hospital at Richmond, Virginia. Possessions at time of death were: 1 blanket, 1 jacket, 1 pair shoes, 1 pair socks and 1 hat valued at $6.00. He is buried in Hollywood Cemetery at Richmond, Virginia. November 28, 1864 death benefit claim was filed by his mother, Elizabeth Hart.

HART, JOSIAH: Company E, private. August 13, 1862 enlisted as a private in Co. E, 27th Regiment, Georgia Infantry in Randolph County, Georgia. December 1862 roll shows him detailed as a teamster. January 1 to May 24, 1863 detailed as a teamster at a rate of $.25 extra per day. April, May and June 1863 issued clothing. December 31, 1863 received pay. February 20, 1864 wounded at Olustee, Florida. January – February roll shows him absent wounded in action at Olustee, Florida. March 20, 1864 died of wounds.

HART, T. L.: Company G, private. June 28, 1864 returned from duty from Jackson Hospital, Richmond, Virginia.

HARTMAN (HORTMAN), FRANKLIN H.: Company C, private. September 10, 1861 enlisted as a private in Co. C, 27th Regiment, Georgia Infantry at Griffin, Spalding County, Georgia. March 7, 1862 admitted to Chimborazo Hospital No. 5 at Richmond, Virginia with Diarrhoea. March 23, 1862 returned to duty. June 10, 1862 received pay ($55.00). August 30,

1862 received pay ($11.00). January 16, 1863 issued clothing at Winder Division 1 Hospital at Richmond, Virginia. January 24, 1863 returned to duty from Winder Division 1 Hospital at Richmond, Virginia. June 26, 1863 issued clothing. September 30, 1863 issued clothing. December 31, 1863 received pay. February 20, 1864 wounded seriously at Olustee, Florida. January – February 1864 roll shows him absent wounded on February 20, 1864 at Olustee, Florida. February 29, 1864 received pay. March – April 1864 roll shows him present. July 1864 issued clothing. April 26, 1865 surrendered, Greensboro, North Carolina. May 1, 1865 paroled at Greensboro, North Carolina.

HASKINS (HOSKINS), JULIUS: Company C, private. September 10, 1861 enlisted as a private in Co. C, 27th Regiment, Georgia Infantry. March – April 1864 roll shows him present. He was killed in North Carolina.

HASKINS (HOSKINS), WILLIAM: Company C, private. September 10, 1861 enlisted as a private in Co. C, 27th Regiment, Georgia Infantry. April 19, 1862 killed while on picket duty at Yorktown, Virginia.

HASLER, A.: Company A, private. February 5, 1863 admitted to C. S. A. General Hospital at Charlottesville, Virginia with Debility. February 6, 1863 returned to duty.

HAWKINS, SAMUEL G.: Company H, private. He enlisted as a private in Co. H, 27th Regiment, Georgia Infantry.

HAWKS, JAMES T.: Company D, private. He enlisted as a private in Co. D, 27th Regiment, Georgia Infantry. November 6, 1861 admitted to General Hospital at Petersburg, Virginia with Rubeola. December 6, 1861 returned to duty. May 31, 1862 wounded at Seven Pines, Virginia. June 1, 1862 admitted to Episcopal Hospital at Williamsburg, Virginia with a Vulnus Sclopeticum (Gunshot Wound). June 15, 1862 furloughed from Episcopal Hospital at Williamsburg, Virginia. October 19, 1862 admitted to Winder Division 5 Hospital at Richmond, Virginia. October 25, 1862 returned to duty. January 24, 1863 discharged from Guinea Station, Virginia.

HAYES, ELIAS: Company D, private. September 31, 1861 enlisted as a private in Co. D, 27th Regiment, Georgia Infantry at Camp Stephens, Griffin, Spalding County, Georgia. December 18, 1861 admitted to Moore Hospital at General Hospital, No. 1 at Danville, Virginia with Catarrhal and was sent to the General Hospital at Front Royal, Virginia. January 19, 1862 died of double Pneumonia at General Hospital at Front Royal, Virginia. July 10, 1862 death benefit claim was filed by his widow Mary Hayes in Hall County, Georgia. December 4, 1862 death benefit claim paid $130.00 (#2073).

HAYES, WILLIAM H.: Company D, private. September 23, 1861 enlisted as a private in Co. D, 27th Regiment, Georgia Infantry in Griffin, Spalding County, Georgia. June 27, 1862 wounded at Cold Harbor, Virginia. July 2, 1862 received pay ($66.00). April, May and June 1863 issued clothing. December 31, 1863 received pay and clothing at Charleston, South Carolina. April 30, 1864 received pay at the Hospital. March - April

1864 roll shows him present. June 20, 1864 wounded in the right hand by a mini ball at Colquitt's Salient near Petersburg, Virginia. June 20, 1864 admitted to Jackson Hospital at Richmond Virginia with a Vulnus Sclopeticum (Gunshot Wound) to the right hand (mini ball). June 30, 1864 appears on roll of 2nd Division Jackson Hospital at Richmond, Virginia. July 14, 1864 furloughed from Jackson Hospital at Richmond Virginia for 30 days. September 20, 1864 issued clothing. Could not read and write.

HEAD, JAMES J.: Company D, private. September 10, 1861 enlisted as a private in Co. D, 27th Regiment, Georgia Infantry at Camp Stephens, Griffin, Spalding County, Georgia. March 30, 1862 admitted to General Hospital No. 18 (formerly Greaner's Hospital) at Richmond, Virginia with Chronic Diarrhoea. April 26, 1862 transferred and admitted to General Hospital at Petersburg, Virginia with Icterus (Jaundice). April 30, 1862 received pay. May 12, 1862 returned to duty. August 31, 1862 roll of General Hospital No. 1 at Richmond, Virginia shows him present. December 3, 1862 admitted to General Hospital No. 1 at Richmond, Virginia. April, May and June 1863 issued clothing. December 1863 issued clothing. February 29, 1864 received pay. March – April 1864 roll shows him present. July 1864 issued clothing. Was a resident of Gainesville, Hall County, Georgia.

HEAD, WILLIAM H. H.: Company E, private. September 9, 1861 enlisted as a private in Co. E, 27th Regiment, Georgia Infantry. December 6, 1861 died of disease at Camp Pickens near Manassas, Virginia. August 7, 1862 death benefit claim was filed by his widow Nancy Head. Death benefit claim paid $57.26 (#958). He was born in Fayette County, Georgia.

HEARD, BAILEY ARMSTRONG: Company B, private. September 10, 1861 enlisted as a private in Co. B, 27th Regiment, Georgia Infantry at Camp Stephens, Griffin, Spalding County, Georgia. December 1862 roll states "Furlough expired. He was shown as "Reporting to Colonel Wrens"and "Absent without leave". June 27, 1862 wounded, in the finger, resulting in amputation at Cold Harbor, Virginia. July 3, 1862 received pay ($66.00). July 21, 1863 received pay ($153.75) for the collection of stragglers at $.75 each. August 31, 1863 received pay. October 30, 1863 received pay ($22.00). March 14, 1864 was on extra duty at Macon Georgia. January 2, 1864 received pay ($22.00). January – February and March -April 1864 rolls show him "absent from wounds received June 27, 1862". March 4, 1864 received pay ($22.00). July 18, 1864 admitted to Floyd House and Ocmulgee Hospitals at Macon, Georgia with Vulnus Sclopeticum (Gunshot Wound) of the left hand causing amputation of ring finger was furloughed for 60 days. July 27, 1864 admitted to Ocmulgee Hospital at Macon, Georgia with a Vulnus Sclopeticum (Gunshot Wound) and was furloughed. October 5, 1864 admitted to Ocmulgee Hospital at Macon, Georgia with Vulnus Sclopeticum (Gunshot Wound) to hand. December 4, 1864 shown as deserted. December 16, 1864 admitted to Ocmulgee Hospital at Macon, Georgia where finger was amputated from old wound. December 22, 1864 admitted to Ocmulgee Hospital at Macon,

Georgia with Vulnus Sclopeticum (Gunshot Wound) of left hand. Lived in the Rutland District of Bibb County, Georgia.

HEARN, BENJAMIN G. (TOBE): Company H, private. March 4, 1862 enlisted as a private in Co. I, 44th Regiment, Georgia Infantry. July 31, 1863 discharged due to disability. June 1864 enlisted as a private in Co. H, 27th Regiment, Georgia Infantry. He was wounded in head, date and place not given. 1865 captured. 1865 released at Fort Delaware, Delaware. He was born in Henry County, Georgia April 25, 1841.

HEARN, J. W.: Company H, private. He enlisted as a private in Co. H, 27th Regiment, Georgia Infantry. May 3, 1863 wounded at Chancellorsville, Virginia died of wounds.

HEARNDON, URIAH. H.: Company E, private. He enlisted as a private in Co. E, 27th Regiment, Georgia Infantry. December 1861 roll shows him in the Hospital in Richmond, Virginia. August 27, 1862 discharged from service with a certificate from Chimborazo Hospital No. 2 at Richmond, Virginia for Arthisis Pulmonalis and Chronic Diarrhoea.

HEATH, N. W.: Company F, private. He enlisted as a private in Co. F, 27th Regiment, Georgia Infantry. September 7 through September 17 on detailed duty in Savannah, Georgia and was paid $2.00 per day. He surrendered May 18, 1865 at Augusta, Georgia and was paroled on that date.

HEMPERLEY (HEMPLAY) EDWARD T.: Company E, private. September 9, 1861 enlisted as a private in Co. E, 27th Regiment, Georgia Infantry at Camp Stephens, Griffin, Spalding County, Georgia. December 7, 1861 discharged on account of Chronic Rheumatism at Manassas, Virginia. August 1, 1863 reenlisted. August 1, 1863 reenlisted December 31, 1863 received pay. February 21, 1864 detailed nurse at Lake City, Florida after the battle at Olustee Florida. February 29, 1864 received pay. March 11, 1864 admitted to Ocmulgee Hospital at Macon, Georgia with Neuralgia. March – April 1864 roll shows him present. September 20, 1864 issued clothing. October 25, 1864 returned to duty. April 26, 1865 surrendered at Greensboro, North Carolina. May 1, 1865 paroled at Greensboro, North Carolina. Born in Campbell County, Georgia in 1835 and was described in 1861 as six feet high, dark complexion, grey eyes, black hair and was a farmer when he enlisted. He died in 1913. He is buried in Evergreen Baptist Church Cemetery in Miller County, Arkansas.

HEMPERLEY (HEMPLAY), JOEL M.: Company E, private. September 9, 1861 enlisted as a private in Co. E, 27th Regiment, Georgia Infantry. September 17, 1862 killed, Sharpsburg, Maryland. He is buried in Sardis Baptist Church Cemetery in Palmetto, Fulton County, Georgia.

HEMPHILL, JOSEPH M.: Company D, private. February 28, 1862 enlisted as a private in Co. D, 27th Regiment, Georgia Infantry at Chestnut Mountain in Hall County, Georgia. March 25, 1862 received bounty pay ($50.00) at Atlanta, Georgia. July 31, 1862 received pay ($69.00). October 31, 18963 received pay. December 9, 1863 both legs crushed in an explosion at Fort Sumter, South Carolina. December 31, 1863 received pay and issued clothing. December 31, 1863 hospital Muster Roll of First Georgia Hospital at Charleston, South Carolina shows him present. January – February 1864 hospital muster Roll of General Hospital No. 1, Summerville, South Carolina shows him present. March –April 1864 roll shows him on sick furlough. He was born in Georgia November 9, 1829.

HEMPHILL, WILLIAM W.: Company D, private. September 17, 1861 enlisted as a private in Co. D, 27th Regiment, Georgia Infantry at Camp Stephens at Griffin, Spalding County, Georgia. December 11, 1861 admitted to Moore Hospital at General Hospital No. 1 at Danville Virginia with Pneumonia and was transferred to General Hospital at Richmond, Virginia. December 1861 roll shows him in the hospital in Richmond, Virginia. April 3, 1862 admitted to General Hospital at Orange Court House, Virginia with Pneumonia. April 14, 1862 admitted to General Hospital No. 21 at Richmond, Virginia with Diarrhoea. May 6, 1862 transferred to hospital at Danville, Virginia. June 27, 1862 killed at Mechanicsville, Virginia. December 16, 1862 death benefit claim was filed by his widow Ophelia Hemphill. September 18, 1863 death benefit claim paid of $139.90 (#8902).

HENNI, G. W.: Company K, private. September 19, 1863 Roll of Prisoners of War show him captured at Chickamauga, Georgia (the 27th Georgia was not at Chickamauga but the 37th Georgia was). October 24, 1863 he is shown as being a Prisoner of War at Nashville, Tennessee. October 25, 1863 received at Military Prison, Louisville, Kentucky. October 26, 1863 roll shows him discharged from Camp Morton.

HENNIGAR (HENEGAR), HENRY: Company B, private. September 10, 1861 enlisted as a private in Co. B, 27th Regiment, Georgia Infantry at Camp Stephens at Griffin, Spalding County, Georgia. June 30 1863 received pay. January – February and March - April 1864 rolls show him in jail in Charleston, South Carolina for desertion. July 1864 issued clothing. August 19, 1864 captured at Weldon Railroad near Petersburg, Virginia. August 24, 1864 received at Point Lookout, Maryland as Prisoner of War. March 14, 1865 paroled at Point Lookout, Maryland and transferred to Aiken's landing, Virginia for exchange. March 16, 1865 received at Boulware and Cox's Wharves, James River, Virginia.

HENNIGAR (HENEGAR), MICHAEL C.: Company B, private. September 10, 1861 enlisted as a private in Co. B, 27th Regiment, Georgia Infantry. March 16, 1862 admitted to Chimborazo Hospital No.4, Richmond, Virginia with Typhoid Fever. March 30, 1862 returned to duty. June 18, 1862 died in Virginia. July 30, 1862 death benefit claim was filed by his widow Elizabeth J. Heniger. January 6, 1863 Death benefit claim was paid $136.60 (#2483).

HENRY, AARON F.: Company H, private. September 9, 1861 enlisted as a private in Co. H, 27th Regiment, Georgia Infantry at Camp Stephens at Griffin, Spalding County, Georgia. September 17, 1862 wounded in the left thigh and captured at Sharpsburg, Maryland. September 27, 1862 paroled by the Army of the Potomac. October 1, 1862 admitted to Summit House U. S. A. Hospital at Philadelphia, Pennsylvania. November 24, 1862 returned to duty from Summit House U. S. A. Hospital at Philadelphia, Pennsylvania. December 15, 1862 sent from Fort Delaware, Delaware to Fortress Monroe, Virginia for exchange. December 31, 1863 received pay. January – February 1864 roll shows him present. February 29, 1864 received pay. March – April 1864 roll shows him present. May 31, 1864 issued clothing. July 1864 issued clothing. September 20, 1864 issued clothing. April 11, 1865 captured at Pineville, North Carolina. April 22, 1865 took Oath of Allegiance at Raleigh, North Carolina.

HENRY, S. M.: Company H, private. September 9, 1861 enlisted as a private in Co. H, 27th Regiment, Georgia Infantry at Camp Stephens at Griffin, Spalding County, Georgia. March 21, 1862 admitted to Chimborazo Hospital No. 1 at Richmond Virginia with Dysentery. March 25, 1862 returned to duty. June 1, 1862 captured at Seven Pines, Virginia. July 9, 1862 paroled at Fort Delaware, Delaware. July 31, 1864 admitted to Jackson Hospital at Richmond, Virginia with Hepatitis and Bronchitis. August 5, 1862 exchanged at Aikens Landing, Virginia. August 10, 1864 furloughed for 30 days. October 23, 1863 received pay ($22.00). December 11, 1863 received at James Island, South Carolina ($13.27) in commutation for rations. December 31, 1863 received pay. January – February 1864 and March – April 1864 rolls show him present. May 12, 1864 issued clothing. May 31, 1864 admitted to Confederate States Hospital at Petersburg, Virginia. June 5, 1864 transferred to hospital at Raleigh, North Carolina. July 1864 issued clothing. July 31, 1864 admitted to Jackson Hospital at Richmond, Virginia with Hepatitis and Bronchitis. August 8, 1864 issued clothing at Jackson Hospital at Richmond, Virginia. August 10, 1864 furloughed for 30 days. October 31, 1864 hospital muster rolls of 2nd Georgia Hospital at Augusta, Georgia show him present. November 17, 1864 issued clothing. Parole records show him as born in Georgia in 1841, 5 feet 9 inches high, light brown hair, grey eyes, fair complexion.

HENRY THOMAS: Company B, private. He enlisted as a private in Co. B, 27th Regiment, Georgia Infantry. May 2, 1862 died at Manassas, Virginia.

HERN, G. M.: Company H, private. Record of Camp Morton, Indianapolis, Indiana shows him captured at Chickamauga, Georgia September 19, 1863 (the 27th Georgia was not at Chickamauga but the 37th Georgia was). Camp Morton records show he escaped August 17, 1864.

HERNDON, ENOCH M.: Company E, private. September 9, 1861 enlisted as a private in Co. E, 27th Regiment, Georgia Infantry. March 8, 1862 admitted to Chimborazo Hospital No. 2 at Richmond, Virginia with Bronchitis. May 27, 1862 died of Typhoid Fever at Chimborazo Hospital No. 2 at Richmond, Virginia. He is most likely buried in Oakwood Cemetery at Richmond Virginia. August 1862 and February 16, 1863 death benefit claim was filed by father Enoch Herndon.

HERNDON, RICHARD: Company E, private. September 9, 1861 enlisted as a private in Co. E, 27th Regiment, Georgia Infantry.

HERNDOON, URIAH H.: Company E, private. September 25, 1861 enlisted as a private in Co. E, 27th Regiment, Georgia Infantry at Camp Stephens at Griffin, Spalding County, Georgia. February 1862 roll shows him detailed as Provost Marshals Guard at Headquarters Post. March 30, 1862 admitted to General Hospital No. 18 (formerly Greaner's Hospital) at Richmond, Virginia with Typhoid Fever. April 11, 1862 transferred to Chimborazo Hospital at Richmond Virginia. April 11, 1862 admitted to Chimborazo Hospital No. 3 at Richmond, Virginia with Debility (Phtisis Pulmonalis and Chronic Diarrhoea) Tuberculosis. August 23, 1862 Certificate of Disability granted in Richmond, Virginia. October 9, 1862 he died at his father's home in Cherokee County, Georgia. November 25, 1862 death benefit claim was filed by his father Enoch Herndon September 18, 1863 death benefit claim was paid $166.36 (#89.60). He lived in Woodstock, Cherokee County, Georgia. Description is born in Georgia in 1842. He is described as blue eyes, dark hair, fair complexion and 5 foot 8 inches high.

HERRICK (HERRICKS), J. (T.) G.: Company F, private. September 9, 1861 enlisted as a private in Co. F, 27th Regiment, Georgia Infantry. July 5, 1862 admitted to Chimborazo Hospital No. 4 with Continua Fever. July and August 1863 issued clothing. August 26, 1862 furloughed from this date to October 6, 1862 by board examiners. August 24, 1863 received ($13.20) in commutation of rations. 1863 died in Richmond, Virginia. He was owed ($80.00) in back pay.

HERRICK (HERRICKS), WILLIS: Company F, private. September 20, 1861 enlisted as a private in Co. F, 27th Regiment, Georgia Infantry at Camp Stephens at Griffin, Spalding County, Georgia. January 7, 1862 admitted to Moore Hospital at General Hospital No.1 at Danville, Virginia with Pneumonia and was sent to the General Hospital 9th ward. January and February 1862 rolls show him in Moore Hospital since January 7, 1862. May 15, 1862 admitted to C. S. A. General Hospital at Danville, Virginia with Typhoid Fever. July 4, 1862 returned to duty. September 17, 1862 wounded at Sharpsburg, Maryland. September 1862 died of wounds at the United States Army Antietam Hospital Sharpsburg, Maryland. January 23, 1863 death benefit claim was filed by widow Missouri H. Hendricks of Taylor County, Georgia.

HERRIN (HERRING), D. H.: Company F, private. August 7, 1862 enlisted as a private in Co. F, 27th Regiment, Georgia Infantry. September 17, 1862 wounded at Sharpsburg, Maryland. December 1862 roll shows him absent wounded at Sharpsburg, Maryland September 17, 1862. September 28, 1862 admitted to General Hospital No. 8 (St. Charles Hospital) at Richmond, Virginia with a Vulnus Sclopeticum (Gunshot Wound) in his side. October 10(12), 1862 furloughed for 30 days from hospital. August 1863 issued clothing. December 31, 1863 received pay. January – February roll shows him present. February 29, 1864 received pay. March – April, 1864 roll shows him present. July 1864 and September 20, 1864 issued clothing. April 26, 1865 surrendered, Greensboro, North Carolina. He was born in North Carolina in 1823.

HERRON, B. F.: Company H, private. He enlisted as a private in Co. H, 27th Regiment, Georgia Infantry. June 20, 1864 wounded in forearm at Colquitt's Salient near Petersburg, Virginia. June 20, 1864 admitted to C. S .A. General Hospital at Farmville, Virginia. July 5, 1864 furloughed for 60 days.

HESTER (HESTERS), DAVID: Company I, private. September 10, 1861 enlisted as a private in Co. I, 27th Regiment, Georgia Infantry. December 10, 1861 discharged, on account of Hernia at Camp Pickens near Manassas, Virginia. May 10, 1862 enlisted as a private in Co. F, 47th Regiment, Georgia Infantry. May 25, 1863 captured at Missionary Ridge, Tennessee. December 20, 1863 died of Diarrhoea and Pneumonia at Rock Island, Illinois.

HESTER (HESTERS), DAVID JACK (J. D.): Company I, private. September 10, 1861 enlisted as a private in Co. I, 27th Regiment, Georgia Infantry. November 15, 1861 admitted to General Hospital No. 18 (formerly Greaner's Hospital) at Richmond, Virginia with Pneumonia. November 22, 1861 died of Pneumonia at Richmond, Virginia. His body was accompanied to Appling County, Georgia by Private Henry Mann, Jr. of Co. I.

HESTER (HESTERS), FRANCIS M.: Company I, private. September 10, 1861 enlisted as a private in Co. I, 27th Regiment, Georgia Infantry. November 15, 1861 admitted to General Hospital No. 18 at Richmond, Virginia. November 1861 roll shows him either sick or wounded. December 1861 roll shows him in the hospital in Richmond, Virginia. September 17, 1862 killed at Sharpsburg, Maryland. March 25, 1864 death benefit claim was filed by mother, Elizabeth Hesters.

HESTER (HESTERS), GEORGE W.: Company I, private. September 10, 1861 enlisted as a private in Co. I, 27th Regiment, Georgia Infantry at Camp Stephens at Griffin, Spalding County, Georgia. November 15, 1861 admitted to General Hospital No. 18 (formerly Greaner's Hospital), Richmond, Virginia. January 1862 roll shows him in the Hospital at Richmond, Virginia. February 26, 1862 furloughed for 60 days. February 1862 roll shows him on sick furlough for 20 days from February 20 or 24. September 17, 1862 severely wounded at Sharpsburg, Maryland. September 30, 1862 paroled by the Army of the Potomac. October 31, 1862 received pay. November 1, 1862 wounded while destroying railroads at Staunton and Strasburg, Virginia. November 2, 1862 admitted to Chimborazo Hospital No. 1 at Richmond, Virginia with wound in hand and thigh. November 6, 1862 furloughed for 35 days in Richmond, Virginia. December 1862 roll shows him on furlough. January – February 1864 and March – April 1864 rolls show him present. May 30, 1864, July and September 1864 issued clothing. April 26, 1865 surrendered, Greensboro, North Carolina. May 1, 1865 paroled at Greensboro, North Carolina. He was born in 1820 and died in 1890 in Appling County, Georgia. He is buried at Mt. Zion Church Cemetery, Jeff Davis County, Georgia.

HEWETT, GEORGE W.: Company A, private. May 27, 1862 enlisted as a private in Co. A, 27th Regiment, Georgia Infantry. June 5, 1862 admitted to General Hospital Camp Winder at Richmond, Virginia with Typhoid Fever. June 29, 1862 died of Typhoid Fever at either C. S. A. General Hospital at Farmville, Virginia of at General Hospital Camp Wider Hospital at Richmond, Virginia (Records Conflict). July 1, 1863 Death benefit claim was filed. April 28, 1864 Death benefit claim paid to father William M. Hewett. Lived in Buena Vista, Marion County, Georgia.

HEWFERTY, JOEL M.: Company E, private. He enlisted as a private in Co. E, 27th Regiment, Georgia Infantry. September 17, 1862 wounded and captured at Sharpsburg, Maryland. He died of wounds at Lewis Farm Hospital.

HICKS, J.: Company C, private. He enlisted as a private in Co. C, 27th Regiment, Georgia Infantry. October 13, 1862 admitted to Receiving and Wayside Hospital or General Hospital at Richmond, Virginia and transferred to General Hospital No. 10.

HIGGINS, T. B.: Company G, private. He enlisted as a private in Co. G, 27th Regiment, Georgia Infantry. June 4, 1864 wounded in the shoulder at Cold Harbor, Virginia. June 4, 1864 admitted to C. S. A. General Hospital at Danville, Virginia with a Vulnus Sclopeticum (Gunshot Wound) in the shoulder. June 21, 1864 transferred from C. S. A. General Hospital at Danville, Virginia.

HIGHSMITY (HYSMITH), D.: Company A, private. He enlisted as a private in Co. A, 27th Regiment, Georgia Infantry. December 1862 roll shows him absent sick since August 1862.

HIGHSMITH, E.J.: Company A, private. September 10, 1861 enlisted as a private in Co. A, 27th Regiment, Georgia Infantry at Camp Stephens at Griffin, Spalding County, Georgia. December 1861 roll shows he was left sick in Georgia on October 31, 1861.. April 1963 and June 1863 issued clothing. December 31, 1863 received pay. January – February and March - April, 1864 rolls show him present. July and September 20, 1864 issued clothing.

HIGHSMITH, G.: Company A, private. January 18, 1862 sent to Moore Hospital at General Hospital, No. 1 at Danville, Virginia. January 1862 roll shows him sent to Moore Hospital at General Hospital, No. 1 at Danville, Virginia.

HIGHSMITH, J. T.: Company A, private. September 10, 1861 enlisted as a private in Co. A, 27th Regiment, Georgia Infantry at Camp Stephens at Griffin, Spalding County, Georgia. January 1862 roll shows he was left sick in Georgia October 31, 1861. June, July, August and September 1863 issued clothing. December 31, 1863 received pay. January – February and

March – April 1864 rolls show him present. May 30 1864 issued clothing. August 5, 1864 killed at Colquitt's Salient near Petersburg, Virginia.

HIGHSMITH, SAMUEL D.: Company A, private. October 23, 1863 enlisted as a private in Co. A, 27th Regiment, Georgia Infantry, at James Island, South Carolina. January 17, 1862 admitted to Moore Hospital at General Hospital, No. 1 at Danville, Virginia with Fever and was sent to hospital at Front Royal, Virginia. March 9, 1862 admitted to Chimborazo Hospital No.5 at Richmond, Virginia with Rheumatism. April 6, 1862 returned to duty. December 31, 1863 received pay. January - February 1864 roll shows him present. July 1864, returned to duty from Jackson Hospital at Richmond, Virginia. September 28, 1864 issued clothing at Jackson Hospital at Richmond, Virginia. September 29, 1864 received pay ($49.13). September 30, 1864 furloughed for 30 days from Jackson Hospital at Richmond, Virginia.

HIGHTOWER, ISAAC (J.): Company B, private. September 10, 1861 enlisted as a private in Co. B, 27th Regiment, Georgia Infantry at Camp Stephens, Griffin, Spalding County, Georgia. July 7, 1862 admitted to U. S. A. General Hospital at Portsmouth Grove, Rhode Island. September 17, 1862 appears on list of Prisoners of War forwarded from U. S. A. General Hospital at Portsmouth Grove, Rhode Island to Fortress Monroe, Virginia. September 18, 1862 appears on a Prisoner of War list received at Fort Columbus, New York Harbor from U. S. General Hospital at Portsmouth Grove, Rhode Island. September 22, 1862 paroled at Fortress Monroe, Virginia for exchange. October 21, 1862 furloughed for 30 days from Richmond, Virginia. October 29, 1862 received pay ($160.00). December 1862 roll shows him detailed collecting stragglers. April 8, 1863 received ($40.00) in commutation for rations. October, November and December 1863 issued clothing. December 31, 1863 received pay. January – February roll shows him present. February 29, 1864 received pay. March - April 1864 roll shows him present. May 30, 1864 issued clothing. June 5, 1864 wounded in the left hand by a mini ball at Cold Harbor, Virginia. June 5, 1864 admitted to Receiving and Wayside Hospital or General Hospital No. 9 at Richmond, Virginia. June 6, 1864 transferred to Jackson Hospital at Richmond, Virginia from Receiving and Wayside Hospital or General Hospital No. 9 at Richmond, Virginia with a Vulnus Sclopeticum (Gunshot Wound) to his left hand (mini ball). July 23 1864 issued clothing at Jackson Hospital at Richmond, Virginia. He was born in Bibb County, Georgia March 27, 1840.

HIGHTOWER, JAMES: Company B, private. He enlisted as a private in Co. B, 27th Regiment, Georgia Infantry. November 15, 1861 admitted to General Hospital No. 18 (formerly Greaner's Hospital) at Richmond, Virginia. November 1861 roll from Manassas, Virginia shows he was sick with Pneumonia and discharged. December 3, 1861 he was discharged and received pay. December 1861 roll shows him in the hospital in Richmond, Virginia. January 1862 roll shows he was discharged for disability December

3, 1861.

HILL, BRYANT (BEVERLY) D.: Company F, private. He enlisted as a private in Co. F, 27th Regiment, Georgia Infantry. January 15 1862 discharged for disability. January 1862 Camp Pickens near Manassas, Virginia roll shows him discharged for disability because of deafness.

HILL, D.: Company F, private. September 9, 1861 enlisted as a private in Co. F, 27th Regiment, Georgia Infantry.

HILL H.: Company F, private. He enlisted as a private in Co. F, 27th Regiment, Georgia Infantry. October 22, 1862 admitted to No. 1, U. S. A. General Hospital at Frederick, Maryland with a Vulnus Sclopeticum (Gunshot Wound). December 13, 1862 returned to duty.

HILL, JAMES (JOHN): Company E, private. September 9, 1861 enlisted as a private in Co. E, 27th Regiment, Georgia Infantry. July, 5, 1865 died of Typhoid Fever in C. S. A. General Hospital at Farmville, Virginia.

HILL, JOHN W.: Company E, private. May 5, 1862 enlisted as a private in Co. E, 27th Regiment, Georgia Infantry. June 3, 1862 admitted to General Hospital Camp Winder, Richmond, Virginia with Typhoid Fever. July 4, 1862 died of Typhoid Fever at General Hospital Camp Winder, Richmond, Virginia. He is buried in Hollywood Cemetery at Richmond, Virginia. August 7, 1862 death benefit claim was filed by his father, John Hill. August 7, 1862 death benefit claim paid of $98.10 (#943). He was born in Fayette County, Georgia.

HILL, JOEL: Company F, private. He enlisted as a private in Co. F, 27th Regiment, Georgia Infantry. April 25, 1862 admitted to Chimborazo Hospital No.4 at Richmond, Virginia with Measles. July 31, 1862 died. November 2, 1862 death benefit claim was filed.

HILL, JOSEPH W.: Company F, private. May 2, 1862 enlisted as a private in Co. F, 27th Regiment, Georgia Infantry in Butler, Taylor County, Georgia. September 16, 1862 admitted to General Hospital No. 12 at Richmond, Virginia. September 26, 1862 records of General Hospital No. 12 at Richmond, Virginia shows he was transferred to another hospital. September 26, 1862 admitted to Division No.1 General Hospital Camp Winder at Richmond, Virginia. July 12, 1863 admitted to C. S. A. General Hospital No. 4 at Wilmington, North Carolina with Typhoid Fever. November 6, 1863 returned to duty. November 6, 1863 detailed as a nurse in the General Hospital No. 4 at Wilmington, North Carolina and was furloughed for 20 days. March 24, 1864 deserted from Camp Milton, Florida. January – February and March – April 1864 rolls indicate he deserted from Camp Milton, Florida on March 24, 1864. July 1864 issued clothing. He was from Crawford County, Georgia.

HILL LEWIS: Company F, private. September 9, 1861 enlisted as a private in Co. F, 27th Regiment, Georgia Infantry at Camp Stephens, Griffin, Spalding County, Georgia. February 21, 1862 furloughed for 20 days. February 1862 roll shows him on furlough. March 31, 1862 wounded at Seven Pines, Virginia. May 3, 1862 wounded slightly at Chancellorsville,

Virginia. December 1862 roll shows him absent sick since June 3, 1862. December 31, 1863 received pay. January – February and March – April 1864 rolls show him absent without leave beginning March 28, 1864. March 28, 1864 - April 30, 1864 he was absent without leave.

HILL, REUBEN G.: Company E, private. He enlisted as a private in Co. F, 27th Regiment, Georgia Infantry. November 18, 1861 admitted to Chimborazo Hospital No.4 at Richmond, Virginia with Measles and was transferred to General Hospital No. 24. December 9, 1861 discharged for disability and received pay in Richmond, Virginia. December 1861 roll show he was discharged for disability in Richmond.

HILL, SLAUGHTER: Company F, private. September 9, 1861 enlisted as a private in Co. F, 27th Regiment, Georgia Infantry. March 7, 1862 admitted to Chimborazo Hospital No.4 at Richmond, Virginia with Icterus (Jaundice). April 9, 1862 returned to duty. September 17, 1862 wounded (5 wounds) and captured, Sharpsburg, Maryland. December 1862 roll shows him absent wounded since September 17, 1862. December 14, 1862 paroled at Fort McHenry, Baltimore, Maryland. December 18, 1862 exchanged at City Point, Virginia. December 18, 1862 admitted to General Hospital at Petersburg, Virginia with 5 Vulnus Sclopeticum (Gunshot Wound)s and is listed as a paroled prisoner. He was wounded in right hip. January 22, 1863 furloughed for 50 days by the Medical Examiners Board. January 26, 1863 furloughed for 30 days. March 18, 1863 admitted to Hospital and transferred to Petersburg, Virginia hospital April 20, 1863. April 18, 1863 admitted to hospital in Richmond, Virginia with a Vulnus Sclopeticum (Gunshot Wound) to right leg. January – February and March – April 1864 rolls show him absent since September 17, 1862. July 18, 1864 in Floyd House and Ocmulgee Hospitals at Macon, Georgia, with conjunctivitis and general disability, disposition "Ap. 60 days". He died in Reynolds, Georgia January 1, 1916.

HILLEY, JAMES PIERCE: Company H, private. September 9, 1861 enlisted as a private in Co. H, 27th Regiment, Georgia Infantry at Camp Stephens, Griffin, Spalding County, Georgia. January 14, 1862 detailed as regimental ambulance driver. January 1862 roll shows him on extra duty as regimental ambulance driver. December 1862 roll shows him detailed on extra duty as a teamster. October 31, 1863 received pay. December 31, 1863 received pay. January – February 1864 and March – April 1864 rolls show him present. June 1, 1864 wounded in left arm at Cold Harbor, Virginia. June 1 1864 admitted to Receiving and Wayside Hospital or General Hospital No. 9 at Richmond, Virginia. June 2, 1864 admitted to Jackson Hospital at Richmond, Virginia with a Vulnus Sclopeticum (Gunshot Wound) (mini ball) to the left arm. June 13, 1864 died of Vulnus Sclopeticum (Gunshot Wound) in Division No. 2, Jackson Hospital at Richmond, Virginia. He is buried in Hollywood Cemetery at Richmond, Virginia.

HILLEY (HILLERY), J. W.: Company H, private. March 1, 1862 enlisted as a private in Co. H, 27th Regiment, Georgia Infantry at McDonough, Henry County, Georgia. December 31, 1864 received pay. January – February 1864 roll shows him present. February 29, 1864 received pay. March – April 1864 roll shows him present. July 1864 and September 20, 1864 issued clothing.

HILLMAN, COLEMAN W.: Company A, private. April 26, 1862 enlisted as a private in Company A, 27th Regiment, Georgia Infantry in Marion County, Georgia. November 20, 1862 received $50.00 bounty pay at Richmond, Virginia. January 3, 1863 died (He had $1.00 on his person at time of death). July 1, 1863 death benefit claim was filed by his father George W. Hillman.

HILLMAN, WILLIAM H. H.: Company A, private. February 24, 1862 enlisted as a private in Company A, 27th Regiment, Georgia Infantry in Marion County, Georgia. November 20, 1862 received $50.00 bounty pay at Richmond, Virginia. April 6 (7), 1862 admitted to General Hospital at Orange Court House, Virginia with Measles. April 15 (19), 1862 died in General Hospital at Orange Court House, Virginia. July 1, 1863 death benefit claim was filed.

HINDMAN, JAMES F.: Company E, private. September 9, 1861 enlisted as a private in Co. E, 27th Regiment, Georgia Infantry. July 12, 1862 received pay of $91.00 at Richmond, Virginia. 1862 died in Virginia.

HINSLEY (HINESLEY), W. M.: Company G, private. February 20, 1864 enlisted as a private in Co. G, 27th Regiment, Georgia Infantry at Olustee, Florida. March – April 1964 roll shows him present. September 20, 1864 issued clothing. April 26, 1865 surrendered, Greensboro, North Carolina. May 1, 1865 paroled at Greensboro, North Carolina.

HOBBS, J. B.: Company A, private. 1864 enlisted as a private in Co. A, 27th Regiment, Georgia Infantry. April 23, 1864 he is shown on register as being in Jackson, Hospital at Richmond, Virginia. June 25, 1864 admitted into General Hospital at Petersburg, Virginia with Rubeola. June 29, 1864 was transferred to Richmond, Virginia. June 29, 1864 admitted to Receiving and Wayside Hospital or General Hospital No. 9 at Richmond, Virginia and was transferred to Jackson Hospital at Richmond, Virginia. June 30, 1864 admitted to Jackson Hospital at Richmond, Virginia with Rubeola. August 18, 1864 furloughed for 30 days from Jackson Hospital at Richmond, Virginia destination Butler, Georgia. April 28, 1865 admitted to C. S. A. Hospital No.11, at Charlotte, North Carolina with Diarrhoea. April 29, 1865 transferred to another hospital. He was born in Georgia July 1846. He lived in Butler, Georgia.

HOBBS, JESSE W.: Company K, private. September 10, 1861 enlisted as a private in Co. K, 27th Regiment, Georgia Infantry at Griffin, Spalding County, Georgia. December 1861, January 1862 and February 1862 rolls show he was left in Georgia sick on October 31, 1861. September 17, 1862 wounded, through right wrist and hand, permanently disabled, at Sharpsburg, Maryland. September 20, 1862 captured at Sharpsburg,

319

Maryland. September 27, 1862 and October 30, 1862 appears of roll of Prisoners of War paroled by the Army of the Potomac. October 4, 1862 admitted to No. 5, U. S. A. General Hospital at Frederick, Maryland with Vulnus Sclopeticum (Gunshot Wound) to the left thigh, fisure broken. December 1862 roll shows him missing since September 17, 1862. December 29, 1862 sent to No. 1, U. S. A. General Hospital at Frederick, Maryland. February 9, 1862 records at No. 1, U. S. A. General Hospital at Frederick, Maryland show he was returned to duty (POW). February 10, 1863 admitted to U. S. A. General Hospital, Camden Street at Baltimore, Maryland with a Vulnus Sclopeticum (Gunshot Wound). February 18, 1863 returned to duty (POW). February 17, 1863 roll of Confederate Prisoners of War show he was received at Fort McHenry, Maryland. (Other records show he was exchanged February 18, 1863). February 18, 1863 admitted to General Hospital at Petersburg, Virginia with Vulnus Sclopeticum (Gunshot Wound)s to the left thigh and right hand and he was a paroled prisoner. March 2, 1863 furloughed for 60 days. July 10, 1863 discharged. July 11, 1863 received pay ($257.64). Description: 5 foot 11 inches high, light complexion, blue eyes and was a farmer by occupation. He was born in Georgia in 1836 (1838).

HOBBS, S. R.: Company A, private. September 21, 1861 enlisted as a private in Co. A, 27th Regiment, Georgia Infantry. December 1861 and January 1862 rolls show he was left in Georgia sick on October 31, 1861. February 22, 1862 placed on sick leave for 30 days. February 22, 1862 received pay ($59.83) in commutation for rations and clothing. February 1862. Roll shows him on sick leave since February 22, 1862. December 1862 roll shows him absent sick since July, 1862. November 1, 1862 discharged from service. November 21, 1862 received pay. October 13, 1863 admitted to Floyd House and Ocmulgee Hospitals at Macon Georgia with Chronic Rheumatism (shown stationed at Charleston, South Carolina).

HOBBS, THOMAS J.: Company A, private. September 10, 1861 enlisted as a private in Co. A, 27th Regiment, Georgia Infantry at Camp Stephens, Griffin, Spalding County, Georgia. April 1 (3), 1862 admitted to General Hospital at Orange Court House, Virginia with Dysentery. April 3 (5), 1862 died at either Orange Court House, Virginia or C. S. A. General Hospital at Farmville, Virginia. October 19, 1863 death benefit claim was filed by his father Thomas Hobbs. He was born in Marion County, Georgia.

HOBSON, C. A.: Company E, private. September 9, 1861 enlisted as a private in Co. E, 27th Regiment, Georgia Infantry. June 1, 1864 to the close of the war he was on detail duty as Surgeon in Chimborazo Hospital at Richmond, Virginia according to pension records.

HODGES (HODGES), SAMUEL H.: Company H, sergeant. 1861 enlisted as a private in Co. H, 27th Regiment, Georgia Infantry. He was appointed sergeant Co. H, 27th Regiment, Georgia Infantry. November 17, 1864 captured in Butts County, Georgia. February 1, 1865 arrived at

Hilton Head, South Carolina. June 13, 1865 took the oath of allegiance and was released at Point Lookout, Maryland. Description: dark complexion, brown hair, dark hazel eyes, 5 foot 8 3/4 inches high. He lived in Butts County, Georgia.

HODGES (HODGES), S.: Company H, private. September 9, 1861 enlisted as a private in Co. H, 27th Regiment, Georgia Infantry at Griffin, Spalding County, Georgia. December 11, 1863 wounded at Fort Sumter, Charleston, South Carolina. December 31, 1863 received pay. January – February and March - April 1864, rolls show him present. August 15, 1864 admitted to Jackson Hospital at Richmond, Virginia with Febris Remit (Malaria). July 1864 issued clothing. August 18, 1864 furloughed for 30 days from Jackson Hospital at Richmond, Virginia to Covington, Georgia.

HOGG, ANDREW: Company K, private. September 10, 1861 enlisted as a private in Co. K, 27th Regiment, Georgia Infantry at Camp Stephens, Griffin, Spalding County, Georgia. November 21 (22), 1861 died of disease in Griffin, Spalding County, Georgia. December 1861 roll shows he died on November 21, 1861 in Georgia. October 23, 1863 death benefit claim was filed. He was a son of Lewis Hogg of Marion County, Georgia. He was born in 1830. He lived in Marion County, Georgia.

HOGG, GEORGE: Company K, private. September 10, 1861 enlisted as a private in Co. K, 27th Regiment, Georgia Infantry at Griffin, Spalding County, Georgia. January 16, 1862 admitted to Moore Hospital at General Hospital No. 1, Danville, Virginia with Dysphasia and was sent to General Hospital at Orange Court House, Virginia. January 17, 1862 admitted to General Hospital at Orange Court House, Virginia with Debilitas. February 4, 1862 died of congestion of the brain at General Hospital at Orange Court House, Virginia. February 1862 roll shows he died of disease on February 6, 1862 in General Hospital at Orange Court House, Virginia. October 28, 1863 death benefit claim was filed by father Lewis Hogg. He lived in Marion County, Georgia. He was born in 1840.

HOGG, PETER P.: Company K, private. September 10, 1861 enlisted as a private in Co. K, 27th Regiment, Georgia Infantry at Griffin, Spalding County, Georgia. March 7, 1862 admitted to in Chimborazo Hospital No. 5 at Richmond, Virginia with Diarrhoea. April 22, 1862 died of Diarrhoea in Chimborazo Hospital No. 5 at Richmond, Virginia. He is most likely buried in Oakwood Cemetery at Richmond Virginia. His personal effects at the time of death were $.50. October 28, 1863 death benefit claim was filed by his father Lewis Hogg. December 15, 1864 death benefit claim was filed. Death benefit claim was paid $25.00. He lived in Marion County, Georgia. He was born in 1843.

HOLLAND (HOLLIS) GREEN: Company F, private. March 7, 1862 enlisted as a private in Co. F, 27th Regiment, Georgia Infantry in Butler, Georgia. December 31, 1863 received pay. January – February 1864 roll shows he was killed in action at Olustee, Florida February 20, 1864. February 20, 1864 killed at Olustee, Florida.

HOLLAWAY, JESSE S.: Company C, private. January 2, 1865 roll of prisoners of War for Louisville, Kentucky shows he was transferred to Camp Chase, Ohio and on December 16, 1864 was captured at Nashville, Tennessee. (The 27th Georgia was not at Nashville but the 37th Georgia was).

HOLLERMIN, GUS A.: Company C, private. He enlisted as a private in Co. C, 27th Regiment, Georgia Infantry. April 26, 1865 surrendered, Greensboro, North Carolina. May 1, 1865 paroled, Greensboro, North Carolina.

HOLLIDAY (HOLIDAY), HENRY B.: Field Staff, major. September 2, 1861 enlisted and elected Assistant Quartermaster 27th Regiment, Georgia Infantry at Griffin, Spalding County, Georgia. December 25, 1861 appointed major of the 27th Regiment, Georgia Infantry at Camp Stephens, Griffin in Spalding County, Georgia. December 1861 roll shows him present at Camp Pickens near Manassas, Virginia. January 1862 roll shows him present with a note that he rejoined the regiment at Camp Pickens near Manassas, Virginia on the first day of January. February 1962 roll indicates him at Camp Pickens near Manassas, Virginia. January 24, 1862 leave granted. June 14, 1862 received pay ($897.00). August 28, 1862 resigned his commission.

HOLLIS, WILLIAM T.: Company E, private. September 9, 1861 enlisted as a private in Co. E, 27th Regiment, Georgia Infantry. November 6, 1861 admitted to General Hospital at Petersburg, Virginia. . December 1861 roll shows him in the Hospital at Petersburg, Virginia with Rubeola. December 10, 1861 returned to duty. December 13, 1861 appears on roll of discharged soldiers and was paid on that date. January and February 1862 rolls show he was left sick at Petersburg on November 6, 1861. 1862 died in Virginia.

HOLLOMAN, JAMES A.: Company C, private. April 7, 1864 enlisted as a private in Co. C, 27th Regiment, Georgia Infantry at Macon, Georgia. March - April 1864 roll shows him present. July 1864 issued clothing. He was captured at the General Hospital, Thomasville, North Carolina. May 1, 1865 paroled as a prisoner of war at General Hospital, Thomasville, North Carolina. He was born in Crawford County, Georgia in 1845.

HOLT, DAVID B.: Company A, private. 1861 enlisted as a private in Co. A, 27th Regiment, Georgia Infantry. November 9 admitted to General Hospital No. 18 (Formerly Greaner's Hospital) at Richmond, Virginia. December 11, 1861 appears on a register of soldiers discharged for disability and paid. February 10, 1863 enlisted as a private in Co. E, 63rd Regiment, Georgia Infantry. April 9, 1865 surrendered at Appomattox, Virginia. He was born in Taylor County, Georgia January 15, 1845.

HOPE, CHARLES M.: Company D, private. February 24, 1862 enlisted as a private in Co. D, 27th Regiment, Georgia Infantry at Hopewell Church, Hall County, Georgia. March 25, 1862 received bounty pay $50.00 in Atlanta, Georgia. July 4, 1862 received pay ($44.00). September 17,

1862 wounded and captured, Sharpsburg, Maryland. Died of wounds in Antietam Hospital of Vulnus Sclopeticum (Gunshot Wounds), date unknown. December 1862 roll shows he was captured at Sharpsburg, Maryland.

HOPE, J. T.: Company D, private. September 10, 1861 enlisted as a private in Co. D, 27th Regiment, Georgia Infantry at Griffin, Spalding County, Georgia. February 29, 1864 received pay. March - April 1864 roll shows him present. April, May, June and December 1864 issued clothing. July 1864 and September 20, 1864 issued clothing.

HORTON, JAMES H.: Company G, private. September 9, 1861 enlisted as a private in Co. G, 27th Regiment, Georgia Infantry at Camp Stephens, Griffin, Spalding County, Georgia. November 11, 1861 admitted to General Hospital No. 18 (formerly Greaner's Hospital) at Richmond, Virginia. November 15, 1861 returned to duty. November 29, 1861 admitted to General Hospital No. 18 (formerly Greaner's Hospital) at Richmond, Virginia. December 16, 1861 returned to duty. May 31, 1862 wounded at Seven Pines, Virginia. July 3, 1862 received pay ($84.50). December 4, 1862 admitted to Chimborazo Hospital No. 3 at Richmond, Virginia with Rheumatism. December 16, 1862 transferred to Chimborazo Hospital No. 2 at Richmond, Virginia with Diarrhoea. December 31, 1862 returned to duty. June 26, 1863 issued clothing. October 30, 1863 and November 24, 1863 issued clothing. December 31, 1863 issued clothing. January – February 1864 roll shows him present. February 29, 1864 received pay. March – April 1864 roll shows him present. July 1864 issued clothing. October 2, 1864 admitted to Jackson Hospital, Richmond, Virginia with Debilitas. October 19, 1864 died of Chronic Diarrhoea and Neuralgia in Jackson Hospital at Richmond, Virginia. He is buried in Hollywood Cemetery in Richmond, Virginia. His effects are shown as 1 oil cloth, 1 Cap, 1 pair drawers, 1 shirt and 1 blanket. His Post Office is shown as Griffin, Spalding County, Georgia.

HORTON, T. J.: Company E, private. September 1, 1862 enlisted as a private in Co. E, 27th Regiment, Georgia Infantry in Fairburn, Georgia. May 31, 1862 wounded through right side of head, fracturing skull and injuring eye and captured at Seven Pines, Virginia. June 5, 1862 appears on list of POWs sent to Fort Monroe, Virginia. Description: was born in Georgia, 19 years old, 6 feet high, dark brown hair, gray eyes, fair complexion and a note states that he was sent up the James River for exchange on August 2, 1862. August 2, 1862 he is shown as POW at Fort Wool near Monroe, Virginia. August 5, 1862 paroled. August 12, 1862 received pay ($69.00). May 3, 1863 wounded and disabled at Chancellorsville, Virginia. May 11, 1863 admitted to Chimborazo Hospital No. 2 at Richmond, Virginia with a mini ball wound to the right thigh. June 6, 1863 furloughed for 30 days. July 7, 1863 received pay ($22.00). December 31, 1863 received pay. January – February 1864 and March – April 1864 rolls show him present. June 20, 1864 wounded in the right thigh at Colquitt's Salient near Petersburg, Virginia. June 20, 1864 admitted to Jackson Hospital at Richmond, Virginia with a Vulnus Sclopeticum (Gunshot Wound) (mini ball) to the right thigh. June 30, 1864 roll of Division 2, Jackson Hospital at Richmond, Virginia shows him present. July 16, 1864 issued clothing at Jackson Hospital at Richmond, Virginia. July 18, 1864 furloughed for 30 days. He was born in 1844 in Georgia.

HORTON, T. W.: Company E, private. August 13, 1862 enlisted as a private in Co. E, 27th Regiment, Georgia Infantry at Camp Randolph, Georgia. April, May and June 1863 issued clothing. December 31, 1863 received pay. January – February 1864 roll shows him present. February 29, 1864 received pay. March – April 1864 roll shows him present. October 2, 1864 admitted to Receiving and Wayside Hospital or General Hospital No. 9 at Richmond, Virginia and was transferred to Jackson Hospital on October 3, 1864. October 1, 1864 admitted to Jackson Hospital at Richmond, Virginia with int. Febris. November 9, 1864 returned to duty. April 26, 1865 surrendered, Greensboro, North Carolina. May 1, 1865 paroled at Greensboro, North Carolina.

HORTON, W. L.: Company E, private. February 17, 1864 enlisted as a private in Co. E, 27th Regiment, Georgia Infantry at Decatur Georgia. January – February 1864 roll shows him absent en-route to command. March - April 1864 roll shows him present.

HOSKINS, JULIUS: Company C, private. September 1, 1862 enlisted as a private in Co. E, 27th Regiment, Georgia Infantry in Griffin, Spalding County, Georgia. November 26, 1861 admitted to hospital at Richmond, Virginia. December 24, 1861 discharged. December 26, 1861 paid. December 1861 roll shows him in hospital at Richmond, Virginia since November 26, 1861. May 31, 1862 captured at Seven Pines, Virginia. June 9, 1862 delivered to Fort Monroe, Virginia. He is described as being born in Georgia, age 30, height 5 feet 10 inches, black hair, grey eyes with sallow complexion. He is shown on roll of Prisoners of War sent from Fort Delaware, Delaware and exchanged at Akins Landing, Virginia on August 5, 1862. August 14, 1862 received pay ($38.86). June 26 and September 30, 1863 issued clothing. December 31, 1863 received pay. February 20, 1864 wounded slightly at Olustee, Florida. January - February and March -April 1864 rolls show him present. July 1864 issued clothing. He was born in Georgia in1832.

HOSKINS, WILLIAM: Company C, private. September 10, 1862 enlisted as a private in Co. E, 27th Regiment, Georgia Infantry in Griffin, Spalding County, Georgia. April 19, 1862 killed while on Picket duty at Yorktown, Virginia. July 28, 1862 death benefit claim was filed by his widow Emily A. Hoskins. November 5, 1862 death benefit claim paid $114.96 (#1769).

HOWARD, ANDREW C.: Company K, private. September 10, 1861 enlisted as a private in Co. K, 27th Regiment, Georgia Infantry in Griffin, Spalding County, Georgia. November 17, 1861 admitted to Chimborazo

Hospital No.1 at Richmond, Virginia and was transferred to the hospital at Petersburg, Virginia. December 18, 1861 he was in Petersburg, Virginia hospital. December 1861 roll shows him in the hospital at Petersburg, Virginia since December 18, 1861. June 2, 1862 is shown on roll of General Hospital No. 13 at Richmond, Virginia. June 11, 1862 died, in General Hospital No. 13 at Richmond, Virginia. August 13, 1863 death benefit claim was filed by his father John Howard. September 9, 1862 death benefit claim paid $156.16 (#4538). He was born in Talbot County, Georgia. Post Office is shown as Talbotton, Talbot County, Georgia.

HOWARD, T. JEFFERSON: Company G, private. September 9, 1861 enlisted as a private in Co. G, 27th Regiment, Georgia Infantry at Camp Stephens in Griffin, Spalding County, Georgia. January 6, 1862 admitted to General Hospital No. 18 (formerly Greaner's Hospital) at Richmond, Virginia. January 9, 1862 admitted to Moore Hospital at General Hospital, No. 1 at Danville, Virginia with Rheumatism and sent to General Hospital at Richmond, Virginia. January 10, 1862 admitted to General Hospital No. 18 (formerly Greaner's Hospital) at Richmond, Virginia with acute Rheumatism. January 21, 1862 furloughed for 30 days. January 20, 1862 received $6.60 for commutation of rations for furlough. January 1862 and February 1862 rolls show him in Hospital in Richmond, Virginia since January 9, 1862. May 14, 1862 admitted to Chimborazo Hospital No.1 at Richmond, Virginia. May 29, 1862 returned to duty. May 31, 1862 captured at Seven Pines, Virginia. June 7, 1862 admitted to Chesapeake U. S. A. General Hospital at Fort Monroe, Virginia with a Vulnus Sclopeticum (Gunshot Wound) in the thigh. July 15, 1862 sent to General Hospital. July 16, 1862 delivered to Aikens landing, Virginia by a detachment of New York Volunteers. August 5, 1862 is shown as a Prisoner of War on the Steamer Katskill and exchanged at Aikens Landing, Virginia. August 15, 1862 received pay ($113.00). August 26, 1862 admitted to General Hospital at Camp Winder at Richmond, Virginia. November 10, 1862 issued clothing. November 27(28), 1862 returned to duty from admission to General Hospital at Camp Winder Division No.2 Hospital at Richmond, Virginia. October 30 and November 24, 1863 issued clothing. December 31, 1863 received pay. January – February 1864 and March – April 1864 rolls show him present. June 1, 1864 killed at Cold Harbor, Virginia. Post Office is shown as Zebulon, Pike County, Georgia.

HOWARD, JOHN: Company K, private. March 4, 1862 enlisted as a private in Co. K, 27th Regiment, Georgia Infantry at Talbotton, Talbot County, Georgia. April 30, 1862 received pay. September 17, 1862 he was missing in action at Sharpsburg, Maryland. December 1862 roll shows him missing in action at Sharpsburg, Maryland since September 17, 1862. October 30, 1863 death benefit claim was filed by his widow, Mary E. Howard (stating he died September 17, 1862 at Sharpsburg, Maryland). He was a resident of Talbot, County, Georgia. He was born in 1836. Shown as having gray eyes, light hair, light complexion and was 5 feet 9 ½ inches high.

HOWARD, WILLIAM: Company B, private. December 31, 1861 admitted to Moore Hospital at General Hospital No. 1 at Danville, Virginia with Parotitis (Mumps) and was sent to the Hospital at Richmond, Virginia.

HOWINGTON (HARRINGTON), JAMES D.: Company D, private. September 23, 1861 enlisted as a private in Co. D, 27th Regiment, Georgia Infantry at Camp Stephens, Griffin, Spalding County, Georgia. March 31, 1862 admitted to Chimborazo Hospital, No. 2 at Richmond, Virginia. May 7, 1862 transferred from Chimborazo Hospital, No. 2 at Richmond, Virginia and admitted to C. S. A. General Hospital at Farmville, Virginia with Diarrhoea. May 23, 1862 returned to duty. September 2, 1862 admitted to General Hospital Camp Winder at Richmond, Virginia. October 10, 1862 received pay including $50.00 bounty. October 11, 1862 was furloughed from General Hospital Camp Winder Division 2 at Richmond, Virginia for 20 days. December 1862 roll shows him in the hospital since July. April, May and June and the 4th Quarter 1863 issued clothing. February 29, 1864 received pay. March - April 1864 roll shows him present. May 30, 1864 and July 1864 issued clothing. April 26, 1865 surrendered, Greensboro, North Carolina. May 1, 1865 paroled in Greensboro, North Carolina. He was born in Walker County, Georgia February 9, 1844.

HOWINGTON (HARRINGTON), M. B.: Company D, private. September 10, 1861 enlisted as a private in Co. D, 27th Regiment, Georgia Infantry at Camp Stephens, Griffin, Spalding County, Georgia. April, May, June and 4th Quarter 1863 issued clothing. February 29, 1864 received pay. March - April 1864 roll shows him present. July 1864 and September 20, 1864 issued clothing.

HOWINGTON (HARRINGTON), M. R.: Company D, private. He enlisted as a private in Co. D, 27th Regiment, Georgia Infantry. November 26, 1862 died of Diarrhoea and Pneumonia in General Hospital No. 26, Richmond, Virginia.

HOWINGTON, N. H.: Company D, private. He enlisted as a private in Co. D, 27th Regiment, Georgia Infantry. December 1862 roll shows him in hospital since July.

HOWINGTON (HARRINGTON), WILSON R. (ROBERT): Company D, private. February 22, 1862 enlisted as a private in Co. D, 27th Regiment, Georgia Infantry at Hopewell, Hall County, Georgia. March 25, 1862 received bounty pay ($50.00). May 4, 1862 admitted to Chimborazo Hospital, No. 3 at Richmond, Virginia with Typhoid. May 18, 1862 transferred to Huguenot Springs Hospital. November 2, 1862 admitted to General Hospital No. 26 at Richmond Virginia. November 26, 1862 died in General Hospital No. 26 at Richmond Virginia. Effects included $76.00.

HUBBARD, ROBERT H. (J.): Company H, private. September 9, 1861 enlisted as a private in Co. H, 27th Regiment, Georgia Infantry at Camp Stephens, Griffin, Spalding County, Georgia. January 30, 1862 admitted to Moore Hospital at General Hospital No. 1 at Danville, Virginia. January

1862 roll shows him at Moore Hospital. September 15, 1862 admitted and appears on register of C. S. A. General Hospital at Danville, Virginia with Diarrhoea. October 1, 1862 died at General Hospital, No. 1 at Danville, Virginia of Variola (Small Pox). January 31, 1863 death benefit claim was filed by his father Matthew Hubbard.

HUBBARD, W. B.: Company D, private. August 1, 1862 enlisted as a private in Co. D, 27th Regiment, Georgia Infantry in Gordon County, Georgia. November 28, 1862 admitted to Chimborazo Hospital, No. 4 at Richmond, Virginia with Rheumatism. December 16, 1862 admitted to General Hospital, Farmville, Virginia with Rheumatism. January 27, 1863 returned to duty. April, May, June and December 1863 issued clothing. December 1, 1863 to December 31, 1863 employed in extra duty as a teamster at James Island, South Carolina. February 7, 1864 received pay for extra duty as a teamster from January 1, 1864 to January 31, 1864 at a rate of $.25 extra per day. February 1, 1864 to February 29, 1864 employed in extra duty as a teamster. February 29, 1864 received pay. March – April 1864 roll shows him present detailed as a teamster. May 1, 1864 to May 31, 1864 employed on extra duty as a teamster. September 20, 1864 received pay at Petersburg, Virginia for extra duty as a teamster from February 1, 1864 to June 9, 1864 at a rate of $.25 extra per day. September 20, 1864 issued clothing. April 26, 1865 surrendered, Greensboro, North Carolina. May 1, 1865 paroled at Greensboro, North Carolina. He was born in Georgia.

HUDGINS, R. B.: Company D, private. September 23, 1861 enlisted as a private in Co. D, 27th Regiment, Georgia Infantry at Camp Stephens, Griffin, Spalding County, Georgia. April, May, June and December 1863 issued clothing. February 29, 1864 received pay. March - April 1864 roll shows him present. July 4, 1864 issued clothing. September 1864 issued clothing. January 3, 1865 died of Pneumonia in General Hospital No. 8 at Raleigh, North Carolina hospital. He was buried in the Confederate Cemetery, Raleigh, North Carolina. His effects included $72.50.

HUDGINS, ZACHARIAH (ZACUS) W.: Company D, private. February 23, 1862 enlisted as a private in Co. D, 27th Regiment, Georgia Infantry at Hopewell, Hall County, Georgia. March 25, 1862 received bounty pay ($50.00). May 13, 1862 admitted to Chimborazo Hospital, No. 3 at Richmond, Virginia with Parotitis (Mumps). May 16, 1862 transferred to Camp Winder Hospital, Richmond, Virginia. June 24, 1862 admitted to General Hospital Camp Winder at Richmond, Virginia with Diarrhoea. July 1, 1862 admitted to General Hospital No. 1 at Danville, Virginia with Variola (Small Pox). December 26, 1862 died, at General Hospital No. 1 at Danville, Virginia of Variola (Small Pox).

HUDSON, A. R.: Company F, private. September 9, 1861 enlisted as a private in Co. F, 27th Regiment, Georgia Infantry. March 1862 died, Clarke Mountain, Virginia.

HUDSON (HUTSON), ALLEN: Company F, private. He enlisted as a private in Co. F, 27th Regiment, Georgia Infantry. Died at Rappahannock River, Virginia. June 20, 1862 death benefit claim was filed by John Hudson, Father. Death benefit claim paid $52.50. He lived in Marion County, Georgia.

HUDSON, JAMES W.: Company C, private. September 10, 1861 enlisted as a private in Co. C, 27th Regiment, Georgia Infantry. April 18, 1862 died of disease. July 19, 1862 death benefit claim was filed by his widow Mary Jane Hudson (resident of Crawford County, Georgia). November 5, 1862 death benefit claim paid of $114.60 (#1770).

HUDSON, JOHN: Company F, private. September 9, 1861 enlisted as a private in Co. F, 27th Regiment, Georgia Infantry. He was appointed sergeant in Co. F, 27th Regiment, Georgia Infantry. January 15, 1862 admitted to Moore Hospital at General Hospital No. 1 at Danville, Virginia. January 27, 1862 discharged, age (60) and disability, at Camp Pickens near Manassas, Virginia and paid. He is described as 6 feet high, fair complexion, gray eyes, white hair and by occupation was a farmer. He was paid $64.43. He was born in Rockingham County, North Carolina in 1802.

HUDSON, JOSEPH E.: Company C, private. He enlisted as a private in Co.C, 27th Regiment, Georgia Infantry. March 30, 1862 admitted to General Hospital No. 18 (formerly Greaner's Hospital) at Richmond, Virginia with Debility. July 1, 1862 wounded at Malvern Hill near Richmond, Virginia. July 3, 1862 admitted to Moore Hospital No. 24 at Richmond, Virginia with a Vulnus Slopeticum (Gunshot Wound). September 23, 1862 received pay ($216.30). September 23, 1863 discharged disability. Described as 32 years old, 5 feet 10 inches high, dark complexion, dark eyes, dark hair and by occupation was a farmer. September 25, 1863 received pay and allowances of $ 163.00. December 1862 roll shows him absent on sick furlough since July 25, 1862 for 30 days. Post Office was Powersville, Georgia.

HUDSON R. B.: Company D, private. He enlisted as a private in Co. D, 27th Regiment, Georgia Infantry. March 1, 1865 died, Raleigh, North Carolina.

HUFF, AUGUSTUS: Company K, private. He enlisted as a private in Co. K, 27th Regiment, Georgia Infantry. January 12, 1862 admitted to Moore Hospital at General Hospital No. 1, Danville, Virginia with Pneumonia and was sent to General Hospital at Front Royal, Virginia. January 27, 1862 died of Typhoid Fever at Moore Hospital at Manassas Junction, Virginia. January 1862 roll at Camp Pickens near Manassas, Virginia indicates his death.

HUFF, JOHN D.: Company K, private. He enlisted as a private in Co. K, 27th Regiment, Georgia Infantry. September 17, 1862 killed at Sharpsburg, Maryland. December 1862 roll shows he was killed at Sharpsburg, Maryland. July 15, 1864 his death benefit claim was filed by Donaldson Huff Administrator. He is described as 28 years old, black eyes, black hair, dark complexion and was by occupation a farmer.

HUGHES HUGHS), ELIAS: Company D, private. He enlisted as a private in Co. D, 27th Regiment, Georgia Infantry. December 1861 roll shows him in the hospital.

HUGHES (HUGHS), JOHN A.: Company I, private. September 10, 1861 enlisted as a private in Co. I, 27th Regiment, Georgia Infantry. November 21, 1861 died of disease at Raleigh, North Carolina. December 1861 roll shows he died of disease in Raleigh, North Carolina on November 21, 1861. March 14, 1862 death benefit claim was filed by his Mother Beady Hughes. Death benefit claim paid of $51.40 (#398).

HUGHES WILLIAM H.: Company I, private. February 8, 1864 enlisted as a private in Co. I, 27th Regiment, Georgia Infantry at Fort Johnson on James Island, South Carolina. January - February 1864 roll shows him present. February 29, 1864 received pay. March – April 1864 roll shows him present. July 1864 and September 20, 1864 issued clothing. April 26, 1865 surrendered, Greensboro, North Carolina. May 1, 1865 paroled at Greensboro, North Carolina.

HULL, B.: Company I, private. He enlisted as a private in Co. I, 27th Regiment, Georgia Infantry. December 28, 1861 admitted to Moore Hospital at General Hospital No. 1 at Danville, Virginia with Catarrah and was sent to the General Hospital at Mt. Jackson, Virginia.

HUMPHRIES, JOHN M.: Company F, private. September 9, 1861 enlisted as a private in Co. F, 27th Regiment, Georgia Infantry. February 13, 1862 was on recruiting service for 30 days. February 1862 roll indicates him on recruiting service. April 10, 1862 admitted to Chimborazo Hospital No. 5 at Richmond, Virginia with Bronchitis. May 12, 1862 transferred to hospital at Camp Winder at Richmond, Virginia. June 27, 1862 killed, Cold Harbor, Virginia.

HUNLEY (HUNDLEY), JOHN JAMES: Company A, private. March 10, 1862 enlisted as a private in Co. A, 27th Regiment, Georgia Infantry at Marion County, Georgia. April 25, 1862 admitted to Chimborazo Hospital No. 2 at Richmond, Virginia with Rubeola (Measles). May 29, 1862 returned to duty. November 20, 1862 received bounty pay ($50.00) at Richmond, Virginia. June 1863 issued clothing. December 31, 1863 received pay. January – February 1864 roll shows him present. February 29, 1864 received pay. March – April 1864 roll shows him present. July 1864 and September 30, 1864 issued clothing. April 26, 1865 surrendered, Greensboro, North Carolina. May 1, 1865 paroled at Greensboro, North Carolina. He was born in Pleasant Hill, Georgia in 1838.

HUNTER, ABNER: Company D, private. September 10, 1861 enlisted as a private in Co. D, 27th Regiment, Georgia Infantry at Camp Stephens, Griffin, Spalding County, Georgia. September 17(28), 1862 captured at Sharpsburg, Maryland. November 10, 1862 exchanged at Aikens Landing, Virginia. April, May, June and December 1863 issued clothing. December 1, 1863 through December 31, 1863 employed on extra duty as a laborer at James Island, South Carolina. December 24, 1864 issued clothing.

December 31, 1863 received pay. 1864 detailed with Co. G, 2nd Regiment, Engineer Troops as artificer. February 1, 1864 through February 14, 1864 employed on extra duty as a teamster at Charleston, South Carolina. February 13, 1864 issued clothing. March – April 1864 roll shows him present. July 1864 and September 20, 1864 issued clothing. April 14 (17), 1865 paroled, Burkeville, Virginia.

HUNTER, W. L.: Company E, private. He enlisted as a private in Co. E, 27th Regiment, Georgia Infantry. June 20, 1864 wounded at Colquitt's Salient near Petersburg, Virginia. June 20, 1864 admitted to Receiving and Wayside Hospital or General Hospital No. 9 at Richmond, Virginia. June 22, 1862 transferred to Petersburg, Virginia.

HUTTO, B. E.: Company C, private. September 10, 1861 enlisted as a private in Co. C, 27th Regiment, Georgia Infantry at Camp Stephens, Griffin, Spalding County, Georgia. May 15, 1862 admitted to Chimborazo Hospital No. 2 at Richmond, Virginia with Intermittent Fever (Malaria). May 18, 1862 returned to duty. July 1, 1862 wounded in the leg at Malvern Hill near Richmond, Virginia. July 3, 1862 admitted to Chimborazo Hospital No. 1 at Richmond, Virginia with a wound of the leg. April 19, June 30 and September 30, 1863 issued clothing. December 31, 1863 received pay. January – February 1864 roll shows him present. February 29, 1864 received pay. March – April 1864 roll shows him present. July 1864 issued clothing. September 30, 1864 admitted to Jackson Hospital at Richmond, Virginia with Chronic Diarrhoea. October 11, 1864 died of Chronic Diarrhoea in Jackson Hospital at Richmond, Virginia. Inventory of effects: 1 blanket, 2 pair drawers, 1 pair pants and 1 jacket. He was buried in Hollywood Cemetery at Richmond, Virginia.

HUTTO, BENJAMIN F.: Company I, sergeant. September 10, 1861 elected 5th sergeant of Co. I, 27th Regiment, Georgia Infantry at Camp Stephens, Griffin, Spalding County, Georgia. December 1861 roll shows him in the hospital in Richmond, Virginia. January 1862 and February 1862 rolls show him in the Mt. Jackson Hospital. March 30, 1862 admitted to Chimborazo Hospital No. 1 at Richmond, Virginia with Diarrhoea. April 23, 1862 returned to duty. July 5, 1862 admitted to Chimborazo Hospital No. 4 at Richmond, Virginia with Remittent Fever (Malaria). July 28, 1862 returned to duty. October 21, 1862 received pay ($127.00). November 10, 1862 received commutation for rations of $13.33 1/3. December 1862 roll shows him absent on furlough. December 31, 1863 received pay. January – February 1864 roll shows him present. February 20, 1864 slightly wounded at Olustee, Florida. February 29, 1864 received pay. March – April 1864 roll shows him present. June 27 and July 1864 issued clothing. August 26, 1864 admitted to Jackson Hospital, at Richmond, Virginia, with Typhoid Fever. September 5 1864 died in Jackson Hospital, at Richmond, Virginia. He is buried in Hollywood Cemetery at Richmond, Virginia.

HUTTO, FREDERICK: Company C, corporal. September 10, 1861 elected 4th corporal in Co. C, 27th Regiment, Georgia Infantry at Camp

Stephens, Griffin, Spalding County, Georgia. June 28, 1862 wounded in the Seven days Around Richmond. June 28, 1862 admitted to 2nd Division General Hospital Camp Winder at Richmond, Virginia with wound in the hand. July 7, 1862 furloughed for 30 days from 2nd Division General Hospital Camp Winder at Richmond, Virginia. September 8, 1862 admitted to 2nd Division General Hospital Camp Winder at Richmond, Virginia with Typhoid Fever. September 30 1862 returned to duty from 2nd Division General Hospital Camp Winder at Richmond, Virginia. May 9, 1863 admitted to C. S. A. General Hospital at Charlottesville, Virginia with Debilitis. June 30 and September 30, 1863 issued clothing. December 31, 1863 received pay. January – February 1864 roll shows him present. March – April 1864 roll shows him present. June 18, 1864 wounded at Colquitt's Salient near Petersburg, Virginia. June 20, 1864 died of Vulnus Sclopeticum (Gunshot Wound)s in Virginia Hospital at Petersburg, Virginia.

HUTTO, REUBEN: Company C, private. March 10, 1862 enlisted as a private in Co. C, 27th Regiment, Georgia Infantry at Knoxville, Georgia. December 23, 1862 admitted to C. S. A. General Hospital at Charlottesville, Virginia with Debility. December 24, 1862 returned to duty. May 7, 1862 admitted to Camp Winder Hospital at Richmond, Virginia with Debilitas. June 3, 1862 returned to duty. June 16, 1863 issued clothing. December 31, 1863 received pay. January – February 1864 roll shows him as absent on sick furlough since January 20, 1864. February 1, 1864 - April 30, 1864 was on sick furlough. March – April 1864 roll shows him absent on sick furlough since February 1, 1864.

HYATT, J. M.: Company C, private. He enlisted as a private in Co. C, 27th Regiment, Georgia Infantry. December 23, 1861 admitted to Moore Hospital at General Hospital No. 1 at Danville, Virginia with Diarrhoea and was sent to Charlottesville, Virginia General Hospital.

HYLER, A. J.: Company A, private. He enlisted as a private in Co. A, 27th Regiment, Georgia Infantry. December 1862 roll dated January 31, 1863 shows him absent sick since January 1863.

HYLER, G. W.: Company A, private. He enlisted as a private in Co. A, 27th Regiment, Georgia Infantry. December 1862 roll dated January 31, 1863 shows him absent sick since January 1863. November 17, 1862 admitted to Camp Winder Division No.1 Hospital at Richmond, Virginia.

IDISON, R. R. J.: Company D, private. He enlisted as a private in Co. D, 27th Regiment, Georgia Infantry. January 6, 1862 died of Typhoid Fever. January 1862 roll indicates his death on January 6, 1862 of Typhoid Fever.

INGRAM. H. N. L.: Company F, private. 1862 enlisted as a private in Co. F, 27th Regiment, Georgia Infantry.

INGRAM, JAMES: Company K, private. July 2, 1863 enlisted as a private in Co. K, 27th Regiment, Georgia Infantry in Macon, Bibb County, Georgia. June 16, 1864 discharged, on account of deafness. March

– April 1864 roll shows him as being discharged on account of deafness June 16, 1864.

JACKSON, J. K.: Company B, private. March 17, 1864 enlisted as a private in Co. B, 27th Regiment, Georgia Infantry in Macon, Georgia. March – April 1864 roll shows him present. September 20, 1864 issued clothing. April 26, 1865 surrendered, Greensboro, North Carolina. May 1, 1865 paroled at Greensboro, North Carolina. He moved to Texas after the war.

JACKSON, JAMES: Company B, private. September 10, 1861 enlisted as a private in Co. B, 27th Regiment, Georgia Infantry. December 1861 roll shows him in the hospital in Richmond, Virginia since November 15, 1861. December 4, 1861 discharged due to disability, at Richmond, Virginia. December 5, 1861 received pay. January 1862 roll shows his discharge.

JARRELL, THOMAS J. (T): Company K, private. September 20, 1861 enlisted as a private in Company K, 27th Georgia infantry at Camp Stephens, Griffin, Spalding County, Georgia. January 15, 1862 discharged, on account of double Hernia, at Camp Pickens near Manassas, Virginia. August 6, 1863 enlisted as a private in Co. K, 27th Regiment, Georgia Infantry at Macon, Georgia. October 31, 1863 received pay. March – April 1864 roll shows him absent sick and was sent to the hospital April 17, 1864. April 28, 1864 admitted to Ocmulgee Hospital at Macon, Georgia with Bronchitis and was transferred May 16, 1864. December 3, 1864 received pay ($ 93.73).

JARRELL, T. G.: Company F, private. He enlisted as a private in Co. F, 27th Regiment, Georgia Infantry. December 20, 1861 admitted to Moore Hospital at General Hospital No. 1 at Danville, Virginia with Pneumonia and was sent to the General Hospital by Dr. Ashby. February 18, 1862 discharged from Moore Hospital at Manassas Junction, Virginia discharged due to Pneumonia.

JENKINS, THOMAS H.: Company D, private. February 23, 1863 enlisted as a private in Co. D, 27th Regiment, Georgia Infantry in Hall County, Georgia. May 3, 1863 transferred from Receiving and Wayside Hospital or General Hospital No. 9 at Richmond, Virginia to Chimborazo Hospital at Richmond, Virginia. May 3, 1863 admitted to Chimborazo Hospital No. 2 at Richmond, Virginia with Rheumatism. May 11, 1863 transferred to Lynchburg, Virginia. December 1863 issued clothing. February 29, 1864 received pay. March - April 1864 roll shows him present. May 30, 1864 issued clothing.

JENNINGS, D. T.: Company E, corporal. September 9, 1861 elected 4th corp. Co. E, 27th Regiment, Georgia Infantry at Camp Stephens, Griffin, Spalding County, Georgia. June 30, 1862 admitted to Chimborazo Hospital No. 3 at Richmond, Virginia with Diarrhoea. July 3, 1862 transferred to Lynchburg, Virginia. July 6, 1862 admitted to C. S. A. General Hospital at Farmville, Virginia with Diarrhoea. November 20, 1862 returned to duty.

April, May and June 1863 issued clothing. October 22, 1863 received pay ($138.00). December 31, 1863 received pay. February 20, 1864 wounded at Olustee, Florida. March 9, 1864 furloughed for 30 days. January – February 1864 roll shows him absent wounded at Olustee Florida. March 9, 1864 placed on 30 days sick furlough. March - April 1864 roll shows him absent on sick furlough for 30 days from March 9, 1864 now shown absent without leave. March 19, 1865 killed, Bentonville, North Carolina.

JEWIS, J. H.: Company H, private. He enlisted as a private in Co. H, 27th Regiment, Georgia Infantry. January 27, 1862 admitted to Moore Hospital at General Hospital, No. 1 at Danville, Virginia with Fever and was sent to Front Royal, Virginia.

JINKS (JENKS), T. L.: Company F, sergeant. September 9, 1861 enlisted as a private in Co. F, 27th Regiment, Georgia Infantry at Camp Stephens, Griffin, Spalding County, Georgia. December 31, 1863 received pay. January – February 1864 and March – April 1864 rolls show him present. September 20, 1864 issued clothing. April 26, 1865 surrendered, Greensboro, North Carolina. He was born in Taylor County, Georgia November 7, 1843.

JOHNSON, ALEXANDER W.: Company I, lieutenant. September 10, 1861 enlisted as a private in Co. I, 27th Regiment, Georgia Infantry at Camp Stephens, Griffin, Spalding County, Georgia. June 10 1862 was elected 2nd lieutenant of Co. I, 27th Regiment, Georgia Infantry. July 19, 1862 received pay ($80.00). September 17, 1862 killed at Sharpsburg, Maryland. December 1862 roll shows him missing in action at Sharpsburg, Maryland.

JOHNSON, DARNELL: Company C, private. He enlisted as a private in Co. C, 27th Regiment, Georgia Infantry.

JOHNSON, G. W.: Company E, private. August 7, 1862 admitted to Chimborazo Hospital No.5 at Richmond, Virginia with Congestive Fever. September 4, 1862 transferred to Huguenot Springs, Virginia.

JOHNSON, HORSEY T.: Company K, private. April 18, 1862 died in Banner Hospital at Richmond, Virginia. September 3, 1863 death benefit claim was filed by his widow, Pricilla J. Johnson, from Talbotton, Talbot County, Georgia. He was born in Georgia in 1827 (1832).

JOHNSON, JACKSON E. (E. J.): Company C, private. August 29, 1863 enlisted as a private in Co. C, 27th Regiment, Georgia Infantry at Knoxville, Georgia. December 31, 1863 received pay. January – February 1864 roll shows him present. February 29, 1864 received pay. March – April 1864 roll shows him present. May 30, 1864, July 1864 and September 20, 1864 issued clothing. April 26, 1865 surrendered, Greensboro, North Carolina. May 1, 1865 paroled at Greensboro, North Carolina.

JOHNSON JAMES A.: Company B, private. September 21, 1861 enlisted as a private in Co. B, 27th Regiment, Georgia Infantry. November 11, 1861 admitted to General Hospital No. 18 (Formerly Greaner's Hospital) at Richmond, Virginia with Typhoid Pneumonia. November 15, 1861 sent to Hospital in Richmond, Virginia with Pneumonia. November 18, 1861 died of Pneumonia in Richmond, Virginia Hospital. December 1861 roll shows him in the hospital in Richmond, Virginia. January 1862 roll shows his death of disease on November 17, 1861 in Richmond, Virginia. August 8, 1862 death benefit claim was filed by his widow Eliza Johnson of Bibb County, Georgia. September 18, 1863 death benefit claim was paid $97.80 (#8936).

JOHNSON JAMES M.: Company K, private. August 10, 1863 enlisted as a private in Co. K, 27th Regiment, Georgia Infantry in Talbotton, Talbot County, Georgia. October 22 and 29, November 24 and December 28, 1863 issued clothing. December 31, 1863 received pay. March – April 1864 roll shows him present with a note that he was shown as being absent without leave for 29 days on last roll. July 1864 and September 20, 1864 issued clothing. October 3, 1864 admitted to Receiving and Wayside Hospital or General Hospital No. 9 at Richmond, Virginia and transferred and admitted to Jackson Hospital at Richmond, Virginia with right foot scalded. November 15, 1864 returned to duty. April 26, 1865, surrendered at Greensboro, North Carolina. May 1, 1865 paroled at Greensboro, North Carolina.

JOHNSON, JAMES P.: Company A, private. January 1862 roll shows he was left sick in Georgia October 31, 1861 and was sent to Moore Hospital January 22, 1862. February 1862 roll shows that he died in Moore Hospital on February 9, 1862 of disease. March 19, 1863 death benefit claim was filed by his widow, Lovica Johnson of Schley County, Georgia. November 30, 1863 death benefit claim was paid $89.30 (#11380R).

JOHNSON, L.: Company I, private. He enlisted as a private in Co. I, 27th Regiment, Georgia Infantry. December 17, 1862 admitted to Winder Division No. 1 Hospital at Richmond, Virginia. May 14, 1862 admitted to Chimborazo Hospital No. 4 at Richmond, Virginia. June 1, 1862 returned to duty. March 10, 1863 returned to duty. November 19, 1862 admitted to General Hospital No. 16 at Richmond, Virginia. February 2, 1863 issued clothing at Winder Division No. 1 Hospital at Richmond, Virginia. May 3, 1863 wounded at Chancellorsville, Virginia. July 1864 issued clothing.

JOHNSON, LAFAYETTE H.: Company I, corporal. September 10, 1861 elected 2nd corporal of Co. I, 27th Regiment, Georgia Infantry at Camp Stephens, Griffin, Spalding County, Georgia. He was appointed 3rd corporal of Co. I, 27th Regiment, Georgia Infantry. February 1862 roll shows him on recruiting service for 30 days from February 18, 1862. December 1862 roll shows him in the hospital. May 3, 1863 wounded at Chancellorsville, Virginia. December 31, 1863 received pay. January – February 1864 roll shows him present. February 29, 1864 received pay. March - April 1864 roll shows him present. October 5, 1864 admitted to Jackson Hospital at Richmond, Virginia with Diarrhoea and Rheumatism. October 15, 1864 returned to duty. April 26, 1865 pension records show he surrendered, Greensboro, North Carolina. He was born March 18, 1863 in Appling County, Georgia. He died June 21, 1915 in Appling County, Georgia. He is buried in Zoar Cemetery, Appling County, Georgia.

JOHNSON, LEVI: Company I, private. August 10, 1861 enlisted as a private in Co. I, 27th Regiment, Georgia Infantry Camp Stephens, Griffin, Spalding County, Georgia. December 28, 1861 admitted to Moore Hospital at General Hospital, No. 1 at Danville, Virginia with Typhoid Fever and was transferred to Mt. Jackson Hospital at Mt. Jackson, Virginia. January and February 1862 rolls show him in Mt. Jackson Hospital at Mt. Jackson, Virginia. April 30, 1862 received pay. September 17, 1862 killed at Sharpsburg, Maryland. December 1862 roll shows him as being killed at Sharpsburg, Maryland and missing in action. May 25, 1864 death benefit claim was filed by his mother Justen Johnson of Appling County, Georgia.

JOHNSON, LUTHER R.: Company B, lieutenant. June 27, 1861 elected 2nd lieutenant in Co. B, 27th Regiment, Georgia Infantry. November 29 (December 10,) 1861 resigned. December 1861 roll indicates he resigned on December 10, 1861.

JOHNSON, SAMUEL M.: Company I, private. September 10, 1861 enlisted as a private in Co. I, 27th Regiment, Georgia Infantry. December 28, 1861 admitted to Moore Hospital at General Hospital, No. 1 at Danville, Virginia with Dyspepsia and was sent to Mt. Jackson Hospital at Mt. Jackson, Virginia. December 1861 roll shows him in Hospital in Richmond, Virginia. March 30, 1862 admitted to Chimborazo Hospital No. 1 at Richmond, Virginia with Diarrhoea. April 19, 1862 returned to duty. June 1, 1862 received pay. June 25, 1862 admitted to Episcopal Church Hospital at Williamsburg, Virginia for convalescence. June 25, 1862 returned to duty. July 11, 1862 received pay ($113.00). 1862 captured. September 30, 1862 paroled. December 1862 roll shows him in Hospital in Richmond, Virginia. January 1, 1863 received pay. January 15, 1863 admitted to Camp Winder Division No. 4 Hospital at Richmond, Virginia. April 4, 1863 admitted to Camp Winder General Hospital at Richmond, Virginia with Ascites. April 21, 1863 admitted to Camp Winder Hospital, Richmond, Virginia. May 1, 1863 returned to duty. June 16 and 27, 1863 issued clothing. December 31, 1863 received pay. January – February 1864 roll shows him present. February 29, 1864 received pay. March - April 1864 roll shows him present. July 1864 and September 20, 1864 issued clothing.

JOHNSON, SIMON: Company C, private. September 10, 1861 enlisted as a private in Co. C, 27th Regiment, Georgia Infantry at Camp Stephens at Griffin, Spalding County, Georgia. January 1862 roll shows him January 16, 1862 discharged due to disability, at Camp Pickens, Virginia. May 7, 1862 admitted to Camp Winder General Hospital Richmond, Virginia with Diarrhoea. July 10, 1862 returned to duty. November 1, 1862 wounded in the thigh while regiment was destroying railroads at Staunton and Strasburg, Virginia. November 2, 1862 admitted to Chimborazo Hospital No. 1 at

335

Richmond, Virginia with wound to thigh. December 17, 1862 returned to duty. June 30 and September 3, 1863 issued clothing. December 18, 1863 received payment for commutation for rations ($6.662/3). December 31, 1863 received pay. January – February 1864 roll shows him present. February 29, 1864 received pay. March - April 1864 roll shows him present. May 30, 1864 and July 1864 issued clothing. August 31, 1864 received pay. December 7, 1864 admitted to Receiving and Wayside Hospital or General Hospital No. 9 at Richmond, Virginia and transferred to Jackson Hospital. December 7, 1864 admitted to Jackson Hospital at Richmond, Virginia with Diarrhoea. December 9, 1864 shown as present on roll of Jackson Hospital at Richmond, Virginia. December 16, 1864 furloughed for 60 days and issued passport to Hamburg, South Carolina.

JOHNSON, W.: Company F, private. He enlisted as a private in Co. F, 27th Regiment, Georgia Infantry. April 25, 1862 admitted to Chimborazo Hospital No. 1 at Richmond, Virginia for convalescence (note on card - left without permission).

JOHNSON, WILLIAM M.: Company K, private. February 23, 1864 enlisted as a private in Co. K, 27th Regiment, Georgia Infantry at Macon, Georgia. March 15, 1864 transferred to Co. D, 28th Battalion, Georgia Siege Artillery (Bonaud's Battalion). March – April 1864 indicate his exchange and transfer. August 18, 1864 sent to hospital. December 9, 1864 furloughed for 60 days.

JOHNSON, WILLIAM W.: Company C, captain. July 6, 1861 elected Jr. 2nd lieutenant Co. C, 27th Regiment, Georgia Infantry at Camp Stephens at Griffin, Spalding County, Georgia. December 1861 roll shows him present at Camp Pickens near Manassas, Virginia. January 1862 roll shows him absent sent to Moon Hospital Memphis January 15, 1862. February 17, 1862 received pay ($160.00). February 1862 roll shows him present and that he had rejoined his company from Hospital February 8, 1862 at Camp Pickens near Manassas, Virginia. March 1, 1862 received pay ($160.00). July 1, 1862 received pay ($320.00). August 1, 1862 received pay ($80.00). September 17, 1862 promoted to 2nd lieutenant Co. C, 27th Regiment, Georgia Infantry. December 1862 roll shows him present near Guinea Station, Virginia. February 12, 1863 elected 1st lieutenant Co. C, 27th Regiment, Georgia Infantry. September 30, 1863 appears on Roster of officers in Colquitt's Brigade. December 31, 1863 received pay. January – February 1864 and March – April 1864 rolls show him present. July 11, 1864 promoted to captain Co. C, 27th Regiment, Georgia Infantry. August 14, 1864 appears on report of Colquitt's Brigade as being absent in Hospital. August 19, 1864 received pay ($180.00). September 30, 1864 admitted to Jackson Hospital at Richmond, Virginia with Dysenteria. October 7 (9), 1864 furloughed to A. A. G. from Jackson Hospital at Richmond, Virginia for 30 days. April 26, 1865 surrendered at Greensboro, North Carolina. May 1, 1865 paroled at Greensboro, North Carolina. Born in Crawford County, Georgia May 26, 1830 and died there February 17, 1913.

JOHNSTON BRADFORD AUGUSTUS: Company C, private. September 10, 1861 enlisted as a private in Co. C, 27th Regiment, Georgia Infantry at Camp Stephens, Griffin, Spalding County, Georgia. January 1, 1862 assigned to Provost Marshalls guard. January 1862 roll shows his duty as Provost Marshall's guard. February 9, 1862 sent to post Hospital. February 1862 roll shows him being sent to post hospital. February 1862 surgeons found him disabled due to Vulnus Sclopeticum (Gunshot Wound) in the right leg and the Surgeon General issued him a certificate of Disability. June 10, 1862 received pay ($55.00). November 14, 1862 received pay ($130.00). December 1862 roll shows him absent sick since November 20, 1862. December 2, 1862 admitted to C. S. A. General Hospital at Charlottesville, Virginia with Pneumonia. December 18, 1862 sent to General Hospital at Lynchburg, Virginia. July 12, 1863 admitted to C. S. A. General military Hospital, No. 4, Wilmington, North Carolina with Diarrhoea. July 27, 1863 returned to duty. September 21, 1863 to January 31, 1864 detailed on extra duty in Macon, Georgia as a Conductor. December 31, 1863 received pay. January – February 1864 roll shows him absent without leave. July 6, 1864 returned to duty from Jackson Hospital at Richmond, Virginia. March 7, 1864 detailed for extra duty at Macon, Georgia through April 30, 1864 at a rate of $3.00 per day. March 14, 1864 received pay ($22.00). March - April 1864 roll shows him absent without leave since February 15, 1864. May 1, 1864 – May 11, 1864 detailed for extra duty in Macon, Georgia at a rate of $3.00 per day. May 18, 1864 received pay. June 5, 1864 wounded in the right leg at Cold Harbor, Virginia. June 5, 1864 admitted to Receiving and Wayside Hospital or General Hospital No. 9 at Richmond, Virginia and transferred to Jackson Hospital. June 5, 1864 admitted to Jackson Hospital at Richmond, Virginia with a Vulnus Sclopeticum (Gunshot Wound) to Right leg (mini ball). June 21, 1864 admitted to Jackson Hospital at Richmond, Virginia with a Vulnus Sclopeticum (Gunshot Wound) to the right leg (old wound). July 6, 1864 returned to duty and received pay ($22.00). February 22, 1865 captured near Wilmington, North Carolina. March 13, 1865 sent from Wilmington, North Carolina to Point Lookout, Maryland. June 4, 1865 released at Point Lookout, Maryland. He was born in North Carolina in 1832. He was a resident of Knoxville, Georgia.

JONES, EVAN FRANKLIN: Company I, private. September 10, 1861 enlisted as a private in Co. I, 27th Regiment, Georgia Infantry at Camp Stephens, Griffin, Spalding County, Georgia. December 1861 roll shows him in the hospital at Manassas, Virginia. January 11, 1862 admitted to Moore Hospital at General Hospital, No. 1 at Danville, Virginia with Pneumonia. January 21, 1862 died of Pneumonia at Camp Pickens near Manassas, Virginia. January 1862 roll indicates his death due to disease in January. October 29, 1862 death benefit claim was filed by his father Elias B. Jones. January 18, 1865 death benefit claim paid $7.70 (#21813). He was a resident of Appling County, Georgia.

JONES, H. J.: Company E, private. He enlisted as a private in Co. E, 27th Regiment, Georgia Infantry. April 26, 1865 surrendered at Greensboro, North Carolina. May 1, 1865 paroled at Greensboro, North Carolina.

JONES, JOHN D.: Company G, lieutenant. September 9, 1861 enlisted as a private in Co. G, 27th Regiment, Georgia Infantry at Camp Stephens, Griffin, Spalding County, Georgia. April 25, 1862 admitted to Chimborazo Hospital, No. 1 at Richmond, Virginia with Pneumonia. May 2, 1862 returned to duty. September 17, 1862 elected Jr. 2nd lieutenant of Co. G, 27th Regiment, Georgia Infantry. September 30, 1862 elected 2nd lieutenant of Co. G, 27th Regiment, Georgia Infantry. December 1862 roll shows him present near Guinea Station, Virginia. June 26, 1863 issued clothing. September 30, 1863 Roster of the officers of A. H. Colquitt's Brigade shows him as a 2nd lieutenant. June 1, 1864 elected 1st lieutenant of Co. G, 27th Regiment, Georgia Infantry. August 22, 1864 received pay ($80.00). March 19, 1865 wounded at Bentonville, North Carolina. He was in Greensboro, North Carolina hospital at the close of the war. He was born in Pike County, Georgia, December 24, 1837.

JONES JOHN T.: Company A, private. September 9, 1863 enlisted as a private in Co. A, 27th Regiment, Georgia Infantry. November – December 1864 roll shows him present.

JONES, JOSEPH: Company I, private. September 10, 1861 enlisted as a private in Co. I, 27th Regiment, Georgia Infantry at Camp Stephens, Griffin, Spalding County, Georgia. December 1861 died at Raleigh, North Carolina.

JONES, LLOYD: Company E, sergeant. September 9, 1861 enlisted as a private in Co. E, 27th Regiment, Georgia Infantry at Camp Stephens, Griffin, Spalding County, Georgia. January 1862 appointed 1st sergeant in Co. E, 27th Regiment, Georgia Infantry. February 1862 roll shows him on recruiting service since February 13, 1862. April 6, 1862 admitted to General Hospital at Orange Court House, Virginia with Catarrh. August 30, 1862 admitted to General Hospital, Camp Winder at Richmond, Virginia with Typhoid Fever. September 1, 1862 received $25.00 as clothing allowance. September 9, 1862 received pay ($105.00). October 15, 1862 received $50.00 bounty pay. October 15, 1862 returned to duty. March 18, 1863 received $10.00 in commutation for rations. July 2, 1863 received $9.90 in commutation for rations. December 1863 detailed on detached duty at Fort Sumter, Charleston, South Carolina. December 31, 1863 received pay. January 4, 1864 - April 30, 1864 was on detached duty as a mechanic and a carpenter at Fort Sumter, South Carolina. He received $2.00 per day extra for 48 days on February 29, 1864. January – February 1864 roll shows him on detached duty at Fort Sumter, Charleston, South Carolina as a carpenter since January 4, 1864. February 29, 1864 received pay. March – April 1864 shows him on detached duty at Fort Sumter, Charleston, South Carolina as a mechanic since January 4, 1864. March 5, 1864 and May 1, 1864 detached detail at Fort Sumter, Charleston, South Carolina extended.

May 8, 1864 he was relieved from detail at Fort Sumter, Charleston, South Carolina. 1864 died in Charleston, South Carolina.

JONES, S. J.: Company E, private. August 1, 1862 enlisted as a private in Co. E, 27th Regiment, Georgia Infantry at Milledgeville, Georgia. September 14, 1862 wounded at Turner's Gap on South Mountain, Maryland. December 31, 1863 received pay. January – February 1864 roll shows him present. February 29, 1864 received pay. March -April 1864 roll shows him present. September 1864 issued clothing.

JONES, SAMUEL W.: Company F, private. September 9, 1861 enlisted as a private in Co. E, 27th Regiment, Georgia Infantry at Camp Stephens, Griffin, Spalding County, Georgia. December 23, 1861 admitted to Moore Hospital at General Hospital, No. 1 at Danville, Virginia with Rheumatism and was sent to Charlottesville, Virginia. December 24, 1861 admitted to C. S. A. General Hospital at Charlottesville, Virginia with Catarrh and with Rheumatism. December 30, 1861 returned to duty. December 1862 roll indicates he "Straggled on March in August". August 31, 1862 received pay. April 21, 1863 discharged due to age. April 22, 1863 received payment ($86.20) upon discharge. He was born in Jones County, Georgia in1813. He is described on his disability certificate as being 50 years of age, 5 foot 8 inches high, dark complexion, blue eyes, and black hair and was by occupation a farmer.

JONES, SIMEON T.: Company E, private. August 13, 1862 enlisted as a private in Co. E, 27th Regiment, Georgia Infantry at Camp Randolph, Georgia. April, May and June 1863 was issued clothing. November 28, 1862 received pay at Division 4, General Hospital, Camp Winder at Richmond, Virginia. December 31, 1863 received pay. January – February 1864 roll shows him present. February 29, 1864 received pay. March – April 1864 roll shows him present. September 20, 1864 issued clothing. April 26, 1865 surrendered, Greensboro, North Carolina. May 1, 1865 paroled at Greensboro, North Carolina. He was born in Baldwin County, Georgia in 1836.

JONES, T. J.: Company A, private. September 10, 1861 enlisted as a private in Co. A, 27th Regiment, Georgia Infantry. November 9, 1861 died of Typhoid Fever at Griffin, Georgia. December 1861 roll shows he died in Griffin, Georgia of disease.

JONES, THOMAS ZACHARY: Company G, private. 1864 enlisted as a private in Co. G, 27th Regiment, Georgia Infantry. February 20, 1864 wounded at Olustee, Florida. August 19, 1864 wounded at Weldon Railroad, Virginia. August 20, 1864 admitted to Jackson Hospital at Richmond, Virginia with a Vulnus Sclopeticum (Gunshot Wound) in the right thigh. September 12, 1864 furloughed to Barnesville, Georgia for 30 days. April 26, 1865, surrendered at Greensboro, North Carolina. May 1, 1865 paroled at Greensboro, North Carolina.

JONES, WESLEY: Company F, private. September 9, 1861 enlisted as a private in Co. F, 27th Regiment, Georgia Infantry. January 11, 1862 admitted to Moore Hospital at General Hospital, No. 1, at Danville, Virginia with Neuralgia and was sent to General Hospital at Richmond, Virginia. June 2, 1862 admitted to Chimborazo Hospital No.1 at Richmond, Virginia, on account of general disability. June 3, 1862 transferred to Lynchburg, Virginia. June 4, 1862 admitted to Moore Hospital at General Hospital, No. 1 at Danville, Virginia with Ebrietas. June 8, 1862 returned to duty.

JONES, WILLIAM D.: Company B, private. February 16, 1864 enlisted as a private in Co. B, 27th Regiment, Georgia Infantry at Decatur, Georgia. January – February 1864 and March – April 1864 rolls show him present.

JONES, WILLIAM J.: Company K, lieutenant. September 10, 1861 enlisted as a private in Co. K, 27th Regiment, Georgia Infantry. September 10, 1861 elected 2nd lieutenant. December 19, 1861 received pay ($173.30). December 1861, January 1862 and February 1862 rolls show him present at Camp Pickens near Manassas, Virginia and that he was assigned as acting Post Adjutant. March 7, 1862 received pay ($80.00). March 15, 1862 elected Jr. 2nd lieutenant of Co. K, 27th Regiment, Georgia Infantry. June 4, 1862 received pay ($240.00). July 4, 1862 and July 10, 1862 received pay ($80.00 each date). July 10, 1862 died.

JONES, WILLIAM R. M.: Company G, private. September 17, 1861 enlisted as a private in Co. G, 27th Regiment, Georgia Infantry at Camp Stephens, Griffin, Spalding County, Georgia. March 16, 1862 admitted to Chimborazo Hospital, No. 1 at Richmond, Virginia for Convalescent. April 2, 1862 sent to hospital. May 31, 1862 wounded at Seven Pines, Virginia. June 1862 received pay ($39.00). June 1, 1862 returned to duty. September 20, 1862 attached to Old School Presbyterian Church and Market House Hospitals at Winchester, Virginia as a nurse. June 26, 1863, October 30, 1863 and November 24, 1863 issued clothing. October 31, 1863 received pay. December 31, 1863 received pay. January 10, 1864 stationed at James Island, South Carolina. Description as follows: Age 21, yellow eyes, light hair, fair complexion 5 feet 10 inches high and a resident of Pike County, Georgia by occupation a farmer. February 20, 1864 wounded at Olustee, Florida. January – February 1864 roll shows him absent due to wounds at Olustee, Florida. February 29, 1864 received pay ($22.00). March 2, 1864 received pay. March – April 1864 roll shows him present. May 31, 1864, July 1864 and September 20, 1864 issued clothing. March 19, 1865 wounded through the shoulder at Bentonville, North Carolina. He was born in Pike County, Georgia in 1842.

JORDAN, A. L.: Company A, sergeant. He enlisted as a private in Co. A, 27th Regiment, Georgia Infantry. May 15, 1862 admitted to Chimborazo Hospital, No. 2 at Richmond, Virginia with Diarrhoea. He was elected 2nd sergeant Co. A, 27th. Regiment, Georgia Infantry. September 1, 1862 received pay ($93.00). December 30, 1862 received pay ($84.00).

JORDAN J.: Company B, private. September 21, 1861 enlisted as a private in Co. B, 27th Regiment, Georgia Infantry.

JORDAN, JAMES M.: Company A, private. September 28, 1862 enlisted as a private in Co. A, 27th Regiment, Georgia Infantry at Camp Randolph, Georgia. July, August and September 1863 issued clothing. December 31, 1863 received pay. January – February 1864 roll shows him present. March - April 1864 roll shows him present. June 18, 1864 captured at Colquitt's Salient near Petersburg, Virginia. June 24, 1864 arrived at Point Lookout, Maryland from City Point, Virginia. July 25, 1864 transferred to Elmira Prison, Elmira, New York. January 26, 1865 he died of Chronic Diarrhoea, at Elmira Prison, New York. He is buried in grave No.1628 Woodlawn National Cemetery at Elmira, New York.

JORDAN, JAMES R.: Company G, sergeant. September 9, 1861 enlisted as a private in Co. F, 27th Regiment, Georgia Infantry. September 9, 1861 enlisted as a private in Co. G, 27th Regiment, Georgia Infantry. He was elected corporal. March 31, 1862 wounded at Seven Pines, Virginia. June 26, 1863, October 30, 1863 and November 24, 1863 issued clothing. December 31, 1863 received pay. January – February and March – April 1864 rolls show him present. May 30, 1864 issued clothing. June 1, 1864 wounded at Cold Harbor, Virginia. June 20, 1864 wounded in the neck at Colquitt's Salient near Petersburg, Virginia June 20, 1864 admitted to Receiving and Wayside Hospital or General Hospital No. 9 at Richmond, Virginia. June 21, 1864 admitted to Jackson Hospital with a Vulnus Sclopeticum (Gunshot Wound) (mini ball) to the neck. June 30, 1864 shown as present at 2nd Division, Jackson Hospital at Richmond, Virginia. July 18, 1864 furloughed from Jackson Hospital at Richmond, Virginia for 40 days. 1864 he was appointed sergeant. March 19, 1865 captured at Bentonville, North Carolina. April 3, 1865 arrived at Point Lookout Maryland from New Bern, North Carolina. June 28, 1865 released from Point Lookout, Maryland. Described at Point Lookout as being a resident of Pike County, Georgia with light complexion, dark brown hair, hazel eyes and being 5 feet 6 ¾ inches high at the time he took the oath of allegiance. He was born in Upson County, Georgia April 1, 1845. March 11, 1937 died of Pneumonia at soldiers Home in Atlanta, Georgia. March 13, 1837 buried in Confederate Cemetery at Marietta, Georgia.

JORDAN, WILLIAM G.: Company C, private. September 10, 1861 enlisted as a private in Co. C, 27th Regiment, Georgia Infantry at Camp Stephens, Griffin, Spalding County, Georgia. March 16, 1862 admitted to Chimborazo Hospital No. 3 at Richmond, Virginia with Rheumatism. March 23, 1862 returned to duty. September 17, 1862 wounded through the right hip joint and permanently disabled at Sharpsburg, Maryland. December 31 1862 received $.33 per day for commutation for rations from September 17, 1862 to December 21, 1862. December 1862 roll shows he was wounded on September 17 and was on furlough. December 31, 1863 received pay. January – February and March –April 1864 rolls show him present. April 30, 1864 received pay. May 30, 1864 issued clothing. June 30, 1864 shown as present on roll of 2nd Division Jackson Hospital at Richmond, Virginia. June 30, 1864 admitted to Receiving and Wayside

Hospital or General Hospital No. 9 at Richmond, Virginia and transferred to Jackson Hospital at Richmond, Virginia. July 1, 1864 admitted to Jackson Hospital at Richmond, Virginia with Chronic Diarrhoea. July 24, 1864 furloughed for 30 days from Jackson Hospital at Richmond, Virginia. October 19, 1864 issued clothing at Buckner and Gamble Hospital at Fort Valley, Georgia. He was born in Georgia May 1, 1841.

KELLUM, ROBERT H.: Company K, sergeant. September 10, 1861 elected 1st corporal of Co. K, 27th Regiment, Georgia Infantry at Camp Stephens, Griffin, Spalding County, Georgia. October 29, 1863 issued clothing. October 31, 1863 received pay. November 24, 1863 issued clothing. March – April 1864 roll shows him present. He was appointed sergeant of Co. K, 27th Regiment, Georgia Infantry. June 1864 and July 1864 issued clothing. July 30, 1864 pension records show he was wounded in the toe, necessitating amputation at Petersburg, Virginia. July 31, 1864 admitted to Jackson Hospital at Richmond, Virginia with Vulnus Sclopeticum (Gunshot Wound) to right foot. August 7, 1864 furloughed for 40 days. April 26, 1865 surrendered at Greensboro, North Carolina. May 1, 1865 paroled at Greensboro, North Carolina. He was born in Georgia September 22, 1841.

KELLUM, WILLIAM ROBINSON: Company K, sergeant. March 4, 1862 enlisted as a private in Co. K, 27th Regiment, Georgia Infantry at Talbotton, Georgia at the age of 21. September 23, 1862 admitted to 3rd Division, General Hospital Camp Winder at Richmond, Virginia. October 8, 1862 received pay ($69.00). October 9, 1862 furloughed for 30 days. October 29, 1863 issued clothing. December 31, 1863 received pay. March – April 1864 roll shows him present. May 30, 1864, July 1864 and September 20, 1864 issued clothing. He was appointed sergeant in Co. K, 27th Regiment, Georgia Infantry. February 22, 1865 captured near Wilmington, North Carolina. March 13, 1865 arrived at Point Lookout, Maryland from Wilmington, North Carolina. June 28, 1865 released at Point Lookout, Maryland after taking oath of Allegiance. He is described as being a resident of Talbot County, Georgia, light complexion, brown hair, blue eyes and 5 feet 3 ½ inches high.

KELLY (KELLEY), WILLIAM: Company F, private. August 1, 1863 enlisted as a private in Co. F, 27th Regiment, Georgia Infantry at Butler, Georgia. August 25, 1863 issued clothing. December 31, 1863 received pay. January – February and March – April 1864 rolls show him present. March 5, 1864 issued 'drawers" at Camp Milton, Florida. July 1864 issued clothing. August 17, 1864 admitted to Jackson Hospital at Richmond, Virginia with Remitting Fever (Malaria). August 28, 1864 furloughed for 30 days to Macon, Georgia. March 19, 1865 captured, Bentonville, North Carolina. April 3, 1865 arrived at Point Lookout, Maryland from New Bern, North Carolina. June28, 1865 released at Point Lookout, Maryland after taking the oath of allegiance. Described as being a resident of Taylor

County, Georgia with fair complexion, light brown hair, light blue eyes and was 5 feet 5 inches tall.

KEMP, PETER D.: Company I, private. September 10, 1861 enlisted as a private in Co. I, 27th Regiment, Georgia Infantry at Camp Stephens, Griffin, Spalding County, Georgia. December 31, 1861 received pay. July 5, 1862 admitted to Chimborazo Hospital No. 4 at Richmond, Virginia with Fever. August 1(4), 1862 died of Typhoid Fever in Chimborazo Hospital No.4 at Richmond, Virginia. August 6, 1862 buried in Oakwood Cemetery at Richmond, Virginia. August 4, 1863 death benefit claim was filed by Instance Cook, administrator of his estate. Claim paid at $25.00. He was born in Tattnall County, Georgia. He was the son of James Kemp and Flora Hall Kemp.

KENDRICK, H. H.: Company A, private. September 1, 1862 enlisted as a private in Co. A, 27th Regiment, Georgia Infantry at Camp Randolph, Georgia. December 31, 1863 received pay. January – February 1864 roll shows him present. February 29, 1864 received pay. March – April 1864 roll shows him present. July 1864 issued clothing. April 26, 1865 surrendered, Greensboro, North Carolina. May 1, 1865 paroled at Greensboro, North Carolina. He was born in Georgia 1845.

KENDRICH, THOMAS S.: Company A, corporal. September 1, 1862 enlisted as a private in Co. A, 27th Regiment, Georgia Infantry and was elected 1st corporal. December 1861 and January 1862 rolls show he was left in Georgia sick on October 31, 1861. April 30, 1862 received pay. September 17, 1862 killed at Sharpsburg Maryland. December 27, 1862 death benefit claim was filed by his father, Paton K. Kendrick. He was a resident of Schley County, Georgia.

KENDRICK, WILLIAM F.: Company A, private. April 15, 1863 enlisted as a private in Co. A, 27th Regiment, Georgia Infantry. April 26, 1865 surrendered, Greensboro, North Carolina. He was born in Georgia.

KENNEDY, BENJAMIN F.: Company C, sergeant. September 10, 1861 elected 3rd corporal in Co. C, 27th Regiment, Georgia Infantry at Camp Stephens at Griffin, Spalding County, Georgia. He was appointed sergeant in Co. C, 27th Regiment, Georgia Infantry. March 31, 1862 admitted to Chimborazo Hospital No. 2, at Richmond, Virginia with Dysentery. April 10, 1862 returned to duty. June 26, 1863 issued clothing. July 25, 1863 received $29.33 in commutation for rations. December 31, 1863 received pay and was issued clothing. February 20, 1864 wounded through both hips and head at Olustee, Florida. January – February 1864 roll shows him absent wounded of February 20, 1864 at Olustee, Florida. February 29, 1864 received pay. March – April 1864 roll shows him present. September 20, 1864 issued clothing. April 26, 1865 surrendered, Greensboro, North Carolina. May 1, 1865 paroled at Greensboro, North Carolina. He was born in Crawford County, Georgia in 1845.

KENNEDY, HARRISON: Company D, private. March 4, 1862 enlisted as a private in Co. D, 27th Regiment, Georgia Infantry in Gainesville, Hall

County, Georgia. March 25, 1862 paid $50.00 bounty in Atlanta, Georgia. June 5, 1862 received pay ($45.16 2/3). July 7, 1863 admitted to Receiving and Wayside Hospital or General Hospital No. 9 at Richmond, Virginia and was transferred to Chimborazo Hospital No. 2, at Richmond, Virginia. July 8, 1863 admitted to Chimborazo Hospital No. 2 at Richmond, Virginia with Debility. July 22, 1863 returned to duty. August 16, 1863 through October 22, 1863 held for mutiny. December 1863 issued clothing. February 29, 1864 received pay. March - April 1864 roll shows him present. May 30, 1864, July 1864 and September 1864 issued clothing.

KENNEDY, HENRY C.: Company D, private. March 18, 1863 enlisted as a private in Co. D, 27th Regiment, Georgia Infantry in Hall County, Georgia. December 31, 1863 received pay. March – April 1864 roll shows him present.

KENNEDY, JOHN C.: Company C, private. 1864 enlisted as a private in Co. C, 27th Regiment, Georgia Infantry. April 26, 1865 surrendered, Greensboro, North Carolina. May 1, 1865 paroled at Greensboro, North Carolina.

KENNEDY (KENEDAY) (KENNANA), WILLIAM: Company D, lieutenant. September 10, 1861 elected 1st lieutenant Co. D, 27th Regiment, Georgia Infantry at Camp Stephens, Griffin, Spalding County, Georgia. December 19, 1861 received pay ($ 183.00). December 1861 and January 1862 rolls show him present at Camp Pickens near Manassas, Virginia. February 1862 roll shows him absent on Recruiting Service beginning February 13, 1862. June 14, 1862 died in Richmond, Virginia. June 10, 1863 death benefit claim was filed by his father Ambrose Kennedy of Hall County, Georgia.

KERLIN, F. M.: Company E, private. September 9, 1861 enlisted as a private in Co. E, 27th Regiment, Georgia Infantry. May 7, 1862 admitted to General Hospital at Camp Winder at Richmond, Virginia with Diarrhoea. June 8, 1862 returned to duty. August 25, 1862 admitted to General Hospital at Camp Winder at Richmond, Virginia. September 9, 1862 received pay ($69.00). September 15, 1862 died of Chronic Diarrhoea in General Hospital at Camp Winder at Richmond, Virginia.

KERLIN, J.: Company E, private. September 10, 1861 enlisted as a private in Co. E, 27th Regiment, Georgia Infantry. September 7, 1862 died in Richmond, Virginia. He is buried in Hollywood Cemetery at Richmond, Virginia.

KILCREASE, DANIEL: Company A, corporal. March 4, 1862 enlisted as a private in Confederate States Army. December 1863 appointed 3rd corporal. April 1, 1865 transferred to Co. A, 27th Regiment, Georgia Infantry. April 26, 1865 surrendered, Greensboro, North Carolina. May 1, 1865 paroled at Greensboro, North Carolina.

KIMBERLY, CHARLES EDWARD: Company E, private. September 9, 1861 enlisted as a private in Co. E, 27th Regiment, Georgia Infantry. December 1861 roll shows he was left sick in Georgia. January 1862 roll shows him on furlough for 30 days since January 10, 1862. February 1862 roll shows he was left sick in Georgia October 31, 1861. May 7, 1862 detailed as a nurse in 2nd Division, General Hospital Camp Winder at Richmond, Virginia. May 16, 1862 "Special Order No. 85" from the Secretary of War directs him to report to Camp Winder Hospital as a nurse. August 4, 1862 he is shown on furlough. November 1, 1862 received pay. December 1862 roll of 2nd Division, General Hospital Camp Winder at Richmond, Virginia shows him present detailed as a nurse since May 7, 1862 and due two months extra duty pay. December 1862 roll shows him absent sick since May. January 1, 1863 received pay. January – February 1863 roll of 2nd Division, General Hospital, Camp Winder at Richmond, Virginia shows him present detailed by the Secretary of War. August 31, 1863 received pay. January – February 1864 roll shows him absent detailed in Hospital at Richmond, Virginia since May of 1862. March – April 1864 roll shows he was discharged by order of General Beauregard January 30, 1864. January 30, 1864 discharged due to disability, at Atlanta, Georgia. February 5, 1864 discharged. February 20, 1864 received pay. Described on disability Certificate as being born in the Union District, South Carolina and is 38 years of age (January 1864), 6 feet 6 inches high, ruddy complexion, blue eyes, dark hair and by occupation was a farmer. He was a resident of Fayetteville, Georgia. He was born in 1826.

KIMBREW, JAMES M.: Company B, private. September 10, 1861 enlisted as a private in Co. B, 27th Regiment, Georgia Infantry at Camp Stephens, Griffin, Spalding County, Georgia. He was appointed 4th corporal. April 3, 1862 admitted to General Hospital at Orange Court House with Febris (Fever). April 7, 1862 died of Pneumonia in General Receiving Hospital (also known as Charity Hospital) at Gordonsville, Virginia. His effects were $0.95 in monies.

KING, DAVID: Company H, private. August 1, 1862 enlisted as a private in Co. H, 27th Regiment, Georgia Infantry at McDonough, Henry County, Georgia. December 31, 1863 received pay. January – February 1864 roll shows him present. February 29, 1864 received pay. March – April 1864 roll shows him present. July 1864 and September 20, 1864 issued clothing, March 19, 1865 captured at Bentonville, North Carolina. March 30, 1865 received at Point Lookout, Maryland from New Bern, North Carolina. June 28, 1865 released at Point Lookout, Maryland after taking the Oath of Allegiance. Described as being a resident of Henry County, Georgia with fair complexion, brown hair, blue eyes, 5 feet 6 ¼ inches high.

KING, DAVID: Company H, private. He enlisted as a private in Co. H, 27th Regiment, Georgia Infantry. March 21, 1862 admitted to Chimborazo Hospital No. 1 at Richmond, Virginia for convalescent. May 9, 1862 transferred to Lynchburg. June 1862 was in General Hospital No. 2, Lynchburg, Virginia with diseased lungs. June 6 1862 discharged disability for Phthisis Pulmonalis (Tuberculosis).

KING, JOHN LEWIS: Company E, sergeant. March 1, 1862 elected

5th sergeant, Co. E, 27th Regiment, Georgia Infantry at Fairburn, Georgia. May 7, 1862 admitted to General Hospital Camp Winder at Richmond, Virginia with Febris Typhoides. May 15, 1862 admitted to Chimborazo Hospital No. 2 at Richmond, Virginia with Diarrhoea. May 16, 1862 admitted to General Hospital Camp Winder at Richmond, Virginia with Febris Typhoides. July 4, 1862 returned to duty. May 23, 1862 returned to duty. August 23, 1862 admitted to General Hospital No. 13 at Richmond, Virginia with Bronchitis. August 29, 1862 admitted to General Hospital Camp Winder at Richmond, Virginia. August 30, 1862 transferred to Mayo Island. September 6, 1862 received pay ($69.00). October 11, 1862 furloughed for 30 days from 2nd Division, General Hospital Camp Winder at Richmond, Virginia. November 31, 1862 received commutation for rations ($10.13). December 1862 roll shows him absent without leave. December 31, 1863 received pay. January – February 1864 roll shows him present. February 29, 1864 received pay. March - April 1864 roll shows him present. June 14, 1864 admitted to Jackson Hospital at Richmond, Virginia with Chronic Diarrhoea. June 20, 1864 received pay ($34.00) and returned to duty. July 1864 appointed 2nd sergeant Co. E, 27th Regiment, Georgia Infantry. October 1, 1864 admitted to Jackson Hospital at Richmond, Virginia with Chronic Diarrhoea. November 25, 1864 issued clothing at Jackson Hospital at Richmond, Virginia. November 28, 1864 returned to duty. April 26, 1865 surrendered Greensboro, North Carolina. May 1, 1865 paroled at Greensboro, North Carolina. He was a resident of Locust Grove, Henry County, Georgia.

KING, JOSEPH L.: Company H, private. He enlisted as a private in Co. H, 27th Regiment, Georgia Infantry. July 2, 1863 died in hospital at Goldsboro, North Carolina of Febris Typhoides and Chronic Diarrhoea. August 25, 1863 death benefit claim was filed by his father Joseph King. He was a resident of Lovejoy Station, McDonough, Henry County, Georgia.

KING, JOSHUA S.: Company E, private. He enlisted as a private in Co. E, 27th Regiment, Georgia Infantry. January and February 1862 rolls show he was Provost Marshals guard at headquarters post. July 2, 1863 he died in North Carolina of Febris Typhoides (Typhoid Fever).

KING, LEMON: Company H, private. He enlisted as a private in Co. H, 27th Regiment, Georgia Infantry.

KING, LEWIS W.: Company E, private. September 9, 1861 enlisted as a private in Co. E, 27th Regiment, Georgia Infantry at Camp Stephens, Griffin, Spalding County, Georgia. October 1, 1861 left sick in Georgia. December 1861, January 1862 and February 1862 rolls show he was left sick in Georgia October 31, 1861. May 23, 1862 discharged at Richmond, Virginia and received pay of $119.01. He was born in Putnam County, Georgia in 1811. He was a resident of Fayette County, Georgia. he is described on his certificate as being 51 years of age, 5 feet 10 inches high, fair complexion, blue eyes light hair and was by occupation a farmer.

KING, SOLOMON: Company H, private. March 1, 1862 enlisted as a private in Co. H, 27th Regiment, Georgia Infantry at McDonough, Henry County, Georgia. March 21, 1862 admitted to Chimborazo Hospital No. 1 at Richmond, Virginia convalescent record shows he left hospital without permission. February 20, 1864 wounded at Olustee, Florida. November 15, 1863 received $9.90 for commutation for rations. December 31, 1863 received pay. January – February 1864 and March – April 1864 rolls show him absent wounded in hospital at Quincy, Florida. September 2, 1864 received pay ($44.00). October 11, 1864 admitted to Receiving and Wayside Hospital or General Hospital No. 9, Richmond, Virginia and was transferred to Jackson Hospital on October 12, 1864. October 12, 1864 admitted to Jackson Hospital at Richmond, Virginia with Nyctalopia. October 28, 1864 returned to duty. February 21, 1865 admitted to C. S. A. General Hospital, No. 3, Greensboro, North Carolina with Rubeola. February 23, 1865 transferred to and admitted to Pettigrew General Hospital at Raleigh, North Carolina with a complaint of a Vulnus Sclopeticum (Gunshot Wound) to the scalp. February 27, 1865 returned to duty. February 28, 1865 issued clothing at Pettigrew General Hospital at Raleigh, North Carolina. March 18, 1865 wounded in the arm necessitating amputation at Bentonville, North Carolina. He was born in Georgia January 24, 1838. He was a resident of McDonough, Henry County, Georgia.

KING, THOMAS H.: Company E, private. January 1, 1864 enlisted as a private in Co. E, 27th Regiment, Georgia Infantry in Charleston, South Carolina. January – February 1864 roll shows him present and due $50.00. March 29, 1864 sent to Lake City, Florida hospital. March - April 1864 roll shows him absent sick.

KING, THOMAS J. M.: Company G, private. September 9, 1861 enlisted as a private in Co. G, 27th Regiment, Georgia Infantry. February 1862 roll shows him as a courier for the garrison court martial. May 21, 1862 died at Richmond, Virginia. He was buried in Hollywood Cemetery at Richmond, Virginia. July 23, 1862 death benefit claim was filed. February 22, 1864 death benefit claim paid $ 124.50 (#13524).

KING, WILLIAM MILLIGAN: Company E, private. September 9, 1861 enlisted as a private in Co. E, 27th Regiment, Georgia Infantry at Camp Stephens, Griffin, Spalding County, Georgia. October 25 (November (15) 27), 1861 died of disease at Camp Stephens, Georgia. December 1861 roll shows he died of disease at Camp Stephens. August 16, 1862 death benefit claim was filed Lewis W. King, father. He is described as 20 years old, dark eyes, light hair, light complexion, 6 foot 0 inches high, born in Henry County, Georgia and by occupation was a farmer.

KINNEY, GEORGE: Company G, private. February 23, 1864 enlisted as a private in Co. G, 27th Regiment, Georgia Infantry in Decatur, Georgia. March - April 1864 roll shows him present. July 1864 and September 20, 1864 issued clothing. April 26, 1865 surrendered, Greensboro, North Carolina. May 1, 1865 paroled at Greensboro, North Carolina.

KISER (KIZER), CHRISTOPHER: Company D, private. He enlisted as a private in Co. D, 27th Regiment, Georgia Infantry. He died in Strasburg, Virginia. November 17, 1862 death benefit claim was filed.

KITCHENS, B. F.: Company H, private. He enlisted as a private in Co. H, 27th Regiment, Georgia Infantry. November 8, 1861 died of disease at Griffin, Georgia. December 1861 roll shows he died of disease (Pneumonia) in Griffin, Georgia.

KITCHENS, T. JEFFERSON: Company H, corporal. September 9, 1861 elected 3rd corporal of Co. H, 27th Regiment, Georgia Infantry at Camp Stephens at Griffin, Spalding County, Georgia. May 18, 1862 admitted to General Hospital No. 18 (formerly Greaner's Hospital) at Richmond, Virginia with Diarrhoea. June 12, 1862 received pay ($80.00). June 16, 1862 returned to duty. December 31, 1863 received pay. January – February 1864 roll shows him present. February 29, 1864 received pay. March - April 1864 roll shows him present. July 1864 and September 20, 1864 issued clothing. September 26, 1864 admitted to Jackson Hospital at Richmond, Virginia. October 1, 1864 admitted to Jackson Hospital at Richmond, Virginia with Chronic Diarrhoea. October 9, 1864 furloughed for 30 days.

KITE, A. J.: Company E, private. March 1, 1864 enlisted as a private in Co. K, 27th Regiment, Georgia Infantry at Atlanta, Georgia. June 30, 1864 his name appears on Hospital Muster Roll of Stuart Hospital at Richmond, Virginia. July 3, 1864 admitted to Stuart Hospital, Richmond at Virginia with Chronic Diarrhoea. July 16, 1864 issued clothing at Stuart Hospital at Richmond, Virginia. July 26, 1864 received pay.

KITE, BENJAMIN S.: Company E, private. May 1, 1862 enlisted as a private in Co. C, 53rd Regiment, Georgia Infantry. July 2, 1863 wounded and captured at Gettysburg, Pennsylvania. September 23, 1863 exchanged at City Point, Virginia. July 9, 1864 transferred to Co. E, 27th Regiment, Georgia Infantry. April 26, 1865 surrendered, Greensboro, North Carolina

KITE, D.: Company E, private. February 26, 1862 enlisted as a private in Co. E, 27th Regiment, Georgia Infantry at Clayton, Georgia. May 1, 1863 received pay. June 30, 1863 his name appears on the hospital roll for 1st Division, General Hospital, Camp Winder at Richmond, Virginia. October 31, 1863 received pay. September 20, 1864 issued clothing.

KITE, DAVID: Company E, private. March 1, 1862 enlisted as a private in Co. E, 27th Regiment, Georgia Infantry at Fairburn, Georgia. May 16, 1862 admitted to General Hospital, Camp Winder at Richmond, Virginia. May 17, 1862 returned to duty. May 3, 1863 wounded severely at Chancellorsville, Virginia. December 31, 1863 received pay.
January – February 1864 roll shows him present. February 29, 1864 received pay.
March - April 1864 roll shows him present. April 26, 1865 surrendered Greensboro, North Carolina. May 1, 1865 paroled at Greensboro, North Carolina.

348

KITE, GEORGE W.: Company E, private. February 1, 1864 enlisted as a private in Co. E, 27th Regiment, Georgia Infantry at Charleston, South Carolina and received pay. January – February 1864 roll shows him present and due $50.00 bounty. March - April 1864 roll shows him present. July 13, 1864 admitted to Jackson Hospital at Richmond, Virginia with Int. Febris (Intermittent Fever). August 17, 1864 admitted to Jackson Hospital at Richmond, Virginia with Chronic Diarrhoea. August 24, 1864 issued clothing at Jackson Hospital at Richmond, Virginia. August 25, 1864 returned to duty. August 27, 1864 furloughed for 30 days to Jonesboro, Georgia. September 20, 1864 admitted to Jackson Hospital at Richmond, Virginia with Chronic Diarrhoea. September 1864 issued clothing. April 26, 1865 surrendered Greensboro, North Carolina. May 1, 1865 paroled at Greensboro, North Carolina. He was born in Fayette County, Georgia August 30, 1842.

KITE, JOSIAH: Company E, private. August 1, 1863 enlisted as a private in Co. E, 27th Regiment, Georgia Infantry at Fairburn, Georgia. October 31, 1863 received pay. November 14, 1863 received pay ($22.00). December 31, 1863 received pay. January – February 1864 roll shows him present and owed $50.00 bounty. March - April 1864 roll shows him present. July 13, 1864 admitted to Jackson Hospital at Richmond, Virginia with Febris Congestive (Malaria). August 24, 1864 returned to duty. August 24, 1864 received pay ($22.00). August 29, 1864 received pay ($22.00). September 20, 1864 admitted to Jackson Hospital at Richmond, Virginia with Chronic Diarrhoea. October 12, 1864 furloughed for 30 days. October 13, 1864 admitted to C. S. A. General Hospital, No. 11 at Charlotte, North Carolina with Chronic Diarrhoea. October 22, 1864 died in C. S. A. General Hospital, No. 11 at Charlotte, North Carolina.

KITE, RENFROE: Company E, private. He enlisted as a private in Co. E, 27th Regiment, Georgia Infantry.

KIZER (KISER), J.AMES H.: Company D, private. September 10, 1861 enlisted as a private in Co. D, 27th Regiment, Georgia Infantry at Camp Stephens, Griffin, Spalding County, Georgia. January and February 1862 rolls show him fatigue duty at Headquarters Post since December 14, 1861. Roll shows him at Lynchburg Virginia Hospital in 1862. December 1862 roll shows him in the hospital since August. March 6, 1863 released from hospital duty. April, May and June 1863 issued clothing. October 21, 1863 received $5.94 in commutation for rations. December 1863 issued clothing. February 29, 1864 received pay. March - April 1864 roll shows him present. July and September 1864 issued clothing. May 1, 1865 paroled at General Hospital at Thomasville, North Carolina.

KIZER, SIMPSON W.: Company D, private. September 10, 1861 enlisted as a private in Co. D, 27th Regiment, Georgia Infantry at Camp Stephens at Griffin, Spalding County, Georgia. January 1862 roll shows him on fatigue duty at Headquarters Post since January 30, 1862. December 31, 1863 received pay and was issued clothing.

March - April 1864 roll shows him present. April 26, 1865 pension records show he surrendered Greensboro, North Carolina. He was born in Gainesville, Georgia August 24, 1833.

KNIGHT, H.: Company F, private. June 5, 1865 surrendered at Augusta, Georgia and was paroled that date.

LAMBERT, GREEN LEWIS: Company B, private. February 20, 1864 enlisted as a private in Co. B, 27th Regiment, Georgia Infantry at Decatur, Georgia. January – February 1864 roll shows him present. March - April 1864 roll shows him present. June 1, 1864 wounded (Shot through the chest by a Yankee sharpshooter) and captured, Cold Harbor, Virginia. June 11, 1864 arrived at Point Lookout, Maryland from White House, Virginia. July 12, 1864 transferred to Elmira Prison, Elmira, New York. December 28, 1864 died of Pneumonia at Elmira Prison, New York. He is buried in grave No.1291 (1306), Woodlawn National Cemetery at Elmira, New York.

LAMPKIN: Company K, private. September 10, 1861 enlisted as a private in Co. K, 27th Regiment, Georgia Infantry Camp Stephens, Griffin, Spalding County, Georgia.

LAMPKIN, JOSEPH: Company K, private. April 27, 1862 enlisted as a private in Co. K., 27th Regiment, Georgia Infantry in Virginia. August 13, 1862 died in Virginia.

LANCASTER, JESSE FRANCIS: Company B, private. September 10, 1861 enlisted as a private in Co. B., 27th Regiment, Georgia Infantry. November 13, 1861 died of disease at Macon, Bibb County, Georgia. October 27, 1862 death benefit claim was filed by Martha S. Lancaster, widow. January 20, 1864 death benefit claim paid $98.46 (#11803).

LANCASTER, THOMAS C.: Company B, corporal. June 12, 1861 elected 1st corporal Co. B, 27th Regiment, Georgia Infantry. December 1861 roll shows him in the Hospital in Richmond, Virginia since November 15, 1861. December 16, 1861 discharged due to disability at Richmond, Virginia and received pay. January 1862 roll shows he was discharged due to disability December 16, 1861. He was born in Hancock County, Georgia in 1828.

LANDEN, B. M.: Company D, private. He enlisted as a private in Co. D, 27th Regiment, Georgia Infantry. December 1862 roll shows him at the hospital December 1, 1862.

LANGFORD, H. M.: Company D, private. September 10, 1861 enlisted as a private in Co. D, 27th Regiment, Georgia Infantry at Camp Stephens, Griffin, Spalding County, Georgia. May 31, 1862 wounded at Seven Pines, Virginia. June 3, 1862 died in the Hospital in Richmond, Virginia. July 10, 1862 death benefit claim was filed by Susannah Langford, his mother. December 4, 1862 death benefit claim paid $131.10 (#2074).

LANGFORD, W. G.: Company D, private. September 1, 1862 enlisted as a private in Co. D, 27th Regiment, Georgia Infantry at Camp Randolph, Georgia. December 1862 roll shows him in the hospital since August.

December 1863 issued clothing. January 28, 1864 discharged due to disability (blindness of left eye and weakness of right eye). January 28, 1864 received pay ($27.23). He is described on his certificate of disability as being born in Hall County, Georgia, aged 24 years, 6 feet 1 inch high, fair complexion, blue eyes, light hair and by occupation a farmer.

LASLIE (LESLIE), A. D.: Company I, private. September 17, 1863 enlisted as a private in Co. I, 27th Regiment, Georgia Infantry at Macon, Georgia. December 31, 1863 received pay. January – February 1864 roll shows him present. February 29, 1864 received pay. March - April 1864 roll shows him present. He is listed in the personal papers of Major James Gardner as "Men for Gallantry". July 1864 and September 20, 1864 issued clothing. April 26, 1865, surrendered at Greensboro, North Carolina. May 1, 1865 paroled at Greensboro, North Carolina.

LASITER (LASETER) (LASSITER), HIRAM M.: Company E, private. September 9, 1861 enlisted as a private in Co. E, 27th Regiment, Georgia Infantry Camp Stephens, Griffin, Spalding County, Georgia. June 18, 1864 wounded at Colquitt's Salient at Petersburg, Virginia in the hand necessitating amputation of finger. September 20, 1864 issued clothing. April 26, 1865 surrendered at Greensboro, North Carolina. May 1, 1865 paroled at Greensboro, North Carolina.

LASITER (LASETER) (LASSITER), J. A.: Company E, private. September 9, 1861 enlisted as a private in Co. E, 27th Regiment, Georgia Infantry at Camp Stephens at Griffin, Spalding County, Georgia. January 1863 transferred to Co. I, 10th Regiment, Georgia Infantry. July 3, 1863 captured at Gettysburg, Pennsylvania. May 12, 1865 released at Fort Delaware, Delaware. He was born in Coweta County, Georgia May 31, 1838.

LASITER (LASETER) (LASSITER) (LASTER), JAMES: Company E, private. September 9, 1861 enlisted as a private in Co. E, 27th Regiment, Georgia Infantry at Camp Stephens at Griffin, Spalding County, Georgia. November 24, 1863 received $6.60 for commutation for rations. April, May and June 1863 issued clothing. December 31, 1863 received pay. January – February 1864 roll shows him present. February 29, 1864 received pay. March - April 1864 roll shows him present. May 30, 1864 and September 1864 issued clothing. April 26, 1865 surrendered Greensboro, North Carolina. May 1, 1865 paroled at Greensboro, North Carolina. He was born in Walton County, Georgia in 1831.

LASITER (LASETER) (LASSITER), JOEL: Company E, private. September 9, 1861 enlisted as a private in Co. E, 27th Regiment, Georgia Infantry at Camp Stephens at Griffin, Spalding County, Georgia. December 1861 roll shows him in the hospital at Petersburg, Virginia. January 1862 roll shows he was left sick at Petersburg on November 6, 1861. March 29, 1863 transferred to Co. I, 10th Georgia Infantry. April 26, 1865 surrendered Greensboro, North Carolina.

LASITER (LASETER) (LASSITER, RICHARD V.: Company E,

private. September 9, 1861 enlisted as a private in Co. E, 27th Regiment, Georgia Infantry at Camp Stephens at Griffin, Spalding County, Georgia. November 6, 1861 admitted to General Hospital at Petersburg, Virginia with Rubeola. November 13, 1861 died of Rubeola at Petersburg, Virginia. December 1861 roll shows he died of disease November 13, 1861 at Petersburg, Virginia.

LASITER (LASETER) (LASSITER, S.: Company E, private. June 3, 1861 enlisted as a private in Co. E, 27th Regiment, Georgia Infantry at Fayetteville, Georgia. December 31, 1863 received pay. June 20, 1864 wounded at Colquitt's Salient near Petersburg, Virginia. June 20, 1864 admitted to Receiving and Wayside Hospital or General Hospital No. 9 at Richmond, Virginia. June 21, 1864 transferred to Jackson Hospital at Richmond, Virginia. June 21, 1864 admitted to Jackson Hospital at Richmond, Virginia with a Vulnus Sclopeticum (Gunshot Wound) to the left hand by a mini ball. June 30, 1864 shown on rolls of Division 2, Jackson Hospital at Richmond, Virginia as present. July 18(19), 1864 furloughed for 30 days from Jackson Hospital at Richmond, Virginia.

LATHAM, GEORGE W.: Company D, captain. September 10, 1861 enlisted as a private in Co. D, 27th Regiment, Georgia Infantry at Camp Stephens at Griffin, Spalding County, Georgia. June 21, 1861 elected 1st lieutenant Co. D, 27th Regiment, Georgia Infantry. July 4, 1862 received pay ($99.00). September 15, 1862 received pay ($207.00). December 1862 roll shows him present near Guinea Station, Virginia. July 1, 1862 wounded at Malvern Hill, Virginia. January 10, 1863 elected captain Co. D, 27th Regiment, Georgia Infantry. August 7, 1863 admitted to the C. S. A. General Military Hospital, No. 4 at Wilmington, North Carolina with "Ulcus". August 11, 1863 returned to duty. March – April 1864 roster shows him present. July 1864 stationed in Petersburg, Virginia. July 24, 1864 admitted to General Hospital No. 4 at Richmond, Virginia with Intermittent Fever. August 1, 1864 sent from General Hospital No. 4 at Richmond, Virginia to Gainesville, Hall County, Georgia for 30 days. (He had been hospitalized for 4 weeks with Chronic Dysentery). September 30, 1864 he is shown on roster of officers of Gen. A. H. Colquitt's Brigade. November 1, 1864 appears on roster. November 8, 1864 received pay ($260.00). April 26, 1865 surrendered Greensboro, North Carolina. May 1, 1865 paroled at Greensboro, North Carolina. He was born in Georgia March 23, 1839.

LATHEM, JAMES S.: Company D, sergeant. September 10, 1861 enlisted as a private in Co. D, 27th Regiment, Georgia Infantry at Camp Stephens at Griffin, Spalding County, Georgia. December 1861 roll shows he was left sick in Richmond, Virginia. January 1862 and February 1862 rolls shows he was in the hospital in Richmond, Virginia. March 30, 1862 admitted to General Hospital No. 18 (formerly Greaner's Hospital) at Richmond, Virginia with Tonsillitis. April 14, 1862 returned to duty. July 4, 1862 received pay ($78.00). August 30, 1862 admitted to Camp

Winder Division No. 2 Hospital at Richmond, Virginia with Typhoid Fever. September 15, 1862 transferred to 1st Georgia Hospital at Richmond, Virginia. September 24, 1862 admitted to Camp Winder Division No. 2 Hospital at Richmond, Virginia with Typhoid Fever. September 30, 1862 he was returned to duty from Winder, Division 2 Hospital at Richmond, Virginia. April, May and June 1863 issued clothing. October 23, 1863 arrested and sent to court martial for untying a private that had been bucked and gaged for stealing a watermelon. December 1863 issued clothing. February 29, 1864 received pay. Received pay for extra duty as a teamster in Charleston, South Carolina from February1 through February 14, 1864. March - April 1864 roll shows him present. July 1864 and September 20, 1864 issued clothing. April 26, 1865 surrendered Greensboro, North Carolina. May 1, 1865 paroled at Greensboro, North Carolina.

LATIMER, CORNELIUS: Company D, private. He enlisted as a private in Co. D, 27th Regiment, Georgia Infantry. May 31, 1862 captured at Seven Pines, Virginia. June 14, 1862 sent from Fort Monroe, Virginia to Fort Delaware, Delaware. Described as being born in South Carolina, age 23, height 5 feet 10 inches high, light hair, blue eyes and fair complexion. August 5, 1862 sent from Fort Delaware, Delaware and exchanged at Aikens Landing, Virginia. September 17, 1862 killed at Sharpsburg, Maryland. June 10, 1863 death benefit claim was filed by J. E. Redwine, atty.

LAVENDER, ANTHONY: Company F, private. September 9, 1861 enlisted as a private in Co. F, 27th Regiment, Georgia Infantry at Camp Stephens at Griffin, Spalding County, Georgia. December 1861 roll shows him in the hospital in Culpepper, Virginia. December 29, 1861 admitted to Moore Hospital at General Hospital, No. 1 at Danville, Virginia with Congestive Fever (Malaria) and was sent to the General Hospital at Culpepper, Virginia. January 1862 roll shows him in Moore Hospital. March 9, 1863 received commutation of rations while on furlough ($10.00). October 31, 1863 received pay. December 31, 1863 received pay and is shown on roll of First Georgia Hospital at Charleston, South Carolina. January – February 1864 roll shows him present. March - April 1864 roll shows him present. June 25, 1864 admitted to General Hospital at Petersburg, Virginia with Typhoid Fever. June 29, 1864 transferred to Richmond, Virginia. July 2, 1864 died in Richmond, Virginia. February 28, 1865 death benefit claim was filed by his widow, Nancy Lavender.

LAWHORN (LAWHORNE), SIMEON P.: Company A, private. April 25, 1864 enlisted as a private in Co. A, 27th Regiment, Georgia Infantry. March - April 1864 roll shows him absent with leave. May 30, 1864 issued clothing. July 1864 issued clothing. July 11, 1864 admitted to Jackson Hospital at Richmond, Virginia with Rubeola. August 1, 1864 died of Measles (Rubeola) in Jackson Hospital at Richmond, Virginia. He was buried in Hollywood Cemetery at Richmond, Virginia. October 27, 1864 death benefit claim was filed by his widow Martha Lawhorn of Buena Vista, Marion County, Georgia.

LAWSON, D. B. M.: Company F, private. August 7, 1862 enlisted as a private in Co. F, 27th Regiment, Georgia Infantry in Randolph, County, Georgia. December 1862 roll shows he was sent to hospital in November 1862. January 19, 1863 received pay ($52.80). August 1863 issued clothing. January-February 1864 and March-April 1864 rolls show him absent in the hospital in Savannah, Georgia since February 13, 1864. February 13, 1864 - April 30, 1864 sick in Savannah, Georgia hospital.

LAWSON, JAMES P.: Company F, private. August 3, 1862 enlisted as a private in Co. F, 27th Regiment, Georgia Infantry at Camp Randolph in Butler, Georgia. September 30, 1862 admitted to 4th Division, General Hospital Camp Winder at Richmond, Virginia. October 7, 1862 returned to duty. October 31, 1862 received pay. November 15, 1862 admitted to 4th Division, General Hospital Camp Winder at Richmond, Virginia. December 4, 1862 returned to duty. December 1862 roll shows he was sent to hospital in November 1862. December 28, 1862 admitted to General Hospital No. 19 at Richmond, Virginia. January 22, 1863 admitted to General Hospital No. 1, Camp Winder at Richmond, Virginia. December 31, 1863 received pay. February 20, 1864 wounded at Olustee, Florida. January – February 1864 roll shows him absent wounded. March - April 1864 roll shows him on wounded furlough.

LAWSON, JULIUS: Company F, private. He enlisted as a private in Co. F, 27th Regiment, Georgia Infantry. March - April 1864 roll shows him present.

LAYFIELD, DRURY: March 4, 1862 enlisted as a private in Co. F, 27th Regiment, Georgia Infantry. July 20, 1862 died 1st Georgia Hospital, Richmond, Virginia. March 12, 1863 death benefit claim was filed by George Layfield, father. He was born in Talbot County, Georgia June 14, 1843.

LAYFIELD, FLOYD P.: Company F, sergeant. September 9, 1861 enlisted as a private in Co. F, 27th Regiment, Georgia Infantry. April 10, 1862 admitted to Chimborazo Hospital at Richmond, Virginia with Pneumonia. April 21, 1862 died of Pneumonia in Chimborazo Hospital No. 5 at Richmond, Virginia. He is most likely buried in Oakwood Cemetery at Richmond Virginia.
May 15, 1862 death benefit claim was filed by George Layfield of Taylor County, father. July 19, 1862 death benefit claim paid $83.90 (#741). He is described as a farmer, fair complexion, light hair, blue eyes, 5 foot 9 inches and was age 21.

LAYFIELD, JOHN H.: Company F, private. September 20, 1861 enlisted as a private in Co. F, 27th Regiment, Georgia Infantry at Camp Stephens, Griffin, Spalding County, Georgia. January 7, 1862 admitted to Moore Hospital at General Hospital, No. 1 at Danville, Virginia with Pneumonia and was sent to the 9th ward. January 1862 and February 1862 rolls show he was sent to Moore Hospital on January 7. April 10, 1862 admitted to Chimborazo Hospital No. 5, at Richmond, Virginia with Pneumonia.

May 9, 1862 transferred to Lynchburg. June 19, 1862 died of disease in Richmond, Virginia hospital. February 20, 1863 death benefit claim was filed by Josephine Layfield, his widow.

LAYFIELD, W. H.: Company F, private. September 20, 1861 enlisted as a private in Co. F, 27th Regiment, Georgia Infantry at Camp Stephens, Griffin, Spalding County, Georgia. September 30, 1862 admitted to General Hospital No. 16, Richmond, Virginia. September 29, 1862 received pay ($113.00). October 4, 1862 admitted to Camp Winder Division No. 1 Hospital Richmond, Virginia. August 1863 and September 1863 issued clothing. December 31, 1863 received pay. January – February 1864 roll shows him present. March - April 1864 roll shows him present. July 1864 issued clothing. April 26, 1865 surrendered Greensboro, North Carolina. May 1, 1865 paroled at Greensboro, North Carolina.

LECKIE, JAMES: Company D, private. February 23, 1862 enlisted as a private in Co. D, 27th Regiment, Georgia Infantry in Hall County, Georgia. March 25, 1862 received bounty pay ($50.00) in Atlanta, Georgia. June 1863 issued clothing. December 1863 issued clothing. February 29, 1864 received pay. March - April 1864 roll shows him present. July, 31, 1864 and September 20, 1864 issued clothing. December 1864 pension records show he enlisted in Graham's Battalion, Georgia Militia and served until the close of the war. He was born in Georgia in 1845.

LEE, J. D.: Company G, private. May 19, 1862 enlisted as a private in Co. G, 27th Regiment, Georgia Infantry in Pike County, Georgia. July 24, 1862 admitted to Jackson Hospital at Richmond, Virginia with Dysentery. June 26, 1863, October 30, 1863 and November 21, 1863 issued clothing. December 31, 1863 received pay. January – February 1864 roll shows him present. March 5, 1864 issued clothing. March - April 1864 roll shows him present. July 24, 1864 admitted to Jackson Hospital at Richmond, Virginia with Dysentery. June 30, 1864 roll of 1st Division, Jackson Hospital at Richmond, Virginia shows him present. July 31, 1864 furloughed for 30 days.

LEE, JAMES M.: Company G, private. September 9, 1861 enlisted as a private in Co. G, 27th Regiment, Georgia Infantry at Camp Stephens, Griffin, Spalding County, Georgia. January 7, 1862 admitted to Moore Hospital at General Hospital, No. 1 at Danville, Virginia with Pneumonia and was transferred to General Hospital at Front Royal, Virginia. January 1862 roll shows he was in the hospital in Richmond, Virginia. February 1862 roll shows he was reported absent without leave because furlough had expired. September 17, 1862 killed at Sharpsburg, Maryland. November 20, 1862 death benefit claim was filed by his widow, Mary M. Lee. August 6, 1863 death benefit paid $125.23 (#7261).

LEE, OSGOOD A.: Company I, captain. July 6, 1861 elected captain of the Appling Grays in Appling County, Georgia. September 10, 1861 became captain of Co. I, 27th Regiment, Georgia Infantry at Camp Stephens, Griffin, Spalding County, Georgia. September - December 1861 and

January 1862 rolls show him present at Camp Pickens, Virginia. February 13, 1862 granted 30 day sick furlough at Camp Pickens near Manassas Junction, Virginia. February 1862 roll shows him absent sick. May 31, 1862 killed at Seven Pines, Virginia. He is buried at Richmond, Virginia (Seven Pines, Virginia according to historian at the Richmond Battlefield he was most likely buried where he fell).

LEGGETT, BENJAMIN: Company I, private. September 10, 1861 enlisted as a private in Co. I, 27th Regiment, Georgia Infantry at Camp Stephens, Griffin, Spalding County, Georgia. October 16, 1862 returned to duty from Camp Winder Division No. 3 Hospital Richmond, Virginia. December 31, 1863 received pay. February 20, 1864 wounded at Olustee, Florida. January – February 1864 and March-April 1864 rolls show him absent wounded. June 16, June 27, July 1864 and September 20, 1864 issued clothing. March 19, 1865 captured at Bentonville, North Carolina. April 3, 1865 arrived at Point Lookout, Maryland from Newbern, North Carolina. June 29, 1865 released at Point Lookout, Maryland. Described as being from Appling County, Georgia with a light complexion, auburn hair, blue eyes and was 6 foot and ½ inches tall.

LEGGETT, WILLIAM: Company I, private. March 8, 1862 enlisted as a private in Co. I, 27th Regiment, Georgia Infantry at Waynesville, Wayne County, Georgia. December 31, 1863 received pay. January – February 1864 roll shows him present. February 29, 1864 received pay. March - April 1864 roll shows him present.
June 16, June 27, July 1864 and September 20, 1864 issued clothing.

LESNER, ADOLPH S.: Company I, sergeant. September 10, 1861 enlisted as a private in Co. I, 27th Regiment, Georgia Infantry at Camp Stephens, Griffin, Spalding County, Georgia. He was appointed 1st sergeant in Co. I, 27th Regiment, Georgia Infantry. September 17, 1862 he is shown as killed (missing in action) at Sharpsburg, Maryland. December 1862 roll shows him missing in action at Sharpsburg, Maryland .

LESSINGER (LESUEUR), SEABORN S.: Company G, private. September 9, 1861 enlisted as a private in Co. G, 27th Regiment, Georgia Infantry at Camp Stephens, Griffin, Spalding County, Georgia. March 7, 1862 admitted to Chimborazo Hospital No. 1 at Richmond, Virginia with Jaundice. May 29, 1862 furloughed for 60 days. October 4, 1862 admitted to Camp Winder Division No. 5, Hospital at Richmond, Virginia. October 21, 1862 returned to duty. October 26, 1862 admitted to Receiving and Wayside Hospital or General Hospital No. 9 at Richmond, Virginia and transferred to General Hospital, No. 20 at Richmond, Virginia. October 28, 1862 transferred to Amelia I St. December 1862 roll shows him absent sick. March 13 1863 received pay ($66.00). June 26, 1863 received pay ($22.00). September 17, 1863 received pay ($44.00). December 31, 1863 received pay. January – February 1864 roll shows him present. March – April 1864 roll shows him present. June 2, 1864 wounded at the battle of Cold Harbor. June 2, 1864 admitted to Receiving and Wayside Hospital or General Hospital No. 9 at Richmond, Virginia and was transferred to Petersburg, Virginia. June 3, 1864 pension records show second finger on left hand was shot off at Cold Harbor, Virginia, also hearing and sight practically destroyed by small-pox. June 20, 1864 admitted to Receiving and Wayside Hospital or General Hospital No. 9, Richmond, Virginia. June 22, 1864 transferred to Petersburg, Virginia. He was born in Georgia December 22, 1838.

LEWIS, DANIEL R.: Company H, private. November 1, 1863 enlisted as a private in Co. H, 27th Regiment, Georgia Infantry at McDonough, Georgia. December 31, 1863 received pay. January – February 1864 roll shows him present. February 29, 1864 received pay. March - April 1864 roll shows him present. February 20, 1864 wounded at Olustee Florida. May 31, 1864 admitted to Receiving and Wayside Hospital or General Hospital No. 9 at Richmond, Virginia. June 1, 1864 transferred to Jackson Hospital at Richmond, Virginia. June 14, 1864 returned to duty. July 1864 issued clothing. April 26, 1865 surrendered Greensboro, North Carolina. May 1, 1865 paroled at Greensboro, North Carolina.

LEWIS, J. H.: Company H, private. September 9, 1861 enlisted as a private in Co. H, 27th Regiment, Georgia Infantry at Camp Stephens, Griffin, Spalding County, Georgia. January 27, 1862 admitted to hospital at Front Royal, Virginia. January 1862 roll shows him in Front Royal Hospital. July 19, 1862 received pay ($91.00). December 31, 1863 received pay. January – February 1864 roll shows him present. February 29, 1864 received pay. March - April 1864 roll shows him present. May 31, 1864 issued clothing. June 14, 1864 admitted to Jackson Hospital at Richmond, Virginia with Dysentery. July 9, 1864 issued clothing at Jackson Hospital at Richmond, Virginia. July 13, 1864 returned to duty. April 26, 1865 surrendered Greensboro, North Carolina. May 1, 1865 paroled at Greensboro, North Carolina.

LEWIS, J. T.: Company H, private. March 1, 1862 enlisted as a private in Co. H, 27th Regiment, Georgia Infantry at McDonough, Henry County, Georgia. June 30, 1863 received pay. July 18, 1863 received commutation for rations while on furlough ($6.66). January – February 1864 roll shows him absent without leave. March - April 1864 roll shows him present (shows he was absent without leave from October 31, 1863 to January 31, 1864). April 26, 1865 surrendered Greensboro, North Carolina. May 1, 1865 paroled at Greensboro, North Carolina.

LEWIS, J. W.: Company H, sergeant, major. September 9, 1861 enlisted as a corporal in Co. H, 27th Georgia Infantry, Camp Stephens, Griffin, Spalding County, Georgia. December 1861 roll shows he was left in Griffin, Georgia sick on October 31, 1861. January 1862 roll shows him absent with leave. March 10, 1862 admitted to Chimborazo Hospital No. 5 at Richmond, Virginia with Debility. April 7, 1862 returned to duty. April 25, 1862 received pay ($99.53). April 30, 1862 elected sergeant Co. H, 27th Georgia Infantry. October 5, 1862 admitted to General Hospital, No. 17

at Richmond, Virginia. October 6, 1862 received pay ($143.00). January 1, 1863 elected sergeant major 27th Regiment, Georgia Infantry. January 2, 1863 received pay ($68.00). January 23, 1863 paid for commutation of rations in Atlanta, Georgia. December 31, 1863 received pay. February 18, 1864 returned to Co. H as a private. February 29, 1864 received pay. January – February 1864 roll shows him present. March - April 1864 roll shows him present. July 1864 and September 20, 1864 issued clothing. October 8, 1864 admitted to Jackson Hospital at Richmond, Virginia with Chronic Diarrhea. October 27, 1864 furloughed to Griffin, Georgia for 30 days.

LEWIS, JOHN KING: Co. E, sergeant. He enlisted as a private in Co. H, 27th Regiment, Georgia Infantry. January 3, 1862 elected 5th sergeant of Co. E, 27th Regiment, Georgia Infantry.

LEWIS, L. H. (LITT): Company H, private. He enlisted as a private in Co. H, 27th Regiment, Georgia Infantry. June 2, 1862 received pay ($69). September 17, 1862 missing in action at Sharpsburg, Maryland. December 1862 roll shows him missing in action at Sharpsburg, Maryland.

LEWIS, SANFORD: Company H, private. He enlisted as a private in Co. H, 27th Regiment, Georgia Infantry.

LEWIS, S. P. J.: Company H, private. He enlisted as a private in Co. H, 27th Regiment, Georgia Infantry. May 18, 1862 admitted to General Hospital No. 18 (formerly Greaner's Hospital) at Richmond, Virginia with Diarrhoea. June 11, 1862 returned to duty.

LIFSEY, BENJAMIN HAWKINS: Company G, private. September 21, 1862 enlisted as a private in Co. G, 27th Regiment, Georgia Infantry. December 1862 roll shows him absent sick. June 16, 1863, June 26, 1863, October 30, 1863 and November 1863 issued clothing. December 31, 1863 received pay. January – February 1864 roll shows him present. February 29, 1864 received pay. March - April 1864 roll shows him present. July 1864 issued clothing. April 26, 1865 surrendered Greensboro, North Carolina. May 1, 1865 paroled at Greensboro, North Carolina. He was born in Pike County, Georgia in 1832.

LIFSEY, HENRY THOMAS: Company G, lieutenant. September 9, 1861 enlisted as a private in Co. G, 27th Regiment, Georgia Infantry at Camp Stephens, Griffin, Spalding County, Georgia. November 14, 1861 admitted to General Hospital No. 18 (formerly Greaner's Hospital) at Richmond, Virginia. December 1861 roll shows him in the hospital in Richmond, Virginia. December 1861 hospital muster roll for General Hospital No. 18 (formerly Greaner's Hospital) at Richmond, Virginia shows him present. January 27, 1862 returned to duty. September 17, 1862 wounded at Sharpsburg, Maryland. September 30, 1862 elected Jr. 2nd lieutenant of Co. G, 27th Regiment, Georgia Infantry. December 1862 roll shows him present near Guinea Station, Virginia. February 20, 1864 wounded at Olustee, Florida. January – February 1864 and March – April 1864 rolls do not indicate him present or not. June 1, 1864 wounded at Cold Harbor, Virginia. June 2, 1864 admitted to Receiving and Wayside Hospital or General Hospital No. 9 at Richmond, Virginia and then transferred to Jackson Hospital at Richmond, Virginia with a Vulnus Sclopeticum (Gunshot Wound) to both hips (mini ball). June 2, 1864 died of wounds in Jackson Hospital at Richmond, Virginia. He is buried in Hollywood Cemetery at Richmond, Virginia. He was born in Pike County, Georgia and was a resident of Zebulon, Pike County, Georgia.

LIFSEY, JAMES S.: Company G, corporal. May 19, 1862 enlisted as a private in Co. G, 27th Regiment, Georgia Infantry in Richmond, Virginia. May 31, 1862 wounded in finger necessitating amputation at Seven Pines, Virginia. June 2, 1862 received pay ($29.40). October 29, 1862 admitted to Camp Winder Division No. 1 Hospital at Richmond, Virginia. December 1, 1862 returned to duty. June 16, 1863, October 30, 1863 and November 1863 issued clothing. December 31, 1863 received pay. January – February 1864 roll shows him present. February 29, 1864 received pay. March - April 1864 roll shows him present. June 1, 1864 wounded at Cold Harbor, Virginia. June 2, 1864 admitted to Receiving and Wayside Hospital or General Hospital No. 9 at Richmond, Virginia and then transferred to and admitted to Jackson Hospital at Richmond, Virginia with Vulnus Sclopeticum (Gunshot Wound) to the right shoulder (mini ball). June 8, 1864 furloughed for 30 days. September 20, 1864 issued clothing. March 19, 1865 wounded at Bentonville, North Carolina. April 26, 1865 surrendered Greensboro, North Carolina. May 1, 1865 paroled at Greensboro, North Carolina. He was born in Pike County, Georgia May 21, 1840 and died in Pike County, Georgia in 1921.

LIFSEY, JOHN: Company G, private. June 6, 1863 enlisted as a private in Co. G, 27th Regiment, Georgia Infantry. December 31, 1863 received pay. January – February 1864 roll shows him discharged. January 26, 1864 discharged due to disability, at Fort Johnson, South Carolina. He was born in Monroe County, Georgia on February 14, 1822. He died in Pike County, Georgia January 24, 1896. He was buried in Fincher's Cemetery in Pike County, Georgia near Zebulon.

LIGHTNER, P. A.: Company A, corporal. He enlisted as a private in Co. A, 27th Regiment, Georgia Infantry. December 1861 and January 1862 rolls show he was left sick in Georgia October 31, 1861. He died August 1862. January 8, 1863 death benefit claim was filed by his widow, Caroline Lightner.

LINDER, JERRY E: Company E, private. September 9, 1861 enlisted as a private in Co. E, 27th Regiment, Georgia Infantry. He was captured date and place not given. June 1865 released at Johnson's Island, Ohio.

LINDSEY, DANIEL N.: Company H, private. March 1, 1862 enlisted as a private in Co. H, 27th Regiment, Georgia Infantry at McDonough, Henry County, Georgia. May 3, 1863 wounded at Chancellorsville, Virginia. December 31, 1863 received pay. February 20, 1864 wounded at Olustee, Florida. January – February 1864 roll shows him absent wounded at

Tallahassee, Florida. February 29, 1864 received pay. March - April 1864 roll shows him present. September 20, 1864 issued clothing. April 26, 1865 surrendered Greensboro, North Carolina. May 1, 1865 paroled at Greensboro, North Carolina.

LINDSEY, J. M: Company H, private. September 9, 1861 enlisted as a private in Co. H, 27th Regiment, Georgia Infantry at Camp Stephens at Griffin, Spalding County, Georgia. February 20, 1864 wounded at Olustee, Florida. December 31, 1863 received pay. January – February 1864 roll shows him present. February 29, 1864 received pay. March - April 1864 roll shows him present. May 31, 1864, July 1864 and September 20, 1864 issued clothing. He was born in Henry County, Georgia in 1839.

LINLER (LINDLER), ISRAEL E.: Company E, private. September 9, 1861 enlisted as a private in Co. E, 27th Regiment, Georgia Infantry at Camp Stephens at Griffin, Spalding County, Georgia. December 1861 roll shows him sick in hospital in Richmond, Virginia. February 19, 1862 furloughed for 30 days. February 1862 roll shows him on furlough for 30 days from February 19. April, May and June 1863 issued clothing. December 31, 1863 received pay. January 2, 1864 through January 31, 1864 on detached duty at Fort Johnson, South Carolina as an oarsman at a rate of $.25 per day. January – February 1864 roll shows him present. February 29, 1864 received pay. March - April 1864 roll shows him present. September 20, 1864 issued clothing. 1865 furloughed at Sugar Loaf, North Carolina. He died at Lovejoy, Georgia January 11, 1914.

LISLE, W. M.: Company G, private. He enlisted as a private in Co. G, 27th Regiment, Georgia Infantry. February 14, 1865 admitted to C. S. A. General Military Hospital at Charlotte, North Carolina with Chronic Diarrhea. May 3, 1865 paroled at Charlotte, North Carolina.

LITTLE, ABRAHAM: Company D, private. September 10, 1861 enlisted as a private in Co. D, 27th Regiment, Georgia Infantry. December 1863 wounded in the left hand necessitating amputation of finger at Fort Sumter, South Carolina. December 31, 1863 received pay and issued clothing at Hospital. January – February 1864 roll of General Hospital No. 1, Summerville, South Carolina shows him present. March - April 1864 roll shows him on sick furlough. He was born in Georgia in 1832.

LITTLE, EDWARD O.: Company A, private. May 12, 1862 enlisted as a private in Co. A, 27th Regiment, Georgia Infantry in Schley County, Georgia. September 17, 1862 wounded in the right leg at Sharpsburg, Maryland. October 14, 1863 received commutation for rations for 9 months ($202.00). November 20, 1862 received bounty pay ($50.00). November 21, 1862 received pay ($61.96). December 1862 roll shows him wounded (September) in Georgia. December 31, 1863 received pay and issued clothing. January – February 1864 roll shows him present. March - April 1864 roll shows him present. July 1, 1864 issued clothing. July 21, 1864 admitted to Jackson Hospital at Richmond, Virginia with acute Dysentery. August 18, 1864 issued clothing at Jackson Hospital,

360

Richmond, Virginia. October 1864 Hospital Muster Roll for Jackson Hospital at Richmond, Virginia shows him present as a nurse. October 24, 1864 attached to Jackson Hospital, Richmond, Virginia as a nurse due to unfitness for duty. December 14, 1864 issued clothing at Jackson Hospital at Richmond, Virginia. December 1864 Hospital Muster Roll for Jackson Hospital at Richmond, Virginia shows him present as a nurse. January 15, 1865 furloughed for 30 days from Jackson Hospital, Richmond, Virginia. May 10, 1865 surrendered at Tallahassee, Florida. May 18, 1865 paroled at Albany, Georgia.

LITTLE, J. M.: Company D, private. September 10, 1861 enlisted as a private in Co. D, 27th Regiment, Georgia Infantry. December 23, 1862 received pay ($66.00). April, May, June and December 1863 issued clothing. February 29, 1864 received pay. March - April 1864 roll shows him present. May 30, 1864, July 1864 and September 20, 1864 issued clothing. January 1865 pension records show he was at home on furlough from this date until the close of the war. He was born in Hall County, Georgia January 25, 1840.

LITTLE, JOSEPH HARRISON: Company A, lieutenant. September 10, 1861 enlisted as a private in Co. A, 27th Regiment, Georgia Infantry. July 17, 1862 received pay ($91.00). He was appointed sergeant for Co. A, 27th Regiment, Georgia Infantry. August 26, 1862 admitted to General Hospital No. 7, Richmond, Virginia. August 27, 1862 returned to duty. November 21, 1862 received pay ($130.00). July 20, 1863 elected 2nd lieutenant in Co. A, 27th Regiment, Georgia Infantry. August 22, 1864 received pay ($160.00). March 18, 1865 pension records indicate he was wounded at Bentonville, North Carolina and was in Charlotte, North Carolina Hospital, wounded at the close of the war. He was born in Jones County, Georgia December 5, 1840.

LITTLE, W. H.: Company D, private. February 20, 1863 enlisted as a private in Co. D, 27th Regiment, Georgia Infantry. April, May, June and December 1863 issued clothing. December 31, 1863 received pay. March - April 1864 roll shows him present.

LITTLE, ZEDEKIAH W.: Company I, lieutenant. September 10, 1861 elected Jr. 2nd lieutenant of Co. I, 27th Regiment, Georgia Infantry. December 1861 roll states he joined his company from Georgia on December 10, 1861 and is present at Camp Pickens, near Manassas, Virginia. January 7, 1862 received pay ($245.00). January 1862 roll shows him absent without leave. February 1862 roll shows him absent sick. December 1862 roll shows him present near Guinea Station, Virginia. June 10, 1862 promoted to 2nd lieutenant. July 11, 1862 received pay ($160.00). August 19, 1862 received pay ($80.00). September 2, 1862 received pay ($80.00). September 21, 1862 received commutation for rations ($7.50). April 30, 1863 elected 1st lieutenant of Co. I, 27th Regiment, Georgia Infantry. He was detailed assistant surgeon 27th Regiment, Georgia Infantry. August 19, 1865 received pay ($360.00). September 20, 1864 tenders his resignation.

361

September 27, 1864 report shows him as being on sick furlough. September 30, 1864 admitted to Jackson Hospital, Richmond, Virginia with Bronchitis. October 17, 1864 furloughed from Jackson Hospital, Richmond, Virginia for 30 days. December 31, 1864, a report from Camp Whiting, North Carolina from General Colquitt's Brigade and General Hoke's Division that he was furloughed by General Lee on October 15, 1864.

March 15, 1865 dropped from rolls for prolonged absence without leave.

LIVINGSTON, D. M.: Company I, sergeant. September 9, 1861 elected 1st sergeant of Co. I, 27th Regiment, Georgia Infantry at Camp Stephens, Griffin, Spalding County, Georgia. September 26, 1862 furloughed from General Hospital, Camp Winder, Richmond, Virginia. November 1862 received for commutation of rations while on furlough ($13.33). June 16 and June 27, 1863 issued clothing. July 12, 1863 admitted to C. S. A. General Military Hospital, No. 4, Wilmington, North Carolina with Catarrh. July 20, 1863 returned to duty. December 31, 1863 received pay. January – February 1864 roll shows him present. February 29, 1864 received pay. March - April 1864 roll shows him present. June 1864 wounded at Petersburg, Virginia. June 20, 1864 wounded at Cold Harbor, Virginia. June 20, 1864 admitted to Jackson Hospital at Richmond, Virginia, Vulnus Sclopeticum (Gunshot Wound) to the head (mini ball). June 27, 1864 died in Jackson Hospital at Richmond, Virginia. He is buried in Hollywood Cemetery at Richmond, Virginia. His inventory of effects was: 1 pair pants, 1 pair shoes and 1 jacket.

LONG, GREEN W.: Company C, private. September 10, 1861 enlisted as a private in Co. C, 27th Regiment, Georgia Infantry at Camp Stephens, Griffin, Spalding County, Georgia. September 28, 1862 admitted to Chimborazo Hospital No. 3 at Richmond, Virginia with a Hernia from shell bruise and irritation of bladder. December 1862 roll shows him absent on sick furlough. June 16 and June 26, 1863 issued clothing. January 31, 1864 transferred to Co. E. 22 Battery Georgia Artillery.

LOWNSBURY, J. H.: Company C, private. He enlisted as a private in Co. C, 27th Regiment, Georgia Infantry. June 3, 1864 transferred from Jackson Hospital at Richmond, Virginia to Staunton, Virginia.

LOWERY, ASBURY S.: Company D, private. He enlisted as a private in Co. D, 27th Regiment, Georgia Infantry. December 28, 1861 admitted to Moore Hospital at General Hospital, No. 1 at Danville, Virginia with Congestive Fever (Malaria) and was transferred to General Hospital at Richmond, Virginia. December 1861, January 1862 and February 1862 rolls show him in the hospital in Richmond, Virginia. June 7, 1862 received pay ($131.83). He died in Richmond, Virginia. May 18, 1863 death benefit claim was filed by John D. Lowery, father.

LOWERY (LOWRY), H. A.: Company D, private. March 25, 1864 enlisted as a private in Co. D, 27th Regiment, Georgia Infantry in Florida. March - April 1864 roll shows him present. August 11, 1864 admitted to Jackson Hospital at Richmond, Virginia with a Vulnus Sclopeticum

(Gunshot Wound) to the left leg (exploding shell). August 18, 1864 furloughed for 30 days from Jackson Hospital at Richmond, Virginia.

LOWERY (LOWRY), ROBERT S. (H.): Company D, private. February 25, 1862 enlisted as a private in Co. D, 27th Regiment, Georgia Infantry in Gainesville, Hall County, Georgia. March 25, 1862 received bounty pay ($50.00) in Atlanta, Georgia. April 6, 1862 admitted to General Hospital at Orange Court House, Virginia with Fever. December 1863 issued clothing. February 29, 1864 received pay. March - April 1864 roll shows him present. April 26, 1865 surrendered Greensboro, North Carolina. May 1, 1865 paroled at Greensboro, North Carolina.

LOVEJOY, W.: Company A, private. September 10, 1861 enlisted as a private in Co. A, 27th Regiment, Georgia Infantry at Camp Stephens, Griffin, Spalding County, Georgia. January 1862 roll shows he was left in Georgia sick on October 31, 1861.

LOVETT, T. Y.: Company D, private. October 12, 1864 enlisted as a private in Co. D, 27th Regiment, Georgia Infantry. December 30, 1864 returns show him present.

LYLE, WILLIAM H.: Company H, private. September 9, 1861 enlisted as a private in Co. H, 27th Regiment, Georgia Infantry. November 15, 1861 admitted to General Hospital No. 18 (formerly Greaner's Hospital) at Richmond, Virginia with congestion of lungs and that he died November 30, 1861. November 1861 roll shows that on November 30, 1861 he died of Pneumonia at Richmond, Virginia. December 1861 roll shows he died in Richmond.

LYNCH, EDWARD H. (A.): Company G, private. September 9, 1861 enlisted as a private in Co. G, 27th Regiment, Georgia Infantry. January 7, 1862 admitted to Moore Hospital, General Hospital No.1 at Danville, Virginia. January 7 (8), 1862 sent to General Hospital, Ward 9 at Danville, Virginia, where he died of Typhoid Pneumonia. December 20, 1862 death benefit claim was filed by Zacharias Lynch, his father. November 24, 1863 death benefit claim paid $74.56 (#10823).

LYNN, DANIEL E.: Company I, private. September 10, 1861 enlisted as a private in Co. I, 27th Regiment, Georgia Infantry at Camp Stephens, Griffin, Spalding County, Georgia. December 1861 roll shows him in the hospital in Richmond, Virginia. January 1862 roll shows him on furlough. February 1862 roll shows him absent sick since November 14, 1861 in Richmond, Virginia. June 16 and June 27, 1863 issued clothing. December 31, 1863 received pay. January – February 1864 roll shows him present. February 29, 1864 received pay. March - April 1864 roll shows him present. July 1864 issued clothing. October 18, 1864 received pay ($47.12).

LYNN, PATRICK: Company I, private. September 10, 1861 enlisted as a private in Co. I, 27th Regiment, Georgia Infantry at Camp Stephens, Griffin, Spalding County, Georgia. November 2, 1861 died of Typhoid Fever at Griffin, Georgia. November Report of Sick and Wounded shows he died of Typhoid Fever on November 2, 1861. December 1861 roll stated

363

he died November 2 in Griffin Georgia.

LYNN, J. W.: Company F, private. He enlisted as a private in Co. F, 27th Regiment, Georgia Infantry. March 31, 1862 admitted to Chimborazo Hospital No. 2, at Richmond, Virginia. May 9, 1862 transferred to Lynchburg, Virginia.

LYNN (LINN), WILLIAM: Company I, private. He enlisted as a private in Co. I, 27th Regiment, Georgia Infantry. March 25, 1862 died of Typhoid Fever at General Receiving Hospital (also known as Charity Hospital) at Gordonsville, Virginia (he had $20.00).

LYNN, WILLIAM: Company I, private. September 10, 1861 enlisted as a private in Co. I, 27th Regiment, Georgia Infantry at Camp Stephens, Griffin, Spalding County, Georgia. April 1862 died in Virginia.

LYON (LYONS, J. B.: Company F, private. September 9, 1861 enlisted as a private in Co. F, 27th Regiment, Georgia Infantry at Camp Stephens, Griffin, Spalding County, Georgia. June 27, 1862 killed, Cold Harbor, Virginia.

LYON (LYONS J. W.: Company F, private. September 10, 1861 enlisted as a private in Co. I, 28th Regiment, Georgia Infantry at Camp Stephens, Griffin, Spalding County, Georgia. 1861 transferred as a private in Co. F, 27th Regiment, Georgia Infantry. March 31, 1862 admitted to Chimborazo Hospital No.2 at Richmond, Virginia. May 9, 1862 transferred to Lynchburg, Virginia.

MABRY (MABARY), DAVID A.: Company D, private. February 24, 1862 enlisted as a private in Co. D, 27th Regiment, Georgia Infantry at Gainesville, Hall County, Georgia. March 25, 1862 received bounty pay ($50.00) at Atlanta, Georgia. September 19, 1862 died of Typhoid Fever at General Hospital at Scottsville, Virginia. December 24, 1862 death benefit claim was filed by Eli L. Mabry, his father. January 11, 1865 death benefit claim paid $100.96 (#21811).

MABRY, M. W.: Company D, corporal. September 10, 1861 enlisted as a private in Co. D, 27th Regiment, Georgia Infantry at Camp Stephens, Griffin, Spalding County, Georgia. He was elected 2nd corporal of Company D. April, May, June and December 1863 issued clothing. November 26, 1863 received commutation for rations $15.00. December 31, 1863 received pay. March - April 1864 roll shows him present. September 1864 issued clothing.

MABRY (MABRA), W. N.: Company G, private. He enlisted as a private in Co. G, 27th Regiment, Georgia Infantry. October 8, 1862 admitted to Receiving and Wayside Hospital or General Hospital No. 9 at Richmond, Virginia and was sent to Hospital No. 25 at Richmond, Virginia. June 16, June 23, October 30 and November 18, 1863 issued clothing.

MACKEY, ELI: Company A, private. September 10, 1861 enlisted as a private in Co. A, 27th Regiment, Georgia Infantry at Camp Stephens, Griffin, Spalding County, Georgia. December 1861, January 1862 and February 1862 rolls show he was left in Georgia sick on October 31,

1861. May 17, 1862 admitted to Chimborazo Hospital No. 2 at Richmond, Virginia with Debility. May 27, 1862 transferred to Lynchburg, Virginia or Farmville, Virginia. December 1862 roll shows he was detailed as a pioneer. May 5, 1863 killed at Chancellorsville, Virginia. October 24, 1865 death benefit claim was filed by John Mackey, father.

MADDOX, W. ROE: Company H, private. He enlisted as a private in Co. H, 27th Regiment, Georgia Infantry. September 17, 1862 captured at Sharpsburg, Maryland. September 27, 1862 paroled.

MALEN, J. W.: Company C, private. He enlisted as a private in Co. C, 27th Regiment, Georgia Infantry. February 22, 1865 transferred from Kinston, North Carolina and admitted to C. S. A. General Hospital, No. 3 at Greensboro, North Carolina with Pneumonia. February 23, 1865 sent to other hospital. He lived in Byron, Georgia.

MALLORY, WILLIAM H.: Company K, private. September 10, 1861 enlisted as a private in Co. A, 27th Regiment, Georgia Infantry at Camp Stephens, Griffin, Spalding County, Georgia. November 6, 1861 admitted to General Hospital at Petersburg, Virginia with Rubeola. November 19, 1861 he died in General Hospital at Petersburg, Virginia of Rubeola. November 1861 Report of Sick and Wounded shows he died of Pneumonia. December 1861 roll indicates he died at Petersburg of disease. September 15, 1862 death benefit claim was filed by his father Absalom Mallory. He lived in Talbotton, Talbot County, Georgia.

MANCY, JAMES: Company E, lieutenant. He enlisted as a private in Co. E, 27th Regiment, Georgia Infantry. September 17, 1862 wounded and captured at Sharpsburg, Maryland. October 3, 1862 died of Vulnus Sclopeticum (Gunshot Wound) at Smoketown, Maryland.

MANGHAM, WILEY JAMES: Company G, sergeant. September 9, 1861 enlisted as a private in Co. G, 27th Regiment, Georgia Infantry at Camp Stephens, Griffin, Spalding County, Georgia. He was appointed sergeant of Co. G, 27th Regiment, Georgia Infantry. February 14, 1862 died of Typhoid Pneumonia, at Camp Pickens, near Manassas, Virginia. February 1862 roll shows he died of disease at Camp Pickens on February 14, 1862. August 4, 1862 death benefit claim was filed by his widow, Susan G. Mangham. November 20, 1863 death benefit claim paid $71.53 (#10827). He was a resident of Pike, County, Georgia.

MANN JR., HENRY: Company I, sergeant. September 10, 1861 enlisted as a private in Co. I, 27th Regiment, Georgia Infantry at Camp Stephens, Griffin, Spalding County, Georgia. November 15, 1861 admitted to General Hospital No. 18 (formerly Greaner's Hospital), Richmond, Virginia. November 28, 1861 sent home with the corpse of David Tuten. December 1861 roll shows him in the hospital in Richmond, Virginia. January 1862 roll shows him on furlough. March 1862 received payment for commutation of rations ($7.50). June 27, 1862 wounded at Cold Harbor, Virginia. July 28, 1862 received pay ($128.00). December 31, 1863 received pay. February 20, 1864 wounded in arm at Olustee, Florida. January – February 1864 roll shows him present. February 29, 1864 received pay. March - April 1864 roll shows him present. June 8, 1864 and July 1864 issued clothing. July 9, 1864 wounded in the left elbow by exploding shell at Colquitt's Salient, near Petersburg, Virginia. July 9, 1864 admitted to Jackson Hospital at Richmond, Virginia with a Vulnus Sclopeticum (Gunshot Wound) to the left elbow from a shell. July 14, 1864 returned to duty. March 1865 appointed 1st. sergeant of Co. I, 27th Regiment, Georgia Infantry. April 26, 1865 surrendered Greensboro, North Carolina. May 1, 1865 paroled at Greensboro, North Carolina. He was born October 30, 1864 in Appling County, Georgia. He died August 15, 1911 in Toombs County, Georgia and is buried in the Henry Mann Cemetery on State Route 147 in Toombs County, Georgia.

MARD, W. S. D: Company A, private. September 9, 1861 enlisted as a private in Co. A, 27th Regiment, Georgia Infantry at Camp Stephens, Griffin, Spalding County, Georgia. He was sent home sick to Schley County, Georgia. Died there of disease November 18, 1861.

MARBRY, M. W.: Company D, corporal. September 10, 1861 elected 2nd corporal in Co. D, 27th Regiment, Georgia Infantry at Camp Stephens, Griffin, Spalding County, Georgia. March -April 1864 roll shows him present.

MARFIELD, ENOCH: Company F, private. He enlisted as a private in Co. F, 27th Regiment, Georgia Infantry. May 20, 1862 admitted to General Hospital, Camp Winder at Richmond, Virginia with Diarrhoea. June 5, 1862 discharged for duty.

MARSHALL, C. H.: Company C, private. May 15, 1862 enlisted as a private in Co. C, 27th Regiment, Georgia Infantry in Knoxville, Georgia. June 26, June 30 and September 30, 1863 issued clothing. December 31, 1863 received pay. January – February 1864 roll shows him present. February 29, 1864 received pay. March - April 1864 roll shows him present. July 1864 and September 20 issued clothing. April 26, 1865 surrendered Greensboro, North Carolina. May 1, 1865 paroled at General Hospital at Thomasville, North Carolina. He died in Crawford County, Georgia November 24, 1904.

MARSHALL, JAMES G.: Company K, private. He enlisted as a private in Co. K, 27th Regiment, Georgia Infantry. December 1862 roll shows him in Richmond, Virginia in July.

MARSHALL, SAMUEL: Company K, sergeant. He enlisted as a private in Co. K, 27th Regiment, Georgia Infantry. July 18, 1862 received pay ($120.50).

MARTIN, G. L.: Company E, private. He enlisted as a private in Co. E, 27th Regiment, Georgia Infantry. April 4, 1862 discharged from service due to Epilepsy at General Hospital No. 1, Lynchburg, Virginia. He was born in Caldwell, County, North Carolina in 1832. He is described as being 6 feet high, dark complexion, black eyes and black hair. And he was by profession a farmer.

MARTIN, J. J.: Company D, private. September 10, 1861 enlisted as a private in Co. D, 27th Regiment, Georgia Infantry at Camp Stephens, Griffin, Spalding County, Georgia. November 6, 1861 admitted to General Hospital at Petersburg, Virginia with Rubeola. November 15, 1861 returned to duty. May 11, 1862 admitted to Chimborazo Hospital No. 2 at Richmond, Virginia with Debility. May 13, 1862 returned to duty. August 21, 1862 admitted to General Hospital at Farmville, Virginia with Debilitas. September 12, 1862 returned to duty. April, May, June and December 1863 issued clothing. February 29, 1864 received pay. March - April 1864 roll shows him present. July 1864 and September 20, 1864 issued clothing. April 26, 1865 surrendered Greensboro, North Carolina. May 8, 1865 appears on a roll of Prisoners of War and was paroled on that date at Greensboro, North Carolina. May 9, 1865 took oath of allegiance to the United States.

MARTIN, W. D.: Company D, private. He 1861 enlisted as a private in Co. D, 27th Regiment, Georgia Infantry. December 1862 roll shows he died on December 20, 1862 in Georgia.

MARTIN, WILLIAM A.: Company D, private. March 4, 1862 enlisted as a private in Co. D, 27th Regiment, Georgia Infantry in Gainesville, Hall County, Georgia. March 25, 1862 received pay ($50.00). April 30, 1862 received pay. August 1862 he is shown on roll for General Hospital, Richmond, Virginia. September 17, 1862 wounded at Sharpsburg, Maryland. October 5, 1862 admitted to General Hospital No. 21, Richmond, Virginia with a Vulnus Sclopeticum (Gunshot Wound). October 10, 1862 furloughed for 30 days.

MARTIN, WILLIAM: Company I, private. September 10, 1861 enlisted as a private in Co. I, 27th Regiment, Georgia Infantry at Camp Stephens, Griffin, Spalding County, Georgia. December 1862 roll shows that on November 12, 1861 he died of disease in Raleigh, North Carolina. March 25, 1864 death benefit claim was filed by his mother, Sidney Martin.

MASON, J. R.: Company D, private. August 30, 1862 enlisted as a private in Co. D, 27th Regiment, Georgia Infantry in Hall County, Georgia. January 10, 1863 transferred from Camp Lee and admitted to Howards Grove Hospital at Richmond, Virginia with Variola. February 28, 1863 he is shown as sick on the rolls of General Hospital No. 28 at Richmond, Virginia. April 4, 1863 transferred to and admitted to General Hospital No. 26 at Richmond, Virginia. March 4, 1863 admitted to C. S. A. General Hospital at Danville, Virginia with Debilitas. May 5, 1863 admitted to General Hospital No. 26, Richmond, Virginia. May 26, 1863 returned to duty. April, May, June and December 1863 issued clothing. May 21, 1863 issued clothing. February 29, 1864 received pay. March - April 1864 roll shows him present. July 1864 issued clothing. March 19, 1865 killed, Bentonville, North Carolina.

MASON, JAMES MILES: Company E, private. September 9, 1861 enlisted as a private in Co. E, 27th Regiment, Georgia Infantry at Camp

Stephens, Griffin, Spalding County, Georgia. December 1861 roll shows him in Georgia sick. January 1862 roll shows he was left sick in Georgia October 31, 1861. June 27, 1862 wounded, Cold Harbor, Virginia. July 12, 1862 received pay ($156.70 including a $50.00 clothing allowance). September 9, 1862 received pay ($47.00). December 1862 roll shows he was wounded in June and September 1862. January 26, 1863 received pay for commutation of rations in Atlanta, Georgia for 30 days. April 3, 1863 detailed by General Lee to Empire Hotel Hospital in Atlanta, Georgia as a nurse at an extra $.25 per day did not arrive until June 1, 1863. April 17, 1863 admitted to Camp Winder Hospital, Richmond, Virginia with Chronic Rheumatism. May 7, 1863 transferred to Division 5. February 28, 1864 received pay. February 9, 1864 received detail pay ($15.25). April 3, 1863 detailed nurse in Atlanta, Georgia Hospital. April 15, 1865 captured at West Point, Georgia. April 23, 1865 transferred to Captain Hathaway, Commanding military Prison at Macon, Georgia. March – April 1964 roll shows him absent detailed in hospital in Atlanta, Georgia since April 23, 1863. March 17, 1864 issued clothing. April 16, 1865 he was captured and transferred to prison on April 23, 1865.

MASON, JASPER WILLIAM L.: Company H, musician. September 9, 1861 enlisted as a private in Co. H, 27th Regiment, Georgia Infantry at Camp Stephens, Griffin, Spalding County, Georgia. December 1861 roll shows he was left sick in Georgia October 31, 1861. April 22, 1862 furloughed for 30 days and received pay ($88.06). October 10, 1862 received pay ($119.00). He was appointed Musician (Drummer) of Co. H, 27th Regiment, Georgia Infantry. June 15, 1863 received $7.50 for commutations of rations. December 31, 1863 received pay. January – February 1864 roll shows him present. March - April 1864 roll shows him present. June 20, 1864 wounded at Colquitt's Salient near Petersburg, Virginia. June 22, 1864 died in Virginia Hospital at Petersburg, Virginia of a Vulnus Slopeticum (Gunshot Wound).

MASON, JOHN N.: Company H, lieutenant. September 9, 1861 elected corporal of Co. H, 27th Regiment, Georgia Infantry at Camp Stephens, Griffin, Spalding County, Georgia. June 26, 1862 wounded by fall into ditch, producing Hernia, at Mechanicsville, Virginia. June 27, 1862 wounded in left thigh, causing partial paralysis of leg, and in the back and head, at Cold Harbor, Virginia. June 28, 1862 admitted to General Hospital, Howard's Grove at Richmond, Virginia. August 30, 1862 admitted to General Hospital, Camp Winder at Richmond, Virginia with a Hernia. September 2, 1862 received pay ($26.00). October 10, 1862 furloughed from General Hospital, Camp Winder at Richmond, Virginia. January 14, 1863 listed as a deserter. December 31, 1863 received pay. He was elected 5th Sergeant. January – February 1864 roll shows him present. February 29, 1864 received pay. March - April 1864 roll shows him present. May 31, 1864 and July 1864 issued clothing. August 18, 1864 elected 2nd lieutenant of Co. H, 27th Regiment, Georgia Infantry.

1865 paroled at Macon, Georgia. He was born February 14, 1842.

MASON, ROBERT W.: Company E, sergeant. February 17, 1864 enlisted as a private in Co. E, 27th Regiment, Georgia Infantry at Decatur, Georgia. January – February 1864 roll shows him absent detailed as guard for command. February 29, 1864 received pay. March - April 1864 roll shows him present. June 24, 1864 appointed first sergeant in Co. E, 27th Regiment, Georgia Infantry. September 20, 1864 issued clothing. April 26, 1865 surrendered Greensboro, North Carolina. May 1, 1865 paroled at Greensboro, North Carolina.

MASON, WILLIAM J.: Company H, private. September 9, 1861 enlisted as a private in Co. H, 27th Regiment, Georgia Infantry at Camp Stephens, Griffin, Spalding County, Georgia. December 1861 roll shows he was left sick in Georgia October 31,1861. April 17, 1862 died of Typhoid Fever at General Receiving Hospital (also known as Charity Hospital) at Gordonsville, Virginia. November 16, 1863 death benefit claim was filed by father, L. B. Mason, of Sandy Ridge, Henry County, Georgia. November 21, 1863 death benefit claim paid $133.30 (8893) plus $21.26 (#10885) supplemental (November 21, 1863).

MASSEY, GREEN: Company F, private. September 9, 1861 enlisted as a private in Co. F, 27th Regiment, Georgia Infantry at Camp Stephens, Griffin, Spalding County, Georgia. March 20, 1862 admitted to Chimborazo Hospital No. 4, at Richmond, Virginia with Chronic Diarrhoea. May 8, 1862 returned to duty. May 31, 1862 wounded in left shoulder at Seven Pines, Virginia. August 5, 1863 issued clothing. December 31, 1863 received pay. January – February 1864 roll shows him present. February 29, 1864 received pay. March - April 1864 roll shows him present. June 16, 1864 admitted to Confederate States Hospital at Petersburg, Virginia. July 3, 1864 returned to duty. September 20, 1864 issued clothing.

MASSEY, WILLIAM M.: Company F, private. August 1, 1863 enlisted as a private in Co. F, 27th Regiment, Georgia Infantry at Camp Stephens, Griffin, Spalding County, Georgia. June 1862 wounded in the left arm, resulting in amputation, at James Island, South Carolina. January – February 1864 and March – April 1864 rolls show him absent without leave since February 15, 1864. June 21, 1864 issued clothing at Floyd House Hospital at Macon Georgia.

MATHEWS, CULLEN: Company B, private. March 4, 1862 enlisted as a private in Co. B, 27th Regiment, Georgia Infantry. March - April 1864 roll shows him present.

MATHEWS, FREEMAN: Company K, private. September 10, 1861 enlisted as a private in Co. K, 27th Regiment, Georgia Infantry at Camp Stephens, Griffin, Spalding County, Georgia. December 1861 roll shows him in the hospital at Richmond, Virginia since December 18, 1861. June 7, 1862 received pay ($55.00). June 1863 issued clothing. October 29, November 8 and November 24, 1863 issued clothing. December 31, 1863 received pay. March - April 1864 roll shows him present. July 1864 and

September 20 1864 issued clothing.

MATHEWS, G. E.: Company H, private. He enlisted as a private in Co. H, 27th Regiment, Georgia Infantry. January 15, 1865 transferred from General Hospital No. 4 at Wilmington, North Carolina to General Hospital No. 3 at Goldsboro, North Carolina with Pneumonia.

MATHEWS, GEORGE H.: Company K, private. September 10, 1861 enlisted as a private in Co. K, 27th Regiment, Georgia Infantry at Camp Stephens, Griffin, Spalding County, Georgia. November 17, 1861 admitted to Chimborazo Hospital No.3 at Richmond, Virginia with Measles. December 2, 1861 returned to duty. June 7, 1862 received pay at Richmond, Virginia ($55.00). June 1863 issued clothing. October 6, 1863 received pay ($22.00). October 29, 1863 issued clothing. December 31, 1863 received pay. March - April 1864 roll shows him present. June 9, 1864 killed at Cold Harbor, Virginia.

MATHEWS, SAMUEL: Company B, private. September 10, 1861 enlisted as a private in Co. B, 27th Regiment, Georgia Infantry at Camp Stephens, Griffin, Spalding County, Georgia. December 23, 1861 discharged due to disability. March 4, 1862 reenlisted. March – April 1864 roll shows him present.

MATHEWS, WILLIAM W.: Company F, sergeant. September 9, 1861 enlisted as a private in Co. F, 27th Regiment, Georgia Infantry. He was appointed sergeant in Co. F, 27th Regiment, Georgia Infantry. February 21, 1865 captured at Wilmington, North Carolina. June 29, 1865 released at Point Lookout, Maryland.

MATHIS, E.: He enlisted as a private in the 27th Regiment, Georgia Infantry. May 16, 1865 paroled at Tallahassee, Florida. He is described as 5 feet 8 inches high, dark hair, blue eyes and light complexion.

MAXEY, JAMES F.: Company G, lieutenant. September 10, 1861 enlisted as a private in Co. G, 27th Regiment, Georgia Infantry. November 6, 1861 admitted to General Hospital, Petersburg, Virginia with Rubeola. December 17, 1861 returned to duty. December 20, 1861 admitted to General Hospital No. 18 (formerly Greaner's Hospital) at Richmond, Virginia. December 1861 and January 1862 rolls show him absent in the hospital in Richmond, Virginia. January 4, 1864 furloughed for 30 days. He was appointed sergeant of Co. G, 27th Regiment, Georgia Infantry. He was elected 1st lieutenant of Co. G, 27th Regiment, Georgia Infantry. April 3, 1862 admitted to General Hospital at Orange Court House, Virginia with Diarrhoea. April 23, 1862 admitted to C. S. A. General Hospital at Charlottesville, Virginia with Erysipelas. May 26, 1862 returned to duty. September 17, 1862 wounded in the breast and captured at Sharpsburg, Maryland. September 27, 1862 his name appears on a roll as a prisoner of War being held by the Army of the Potomac. October 5, 1862 admitted to U. S. A. Field Hospital at Smoketown, Maryland. October 13, 1863 died of wounds in Antietam General Hospital at Smoketown Maryland of wound in breast, leg, arm and back. He is buried in Confederate Cemetery at Hagerstown, Maryland.   He was a resident of Zebulon, Pike County, Georgia.

MCBRIDE, ISAAC: Company H, private. He enlisted as a private in Co. H, 27th Regiment, Georgia Infantry.

MCBRIDE (MCBRYDE), J. N.: Company H, private. He enlisted as a private in Co. H, 27th Regiment, Georgia Infantry. December 1862 roll shows him detailed as a teamster. October 7, 1863 received pay ($22.00). January 1, 1863 to May 24, 1863 detailed as a teamster at and additional $.25 per day. August 20, 1864 received pay.

MCBRIDE (MCBRYDE), ROBERT W.: Company H, private.   He enlisted as a private in Co. H, 27th Regiment, Georgia Infantry. February 1862 roll shows him in Moore Hospital at Danville, Virginia.   February 26, 1862 sent to Moore Hospital at Danville, Virginia.   February 28, 1862 died of Pneumonia in Moore Hospital at Danville, Virginia (Manassas Junction).

MCCLENDON, FRANK W.: Company H, private.   September 9, 1861 enlisted as a private in Co. H, 27th Regiment, Georgia Infantry at Camp Stephens, Griffin, Spalding County, Georgia.   May 30, 1862 wounded and captured at Seven Pines, Virginia.   October 6, 1862 received at Aiken's Landing, Virginia.   November 10, 1862 exchanged at Aiken's Landing, Virginia.   March – April 1864 roll shows him absent without leave.

MCCLENDON, JOHN C.: Company H, private.   September 9, 1861 enlisted as a private in Co. H, 27th Regiment, Georgia Infantry at Camp Stephens, Griffin, Spalding County, Georgia. February 20, 1864 wounded at Olustee, Florida.   April 26, 1865 surrendered Greensboro, North Carolina.

MCCLUNG, ROYAL: Company K, private.   September 10, 1861 enlisted as a private in Co. K, 27th Regiment, Georgia Infantry at Camp Stephens, Griffin, Spalding County, Georgia.   April 26, 1865 surrendered Greensboro, North Carolina.

MCCLURE, JOHN C. (JAMES C.): Company G, private.   September 9, 1861 enlisted as a private in Co. G, 27th Regiment, Georgia Infantry at Camp Stephens, Griffin, Spalding County, Georgia.   June 13, 1862 admitted to General Hospital No.18 at Richmond, Virginia with Typhoid Fever.   June 15 (22), 1862 died in General Hospital No.18 at Richmond, Virginia.

MCCRAY, J. H.: Company G, private. He enlisted as a private in Co. G, 27th Regiment, Georgia Infantry. May 26, 1865 surrendered at New Orleans, Louisiana. June 8, 1865 was paroled at Shreveport, Louisiana. Home was De Soto Parrish, Louisiana.

MCCRARY (MCCRORIE) (MCCROREY) L. Q. C.: Company F, lieutenant. September 9, 1861 elected 2nd lieutenant Co. F, 27th Regiment, Georgia Infantry at Camp Stephens, Griffin, Spalding County, Georgia. September 11, 1861 elected 1st lieutenant in Co. F, 27th Regiment, Georgia Infantry. December 1861 roll at Camp Pickney, Virginia shows him present.

January 1862 roll shows him absent without leave beginning January 10, 1862. February 1862 roll at Camp Pickney, Virginia shows him present. March 16, 1862 admitted to Chimborazo Hospital No. 3 at Richmond, Virginia. March 20, 1862 returned to duty (transferred to private quarters). April 22, 1862 surgeon recommended a 20 day furlough due to Bronchitis. May 22, 1862 received pay ($90). May 31, 1862 wounded at Seven Pines, Virginia. June 22 1862 furloughed. December 1862 roll shows him absent on furlough since June 22, 1862. July 11, 1862 admitted to Moore Hospital at General Hospital No. 1 at Danville, Virginia with Pneumonia and transferred to Richmond. February 23, 1863 resigned due to disability. He was born in Baldwin County, Georgia July 22, 1826.

MCCROREY (MCCRORIE) (MCCRARY) ADGER C.: Company K, lieutenant. September 10, 1861 enlisted as a private in Co. K, 27th Regiment, Georgia Infantry at Camp Stephens, Griffin, Spalding County, Georgia. January 1862 roll shows him detailed as courier for headquarters post. February 8, 1862 received $14 additional pay for services as courier for headquarters post. February 1862 roll shows him on recruiting service for 30 days beginning February 13, 1862. July 10, 1862 elected Jr. 2nd lieutenant of Co. K, 27th Regiment, Georgia Infantry. September 13, 1862 captured at South Mountain, Maryland. October 6, 1862 appears on the list of lieutenants, C. S. A. delivered to Akins Landing, Virginia and exchanged for federal lieutenants. December 1862 roll shows him present station near Guinea Station, Virginia. March 16, 1863 elected 2nd lieutenant of Co. K, 27th Regiment, Georgia Infantry. March-April 1864 roll shows him present May 1, 1864 elected 1st lieutenant of Co. K, 27th Regiment, Georgia Infantry. September 23, 1864 near Petersburg, Virginia he tendered his resignation. October 5, 1864 admitted to Receiving and Wayside Hospital, or General Hospital No. 9 at Richmond, Virginia and transferred to Jackson Hospital at Richmond, Virginia with spinal affection. October 13, 1863 returned duty. October 30, 1863 granted a 30 day leave of absence from Charleston, South Carolina. May 3, 1864 he requested 30 days leave of absence due to bouts of Pneumonia and exposure at the battle of Olustee, Florida. August 23, 1864 received pay ($490.00). March 19, 1865 captured at Bentonville, North Carolina. April 3, 1865 arrived as a prisoner of war at Point Lookout, Maryland from New Bern, North Carolina. April 3, 1865 transferred to Washington D. C. from Point Lookout, Maryland. April 4, 1865 committed to Old Capital Prison, Washington, D. C. April 11, 1865 received at Depot Prisoners of War, near Sandusky, Ohio. June 17, 1865 released after taking oath of allegiance to the United States. He is described as being a resident of Bellevue, Georgia. He is age 35 with dark complexion, dark hair, blue eyes and his 6 foot one inch high.

MCCULLERS, BARWELL: Company F, private. September 9, 1861 enlisted as a private in Co. F, 27th Regiment, Georgia Infantry at Camp Stephens, Griffin, Spalding County, Georgia. March 30, 1862 admitted to Chimborazo Hospital No. 4 at Richmond, Virginia with acute Diarrhea.

April 16, 1862 died with Diarrhoea and Typhoid Fever, in Chimborazo, Hospital No.4 at Richmond, Virginia. He is most likely buried in Oakwood Cemetery at Richmond Virginia. January 23, 1863 death benefit claim was filed by his widow, Keziah McCullers. September 24, 1863 death benefit claim paid $113.13 (#8993). He was a resident of Taylor County, Georgia.

MCCULLERS, HENRY: Company F, private. September 9, 1861 enlisted as a private in Co. F, 27th Regiment, Georgia Infantry at Camp Stephens, Griffin, Spalding County, Georgia. May 2 (3), 1862 killed at Chancellorsville, Virginia. January 22, 1864 death benefit claim was filed by Mary McCullers, his mother.

MCCULLOUGH, ROBERT J. (J. ROBERT): Company H, private. August 1, 1863 enlisted as a private in Co. H, 27th Regiment, Georgia Infantry at McDonough, Henry County, Georgia. December 31, 1863 received pay. February 20, 1864 wounded at Olustee, Florida. February 24, 1864 January – February 1864 roll shows him absent, wounded, in the hospital at Whitesville, Georgia. January - February 1864 Hospital muster roll of General Hospital at Guyton, Georgia shows him present. March-April 1864 roll shows him present. June 30, 1864 Hospital Muster Roll for General Hospital No. 1 at Summerville, South Carolina shows him present. September 20, 1864 issued clothing. October 1, 1864 admitted to Jackson Hospital at Richmond, Virginia with Jaundice. December 5, 1864 received pay at Jackson Hospital at Richmond, Virginia. January 5, 1865 returned to duty. February 21, 1865 transferred from Wilmington, North Carolina to C. S. A. General Hospital No. 1 at Greensboro, North Carolina. February 23, 1865 transferred from Greensboro North Carolina and admitted to Pettigrew General Hospital No.13 at Raleigh, North Carolina, on account of Debility from Pneumonia. February 24, 1865 transferred to another hospital at Raleigh, North Carolina. 1865 died in Raleigh, North Carolina. He was buried in the Confederate Cemetery at Raleigh, North Carolina. His post office was listed as Jonesboro Georgia.

MCCULLOUGH, W. PERRY: Company H, private. September 10, 1863 enlisted as a private in Co. H, 27th Regiment, Georgia Infantry at Camp Stephens, Griffin, Spalding County, Georgia. December 31, 1863 received pay. January – February and March-April 1864 rolls show him present. June 30, 1864 muster roll for 1st Division Jackson Hospital at Richmond, Virginia shows him present. July 1864 issued clothing. July 21, 1864 admitted to Jackson Hospital at Richmond, Virginia with Fever. July 28, 1864 furloughed for 40 days. February 22, 1865 admitted to C. S. A. General Hospital, No. 3 at Greensboro, North Carolina, with Intermittent Fever. February 23, 1865 transferred to Pettigrew General Hospital No. 13 at Raleigh, North Carolina with Debilitas from Pneumonia. February 24, 1865 he was issued clothing and it appears he was transferred to Wake Forest, North Carolina. May 11, 1865 captured near Raleigh, North Carolina. May 12, 1865 paroled at Raleigh, North Carolina. He is shown as being from

Henry County, Georgia with a post office in Jonesboro, Georgia

MCDONALD, J. W.: Company K, private. He enlisted as a private in Co. K, 27th Regiment, Georgia Infantry. March 7, 1862 death benefit claim was filed by Catherine McDonald, his mother.

MCDONALD, JAMES B.: Company B, private. September 10, 1861 enlisted as a private in Co. B, 27th Regiment, Georgia Infantry at Camp Stephens, Griffin, Spalding County, Georgia. January 7, 1862 admitted to Moore Hospital at General Hospital, No. 1 at Danville, Virginia with Dysentery. January 1862 roll shows him absent in the hospital in Richmond, Virginia since January 7, 1862. April 6, 1862 admitted to General Hospital at Orange Court House, Virginia with Fever. April 9, 1862 died of Typhoid Pneumonia in General Hospital at Orange Court House, Virginia (Farmville Virginia). September 9, 1862 death benefit claim was filed by Middleton McDonald, his father. September 22, 1863 death benefit claim paid $61.30 (#4865). He was a resident of Bibb County, Georgia.

MCDOWELL, GEORGE Y.: Company K, private. June 23, 1863 enlisted in Howard's Battalion of non-conscripts at Columbus, Georgia. March 15, 1864 transferred as a private to Co. K, 27th Regiment, Georgia Infantry. December 31, 1863 received pay. February 20, 1864 wounded at Olustee, Florida. March-April 1864 roll shows him present. June 9, 1864 wounded through the left lung and spinal column, at Cold Harbor, Virginia. June 20, 1864 admitted to General Hospital at Petersburg, Virginia with a Vulnus Sclopeticum (Gunshot Wound) and given a 60 day furlough. July 2, 1864 he was on list of men remaining in the General Hospital at Petersburg, Virginia. March 30, 1865 furlough extended for 30 days, on account of wounds. He was born in Georgia November 20, 1845.

MCDOWELL, ROBERT A.: Company K, private. September 10, 1861 enlisted as a private in Co. K, 27th Regiment, Georgia Infantry at Camp Stephens, Griffin, Spalding County, Georgia. December 1861. January 1862 and February 1862 rolls show he was left in Griffin, Georgia sick on October 31, 1861. March 9, 1862 hospital records show he was sick located in a private residence owned by Mrs. Everett on Main Street in Richmond, Virginia. July 4, 1862 received pay ($106.33). July 9, 1862 he was transferred to Lynchburg, Virginia. December 1862 roll (dated January 31, 1863) indicates he was admitted to the hospital January 14, 1863. October 29, 1863 issued clothing. December 31, 1863 received pay. March 17, 1864 appears on the roster of General Hospital No. 1 at Savannah, Georgia (General Hospital, Oglethorpe Barracks) indicating General Hospital No. 2 on report. March-April 1864 roll shows him present. September 24, 1864 issued clothing. April 26, 1865, surrendered at Greensboro, North Carolina. May 1, 1865 paroled at Greensboro, North Carolina. He was born in South Carolina October 30, 1830. His Post Office is listed as Bellevue, Talbot County, Georgia.

MCDOWWELL, ROBERT A.: Company K, private. He enlisted as a private in Co. K, 27th Regiment, Georgia Infantry. April 26, 1865

surrendered Greensboro, North Carolina.

MCDOWELL, TELEMACHUS P.: Company K, private. June 23, 1863 enlisted in Howard's Battalion of non-conscripts at Columbus, Georgia. December 31, 1863 received pay. March 15, 1864 transferred as a private to Co. K, 27th Regiment, Georgia Infantry. March-April 1864 roll shows him present. September 24, 1864 issued clothing. October (November) 1864 pension records show he was sent to hospital, with Chronic Diarrhoea. He was in Columbus, Georgia Hospital at the close of the war. He was born in Georgia June 9, 1845.

MCELMURRAY, ANDREW J.: Company A, private. February 28, 1862 enlisted as a private in Co. A, 27th Regiment, Georgia Infantry in Schley County, Georgia. May 7, 1862 admitted to General Hospital Camp Winder, Richmond, Virginia with Diarrhea. May 16, 1862 furloughed for 30 days. October 12, 1862 admitted to General Hospital Camp Winder at Richmond, Virginia with Dysentery. October 31, 1862 returned to duty. November 5, 1862 received pay in the amount of $68.93. November 20, 1862 issued clothing and received a $50.00 bounty pay. June, July, August, September and December 1863 issued clothing. June 16, 1864 captured, Petersburg, Virginia. June 24, 1864 arrived at Point Lookout, Maryland from City Point, Virginia. July 27, 1864 transferred to Elmira prison in New York from Point Lookout, Maryland. July 30, 1864 received at Elmira Prison, New York. June 16, 1865 released at Elmira Prison, New York. He is described upon his release as being a resident of Butler, Georgia with fair complexion, light hair, hazel eyes and being 5'6" high. He was born in Bibb County, Georgia April 12, 1840.

MCGAHEE, SAMUEL F.: Company A, private. July 29, 1863 enlisted as a private in Co. A, 27th Regiment, Georgia Infantry in Decatur, Georgia. January-February 1864 roll shows him present. February 29, 1864 received pay. March - April 1864 roll shows him present. May 30, 1864 issued clothing. July 1864 issued clothing. September 30, 1864 issued clothing.

MCGAULEY (MCGALLEY), JAMES: Company I, private. September 10, 1861 enlisted as a private in Co. I, 27th Regiment, Georgia Infantry at Camp Stephens, Griffin, Spalding County, Georgia. December 23, 1861 admitted to Moore Hospital at General Hospital, No. 1 at Danville, Virginia with Pneumonia. December 1861 roll shows him in the hospital at Manassas, Virginia. January 1862 roll shows him in Moore Hospital at Manassas, Virginia. June 27, 1862 killed at Cold Harbor, Virginia (some records erroneously state that he was killed at Seven Pines but date would be incorrect). April 14, 1863 death benefit claim was filed by James Tillman, administrator of estate.

MCGINTY, GEORGE: Company F, private. September 9, 1861 enlisted as a private in Co. F, 27th Regiment, Georgia Infantry at Camp Stephens, Griffin, Spalding County, Georgia.

MCGINTY, H.: Company F, private. He enlisted as a private in Co. F, 27th Regiment, Georgia Infantry. December 26, 1861 admitted to Moore

Hospital at Danville, Virginia with Fever and sent to Charlottesville, Virginia. December 1861 roll shows him in the hospital at Charlottesville, Virginia.

MCGINTY, RICHARD H.: Company F, private. September 9, 1861 enlisted as a private in Co. F, 27th Regiment, Georgia Infantry at Camp Stephens, Griffin, Spalding County, Georgia. December 24, 1861 sent to Moore Hospital at Danville, Virginia. December 26, 1861 admitted to Moore Hospital at Danville, Virginia with Fever. January 2, 1862 discharged and received payment. January 1862 and February 1862 rolls show him in Moore Hospital at Danville, Virginia.

MCGINTY, J. B.: Company B, private. He enlisted as a private in Co. B, 27th Regiment, Georgia Infantry. March 30, 1862 admitted to General Hospital No. 18 (formerly Greaner's Hospital) at Richmond, Virginia with Chronic Rheumatism. His Post Office is shown as Geneva, Georgia. April 11, 1862 transferred to Amelia Court House. September 23, 1862 received pay ($69.00).

MCGLAMRY, JNO. M.: Company F, private. April 18, 1864 enlisted as a private in Co. F, 27th Regiment, Georgia Infantry in Charleston, South Carolina. January – February 1864 roll shows him present. March - April 1864 roll shows him present. July 1864 wounded and permanently disabled at Mortar Hill, near Petersburg, Virginia. July 1864 and September 20, 1864 issued clothing. April 26, 1865 surrendered at Greensboro, North Carolina. May 1, 1865 paroled at Greensboro, North Carolina. He was born in Georgia October 1, 1846.

MCGLAMERY (MCGLARNEY) (MCGLAMMRY), WILLIAM G.: Company F, corporal. September 9, 1861 elected 3rd corporal in Co. F, 27th Regiment, Georgia Infantry at Camp Stephens, Griffin, Spalding County, Georgia. December 1861, January 1862 and February 1862 rolls show he was left sick in Georgia October 31. May 17, 1862 admitted to Chimborazo Hospital No. 4 at Richmond, Virginia with acute Diarrhea and Nephritis. May 30, 1862 returned to duty. August 1863 issued clothing. December 31, 1863 received pay. January – February 1864 and March - April 1864 rolls show him present.

MCINTYRE, DANIEL: Company A, private. He enlisted as a private in Co. A, 27th Regiment, Georgia Infantry. January 31, 1863 roll shows him absent sick since January 24, 1863.

MCILVANE, A. J.: Company A, private. He enlisted as a private in Co. A, 27th Regiment, Georgia Infantry. December 1862 roll indicates he strayed from the ranks on September 24, 1862.

MCINVALE, JOHN M.: Company F, private. He enlisted as a private in Co. F, 27th Regiment, Georgia Infantry. February 1862 roll shows him on detached duty as regimental Teamster. April 11, 1862 died of Pneumonia in the General Hospital at Orange Court House, Virginia (CSA General Hospital at Farmville, Virginia).

MCINVALE, T. M.: Company F, private. September 9, 1861 enlisted as a private in Co. F, 27th Regiment, Georgia Infantry at Camp Stephens, Griffin, Spalding County, Georgia.

MCINVALE, W. H.: Company F, private.   September 9, 1861 enlisted as a private in Co. F, 27th Regiment, Georgia Infantry at Camp Stephens, Griffin, Spalding County, Georgia.   December 1861 and January 1862 rolls show he was left sick in Georgia October 31, 1861.   April 14, 1862 admitted to General Hospital No. 21 at Richmond, Virginia with Typhoid Fever. May 1, 1862 received pay. May 5, 1862 admitted to C. S. A. General Hospital at Danville, Virginia with Pneumonia. May 24, 1862 returned to duty. November 17, 1862 admitted to Fourth Division, General Hospital Camp Winder at Richmond, Virginia. Roll dated November 20, 1862 of Fourth Division, General Hospital Camp Winder at Richmond, Virginia shows him present. December 2, 1862 returned to duty. December 31, 1863 received pay. January – February 1864 roll shows him present. February 29, 1864 received pay. March - April 1864 roll shows him present.   June 8, 1864 and July 1864 issued clothing.

MCKEE, JOSEPH: Company E, private.   April 1, 1863 enlisted as a private in Co. E, 27th Regiment, Georgia Infantry at Fairburn, Georgia. December 31, 1863 received pay.

January – February 1864 roll shows him present. March - April 1864 roll shows him present.   August 19, 1864 admitted to Receiving and Wayside Hospital or General Hospital No. 9 at Richmond, Virginia. August 20, 1864 admitted to Jackson Hospital at Richmond, Virginia with Chronic Diarrhea. September 1864 issued clothing. August 25, 1864 furloughed for 30 days. His address is shown as Fairburn, Georgia. Pension records show he was captured, date and place not given.   1865 released from prison.

MCKINLEY, COLBERT: Company G, private.   September 9, 1861 enlisted as a private in Co. G, 27th Regiment, Georgia Infantry at Camp Stephens, Griffin, Spalding County, Georgia. November 9, 1861 admitted to General Hospital No. 18 (formerly Greaner's Hospital) at Richmond, Virginia. December 16, 1861 returned to duty.

May 8, 1862 died in Richmond, Virginia. July 25, 1862 death benefit claim was filed by his father, M. L. McKinley. July 25, 1862 death benefit claim paid $68.43 (#807). He is buried in Hollywood Cemetery at Richmond, Virginia.

MCKINLEY, JOHN W.: Company G, private. September 9, 1861 enlisted as a private in Co. G, 27th Regiment, Georgia Infantry at Camp Stephens, Griffin, Spalding County, Georgia. April 11, 1862 he died in Richmond, Virginia. May 25, 1863 death benefit claim was filed by his father, Charles L. McKinley.

MCKINNEY (MCKENNEY), A. C.: Company A, private.   December 28, 1863 enlisted as a private in Co. A, 27th Regiment, Georgia Infantry in Atlanta, Georgia.   January – February 1864 roll shows him present. February 29, 1864 received pay.   March - April 1864 roll shows him present. September 30, 1864 issued clothing. April 26, 1865 surrendered

Greensboro, North Carolina. May 1, 1865 paroled at Greensboro, North Carolina.

MCKINNEY (MCKENNEY), JOSHUA A.: Company D, private. August 4, 1862 enlisted as a private in Co. D, 27th Regiment, Georgia Infantry in Richmond, Virginia. April, May, June and December 1863 issued clothing. February 29, 1864 received pay. March - April 1864 roll shows him present. September 20, 1864 issued clothing. April 26, 1865 surrendered Greensboro, North Carolina. May 1, 1865 paroled at Greensboro, North Carolina.

MCKINNEY (MCKENNEY), H.: Company D, private. He enlisted as a private in Co. D, 27th Regiment, Georgia Infantry. June 1, 1862 admitted to General Hospital No. 21 at Richmond, Virginia with a Vulnus Slopeticum (Gunshot Wound). June 4, 1862 transferred to the Georgia Hospital, in Virginia.

MCKINNEY (MCKENNEY), STEPHEN P.: Company D, private. September 10, 1861 enlisted as a private in Co. D, 27th Regiment, Georgia Infantry at Camp Stephens, Griffin, Spalding County, Georgia. September 17, 1862 wounded and captured at Sharpsburg, Maryland. December 1862 roll shows he was captured at Sharpsburg, Maryland September 17, 1862. September 27, 1862 he is shown as being paroled by the office of the Provost Marshal General, Army of the Potomac at Fort Delaware, Delaware. October 1, 1862 he was admitted to U. S. A General Hospital at Germantown (Philadelphia), Pennsylvania with a Vulnus Slopeticum (Gunshot Wound) to the right thigh (remark: prisoner sent from Hospital January 1, 1863). April, May and June 1863 issued clothing. November 1, 1863 detailed as a Teamster at San Andrews near Charleston , South Carolina. November 25, 1863 received pay and clothing allowance totaling $162.75. November 1863 roll of noncommissioned officers and privates employed on extra duty at San Andrews indicates he was assigned to Teamster duty from October 9, 1863 until January 31, 1864 at a rate of pay of $.25 per day additional. December 18, 1863 issued clothing. February 29, 1864 received pay. Records show he was on detached duty as a Teamster (ambulance driver) paid at Petersburg, Virginia from February 1, 1864 to June 9, 1864 at a rate of pay of $.25 additional per day. March - April 1864 roll shows him present detailed as a Teamster. July 1864 issued clothing

MCKINNEY (MCKENNEY), WILLIAM H.: Company C, private. September 10, 1861 enlisted as a private in Co. C, 27th Regiment, Georgia Infantry. September 1862 and October 20, 1862 received pay plus $50 bounty at Richmond, Virginia. December 16, 1862 returned to duty from Camp Winder Division No. 1 Hospital at Richmond, Virginia. May 14, 1862 admitted to Chimborazo Hospital No. 4, at Richmond, Virginia with Debility. May 31, 1862 wounded at Seven Pines, Virginia. May 31, 1862 admitted to General Hospital Number 21 at Richmond, Virginia with a Vulnus Slopeticum (Gunshot Wound). July 9, 1862 transferred to

Farmville Hospital and furloughed for 30 days. February 1, 1863 attached to the Hospital 2d Corps, Army of Northern Virginia at Guinea Station, Virginia as a cook. April 1, 1863 attached to the Hospital 2d Corps, Army of Northern Virginia, Guinea Station, Virginia as a nurse. May 31, 1863 received pay. July 31, 1863 muster roll of Hospital 2nd Corps, Army of Northern Virginia at Liberty Mills, Virginia shows that he is absent (remarks: left with assistant surgeon Gresham on June 5, 1863). December 31, 1863 received pay. January – February 1864 roll shows him present. March 5, 1864 transferred to Co. H, 1st Regiment, Georgia Regulars. April 4, 1864 transferred to Confederate States Navy. 1864 served at Shreveport Station. February 22, 1865 captured at Wilmington, North Carolina. April 27, 1865 died of Pneumonia in Point Lookout, Maryland Hospital of Infection of the lungs. He is buried in grave #1595 of the prisoner of war grave yard in Point Lookout, Maryland.

MCKEW, W. H.: Company C, private. He enlisted as a private in Co. C, 27th Regiment, Georgia Infantry. December 1862 roll shows him absent sick since December 24, 1862.

MCLENDON, JAMES M.: Company I, corporal. September 10, 1861 elected 3rd corporal of Co. I, 27th Regiment, Georgia Infantry at Camp Stephens, Griffin, Spalding County, Georgia. November 15, 1861 admitted to General Hospital No. 18(formerly Greaner's Hospital) at Richmond, Virginia. December 13, 1861 returned to duty. June 27, 1862 wounded at Cold Harbor, Virginia. December 1862 roll shows him absent without leave since December 1, 1862. December 31, 1863 received pay. February 20, 1864 wounded at Olustee, Florida. January – February 1864 roll shows him on detached service since. February 29, 1864 received pay. March - April 1864 roll shows him on the attached service since April 13, 1864. May 6, 1864 wounded at Wilderness, Virginia. June 10, 1864 wounded through the left breast and ankle at Cold Harbor, Virginia. July 1864 and September 20, 1864 issued clothing. April 26, 1865 surrendered Greensboro, North Carolina. November 3, 1864 received pay ($541.26). May 1, 1865 paroled at Greensboro, North Carolina. He was born in July 6, 1827.

MCLEROY (MCCRAY), PITT M.: Company E, corporal. July 1, 1863 enlisted as a private in Co. E, 27th Regiment, Georgia Infantry at Fairburn, Georgia. He was elected 2nd corporal of Co. E, 27th Regiment, Georgia Infantry. December 31, 1863 received pay. January – February 1864 roll shows him present. March - April 1864 roll shows him present. June 30, 1864 name appears on Hospital Muster Roll for Stuart Hospital at Richmond, Virginia. July 1, 1864 wounded behind right ear at Petersburg, Virginia. July 2, 1864 sent to and admitted to Stuart Hospital at Richmond, Virginia with Diarrhoea. July 21, 1864 issued clothing at for Stuart Hospital at Richmond, Virginia. July 29, 1864 received pay and furloughed. September 20, 1864 issued clothing. April 26, 1865 surrendered Greensboro, North Carolina. May 1, 1865 paroled at Greensboro, North Carolina. He was born in Georgia July 5, 1845.

MCMICHAEL, LEROY B.: Company C, private. September 10, 1861 enlisted as a private in Co. C, 27th Regiment, Georgia Infantry at Camp Stephens, Griffin, Spalding County, Georgia. February 18, 1862 sent to Richmond, Virginia, sick. February 1862 roll shows he was sent to Richmond sick. April 4, 1862 received pay ($22). May 7, 1862 admitted to General Hospital Camp Winder at Richmond, Virginia with Typhoid Fever.

MCMILLAN, JAMES: Company A, private. He enlisted as a private in Co. A, 27th Regiment, Georgia Infantry. April 26, 1865, surrendered at Greensboro, North Carolina. May 1, 1865 paroled at Greensboro, North Carolina.

MCMULLIN (MCMULLEN), L. O. (C.): Company H, private. September 9, 1861 enlisted as a private in Co. H, 27th Regiment, Georgia Infantry at Camp Stephens, Griffin, Spalding County, Georgia. December 1861 roll shows he was left sick in Georgia October 31. April 23, 1862 received pay ($88.06). May 7, 1862 assigned as nurse to 2d Division, General Hospital Camp Winder at Richmond, Virginia. November 1, 1862 and January 1, 1863 received pay. December 1862 roll shows him detailed as a nurse in the hospital. November-December 1862 roll from 2d Division, General Hospital Camp Winder at Richmond, Virginia shows him present and due two months' pay for extra duty. March 1, 1863 ordered to report to regular duty. May 3, 1863 wounded near Chancellorsville, Virginia. May 9, 1863 admitted to Receiving and Wayside Hospital or General Hospital No. 9 at Richmond, Virginia. December 31, 1863 received pay. January – February 1864 roll shows him absent without leave since February 9, 1864. March-April 1864 roll shows him present.

MCNEICE, W. S.: Company C, corporal. September 10, 1861 enlisted as a private in Co. C, 27th Regiment, Georgia Infantry at Camp Stephens, Griffin, Spalding County, Georgia. He was appointed corporal of Co. C, 27th Regiment, Georgia Infantry. June 27, 1862 wounded in Virginia (most likely at Gaines Mill or Cold Harbor). June 28, 1862 admitted to General Hospital Camp Winder at Richmond, Virginia, wounded in the hand. July 7, 1862 furloughed for 30 days. He was appointed sergeant of Co. C, 27th Regiment, Georgia Infantry. May 3, 1863 killed at Chancellorsville, Virginia.

MCSWAIN, DANIEL: Company A, private. September 28, 1862 enlisted as a private in Co. A, 27th Regiment, Georgia Infantry at Camp Randolph, Georgia. November 17, 1862 admitted to Camp Winder Division No. 1 Hospital at Richmond, Virginia. December 26, 1862 transferred to Danville, Virginia. January 30 1863 admitted to Lynchburg No. 3 Hospital at Lynchburg, Virginia with Erysipelas. April 30, 1863 granted 30 day furlough. May 5, 1863 paid for commutation of rations. June 8, 1863 issued clothing. July, August, September and December 1863 issued clothing. December 31, 1863 received pay. January – February 1864 roll shows him present. February 29, 1864 received pay. March-April 1864 roll shows him present. July and September 30, 1864 issued clothing.

MEADOWS, B.: Company D, private. December 25, 1862 enlisted as a private in Co. D, 27th Regiment, Georgia Infantry at Guinea Station, Virginia. December 1862 roll shows his enlistment.

MEANS H.: Company I, private. He enlisted as a private in Co. I, 27th Regiment, Georgia Infantry. February 1862 roll shows him absent sick since November 14, 1861 in Richmond, Virginia.

MEANS, W. H.: Company G, private. September 9, 1861 enlisted as a private in Co. G, 27th Regiment, Georgia Infantry at Camp Stephens, Griffin, Spalding County, Georgia. March 30, 1862 admitted to Chimborazo Hospital No.4 at Richmond, Virginia with Diarrhoea. April 13, 1862 admitted to Chimborazo Hospital No.1 at Richmond, Virginia with Diarrhoea. May 13, 1862 returned to duty. May 24, 1862 received pay ($44.00).

MELVIN, J. W.: Company F, private. He enlisted as a private in Co. F, 27th Regiment, Georgia Infantry. December 1862 morning report of General Hospital Howard Grove at Richmond, Virginia shows he was transferred to Chimborazo Hospital at Richmond, Virginia.

MENTS, WILLIAM: Company H, private. He enlisted as a private in Co. H, 27th Regiment, Georgia Infantry. November 14, 1863 wounded at Fort Sumter, South Carolina.

MERRETT, ELBERT: Company C, private. September 10, 1861 enlisted as a private in Co. C, 27th Regiment, Georgia Infantry at Camp Stephens, Griffin, Spalding County, Georgia. June 29, 1862 admitted to Chimborazo Hospital No. 3 at Richmond, Virginia with Pneumonia. July 29, 1862 transferred to Lynchburg hospital. July 30, 1862 admitted to C. S. A. General Military Hospital at Danville, Virginia with Chronic Diarrhoea. September 16(18), 1862 returned to duty. January 1, 1863 detailed as a teamster at an additional $.25 per day through May 24, 1863. June 30- September 30, 1863 issued clothing. December 31, 1863 received pay. January – February 1864 roll shows him absent without leave under General Order No. 26. March - April 1864 roll shows him present. June 1, 1864 wounded in the right hand at Cold Harbor, Virginia. June 2, 1864 admitted to Jackson Hospital at Richmond, Virginia with Vulnus Sclopeticum (Gunshot Wound) of the right hand. June 5, 1864 furloughed for 30 days. July 1864 register of Floyd House and Ocmulgee Hospitals at Macon, Georgia shows him admitted with a Vulnus Sclopeticum (Gunshot Wound) to the finger of the left hand. July 29, 1864 received pay ($44.00). He was a resident of Knoxville, Georgia.

MERRETT, MATTHEW: Company A, private. September 10, 1861 enlisted as a private in Co. A, 27th Regiment, Georgia Infantry at Camp Stephens, Griffin, Spalding County, Georgia. November 6, 1861 admitted to General Hospital at Petersburg, Virginia with Rubeola. November 15, 1861 died of Typhoid Fever at Petersburg, Virginia. December 1861 roll shows he died of Typhoid Fever at Petersburg, Virginia on November 15, 1861.

MERRETT, MICHAEL: Company C, private.   September 10, 1861 enlisted as a private in Co. C, 27th Regiment, Georgia Infantry at Camp Stephens, Griffin, Spalding County, Georgia. June 30, 1862 and September 30, 1862 issued clothing. April 19, 1863 and June 16, 1863 issued clothing. December 31, 1863 received pay.   February 20, 1864 killed, Olustee, Florida.   January – February 1864 roll shows he was killed in action at Olustee, Florida on February 20, 1864.

MERRETT, RILEY: Company C, private.   He enlisted as a private in Co. C, 27th Regiment, Georgia Infantry.   December 1862 roll shows him absent sick since December 24, 1862.

MERRETT, WILLIAM R.: Company C, private.   He enlisted as a private in Co. C, 27th Regiment, Georgia Infantry. June 29, 1862 admitted to Chimborazo Hospital No. 3 at Richmond, Virginia with remittent Fever. July 30, 1862 admitted to C. S. A. General Military Hospital at Danville, Virginia with Chronic Diarrhoea.   September 16, 1862 returned to duty. November 20, 1862 died.   July 11, 1863 death benefit claim was filed by Nancy Merritt. His address was Knoxville, Georgia.

MICHAELS, JOHN A.: Company K, private. He enlisted as a private in Co. K 27th Regiment, Georgia Infantry.   September 17, 1862 wounded and captured at Sharpsburg Maryland.   October 16, 1862 died of wounds at Frederick, Maryland. He is buried in Mt. Olivet Cemetery at Frederick, Maryland (grave # 123).

MILAM, JAMES W.: Company E, private.   September 9, 1861 enlisted as a private in Co. E, 27th Regiment, Georgia Infantry at Camp Stephens, Griffin, Spalding County, Georgia.   February 1862 roll shows him absent on sick leave beginning February 27, 1862.   June 9, 1862 paid ($6.25) commutation of rations.   August 30, 1862 admitted to General Hospital Camp Winder at Richmond, Virginia with Diarrhoea.   September 9, 1862 received pay ($77.00).   October 2, 1862 received bounty pay ($50.00). October 1862 furloughed for 16 days from General Hospital Camp Winder Division No. 2 Hospital at Richmond, Virginia.   December 1862 roll shows him absent without leave. December 31, 1863 received pay. February 20, 1864 wounded at Olustee, Florida. January – February 1864 roll shows him present.   March-April 1864 roll shows him present.   May 30, 1864 issued clothing. August 19, 1864 wounded in the right foot at Weldon Railroad, Virginia. August 20, 1864 admitted to Jackson Hospital at Richmond, Virginia with a Vulnus Sclopeticum (Gunshot Wound) to the right foot. August 25, 1864 furloughed for 30 days. September 1864 issued clothing. Pension records show he was wounded in right foot, date and place not given, and was at home at Fayette, Georgia on wounded furlough at the close of the war. He lived in Fayette, Georgia. He was born in Pike County, Georgia March 10, 1839.

MILLER, HENRY H.: Company H, private.   September 9, 1861 enlisted as a private in Co. H, 27th Regiment, Georgia Infantry at Camp Stephens, Griffin, Spalding County, Georgia. September 17, 1862 killed at Sharpsburg, Maryland. February 2, 1863 death benefit claim was filed by his father, William G. Miller resident of Spring, Georgia. September 26, 1863 death benefit claim paid $75.23 (#9123).

MILIKIN (MILLIKEN) (MIILLIGAN) (MILLICAN), BENJAMIN: Company I, sergeant. September 10, 1861 enlisted as a private in Co. I, 27th Regiment, Georgia Infantry at Camp Stephens, Griffin, Spalding County, Georgia. He was appointed corporal. December 1861 roll shows him sick in hospital. January 1862 roll shows him on sick leave. January 1862 appointed 4th sergeant, Co. I, 27th Regiment, Georgia Infantry. February 1862 roll shows him absent sick. September 17, 1862 wounded through the right foot in the cornfield and captured, Sharpsburg, Maryland. September 27, 1862 appears on list of prisoners paroled. October 27, 1862 sent from Frederick, Maryland to Baltimore, Maryland with other prisoners. November 4, 1862 admitted to General Hospital, Howard's Grove at Richmond, Virginia with a Vulnus Sclopeticum (Gunshot Wound). November 4, 1862 exchanged at Aiken's Landing, James River, Virginia. November 11, 1862 furloughed for 40 days. December 1862 roll shows him on furlough. October 1863 discharged due to disability. April 26, 1864 elected captain of Co. F, 1st Regiment, Georgia Reserve Infantry (Symon's). December 21, 1864 captured at Savannah, Georgia. June 17, 1865 released at Fort Delaware, Delaware. He was born in Appling County, Georgia in 1842. He is buried in the Jesup City Cemetery, Wayne County, Georgia.

MILLING, ROBERT: Company K, private. September 24, 1863 enlisted as a private in Co. K, 27th Regiment, Georgia Infantry at Columbus, Georgia. December 31, 1863 received pay. March - April 1864 roll shows him present. July 1864 issued clothing. April 26, 1865, surrendered at Greensboro, North Carolina. May 1, 1865 paroled at Greensboro, North Carolina.

MILLRONS, GEORGE W.: Company F, private. He enlisted as a private in Co. F, 27th Regiment, Georgia Infantry. January 13, 1862 died of Diphtheria at Camp Pickens near Manassas, Virginia. January 1862 roll shows his death on January 13, 1862.

MILLER, HENRY H.: Company H, private. September 9, 1861 enlisted as a private in Co. H, 27th Regiment, Georgia Infantry at Camp Stephens, Griffin, Spalding County, Georgia. September 17, 1862 killed at Sharpsburg, Maryland.

MILLING, ROBERT H.: Company K, private. September 24, 1864 enlisted as a private in Co. K, 27th Regiment, Georgia Infantry. April 26, 1865 surrendered Greensboro, North Carolina.

MILLS, G. F.: Company A, private. He enlisted as a private in Co. A, 27th Regiment, Georgia Infantry. April 28, 1865 admitted to C. S. A. General Hospital, No. 11 at Charlotte, North Carolina with Fever.

MIMBS, SEABORN S.: Company E, sergeant.   He enlisted as a private in Co. E, 27th Regiment, Georgia Infantry. July 4, 1864 captured at Marietta, Georgia.   June 20, 1865 discharged from Camp Douglas, Illinois prison camp. He was a resident of Houston County, Georgia.

MINCHEW (MINSHEW), MORTIMOER (MARTIMORE) M.: Company B, private.   September 10, 1861 enlisted as a private in Co. B, 27th Regiment, Georgia Infantry at Camp Stephens, Griffin, Spalding County, Georgia. December 28, 1861 discharged due to disability (Hernia) at Camp Pickens near Manassas, Virginia. December 1861 roll shows he was discharged due to disability. April 11, 1864 enlisted as a private in Co. B, 27th Regiment, Georgia Infantry at Macon, Georgia.   March - April 1864 roll shows him "absent with leave until May 1, 1864". June 3, 1864 wounded at Cold Harbor, Virginia. June 3, 1864 admitted to Receiving and Wayside Hospital or General Hospital No. 9 at Richmond, Virginia and sent to Danville, Virginia.   June 4, 1864 admitted to C. S. A. General Hospital at Danville, Virginia with a Vulnus Sclopeticum (Gunshot Wound) in the back. June 7, 1864 furloughed.

MISE (MIZE), JACK: Company B, private.   January 14, 1864 enlisted as a private in Co. B, 27th Regiment, Georgia Infantry. January – February 1864 roll shows him present. February 29, 1864 received pay. March - April 1864 roll shows him present. July 1864 and September 20, 1864 issued clothing. He was born in Butts County, Georgia in 1833.

MITCHELL, J. M.: Company A, private.   He enlisted as a private in Co. A, 27th Regiment, Georgia Infantry. April 18, 182 died of Typhoid Fever at General Receiving Hospital (also known as Charity Hospital) at Gordonsville, Virginia. April 1862 report from General Receiving Hospital (also known as Charity Hospital) at Gordonsville, Virginia reports his death.

MITCHELL, JOHN WESLEY: Company C, private.   May 1, 1862 enlisted as a private in Co. C, 27th Regiment, Georgia Infantry at Richmond, Virginia. June 15, 1863, June 30, 1863 and September 30, 1863 issued clothing. December 31, 1863 received pay. January – February 1864 roll shows him present.   March - April 1864 roll shows him present. July 9, 1864 killed, Petersburg, Virginia.

MITCHELL, JAMES T.: Company K, private.   September 10, 1861 enlisted as a private in Co. K, 27th Regiment, Georgia Infantry at Camp Stephens, Griffin, Spalding County, Georgia. December 1861 roll shows he was left in Georgia sick on October 31, 1861.

MITCHELL, THOMAS J.: Company K, private.   September 10, 1861 enlisted as a private in Co. K, 27th Regiment, Georgia Infantry at Camp Stephens, Griffin, Spalding County, Georgia. January and February 1862 rolls show he was left in Georgia sick on October 31, 1861.

MITCHELL, THOMAS W.: Company A, corporal.   September 10, 1861 elected 3rd corporal Co. A, 27th Regiment, Georgia Infantry at Camp Stephens, Griffin, Spalding County, Georgia. January 17, 1862 admitted to

Moore Hospital at General Hospital, No. 1 at Danville, Virginia. January 1862 roll shows him sent to Moore Hospital on January 18, 1862. June 9, 1862 received pay ($65.00). June, July, August and September 1863 issued clothing. December 31, 1863 received pay. January – February 1864 roll shows him present. February 29, 1864 received pay. March - April 1864 roll shows him present. May 30, 1864, July 1864 and September 1864 issued clothing.

MITCHELL, WILLIAM J.: Company E, private. August 1, 1863 enlisted as a private in Co. E, 27th Regiment, Georgia Infantry at Fairburn, Georgia. December 31, 1863 received pay. January – February 1864 roll shows him present. March - April 1864 roll shows him present. June 14, 1864 admitted to Jackson Hospital at Richmond, Virginia with Diarrhoea (record indicates he died of Chronic Diarrhoea at Jackson Hospital at Richmond, Virginia on this date- may be a conflict). June 30, 1864 roll of 1st Division, Jackson Hospital at Richmond, Virginia shows him present. July 28, 1864 furloughed for 30 days. Pension records show he was at home on sick furlough at the close of the war.

MITCHELL, WILLIAM J.: Company F, sergeant. September 9, 1861 elected 3rd sergeant in Co. F, 27th Regiment, Georgia Infantry at Camp Stephens, Griffin, Spalding County, Georgia. January 6, 1862 died of Pneumonia at Camp Pickens near Manassas, Virginia. January 1862 roll indicates his death. March 15, 1862 death benefit claim was filed by his mother Casamaia Albritton. October 2, 1862 death benefit claim paid $36.83 (#1372). Records indicate he was born in Marion County, Georgia. He was a resident of Schley County, Georgia.

MIZE, JACK: Company B, private. January 14, 1864 enlisted as a private in Co. B, 27th Regiment, Georgia Infantry. March - April 1864 roll shows him present.

MOLEN, JAMES WILLIAM: Company C, private. September 20, 1863 enlisted as a private in Co. C, 27th Regiment, Georgia Infantry in Charleston, South Carolina. January – February 1864 roll shows him absent with leave since October 1863. February 29, 1864 received pay. March - April 1864 roll shows him present. January 7, 1865 admitted to C. S. A. General Military Hospital, No. 4 at Wilmington, North Carolina with Pneumonia. February 18, 1865 returned to duty. April 26, 1865 pension records show he surrendered Greensboro, North Carolina.

MOLAND (MOLEN), JAMES EUDOCHES: Company C, private. He enlisted as a private in Co. C, 27th Regiment, Georgia Infantry. April 7, 1862 admitted to General Hospital at Orange Court House, Virginia. April 18, 1862 admitted to General Hospital at Charlottesville, Virginia with Debility. May 7, 1862 died of Pneumonia at General Hospital No. 2 at Lynchburg, Virginia. May 7, 1862 burial recorded (must be buried at Lynchburg, Virginia). May 9, 1862 he is on report from General Hospital at Charlottesville, Virginia as being absent without leave or notice. May 10, 1862 on report from General Hospital at Charlottesville, Virginia (has been the subject of special communication to the Medical Director).   August 12, 1862 death benefit claim was filed.   November 5, 1862 death benefit claim paid to Martha Moland, widow $55.06 (#1773).

MOORE, B. B.: Company A, private. He enlisted as a private in Co. A, 27th Regiment, Georgia Infantry.   December 1862 roll shows him on furlough sick in Georgia.

MOORE, FRELING HUSEN: Company D, private.   August 26, 1863 enlisted as a private in Co. D, 27th Regiment, Georgia Infantry in Hall County, Georgia.   November 6, 1861 admitted to General Hospital at Petersburg, Virginia with Rubeola.   December 1861, January 1862 and February 1862 rolls show him in the hospital at Petersburg, Virginia. March 7, 1862 returned to duty.   March 30, 1862 admitted to General Hospital No. 18(formerly Greaner's Hospital) at Richmond, Virginia with Chronic Diarrhoea.   December 1862 roll shows him absent without leave. December 1863 issued clothing. February 29, 1864 received pay. March - April 1864 roll shows him present.   May 30, 1864 and July 1864 issued clothing. January 1865 carried to Mrs. Avery's home at Wilmington, North Carolina with a frozen foot.   May 1865 went home.   He was born in Hall County, Georgia in 1844.   He was a resident of Gainesville, Georgia.

MOORE, J. B. C.: Company B, sergeant.   September 27, 1862 admitted to General Hospital No. 21 (Maryland Hospital, Gwathmey Hospital) at Richmond, Virginia with a Vulnus Sclopeticum (Gunshot Wound). February 21, 1863 received pay ($211.00).   October 2, 1864 admitted to Receiving and Wayside Hospital or General Hospital No. 9 at Richmond, Virginia.   October 3, 1864 transferred to Jackson Hospital at Richmond, Virginia.

MOORE, JAMES: Company A, private.   September 10, 1861 enlisted as a private in Co. A, 27th Regiment, Georgia Infantry at Camp Stephens, Griffin, Spalding County, Georgia.   December 1861 and January 1862 rolls show he was left in Georgia sick on October 31, 1861. April 18, 1862 died of Dysentery at Chimborazo Hospital No. 5 at Richmond, Virginia. He is most likely buried in Oakwood Cemetery at Richmond Virginia.

MOORE, JESSE: Company A, private.   He enlisted as a private in Co. A, 27th Regiment, Georgia Infantry.   December 1861 and January 1862 rolls show he was left in Georgia sick on October 31, 1861.   March 30, 1862 admitted to Chimborazo Hospital No. 2 at Richmond, Virginia with Diarrhoea. July 2, 1862 died at Chimborazo Hospital No. 2 at Richmond, Virginia.   He is most likely buried in Oakwood Cemetery at Richmond Virginia.

MOORE, JOHN C.: Company G, private.   September 9, 1861 enlisted as a private in Co. G, 27th Regiment, Georgia Infantry at Camp Stephens, Griffin, Spalding County, Georgia. March 7, 1862 admitted to Chimborazo Hospital No. 4 at Richmond, Virginia with Debility. April 10, 1862 returned to duty.   July 1, 1862 wounded at Malvern Hill, Virginia. September 20, 1862 admitted to General Hospital No. 12 at Richmond, Virginia. September

26, 1862 furloughed for 30 days. The record of General Hospital No. 12 at Richmond, Virginia (Age 18, Farmer wounded July 1 through lower third of thigh). He was admitted from General Hospital No. 15 at Richmond, Virginia. Wound healed but biceps tendons so retracted as to render him unable to straighten the leg (Gone on furlough for 30 days). September 26, 1862 furloughed for 30 days at Richmond, Virginia. December 1862 roll shows him absent sick. July 4, 1863 paid commutation of rations ($7.50). December 31, 1863 received pay. January – February 1864 and March - April 1864 rolls show him absent on furlough from December 1, 1862 for 30 days – furlough extended.

MOORE, JOHN K.: Company D, corporal. September 10, 1861 elected 3rd corporal in Co. D, 27th Regiment, Georgia Infantry at Camp Stephens, Griffin, Spalding County, Georgia. May 4, 1862 admitted to Chimborazo Hospital No. 5 at Richmond, Virginia with Fever. June 10, 1862 received pay ($55.00). June 26 1862 transferred from Chimborazo Hospital No. 5 at Richmond, Virginia to either Danville or Lynchburg, Virginia. October 1, 1862 admitted to Camp Winder Division No. 2 Hospital at Richmond, Virginia with a Vulnus Sclopeticum (Gunshot Wound). October 10, 1862 furloughed for 30 days. October 17, 1862 received pay ($119.00). April, May, June and December 1863 issued clothing. February 29, 1864 received pay. March - April 1864 roll shows him present. July 1864 and September 20, 1864 issued clothes. April 26, 1865 surrendered Greensboro, North Carolina. May 1, 1865 paroled at Greensboro, North Carolina.

MOORE, JOSEPH: Company D, private. August 29, 1862 enlisted as a private in Co. D, 27th Regiment, Georgia Infantry at Gordon County, Georgia. December 11, 1862 admitted to Camp Winder Division No. 4 Hospital at Richmond, Virginia. November 19, 1862 admitted to General Hospital No. 16 at Richmond, Virginia. November 1862 roll of General Hospital No. 16 at Richmond, Virginia shows him present. December 19, 1862 returned to duty. April, May, June and December 1863 issued clothing. December 31, 1863 received pay. March 1, 1864 killed, Cedar Creek, Florida. March - April 1864 roll shows he was killed at Cedar Creek, Florida.

MOORE, MALACHI: Company D, private. September 10, 1861 enlisted as a private in Co. D, 27th Regiment, Georgia Infantry at Camp Stephens, Griffin, Spalding County, Georgia. December 21, 1861 admitted to Moore Hospital at General Hospital, No. 1 at Danville, Virginia with Pneumonia and sent to General Hospital at Richmond, Virginia. December1861 roll shows him in hospital at Richmond, Virginia. April 30, 1862 received pay. June 5, 1862 received pay ($69.00). August 4, 1862 died. December 13, 1862 death benefit claim was filed by his father, Moren Moore. September 18, 1863 death benefit claim paid $84.46 (#8797).

MOORE, SCOTT: Company D, private. May 1864 enlisted as a private in Co. D, 27th Regiment, Georgia Infantry. April 26, 1865 surrendered Greensboro, North Carolina. He was born in Georgia.

MOORE, W. S.: Company D, private. He enlisted as a private in Co. D, 27th Regiment, Georgia Infantry. July 1864 issued clothing. April 26, 1865, surrendered at Greensboro, North Carolina. May 1, 1865 paroled at Greensboro, North Carolina.

MOORE, WILLIAM H.: Company F, private. May 22, 1862 enlisted as a private in Co. F, 27th Regiment, Georgia Infantry in Butler, Georgia. May 1, 1862 received pay. July 5, 1862 admitted to Chimborazo Hospital No. 4 at Richmond, Virginia with acute Diarrhoea. July 22, 1862 transferred to Danville, Virginia hospital. July 23, 1862 admitted to C. S. A. General Military Hospital at Danville, Virginia with Rheumatism. October 8, 1862 furloughed for 60 days. December 1862 roll shows him absent sick since June 1862. February 27, 1863 admitted to Camp Winder Division No. 2 Hospital at Richmond, Virginia with Chronic Rheumatism. July 30, 1863 furloughed for 30 days. February 27, 1863 name is on a report of Camp Winder Division No. 2 Hospital at Richmond, Virginia as having deserted on February 7, 1863 and shown as being detailed and ordered on hospital duty there by General Lee. March -April 1864 roll shows him on detached duty at Camp Winder Hospital at Richmond, Virginia by order of General Lee. February 20, 1865 is shown in Floyd House Hospital at Macon, Georgia Hospital with Chronic Rheumatism.

MORELAND, WILLIAM A.: Company G, private. September 9, 1861 enlisted as a private in Co. G, 27th Regiment, Georgia Infantry at Camp Stephens, Griffin, Spalding County, Georgia. January 9, 1862 admitted to Moore Hospital at General Hospital, No. 1 at Danville, Virginia with Pneumonia and was sent to Richmond, Virginia. January 10, 1862 admitted to General Hospital No. 18 (formerly Greaner's Hospital) at Richmond, Virginia with Constipation. February 6, 1862 furloughed for 30 days. March 23, 1862 returned to duty. June 27, 1862 wounded at Malvern Hill near Richmond, Virginia. June 28, 1862 admitted to General Hospital No. 18 (formerly Greaner's Hospital) at Richmond, Virginia with a Vulnus Sclopeticum (Gunshot Wound). June 30, 1862 transferred to Camp Winder Division No. 1 Hospital at Richmond, Virginia. September 17, 1862 wounded at Sharpsburg, Maryland. October 15, 1862 furloughed for 60 days. March 17, 1863 received pay ($20.00) for commutation of rations. His home Post office was Zebulon, Georgia. He was born in Georgia June 20, 1836.

MORGAN, E. R.: Company K, private. He enlisted as a private in Co. K, 27th Regiment, Georgia Infantry. February 20, 1865 captured near Wilmington, North Carolina. March 13, 1865 he arrived at Point Lookout, Maryland as a prisoner of war. May 15, 1865 released from Point Lookout, Maryland.

MORGAN, ISAIAH D.: Field Staff, Assistant Surgeon. September 10, 1861 enlisted as an assistant surgeon in the 27th Regiment, Georgia Infantry at Camp Stephens, Griffin, Spalding County, Georgia. August 28, 1862 received pay ($110.00). December 1862 roll shows him present near Guinea Station, Virginia. November 1864 appears on roster 27th Regiment, Georgia Infantry.

MORGAN, STANLEY R.: Company D, private. September 10, 1861 enlisted as a private in Co. D, 27th Regiment, Georgia Infantry at Camp Stephens, Griffin, Spalding County, Georgia. December 1861, January 1862 and February 1862 rolls show him in the hospital in Warrenton, Virginia. March 1, 1862 admitted to C. S. A. General Hospital at Charlottesville, Virginia with Pneumonia. March 3, 1862 returned to duty. March 30, 1862 admitted to Chimborazo Hospital No. 1 at Richmond, Virginia as a convalescent (also states he left without permission). June 1, 1862 admitted to C. S. A. General Military Hospital, No. 4 at Wilmington, North Carolina with Congestive Fever. June 1862 roll of General Hospital at Wilmington, North Carolina shows he died on June 11 of Typhoid Fever. His effects and body were returned home to Georgia. August 29, 1864 death benefit claim was filed stating he died in Wilmington, North Carolina. He was a resident of Browns Bridge, Georgia.

MORIARTY, E.: Company C, private. He enlisted as a private in Co. C, 27th Regiment, Georgia Infantry. December 1862 roll shows him detailed as a teamster.

MORRIS, B. F.: Company H, private. He enlisted as a private in Co. H, 27th Regiment, Georgia Infantry. November 25, 1863 wounded at Fort Sumter, South Carolina.

MORRIS, J. M.: Company A, private. September 10, 1861 enlisted as a private in Co. A, 27th Regiment, Georgia Infantry at Camp Stephens, Griffin, Spalding County, Georgia. October 17, 1861 died of disease at Spalding, County, Georgia. December 1861 roll shows his death in Georgia. January 27, 1863 death benefit claim was filed by his father, J. W. Morris.

MORRIS, J. R.: Company E, private. He enlisted as a private in Co. E, 27th Regiment, Georgia Infantry.

MORRISON, J. M: Company D, private. September 10, 1861 enlisted as a private in Co. D, 27th Regiment, Georgia Infantry at Camp Stephens, Griffin, Spalding County, Georgia. June 22, 1864 wounded in finger necessitating amputation at Kennesaw Mountain, Georgia.

MORSE, l.: Company A, private. August 10, 1862 enlisted as a private in Co. A, 27th Regiment, Georgia Infantry at Savannah, Georgia. December 31, 1863 received pay. November-December 1864 roll of Co. E, 2nd Battalion Troops and Defences, Macon, Georgia absent detailed as Provost Marshall Guard.

MOSS, EPHRAIM: Company D, private. August 18, 1862 enlisted as a private in Co. D, 27th Regiment, Georgia Infantry in Calhoun County, Georgia. September 30, 1862 admitted to South Carolina Hospital at Manchester, Virginia with Rubeola. November 16, 1862 discharged from service due to Amaurosis. November 21, 1862 discharged and received pay. November 1862 roll of South Carolina Hospital at Manchester, Virginia shows he was discharged due to Amaurosis (lack of vision) from

389

disease. His discharge states he was born in Morgan County, Georgia. He was 30 years of age, 6 feet 2 inches high, dark complexion, blue eyes and dark hair. He was a farmer by occupation.

MULLINS, SEABORN GEORGE W.: Company F, private. September 22, 1861 enlisted as a private in Co. K, 27th Regiment, Georgia Infantry. December 1861 and January 1862 roll shows he was left in Georgia sick on October 31, 1861. February 11, 1862 sent to Moore Hospital at General Hospital, No. 1 at Danville, Virginia. February 25, 1862 admitted to C. S. A. General Hospital at Charlottesville, Virginia for convalescence from Measles. April 12, 1862 returned to duty. September 17, 1862 captured at Sharpsburg, Maryland. September 30, 1862 paroled by the Army of the Potomac and sent to Aikens Landing, Virginia for exchange. October 27, 1862 sent from Fort McHenry, Maryland to Fortress Monroe, Virginia for exchange. November 4, 1862 admitted to General Hospital, Howards Grove at Richmond, Virginia with Asthma. November 1862 roll of General Hospital, Howards Grove at Richmond, Virginia shows him present. December 11, 1862 transferred to Chimborazo Hospital at Richmond, Virginia. December 12, 1862 admitted to Chimborazo Hospital No. 3 at Richmond, Virginia. December 16, 1862 transferred to Chimborazo Hospital No. 2 at Richmond, Virginia. December 18, 1862 returned to duty. February 14, 1863 discharged at Receiving and Wayside Hospital or General Hospital No. 9 at Richmond, Virginia. February 17, 1863 received pay ($64.01). Born in Houston, County, Georgia, 16 years of age is shown on his certificate of discharge as being 5 feet 9 inches high, fair complexion, blue eyes, and auburn hair.

MURCHISON, JOHN C.: Company C, sergeant. September 10, 1861 elected 2nd sergeant in Co. C, 27th Regiment, Georgia Infantry at Camp Stephens, Griffin, Spalding County, Georgia. April 10, 1862 admitted to Chimborazo Hospital No. 5 at Richmond, Virginia with Dysentery. May 12, 1862 transferred to Camp Winder Hospital at Richmond, Virginia. July 7, 1862 admitted to U. S. Hospital at Portsmouth Grove, Rhode Island with a Vulnus Sclopeticum (Gunshot Wound). September 17, 1862 sent from U. S. Hospital at Portsmouth Grove, Rhode Island to Fortress Monroe, Virginia and was received on September 18, 1862. September 18, 1862 Prisoner of War report shows him received at Fort Columbus, New York Harbor, New York from U. S. Hospital at Portsmouth Grove, Rhode Island. September 22, 1862 paroled for exchange at Fort Monroe, Virginia. October 25, 1862 furloughed from Richmond, Virginia for 30 days. October 29, 1862 received pay ($220.00). June 26, 1863 issued clothing. December 31, 1863 received pay. January – February 1864 roll shows him present. February 20, 1864 wounded at Olustee, Florida. March - April 1864 roll shows him present. June 1, 1864 wounded at Cold Harbor, Virginia. June 3, 1864 admitted to Receiving and Wayside Hospital or General Hospital No. 9 at Richmond, Virginia with Vulnus Sclopeticum (Gunshot Wound) to the elbow with a mini ball resulting in amputation and was transferred to Jackson Hospital at Richmond, Virginia. June 23, 1864 admitted to Jackson Hospital at Richmond, Virginia where right arm was amputated. June 25, 1864 died of wounds in Jackson Hospital at Richmond, Virginia. He is buried in Hollywood Cemetery at Richmond, Virginia.

MURPHEY(MURPHY), E. M.: Company A, private. He enlisted as a private in Co. A, 27th Regiment, Georgia Infantry. July 1864 and September 20, 1864 issued clothing. May 1, 1865 paroled at Greensboro, North Carolina.

MURPHEY (MURPHY), GEORGE T.: Company A, private. February 23, 1862 enlisted in Co. A, 27th Regiment, Georgia Infantry at Marion County, Georgia. March 20, 1862 received bounty pay ($50.00) at Richmond, Virginia. October 15, 1862 issued clothing. October 18, 1862 admitted to Receiving and Wayside Hospital or General Hospital No. 9 at Richmond, Virginia and was transferred to Camp Winder Division Hospital Richmond, Virginia. October 19, 1862 admitted to Camp Winder Division No. 5 Hospital at Richmond, Virginia. October 25, 1862 returned to duty. June 1863 issued clothing. July, August and September 1863 issued clothing. September 22, 1863 received pay ($22.00). December 1863 issued clothing. December 31, 1863 received pay. January – February 1864 roll shows him present. March - April 1864 roll shows him present. June 17, 1864 captured at Colquitt's Salient near Petersburg, Virginia. June 23, 1864 arrived at Fortress Monroe, Virginia. June 25, 1864 transferred to Elmira Prison, New York. July 18, 1864 arrived at Elmira Prison, New York. June (May) 19, 1865 signed oath of allegiance to the United States of America and was released from Elmira Prison, New York. He is described as being a resident of Columbus, Georgia and having dark complexion, dark hair and dark eyes. He is shown as being 5 feet 11 inches high.

MURPHEY (MURPHY), JOHN: Company E, private. September 9, 1861 enlisted as a private in Co. E, 27th Regiment, Georgia Infantry at Camp Stephens, Griffin, Spalding County, Georgia. April 6, 1862 admitted to General Hospital at Orange Court House, Virginia. September 17, 1862 wounded and captured at Sharpsburg, Maryland. October 21 (20), 1862 died of wounds in United States Hospital at Frederick, Maryland. He is buried at Mt. Olivet Cemetery at Frederick, Maryland (grave # 137).

MURPHEY (MURPHY), JOHN M., JR.: Company K, corporal. September 10, 1861 enlisted as a private in Co. K, 27th Regiment, Georgia Infantry at Camp Stephens, Griffin, Spalding County, Georgia. December 17, 1861 admitted to Moore Hospital at General Hospital, No. 1 at Danville, Virginia and was sent to Richmond, Virginia. September 27, 1862 paroled. December 31, 1863 received pay. March - April 1864 roll shows him present. August 10, 1864 admitted to Jackson Hospital at Richmond, Virginia with Dyspepsia. August 20, 1864 returned to duty. September 12, 1864 admitted to Jackson Hospital at Richmond, Virginia with Dyspepsia. September 30, 1864 furloughed for 30 days.

MURPHEY (MURPHY), JOSEPH M.: Company K, private. September

10, 1861 enlisted as a private in Co. K, 27th Regiment, Georgia Infantry at Camp Stephens, Griffin, Spalding County, Georgia. January 16, 1862 admitted to Moore Hospital at General Hospital, No. 1 at Danville, Virginia and sent to Orange Court House, Virginia hospital. January 17, 1862 admitted to General Hospital at Orange Court House, Virginia with Pleuritis. January and February1862 rolls show him in Hospital at Orange Court House, Virginia. March 15, 1862 returned to duty. June 30 1862 returned to duty from General Hospital No. 13, Richmond, Virginia. June 1863 issued clothing. July 7, 1863 received pay ($88.00). August 24, 1863 - October 24, 1863 on furlough. November 21, 1863 received commutation for rations pay ($16.50). October 29, 1863, November 24, 1863 and December 18, 1863 issued clothing. January – February 1864 roll shows him absent in hospital at Orange Court house, Virginia. July 1864 issued clothing. September 28, 1864 issued clothing at Jackson Hospital at Richmond, Virginia. September 29, 1864 received pay ($63.13). He died in service. He was a resident of Talbotton, Georgia.

MURPHEY (MURPHY), MICHAEL: Company K, private. September 10, 1861 enlisted as a private in Co. K, 27th Regiment, Georgia Infantry at Camp Stephens, Griffin, Spalding County, Georgia.

MURPHEY (MURPHY), R. H.: Company K, private. September 10, 1861 enlisted as a private in Co. K, 27th Regiment, Georgia Infantry at Camp Stephens, Griffin, Spalding County, Georgia.

MURPHEY (MURPHY), MIKE: Company A, private. 1862 enlisted as a private in Co. A, 27th Regiment, Georgia Infantry. April 26, 1865 surrendered, Greensboro, North Carolina.

MURRAY, D. M.: Company D, private. September 2, 1862 enlisted as a private in Co. D, 27th Regiment, Georgia Infantry. October 21, 1862 died of Measles.

MURRAY, H. ALLEN: Company A, sergeant. September 9, 1861 enlisted as a private in Co. E, 27th Regiment, Georgia Infantry at Camp Stephens, Griffin, Spalding County, Georgia. December 1861 and January 1862 rolls show he was left sick in Georgia October 31, 1861. February 16, 1863 death benefit claim was filed by Stephen Murray, attorney.

MURRAY, JAMES W.: Company C, captain. September 10, 1861 enlisted as a private in Co. C, 27th Regiment, Georgia Infantry at Camp Stephens, Griffin, Spalding County, Georgia. July 6, 1861 elected 1st. lieutenant in Co. C, 27th Regiment, Georgia Infantry. December 1861, January and February 1862 rolls show him present at Camp Pickens near Manassas, Virginia. September 17, 1862 elected captain Co. C, 27th Regiment, Georgia Infantry. October 31, 1862 admitted to General Hospital No. 4 at Richmond, Virginia. February 15, 1862 received $750.00 for recruiting duty. March 25, 1862 received $400.00 for recruiting duty. May 21, 1862 received pay ($270.00). June 9, 1862 received pay ($90.00). June 21, 1862 received pay ($ 270.00). July 19, 1862 received pay ($90.00). November 4, 1862 granted 30 days furlough from Richmond,

Virginia. December 1862 received pay ($195.00). January 4, 1863 he is shown as absent without leave. January 1863 roll shows him AWOL since January 4, 1863. February 12, 1863 resigned his commission. March 10, 1863 issued clothing. March 17, 1863 Medical Examining Board of Richmond, Virginia found him to have Hemophthis (Spitting of Blood) and was admitted to General Hospital No. 4 at Richmond, Virginia. March 17, 1863 received pay ($390.00).

MURRAY (MURRY), LESEUR L.: Company B, private. September 10, 1861 enlisted as a private in Co. B, 27th Regiment, Georgia Infantry at Camp Stephens, Griffin, Spalding County, Georgia. November 6, 1861 admitted to General Hospital at Petersburg, Virginia with Rubeola. December 17, 1861 returned to duty. May 15, 1862 admitted to Chimborazo Hospital No.2 at Richmond, Virginia with Diarrhoea. May 18, 1862 returned to duty. July 6, 1862 admitted to General Hospital at Farmville, Virginia with Rheumatism. October 18, 1862 returned to duty. He was appointed corporal in Co. B, 27th Regiment, Georgia Infantry. May 3, 1863 wounded at Chancellorsville, Virginia. August 6 - August 24, 1863 on furlough. August 1863 received $5.96 in commutation for rations while on furlough. October, November and December 1863 issued clothing. December 1863 died. April 5, 1864 death benefit claim was filed.

MURRAY, STEPHEN: Company A, private. September 10, 1861 enlisted as a private in Co. A, 27th Regiment, Georgia Infantry. August 20, 1862 received pay ($59.00). November 21, 1862 received pay ($84.00). December 9, 1862 admitted to General Hospital No. 16 at Richmond, Virginia. December 1862 roll shows he was sent off sick in December. January 10, 1863 roll of General Hospital No. 16 at Richmond, Virginia shows him present. February 16, 1863 furloughed for 35 days from Richmond, Virginia. March 2, 1863 received pay ($34.00). July 25, 1862 received $5.00 in commutation for rations while on furlough. October 31, 1863 received pay. December 1863 issued clothing. January – February 1864 roll shows him present. March - April 1864 roll shows him present. October 31, 1864 he was subject of a court martial. April 26, 1865 surrendered Greensboro, North Carolina. May 1, 1865 paroled at Greensboro, North Carolina.

MURRAY, WILLIAM M.: Company F, private. September 10, 1861 enlisted as a private in Co. F, 27th Regiment, Georgia Infantry at Camp Stephens, Griffin, Spalding County, Georgia. January 10, 1862 discharged and paid $70.58. July 15, 1864 furloughed from Floyd House Hospital at Macon, Georgia after amputation of the left forearm. His Post Office was Butler, Taylor County, Georgia.

MYRICK, NATHAINEL WESLEY: Company A, corporal. May 12, 1862 enlisted as a private in Co. A, 27th Regiment, Georgia Infantry in Schley County, Georgia. June 1, 1862 wounded at Seven Pines, Virginia. June 1, 1862 admitted to Chimborazo Hospital No. 1 at Richmond, Virginia with a Vulnus Sclopeticum (Gunshot Wound). He was appointed corporal in Co. A, 27th Regiment, Georgia Infantry. November 20, 1862 received bounty pay ($50.00). October 31, 1863 received pay. December 31, 1863 received pay and issued clothing. January – February 1864 roll shows him absent without leave since April 24, 1863. February 28, 1864 received pay. March - April 1864 roll shows him present. August 19, 1864 wounded and captured at Weldon Railroad, Virginia. August 20, 1864 left thigh amputated in the field Hospital. August 27, 1864 sent to City Point, Virginia. August 30, 1864 admitted to the Carver U. S. A. General Hospital at Washington D. C. with a Vulnus Sclopeticum (Gunshot Wound) (a fracture of patella and head of the tibia) necessitating amputation. October 18, 1864 transferred to Lincoln U. S. A. General Hospital at Washington D. C. November 23, 1864 transferred Old Capital Prison at Washington, D. C. December 16, 1864 sent to Elmira prison, New York from Old Capital Prison at Washington, D. C. December 17, 1864 arrived at Elmira Prison, New York. February 13, 1865 paroled at Elmira Prison, New York and sent to James River, Virginia for exchange. February 20-21, 1865 received at Boulware and Cox's Wharves, James River, Virginia. February 20, 1865 admitted to Receiving and Wayside Hospital or General Hospital No. 9 at Richmond, Virginia and transferred to Jackson Hospital. February 22, 1865 received at Receiving and Wayside Hospital at Richmond, Virginia and sent to Jackson Hospital there the same date and was in said hospital March 16, 1865 as a paroled prisoner and was issued clothing. March 18, 1865 furloughed for 60 days from Jackson Hospital at Richmond, Virginia.

MYRICK (MURICK), SEPTIMUS WHEATHERSBY: Company A, corporal. September 10, 1861 enlisted as a private and elected 1st corporal in Co. C, 27th Regiment, Georgia Infantry at Camp Stephens, Griffin, Spalding County, Georgia. September 30, 1862 admitted to Camp Winder Division No. 3 Hospital at Richmond, Virginia. October 9, 1862 received pay ($94.00). October 10, 1862 returned to duty. October 31, 1863 received pay. January – February 1864 roll shows him present. February 29, 1864 received pay. March- April 1864 roll shows him present. July 1864 issued clothing. March 25, 1865 wounded at Bentonville, North Carolina and in the hospital there at the close of the war. He was born in Georgia in 1837.

MYRNE, W. A.: Company D, private. He enlisted as a private in Co. D, 27th Regiment, Georgia Infantry. October 1862 admitted to Receiving and Wayside Hospital or General Hospital No. 9 at Richmond, Virginia. October 8, 1862 transferred to General Hospital No. 21 or 22 at Richmond, Virginia.

NAIL, B. W.: Company H, private. September 9, 1861 enlisted as a private in Co. H, 27th Regiment, Georgia Infantry at Camp Stephens, Griffin, Spalding County, Georgia. November 21, 1863 received pay at James Island, South Carolina. December 31, 1863 received pay. January – February 1864 roll shows him present. February 29, 1864 received pay. March - April 1864 roll shows him present. July 1864 and September

20, 1864 issued clothing. April 26, 1865 surrendered Greensboro, North Carolina. May 1, 1865 paroled at Greensboro, North Carolina.

NAIL, F. M.: Company H, private. September 9, 1861 enlisted as a private in Co. H, 27th Regiment, Georgia Infantry at Camp Stephens, Griffin, Spalding County, Georgia. March 1, 1864 killed at Cedar Creek, Florida. March - April 1864 roll shows he was killed at Cedar Creek, Florida on March 1, 1864.

NAIL, R. J.: Company H, private. September 9, 1861 enlisted as a private in Co. H, 27th Regiment, Georgia Infantry at Camp Stephens, Griffin, Spalding County, Georgia. December 21, 1861 admitted to Moore Hospital at General Hospital, No. 1, Danville, Virginia with Neuralgia and was sent to the Hospital in Richmond, Virginia. August 30, 1862 admitted to Camp Winder Division Hospital at Richmond, Virginia. October 7, 1862 admitted to Camp Winder Division No. 2 Hospital at Richmond, Virginia. October 17, 1862 returned to duty. December 31, 1863 received pay. January – February 1864 roll shows him present. February 29, 1864 received pay. March - April 1864 roll shows him present. May 21, 1864 returned to duty from Pettigrew General Hospital No. 13 at Raleigh, North Carolina. May 31, 1864 issued clothing. June 9, 1864 wounded in right shoulder and hand, at Petersburg, Virginia. September 20, 1864 issued clothing. January 1865 was on detached duty at Lexington, North Carolina to the close of the war. April 26, 1865 surrendered at Greensboro, North Carolina. May 1, 1865 paroled at Greensboro, North Carolina. He was born in Georgia.

NAIL, RUBIN W. J.: Company H, private. August 1, 1862 enlisted as a private in Co. H, 27th Regiment, Georgia Infantry at McDonough, Georgia. October 13, 1863 wounded, spine broken in fall over breast works at Fort Johnson, South Carolina. December 31, 1863 received pay. January – February 1864 roll shows him present. February 29, 1864 received pay. March - April 1864 roll shows him present. March 5, 1864 issued clothing at Camp Milton, Florida. July a1864 and September 20, 1864 issued clothing. April 26, 1865 surrendered Greensboro, North Carolina. May 1, 1865 paroled at Greensboro, North Carolina. He was born in Georgia October 14, 1847.

NAIL, THOMAS J.: Company H, private. September 9, 1861 enlisted as a private in Co. H, 27th Regiment, Georgia Infantry at Camp Stephens, Griffin, Spalding County, Georgia. July 5, 1862 received pay ($91.00). December 31, 1863 received pay. January – February 1864 roll shows him present. February 29, 1864 received pay. March - April 1864 roll shows him present. September 20, 1864 issued clothing. March 19, 1865 wounded, bone in right hip shattered, at Bentonville, North Carolina. April 5, 1865 admitted to Pettigrew General Hospital No. 13 at Raleigh, North Carolina. April 6 and April 17, 1865 issued clothing at Pettigrew General Hospital No. 13 at Raleigh, North Carolina. April 13, 1865 captured in the hospital at Raleigh, North Carolina at the close of the war. May 5, 1865 paroled at Raleigh, North Carolina. He was born in Georgia February 19, 1839. His home was McDonough, Henry County, Georgia.

NASH, D. L.: Company H, private. He enlisted as a private in Co. H, 27th Regiment, Georgia Infantry.

NASH, ELIHU C.: Company H, private. September 9, 1861 enlisted as a private in Co. H, 27th Regiment, Georgia Infantry at Camp Stephens, Griffin, Spalding County, Georgia. February 3, 1862 sent to Moore Hospital at Danville, Virginia. February 1862 roll shows he was sent to Moore Hospital on February 9. May 8, 1862 died near Richmond, Virginia. September 9, 1862 death benefit claim was filed by T (J) E. Nash, father. September 22, 1863 death benefit claim paid $71.43 (#4871). He was born in Henry County, Georgia.

NASH, JOHN PLEASANT SHAW: Company H, sergeant. May 13, 1862 enlisted in Co. H, 27th Regiment, Georgia Infantry at Richmond, Virginia. June 30, 1862 received pay. July 2, 1862 admitted to C. S. A. General Military Hospital at Danville, Virginia with Debilitas. August 1, 1862 returned to duty. August 29, 1862 admitted to Camp Winder Division Hospital at Richmond, Virginia with Remittent Fever. September 2, 1862 returned to duty. September 6, 1862 admitted to Chimborazo Hospital No. 1 at Richmond, Virginia with Remittent Fever. September 18, 1862 returned to duty. October 4, 1862 admitted with Remittent Fever to Confederate Hospital at Culpepper, Virginia. October 31, 1862 roll of General Hospital No. 11 at Richmond, Virginia shows him present. November 6, 1862 admitted to General Hospital No. 11 at Richmond, Virginia. November 22, 1862 admitted to Chimborazo Hospital No. 4 at Richmond, Virginia with Debility. December 1862 roll shows him absent with leave. April 27, 1863 returned to duty from Chimborazo Hospital No. 4 at Richmond, Virginia. He was elected 4th corporal of Co. H, 27th Regiment, Georgia Infantry. December 31, 1863 received pay. January – February 1864 roll shows him present. March - April 1864 roll shows him absent with leave. March 19, 1865 wounded in hip at Bentonville, North Carolina. May 1, 1865 paroled at General Hospital at Thomasville, North Carolina. He was born in Georgia.

NASH, JAMES HAMBREE: Company H, private. September 9, 1861 enlisted as a private in Co. H, 27th Regiment, Georgia Infantry at Camp Stephens, Griffin, Spalding County, Georgia. January 25, 1862 admitted to Moore Hospital at General Hospital, No. 1 at Danville, Virginia with Pneumonia and sent to Jackson Hospital. June 25, 1862 admitted to Episcopal Church Hospital at Williamsburg, Virginia with Fistula. August 19, 1862 returned to duty. August 22, 1862 discharged, furnished substitute. He was born in Georgia.

NASH, JOHN ADAM: Company H, private. September 9, 1861 enlisted as a private in Co. H, 27th Regiment, Georgia Infantry at Camp Stephens, Griffin, Spalding County, Georgia. January 25, 1862 admitted to Mt. Jackson Hospital at Mt. Jackson, Virginia. January and February 1862 rolls show him in hospital at Mt. Jackson since January 25, 1862. July 12, 1862 received pay ($91.00). August 25, 1862 received pay ($22.00). August 30, 1862 admitted to Camp Winder Division Hospital at Richmond, Virginia with Rheumatism. September 30, 1862 returned to duty from Camp Winder Division No. 2 Hospital at Richmond, Virginia. February 3, 1863 furloughed for 30 days. March 23, 1863 received pay ($22.00). April 4, 1863 received $9.90 in commutation for rations while on furlough. December 31, 1863 received pay. January – February 1864 roll shows him present. February 29, 1864 received pay. March - April 1864 roll shows him present. June 18, 1864 wounded in the neck by a mini ball at Colquitt's Salient near Petersburg, Virginia. June 20, 1864 admitted to Jackson Hospital at Richmond, Virginia with a Vulnus Sclopeticum (Gunshot Wound) to the neck. August 29, 1864 issued clothing at Jackson Hospital, Richmond, Virginia. August 31, 1864 returned to duty from Jackson Hospital at Richmond, Virginia and received pay ($22.00). September 20, 1864 issued clothing. October 3, 1864 admitted to Receiving and Wayside Hospital or General Hospital No. 9 at Richmond, Virginia with a mini ball wound in the left leg (left arm) and sent to Jackson Hospital at Richmond, Virginia. January 20, 1864 returned to duty. April 26, 1865 surrendered Greensboro, North Carolina. May 1, 1865 paroled at Greensboro, North Carolina.

NASH, Q. L.: Company H, private. September 1, 1863 enlisted as a private in Co. H, 27th Regiment, Georgia Infantry at McDonough, Georgia. December 31, 1863 received pay. January – February 1864 roll shows him present. March - April 1864 roll shows him present. July 1864 issued clothing. August 18, 1864 admitted to Jackson Hospital at Richmond, Virginia with Jaundice. October 3, 1864 returned to duty. April 26, 1865 surrendered Greensboro, North Carolina. May 1, 1865 paroled at Greensboro, North Carolina. He was born in New Bern, North Carolina in 1844.

NEELEY, ANDREW J.: Company C, private. He enlisted as a private in Co. C, 27th Regiment, Georgia Infantry. December 29, 1861 died. September 27, 1862 death benefit claim was filed by his mother, Mary Neeley.

NELSON, WILLIAM: Company E, private. September 9, 1861 enlisted as a private in Co. E, 27th Regiment, Georgia Infantry at Camp Stephens, Griffin, Spalding County, Georgia. June 6, 1862 admitted to General Hospital at Farmville, Virginia with Remitting Fever (Malaria). August 14, 1862 returned to duty. August 16, 1862 received pay ($69.00). September 26, 1862 admitted to General Hospital No. 20 at Richmond, Virginia. October 23, 1862 died of disease in hospital. December 1862 roll shows him in the hospital.

NELSON, WILLIAM H.: Company I, private. September 10, 1861 enlisted as a private in Co. I, 27th Regiment, Georgia Infantry at Camp Stephens, Griffin, Spalding County, Georgia. June 16 and June 27, 1863 issued clothing. December 31, 1863 received pay. January – February 1864 roll shows him present. February 29, 1864 received pay. March - April 1864 roll shows him present. June 20, 1864 wounded in the head at Colquitt's Salient near Petersburg, Virginia. June 26, 1864 died of wounds at Confederate States Hospital at Petersburg, Virginia. October 22, 1864 death benefit claim was filed by his father, William A. Nelson. Shown in death record as being 23 years of age and was a farmer and being in possession of $11.15.

NELSON, WILLIAM M.: Company E, private. September 9, 1861 enlisted as a private in Co. E, 27th Regiment, Georgia Infantry at Camp Stephens, Griffin, Spalding County, Georgia. September 17, 1862 killed at Sharpsburg, Maryland.

NEWBERRY, B. F.: Company C, private. March 15, 1862 enlisted as a private in Co. C, 27th Regiment, Georgia Infantry in Knoxville, Georgia. June 27, 1862 admitted to Chimborazo Hospital No. 5 at Richmond, Virginia with Congestive Fever (Malaria). July 5, 1862 transferred to C. S. A. General Hospital at Farmville, Virginia. July 6, 1862 admitted to C. S. A. General Hospital at Farmville, Virginia with Ascites. August 2, 1862 returned to duty from C. S. A. General Hospital at Farmville, Virginia. May 9, 1863 admitted to C. S. A. General Hospital at Charlottesville, Virginia with Hydrothroax (dropsy in the chest). June 11, 1863 returned to duty. June 27, 1863 issued clothing. June 30, 1863 received pay and issued clothing. July 5, 1862 transferred from Chimborazo Hospital No. 5 at Richmond, Virginia to either Farmville, Danville or Lynchburg hospital. September 30, 1863 issued clothing. January – February 1864 roll shows him present. March 5, 1864 issued clothing at Camp Milton, Florida. March - April 1864 roll shows him present. June 21, 1864 admitted to Receiving and Wayside Hospital or General Hospital No. 9 at Richmond, Virginia. June 2, 1864 admitted to Receiving and Wayside Hospital or General Hospital No. 9 at Richmond, Virginia. June 2, 1864 admitted to Jackson Hospital at Richmond, Virginia with a Vulnus Sclopeticum (Gunshot Wound) (mini ball). June 9, 1864 roll of Jackson Hospital, Richmond, Virginia shows he deserted. June 22, 1864 transferred to Jackson Hospital at Richmond, Virginia. August 27, 1864 admitted to Ocmulgee Hospital at Macon, Georgia with Rubeola. October 1864 pension records show he was wounded this month. Continuingracted Rheumatism in service and was home on furlough at the close of the war. He was born in Crawford County, Georgia in 1843.

NEWBERRY, COLUMBUS M.: Company C, lieutenant. September 10, 1861 enlisted as a private in Co. C, 27th Regiment, Georgia Infantry at Camp Stephens, Griffin, Spalding County, Georgia. February 12, 1863 elected Jr. 2nd lieutenant Co. C, 27th Regiment, Georgia Infantry. July 11, 1864 promoted to 2nd lieutenant Co. C, 27th Regiment, Georgia Infantry. September 30, 1863 he is shown on roll of officers of Colquitt's Brigade. December 31, 1863 received pay. January – February 1864 roll shows

him present. March - April 1864 roll shows him present. August 28, 1864 received pay ($160.00). November 1864 appears on roster for this month.
NEWBERRY, J. HENRY: Company C, private. September 10, 1861 enlisted as a private in Co. C, 27th Regiment, Georgia Infantry at Camp Stephens, Griffin, Spalding County, Georgia. November 4, 1863 paid commutation of rations for July 24, 1863 to October 27, 1863. November 25, 1863 detailed mechanic at Selma, Alabama. January – February 1864 roll shows him absent on detached service in Selma, Alabama. March - April 1864 roll shows him present. June 18, 1864 wounded in the right arm and sub clavicula region at Colquitt's Salient near Petersburg, Virginia. July 1864 issued clothing. August 5, 1864 furloughed.
NEWTON, D. JEEPTHA: Company F, sergeant. September 9, 1861 enlisted as a private in Co. F, 27th Regiment, Georgia Infantry at Camp Stephens, Griffin, Spalding County, Georgia. December 31, 1863 received pay. January – February 1864 roll shows him present. March - April 1864 roll shows him present. June 30, 1864 roll at Jackson Hospital at Richmond, Virginia shows him present. July and August 1863 issued clothing. June 30, 1864 wounded in the left arm at Colquitt's Salient near Petersburg, Virginia. July 1, 1864 admitted to Jackson Hospital at Richmond, Virginia wounded in the left arm result was that left arm was amputated. July 27, 1864 issued clothing at Jackson Hospital at Richmond, Virginia. July 28, 1864 furloughed for 60 days. He is shown in Richmond, Virginia hospital at the close of the war. He was born in Georgia August 19, 1844.
NEWTON, WILLIAM J.: Company F, corporal. September 9, 1861 enlisted as a private in Co. F, 27th Regiment, Georgia Infantry at Camp Stephens, Griffin, Spalding County, Georgia. January 7, 1862 admitted to Moore Hospital at General Hospital, No. 1 at Danville, Virginia with Diarrhoea and was sent to 9th ward. January and February 1862 rolls show him in Moore Hospital at General Hospital, No. 1 at Danville, Virginia since January 7, 1862. April 30, 1862 received pay. May 8, 1862 admitted to Chimborazo Hospital No. 2 at Richmond, Virginia. May 11, 1862 returned to duty. August 18, 1862 discharged due to disability. Discharge record shows he was born in Crawford County, Georgia and was 5 feet 11 inches high with dark complexion, black eyes and black hair and was a farmer. Disability was Bronchitis, General Debility and Chronic Diarrhoea. August 18, 1862 received pay ($39.00).
NIX, G. W. S.: Company I, private. September 10, 1861 enlisted as a private in Co. I, 27th Regiment, Georgia Infantry at Camp Stephens, Griffin, Spalding County, Georgia. December 26, 1861 died of Pneumonia at Moore Hospital at General Hospital, No. 1, Danville, Virginia. December 1861 roll shows he died December 26, 1861 of disease.
NOLAN (NOLAND) (NOLEN), M. L.: Company H, private. He enlisted as a private in Co. H, 27th Regiment, Georgia Infantry. June 6, 1864 wounded at Cold Harbor, Virginia. June 3, 1864 admitted to Receiving and Wayside Hospital or General Hospital No. 9 at Richmond, Virginia. June

3, 1864 transferred to Jackson Hospital at Richmond, Virginia.

NOLAN, W. CALLAWAY: Company H, sergeant. September 9, 1861 elected 4th sergeant of Co. H, 27th Regiment, Georgia Infantry at Camp Stephens, Griffin, Spalding County, Georgia. July 3, 1862 received pay ($78.00). February 2, 1863 furloughed for 30 days. March 22, 1863 received $10.00 commutation of rations. December 31, 1863 received pay. January – February 1864 roll shows him present. March - April 1864 roll shows him present. June 6, 1864 wounded at Cold Harbor, Virginia. June 7, 1864 admitted to Receiving and Wayside Hospital or General Hospital No. 9 at Richmond, Virginia. June 7, 1864 transferred to Jackson Hospital at Richmond, Virginia. June 7, 1864 admitted to Jackson Hospital at Richmond, Virginia with a Vulnus Sclopeticum (Gunshot Wound) to the left hip (mini ball). June 12, 1864 died in Jackson Hospital at Richmond, Virginia of a Vulnus Sclopeticum (Gunshot Wound) to the thigh. He is buried in Hollywood Cemetery at Richmond, Virginia.

NORMAN, D.: Company C, private. He enlisted as a private in Co. C, 27th Regiment, Georgia Infantry. December 23, 1861 admitted to Moore Hospital at General Hospital, No. 1 at Danville, Virginia with Debility.

NORRIS, BENJAMIN F.: Company H, private. January 25, 1862 enlisted as a private in Co. H, 27th Regiment, Georgia Infantry at Manassas, Virginia. January 1862 roll shows he was received as a substitute on January 27, 1862. March 10, 1862 admitted to C. S. A. General Hospital at Charlottesville, Virginia with acute Bronchitis. May 22, 1862 returned to duty. August 29, 1862 admitted to Camp Winder Division Hospital at Richmond, Virginia with Diarrhoea. September 17, 1862 admitted to Chimborazo Hospital No. 5 at Richmond, Virginia with Diarrhoea. November 7, 1862 furloughed for 60 days from Chimborazo Hospital No. 5 at Richmond, Virginia. December 1862 roll shows him absent without leave. December 31, 1863 received pay. January – February 1864 roll shows him present. March - April 1864 roll shows him present. July 1864 issued clothing. August 19, 1864 captured at Weldon Railroad, Virginia. August 24, 1864 arrived at point Lookout, Maryland from City Point, Virginia. March 15, 1865 paroled at Point Lookout, Maryland and transferred to Aiken's Landing, Virginia. March 18, 1865 received at Boulware and Cox's Wharves, James River, Virginia.

NORRIS, HENRY F.: Company E, private. February 1, 1864 enlisted as a private in Co. E, 27th Regiment, Georgia Infantry in Charleston, South Carolina. January – February 1864 roll shows him present and due $50.00 bounty. March - April 1864 roll shows him present. May 30, 1864 issued clothing. June 1, 1864 killed at Cold Harbor, Virginia.

NORRIS (MORRIS), THOMAS S.: Company F, private. September 9, 1861 enlisted as a private in Co. F, 27th Regiment, Georgia Infantry at Camp Stephens, Griffin, Spalding County, Georgia. December 1861 and January 1862 rolls show he was left in Georgia sick on October 31, 1861. April 10, 1862 admitted to Chimborazo Hospital No. 5 at Richmond,

Virginia with Remitting Fever (Malaria). May 4, 1862 sent to Camp Winder Division Hospital Richmond, Virginia. May 16, 1862 returned to duty. May 5, 1863 wounded severely at Chancellorsville, Virginia. August 1863 issued clothing. December 31, 1863 received pay. January 2, 1864 to January 31, 1864 detailed as an oarsman at Fort Johnson, South Carolina. February 7, 1864 paid $.25 per day extra for duty as an oarsman. February 20, 1864 wounded at Olustee, Florida. January – February 1864 roll shows him present. February 29, 1864 received pay. March - April 1864 roll shows him present. July 1864 issued clothing. August 19, 1864 captured at Weldon Railroad, Virginia. August 24, 1864 received at Point Lookout, Maryland from City Point, Virginia. March 14, 1865 transferred to Aiken's Landing, Virginia. March 16, 1865 received at Boulward and Cox's Wharves, James River, Virginia for exchange. May 19, 1865 paroled at Headquarters, 16th Army Corps at Montgomery, Alabama.

NORTON, J. L.: Company E, private. September 9, 1861 enlisted as a private in Co. E, 27th Regiment, Georgia Infantry at Camp Stephens, Griffin, Spalding County, Georgia.

NORTON, WILLIAM H.: Company E, private. September 9, 1861 enlisted as a private in Co. E, 27th Regiment, Georgia Infantry at Camp Stephens, Griffin, Spalding County, Georgia. June 30, 1862 admitted to General Hospital Camp Winder Hospital at Richmond, Virginia with Typhoid Fever. July 24, 1862 transferred to Lynchburg. December 31, 1863 received pay. February 20, 1864 wounded at Olustee, Florida. January – February 1864 roll shows him present. February 29, 1864 received pay. March - April 1864 roll shows him present. September 20, 1864 issued clothing. April 26, 1865 surrendered Greensboro, North Carolina. May 1, 1865 paroled at Greensboro, North Carolina.

O'CONNER, P. F.: Company I, private. September 10, 1861 enlisted as a private in Co. I, 27th Regiment, Georgia Infantry at Camp Stephens, Griffin, Spalding County, Georgia. February 20, 1864 was missing at Savannah, Georgia (Olustee, Florida?).

ODOM, SAMUEL G. B.: Company B, lieutenant. September 10, 1861 enlisted and elected 2nd sergeant in Co. B, 27th Regiment, Georgia Infantry at Camp Stephens, Griffin, Spalding County, Georgia. December 1861 roll shows him in the hospital in Richmond, Virginia since November 10, 1861. January 1862 roll shows him absent without leave since December 22, 1861. June 10, 1862 elected 2nd lieutenant in Co. B, 27th Regiment, Georgia Infantry. June 27, 1862 killed at Cold Harbor, Virginia. December 24, 1863 death benefit claim was filed by Martha J. Odom, administrator. September 24, 1863 death benefit claim paid $213.10 (#8995).

O'HERN (OHEARN), JOHN C.: Company F, private. September 9, 1861 enlisted as a private in Co. F, 27th Regiment, Georgia Infantry at Camp Stephens, Griffin, Spalding County, Georgia. December 1861 and January 1862 rolls show he was left in Georgia sick on October 31, 1861. March 20, 1862 admitted to Chimborazo Hospital No. 2 at Richmond,

Virginia with Bronchitis. May 9, 1862 transferred to Lynchburg, Virginia. June 30, 1862 wounded in leg at White Oak Swamp, Virginia. July 1, 1862 wounded at Malvern Hill, Virginia. July and August 1863 issued clothing. December 31, 1863 received pay. January 11, 1864 on detached duty at Fort Sumter, South Carolina as a carpenter. January – February 1864 roll shows him on detached service. March 1, 1864 to May 5, 1864 on detached duty as a carpenter at Fort Sumter, South Carolina. May 8, 1864 ordered to return to company. March - April 1864 roll shows him absent on detached duty. July 1864 and September 20, 1864 issued clothing. He was born in Twiggs, County, Georgia April 5, 1834.

ORR, MATTHEW: Company H, private. September 9, 1861 enlisted as a private in Co. H, 27th Regiment, Georgia Infantry at Camp Stephens, Griffin, Spalding County, Georgia. December 12, 1861 discharged due to disability, at Camp Pickens near Manassas, Virginia. December 1861 roll shows he was discharged due to disability on December 12, 1861. He is shown on disability certificate as being twenty-six years of age, six feet one inch high, fair complexion, black eyes and black hair and was a mechanic by occupation. He was a resident of Henry County, Georgia.

OWEN, DANIEL A.: Company K, private. June 23, 1863 enlisted as a private in Co. B, 27th Battalion, Georgia Infantry (non-conscripts) at Camp Howard, Columbus, Georgia. December 31, 1863 received pay. March 15, 1864 transferred as a private to Co. K, 27th Regiment Georgia Infantry. March - April 1864 roll shows him present. July 1864 issued clothing. September 12, 1864 was in Camp Winder Hospital at Richmond, Virginia. September 17, 1864 furloughed from Richmond, Virginia for Geneva, Georgia. January 28, 1865 admitted to Lee Hospital at Columbus, Georgia. January 31, 1865 returned to duty. October 1864 pension records show he was sent to hospital with Chronic Diarrhoea. He was in the hospital at Columbus, Georgia at the close of the war. He was born in Georgia June 9, 1845.

OWEN, J. N.: private. He enlisted as a private in the 27th Regiment, Georgia Infantry.
September 28, 1862 Sixth Corps Headquarters note 'Found sick near Urbana and left where found."

OWEN, JAMES L.: Company B, private. September 10, 1861 enlisted as a private in Co. B, 27th Regiment, Georgia Infantry at Camp Stephens, Griffin, Spalding County, Georgia. September 1, 1862 received pay ($60.00). September 7, 1862 died of Fever in General Hospital No.14 at Richmond, Virginia.

PAGE, JOHN M.: Company B, private. September 10, 1861 enlisted as a private in Co. B, 27th Regiment, Georgia Infantry at Camp Stephens, Griffin, Spalding County, Georgia. March 31, 1862 received pay. September 28, 1862 admitted to General Hospital No. 21 at Richmond, Virginia with a Vulnus Sclopeticum (Gunshot Wound). October 11, 1862 shown on roll of General Hospital No. 21 at Richmond, Virginia.

October 13, 1862 furloughed for 60 days (age shown as 33). December 1862 roll shows that his furlough had expired and he was absent without leave. October, November and December 1863 issued clothing. December 31, 1863 received pay. January – February 1864 roll shows him present. March - April 1864 roll shows him present. May 17, 1863 paid $26.00 in commutation or rations. July 1864 issued clothing. August 19, 1864 wounded and captured, Weldon Railroad, Virginia. September 16, 1864 right thigh amputated and he died from effects of the operation, in Carver U. S. A. Hospital, at Washington, D.C. He was buried in Arlington, Virginia Cemetery. In his possession at the time of death effects were 1 wallet and 1 lock of hair.

PAGE, WILLIAM H.: Company C, private. September 10, 1861 enlisted as a private in Co. C, 27th Regiment, Georgia Infantry at Camp Stephens, Griffin, Spalding County, Georgia. November 3 (4), 1861 died of Pneumonia at Camp Stephens, Georgia.

PARKER, CHRISTOPHER C.: Field Staff, sergeant major. September 1861 enlisted as a private in Co. G, 27th Regiment Georgia Infantry at Camp Stephens, Griffin, Spalding County, Georgia. September 5, 1861 appointed sergeant major of the 27th Regiment Georgia Infantry at Camp Stephens, Griffin, Spalding County, Georgia. May 10, 1862 furloughed home for 30 days due to Chronic Diarrhoea "at the end of which time he will report to General Winder". December 1862 roll shows him absent without leave.

PARKER, G. B.: Company B, private. He enlisted as a private in Co. B, 27th Regiment, Georgia Infantry. July 14, 1862 died in Chimborazo Hospital No. 2 at Richmond, Virginia of Remitting Fever (Malaria). He is most likely buried in Oakwood Cemetery at Richmond Virginia.

PARKER, J. J.: Company E, private. March 8, 1864 enlisted as a private in Co. E, 27th Regiment, Georgia Infantry at Decatur, Georgia. March - April 1864 roll shows him present. September 20, 1864 issued clothing. February 21, 1865 admitted to C. S. A. General Hospital, No. 3 at Greensboro, North Carolina with Rubeola. His Post Office is shown as Fairburn, Georgia. February 23, 1865 transferred to other hospital (note indicates he was transferred there from Wilmington, North Carolina.)

PARKER, JOSHUA: Company G, private. September 10, 1861 enlisted as a private in Co. G, 27th Regiment, Georgia Infantry at Camp Stephens, Griffin, Spalding County, Georgia. November 23, 1861 died of disease at Richmond, Virginia. December 1861 roll shows his death on November 23, 1861 in Richmond, Virginia.

PARKER, JOSIAH BUNKLEY: Company K, lieutenant. September 10, 1861 elected 2nd sergeant of Co. K, 27th Regiment, Georgia Infantry at Camp Stephens, Griffin, Spalding County, Georgia. January 16, 1862 admitted to Moore Hospital at General Hospital, No. 1 at Danville, Virginia with Fever and was sent to Ward #8. January 1862 roll shows him in Moore Hospital at General Hospital, No. 1 at Danville, Virginia since

January 16, 1862. December 1862 roll shows him detailed as a teamster. June 1863 issued clothing. He was recognized in Major James Gardner's report of "Men for Gallantry". August 23, 1863 received pay for extra duty as ambulance driver at a rate of $.25 per day from January1, 1863 to March 31, 1863. October 29, 1863 issued clothing and furloughed. November 21, 1863 received $6.60 in commutation of rations. December 31, 1863 received pay. March - April 1864 roll shows him present. July 1864 issued clothing. September 14, 1864 elected 2nd lieutenant of Co. K, 27th Regiment, Georgia Infantry. April 26, 1865 surrendered Greensboro, North Carolina. May 1, 1865 paroled at Greensboro, North Carolina. He was born in Talbot County, Georgia July 1844.

PARKER, WADE: Company D, private. September 23, 1861 enlisted as a private in Co. D, 27th Regiment, Georgia Infantry. February 1862 roll shows him detailed as the regimental teamster. December 1862 roll shows him detailed as a teamster. April, May, June and December 1863 issued clothing. August 1, 1863 detailed as a teamster in South Carolina. August 18, 1863 received $6.66 2/3 in commutation of rations. October 30, 1863 detailed as Quarter Masters Department on James Island, South Carolina as a teamster by order of Colonel Zachry. November 1, 1863 to December 31, 1863 detailed as a teamster on James Island, South Carolina. January 1, 1864 to January 31, 1864 detailed as a teamster at Fort Johnson, South Carolina. February 1, 1864 through June 9, 1864 detailed as a teamster in South Carolina, Florida and at Petersburg, Virginia at a rate of $.25 per day extra. February 29, 1864 received pay. March - April 1864 roll shows him present detailed as a teamster. July 1864 issued clothing. November 5, 1864 discharged by reason of expiration of term of service. November 8, 1864 received pay ($60.37). Discharge certification states he was born in the Abbeville District, South Carolina, age 51 years, 5 feet 9 inches high, red complexion, blue eyes and sandy hair. He was by occupation a farmer.

PARKER, WILLIAM: Company B, private. September 10, 1861 enlisted as a private in Co. B, 27th Regiment, Georgia Infantry at Camp Stephens, Griffin, Spalding County, Georgia. August 27, 1862 received pay ($85.00). November 6, 1862 admitted to General Hospital at Petersburg, Georgia with Rubeola. December 17, 1862 returned to duty. June 10, 1863 furloughed for 20 days. August 7, 1863 received $6.60 in pay for commutation of rations while on furlough. October, November and December 1863 issued clothing. December 31, 1863 received pay. February 20, 1864 wounded severely at Olustee, Florida. February 28, 1864 died of wounds. He had $1.40 in his possession at time of death. January – February 1864 roll shows he died of wounds February 28, 1864.

PARKER, WILLIAM: Company K, private. September 9, 1861 enlisted as a private in Co. K, 27th Regiment, Georgia Infantry at Camp Stephens, Griffin, Spalding County, Georgia. November 7, 1861 died of Pneumonia at Raleigh, North Carolina. December 1861 roll shows he died on November

7, 1861 at Raleigh, North Carolina.

PARKER, WILLIAM J.: Company D, private. February 28, 1862 enlisted as a private in Co. D, 27th Regiment, Georgia Infantry. April, May, June and December 1863 issued clothing. March 22, 1865 captured, Bentonville, North Carolina. April 10, 1865 received at Hat's Island, New York Harbor from New Bern, North Carolina. June 15, 1865 took Oath of Allegiance. June 18, 1865 released at Hart's Island, New York Harbor. Parole describes him as being a resident of Hall County, Georgia, fair complexion, light hair, gray eyes and 5 foot 7 1/2 inches high.

PARKS, JAMES MONROE: Company F, private. September 9, 1861 enlisted as a private in Co. F, 27th Regiment, Georgia Infantry at Camp Stephens, Griffin, Spalding County, Georgia. January 20, 1862 admitted to Moore Hospital at General Hospital, No. 1 at Danville, Virginia with Pneumonia and was sent to Ward #8. January and February 1862 rolls show he was in Moore Hospital. May 31, 1862 wounded, Seven Pines, Virginia. May 31, 1862 the following remarks appearing relative to him "wounded in chest and hemorrhage of lungs". July 29, 1864 detailed nurse at Jackson Hospital at Richmond, Virginia.

PARKS, WALTER: Company C, private. September 9, 1861 enlisted as a private in Co. C, 27th Regiment, Georgia Infantry at Camp Stephens, Griffin, Spalding County, Georgia. December 4, 1861 discharged due to disability, Camp Pickens near Manassas, Virginia. December 6, 1862 received pay.

PARKS, WALTER: Company G, private. September 9, 1861 enlisted as a private in Co. G, 27th Regiment, Georgia Infantry at Camp Stephens, Griffin, Spalding County, Georgia. October 28, 1861 transferred to Co. G, 27th Regiment, Georgia Infantry.

PARKS, WILLIAM HENRY: Company F, private. September 9, 1861 enlisted as a private in Co. F, 27th Regiment, Georgia Infantry at Camp Stephens, Griffin, Spalding County, Georgia. May 31, 1862 wounded in the chest at Seven Pines, Virginia. He was detailed by General Lee to Camp Winder Hospital at Richmond, Virginia. September 20, 1862 received pay ($113.00). December 1862 roll shows him absent sick since June 3, 1862. June 26, 1862 - April 30, 1864 was on detached duty in Georgia. March 15, 1863 transferred from Receiving and Wayside Hospital or General Hospital No. 9 at Richmond, Virginia to General Hospital No. 1. March 30, 1863 appears on roll of Camp Winder Division No. 5 Hospital at Richmond, Virginia. April 4, 1863 admitted to Camp Winder Division No. 2 Hospital at Richmond, Virginia with a Vulnus Sclopeticum (Gunshot Wound). May 7, 1863 furloughed for 30 days. October 14, 1863 received pay ($44.00). November 28, 1863 admitted from Charleston, South Carolina to Floyd House and Ocmulgee Hospitals at Macon Georgia with a Vulnus Sclopeticum (Gunshot Wound) to the breast. (His home was Butler, Georgia). November 28, 1863 received pay ($22.00). January – February 1864 roll shows him sick in the Hospital at Macon, Georgia. March - April

1864 roll shows him on detached duty in Georgia since June 26, 1862. June 1, 1864 wounded Cold Harbor, Virginia. June 2, 1864 admitted to Receiving and Wayside Hospital or General Hospital No. 9 at Richmond, Virginia. June 2, 1864 admitted to Jackson Hospital at Richmond, Virginia with Vulnus Sclopeticum (Gunshot Wound) to the breast (mini ball). June 21, 1864 admitted to Receiving and Wayside Hospital or General Hospital No. 9 at Richmond, Virginia. June 22, 1864 transferred to Jackson Hospital at Richmond, Virginia. July 29, 1864 admitted to Jackson Hospital at Richmond, Virginia with old Vulnus Sclopeticum (Gunshot Wound) from May 31, 1862 and hemorrhaging from the lungs detailed as a nurse. August 1, 1864 issued clothing at Jackson Hospital at Richmond, Virginia. August 18, 1864 issued clothing at Richmond, Virginia. September 7, 1864 detailed as a nurse at Jackson Hospital at Richmond, Virginia. It was stated on report that he had Emphysema of both lungs result of shell wound of chest on May 31, 1862. September 20, 1864 or September 21, 1864 returned to duty. September 21, 1864 wounded near Petersburg, Virginia. September 21, 1864 admitted to Receiving and Wayside Hospital or General Hospital No. 9 at Richmond, Virginia. September 22, 1864 transferred and admitted to Jackson Hospital at Richmond, Virginia with a Vulnus Sclopeticum (Gunshot Wound) to his breast by a mini ball. October 22, 1864 issued clothing a t Jackson Hospital at Richmond, Virginia. October 23, 1864 furloughed for 60 days destination Butler, Georgia.

PATE, FRANCIS MARION: Company E, private. March 1, 1862 enlisted as a private in Co. E, 27th Regiment, Georgia Infantry at Fayetteville, Georgia. May 14, 1862 admitted to Chimborazo Hospital No.1 at Richmond, Virginia with Typhoid Dysentery. July 1, 1862 transferred to Danville, Virginia. July 2, 1862 admitted to C. S. A. General Military Hospital, Danville, Virginia with Nephritis. October 31, 1862 roll of General Hospital No, 14 at Richmond, Virginia shows him present. November 3, 1862 returned to duty. November 6, 1862 admitted to General Hospital No, 14 at Richmond, Virginia. April 6, 1863 died in Richmond, Virginia. February 18, 1864 death benefit claim was filed by his father, Herrod Pate.

PATE, T. G.: Company B, private. September 10, 1861 enlisted as a private in Co. B, 27th Regiment, Georgia Infantry at Camp Stephens, Griffin, Spalding County, Georgia. June 4, 1864 wounded in the right thigh at Cold Harbor, Virginia. June 4, 1864 admitted to Receiving and Wayside Hospital or General Hospital No. 9 at Richmond, Virginia and transferred to Jackson Hospital at Richmond, Virginia. June 6, 1864 admitted to Jackson Hospital at Richmond, Virginia with a Vulnus Sclopeticum (Gunshot Wound) to the right thigh (mini ball). June 25, 1864 died in Division No.1 Jackson Hospital at Richmond, Virginia. His effects were: 1 blanket, 1 coat, 1 pr. socks, 1 shirt, 1 jacket, 1blanket, 1 cap and 1 pr. of shoes worth $19.25. He is buried in Hollywood Cemetery at Richmond, Virginia.

PATTILLO, GEORGE HENRY: Field Staff, Chaplin. October 10, 1861 appointed Chaplin 27th Georgia Infantry. November 1861 resigned as Chaplin 27th Georgia Infantry.

PATTON (PATTEN), ROBERT: Company A, captain. June 10, 1862 elected 2nd lieutenant Co. A, 27th Regiment, Georgia Infantry. December 1, 1861, January and February 1862 rolls show him present at Camp Pickens near Manassas, Virginia. March 3, 1862 received pay ($160.00). April 22, 1862 received 20 days furlough due to illness. June 10, 1862 promoted to 1st lieutenant Co. A, 27th Regiment, Georgia Infantry. July 7, 1862 received pay ($240.00). August 2, 1862 received pay ($90.00). October 2, 1862 admitted to General Hospital No. 16 at Richmond, Virginia. December 19, 1862 received pay ($157.34). December 1862 roll shows him absent sick since December 28, 1862 from near Guinea Station, Virginia. February 3, 1863 issued clothing. April 20, 1863 paid $13.00 for commutation of rations. July 20, 1863 elected captain Co. A, 27th Regiment, Georgia Infantry. December 1863 issued clothing. February 20, 1864 wounded at Olustee, Florida. January – February 1864 roll shows him absent with leave since February 20, 1864. June 16, 1864 captured at Petersburg, Virginia. June 25, 1864 received at Ft. Delaware, Delaware from City Point, Virginia. August 1864 report of commissioned officers of Colquitt's Brigade shows him missing in action. October 21, 1864 received at Point Lookout, Maryland from Ft. Delaware, Delaware. October 31, 1864 exchanged. November 15, 1864 received at Venus Point, Savannah. April 26, 1865 surrendered at Greensboro, North Carolina. May 1, 1865 paroled at Greensboro, North Carolina.

PEACOCK, KINCHIN: Company F, private. September 9, 1861 enlisted as a private in Co. F, 27th Regiment, Georgia Infantry at Camp Stephens, Griffin, Spalding County, Georgia. January 15, 1861 admitted to Moore Hospital at Danville, Virginia and transferred to Mount Jackson. January 1862 roll shows he was in Moore Hospital at Danville, Virginia since January 15, 1861. April 14, 1862 admitted to General Hospital No.21 at Richmond, Virginia with Typhoid Fever. April 27, 1862 died in General Hospital No.21 at in Richmond, Virginia. February 20, 1863 death benefit claim was filed by Martha Peacock, his widow. He was resident of Taylor County, Georgia.

PEACOCK, MOLTON A.: Company F, private. September 9, 1861 enlisted as a private in Co. F, 27th Regiment, Georgia Infantry. November 30, 1861 died of Pneumonia at General Hospital at Manassas, Virginia. December 1861 roll shows he died of disease on November 30, 1861 at Camp Pickens near Manassas, Virginia. March 15, 1862 death benefit claim was filed by Asa Peacock. October 28, 1863 death benefit claim paid $105.00 (#9103).

PEACOCK, R.: Company D, private. September 10, 1861 enlisted as a private in Co. D, 27th Regiment, Georgia Infantry at Camp Stephens, Griffin, Spalding County, Georgia. April 28, 1862 died at Richmond, Virginia. He is buried in Hollywood Cemetery, Richmond, Virginia.

PEAVY, JOSEPH F.: Company B, private. September 10, 1861 enlisted as a private in Co. B, 27th Regiment, Georgia Infantry at Camp Stephens, Griffin, Spalding County, Georgia. December 1862 roll shows him present and he was the regimental teamster. January 1, 1863 - May 24, 1863 detailed as teamster. May 19, 1863 received $10.00 in commutation of rations. August 20, 1863 received pay (at a rate of $.25 per day) as teamster. August 1, 1863 – September 30, 1863 detailed as teamster at James Island, South Carolina. October, November and December 1863 issued clothing. October 11 – December 31, 1863 detailed as a teamster on James Island, South Carolina (absent on furlough for 8 days in December). December 31, 1863 received pay plus $.25 per day additional as teamster from August 1, 1863 through November 20, 1863. January 1, 1864 – February 29, 1864 detailed as a teamster on James Island, South Carolina. January – February 1864 roll shows him present detailed as a teamster. February 29, 1864 received pay. March 1, 1864 – March 31, 1864 detailed as a teamster at Camp Milton, Florida. March - April 1864 roll shows him present detailed as a teamster. July 1864 issued clothing. April 26, 1865 surrendered Greensboro, North Carolina. May 1, 1865 paroled at Greensboro, North Carolina.

PEEDE, URIAH: Company A, private. He enlisted as a private in Co. A, 27th Regiment, Georgia Infantry. December 10, 1862 died in the Hospital. April 15, 1863 death benefit claim was filed by his father, William Peede.

PEEK, AUGUSTUS J. W.: Company H, private. September 9, 1861 enlisted as a private in Co. H, 27th Regiment, Georgia Infantry at Camp Stephens, Griffin, Spalding County, Georgia. September 17, 1862 captured at Sharpsburg, Maryland. October 10, 1862 admitted to U. S. A. General Hospital No. 5 at Frederick, Maryland and sent to General Hospital on October 11, 1862. October 13, 1862 paroled and sent from Fort McHenry, Maryland to Fort Monroe, Virginia for exchange. October 20, 1862 admitted to Chimborazo Hospital No. 4 at Richmond, Virginia with a Vulnus Slopeticum (Gunshot Wound). November 2, 1862 furloughed for 25 days. March 12, 1863 received $4.64 in commutations of rations. December 31, 1863 received pay. February 20, 1864 wounded at Olustee, Florida. January – February 1864 and March - April 1864 rolls show him present. June 1, 1864 wounded at Cold Harbor, Virginia. June 3, 1864 admitted to Receiving and Wayside Hospital or General Hospital No. 9 at Richmond, Virginia and transferred to Jackson hospital at Richmond, Virginia. June 7, 1864 admitted to Jackson Hospital at Richmond, Virginia with a Vulnus Slopeticum (Gunshot Wound) to the bowels by a mini ball. August 10, 1864 furloughed for 30 days, on account of wounds. November 22, 1864 issued clothing. He was born in Georgia June 22, 1844.

PENLEY (PENDLEY), BENJAMIN F.: Company E, private. September 9, 1861 enlisted as a private in Co. E, 27th Regiment, Georgia Infantry at Camp Stephens, Griffin, Spalding County, Georgia. December 20, 1861 admitted to Moore Hospital at General Hospital, No. 1 at Danville, Virginia with Debilitas. December 1861 roll shows him in the hospital at Mount Jackson, Virginia. January 1, 1862 died of Pneumonia in General Hospital at Mount Jackson, Virginia. January 1862 roll shows he died of disease at General Hospital at Mount Jackson, Virginia. January 1862 roll of General Hospital at Mount Jackson, Virginia shows he died of Pneumonia on January 1, 1862. He is buried in Soldiers Cemetery at Mt. Jackson, Virginia.

PENNINGTON, H.: Company E, private. March 4, 1864 enlisted as a private in Co. E, 27th Regiment, Georgia at Macon, Georgia. July 8, 1864 admitted to Jackson Hospital at Richmond, Virginia wounded in the leg, mouth and wrists with fragments of a shell. July 21, 1861 furloughed for 30 days. July (June) 30, 1864 shown on roll of Second Division, Jackson Hospital at Richmond, Virginia.

PERDUE (PARDUE), G. W.: Company B, private. January 30, 1864 enlisted as a private in Co. B, 27th Regiment, Georgia Infantry at Macon, Bibb County, Georgia. February 20, 1864 killed at Olustee, Florida. January – February 1864 roll shows he was killed in action February 20, 1864 at Olustee, Florida.

PERDUE, JAMES W.: Company B, private. September 10, 1861 enlisted as a private in Co. B, 27th Regiment, Georgia Infantry at Camp Stephens, Griffin, Spalding County, Georgia. June 27, 1862 killed at Cold Harbor, Virginia. September 3, 1862 death benefit claim was filed.

PERDUE, JOHN T.: Company B, private. September 10, 1861 enlisted as a private in Co. B, 27th Regiment, Georgia Infantry at Camp Stephens, Griffin, Spalding County, Georgia. September 17, 1862 killed at Sharpsburg, Maryland. December 1862 roll shows him missing in action since September 17, 1862 at Sharpsburg, Maryland.

PERKLE, ELIJAH L.: Company D, private. July 30, 1862 enlisted as a private in Co. A, 27th Regiment, Georgia Infantry at Camp Randolph in Gordon, County, Georgia. December 1862 roll shows him in the hospital since November. November 13, 1862 died in Fauquier County, Virginia. November 17, 1863 death benefit claim was filed by his widow, Martha Jane Perkle.

PERRY, CHARLES F.: Company D, private. He enlisted as a private in Co. D, 27th Regiment, Georgia Infantry. January 1862 roll shows him present. February 1862 roll shows he was sent to hospital on February 24, 1862. August 1862 he was furloughed. December 1862 roll shows he was furloughed in August. October 10, 1862 furloughed for 60 days. October 13, 1862 received pay ($163.00). March 16, 1863 received $20.00 for commutation of rations. August 18, 1863 at James Island, South Carolina indicated as desiring to leave the artillery (Boman's Light Battery, Chestatee Artillery) and enter into the infantry. Described on document as age 22, 5 foot 9 inches high, black eyes, black hair, dark complexion and by occupation a farmer in Lumpkin County, Georgia. He was born in 1841.

PERRY, JOSEPH: Company A, corporal. September 10, 1861 enlisted as a private in Co. A, 27th Regiment, Georgia Infantry at Camp Stephens, Griffin, Spalding County, Georgia. He was appointed corporal of Co. A, 27th Regiment, Georgia Infantry. November 9, 1861 admitted to General Hospital No. 18 (formerly Greaner's Hospital) at Richmond, Virginia with Typhoid Fever. November 15, 1861 died of Pneumonia, Richmond, Virginia. November 1861 roll shows he died November 15, 1861. December 27, 1862 death benefit claim was filed by his widow, Mary A. Perry.

PERRY, WILLIAM S.: Company A, private. September 10, 1861 enlisted as a private in Co. A, 27th Regiment, Georgia Infantry at Camp Stephens, Griffin, Spalding County, Georgia. August 1, 1862 died of Measles. October 19, 1863 death benefit claim was filed by his widow, Elizabeth Perry. He was a resident of Marion County.

PETERS, ANDREW JACKSON: Company E, private. March 1, 1862 enlisted as a private in Co. E, 27th Regiment, Georgia Infantry. May 15, 1862 admitted to Chimborazo Hospital No.1 at Richmond, Virginia with Dysentery. June 1, 1862 died in Richmond, Virginia. He is most likely buried in Oakwood Cemetery at Richmond Virginia. August 16, 1862 death benefit claim was filed by his widow, Cynthia C. Peters. August 3, 1863 death benefit claim paid $58.36 (#7207). He was a resident of Fayette County, Georgia.

PETERS, HORSEY: Company E, private. March 1, 1862 enlisted as a private in Co. E, 27th Regiment, Georgia Infantry at Fairburn, Georgia. April 30, 1862 received pay. May 15, 1862 admitted to Chimborazo Hospital No. 2 at Richmond, Virginia with Typhoid Fever. May 28, 1862 transferred to Chimborazo Hospital No. 1 at Richmond, Virginia. June 13, 1862 returned to duty. September 17, 1862 wounded and captured at Sharpsburg, Maryland. October 3, 1862 paroled. October 13, 1862 sent from Fort McHenry, Maryland to Fort Monroe, Virginia for exchange. October (November) 10, 1862 exchanged at Aiken's Landing, Virginia. October 24, 1862 admitted to Chimborazo Hospital No. 4 at Richmond, Virginia with wound to shoulder and back. November 14, 1862 furloughed from Chimborazo Hospital No. 4 at Richmond, Virginia for 25 days. December 1862 roll shows him on furlough since November (September – incorrect) 17, 1862. 1864 wounded in arm, necessitating amputation. January – February 1864 roll shows him absent sick in the hospital in Atlanta, Georgia disabled from field service on account of wounds. March – April 1864 roll shows him "detailed with Lee's Crippled Battalion, at Atlanta, Georgia on October 1, 1863".

PETERS, JOHN B.: Company G, private. September 9, 1861 enlisted as a private in Co. G, 27th Regiment, Georgia Infantry at Camp Stephens, Griffin, Spalding County, Georgia. January 16, 1862 admitted to Moore Hospital at General Hospital, No. 1 at Danville, Virginia with Psora (itch) and sent to General Hospital at Front Royal, Virginia. July 1, 1862 wounded and captured at Malvern Hill, near Richmond, Virginia. July 7, 1862 admitted to U. S. Hospital at Portsmouth Grove,

Rhode Island with a Vulnus Sclopeticum (Gunshot Wound). September 18, 1862 Prisoner of War received at Fort Columbus, New York Harbor from U. S. Hospital at Portsmouth Grove, Rhode Island. September 18, 1862 received at Fortress Monroe, Virginia from U. S. Hospital at Portsmouth Grove, Rhode Island. September 22, 1862 paroled at Fort Monroe, Virginia for exchange. October 1, 1862 received pay. November 6, 1862 admitted to General Hospital at Petersburg, Virginia. December 17, 1862 returned to duty. August 17, 1863 through January 31, 1864 detailed as a teamster for the Quartermasters Department at James Island, South Carolina at an additional $.25 per day. September, 1863, October 30, 1863 and November 24, 1863 issued clothing. December 31, 1863 received pay. January – February 1864 roll shows him present. February 29, 1864 received pay. March - April 1864 roll shows him present detailed as a teamster since February 28, 1864. September 20, 1864 received pay through August 31, 1864 as a teamster at an additional $.25 per day ($124.00). May 4, 1864 issued clothing. April 26, 1865, surrendered at Greensboro, North Carolina. May 1, 1865 paroled at Greensboro, North Carolina.

PHELPS, WILLIAM S.: Company A, private. September 10, 1861 enlisted as a private in Co. A, 27th Regiment, Georgia Infantry at Camp Stephens, Griffin, Spalding County, Georgia. December 13, 1861 admitted to General Hospital No. 18(formerly Greaner's Hospital), Richmond, Virginia. December 1861 roll shows him sick in the Hospital in Richmond, Virginia since November 25. January and February 1862 rolls show he was left sick in Georgia October 31, 1861. October 10, 1862 received pay ($119.00). December 1862 roll shows he strayed from the ranks September 24, 1862. June, July, August and September 1863 issued clothing. December 31, 1863 received pay and issued clothing. January – February 1864 roll shows him absent sent to the hospital on March 8. March 15, 1864 wounded. March - April 1864 roll shows him absent wounded since March 15, 1864. August 5, 1864 in Floyd House Hospital at Macon, Georgia with Vulnus Sclopeticum (Gunshot Wound) resulting in the amputation of two toes on the left foot. 1864 furloughed for 60 days. April 26, 1865 surrendered Greensboro, North Carolina. May 1, 1865 paroled at Greensboro, North Carolina. Shown as a resident of Tazewell, Marion County, Georgia.

PHILLIPS, A. F.: Company H, private. September 9, 1861 enlisted as a private in Co. H, 27th Regiment, Georgia Infantry at Camp Stephens, Griffin, Spalding County, Georgia. July 6, 1864 died in Columbus, Georgia.

PHILLIPS, DANIEL J.: Company I, private. September 1863 enlisted as a private in Co. I, 27th Regiment, Georgia Infantry. January 8, 1864 died in hospital at Charleston, South Carolina.

PHILLIPS, M.: Company C, private. He enlisted as a private in Co. C, 27th Regiment, Georgia Infantry. April 24, 1862 admitted to General Hospital No. 18(formerly Greaner's Hospital), Richmond, Virginia. May

1, 1862 transferred to Petersburg.

PHILLIPS, MADISON: Company H, private. September 9, 1861 enlisted as a private in Co. H, 27th Regiment, Georgia Infantry at Camp Stephens, Griffin, Spalding County, Georgia. March 20, 1862 wounded. April 24, 1862 admitted to General Hospital No.18 at Richmond, Virginia. May 18, 1862 transferred to Petersburg, Virginia.

PIERCE, ELI: Company E, private. August 27, 1861 enlisted as a private in Co. E, 27th Regiment, Georgia Infantry. December 7, 1861 discharged due to disability (Tuberculosis), at Camp Pickens near Manassas, Virginia. December 1861 roll shows him discharged due to disability. February 22, 1864 reenlisted in Co. E, 27th Regiment, Georgia Infantry at Decatur, Georgia. January – February 1864 roll shows him absent on an errand for command. March - April 1864 roll shows him present. May 30, 1864 issued clothing. June 30, 1864 wounded at Colquitt's Salient near Petersburg, Virginia. June 30, 1864 admitted to First Division Jackson Hospital at Richmond, Virginia with a Vulnus Sclopeticum (Gunshot Wound) to the right hip by a mini ball. July 11, 1864 issued clothing. July 21, 1864 furloughed for 30 days. He was born in Walton County, Georgia in 1835. At the time of discharge in December 1861 he was 19 years of age, 5 foot 7 1/2 inches high, fair complexion, blue eyes, light hair and by occupation was a farmer.

PLEDGER, F. M.: Company B, private. February 2, 1864 enlisted as a private in Co. B, 27th Regiment, Georgia Infantry at Decatur, Georgia. January – February 1864 roll shows him present. March - April 1864 roll shows him present. March 5, 1864 issued clothing. He was killed in battle.

POLHILL, J. J.: Company B, private. He enlisted as a private in Co. B, 27th Regiment, Georgia Infantry. May 18, 1865 surrendered and paroled at Augusta, Georgia.

POOLE, ISAAC: Company B, private. October 24, 1863 enlisted as a private in Co. B, 27th Regiment, Georgia Infantry at Decatur Georgia. February 20, 1864 wounded, Olustee, Florida. October, November and December 1863 issued clothing. December 31, 1863 received pay. January – February 1864 roll shows him present. March 10, 1864 died of wounds. March - April 1864 roll shows he died of wounds March 10, 1864.

PORTER, F.: Company K, private. September 10, 1861 enlisted as a private in Co. K, 27th Regiment, Georgia Infantry. December 1861 roll shows he died of disease in Georgia December 28, 1861.

POUND (POUNDS), JAMES M.: Company K, private. July 2, 1862 enlisted as a private in Co. K, 27th Regiment, Georgia Infantry at Calhoun, Georgia. September 14, 1862 captured at South Mountain, Maryland. October 2, 1862 sent for exchange from Fort Delaware, Delaware to Aikens Landing, Virginia. November 10, 1862 exchanged at Aikens Landing, Virginia. December 1862 roll shows him missing since September 17, 1862. November 10, 1862 exchanged at Aikens Landing, Virginia. December

1862 roll shows him missing since September 17, 1862. February 3, 1863 returned to duty. May 5, 1863 captured at Chancellorsville, Virginia. May 8, 1863 paroled. June 1863, October 29, 1863 and November 24, 1863 issued clothing. October 12, 1863 admitted to Camp Winder Division No. 2 Hospital at Richmond, Virginia with Lumbago. December 31, 1863 received pay. March - April 1864 roll shows him present. March 17, 1864 appears on roll of General Hospital No. 1 (General Hospital, Oglethorpe Barracks) at Savannah, Georgia. April 9, 1865 took oath of allegiance at Point Lookout, Maryland.

POUND (POUNDS), JOHN THOMAS: Company K, private. September 10, 1861 enlisted as a private in Co. K, 27th Regiment, Georgia Infantry at Camp Stephens, Griffin, Spalding County, Georgia. March 30, 1862 admitted to Chimborazo Hospital No. 5 at Richmond, Virginia with Congestive Fever. May 1, 1862 returned to duty. July 2, 1862 died of Fever at Chimborazo Hospital No.5 at Richmond, Virginia. He is most likely buried in Oakwood Cemetery at Richmond Virginia. August 7, 1862 death benefit claim was filed by widow, Louisa M. Pound. September 23, 1863 death benefit claim paid $142.10 (#8859). He was a resident of Talbotton, Talbot County, Georgia.

POUND (POUNDS), JOSEPH GIBLERT: Company K, private. February 24, 1862 enlisted as a private in Co. K, 27th Regiment, Georgia Infantry. May 7, 1862 admitted to Camp Winder General Hospital Richmond, Virginia with Febris Continuing. Comm (Malaria). June 1863 issued clothing. October 22 and October 29, 1863 issued clothing. October 31, 1863 received pay. November 13, 1863 wounded, left hip shattered at Fort Sumter, South Carolina. December 31, 1863 roll of First Georgia Hospital at Charleston, South Carolina shows him present. March - April 1864 roll shows him absent wounded at Fort Sumter, South Carolina. November 14, 1863 and was sent to the Hospital at Charleston, South Carolina. Pension records show he was at home, wounded, at the close of the war. He was born in Georgia January 7, 1842.

POUND (POUNDS), MATTHEW J.: Company K, private. July 2, 1862 enlisted as a private in Co. K, 27th Regiment, Georgia Infantry. June 1864 captured at Petersburg, Virginia. 1865 released at Point Lookout, Maryland.

POWELL, AUGUSTUS N. (M.): Company G, private. September 9, 1861 enlisted as a private in Co. G, 27th Regiment, Georgia Infantry at Camp Stephens, Griffin, Spalding County, Georgia. March 7, 1862 admitted to Chimborazo Hospital No. 1 at Richmond, Virginia for convalescent. March 25, 1862 returned to duty. July 16, 1862 admitted to General Hospital at Farmville, Virginia with Debility. August 28, 1862 returned to duty. December 1862 roll shows him absent sick. June 4, 1863 received pay ($44.00). October 30, 1863 and December 16, 1863 issued clothing. December 31, 1863 received pay. January – February 1864 roll shows him present. March - April 1864 roll shows him present. July 1864 issued

413

clothing. August 19, 1864 wounded in the left arm at Weldon Railroad, Virginia. August 21, 1864 admitted to Receiving and Wayside Hospital or General Hospital No. 9 at Richmond, Virginia with a Vulnus Sclopeticum (Gunshot Wound) and sent to Jackson Hospital at Richmond, Virginia. August 22, 1864 admitted to Jackson Hospital at Richmond, Virginia with a Vulnus Sclopeticum (Gunshot Wound) to the left arm. August 25, 1864 furloughed for 30 days. August 24, 1864 issued clothing at Jackson Hospital at Richmond, Virginia. April 26, 1865 surrendered Greensboro, North Carolina. May 1, 1865 paroled at Greensboro, North Carolina. His home was Barnesville, Georgia.

PRESCOTT, HENRY: Company I, private. September 10, 1861 enlisted as a private in Co. I, 27th Regiment, Georgia Infantry at Camp Stephens, Griffin, Spalding County, Georgia. November 12, 1861 admitted to General Hospital No. 18 (formerly Greaner's Hospital) at Richmond, Virginia. January 4, 1862 discharged from service. January 6, 1862 received pay ($89.05). December 1861 and January 1862 rolls show him in Richmond, Virginia hospital. February 24, 1862 furloughed for 20 days, on account of sickness. February 1862 roll shows him furloughed from February 20th or 24th.

PRESCOTT, JOHN A.: Company I, private. September 10, 1861 enlisted as a private in Co. I, 27th Regiment, Georgia Infantry at Camp Stephens, Griffin, Spalding County, Georgia. May 22, 1862 admitted to Chimborazo Hospital No. 5 at Richmond, Virginia and was transferred to Lynchburg, Virginia. May 23, 1862 admitted to General Hospital at Farmville, Virginia with Ulcer on leg. September 12(13), 1862 discharged, on account of injury to ankle joint from General Hospital at Farmville, Virginia. Medical certification sated injury to ankle was a result of a Vulnus Sclopeticum (Gunshot Wound) received in 1846. September 19, 1862 received pay ($87.43) plus clothing allowance of $5.50. He is described as being born in Appling County, Georgia, 34 years of age, 6 feet 5 inches high, fair complexion, blue eyes, light hair and by occupation was a mechanic.

PRESLEY (PRESSLEY), HARVEY S.: Company D, private. February 22, 1862 enlisted as a private in Co. D, 27th Regiment, Georgia Infantry at Gainesville, Georgia. March 25, 1862 received bounty pay ($50.00). June 5, 1862 received pay ($47.00). July 11, 1863 furloughed for 30 days. November 11, 1863 received $7.50 in commutation of rations. April, May, June and November 1863 issued clothing. February 29, 1864 received pay. March - April 1864 roll shows him present. July 1864 issued clothing. He was born in Franklin County, Georgia March 11, 1830.

PROCTOR, EDWARD: Company K, sergeant. September 10, 1861 enlisted as a private in Co. K, 27th Regiment, Georgia Infantry at Camp Stephens, Griffin, Spalding County, Georgia. He was appointed 3rd sergeant in Co. K, 27th Regiment, Georgia Infantry. January 6, 1862 died of Pneumonia at Camp Pickens near Manassas, Virginia. January 1862 roll indicates his death on January 6, 1862.

PRYOR BURRELL P.: Company H, corporal. September 9, 1861 elected 2nd corporal of Co. H, 27th Regiment, Georgia Infantry at Camp Stephens, Griffin, Spalding County, Georgia. December 1861 roll shows he was left sick in Georgia October 31, 1861.
April 25, 1862 received pay ($88.06). May 24, 1863 furloughed for 30 days. July 1, 1863 received pay in commutation of rations ($6.00). December 31, 1863 received pay. January – February 1864 roll shows him present. March - April 1864 roll shows him present.

PUCKETT, JAMES M.: Company I, private. September 15, 1861 enlisted as a private in Co. I, 27th Regiment, Georgia Infantry at Camp Stephens, Griffin, Spalding County, Georgia. November 25, 1861 admitted to Chimborazo Hospital No. 1, at Richmond, Virginia (note: deserted from the hospital without the knowledge of the surgeon).
December 28, 1861 admitted to Moore Hospital at General Hospital, No. 1 at Danville, Virginia and sent to Mt. Jackson Hospital at Mt. Jackson, Virginia. December 1861 roll shows him in hospital at Richmond, Virginia. January 1862 roll shows him in Mt. Jackson Hospital at Mt. Jackson, Virginia. December 1862 roll shows him absent without leave since December 1, 1862. June 5, 1863 received pay ($110.00). July 1, 1862 wounded at Malvern Hill, Virginia. July 28, 1862 received pay ($113.00). August 10, 1863 received pay ($61.00). November 2, 1863 received pay ($33.00). November 3, 1863 and January 30, 1864 issued clothing. December 31, 1863 received pay. January – February 1864 roll shows him absent on detached service since February 23, 1864. February 28, 1864 - April 30, 1864 was on detached duty. March - April 1864 roll shows him absent on detached service since February 28, 1864. June 10, 1864 issued clothing. August 11, 1864 admitted to Jackson Hospital at Richmond, Virginia with a Vulnus Sclopeticum (Gunshot Wound) to the hip by a mini ball. August 22, 1864 returned to duty and received pay ($22.00). September 20, 1864 and October 19, 1864 issued clothing at Jackson Hospital at Richmond, Virginia. October 13, 1864 admitted to Jackson Hospital at Richmond, Virginia with a Vulnus Sclopeticum (Gunshot Wound) to the right hip by a mini ball. October 15, 1864 furloughed for 60 days. April 20 (21), 1865 captured at Macon, Georgia.

PULLIN (PULLING), G. W.: Company F, private. September 9, 1861 enlisted as a private in Co. F, 27th Regiment, Georgia Infantry at Camp Stephens, Griffin, Spalding County, Georgia. December 29, 1861 admitted to Moore Hospital at General Hospital, No. 1, Danville, Virginia with Continuing. Fever and sent to General Hospital at Culpepper, Virginia. September 12, 1862 captured near Frederick, Maryland and admitted to U. S. A. General Hospital there. October 2, 1862 sent for exchange from Fort Delaware, Delaware to Aiken's Landing, Virginia. November 10, 1862 exchanged at Aiken's Landing, Virginia. May 23, 1863 furloughed for 30 days and paid commutation of rations ($7.50). May 31, 1863 issued clothing at Camp Winder Division No. 1 Hospital at Richmond, Virginia.

December 31, 1863 received pay. February 24, 1864 deserted from Camp Milton, Florida. January – February 1864 roll shows he deserted from Camp Milton, Florida on March 24, 1864. March - April 1864 roll shows him as deserted from Camp Milton, Florida February 24, 1864. July 1864 and September 20, 1864 issued clothing. He was born in Taylor County, Georgia in 1838.

PYE, JESSE B.: Field Staff, Adjutant. September 10, 1861 enlisted as a private in Co. K, 27th Regiment, Georgia Infantry at Camp Stephens, Griffin, Spalding County, Georgia. January and February 1862 rolls show him detailed as Colonel's Orderly. December 20, 1862 received pay ($138.10). March 1, 1863 furloughed for 60 days. May 2, 1863 appointed adjutant of 27th Georgia Infantry at James Island. South Carolina. May 16, 1863 received commutations for rations ($36.60). July 30, 1863 received pay ($145.00). September 30, 1863 was shown as adjutant on General Colquitt's staff. December 6, 1864 admitted to Jackson Hospital at Richmond, Virginia with Odontalgioa. December 6, 1864 returned to duty. March 19, 1865 wounded in the knee at Bentonville, North Carolina. March 21, 1865 admitted to Pettigrew General Hospital at Raleigh, North Carolina with a Vulnus Sclopeticum (Gunshot Wound) of the left knee (mini ball). He was a resident of Pleasant Hill, Talbot County, Georgia.

PYLE, E. R.: Company E, private. February 10, 1864 enlisted as a private in Co. E, 27th Regiment, Georgia Infantry at Decatur, Georgia. January – February 1864 roll shows him absent. March - April 1864 roll shows him present. June 1864 issued clothing. June 30, 1864 roll of Jackson Hospital at Richmond, Virginia shows him present. July 13, 1864 admitted to Jackson Hospital at Richmond, Virginia with Dysenteria. July 28, 1864 furloughed for 30 days. April 26, 1865 surrendered Greensboro, North Carolina. May 1, 1865 paroled at Greensboro, North Carolina. He was born in Georgia in 1845.

QUINN, FRANKLIN: Company I, private. He enlisted as a private in Co. I, 27th Regiment, Georgia Infantry. May 31, 1862 killed at Seven Pines, Virginia. December 15, 1862 death benefit claim was filed.

RADCLIFF, RICHARD, JR.: Company K, private. September 10, 1861 enlisted as a private in Co. K, 27th Regiment, Georgia Infantry at Camp Stephens, Griffin, Spalding County, Georgia. June 1863 issued clothing. October 28, 1863 died. April 4, 1864 death benefit claim was filed by Elizabeth Radcliff, mother. He was born in 1843.

RADCLIFF, RICHARD, SR.: Company K, private, September 10, 1861 enlisted as a private in Co. K, 27th Regiment, Georgia Infantry at Camp Stephens, Griffin, Spalding County, Georgia. November 30, 1862 died. April 4, 1864 death benefit claim was filed by Elizabeth Radcliff, widow. He was born in 1813.

RAINES, WILKINS J.: Company K, lieutenant. September 10, 1861 elected 2nd lieutenant of Co. K. 27th Regiment, Georgia Infantry at Camp

Stephens, Griffin, Spalding County, Georgia. September 11, 1861 elected 1st lieutenant of Co. K, 27th Regiment, Georgia Infantry. December 1861 and January 1862 rolls show him present. February 1862 roll shows him absent on recruiting service for 30 days beginning February 12, 1862. March 2, 1862 received pay ($90.00). May 21, 1862 received pay ($90.00). May 31, 1862 wounded in the left leg and permanently disabled at Seven Pines, Virginia. June 1, 1862 received pay ($90.00). December 1862 roll shows him absent without leave due to wound received. January 12, 1863 on roll of Medical Director's office, Richmond, Virginia, under the head of "Assignment for treatment". March 16, 1863 resigned his commission with a certificate of disability. He was born in Georgia May 20, 1833.

RAINEY, JOHN F.: Company G, private. August 27, 1861 enlisted as a private in Co. G, 27th Regiment, Georgia Infantry. November 8, 1861 admitted to General Hospital No. 18 (formerly Greaner's Hospital), Richmond, Virginia. December 1861 roll shows him in the hospital at Petersburg, Virginia. January 1862 roll shows him in hospital at Richmond, Virginia since January 7, 1862. January (3) (4) 6, 1862 discharged due to disability, at Richmond, Virginia and received pay ($72.62). February 1862 roll shows him in hospital since November 1861. His Post Office is shown as Zebulon, Pike County, Georgia.

RAINEY, J. M.: Company K, private. September 10, 1861 enlisted as a private in Co. K, 27th Regiment, Georgia Infantry at Camp Stephens, Griffin, Spalding County, Georgia. November 17, 1861 admitted to Chimborazo Hospital No. 1 at Richmond, Virginia. November 20, 1861 returned to duty.

RAPE, GEORGE W.: Company H, private. September 9, 1861 enlisted as a private in Co. H, 27th Regiment, Georgia Infantry at Camp Stephens, Griffin, Spalding County, Georgia. September 17, 1862 wounded in the arm and left hip and captured at Sharpsburg, Maryland. September 27, 1862 paroled. October 10, 1862 admitted to the No. 5, U. S. A. General Hospital at Frederick Maryland. October 11, 1862 sent to the General Hospital. October 13, 1862 sent to Fort Monroe, Virginia for exchange. October 24, 1862 admitted to Chimborazo Hospital No. 4 at Richmond, Virginia with wound in arm and left hip. November 10, 1862 furloughed for 40 days from Chimborazo Hospital No. 4 at Richmond, Virginia. December 1862 roll shows him absent without leave. November 13, 1863 received in commutation of rations $13.33. December 31, 1863 received pay. January – February 1864 roll shows him present. March - April 1864 roll shows him present. June 9, 1864 wounded in arm, necessitating amputation, at Petersburg, Virginia. July 1864 issued clothing. August 18, 1864 admitted to Jackson Hospital at Richmond, Virginia with an amputated right arm. September 29, 1864 issued clothing at Jackson Hospital at Richmond, Virginia. October 27, 1864 furloughed for 60 days and issued passport to Griffin, Georgia.

REAMS, ROBERT: Company E, private. He enlisted as a private in Co.

E, 27th Regiment, Georgia Infantry. April 14, 1862 admitted to General Hospital No. 21 at Richmond, Virginia with Pneumonia. May 5, 1862 transferred to Lynchburg, Virginia.

REAVES, REUBEN: Company I, private. September 17, 1863 enlisted as a private in Co. I, 27th Regiment, Georgia Infantry at Macon, Georgia. December 31, 1863 received pay. January – February 1864 roll shows him present. February 29, 1864 received pay. March - April 1864 roll shows him present. October 18, 1864 received pay ($44.00). April 26, 1865 pension records show he surrendered Greensboro, North Carolina. He was born in South Carolina in 1820 or 1821.

REAVES, SIMEON: Company G, private. October 14, 1861 enlisted as a private in Co. G, 27th Regiment, Georgia Infantry. October 22, 1861 died of disease at Camp Stephens, Georgia.

REDDING, CHARLES F: Field Staff, Adjutant. September 5, 1861 He enlisted in the 27th Regiment, Georgia Infantry and elected adjutant. November 1861 resigned his commission. August 4, 1863 elected captain of Company D, 8th Battalion, Georgia State Guards Cavalry. February 4, 1864 mustered out near Atlanta, Georgia.

REDDING, WILLIAM DOZIER: Company G, captain. August 21, 1861 elected captain of Co. G, 27th Regiment, Georgia Infantry at Camp Stephens, Griffin, Spalding County, Georgia. December 1861 roll shows him present at Camp Pickens near Manassas, Virginia. January 11, 1862 received pay ($541.00). January 1862 roll shows him absent on sick leave since January 8, 1861 on 40 day furlough. February 1862 roll shows him present at Camp Pickens near Manassas, Virginia. May 17, 1862 received pay ($520.00). July 19, 1862 resigned his commission on certificate of disability and received pay ($249.00). July 24, 1862 received pay ($225.33).

REDMOND, JAMES B.: Company D, corporal. September 10, 1861 elected corporal in Co. D, 27th Regiment, Georgia Infantry at Camp Stephens, Griffin, Spalding County, Georgia. December 1861 roll shows he was left sick at Richmond, Virginia. December 10, 1861 discharged due to disability from Richmond, Virginia and received pay. January 1862 roll shows he was discharged due to disability in Richmond.

REED (REID), BENJAMIN W.: Company D, private. September 10, 1861 enlisted as a private in Co. D, 27th Regiment, Georgia Infantry at Camp Stephens, Griffin, Spalding County, Georgia. December 1861 roll shows him in the hospital in Richmond, Virginia. April 10, 1862 admitted to Chimborazo Hospital No. 1 at Richmond, Virginia, convalescent. May 7, 1862 admitted to General Hospital at Farmville, Virginia with Catarrh. May 23, 1863 returned to duty. May 31, 1862 wounded, Seven Pines, Virginia. July 3, 1862 furloughed for 30 days. April 13, 1863 received for commutation of rations ($7.50). December 1863 issued clothing. February 29, 1864 received pay. March - April 1864 roll shows him present. July and September 1864 issued clothing. April 26, 1865 surrendered Greensboro,

North Carolina. May 1, 1865 paroled at Greensboro, North Carolina. August 22, 1865 took the oath of allegiance at Gainesville, Georgia. He is described as a resident of Hall County, Georgia, fair complexion, light hair, blue eyes and was 6 feet high. He was born in Georgia.

REED (REID), COLUMBUS A.: Company G, private. September 9, 1861 enlisted as a private in Co. G, 27th Regiment, Georgia Infantry at Camp Stephens, Griffin, Spalding County, Georgia. November 18, 1861 admitted to General Hospital No. 18 (formerly Greaner's Hospital), Richmond, Virginia. December 27, 1861 returned to duty. March 7, 1862 admitted to Chimborazo Hospital No.4, at Richmond, Virginia with Debility. April 10, 1862 returned to duty. He was a resident of Zebulon, Pike County, Georgia.

REED (REID), J. A.: Company D, private. August 15, 1863 enlisted as a private in Co. D, 27th Regiment, Georgia Infantry at Camp Stephens, Griffin, Spalding County, Georgia. December 31, 1863 received pay and was issued clothing. March - April 1864 roll shows him present. July 1864 issued clothing. April 26, 1865 surrendered Greensboro, North Carolina. May 1, 1865 paroled at Greensboro, North Carolina.

REED (REID), J. W.: Company D, private. August 1, 1863 enlisted as a private in Co. D, 27th Regiment, Georgia Infantry in Hall County, Georgia. December 1863 issued clothing. February 29, 1864 received pay. March - April 1864 roll shows him present. July 1864 issued clothing. April 26, 1865 surrendered Greensboro, North Carolina. He was born in Georgia in 1844.

REED (REID), JOSIAH R.: Company D, private. September 23, 1861 enlisted as a private in Co. D, 27th Regiment, Georgia Infantry at Camp Stephens, Griffin, Spalding County, Georgia. March - April 1864 roll shows him present. April 26, 1865, surrendered at Greensboro, North Carolina. May 1, 1865 paroled at Greensboro, North Carolina.

REED (REID), JOSEPH R.: Company D, sergeant. September 23, 1861 enlisted as a private in Co. D, 27th Regiment, Georgia Infantry at Camp Stephens, Griffin, Spalding County, Georgia. December 1861, January and February 1862 rolls show he was left sick in Georgia October 31, 1861. May 31, 1862 wounded, Seven Pines, Virginia. June 3, 1862 furloughed for 30 days. June 7, 1862 admitted to C. S. A. General Military Hospital, No. 4 at Wilmington, North Carolina with note (he was wounded at battle around Richmond and wound was dressed and is home on furlough). April 13, 1863 received commutation of rations ($10.00). December 1863 issued clothing. February 29, 1864 received pay. March - April 1864 roll shows him present. July 1864 and September 20, 1864 issued clothing. October 3, 1864 wounded at Fort Harrison near Richmond, Virginia. October 3, 1864 admitted to Receiving and Wayside Hospital or General Hospital No. 9, Richmond, Virginia with a Vulnus Sclopeticum (Gunshot Wound) and sent to Jackson hospital. October 4, 1864 admitted to Jackson Hospital at Richmond, Virginia with a Vulnus Sclopeticum (Gunshot Wound) to his left arm (mini ball). October 31, 1864 returned to duty. April 26, 1865, surrendered at Greensboro, North Carolina. May 1, 1865 paroled at Greensboro, North Carolina. He was born in Hall County, Georgia July 7, 1839.

REED (REID), M. M.: Company D, private. February 20, 1863 enlisted as a private in Co. D, 27th Regiment, Georgia Infantry at Hall County, Georgia. December 1863 issued clothing. February 29, 1864 received pay. March - April 1864 roll shows him present. July 1864 issued clothing. April 26, 1865 surrendered Greensboro, North Carolina. May 1, 1865 paroled at Greensboro, North Carolina. He was born in Hall County, Georgia December 1843.

REEVES, JEREMAIH: Company G, private. He enlisted as a private in Co. G, 27th Regiment, Georgia Infantry. July 18, 1864 admitted to Floyd House Hospital at Macon, Georgia with Chronic Diarrhoea.

REEVES, JAMES B.: Company G, private. September 9, 1861 enlisted as a private in Co. G, 27th Regiment, Georgia Infantry at Camp Stephens, Griffin, Spalding County, Georgia. October 31, 1861 discharged at Camp Stephens, Georgia. He was born in Pike County, Georgia August 2, 1839.

REEVES, JOHN H. (J. S. S.): Company E, private. August 1, 1863 enlisted as a private in Co. E, 27th Regiment, Georgia Infantry at Fairburn, Georgia. December 31, 1863 received pay. January – February 1864 roll shows him present. February 29, 1864 received pay. March - April 1864 roll shows him present. May 30, 1864 issued clothing. August 29, 1864 admitted to Jackson Hospital at Richmond, Virginia with remitting Remitting Fever (Malaria). September 8, 1864 furloughed for 30 days. September 1864 issued clothing.

REEVES, PARTICK: Company B, private. September 10, 1861 enlisted as a private in Co. B, 27th Regiment, Georgia Infantry at Camp Stephens, Griffin, Spalding County, Georgia. He was killed in battle.

REEVES, ROBERT: Company G, private. September 9, 1861 enlisted as a private in Co. G, 27th Regiment, Georgia Infantry at Camp Stephens, Griffin, Spalding County, Georgia. November 11, 1861 admitted to General Hospital No. 18 (formerly Greaner's Hospital) at Richmond, Virginia. December 27, 1861 returned to duty. June 28, 1862 admitted to General Hospital No. 18 (formerly Greaner's Hospital) at Richmond, Virginia with Rheumatism. July 18, 1862 returned to duty. September 17, 1862 wounded and captured at Sharpsburg, Maryland. September 27, 1862 paroled. October 12, 1862 admitted to U. S. A. General Hospital at Frederick, Maryland with a compound fracture of the thigh. May 21, 1863 died in U. S. A. General Hospital at Frederick, Maryland (gangrene). May 23, 1863 he was buried in grave #200 at Mt. Olivet or Hospital Cemetery at Frederick, Maryland. January 23, 1864 death benefit claim was filed by his widow, Mary E. Reeves. January 25, 1864 death benefit claim paid $347.48. His Post Office was Zebulon, Pike County, Georgia. He was born in Louisiana in 1861.

REEVES, SIMON: Company G, private. September 9, 1861 enlisted as a private in Co. G, 27th Regiment, Georgia Infantry at Camp Stephens, Griffin, Spalding County, Georgia. October 22, 1861 died at Camp Stephens. February 4, 1862 death benefit claim was filed by Felecia L. Reeves, mother. March 23, 1863 death benefit claim paid $78.30 (#4191).

REEVES, W. N.: Company E, sergeant. He enlisted as a private in Co. E, 27th Regiment, Georgia Infantry. July 12, 1862 received pay ($127.00).

REEVES, WARREN: Company G, private. September 21, 1862 enlisted as a private in Co. G, 27th Regiment, Georgia Infantry at Randolph County, Georgia. May 3, 1863 admitted to Receiving and Wayside Hospital or General Hospital No. 9 at Richmond, Virginia and transferred to Chimborazo No. 2. May 3, 1863 admitted to Chimborazo Hospital No. 2 at Richmond, Virginia with Dyspepsia. May 11, 1863 transferred to Lynchburg, Virginia. October 1863 issued clothing. December 31, 1863 received pay. January – February 1864 roll shows him present. March - April 1864 roll shows him present. July 1864 issued clothing. August 5, 1864 wounded in the right thigh at Colquitt's Salient near Petersburg, Virginia. August 6, 1864 admitted to Jackson Hospital at Richmond, Virginia with a wound to the right thigh (mini ball). September 4, 1864 died of wounds in Jackson Hospital at Richmond, Virginia.

REEVES, WILLIAM C.: Company E, lieutenant. September 9, 1861 enlisted as a private in Co. E, 27th Regiment, Georgia Infantry at Camp Stephens, Griffin, Spalding County, Georgia. July 12, 1862 received pay ($127.00). April, May and June 1863 issued clothing. November 1, 1863 elected Jr. 2nd lieutenant in Co. E, 27th Regiment, Georgia Infantry. December 31, 1863 received pay. January – February 1864 roll shows him present. March - April 1864 roll shows him present and that he was promoted to rank November 1, 1863. June 28, 1864 promoted to 2nd lieutenant in Co. E, 27th Regiment, Georgia Infantry. August 31, 1864 received pay ($108.00). April 26, 1865 surrendered Greensboro, North Carolina. May 1, 1865 paroled at Greensboro, North Carolina.

RENTFROE (RENFROE), THOMAS: Company E, captain. He enlisted as a private in Co. E, 27th Regiment, Georgia Infantry. August 28, 1864 admitted to General Hospital No. 4 at Richmond, Virginia with Colitis. September 15, 1864 furloughed.

RENTFROE (RENFROE), WILLIAM H.: Field Staff, major. September 10, 1861 elected 2nd lieutenant Co. E, 27th Regiment, Georgia Infantry at Camp Stephens, Griffin, Spalding County, Georgia. December 15, 1861 received pay ($173.24). December 20, 1861 elected captain Co. E, 27th Regiment, Georgia Infantry at Camp Stephens, Griffin, Spalding County, Georgia. December 1861 and January 1862 rolls show him present at Camp Pickens near Manassas, Virginia. February 1862 roll shows him absent on sick leave beginning February 5, 1862. May 4, 1862 received pay. December 1862 roll shows him present at camp near Guinea Station,

Virginia.   January 31, 1864 received pay. January – February 1864 roll shows him absent on recruiting service for 15 days from February 7, 1864 to February 22, 1864 and absent without leave from February 22, 1864 to February 29, 1864 during change of station.   March – April 1864 roll shows him on detached service.   1864 admitted to Pettigrew General Hospital No.13 at Raleigh, North Carolina. May 21, 1864 returned to duty. June 24, 1864 promoted to major of the 27th Regiment, Georgia Infantry. July 1, 1864 admitted to General Hospital No. 4 at Richmond, Virginia with Chronic Dysentery. August 15, 1864 granted sick leave by General Beauregard. August 20, 1864 received pay ($260.00). September 15, 1864 granted 30 days furlough to home in Jonesboro, Georgia. September 16, 1864 received pay ($ 260.00). March 19, 1865 wounded in the thigh at Bentonville, North Carolina.   April 6, 1865 died of wounds at Smithfield, North Carolina.

RENTZ, JACOB S.: Company I, private.   September 10, 1861 enlisted as a private in Co. I, 27th Regiment, Georgia Infantry at Camp Stephens, Griffin, Spalding County, Georgia. November 12, 1861 admitted to General Hospital No. 18 (formerly Greaner's Hospital) at Richmond, Virginia with Typhoid Fever. November 25, 1861 died of Typhoid Fever (Pneumonia) in General Hospital No.18 at Richmond, Virginia. December 1861 roll shows his death. May 24, 1864 death benefit claim was filed by his father, Aaron Rentz of Appling County, Georgia.

REYNOLDS, ANDERSON J.: Company D, private.   September 23, 1861 enlisted as a private in Co. D, 27th Regiment, Georgia Infantry at Camp Stephens, Griffin, Spalding County, Georgia   December 1861 roll shows him in the hospital at Richmond, Virginia. June 29, 1862 admitted to General Hospital No. 18 (formerly Greaner's Hospital) at Richmond, Virginia with a Vulnus Sclopeticum (Gunshot Wound) and was transferred to Camp Winder on June 30, 1862.   September 17, 1862 wounded at Sharpsburg, Maryland. September 30, 1862 admitted to General Hospital Camp Winder at Richmond, Virginia with a Vulnus Sclopeticum (Gunshot Wound).   October 24, 1862 furloughed for 40 days.   October 25, 1862 received pay ($94.00). December 1862 roll shows him wounded (September 17, 1862) on furlough. December 1863 issued clothing. February 29, 1864 received pay. March - April 1864 roll shows him present. July 1864 issued clothing. August 19, 1864 wounded in the right thigh and captured at Weldon Railroad, Virginia.   August 22, 1864 died from wounds and amputation in Field Hospital, 1st Division, 9th Army Corps, Virginia.

REYNOLDS, JOHN B.: Company D, private.   September 23, 1861 enlisted as a private in Co. D, 27th Regiment, Georgia Infantry at Camp Stephens, Griffin, Spalding County, Georgia. March 30, 1862 admitted to Chimborazo Hospital No. 2 at Richmond, Virginia with Typhoid Fever. April 5, 1862 died of Typhoid Fever at Chimborazo Hospital No. 2 at Richmond, Virginia. He is most likely buried in Oakwood Cemetery at Richmond Virginia.   February 25, 1863 death benefit claim was filed by his father, Sharp S. Reynolds. September 24, 1863 death benefit claim paid $109.46 (#9015).

RICKERSON, EMARLD M.: Company K, private. February 9, 1864 enlisted as a private in Co. K, 27th Regiment, Georgia Infantry at Macon, Georgia. March 9, 1864 sent to Lake City, Florida hospital. March - April 1864 roll shows him absent at Lake City, Florida hospital. January 1865 admitted to C. S. A. General Military Hospital, No. 4 at Wilmington, North Carolina with Chronic Diarrhoea and transferred to Goldsboro hospital on January 18, 1865. January 20, 1865 admitted to Goldsboro Hospital No. 3 at Goldsboro, North Carolina. January 22, 1865 died of Pneumonia in Goldsboro Hospital No. 3 at Goldsboro, North Carolina. His Post Office was Knoxville, Georgia.

RISSON, W. G.: Company G, private. He enlisted as a private in Co. G, 27th Regiment, Georgia Infantry. December 9, 1862 admitted to C. S. A. General Hospital at Charlottesville, Virginia with Debility. December 10, 1862 returned to duty remark: (Regularly discharged fourth hospital in Lynchburg and was on his way to his Regiment, but the Central Cars being too much crowded for him to get on he was left here for one day and "Returned to duty").

RITCHIE (RICHEY), ELIJAH N.: Company D, private. March 4, 1862 enlisted as a private in Co. D, 27th Regiment, Georgia Infantry in Gainesville, Georgia. March – April 1864 roll shows him present.

RITCHIE, ELIZAR. N.: Company D, private. March 4, 1862 enlisted as a private in Co. D, 27th Regiment, Georgia Infantry in Gainesville, Georgia. March 25, 1862 received bounty pay in Atlanta, Georgia ($50.00). July 26, 1862 received pay ($42.90). December 1863 issued clothing. February 29, 1864 received pay. March - April 1864 roll shows him present. July 1864 issued clothing.

RIX, SAMUEL: Company H, private. He enlisted as a private in Co. H, 27th Regiment, Georgia Infantry.

ROACH, JOAB: Company B, private. September 20, 1861 enlisted as a private in Co. B, 27th Regiment, Georgia Infantry at Camp Stephens, Griffin, Spalding County, Georgia. August 28, 1862 received pay ($ 47.00). December 1862 roll shows him absent without leave (furlough expired). October, November and December 1863 issued clothing. December 31, 1863 received pay. January 1, 1864 detailed on extra duty on Engineer Corps at Fort Johnson, South Carolina. January – February 1864 roll shows him present. February 7, 1864 received pay at a rate of $.25 per day for detail on the Engineer Corps. February 29, 1864 received pay. March - April 1864 roll shows him present. July 1864 issued clothing. September 20, 1864 at Petersburg, Virginia clothing was issued to him and received extra pay at a rate of $.25 per day as an overseer in January 1864. April 18, 1865 furloughed for 60 days from General Hospital No.10 at Salisburg, North Carolina. May 1, 1865 paroled in Macon, Georgia. He died in Sumter County, Georgia February 11, 1906.

423

ROBERS, BEARS: Company F, private. He enlisted as a private in Co. F, 27th Regiment, Georgia Infantry. December 1862 roll shows he was in Richmond, Virginia sick.

ROBERSON, COLUMBUS: Company C, private. He enlisted as a private in Co. C, 27th Regiment, Georgia Infantry. August 28, 1862 received pay at Richmond, Virginia ($15.76). September 27, 1862 admitted to Camp Winder Division No. 2 Hospital at Richmond, Virginia with Typhoid Fever. December 3, 1862 returned to duty. June 26, 1863 issued clothing. September 6, 1863 wounded in the evacuation of Morris Island (Battery Wagner), South Carolina (resulting in amputation).

ROBERSON, JAMES W.: Company C, lieutenant. He enlisted as a private in Co. C, 27th Regiment, Georgia Infantry. January 11, 1862 admitted to the hospital. January 1862 roll shows him absent in the hospital at Richmond, Virginia. September 30, 1862 elected 2nd lieutenant, Co. C, 27th Georgia Infantry. November 11, 1862 died at Mt. Jackson Hospital of Typhoid Pneumonia. His effects were $6.75 and 1 coat. August 4, 1863 death benefit claim was filed. Death benefit claim paid $119.05 (#7923). He was a resident of Crawford County, Georgia.

ROBERSON, WILLIAM H.: Company C, lieutenant. September 9, 1861 enlisted in Co. C, 27th Regiment, Georgia Infantry at Camp Stephens, Griffin, Spalding County, Georgia. September 10, 1861 was elected 2nd lieutenant of Co. C, 27th Regiment, Georgia Infantry. December 1861 roll shows him present at Camp Pickens near Manassas, Virginia. December 24, 1864 admitted to Moore Hospital at General Hospital, No. 1 at Danville, Virginia and sent to Richmond, Virginia. January 16, 1862 died of disease at Georgia Hospital at Richmond, Virginia. January 1862 roll shows his death in Richmond, Virginia on January 2 (16), 1862. July 22, 1862 death benefit claim was filed by his widow, Susannah C. Roberson. August 20, 1862 death benefit claim was paid $202.06 (#1084).

ROBERTS, BENJAMIN F.: Company F, private. September 9, 1861 enlisted as a private Co. F, 27th Regiment, Georgia Infantry at Camp Stephens, Griffin, Spalding County, Georgia. November 29, 1861 admitted to Chimborazo Hospital No. 1 at Richmond, Virginia. December 1861 and January 1862 rolls show him in the hospital in Richmond, Virginia since November 28, 1861. February 2, 1862 returned to duty. April 25, 1862 admitted to Chimborazo Hospital No. 4 at Richmond, Virginia with Pneumonia. September 8, 1862 received pay ($178.70). October 28, 1862 admitted to Chimborazo Hospital No. 4 at Richmond, Virginia. October 30, 1862 admitted to Camp Winder Division No. 4 Hospital at Richmond, Virginia. November 28, 1862 discharged from service by Surgeon, William A. Davis at Richmond, Virginia. December 1, 1862 discharged from service due to Copious Hemoptysis (coughing up of blood). December 2, 1862 received pay. December roll of Chimborazo Hospital No. 4, at Richmond, Virginia shows his discharge on December 1, 1862. Discharge certificate shows he was born in Crawford County, Georgia in

1843. He was 19 years of age, 5 feet 4 inches high, light complexion, grey eyes, brown hair and was by occupation a farmer.

ROBERTS, GRAVES: Company E, private. September 9, 1861 enlisted as a private in Co. E, 27th Regiment, Georgia Infantry at Camp Stephens, Griffin, Spalding County, Georgia.

ROBERTS, L. E.: Company E, private. September 9, 1861 enlisted as a private in Co. E, 27th Regiment, Georgia Infantry at Camp Stephens, Griffin, Spalding County, Georgia. March 10, 1862 admitted to Chimborazo Hospital No. 5 at Richmond, Virginia with Catarrh. May 12, 1862 transferred to Camp Winder Hospital at Richmond, Virginia. December 31, 1863 received pay. January – February 1864 roll shows him present. February 29, 1864 received pay. March - April 1864 roll shows him present. September 1864 issued clothing. April 28, 1865 admitted to C. S. A. General Hospital at Charlotte, North Carolina with Diarrhoea. April 29, 1865 sent to another hospital. He was born December 2, 1841.

ROBERTS, R.F.: Company G, private. He enlisted as a private in Co. G, 27th Regiment, Georgia Infantry.

ROBERTS, REUBEN: Company B, private. September 10, 1861 enlisted as a private in Co. B, 27th Regiment, Georgia Infantry at Camp Stephens, Griffin, Spalding County, Georgia. February 1, 1862 sent to Moore Hospital at General Hospital, No. 1 at Danville, Virginia. February 26, 1862 admitted to C. S. A. General Hospital at Charlottesville, Virginia. February 1862 roll shows he was sent to Moore Hospital. April 11, 1862 died in C. S. A. General Hospital at Charlottesville, Virginia of Phthisis (Tuberculosis). His effects were $17.37. May 6, 1863 death benefit claim (#6449) was filed by his father, Luke Roberts.

ROBERTSON, C.B.: Company D, private. September 10, 1861 enlisted as a private in Co. D, 27th Regiment, Georgia Infantry at Camp Stephens, Griffin, Spalding County, Georgia. December 23, 1861 admitted to Moore Hospital at General Hospital, No. 1 at Danville, Virginia with Pneumonia and was sent to Charlottesville, Virginia.

ROBERTSON, JAMES: Company B, private. September 10, 1861 enlisted as a private in Co. B, 27th Regiment, Georgia Infantry at Camp Stephens, Griffin, Spalding County, Georgia. January 1862 admitted to General Hospital at Front Royal, Virginia with Pneumonial paralysis. January 27, 1862 died at General Hospital at Front Royal, Virginia.

ROBERTSON, JOHN W.: Company C, corporal. January 27, 1863 issued clothing at General Hospital at Farmville, Virginia. February 11, 1863 furloughed for 30 days. March 17, 1863 received commutation of rations pay. June 26, 1863 issued clothing.

ROBINSON (ROBERSON), A. J.: Company C, private. September 10, 1861 enlisted as a private in Co. C, 27th Regiment, Georgia Infantry at Camp Stephens, Griffin, Spalding County, Georgia. 1863 died in Virginia.

ROBINSON, GEORGE E.: Company D, private. September 10, 1861 enlisted as a private in Co. D, 27th Regiment, Georgia Infantry at Camp

Stephens, Griffin, Spalding County, Georgia. December 1861 roll shows him in the hospital at Richmond, Virginia. January 17, 1862 died of disease at Richmond, Virginia. January 1862 roll shows his death in Richmond, Virginia. August 29, 1862 or April 4, 1864 death benefit claim was filed by John Robinson, father.

ROBINSON (ROBERTSON), JAMES W.: Company C, lieutenant. September 10, 1861 elected 1st corporal in Co. C, 27th Regiment, Georgia Infantry at Camp Stephens, Griffin, Spalding County, Georgia. September 30, 1862 elected Jr. 2nd lieutenant Co. C, 27th Regiment, Georgia Infantry. 1862 wounded. November 25, 1862 died at Mount Jackson, Virginia. He is buried in Soldiers Cemetery at Mt. Jackson, Virginia.

ROBINSON, JOHN: Company H, private. September 9, 1861 enlisted as a private in Co. H, 27th Regiment, Georgia Infantry at Camp Stephens, Griffin, Spalding County, Georgia. April 23, 1862 admitted to C. S. A. General Hospital at Charlottesville, Virginia with Febris Typhoides (Typhoid Fever). May 10, 1862 returned to duty. June 25, 1862 discharged due to disability. June 30, 1862 received pay ($70.25). Discharge Certificate shows he was born December 1830 in Georgia. He is described as 31 years of age, 6 feet 1 inch high, sallow complexion, blue eyes, light hair and by occupation was a farmer.

ROBINSON, JOHN W.: Company C, corporal. September 10, 1861 enlisted as a private in Co. C, 27th Regiment, Georgia Infantry at Camp Stephens, Griffin, Spalding County, Georgia. November 26, 1861 sent to the hospital in Richmond, Virginia. December 1861 roll shows he is in the hospital in Richmond, Virginia. January 11, 1862 admitted to Moore Hospital at General Hospital, No. 1 at Danville, Virginia with and sent to Richmond, Virginia with Fonletis. January 1862 roll shows him sick since December 14, 1861. February 11, 1862 furloughed from General Hospital at Farmville, Virginia with instructions to return to his regiment. February 1862 roll shows him absent without leave since February 20, 1862. July 2, 1862 wounded at Malvern Hill near Richmond, Virginia. July 5, 1862 transferred to Farmville hospital from Chimborazo Hospital No. 5 at Richmond, Virginia. July 5, 1862 received pay ($88.00). July 6, 1862 admitted to General Hospital at Farmville, Virginia with wounds. August 6, 1862 attached to General Hospital at Farmville, Virginia as a nurse. October 20, 1862 received pay ($97.00). December 1862 roll shows him absent on sick furlough. January 1, 1863 received pay. January 27, 1863 issued clothing at General Hospital at Farmville, Virginia. February 2, 1863 furloughed from General Hospital at Farmville, Virginia due to a Vulnus Sclopeticum (Gunshot Wound). February 10, 1863 discharged from General Hospital at Farmville, Virginia as a nurse. December 31, 1863 received pay. January – February 1864 roll shows him present. March - April 1864 roll shows him present. June 19, 1864 admitted to Confederate States Hospital at Petersburg, Virginia (note on report: wounded by a musket ball entering the muscles just external to the spine on the left side ranging downwards wounding the internal carotid artery and probably some branch of the occipital, the occipital, the left carotid trio in the superior triangle). July 5, 1864 died in Confederate States Hospital at Petersburg, Virginia. He was 21 years of age. September 8, 1864 death benefit claim was filed by Lewis R. Robinson.

ROBINSON (ROBERTSON), SAMUEL: Company B, private. September 10, 1861 enlisted as a private in Co. B, 27th Regiment, Georgia Infantry at Camp Stephens, Griffin, Spalding County, Georgia. January 17, 1862 admitted to Moore Hospital at General Hospital, No. 1 at Danville, Virginia. January 18, 1862 sent to hospital at Front Royal, Virginia. January 27, 1862 died of disease in Hospital at Front Royal, Virginia (Deep Bottom, Virginia hospital). January 1862 roll shows him in the hospital at Front Royal. February 1862 roll shows he died of disease.

ROBINSON, TIMOTHY: Company C, private. September 10, 1861 enlisted as a private in Co. C, 27th Regiment, Georgia Infantry at Camp Stephens, Griffin, Spalding County, Georgia. November 6, 1861 admitted to General Hospital at Petersburg, Virginia with Rubeola. November 10, 1861 sent to hospital at Petersburg, Virginia. December 1861 roll shows him in the hospital at Petersburg, Virginia. January 20, 1862 returned to duty. October 17, 1862 furloughed for 30 days from Hospital No. 19. October 17, 1862 received pay ($50.00). December 9, 1862 death benefit claim was filed.

ROBINSON, WILLIAM F: Company H, corporal. September 9, 1861 enlisted as a private in Co. H, 27th Regiment, Georgia Infantry at Camp Stephens, Griffin, Spalding County, Georgia. December 31, 1861 received pay. June 8, 1862 he died in Richmond, Virginia. August 15, 1862 death benefit claim was filed by Susannah C. Robinson, widow.

ROBINSON, WILLIAM H.: Company C, lieutenant. September 10, 1861 elected 2nd lieutenant in Co. C, 27th Regiment, Georgia Infantry at Camp Stephens, Griffin, Spalding County, Georgia. December 19, 1861 received pay ($170.66). December 24, 1861 admitted to Moore Hospital at General Hospital, No. 1 Danville, Virginia with Fever and was transferred to Richmond, Virginia. July 6, 1861 elected 1st lieutenant in Co. C, 27th Regiment, Georgia Infantry. December 1861 roll shows him present at Camp Pickens near Manassas, Virginia. January 16 (2), 1862 died of disease at Georgia Hospital at Richmond, Virginia. July 22, 1862 death benefit claim was filed. Death benefit claim paid $202.06 (#1084).

RODGERS, WILLIAM: Company A, private. He enlisted as a private in Co. A, 27th Regiment, Georgia Infantry. December 1863 issued clothing. February 5, 1864 died in Louisiana Hospital at Charleston, South Carolina.

ROGERS (RODGERS), ANDREW JACKSON: Company A, private. July 10, 1862 enlisted as a private in Co. A, 27th Regiment, Georgia Infantry at Camp Randolph, Georgia. May 5, 1863 wounded at Chancellorsville, Virginia. July, August and September 1863 issued clothing. December 31,

1863 received pay and issued clothing. January – February 1864 roll shows him present. February 29, 1864 received pay. March- April 1864 roll shows him present. July 1864 issued clothing. October 3, 1864 admitted to Jackson Hospital at Richmond, Virginia with Encephalitis (swelling of the brain). November 10, 1864 furloughed for 60 days.

ROGERS, ELI B.: Company F, private. August 7, 1862 enlisted as a private in Co. F, 27th Regiment, Georgia Infantry. November 1, 1862 received pay at Huguenot Springs, Virginia. November 11, 1862 admitted to Camp Winder Division No. 1 Hospital at Richmond, Virginia. November 12, 1862 received pay ($160.00). November 22, 1862 issued clothing at Camp Winder Hospital at Richmond, Virginia. December 16, 1862 transferred to Hospital at Huguenot Springs, Virginia. December 1862 roll shows him sick in Richmond since June or July. December 31, 1862 roll from Hospital at Huguenot Springs, Virginia shows him present. May 27, 1863 admitted to Hospital No. 1 at Lynchburg, Virginia. December 31, 1863 received pay. February 29, 1864 received pay. January – February and March – April 1864 rolls show him absent without leave since March 28, 1864 (dated May 2, 1864). July 1864 issued clothing. March 11, 1865 admitted to Pettigrew General Hospital No. 13 at Raleigh, North Carolina with Catarrhal (allergy). March 12, 1865 issued clothing. March 14, 1865 returned to duty. April 26, 1865 surrendered, Greensboro, North Carolina. May 1, 1865 paroled at Greensboro, North Carolina.

ROGERS (RODGERS), MATTHEW R.: Company A, private. September 10, 1861 enlisted as a private in Co. A, 27th Regiment, Georgia Infantry at Camp Stephens, Griffin, Spalding County, Georgia. December 1861 and January 1862 rolls show he was left in Georgia sick on October 31, 1861. February 1862 roll shows him absent without leave. July 5, 1862 admitted to Chimborazo Hospital No. 4 at Richmond, Virginia with a double Hernia. July 8, 1862 received pay ($150.46). October 24, 1862 admitted to Chimborazo Hospital No. 2 at Richmond, Virginia with a double Hernia. October 31, 1863 received pay in Richmond, Virginia. December 17, 1863 applied for detail at Chimborazo Hospital No. 2 at Richmond, Virginia. January 14, 1864 Special Order Number 11/11 detailed him as a nurse to Chimborazo Hospital No. 2 at Richmond, Virginia. January 22, 1864 sent on furlough. January – February and March – April 1864 rolls show him absent on detached service since November 1862 in Richmond, Virginia. March 1, 1864 and May 1, 1864 received pay. May – June 1864 roll of Chimborazo Hospital No. 2 at Richmond, Virginia shows him present. July 1, 1864, September 11, 1864, November 1, 1864 received pay. November 8 and 22, 1864 issued clothing at Chimborazo Hospital No. 2 at Richmond, Virginia. October 12, 1864 returned to duty from Chimborazo Hospital No. 2 at Richmond, Virginia. January 1864 through January 1865 he is shown on roll of Chimborazo Hospital No. 2 at Richmond, Virginia. January 1865 employed as a cook at Chimborazo Hospital No. 2 at Richmond, Virginia due to a double Hernia. Discharge states he was born in Marion County,

Georgia in 1826. He was 37 years of age 5 feet 9 1/2 inches high, fair complexion, dark eyes, black hair and by occupation was a farmer.

ROGERS (RODGERS), M. W.: lieutenant. He enlisted as a private in the 27th Regiment, Georgia Infantry. February 28, 1864 admitted to General Hospital No. 4 at Richmond, Virginia with a Vulnus Sclopeticum (Gunshot Wound).

ROGERS, WILLIAM B.: Company F, sergeant. August 7, 1862 enlisted as a private in Co. F, 27th Regiment, Georgia Infantry at Camp Randolph, Georgia. August 1863 issued clothing. December 31, 1863 received pay. January – February 1864 roll shows him present. February 29, 1864 received pay. March - April 1864 roll shows him present. May 31, 1864 and July 1864 issued clothing. August 19, 1864 wounded at Weldon Railroad near Petersburg, Virginia. August 20, 1864 admitted to Jackson Hospital at Richmond, Virginia with a Vulnus Sclopeticum (Gunshot Wound) to right arm. August 28, 1864 furloughed for 40 days from Jackson Hospital at Richmond, Virginia and received a passport to Butler, Georgia. August 31, 1864 appointed 3rd in Co. F, 27th Regiment, Georgia Infantry. April 26, 1865 surrendered Greensboro, North Carolina. May 1, 1865 paroled at Greensboro, North Carolina.

ROLAND (ROLAN) (ROWLAND), ROBERT JACKSON: Company C, private. September 10, 1861 enlisted as a private in Co. C, 27th Regiment, Georgia Infantry at Camp Stephens, Griffin, Spalding County, Georgia. July 5, 1862 transferred from Chimborazo Hospital No. 5 at Richmond, Virginia to General Hospital at Farmville, Virginia. July 6, 1862 admitted to General Hospital at Farmville, Virginia. July 22, 1862 returned to duty. June 29, June 30 and September 30, 1863 issued clothing. October 31, 1863 and December 31, 1863 received pay. January – February and March – April 1864 rolls show him present. March 1, 1864 received pay. May 30, 1864 issued clothing. June 1, 1864 his skull was fractured and he was captured at Cold Harbor, Virginia. June 11, 1864 arrived at Point Lookout, Maryland from White House, Virginia. July 17, 1864 received at Elmira Prison, New York from Point Lookout, Maryland. February 9, 1865 paroled at Elmira Prison, New York and was sent to James River, Virginia on February 13, 1865 for exchange. February 22, 1865 admitted to Receiving and Wayside Hospital or General Hospital No. 9 at Richmond, Virginia, transferred to and admitted to Jackson Division 1 Hospital at Richmond, Virginia as a paroled prisoner with Debilitas. February and March 1865 rolls of Jackson Division 1 Hospital at Richmond, Virginia show him present. March 24, 1865 issued clothing at Jackson Hospital at Richmond, Virginia. March 27, 1865 furloughed for 30 days from Jackson Hospital at Richmond, Virginia. He was born in Crawford County, Georgia in 1842.

ROLAN (ROLLINS), WILLIAM: Company H, private. September 9, 1861 enlisted as a private in Co. H, 27th Regiment, Georgia Infantry at Camp Stephens, Griffin, Spalding County, Georgia. September 22, 1862 death benefit claim was filed.

ROOK, SAMUEL L.: Company A, private. He enlisted as a private in Co. A, 27th Regiment, Georgia Infantry. August 19, 1864 wounded in the left arm and captured at Weldon Railroad near Petersburg, Virginia. August 21, 1864 admitted to 2nd Division of Depot Field Hospital 5th A. C. A of P. at City Point, Virginia with a Vulnus Sclopeticum (Gunshot Wound) to the left arm and was sent to General Hospital September 4, 1864.

ROSEBOROUGH, J.: Company H, private. September 9, 1861 enlisted as a private in Co. G, 27th Regiment, Georgia Infantry at Camp Stephens, Griffin, Spalding County, Georgia. December 23, 1861 admitted to Moore Hospital at General Hospital, No. 1 at Danville, Virginia and sent to Charlottesville, Virginia Hospital.

ROSS, DAVID J.: Company C, private. September 10, 1861 enlisted as a private in Co. C, 27th Regiment, Georgia Infantry. July 5, 1862 received pay ($66.00). June 26, 1863 issued clothing. October 1, 1863 detailed for extra duty as a teamster for the Quartermasters Department at Fort Johnson on James Island, South Carolina at an additional $.25 per day. He was wounded date and place not given. December 31, 1863 received pay. October, November, December and January 1864 on rolls shown as a teamster. January – February 1864 roll shows him present. February 29, 1864 received pay. February 7, 1864 received pay as a teamster through January 31, 1864. March - April 1864 roll shows him present. May 30, June 30, July, September 20 and September 30, 1864 issued clothing. September 20, 1864 received pay as a teamster at Petersburg, Virginia. April 26, 1865 surrendered Greensboro, North Carolina. May 1, 1865 paroled at Greensboro, North Carolina.

ROSS, ROBERT H.: Company G, private. September 9, 1861 enlisted as a private in Co. G, 27th Regiment, Georgia Infantry at Camp Stephens, Griffin, Spalding County, Georgia. March 7, 1862 admitted to Chimborazo Hospital No. 1 at Richmond, Virginia with Typhoid Fever. March 27, 1862 admitted to Chimborazo Hospital No. 1 at Richmond, Virginia for convalescent (transferred from 1st General Hospital). April 5(8), 1862 returned to duty. May 31, 1862 killed at Seven Pines, Virginia. August 4, 1862 death benefit claim was filed by his widow, Ann V. Ross. January 8, 1863 death benefit claim paid $130.00 (#2543). He was a resident of Pike County, Georgia.

ROSS, RUSSELL: Company G, private. September 9, 1861 enlisted as a private in Co. G, 27th Regiment, Georgia Infantry at Camp Stephens, Griffin, Spalding County, Georgia. September 17, 1862 captured at Sharpsburg, Maryland. September 27, 1862 paroled from the Army of the Potomac. October 12, 1862 admitted to No. 5, U. S. A. General Hospital at Frederick, Maryland with a Vulnus Sclopeticum (Gunshot Wound) in the back. October 15, 1862 admitted to No. 5, U. S. A. General Hospital at Frederick, Maryland. October 16, 1862 sent to General Hospital. October 18, 1862 sent from Fort Henry, Maryland to Fort Monroe, Virginia for exchange. October 23 (24), 1862 admitted to Chimborazo Hospital No. 4 at Richmond, Virginia with a Vulnus Sclopeticum (Gunshot Wound) to the back. November 10, 1862 furloughed for 35 days from Chimborazo Hospital No. 4 at Richmond, Virginia. December 31, 1862 received pay. December 1862 roll shows him absent without leave. February 7, 1863 furloughed for 30 days. March 12, 1863 furloughed for 30 days from headquarters Military Post at Atlanta, Georgia due to Vulnus Sclopeticum (Gunshot Wound). March 13, 1863 received pay in commutations of rations. December 16, 1863 received pay in commutation of rations ($180.00). December 22, 1863 - April 30, 1864 absent without leave. December 15, 1863 admitted to Floyd House and Ocmulgee Hospitals at Macon, Georgia with a Vulnus Sclopeticum (Gunshot Wound). January 8, 1864 furloughed for 30 days from Floyd House and Ocmulgee Hospitals at Macon, Georgia. January – February and March – April 1864 rolls show him absent without leave from December 22, 1863 and due commutations of $134.13. April 11, 1864 issued clothing. He was a resident of Barnesville, Georgia.

ROSS, WILLIAM M. (G.): Company C, lieutenant. September 10, 1861 enlisted as a private in Co. C, 27th Regiment, Georgia Infantry at Camp Stephens, Griffin, Spalding County, Georgia. December 1861 and January 1862 rolls show him in the Hospital in Richmond since December 30, 1861(January 3, 1862). January 2, 1862 admitted to Moore Hospital at General Hospital, No. 1 at Danville, Virginia with Pneumonia. March 16, 1862 admitted to Chimborazo Hospital No. 3 at Richmond, Virginia with Diarrhoea. March 23, 1862 returned to duty. April 19, 1862 admitted to Chimborazo Hospital No. 5 at Richmond, Virginia with Pneumonia. May 12, 1862 transferred from Chimborazo Hospital No. 5 at Richmond, Virginia to Camp Winder Hospital at Richmond, Virginia. November 25, 1862 elected Jr. 2nd lieutenant Co. C, 27th Regiment, Georgia Infantry. December 1862 roll shows him present in camp near Guinea Station, Virginia. September 30, 1863 roll of officers in Colquitt's Brigade shows him present. February 12, 1863 elected 2nd lieutenant Co. C, 27th Regiment, Georgia Infantry. December 31, 1863 received pay. January – February and March – April 1864 rolls show him present. June 1, 1864 wounded at Cold Harbor, Virginia. June 3, 1864 sent from Receiving and Wayside Hospital or General Hospital No. 9 at Richmond, Virginia to Jackson Hospital at Richmond, Virginia. June 5, 1864 admitted to Jackson Hospital at Richmond, Virginia with a Vulnus Sclopeticum (Gunshot Wound) to the left leg (mini ball). June 14, 1864 received pay ($160.00). July 11, 1864 elected 1st lieutenant Co. C, 27th Regiment, Georgia Infantry. July 13, 1864 furloughed for 30 days from Jackson Hospital at Richmond, Virginia. September 28, 1864 admitted to Ocmulgee Hospital at Macon, Georgia with a Vulnus Sclopeticum (Gunshot Wound) to the flesh of the left leg. (Note; ball passed through tendons destroying muscle). October 30, 1864 Report of Hoke's Division shows him on sick furlough at Knoxville, Georgia. November 1864 roll shows him present. December 31, 1864 roll of Hoke's

Division, Colquitt's Brigade at Camp Whiting, North Carolina shows him absent wounded. April 26, 1865 surrendered Greensboro, North Carolina. May 1, 1865 paroled at Greensboro, North Carolina.

ROUNDTREE, EPHRAIM: Company E, private. August 1, 1863 enlisted as a private in Co. E, 27th Regiment, Georgia Infantry at Fairburn, Georgia. August 31, 1863 received pay. December 31, 1863 received pay. January – February 1864 roll shows him present and due $50.00 bounty. March - April 1864 roll shows him present. May – June 1864 roll of General Hospital No. 1 at Summerville, South Carolina shows him present. April 26, 1865 surrendered, Greensboro, North Carolina. April 28, 1865 admitted to C. S. A. General Hospital, No. 11 at Charlotte, North Carolina with Diarrhoea. May 1865 paroled at Charlotte, North Carolina as a patient.

ROUSE, J. W.: Company D, private. November 20, 1863 enlisted as a private in Co. D, 27th Regiment, Georgia Infantry at Charleston, South Carolina. December 31, 1863 received pay. March - April 1864 roll shows him present. July 1864 issued clothing.

March - April 1864 roll shows him present.

ROUSE, WILEY: Company D, sergeant. September 10, 1861 elected 3rd sergeant. in Co. D, 27th Regiment, Georgia Infantry at Camp Stephens, Griffin, Spalding County, Georgia. April 30, 1862 received pay. June 5, 1862 received pay ($90.00). September 30, 1862 admitted to General Hospital No. 1 at Richmond, Virginia. August 31, 1862 roll of General Hospital No. 1 at Richmond, Virginia shows him present and due $50.00 bounty. April, May, June and November 1863 issued clothing. February 29, 1864 received pay. March - April 1864 roll shows him present. July 1864 issued clothing.

ROLAND, W. C.: Company D, sergeant. He enlisted as a private in Co. D, 27th Regiment, Georgia Infantry. He was appointed sergeant. June 3, 1864 transferred from Receiving and Wayside Hospital or General Hospital No. 9 at Richmond, Virginia to Jackson Hospital at Richmond, Virginia.

RUCKER, J. M.: Company G, private. August 4, 1863 enlisted as a private in Co. G, 27th Regiment, Georgia Infantry at Zebulon, Georgia. October 30, 1863 issued clothing. December 31, 1863 received pay. January – February 1864 roll shows him absent without leave from April 7, 1864. March - April 1864 roll shows him present. March 18, 1865 killed at Bentonville, North Carolina.

RUCKER, JAMES B.: Company G, private. He enlisted as a private in Co. G, 27th Regiment, Georgia Infantry. July 3, 1863 wounded in the arm, necessitating amputation above the elbow at Gettysburg, Pennsylvania (the 27th Georgia was not at Gettysburg). He was born in Pike County, Georgia August 2, 1839.

RUDICIL, J. J.: Company E, private. September 10, 1861 enlisted as a private in Co. E, 27th Regiment, Georgia Infantry at Camp Stephens, Griffin, Spalding County, Georgia. June 6, 1862 died at Richmond,

Virginia. He was buried in Hollywood Cemetery at Richmond, Virginia.
RUSSELL, J. G.: Field Staff, Quartermaster Sergeant. He enlisted in the 27th Regiment, Georgia Infantry. April 9, 1863 promoted to 2nd master sergeant of the Quartermaster's Department by Colonel Charles T. Zachry. June 30, 1863 received pay for commutation of rations ($49.20) from April 9, 1863 to June 30, 1863 at $.60 per day. October 30, 1863 list of detailed men at James Island, South Carolina shows him present. December 31, 1864 - April 30, 1864 roll shows him present. September 1, 1864 issued clothing.
RUSSELL, JAMES: Company H, private. He enlisted as a private in Co. H, 27th Regiment, Georgia Infantry.
RUSSELL, JOHN: Company K, private. March 1, 1862 enlisted at 19 years of age as a private in Co. K, 27th Regiment, Georgia Infantry at Talbotton, Georgia. September 17, 1862 killed at Sharpsburg, Maryland. December 1862 roll shows him missing in action at Sharpsburg, Maryland on September 17, 1862. March 23, 1863 death benefit claim was filed by his father, David R. Russell. August 8, 1863 death benefit claim paid $75.23 (#7315). He was born in 1843. Description is: 19 years of age at enlistment, blue eyes, dark hair, light complexion, 5 feet 10 inches high and was by occupation a farmer.
RUSSELL, L. WHIT: Company H, musician (drummer). March 1, 1862 enlisted as a private in Co. H, 27th Regiment, Georgia Infantry at Chickahominy (Richmond), Virginia. July 26, 1862 received pay for clothing ($25.00). December 31, 1863 received pay. January – February and March – April 1864 rolls show him present as a drummer. June 20, 1864 wounded in the left thigh at Colquitt's Salient. June 20, 1864 admitted to Jackson Hospital at Richmond, Virginia with a Vulnus Sclopeticum (Gunshot Wound) to the left thigh (mini ball). July 1864 issued clothing. August 19, 1864 furloughed to Conyers, Georgia for 30 days from Jackson Hospital at Richmond, Virginia.
RUSSELL, THOMAS C.: Company E, corporal. September 9, 1861 elected 1st corporal Co. E, 27th Regiment, Georgia Infantry at Camp Stephens, Griffin, Spalding County, Georgia. December 1861 roll shows him in the hospital at Richmond, Virginia. January 10, 1862 furloughed for 3 days from hospital and given $6.60 for commutation of rations. January 1862 roll shows him absent on furlough since January 10, 1862. February 1862 roll shows him absent without leave. January 10, 1863 received pay ($71.03). April, May and June 1863 issued clothing. December 31, 1863 received pay. February 20, 1864 wounded through right shoulder and permanently disabled at Olustee, Florida. January – February 1864 roll shows him absent wounded February 20, 1864 at Olustee, Florida. March 9, 1864 furloughed for 30 days. April 9, 1864 furlough extended 30 days. March - April 1864 roll shows him absent on furlough. May 19, 1864 received pay $26.00. Pension Records show he was at home, wounded at the close of the war.

RUSSELL, THOMAS L.: Company H, private. September 9, 1861 enlisted as a private in Co. H, 27th Regiment, Georgia Infantry at Camp Stephens, Griffin, Spalding County, Georgia. December 31, 1863 received pay. January – February 1864 roll shows him present. February 29, 1864 received pay. March - April 1864 roll shows him present. July 1864 issued clothing. September 28, 1864 admitted to Jackson Hospital at Richmond, Virginia with Remitting Febris (Malaria). November 3, 1864 furloughed from Jackson Hospital at Richmond, Virginia for 60 days.

RYDER, WILLIAM: Company B, private. September 10, 1861 enlisted as a private in Co. B, 27th Regiment, Georgia Infantry at Camp Stephens, Griffin, Spalding County, Georgia.

SALLAS, JOHN: Company F, private. He enlisted as a private in Co. D, 27th Regiment, Georgia Infantry. September 20, 1864 issued clothing. April 26, 1865, surrendered at Greensboro, North Carolina. May 1, 1865 paroled at Greensboro, North Carolina.

SAMS WILLIAM J.: Company E, lieutenant. September 10, 1861 elected 1st lieutenant in Co. E, 27th Regiment, Georgia Infantry at Camp Stephens, Griffin, Spalding County, Georgia. December 1861 and January 1861 rolls show him present at Camp Pickens near Manassas, Virginia. February 1862 roll shows him absent on recruiting service for 30 days from February 13, 1861. May 15, 1862 received pay ($90.00). June 13, 1862 died, Richmond, Virginia.

SANDERS, GREEN E.: Company D, private. September 10, 1861 enlisted as a private in Co. D, 27th Regiment, Georgia Infantry at Camp Stephens, Griffin, Spalding County, Georgia. December 29, 1861 died of disease in Richmond, Virginia. December 1861 and January 1862 rolls indicate his death on December 29, 1861 at Richmond, Virginia. December 26, 1862 death benefit claim was filed by his father, William M. Sanders. December 23, 1864 death benefit claim was paid $5.13. He was a resident of Hall County, Georgia.

SANDERS, J. C.: Company D, private. September 10, 1861 enlisted as a private in Co. D, 27th Regiment, Georgia Infantry at Camp Stephens, Griffin, Spalding County, Georgia. May 2, 1863 wounded at Chancellorsville, Virginia. April, May, June and November 1863 issued clothing. February 29, 1864 received pay. March - April 1864 roll shows him present. July 1864 and September 20, 1864 issued clothing. October 1, 1864 wounded at Fort Harrison near Richmond, Virginia. October 1, 1864 admitted to Receiving and Wayside Hospital or General Hospital No. 9 at Richmond, Virginia and sent to Jackson Hospital at Richmond, Virginia. October 1, 1864 admitted to Jackson Hospital at Richmond, Virginia with a Vulnus Sclopeticum (Gunshot Wound) to the left shoulder (mini ball). November 6, 1864 furloughed for 60 days from Jackson Hospital at Richmond, Virginia. March 1, 1865 admitted to Ocmulgee Hospital at Macon, Georgia with a Vulnus Sclopeticum (Gunshot Wound) to the left shoulder. March 28, 1865 returned to duty. April 9, 1865 admitted to Jackson Hospital at Richmond,

Virginia. April 14, 1865 turned over to the Provost Marshal.

SANDERS, ROBERT: Company C, private. He enlisted as a private in Co. C, 27th Regiment, Georgia Infantry. June 3, 1864 wounded, Cold Harbor, Virginia.

SAPP, BUFORD (BLUFORD): Company I, private. September 10, 1861 enlisted as a private in Co. I, 27th Regiment, Georgia Infantry at Camp Stephens, Griffin, Spalding County, Georgia. December 1861 roll shows he was in the hospital at Richmond, Virginia. March 30, 1862 admitted to Chimborazo Hospital No. 1 at Richmond, Virginia with Measles (shows he deserted on July 8, 1862). May 1, 1862 roll of Chimborazo Hospital at Richmond, Virginia shows him present. June 16 and 27, 1863 issued clothing. December 31, 1863 received pay. January – February 1864 roll shows him present. February 29, 1864 received pay. March - April 1864 roll shows him present. July 1864 issued clothing. August 18, 1864 killed at Weldon Railroad, Virginia. (In the memoirs of Benjamin Milikin of Company I, his friend Bluford "Blue" Sapp pulled him up next to a tree at the far end of the cornfield at Sharpsburg, Maryland and propped him up after Milikin was wounded in the leg.)

SAUNDERS, J. C.: Company F, private. September 10, 1861 enlisted as a private in Co. F, 27th Regiment, Georgia Infantry at Camp Stephens, Griffin, Spalding County, Georgia. December 28, 1861 admitted to Moore Hospital at General Hospital, No. 1 at Danville, Virginia with Congestive Fever (Malaria) and was sent to Richmond, Virginia.

SAWYER, D. C.: Company C, private. September 10, 1861 enlisted as a private in Co. C, 27th Regiment, Georgia Infantry at Camp Stephens, Griffin, Spalding County, Georgia. May 31, 1863 captured at Seven Pines, Virginia. Described after capture as 17 years of age, 6 foot 2 inches high, light hair, blue eyes and florid complexion. June 1, 1862 sent to Fort Delaware, Delaware. June 26, 1862 delivered to Aiken's Landing, Virginia for exchange. August 5, 1862 exchanged at Aiken's landing, Virginia. August 13, 1862 received pay ($66.00). September 17, 1862 wounded in the hand at Sharpsburg, Maryland. September 28, 1862 admitted to Chimborazo Hospital No. 5 at Richmond, Virginia with a wound to the hand. November 21, 1862 admitted to Chimborazo Hospital No. 5 at Richmond, Virginia and transferred (to Small Pox Hospital) and admitted to General Hospital No.21 at Richmond, Virginia with Variola. November 30, 1862 died in General Hospital No.21 at Richmond, Virginia (Age 17 years). He was born in Georgia in 1845.

SAWYER, JOHN: Company C, private. June 15, 1862 enlisted as a private in Co. C, 27th Regiment, Georgia Infantry. He died in service.

SAWYER, JULIUS T.: Company C, private. September 10, 1862 enlisted as a private in Co. C, 27th Regiment, Georgia Infantry. March 9, 1862 admitted to Chimborazo Hospital No. 4 at Richmond, Virginia with Jaundice. March 24, 1862 returned to duty. May 7, 1862 admitted to Camp Winder General Hospital at Richmond, Virginia with Debility. May

8, 1862 discharged from hospital. May 16, 1862 became a nurse at Camp Winder General Hospital at Richmond, Virginia. August 21, 1862 received pay ($47.00). October 25, 1862 furloughed for 30 days from Camp Winder Division No. 2 Hospital at Richmond, Virginia. December 1862 roll shows him absent on sick furlough. February 7, 1863 admitted to Camp Winder Division No. 1 Hospital at Richmond, Virginia with Pneumonia. December 7, 1863 returned to duty. June 26, June 30 and September 30, 1863 issued clothing. December 31, 1863 received pay. February 20, 1864 killed, Olustee, Florida. January – February 1864 roll shows him killed in action at Olustee, Florida.

SAXON, CICERO: Company D, private. March 11, 1862 enlisted as a private in Co. D, 27th Regiment, Georgia Infantry at Gainesville, Georgia. March 25, 1862 received bounty pay of $50.00 at Atlanta, Georgia. April 10, 1862 admitted to Chimborazo Hospital No. 5 at Richmond, Virginia with Bronchitis. May 9, 1862 transferred to Lynchburg, Virginia.

SAYE, JAMES G.: Company D, private. September 10, 1861 enlisted as a private in Co. D, 27th Regiment, Georgia Infantry at Camp Stephens, Griffin, Spalding County, Georgia. December 17, 1861 admitted to Moore Hospital at General Hospital No. 1 at Danville, Virginia and was transferred to Richmond, Virginia. December 29, 1861 died. May 29, 1862 death benefit claim was filed by his mother, Elizabeth Saye.

SAYE, JAMES N.: Company D, private. September 23, 1861 enlisted as a private in Co. D, 27th Regiment, Georgia Infantry at Camp Stephens, Griffin, Spalding County, Georgia. May 13, 1862 admitted to Chimborazo Hospital No. 1 at Richmond, Virginia with Diarrhoea. May 27, 1862 transferred to Lynchburg, Virginia. May 28, 1862 admitted to General Hospital at Farmville, Virginia with Typhoid Fever. June 2, 1862 died of Typhoid Fever at General Hospital at Farmville, Virginia. March 23, 1863 death benefit claim was filed by his father, John Saye.

SAYE, WILLIAM L.: Company D, private. He enlisted as a private in Co. D, 27th Regiment, Georgia Infantry. He died in Richmond, Virginia. March 23, 1863, death benefit claim was filed by John Saye.

SCHOFIELD, JACOB: Company B, private. September 10, 1861 enlisted as a private in Co. B, 27th Regiment, Georgia Infantry at Camp Stephens, Griffin, Spalding County, Georgia. April 9, 1862 died at Rapidan River, Virginia date not given. May 27, 1863 death benefit claim was filed. He was born in Bibb County, Georgia in 1845. Description 16 years of age, grey eyes, dark hair, sallow complexion, 5 feet 9 inches high, was from Bibb County, Georgia and was by occupation a farmer.

SCHOFIELD, PHILLIP HARRISON: Company B, private. September 10, 1861 enlisted as a private in Co. B, 27th Regiment, Georgia Infantry at Camp Stephens, Griffin, Spalding County, Georgia. December 1861 and January 1862 rolls show he was left sick in Georgia October 31, 1861. June 30, 1862 received pay ($69.00). December 1862 roll shows him absent without leave – furlough expired. March 25, 1863 received pay for commutation of rations for 90 days plus 20 days furlough from July 28, 1862. July 7, 1863 received pay ($44.00). August 5, 1863 received $94.00 in commutation of rations. November 13, 1863 received pay ($22.00). December 20, 1863 received $40.00 in commutation of rations. December 24, 1863 received $47.00 in commutation of rations. January – February and March – April 1864 rolls show him absent without leave since December 30, 1863. June 6, 1864 wounded in the left ankle at Cold Harbor, Virginia. June 7, 1864 admitted to Receiving and Wayside Hospital or General Hospital No. 9 at Richmond, Virginia. June 8, 1864 transferred and admitted to Jackson Hospital at Richmond, Virginia with a Vulnus Sclopeticum (Gunshot Wound) to the left ankle (mini ball). July 8, 1864 detailed as a nurse at Jackson Hospital at Richmond, Virginia due to Necrosis in the lower portion of the Tibia, the effects of a Vulnus Sclopeticum (Gunshot Wound). August 13, 1864 issued clothing at Jackson Hospital at Richmond, Virginia. August 31, 1864 ordered to report a 6 o'clock in the morning to the sergeant of the guard for assignment of duties at Jackson Hospital at Richmond, Virginia. October 28, 1864 returned to duty. October 28, 1864 attached to Jackson Hospital at Richmond, Virginia as guard (received a pay raise of $5.13). October 31, 1864 received pay. December 14, 1864 issued clothing. December 31, 1864 received pay. December 31, 1864 and February 28, 1865 he is shown on rolls as being on duty at Jackson Hospital. March 8, 1865 elected 4th corporal of Co A, Scott's Battalion at Jackson Hospital at Richmond, Virginia.

SCOTT, JOHN: Company B, private. September 10, 1861 enlisted as a private in Co. B, 27th Regiment, Georgia Infantry at Camp Stephens, Griffin, Spalding County, Georgia.

SCOTT, NATHANIEL W.: Company F, private. August 7, 1862 enlisted as a private in Co. F, 27th Regiment, Georgia Infantry at Camp Randolph, Georgia. September 17, 1862 wounded in the arm and captured at Sharpsburg, Maryland. September 27, 1862 was shown as paroled by the Army of the Potomac. October 1, 1862 admitted to Summit House U. S. A. General Hospital at West Philadelphia, Pennsylvania with a Vulnus Sclopeticum (Gunshot Wound) and Fracture of the left arm. December 5, 1862 returned to duty from Summit House U. S. A. General Hospital at West Philadelphia, Pennsylvania with a Vulnus Sclopeticum (Gunshot Wound) and Fracture of the left arm. December 6, 1862 sent from Provost Barracks, Philadelphia, Pennsylvania to Fort Delaware, Delaware. December 15, 1862 sent from Fort Delaware, Delaware to Fortress Monroe, Virginia for exchange. September 17, 1862 through April 30, 1864 was on detached duty. December 18, 1862 admitted to General Hospital at Petersburg, Virginia with a Vulnus Sclopeticum (Gunshot Wound) (paroled prisoner). December 1862 roll shows him absent wounded since September 17, 1862. January 26, 1863 furloughed for 60 days from General Hospital at Petersburg, Virginia. January – February and March – April 1864 rolls show him absent on wounded furlough since September 17, 1862.

SEALY, A. HOWARD: Company K, private. November 12, 1863, enlisted as a private in Co. B, 27th Battalion, Georgia Infantry (non-conscripts). March 15, 1864 transferred as a private to Co. K, 27th Regiment, Georgia Infantry. March - April 1864 roll shows him present and notes his transfer. June 9, 1864 wounded at Cold Harbor, Virginia. July 1864 issued clothing. November 25, 1864 received pay ($27.13). December 9, 1864 received pay ($22.00). Pension records show he was at home wounded at the close of the war. April 19, 1865 captured at the Flint River Bridge, Georgia.

SEALY (SEALEY) (SEELEY), R. THOMAS: Company G, private. September 9, 1861 enlisted as a private in Co. G, 27th Regiment, Georgia Infantry at Camp Stephens, Griffin, Spalding County, Georgia. January 16, 1862 admitted to Moore Hospital at General Hospital No. 1 at Danville, Virginia with Neuralgia (he was sent to Ward No. 8). January 1862 and February 1862 rolls show him in the hospital since January 16, 1861. October 4, 1862 admitted to Receiving and Wayside Hospital or General Hospital No. 9 at Richmond, Virginia and transferred to Hospital No. 22. October 5, 1862 admitted to General Hospital No. 22 at Richmond, Virginia. October 7, 1862 received pay ($133.00). October 8, 1862 furloughed from General Hospital No. 22 at Richmond, Virginia for 30 days. March 17, 1863 received in commutation of rations ($20.00). June 16, 1863, October 30, 1863 and November 24, 1863 issued clothing. December 31, 1863 received pay. January – February 1864 roll shows him absent sick (at hospital in Savannah, Georgia) since February 14, 1864. February 29, 1864 received pay. March - April 1864 roll shows him present. July 1864 issued clothing. September 4, 1864 admitted to Jackson Hospital at Richmond, Virginia with Febris Remitting. October 2, 1864 furloughed for 30 days from Jackson Hospital at Richmond, Virginia. February 21, 1865 admitted to C. S. A. General Hospital No. 3 at Greensboro, North Carolina with Rubeola (Transferred there from Wilmington, North Carolina). February 23, 1865 admitted to Pettigrew General Hospital No.13 at Raleigh, North Carolina with Chronic Diarrhoea. February 24, 1865 clothing was issued to him at Pettigrew General Hospital No.13 at Raleigh, North Carolina. February 24, 1865 transferred from Pettigrew General Hospital No.13 at Raleigh, North Carolina with remark ("Wake Forest"). April 6, 1865 died in Raleigh, North Carolina Hospital. He was a resident of Zebulon, Pike County, Georgia.

SEALY, ZEPH B.: Company K, private. September 21, 1861 enlisted as a private in Co. K, 27th Regiment, Georgia Infantry at Camp Stephens, Griffin, Spalding County, Georgia. September 17, 1862 killed at Sharpsburg, Maryland. December 1862 roll shows he was killed at Sharpsburg, Maryland September 17, 1862. March 23, 1863 death benefit claim was filed by his father, W. C. Sealy. September 26, 1863 death benefit claim paid $125.23 (#9129). He was a resident of Taylor County, Georgia. He was born in 1844 and was 18 at the time of death.

SEARCY, J. W.: Company F, corporal. September 9, 1861 elected 1st corporal in Co. F, 27th Regiment, Georgia Infantry at Camp Stephens, Griffin, Spalding County, Georgia. November 9, 1861 admitted to General Hospital No. 18 (formerly Greaner's Hospital) at Richmond, Virginia. November 12, 1861 returned to duty. April 10, 1862 admitted to Chimborazo Hospital No. 5 at Richmond, Virginia with Debility. May 9, 1862 transferred to Lynchburg, Virginia. June 3, 1863 furloughed for 30 days.

July 9, 1863 admitted to Receiving and Wayside Hospital or General Hospital No. 9 at Richmond, Virginia (transferred to Chimborazo Hospital No. 2 at Richmond, Virginia). July 10, 1863 admitted to Chimborazo Hospital No. 2 at Richmond, Virginia with Diarrhoea. July 22, 1863 returned to duty. August 26, 1863 received for commutation of rations $7.50. December 31, 1863 received pay. January – February 1864 roll shows him present. March – April 1864 roll shows him present. July 1864 and September 20, 1864 issued clothing. June 12, 1865 paroled at Montgomery, Alabama. He is described on his parole: 6 feet high, dark hair, grey eyes and fair complexion.

SEARS, ALFRED S.: Company D, sergeant. September 10, 1861 elected 1st sergeant, in Co. D, 27th Regiment, Georgia Infantry at Camp Stephens, Griffin, Spalding County, Georgia. June 7, 1862 received pay ($77.00). April, May, June and November 1863 issued clothing. December 31, 1863 received pay. March - April 1864 roll shows him present. July, 1864 and September 20, 1864 issued clothing. August 19, 1864 admitted to Receiving and Wayside Hospital or General Hospital No. 9 at Richmond, Virginia (transferred to Jackson Hospital). August 20, 1864 admitted to Jackson Hospital at Richmond, Virginia with Chronic Diarrhoea. August 25, 1864 furloughed for 30 days to Athens, Georgia.

SELF, JAMES T.: Company B, private. March 1, 1863 enlisted as a private in Co. B, 27th Regiment, Georgia Infantry at Macon, Georgia. Substitute for W. J. Totten. May 2, 1863 wounded at Chancellorsville, Virginia. August 31, 1863 issued clothing at Fairview Hospital at Lexington, Virginia. October, November and December 1863 issued clothing. December 31, 1863 received pay. January – February and March - April 1864 rolls show him present. July 1864 issued clothing. August 16, 1864 admitted to Receiving and Wayside Hospital or General Hospital No. 9 at Richmond, Virginia (transferred to Jackson Hospital). August 17, 1864 admitted to Jackson Hospital at Richmond, Virginia with Ascites. August 25, 1864 furloughed from Jackson Hospital at Richmond, Virginia for 30 days to Marietta, Georgia.

SELLS DANIEL: Company F, private. May 22, 1862 enlisted as a private in Co. F, 27th Regiment, Georgia Infantry at Butler, Georgia. August 14, 1862 received pay ($58.00). December 1862 roll shows him absent since June 3, 1862. January – February and March – April 1864 rolls show him discharged March 25, 1864. November 15, 1864 died at Macon Georgia hospital. December 21, 1864 death benefit claim was filed by Sarah Sells, his widow.

SERGEANT, W. M.: Company E, private.   August 7, 1862 admitted to Chimborazo Hospital No. 5 at Richmond, Virginia with Rheumatism. September 26, 1862 furloughed for 40 days.

SESNOS, J. S.: Company E, private.   September 10, 1861 enlisted as a private in Co. E, 27th Regiment, Georgia Infantry at Camp Stephens, Griffin, Spalding County, Georgia.   February 3, 1865 (March 2, 1865) died at Raleigh, North Carolina.   He is buried in the Confederate Cemetery at Raleigh, North Carolina.

SEXTON, D. C.: Company D, private.   March 12, 1862 enlisted as a private in Co. D, 27th Regiment, Georgia Infantry in Hall County, Georgia. May 9, 1862 transferred from Chimborazo Hospital No. 5 at Richmond, Virginia and admitted to Lynchburg Hospital.   April, May, June and November 1863 issued clothing. December 31, 1863 received pay. March - April 1864 roll shows him present.   July 1864 issued clothing.

SEYMORE, JOHN R.: Company B, sergeant. September 10, 1861 enlisted as a private in Co. B, 27th Regiment, Georgia Infantry at Camp Stephens, Griffin, Spalding County, Georgia.   December 10, 1861 appointed 4th sergeant in Co. B, 27th Regiment, Georgia Infantry. April 30, 1862 received pay. September 17, 1862 wounded in right arm at Sharpsburg, Maryland. September 27, 1862 admitted to General Hospital No. 21 at Richmond, Virginia with a Vulnus Sclopeticum (Gunshot Wound). October 7(10), 1862 furloughed from General Hospital No. 21 at Richmond, Virginia (He was age 22). December 1862 roll shows his furlough had expired. January 14, 1863 paid for commutation of rations for 30 days beginning December 31, 1862. February 6, 1863 received pay ($71.95). August 31, 1863 received pay. October 1863 roll of General Hospital No. 1 at Summerville, South Carolina shows him present.   October, November and December 1863 issued clothing.   December 31, 1863 received pay.   January – February 1864 roll shows him present. February 29, 1864 received pay. March - April 1864 roll shows him present. May 30, 1864, July 1864 and September 20, 1864 issued clothing.   September 30, 1864 wounded in right arm at Fort Harrison, Virginia.   October 1, 1864 admitted to Jackson Hospital at Richmond, Virginia with a Vulnus Sclopeticum (Gunshot Wound) to the right arm (mini ball). November 3, 1864 furloughed for 60 days. April 26, 1865 surrendered Greensboro, North Carolina.   May 1, 1865 paroled at Greensboro, North Carolina. He was born in Putnam County, Georgia in 1834 (1840).

SHAW, S. J.: Company H, private.   He enlisted as a private in Co. H, 27th Regiment, Georgia Infantry.   May 24, 1865 paroled at Talladega, Alabama.

SHEPHERD (SHEPPARD), GEORGE W. (J. W.): Company C, private. September 10, 1861 enlisted as a private in Co. C, 27th Regiment, Georgia Infantry at Camp Stephens, Griffin, Spalding County, Georgia.   January 29, 1863 died in Virginia. March 26, 1863 death benefit claim was filed by Jesse Shepherd, his father (indicating he was 18 years of age). He was born in 1845 and was a resident of Upson, County, Georgia.

SHEPHERD (SHEPPARD), W. F.: Company F, corporal. September 9, 1861 enlisted as a private in Co. F, 27th Regiment, Georgia Infantry at Camp Stephens, Griffin, Spalding County, Georgia. December18, 1862 to August 18, 1863 was on detached service. August 22, 1863 received extra pay for 8 months detached service at $.75 extra per day ($180.00). April 18, 1863 to September 11, 1863 was on detached service and due commutation of rations. September 11, 1863 received $18.00 in commutation of rations. December 31, 1863 received pay. January – February and March - April 1864 roll shows him present. July 1864 issued clothing. April 26, 1865 surrendered Greensboro, North Carolina. May 1, 1865 paroled at Greensboro, North Carolina.

SHEPPARD (SHEPHERD), W. H.: Company F, private. September 9, 1861 enlisted as a private in Co. F, 27th Regiment, Georgia Infantry at Camp Stephens, Griffin, Spalding County, Georgia. September 17, 1862 wounded at Sharpsburg, Maryland. December 1862 roll shows he was wounded at Sharpsburg, Maryland on September 11, 1862.

SHINHOLSTER, JESSE: Company F, private. September 9, 1861 enlisted as a private in Co. F, 27th Regiment, Georgia Infantry at Camp Stephens, Griffin, Spalding County, Georgia. November 14, 1861 admitted to General Hospital No. 18 (formerly Greaner's Hospital) at Richmond, Virginia. December 9, 1861 returned to duty. October 31, 1862 received pay. November 2, 1862 admitted to Hospital No 6 at Richmond, Virginia. December 31, 1862 roll of General Hospital No. 14 at Richmond, Virginia shows him present. December 31, 1862 received pay. December 1862 roll shows him sick in Richmond, Virginia since September. February 13, 1863 admitted to General Hospital No. 16 at Richmond, Virginia. February 28, 1863 roll of General Hospital No. 16 at Richmond, Virginia shows him present. March 12, 1863 furloughed for 45 days from General Hospital No. 16 at Richmond, Virginia. April 7, 1863 wounded in left hip and back at Fort Sumter, South Carolina. August 25, 1863 issued clothing. December 31, 1863 received pay. January – February and March – April 1864 roll shows him absent sick in the Hospital at Tallahassee, Florida since March 10, 1864. February 29, 1864 received pay. June 1864, July 1864 and September 20, 1864 issued clothing. April 26, 1865 surrendered Greensboro, North Carolina. May 1, 1865 paroled at Greensboro, North Carolina. He was born in Georgia March 20, 1831.

SHIPP, JAMES R.: Company A, private. March 6, 1862 enlisted as a private in Co. A, 27th Regiment, Georgia Infantry in Marion County, Georgia. November 20, 1862 paid Bounty $50.00 at Richmond, Virginia. December 9, 1862 admitted to the C. S. A. General Hospital at Charlottesville, Virginia with Debility. December 10, 1862 returned to duty. June, July, August, September and November1863 issued clothing. October 31, 1863 received pay. January – February 1864 roll shows him absent in the Hospital in Macon, Georgia since March 1, 1864.   March 1, 1864 he was in Macon, Georgia Hospital.   March - April 1864 roll shows him present.   July 1864 and September 30, 1864 issued clothing.   April 26, 1865 surrendered Greensboro, North Carolina.   May 1, 1865 paroled at Greensboro, North Carolina.

SHIPP, THOMAS J.: Company A, private.   May 12, 1862 enlisted as a private in Co. A, 27th Regiment, Georgia Infantry at Marion County, Georgia.   December 13, 1862 admitted to the C. S. A. General Hospital at Charlottesville, Virginia with Debility.   December 14, 1862 returned to duty.   June, July, August, September and November 1863 issued clothing.   December 31, 1863 received pay.   January – February 1864 roll shows him present.   February 29, 1864 received pay.   March - April 1864 roll shows him present.   July 1864 and September 30, 1864 issued clothing.   February 21, 1865 captured near Wilmington, North Carolina.   March 13, 1865 arrived at Point Lookout, Maryland from Wilmington, North Carolina.   June 19, 1865 released at Point Lookout, Maryland.   He is described as florid complexion, dark hair, hazel eyes and 5 feet 2 inches high from Marion County, Georgia.

SHIPPEN, T. J.: Company B, private.   He enlisted as a private in Co. B, 27th Regiment, Georgia Infantry.   December 1862 roll shows him absent since January 10, 1863.

SHIRAH, CHARLES: Company F, private.   March 19, 1862 enlisted as a private in Co. F, 27th Regiment, Georgia Infantry.   April 11, 1862 admitted to Chimborazo Hospital No.2 at Richmond, Virginia on account of Debility.   May 12, 1862 died of disease in Richmond, Virginia prior to this date.   March 12, 1863 death benefit claim was filed by his mother, Lucinda (Lourany) Shirah.   February 22, 1864 death benefit claim paid $52.86 (#12661).   He was a resident of Taylor County, Georgia.

SHIRAH, CHRISTOPHER C.: Company F, private.   September 9, 1861 enlisted as a private in Co. F, 27th Regiment, Georgia Infantry at Camp Stephens, Griffin, Spalding County, Georgia.   November 14, 1861 admitted to General Hospital No. 18 (formerly Greaner's Hospital) at Richmond, Virginia.   December 4, 1861 returned to duty.   December 11, 1861 discharged and paid.   December 1861, January and February 1862 rolls show him in the hospital in Richmond, Virginia since November 15.   November 14, 1861 - February 28, 1862 was in General Hospital No.18, at Richmond, Virginia.   September 17, 1862 killed at Sharpsburg, Maryland.   March 12, 1863 death benefit claim was filed by his mother, Lucinda (Lurany) Shirah.   February 19, 1864 death benefit claim was paid $210.30.   He was a resident of Taylor County, Georgia

SHIRAH, JAMES: Company F, lieutenant.   September 20, 1861 enlisted as a private in Co. F, 27th Regiment, Georgia Infantry.   November 29, 1861 admitted to Chimborazo Hospital No. 1 at Richmond, Virginia.   January 20, 1862 admitted to Moore Hospital at General Hospital, No. 1 at Danville, Virginia with a Hernia and sent to the Hospital at Orange Court House.

442

January 21, 1862 admitted to General Hospital at Orange Court House, Virginia with Hernia. January 1862 roll shows him in Moore Hospital since January 20, 1862. February 5, 1862, February 10, 1862 returned to duty. February 15, 1862 discharged with surgeon's certificate of disability due to double Hernia at Camp Pickens near Manassas, Virginia. February 20, 1862 discharged and paid. February 1862 roll shows he was discharged due to disability on February 20, 1862 at Camp Pickens near Manassas, Virginia. He was appointed corporal in Co. F, 27th Regiment, Georgia Infantry. February 20, 1862 discharged due to disability, at Camp Pickens near Manassas, Virginia. July 20, 1862 received pay ($28.81). February 23, 1863 elected 2nd lieutenant in Co. F, 27th Regiment, Georgia Infantry. June 27, 1863 elected 1st lieutenant in Co. F, 27th Regiment, Georgia Infantry. October 24, 1863 granted leave. February 20, 1864 wounded at Olustee, Florida. January – February 1864 roll does not show him present. March - April 1864 roll shows him present. August 11, 1864 died at Petersburg, Virginia. He was born in 1834 in the Richland District, South Carolina. Described in his discharge certificate as age 28 years, 5 feet 7 inches high, fair complexion, blue eyes, dark hair and occupation when enlisted was a farmer.

(Compiler's note: Either there were two James Shirahs or his health improved and he returned to his unit which was not uncommon.)

SHIRAH, JOHN: Company F, private. September 9, 1861 enlisted as a private in Co. F, 27th Regiment, Georgia Infantry at Camp Stephens, Griffin, Spalding County, Georgia. December 1861 roll shows he was discharged due to disability at Richmond, Virginia on December 21, 1861 and paid ($68.22).

SHIRAH, JOHN: Company F, private. September 9, 1861 enlisted as a private in Co. F, 27th Regiment, Georgia Infantry at Camp Stephens, Griffin, Spalding County, Georgia. December 1861 and January 1862 rolls show he was in the Hospital since November 28, 1861 at Richmond, Virginia on December 21, 1861. May 31, 1862 killed at Seven Pines, Virginia. March 12, 1863 death benefit claim was filed by his widow, Lucinda Shirah. September 24, 1863 death benefit claim was paid $196.06 (#9025). He was a resident of Taylor County, Georgia. He was born in 1830.

SHIVER, A. J.: Company B, private. April 26, 1865, surrendered at Greensboro, North Carolina. May 1, 1865 paroled at Greensboro, North Carolina.

SHORT, NOAH: Company K, private. September 10, 1861 enlisted as a private in Co. K, 27th Regiment, Georgia Infantry at Camp Stephens, Griffin, Spalding County, Georgia. December 1861 roll shows he was left sick in Georgia October 31, 1861. January 20, 1862 admitted to Moore Hospital at General Hospital, No. 1 at Danville, Virginia and was transferred to General Hospital at Orange Court House. January 21, 1862 admitted to General Hospital at Orange Court House with Pneumonia.

443

January 1862 report of General Hospital at Orange Court House shows he died of Pneumonia. January 27, 1862. January 1862 roll shows he died of disease at Orange Court House, Virginia on January 27, 1862. August 13, 1862 death benefit claim was filed by his father, Franklin Short. April 7, 1863 death benefit claim was paid $84.90 (#4465). He was a resident of Talbotton, Talbot County, Georgia.

SIBLEY, JOHN K.: Company K, private. September 10, 1861 enlisted as a private in Co. K, 27th Regiment, Georgia Infantry at Camp Stephens, Griffin, Spalding County, Georgia. January 1862 roll shows he was detailed on fatigue duty at the Post headquarters. February 26, 1862 admitted to C. S. A. General Hospital at Charlottesville, Virginia with Rheumatism and Vascular Disease of the Heart. February 1862 roll shows he was sent to the General Hospital at Orange Court House, Virginia on January 20, 1861. April 14, 1862 returned to duty from C. S. A. General Hospital at Charlottesville, Virginia. May 16, 1862 detailed as nurse at Camp Winder General Hospital at Richmond, Virginia. October 12, 1862 roll of Camp Winder General Hospital at Richmond, Virginia shows him employed as a nurse there. June 15, 1864 admitted to Jackson Hospital at Richmond, Virginia with acute Diarrhoea. June 27, 1864 transferred to Camp Winder General Hospital at Richmond, Virginia. June 1863 issued clothing. October 22, October 29, November 24 and December 28, 1863 issued clothing. December 31, 1863 received pay. March - April 1864 roll shows him present. May 30, 1864 issued clothing at Camp Winder General Hospital at Richmond, Virginia. June 27, 1864 report of Jackson Hospital at Richmond, Virginia shows he was transferred to Camp Winder General Hospital at Richmond, Virginia. July 15, and August 10, 1864 issued clothing at Camp Winder General Hospital at Richmond, Virginia.

SIEWERS, W. M.: Company H, private. He enlisted as a private in Co. H, 27th Regiment, Georgia Infantry. November 5, 1862 admitted to Chimborazo Hospital No. 2 at Richmond, Virginia with Dyspepsia. November 14, 1862 transferred to Danville, Virginia.

SIMMONS, W. J.: Company G, private. May 19, 1862 enlisted as a private in Co. G, 27th Regiment, Georgia Infantry. May 5, 1862 wounded and captured at Williamsburg, Virginia. June 7, 1862 admitted to Chesapeake U. S. A. General Hospital at Fort Monroe, Virginia with a Vulnus Sclopeticum (Gunshot Wound) to the thigh and leg. August 5, 1862 exchanged at Aiken's Landing, Virginia. August 28, 1862 received pay ($90.03). December 1962 roll shows him absent without leave. October 30, 1863, November 24 and December 6, 1863 issued clothing. December 31, 1863 received pay. January 13, 1864 discharged due to disability, at Fort Johnson, South Carolina. January – February 1864 roll shows him January 13, 1864 discharged due to disability, at Fort Johnson, South Carolina.

SIMMONS, WILLIAM C.: Company B, private. September 10, 1861 enlisted as a private in Co. B, 27th Regiment, Georgia Infantry at Camp

Stephens, Griffin, Spalding County, Georgia. December 14, 1861 was in Richmond, Virginia hospital. December 1861 roll shows him in the Hospital at Richmond, Virginia since December 14, 1861. January 2, 1862 discharged due to disability, Richmond, Virginia and received pay. January 1862 roll shows him discharged due to disability on January 2 at Richmond, Virginia. March 4, 1862 enlisted as a private in Co. D, 10th Battalion, Georgia Infantry. August 16, 1864 captured at Deep Bottom, Virginia. 1864 paroled at Point Lookout, Maryland. November 15, 1864 received at Venus Point, Savannah River, Georgia for exchange. March 6, 1865 admitted to Ocmulgee Hospital at Macon, Georgia. April 18, 1865 transferred, place not stated. April 1865 captured at Macon, Georgia.

SIMPSON, JOHN W.: Company B, private. September 10, 1861 enlisted as a private in Co. B, 27th Regiment, Georgia Infantry at Camp Stephens, Griffin, Spalding County, Georgia. November 18, 1861 admitted to C. S. A. General Hospital at Charlottesville, Virginia with Catarrh and Mumps. November 28, 1861 Simpson died of Catarrh and Mumps at General Hospital at Charlottesville, Virginia. December 1861 roll shows he died of disease at Charlottesville, Virginia. His effects at time of death are listed as $7.50 and "sundries".

SINLER, ISRAEL E.: Company E, private. September 9, 1861 enlisted as a private in Co. E, 27th Regiment, Georgia Infantry at Camp Stephens, Griffin, Spalding County, Georgia. January 1862 roll shows he was left sick at Richmond, Virginia on November 16, 1861.

SKIPPER, J. W.: Company B, private. September 10, 1861 enlisted as a private in Co. B, 27th Regiment, Georgia Infantry at Camp Stephens, Griffin, Spalding County, Georgia. February 1862 roll shows him 30 days on sick leave from February 21, 1861.

SKIPPER, JUNIUS G.: Company B, private. September 10, 1861 enlisted as a private in Co. B, 27th Regiment, Georgia Infantry at Camp Stephens, Griffin, Spalding County, Georgia. December 1861 and January 1862 rolls show he was left sick at Richmond, Virginia on November 15, 1861. June 30, 1862 received pay ($62.50). September 17, 1862 listed as missing in action (wounded) at Sharpsburg, Maryland. September 18, 1862 died of wounds. December 1862 roll shows him Missing in action at Sharpsburg, Maryland September 17, 1862. February 8, 1864 death benefit claim was filed by his widow, Sarah E. Skipper, stating he died September 18, 1862. Described as age 22, blue eyes, light hair, florid complexion, was 6 feet 1 inch high and by occupation was a farmer. He was born in 1840 in Bibb County, Georgia.

SKIPPER, THOMAS JEFFERSON: Company B, private. September 21, 1861 enlisted as a private in Co. B, 27th Regiment, Georgia Infantry at Camp Stephens, Griffin, Spalding County, Georgia. November 6, 1861 admitted to General Hospital at Petersburg, Virginia with Rubeola. November 15, 1861 returned to duty. November 15, 1861 admitted to C. S. A. General Hospital at Charlottesville, Virginia with Measles and

Rheumatism. December 1861 and January 1862 rolls show him in the hospital at Charlottesville, Virginia since November 11, 1861. February 15, 1862 furloughed for 60 days. August 27, 1862 received pay ($44.00). October 27 (31), 1862 received pay ($72.00) including bounty. November and December 1862 roll of General Hospital at Liberty, Virginia indicate him on list. June 12, 1863 furloughed for 30 days. August 7, 1863 received $9.90 in commutation of rations. October, November and December 1863 issued clothing. December 31, 1863 received pay. January – February 1864 and March - April 1864 rolls show him present. June 1, 1864 wounded in the right shoulder and left lung at Cold Harbor, Virginia. June 2, 1862 admitted to Jackson Hospital at Richmond, Virginia with a Vulnus Sclopeticum (Gunshot Wound) (mini ball) to the right shoulder. June 3, 1864 died of wounds in Jackson Hospital at Richmond, Virginia. He is buried in Hollywood Cemetery at Richmond, Virginia. September 16, 1864 death benefit claim was filed by his widow, Elizabeth Skipper, stating he died June 15, 1864. His effects at the time of death were; 1 blanket, 1 hat, 1 pants and 1 drawers.

SLADE, JAMES M.: Company G, lieutenant. September 9, 1861 enlisted as a private in Co. G, 27th Regiment, Georgia Infantry at Camp Stephens, Griffin, Spalding County, Georgia. November 11, 1861 admitted to General Hospital No. 18 (formerly Greaner's Hospital) at Richmond, Virginia. January 14, 1862 furloughed for 30 days. December 1861 and January 1862 rolls show him in the hospital at Richmond, Virginia since November 13, 1861. August 13, 1862 elected Jr. 2nd lieutenant of Co. G, 27th Regiment, Georgia Infantry. September 17, 1862 elected 1st lieutenant of Co. G, 27th Regiment, Georgia Infantry. October 2, 1862 received pay ($126.33). December 1862 roll shows him present in camp near Guinea Station, Virginia. April 16, 1863 received $8.33 1/3 in commutation of rations from March 14, 1863 to April 9, 1863. January – February 1864 and March - April 1864 rolls do not indicate whether present or absent. August 20, 1864 received pay ($150.00). October 28, 1864 General Colquitt's report from Laurel Hill shows him commanding Division Provost Guard. March 3, 1865 admitted to C. S. A. General Hospital No. 3 at Greensboro, North Carolina. April 26, 1865 surrendered Greensboro, North Carolina with Fistula-in-ano. May 1, 1865 paroled at Greensboro, North Carolina. He was a resident of Zebulon, Pike County, Georgia.

SLADE, WILLIAM H.: Company G, private. August 18, 1864 pension records show he was wounded in the left arm and permanently disabled by bullet passing through his shoulder joint and fracturing same, and middle finger of left hand was shot off at Weldon Railroad, Virginia. August 19, 1864 wounded at Weldon Railroad near Petersburg, Virginia. August 19, 1864 admitted to Jackson Hospital at Richmond, Virginia with a Vulnus Sclopeticum (Gunshot Wound) to the left shoulder. September 1, 1864 furloughed for 30 days and received passport to Griffin, Georgia. 1864 discharged due to disability. He was a resident of Griffin, Georgia,

SLADE, WILLIAM H. C.: Company G, private. March 4, 1862 enlisted as a private in Co. H, 44th Regiment, Georgia Infantry. March 14, 1862 transferred as a private in Co. G, 27th Regiment, Georgia Infantry. December 13, 1862 wounded at Fredericksburg, Virginia. December 16, 1862 admitted to Camp Winder Division No. 1 Hospital at Richmond, Virginia. December 31, 1862 finger amputated. December 1862 roll shows him absent sick. January 16, 1863 admitted to C. S. A. General Hospital at Farmville, Virginia with a Vulnus Sclopeticum (Gunshot Wound). January 27, 1863 issued clothing at C. S. A. General Hospital at Farmville, Virginia. February 9, 1863 returned to duty. April 1863 received $9.90 in commutations of rations. June 26, 1863 issued clothing. September 24, 1863 furloughed for 30 days. October 30, 1863 issued clothing. December 31, 1863 received pay. January – February 1864 roll shows him present. February 29, 1864 received pay. March - April 1864 roll shows him present. May 31, 1864 and July 1864 issued clothing. May 5, 1864 wounded at Chancellorsville, Virginia. April 26, 1865 surrendered Greensboro, North Carolina. May 1, 1865 paroled at Greensboro, North Carolina.

SMALLPIECE, THOMAS: Company A, private. September 10, 1861 enlisted as a private in Co. A, 27th Regiment, Georgia Infantry at Camp Stephens, Griffin, Spalding County, Georgia. March 17, 1862 admitted to Chimborazo Hospital No. 2 at Richmond, Virginia with Rheumatism. April 30, 1862 received pay. June 7, 1862 furloughed for 40 days to Schley County, Georgia. June 12, 1862 received pay ($95.70). August 31, 1862 admitted to Chimborazo Hospital No. 2 at Richmond, Virginia with Nostalgia. October 19, 1862 transferred from Chimborazo Hospital No. 2 at Richmond, Virginia to Hospital at Huguenot Springs, Virginia and shown present on that date. November 1, 1862 received pay. December 1862 roll shows him absent sick since May 1862. December 1862 roll of Hospital at Huguenot Springs, Virginia and shown present. January 1, 1863 received pay. January – February 1863 roll of Hospital at Huguenot Springs, Virginia and shown present. July, August and September 1863 issued clothing. September 25, 1863 discharged and paid ($102.10) in Charleston, South Carolina. He is described on his discharge certificate as being born in Baldwin County, Georgia, 48 years of age, 5 feet 10 inches high, fair complexion, blue eyes, light hair and by occupation was a farmer. He was born in 1815.

SMITH, A. J.: Company E, private. September 9, 1861 enlisted as a private in Co. E, 27th Regiment, Georgia Infantry at Camp Stephens, Griffin, Spalding County, Georgia.

SMITH, ALBINUS: Company D, private. March 4, 1862 enlisted as a private in Co. D, 27th Regiment, Georgia Infantry. March 25, 1862 received bounty pay $50.00 in Atlanta, Georgia. July 1862 received pay ($66.00). April, May, June and November 1863 issued clothing. February 29, 1864 received pay. March - April 1864 roll shows him present. May

447

30, 1864, July 1864 and September 20, 1864 issued clothing. April 26, 1865 pension records show he surrendered Greensboro, North Carolina.

SMITH, C. H.: private.   He enlisted as a private in the 27th Regiment, Georgia Infantry. May 10, 1865 surrendered at Tallahassee, Florida. May 15, 1865 paroled at Thomasville, Georgia. He is described as 5 feet 1/2 inches high, light hair, blue eyes and fair complexion.

SMITH, CHARLES T.: Company K, private. June10, 1863 enlisted as a private in Co. K, 27th Regiment, Georgia Infantry in Talbotton, Talbot County, Georgia. June 10, 1863 furloughed for 21 days. August 8, 1863 received $6.60 in commutation of rations. October 12, October 29 and November 24, 1863 issued clothing. December 31, 1863 received pay. March - April 1864 roll shows him present. June 9, 1864 killed at Cold Harbor, Virginia.

SMITH, C. W.:   Company A, private.   May 14, 1862 admitted to Chimborazo Hospital No. 1 at Richmond, Virginia with Intermittent Febris (Malaria). July 2, 1862 died of Intermittent Febris (Malaria) at Chimborazo Hospital No. 1 at Richmond, Virginia.

SMITH, COLUMBUS W.: Company A, private. February 24, 1862 enlisted as a private in Co. A, 27th Regiment, Georgia Infantry in Schley County, Georgia.   November 20, 1862 received bounty pay of $50.00 at Richmond, Virginia.   December 1862 roll shows him absent sick. February 9, 1863 returned to duty from Chimborazo Hospital No. 1 at Richmond, Virginia. May 5, 1863 wounded severely at Chancellorsville, Virginia. May 9, 1863 admitted to General Hospital, Howard's Grove at Richmond, Virginia with a Vulnus Sclopeticum (Gunshot Wound) of the left shoulder.   June 8, 1863 transferred to General Hospital at Macon, Georgia. September 21, 1863 he is shown on roll as on detached duty at Macon, Georgia as a military conductor (Special Order Number 263/21). December 17, 1863 received pay at Macon, Georgia at a rate of $3.00 per day as a military conductor. January – February 1864 and March - April 1864 rolls show him absent on detached service since May 5, 1863. May 7, 1864 issued clothing. May 18, 1864 received pay (at a rate of $3.00 per day) at Macon, Georgia as a military conductor. June 9, 1864 received pay ($267.13). September 27, 1864 issued clothing. May 10, 1865 surrendered at Tallahassee, Florida.   May 18, 1865 paroled at Albany, Georgia.

SMITH, HIRAM B.: Company D, sergeant.   September 10, 1861 elected 4th sergeant. in Co. D, 27th Regiment, Georgia Infantry at Camp Stephens, Griffin, Spalding County, Georgia. July 1, 1862 wounded at Malvern Hill near Richmond, Virginia.   July 1, 1862 admitted to Chimborazo Hospital No. 4 at Richmond, Virginia with a Vulnus Sclopeticum (Gunshot Wound). September 17, 1862 wounded and captured at Sharpsburg, Maryland. September 27, 1862 paroled by the Army of the Potomac.   October 5, 1862 admitted to U. S. A. Field Hospital at Smoketown, Maryland with a Vulnus Sclopeticum (Gunshot Wound) to the left leg. December 5, 1862 admitted to Summit House U. S. A. General Hospital at West Philadelphia,

Pennsylvania with a Vulnus Sclopeticum (Gunshot Wound). December 6, 1862 sent from Provost Barracks at Philadelphia, Pennsylvania to Fort Delaware, Delaware. December 15, 1862 sent from Fort Delaware, Delaware to Fortress Monroe, Virginia for Exchange. December 19, 1862 admitted to General Hospital at Petersburg, Virginia with a Vulnus Sclopeticum (Gunshot Wound) to the leg (paroled prisoner). December 1862 roll shows he was captured at Sharpsburg, Maryland. January 30, 1863 furloughed for 40 days. April 15, 1863 received $13.33 1/3 in commutation of rations. April, May, June and November 1863 issued clothing. February 29, 1864 received pay. March - April 1864 roll shows him present. May 30, 1864 and July 1864 issued clothing. March 18, 1865 wounded at Bentonville, North Carolina. May 6, 1865 in Charlotte, North Carolina hospital at the close of the war and paroled there. He was born in Georgia in 1849.

SMITH, H.: Company A, private. September 10, 1861 enlisted as a private in Co. A, 27th Regiment, Georgia Infantry at Camp Stephens, Griffin, Spalding County, Georgia. December 1861 and January 1862 rolls show he was left sick in Georgia October 31, 1861. September 1, 1862 receive pay ($94.00). September 30, 1862 admitted to Camp Winder Division No. 3 Hospital at Richmond, Virginia. October 9, 1862 returned to duty and received pay ($36.00). November 19, 1862 admitted to General Hospital No. 16 at Richmond, Virginia. November 1862 roll of General Hospital No. 16 at Richmond, Virginia shows him present. January 2, 1863 transferred to Camp Winder Hospital at Richmond, Virginia. January 16, 1863 issued clothing at Camp Winder Division No. 1 Hospital at Richmond, Virginia. April 13, 1863 furloughed for 60 days. July 25, 1863 received $20.00 in commutation of rations. July, August and September 1863 issued clothing.

SMITH, J. A.: Company A, private. He enlisted as a private in Co. A, 27th Regiment, Georgia Infantry. September 16, 1863 received pay ($22.00).

SMITH, J. W.: Company C, private. September 10, 1861 enlisted as a private in Co. C, 27th Regiment, Georgia Infantry at Camp Stephens, Griffin, Spalding County, Georgia. He was appointed sergeant Co. C, 27th Regiment, Georgia Infantry. September 1, 1862 placed on wounded furlough. March - April 1864 roll shows him absent since September 1, 1862 on wounded furlough. April 26, 1865 surrendered Greensboro, North Carolina. May 8, 1865 paroled at Greensboro, North Carolina.

SMITH, J. Y.: Company C, corporal. September 10, 1861 enlisted as a corporal in Co. C, 27th Regiment, Georgia Infantry at Camp Stephens, Griffin, Spalding County, Georgia. July 3, 1862 admitted to Chimborazo Hospital No. 5 at Richmond, Virginia with Continua Fever (Typhoid Fever). August 5, 1862 died at Chimborazo Hospital No. 5 at Richmond, Virginia with Continua Fever (Typhoid Fever). He is most likely buried in Oakwood Cemetery at Richmond Virginia. February 7, 1863 death benefit claim was filed by his widow, Susanna Smith.

SMITH, JAMES A.: Company D, corporal. September 10, 1861 enlisted as a 1st corporal in Co. D, 27th Regiment, Georgia Infantry at Camp Stephens, Griffin, Spalding County, Georgia. July 11, 1862 admitted to General Hospital at Farmville, Virginia with Diarrhoea and Scorbutis (Scurvy). August 8, 1862 died at General Hospital at Farmville, Virginia of Scorbutis (Scurvy). December 13, 1862 death benefit claim was filed by his father, Wiley C. Smith. September 23, 1863 death benefit claim paid $109.46 (#8997). He was a resident of Hall County, Georgia.

SMITH, JAMES M.: Company K, private. September 10, 1861 enlisted as a private in Co. K, 27th Regiment, Georgia Infantry at Camp Stephens, Griffin, Spalding County, Georgia. July 8, 1862 received pay ($106.33). August 1, 1862 discharged due to disability. August 2, 1862 received pay ($102.00). He is described on his discharge certificate as being born in the Anderson District of South Carolina, 58 years of age, 5 feet 8 inches high, light complexion, blue eyes, light hair and by occupation was a farmer. He was born in 1804.

SMITH, JAMES T. (Y.): Company C, private. July 1861 enlisted as a private in Co. C, 27th Regiment, Georgia Infantry. August 1862 died in hospital.

SMITH JOHN A.: Company A, private. September 10, 1861 enlisted as a private in Co. K, 27th Regiment, Georgia Infantry at Camp Stephens, Griffin, Spalding County, Georgia. December 1861 and January 1862 rolls show he was left in Georgia sick on October 31, 1861. June 1863, July 1863, August 1863, September 1863 and November 1863 issued clothing. September 1863 received pay ($22.00).

SMITH JOHN A.: Company D, private. March 17, 1862 enlisted as a private in Co. D, 27th Regiment, Georgia Infantry at Gainesville, Georgia. March 23, 1862 received bounty pay $50.00 at Atlanta, Georgia. He deserted. September 7, 1863 S. C. Odell received pay ($18.25) for returning him to camp. November 1863 issued clothing. November 25, 1863 wounded at Fort Sumter at Charleston, South Carolina. February 29, 1864 received pay. March - April 1864 roll shows him present. May 30, 1864 and July 1864 issued clothing. April 26, 1865 surrendered Greensboro, North Carolina. July 30, 1864 issued clothing at Jackson Hospital at Richmond, Virginia. May 1, 1865 paroled at Greensboro, North Carolina.

SMITH, JOHN C.: Company A, sergeant. September 10, 1861 elected 2nd sergeant Co. A, 27th Regiment Georgia Infantry at Camp Stephens, Griffin, Spalding County, Georgia. November 1863 issued clothing. December 31, 1863 received pay. January – February 1864 roll shows him present. February 29, 1864 received pay. March - April 1864 roll shows him present. May 30, 1864 and July 1864 issued clothing. January 16, 1865 wounded at Fort Fisher, North Carolina. January 16, 1865 admitted to C. S .A. General Military Hospital No. 4 at Wilmington, North Carolina with a Vulnus Sclopeticum (Gunshot Wound) from a shell to the right shoulder and arm. January 17, 1865 transferred to General Hospital No. 3 at Goldsboro,

North Carolina near Fort Fisher. January 17, 1865 admitted to C. S .A. General Military Hospital No. 3 at Greensboro, North Carolina (Transferred from Wilmington) with a Vulnus Sclopeticum (Gunshot Wound). January 17, 1865 admitted to Pettigrew General Hospital No. 13 at Raleigh, North Carolina with a Vulnus Sclopeticum (Gunshot Wound) to the right shoulder and arm. January 18, 1865 issued clothing at Pettigrew General Hospital No. 13 at Raleigh, North Carolina. January 19, 1865 pension records show he was wounded at Sugar Loaf, North Carolina. February 13, 1865 furloughed for 60 days from Pettigrew General Hospital No. 13 at Raleigh, North Carolina. April 20, 1865 admitted to C. S. A. General Hospital, No. 11 at Charlotte, North Carolina with Febris Intermittent (Malaria). April 26, 1865 transferred to another Hospital. Furlough extended for 60 days. He was a resident of Taswell, Marion County, Georgia.

SMITH, JOHN W.: Company C, private. September 10, 1861 enlisted as a private in Co. C, 27th Regiment, Georgia Infantry at Camp Stephens, Griffin, Spalding County, Georgia. January 17, 1862 admitted to Moore Hospital at General Hospital, No. 1 at Danville, Virginia and sent to Front Royal, Virginia. January 1862 roll shows him in the hospital at Front Royal since January 17, 1862. June 30, 1862 admitted to Chimborazo Hospital No. 5 at Richmond, Virginia with Pneumonia. June 30, 1862 received pay. July 21, 1862 furloughed for 30 days. August 6, 1862 received pay ($66.00). December 1862 roll shows him absent sick since July 20, 1862. February 20, 1864 wounded at Olustee, Florida. January – February 1864 roll shows him absent without leave since February 1864. February 29, 1864 received pay. March - April 1864 roll shows him absent on wounded furlough. September 20, 1864 issued clothing. April 26, 1865, surrendered at Greensboro, North Carolina. May 8, 1865 paroled at Greensboro, North Carolina.

SMITH, LEVI B.: Field Staff, colonel. September 10, 1861 elected captain of Company K, 27th Regiment Georgia Infantry at Camp Stephens, Griffin, Spalding County, Georgia. September 11, 1861 elected colonel, 27th Regiment Georgia Infantry. December 1861, January 1862 and February 1862 rolls show him present at Camp Pickens near Manassas, Virginia. March 4, 1862 received pay ($390.00). June 4, 1862 received pay ($585.00). July 3, 1862 received pay ($195.00). September 17, 1862 wounded in the thigh by a gunshot and died at Sharpsburg, Maryland. December 1, 1862 death benefit claim paid to his widow, Mary M. Smith $695.50 (#782).

SMITH, NEWTON G.: Company E, private. September 10, 1861 enlisted as a private in Co. E, 27th Regiment, Georgia Infantry at Camp Stephens, Griffin, Spalding County, Georgia. November 14, 1861 discharged due to disability (Anemia) at Chimborazo Hospital at Richmond, Virginia. Discharge certificate description: born in Spartanburg, South Carolina, 32 years of age, 5 feet 11 inches high, dark complexion, black eyes, black hair and by occupation was a farmer.

SMITH, REUBEN G.: Company E, private. September 10, 1861 enlisted as a private in Co. C, 27th Regiment, Georgia Infantry at Camp Stephens, Griffin, Spalding County, Georgia. December 7, 1861 discharged due to disability at Richmond, Virginia. December 1861 roll shows his discharge.

SMITH, RUEBEN MARION: Company K, corporal. September 10, 1861 elected 2nd corporal of Co. K, 27th Regiment, Georgia Infantry at Camp Stephens, Griffin, Spalding County, Georgia. September 17, 1862 captured at Sharpsburg, Maryland. October 6, 1862 delivered to Aiken's landing, Virginia for exchange. October 2, 1862 sent from Fort Delaware, Delaware to Aiken's Landing, Virginia for exchange. November 10, 1862 exchanged at Aiken's Landing, Virginia. June 1863 issued clothing. October 31, 1863 received pay. October 22, October 24 and November 24, 1863 issued clothing. March - April 1864 roll shows him present. July 1864 issued clothing. October 13, 1864 admitted to Jackson Hospital at Richmond, Virginia with Debilitas. November 23, 1864 returned to duty. March 19, 1865 captured at Bentonville, North Carolina. April 3, 1865 arrived at New Bern, North Carolina. June 19, 1865 released from Point Lookout, Maryland. Described when he took the oath of allegiance as a resident of Talbot County, Georgia, light complexion, brown hair, hazel eyes and 5 feet 7 inches high.

SMITH, S. Y.: Company C, sergeant. September 10, 1861 enlisted as a sergeant in Co. C, 27th Regiment, Georgia Infantry at Camp Stephens, Griffin, Spalding County, Georgia. December 1861 roll shows him sick in the Hospital at Richmond, Virginia since November 26, 1861. March 25, 1863 death benefit claim was filed by his widow, Susannah Smith.

SMITH, T. Y.: Company C, private. September 10, 1861 enlisted as a private in Co. C, 27th Regiment, Georgia Infantry at Camp Stephens, Griffin, Spalding County, Georgia.

SMITH, THOMAS C.: Company G, private. September 9, 1861 enlisted as a private in Co. G, 27th Regiment, Georgia Infantry at Camp Stephens, Griffin, Spalding County, Georgia. June 4, 1862 died in Richmond, Virginia hospital prior to this date. June 4, 1862 death benefit claim was filed by his father, James A. Smith. September 6, 1863 death benefit claim paid $116.43 (#4449). He was a resident of Pike County, Georgia.

SMITH, WILLIAM MORGAN: Company E, sergeant. March 1, 1862 enlisted as a private in Co. E, 27th Regiment, Georgia Infantry. May 15, 1862 admitted to Chimborazo Hospital No. 2 at Richmond, Virginia with Diarrhoea. May 16, 1862 admitted to Camp Winder General Hospital at Richmond, Virginia. December 1862 roll shows he deserted in July, 1862. December 31, 1863 received pay. January – February 1864 roll shows him present. March - April 1864 roll shows him present. July 9, 1864 transferred to Co. C, 53rd Regiment, Georgia Infantry. He was appointed 2nd corporal Co. C, 53rd Regiment, Georgia Infantry. October 19, 1864 appointed 5th sergeant Co. C, 53rd Regiment, Georgia Infantry. February

1865 roll shows him present.

SMITH, WILLIAM: Company I, private. September 10, 1861 enlisted as a private in Co. I, 27th Regiment, Georgia Infantry at Camp Stephens, Griffin, Spalding County, Georgia. November 15, 1861 admitted to General Hospital No. 18 (formerly Greaner's Hospital) at Richmond, Virginia. December 4, 1861 returned to duty. May 31, 1862 killed at Seven Pines, Virginia. January 10, 1863 death benefit claim was filed by his mother, Emeline Varnadore. He is buried in Hollywood Cemetery at Richmond, Virginia.

SMITH, WILLIAM C.: Company K, 4th sergeant. September 10, 1861 elected 4th sergeant of Co. K, 27th Regiment, Georgia Infantry at Camp Stephens, Griffin, Spalding County, Georgia. May 14, 1862 transferred from Chimborazo Hospital No. 5 at Richmond, Virginia to Lynchburg, Virginia hospital. May 15, 1862 admitted to C. S. A General Hospital at Danville, Virginia with a Vulnus Sclopeticum (Gunshot Wound). June 1, 1862 returned to duty. March 7, 1862 admitted to Chimborazo Hospital No. 5 at Richmond, Virginia with Erysipelas (Contagious skin disease). June, October 22, October 24 and November 24, 1863 issued clothing. December 31, 1863 received pay. March - April 1864 roll shows him present. May 30, 1864 issued clothing. July 15, 1864 admitted to Jackson Hospital at Richmond, Virginia with remit. Febris (Malaria). August 29, 1864 issued clothing at Jackson Hospital at Richmond, Virginia. September 30, 1864 returned to duty. April 26, 1865, surrendered at Greensboro, North Carolina. May 1, 1865 paroled at Greensboro, North Carolina. He was born in Talbot County, Georgia August 8, 1845.

SMITH, WILLIAM H. H.: Company A, private. December 1861 and January 1862 rolls show he was left sick in Georgia October 31, 1861. February 18, 1862 died of Pneumonia at Camp Pickens near Manassas, Virginia. February 1862 roll shows he died of disease at Camp Pickens, near Manassas, Virginia on February 18, 1862.

December 27, 1862 (January 10, 1863) death benefit claim was filed by his father, William Smith. September 26, 1863 death benefit claim was paid $133.30 (#9137).

SNELLGROVES (SMELLGROVE) (SMELLGROVES), J. R.: Company A, sergeant. September 10, 1861 enlisted as a sergeant in Co. A, 27th Regiment, Georgia Infantry at Camp Stephens, Griffin, Spalding County, Georgia. December 1861 and January 1862 rolls show he was left sick in Georgia October 31, 1861. June 14, 1862 received pay ($147.90). August 20, 1862 received pay ($84.00). September 4, 1862 received pay ($59.00). December 26, 1862 received pay ($72.00). September 3, 1863 received pay ($44.00).

SNELLGROVES (SMELLGROVE) (SMELLGROVES), R. A.: Company A, private. February 9, 1862 enlisted as a private in Co. A, 27th Regiment, Georgia Infantry at Macon, Georgia. January – February 1864 roll shows him absent without leave since February 9, 1864. January 18,

1865 admitted to Pettigrew General Hospital, No. 13 at Raleigh, North Carolina with Catarrhs (allergy). February 17, 1865 issued clothing and returned to duty. March 8, 1865 captured, Kinston, North Carolina. March 16, 1865 arrived at Point Lookout, Maryland from New Bern, North Carolina. May 15, 1865 released at Point Lookout, Maryland. He is listed as a resident of De Soto, Schley County and a farmer.

SNIPES, J. T.: Company C, private. September 1, 1861 enlisted as a private in Co. C, 27th Regiment, Georgia Infantry. June 16, June 26, June 30 and September 30, 1863 issued clothing. December 31, 1863 received pay. February 24, 1864 admitted to General Hospital at Guyton, Georgia. January – February 1864 roll of General Hospital at Guyton, Georgia shows him present. January – February 1864 roll shows him absent on sick leave since February 1, 1864. February 29, 1864 received pay. March - April 1864 roll shows him absent sick since February 1, 1864. September 20, 1864 issued clothing. October 3(1), 1863 wounded at Fort Harrison near Richmond, Virginia. October 3, 1864 admitted to Receiving and Wayside Hospital or General Hospital No. 9 at Richmond, Virginia. October 4(1), 1864 admitted to Jackson Hospital at Richmond, Virginia with a Vulnus Sclopeticum (Gunshot Wound) to the right arm (mini ball). November 1, 1864 returned to duty. April 26, 1865 surrendered Greensboro, North Carolina. May 1, 1865 paroled at Greensboro, North Carolina.

SONNEBORN, WILLIAM F.: Company B, private. September 10, 1861 enlisted as a private in Co. B, 27th Regiment, Georgia Infantry at Camp Stephens, Griffin, Spalding County, Georgia. September 21, 1862 attached as a nurse to Camp Winder Division No. 4 Hospital at Richmond, Virginia (note: detailed by examining board regimental pay due from May 1, 1862 – Bounty $50.00). June 7, 1862 received pay ($55.00). October 31, 1862 received pay. November – December roll of Camp Winder Division No. 4 Hospital at Richmond, Virginia shows him as a nurse. December 1862 roll shows him detailed as a nurse at Camp Winder Hospital at Richmond, Virginia. July 1, 1863 received pay at Camp Winder Division No. 4 Hospital at Richmond, Virginia. August 31, 1863 shown on roll of Camp Winder Division No. 4 Hospital at Richmond, Virginia. September 2, 1863 issued clothing. September 3, 1863 furloughed. October 31, 1863 received pay for commutation of rations for 30 days. November 1863 received $9.90 in commutation of rations. December 31, 1863 received pay ($22.00) and was discharged due to disability. February 25, 1864 received pay ($123.13). January – February 1864 and March – April 1864 rolls show him absent detailed as a nurse at hospital at Augusta, Georgia by order of General Beauregard. July 23, 1864 received pay ($44.00). December 31, 1863 he was discharged due to disability. Described on discharge certificate as being born in Germany, 51 years of age, 6 feet 1 inch tall, florid complexion, hazel eyes, sandy hair and by occupation was a farmer March 30, 1865 Macon Georgia Medical Examining Board recommends extension of furlough.

454

SONNEBORN, WILLIAM RILEY: Company B, private. September 10, 1861 enlisted as a private in Co. B, 27th Regiment, Georgia Infantry at Camp Stephens, Griffin, Spalding County, Georgia. July 24, 1862 received pay ($91.00). September 17, 1862 wounded, Sharpsburg, Maryland. September 28, 1862 died from wounds. December 1862 roll shows him missing in action at Sharpsburg, Maryland September 17, 1862. January 26, 1864 death benefit claim was filed by his father, William F. Sonneborn. He is described as being 17 years of age, gray eyes, sandy hair, fallow complexion, was born in Bibb County, Georgia and was a farmer by occupation.

SORRELLS, JAMES B.: Company F, sergeant. September 9, 1861 elected 1st sergeant in Co. F, 27th Regiment, Georgia Infantry at Camp Stephens, Griffin, Spalding County, Georgia. September 17, 1862 wounded at Sharpsburg, Maryland. September 28, 1862 admitted to General Hospital No. 8 (St. Charles Hospital) at Richmond, Virginia with a Vulnus Sclopeticum (Gunshot Wound) to the hand and hip by the bursting of a shell. August 31, 1862 received pay at General Hospital No. 8 at Richmond, Virginia. October 31, 1862 roll of General Hospital No. 8 at Richmond, Virginia shows him. November 4, 1862 furloughed for 60 days. July 15 and August 5, 1863 issued clothing. December 31, 1863 received pay. January – February 1864 roll shows him absent sick since February 13, 1864. February 29, 1864 received pay. March - April 1864 roll shows him absent sick since February 18, 1864. May 31, 1864, July 1864 and September 20, 1864 issued clothing. March 18, 1865 killed, Bentonville, North Carolina.

SPINKS, BENJAMIN F.: Company K, private. September 10, 1861 enlisted as a private in Co. K, 27th Regiment, Georgia Infantry at Camp Stephens, Griffin, Spalding County, Georgia. March 23, 1862 admitted to Chimborazo Hospital No. 5 at Richmond, Virginia with Catarrh. April 23, 1862 returned to duty from Chimborazo Hospital No. 5 at Richmond, Virginia. July 7, 1862 received pay ($66.00). December 16, 1862 admitted to C. S. A. General Hospital at Charlottesville, Virginia with Debility. December 17, 1862 returned to duty (note: returned to duty without regular discharge of this hospital. Was on his way to his regiment from the hospital in Lynchburg, Virginia and was left here yesterday in consequence of the central cars being too much crowded for him to get on). July 1863, October 29, and November 24, 1863 issued clothing. December 31, 1863 received pay. March - April 1864 roll shows him present. January 1864 detailed as oarsman at Fort Johnson near Charleston, South Carolina. February 7, 1864 received pay ($.25 extra per day) for service as an oarsman at Fort Johnson near Charleston, South Carolina. June 12, 1864 admitted to Receiving and Wayside Hospital or General Hospital No. 9 at Richmond, Virginia and transferred to Jackson Hospital at Richmond, Virginia. June 13, 1864 admitted to Jackson Hospital at Richmond, Virginia with Syphilis. August 13, 1864 and September 28, 1864 issued clothing at Jackson Hospital, at

Richmond, Virginia. September 30, 1864 returned to duty from Jackson Hospital, at Richmond, Virginia.

SPINKS, WILLIAM T.: Company K, private. September 10, 1861 enlisted as a private in Co. K, 27th Regiment, Georgia Infantry at Camp Stephens, Griffin, Spalding County, Georgia. May 1, 1862 died in Medical College Hospital at Richmond, Virginia. He is buried in Hollywood Cemetery at Richmond, Virginia. His effects at the time of death were: 1 bed quilt, 1 blanket, 1 coat, 1 vest, 1 pair suspenders, 1 comfort, 1 cap and 1 pair of shoes. April 13, 1863 death benefit claim was filed by his widow, Martha A. Spinks. He was a resident of Talbot County, Georgia was born in 1840.

SPRATLIN, JESSE M.: Company E, captain. August 9, 1861 elected captain Co. E, 27th Regiment, Georgia Infantry. November 26, 1861 died of Pneumonia at Richmond, Virginia. December 1861 roll shows his death. March 15, 1862 death benefit claim was filed by his widow, Mrs. Elizabeth S. Spratlin.

ST JOHN, WILLIAM J.: Company H, private. August 1, 1863 enlisted as a private in Co. H, 27th Regiment, Georgia Infantry at McDonough, Henry County, Georgia. October 1863 his skull was fractured by fragment of a shell at Fort Sumter, South Carolina. December 31, 1863 received pay. January – February 1864 roll shows him present. February 29, 1864 received pay. March - April 1864 roll shows him present. July, 1864 and September 20, 1864 issued clothing. April 26, 1865, surrendered at Greensboro, North Carolina. May 1, 1865 paroled at Greensboro, North Carolina. He and was born in Georgia August 9, 1845.

STALLSWORTH, E. M.: Company H, private. September 9, 1861 enlisted as a private in Co. H, 27th Regiment, Georgia Infantry at Camp Stephens, Griffin, Spalding County, Georgia. December 18, 1861 discharged due to physical inability and received pay. December 1861 roll shows his discharge.

STALLSWORTH, G. FRANK: Company H, corporal. September 9, 1861 enlisted as a private in Co. H, 27th Regiment, Georgia Infantry at Camp Stephens, Griffin, Spalding County, Georgia. July 9, 1862 received pay ($91.00). October 18, 1863 furloughed for 30 days. November 21, 1863 received $6.60 in commutation of rations at James Island, South Carolina. December 31, 1863 received pay. January – February 1864 roll shows him present. February 29, 1864 received pay. March - April 1864 roll shows him present. June 3, 1864 wounded in the arm at Cold Harbor, near Richmond, Virginia. June 3, 1864 admitted to Receiving and Wayside Hospital or General Hospital No. 9 at Richmond, Virginia. June 4, 1864 admitted to C. S. A. General Hospital at Danville, Virginia with a Vulnus Sclopeticum (Gunshot Wound) to the arm. July 25, 1864 issued clothes at General Hospital No. 1 at Columbia, South Carolina. April 26, 1865 surrendered Greensboro, North Carolina. May 1, 1865 paroled at Greensboro, North Carolina.

STANLEY, THOMAS C.: Company G, lieutenant. August 21, 1861 elected 1st lieutenant Co. G, 27th Regiment, Georgia Infantry. December 17, 1861 received pay ($195.00). December 1861 roll shows him present at Camp Pickens near Manassas, Virginia. January 24, 1862 admitted with Fever to Moore Hospital at General Hospital, No. 1 at Danville, Virginia and was transferred to the 3rd Georgia Hospital at Richmond, Virginia. January 1862 roll at Camp Pickens near Manassas, Virginia shows him absent without leave. February 3, 1862 resigned his commission with surgeon's certificate of disability. February 1862 roll shows he resigned his commission (Special Order Adjutant and Inspector General's Office No.).

STARRETT, BENJAMIN J.: Company D, sergeant. September 10, 1861 enlisted as a 2nd sergeant in Co. D, 27th Regiment, Georgia Infantry at Camp Stephens, Griffin, Spalding County, Georgia. January 1862 roll shows him as acting Wagon Master. February 1862 roll shows him on recruiting service for 30 days beginning February 13, 1862. June 13, 1862 died at Camp Winder Hospital at Richmond, Virginia. December 16, 1862 death benefit claim was filed by his widow, Sarah J. Starrett. He was a resident of Hall County, Georgia.

STEARNS, JOHN F.: Company K, private. September 10, 1861 enlisted as a private in Co. K, 27th Regiment, Georgia Infantry at Camp Stephens, Griffin, Spalding County, Georgia. December 25, 1861 discharged due to disability (curved Spine) at Camp Pickens near Manassas, Virginia. December 1861 roll shows his discharge.

STEGER, DAVID R.: Company G, private. September 10, 1861 enlisted as a private in Co. G, 27th Regiment, Georgia Infantry at Camp Stephens, Griffin, Spalding County, Georgia. March 30, 1862 admitted to Chimborazo Hospital No.1, at Richmond, Virginia with Pneumonia. May 7 1862 furloughed at Chimborazo Hospital No.5, at Richmond, Virginia. August 17, 1862 discharged due to disability. October 29, 1862 received pay. February 18, 1863 died of Small-Pox while at home on furlough.

STEINBRIDGE (STEMBRIDGE), WILLIAM W.: Company C, private. April 7, 1864 enlisted as a private in Co. C, 27th Regiment, Georgia Infantry at Macon, Bibb County, Georgia. March - April 1864 roll shows him present. July 1864 and September 20, 1864 issued clothing. March 10, 1865 was killed at Kinston, North Carolina.

STEPHENS (STEVENS), J. F.: Company H, private. September 10, 1861 enlisted as a private in Co. H, 27th Regiment, Georgia Infantry at Camp Stephens, Griffin, Spalding County, Georgia. February 1862 roll shows him detailed at fatigue duty at Post Headquarters since December 15, 1861.

STEPHENS (STEVENS), MILES G.: Company B, lieutenant. He enlisted as a private in Co. B, 27th Regiment, Georgia Infantry. June 12, 1861 elected 1st lieutenant in Co. B, 27th Regiment, Georgia Infantry. September 10, 1861 enlisted as a 2nd lieutenant in Co. B, 27th Regiment,

Georgia Infantry at Camp Stephens, Griffin, Spalding County, Georgia. December 20, 1861 received pay ($170.65) and leave granted for 30 days. December 1861 roll shows him absent from Camp Pickens near Manassas, Virginia (on furlough since December 21, 1861 for 30 days). January 1862 and February 1862 rolls show him present (company reformed on January 26, 1862). March 1, 1862 received pay ($80.00). September 15, 1862 received pay ($80.00). August 13, 1863 surgeon's certificate of disability due to double Hernia. August 24 1862 promoted to 1st lieutenant in Co. B, 27th Regiment, Georgia Infantry. October 6, 1862 resigned commission.

STEWART, ALEX: Company A, private. September 10, 1861 enlisted as a private in Co. A, 27th Regiment, Georgia Infantry at Camp Stephens, Griffin, Spalding County, Georgia. December 1861 and January 1862 rolls show he was left sick in Georgia October 31, 1861. June, July, August and September 1863 issued clothing. September 6, 1863 captured at Morris Island (Battery Wagner), South Carolina. September 7, 1863 was taken to Hilton Head Island, South Carolina. October 6, 1863 arrived at Fort Columbus, New York Harbor. October 9, 1863 transferred to Johnson's Island, Ohio. January 27, 1865 admitted to U. S. A. General Hospital, Point Lookout, Maryland from the camp of Prisoners of war with Chronic Diarrhoea. January 29, 1865 died at Point Lookout, Maryland of Chronic Diarrhoea. He is buried at Point Lookout, Maryland.

STEWART, ELI: Company A, lieutenant. September 10, 1861 enlisted as a private in Co. A, 27th Regiment, Georgia Infantry at Camp Stephens, Griffin, Spalding County, Georgia. January 1862 roll shows him as Provost Marshall's Guard. February 1862 roll shows him on recruiting service for 30 days since February 13, 1861. June 10, 1862 elected 2nd lieutenant Co. A, 27th Regiment, Georgia Infantry. July 8, 1862 received pay ($66.00). July 5, 1862 admitted to Chimborazo Hospital No. 4 at Richmond, Virginia with Diarrhoea. July 8, 1862 received pay ($66.00). July 17, 1862 received pay ($80.00). December 1862 roll shows him present at camp near Guinea Station, Virginia. January 5, 1863 received pay ($80.00). February 16, 1863 shown on register of Receiving and Wayside Hospital or General Hospital No. 9 at Richmond, Virginia (shown as sent to Hospital No. 4). May 5, 1863 wounded at Chancellorsville. Virginia. July 20, 1863 elected 1st lieutenant Co. A, 27th Regiment, Georgia Infantry. September 31, 1863 shown on roll of officers in Colquitt's Brigade. December 22, 1863 leave granted at James Island, South Carolina. January – February 1864 and March - April 1864 roll shows him but does not indicate absent or present. August 22, 1864 received pay ($150.00). August 31, 1864 received pay ($90.00). October 1, 1864 received pay ($53.33). April 26, 1865 surrendered Greensboro, North Carolina. May 1, 1865 paroled at Greensboro, North Carolina.

STEWART, HENRY: Company A, private. September 10, 1861 enlisted as a private in Co. A, 27th Regiment, Georgia Infantry at Camp Stephens, Griffin, Spalding County, Georgia. March 30, 1862 admitted to

Chimborazo Hospital No. 1 at Richmond, Virginia with Pneumonia. April 5, 1862 died of Pneumonia in Chimborazo Hospital No.1 at Richmond, Virginia. He is most likely buried in Oakwood Cemetery at Richmond Virginia. November 21, 1862 death benefit claim was filed. January 23, 1863 death benefit claim was paid $109.83 (#2783).

STEWART, P. F.: Company H, private. September 9, 1861 enlisted as a private in Co. H, 27th Regiment, Georgia Infantry at Camp Stephens, Griffin, Spalding County, Georgia. January 1862 roll shows him detailed on fatigue duty at Post since December 16, 1861. July 10, 1862 received pay ($91.00). December 31, 1863 received pay. February 20, 1864 wounded at Olustee, Florida. January – February 1864 roll shows him present. February 29, 1864 received pay. March - April 1864 roll shows him present. May 31, 1864 issued clothing. March 8, 1865 captured at Kinston, North Carolina. March 16, 1865 arrived at Point Lookout, Maryland from New Bern, North Carolina. May 14, 1865 released at Point Lookout, Maryland. He was a farmer from Henry County, Georgia.

STEWART PETER: Company A, sergeant. September 10, 1861 elected 4th corporal Co. A, 27th Regiment, Georgia Infantry at Camp Stephens, Griffin, Spalding County, Georgia. December 1861 and January 1862 rolls show he was left sick in Georgia October 31, 1861. March 16, 1862 admitted to Chimborazo Hospital No. 1 at Richmond, Virginia Convalescent. May 2, 1863 wounded at Chancellorsville, Virginia. July, August and September 1863 issued clothing. December 31, 1863 received pay. January – February 1864 roll shows him present. February 29, 1864 received pay. March - April 1864 roll shows him present. July 1864 and September 30, 1864 issued clothing. April 26, 1865 surrendered Greensboro, North Carolina. May 1, 1865 paroled at Greensboro, North Carolina.

STEWART, RANDALL: Company A, private. May 12, 1862 enlisted as a private in Co. A, 27th Regiment, Georgia Infantry. June 29, 1862 admitted to General Hospital at Danville, Virginia with Chronic Diarrhoea. August 10, 1862 died of Chronic Diarrhoea at General Hospital at Danville, Virginia (effects $1.00). November 21, 1862 death benefit claim was filed by his wife, Laura R. Stewart. January 22, 1863 death benefit claim paid $58.00 (#2284). His effects at time of death were: 1 suit of clothes, oil cloth, pocket book (wife's letter answer) cash $1.00. He was a resident of Schley, County.

STEWART, WILLIAM B.: Company G, private. February 23, 1864 enlisted as a private in Co. G, 27th Regiment, Georgia Infantry at Decatur, Georgia. March - April 1864 roll shows him present. July 21, 1864 admitted to Jackson Hospital at Richmond, Virginia with Dysenteria. July 1864 issued clothes. August 9, 1864 furloughed for 30 days.

STONE, WILLIAM T.: Company A, private. September 10, 1861 enlisted as a private in Co. A, 27th Regiment, Georgia Infantry at Camp Stephens, Griffin, Spalding County, Georgia. December 1861 and January 1862 rolls show he was left sick in Georgia October 31, 1861. July 5,

1862 admitted to Chimborazo Hospital No. 4 at Richmond, Virginia with Continua Fever. (Malaria). July 14, 1862 returned to duty. October 24, 1862 admitted to Chimborazo Hospital No. 2 at Richmond, Virginia with a double Hernia. November 2, 1862 transferred from Chimborazo Hospital No. 2 at Richmond, Virginia to Danville, Virginia. November 3, 1862 admitted to General Hospital at Danville, Virginia with a Hernia. July 11, 1863 discharged due to Hernia from General Hospital at Danville, Virginia (with surgeon's certificate). July 13, 1863 discharged and paid. July 1864 discharged due to disability, at Danville, Virginia. He was born in Louisiana.

STOREY, WILLIAM: Company I, private. He enlisted as a private in Co. I, 27th Regiment, Georgia Infantry. May 30, 1864 and July 1864 issued clothing. July 30, 1864 admitted to Receiving and Wayside Hospital or General Hospital No. 9 at Richmond, Virginia and transferred to Jackson Hospital at Richmond, Virginia. July 31, 1864 admitted to Jackson Hospital at Richmond, Virginia August 2, 1864 admitted to Receiving and Wayside Hospital or General Hospital No. 9 at Richmond, Virginia and transferred to Jackson Hospital at Richmond, Virginia. August 3, 1864 admitted to Jackson Hospital at Richmond, Virginia with Debilitas. August 23, 1864 returned to duty. August 23, 1864 received pay ($22.00). June 18, 1864 was killed at Colquitt's Salient near Petersburg, Virginia.

STRAWN, P. S. (P. W.): Company E, private. February 1, 1864 enlisted as a private in Co. E, 27th Regiment, Georgia Infantry at Fairburn, Georgia. January – February 1864 roll shows him present (due $50.00 bounty). March - April 1864 roll shows him present.

June 30, 1864 roll of Jackson Hospital at Richmond, Virginia shows him present and never paid. July 8, 1864 wounded at Colquitt's Salient near Petersburg, Virginia. July 8, 1864 admitted to Jackson Hospital at Richmond, Virginia with a Vulnus Sclopeticum (Gunshot Wound) to the right side (shell). July 28, 1864 furloughed for 30 days. April 26, 1865 surrendered Greensboro, North Carolina. May 1, 1865 paroled at Greensboro, North Carolina.

STREETMAN, WILLIAM T.: Company F, sergeant. September 9, 1861 enlisted as a private in Co. F, 27th Regiment, Georgia Infantry at Camp Stephens, Griffin, Spalding County, Georgia. March 7, 1862 admitted to Chimborazo Hospital No. 4 at Richmond, Virginia with Debility. April 28, 1862 returned to duty. September 22, 1862 received pay ($119.00). December 1862 roll shows him on furlough. October 31, 1863 received pay. January – February 1864 roll shows him present. March - April 1864 roll shows him present. September 2, 1864 received pay ($27.13). April 26, 1865 surrendered Greensboro, North Carolina. May 1, 1865 paroled at Greensboro, North Carolina. He died June 16, 1874 and is buried in Bethlehem Primitive Baptist Church Cemetery in Taylor County, Georgia.

STRICKLAND, CAREY: Company G, private. September 9, 1861 enlisted as a private in Co. G, 27th Regiment, Georgia Infantry at Camp

Stephens, Griffin, Spalding County, Georgia.   January 8, 1862 died of Typhoid Pneumonia at Camp Pickens near Manassas, Virginia. January 1862 roll shows his death. February 17, 1862 death benefit claim was filed by his father, Carey Strickland.

STRICKLIN, M. O.: Company D, private.   He enlisted as a private in Co. D, 27th Regiment, Georgia Infantry.   April 11, 1862 admitted to Chimborazo Hospital No. 2 at Richmond, Virginia with Diarrhoea. April 22, 1862 returned to duty.

STUBBS, JOEL G.: Company B, corporal. September 10, 1861 enlisted as a private in Co. B, 27th Regiment, Georgia Infantry at Camp Stephens, Griffin, Spalding County, Georgia. October 31, 1861 received pay. December 26, 1861 he was in hospital. December 1861 roll shows him in the hospital. January 1, 1862 died of disease in Richmond, Virginia. January 1862 roll shows his death on January 1 at Richmond, Virginia. September 3, 1862 death benefit claim was filed his widow, Fannie E. V. Stubbs.   September 30, 1862 death benefit claim paid $23.43 (#1360).

STUBBS, JOHN W.: Field Staff, lieutenant colonel. June 12, 1861 elected captain of the Rutland Grays from Bibb County, Georgia. September 10, 1861 elected captain of Co. B, 27th Georgia Infantry at Camp Stephens, Griffin,   Spalding   County,   Georgia.

   December 20, 1861 received pay ($277.33). December 21, 1861 admitted to Moore Hospital at General Hospital, No. 1 at Danville, Virginia with Catarrh (was sent to Richmond). December 1861 roll shows him absent in the hospital in Richmond, Virginia since December 21, 1861. January 1862 roll shows him absent on sick furlough for 30 days from December 31, 1861. February 1862 roll shows him present at Camp Pickens near Manassas, Virginia. March 1, 1862 received pay ($260.00). May 17, 1862 received pay ($260.00). June 7, 1862 received pay ($130.00). June 17, 1862 received pay ($260.00). July 28, 1862 received pay ($260.00). August 24, 1862, elected major, 27th Georgia Infantry. September 1, 1862 received pay ($130.00). September 17, 1862 elected lieutenant colonel, 27th Georgia Infantry.   September 22, 1862 received pay ($190.00). December 1862 roll (dated January 31, 1863) shows he resigned his commission on January 10, 1863. January 1863 roll of Belleview Hospital at Richmond, Virginia shows surgeon's certificate for discharge due to Chronic Nephritis. January 10, 1863 resigned his commission on account of Chronic Nephritis.

STUBBS, JOSEPH R.: Company B, lieutenant.   April 20, 1861 enlisted as a private in Co. C, 2nd Battalion, Georgia Infantry. 1862 discharged, furnished substitute.   December 11, 1862 elected Jr. 2nd lieutenant in Co. B, 27th Regiment, Georgia Infantry. December 1862 roll shows him present at camp near Guinea Station, Virginia. March 24, 1863 granted a leave of absence. September 30, 1863 roll of Colquitt's Brigade shows him. January - February 1864 and March – April rolls he appears without remark. August 17, 1864 received pay ($80.00). August 19, 1864 promoted to 2nd lieutenant in Co. B, 27th Regiment, Georgia Infantry. August 20, 1864 received pay ($160.00). April 28, 1865 admitted to C. S. A. General Hospital, No. 11 at Charlotte, North Carolina with Branch (Intermittent) Fever. April 29, 1865 sent to other hospital.

STUBBS, THOMAS: Company B, sergeant. September 10, 1861 enlisted as a private in Co. B, 27th Regiment, Georgia Infantry at Camp Stephens, Griffin, Spalding County, Georgia. December 1861 roll shows him in the Hospital in Richmond since November 16. December 7, 1861 discharged due to disability. December 9, 1861 he was discharged and paid. January 1862 roll shows his discharge.

STUBBS, THOMAS Company B, private. March 5, 1864 enlisted as a private in Co. B, 27th Regiment, Georgia Infantry in Macon, Georgia. March - April 1864 roll shows him present. October 17, 1864 asked for a transfer.

SULLIVAN, JAMES M.: Company G, private. August 6, 1864 enlisted as a private in Co. G, 27th Regiment, Georgia Infantry at Macon, Georgia. March - April 1864 roll shows him absent sick at hospital from April 19, 1864. June 30, 1864 roll of General hospital No. 22 (also called Hospital Encampment) at Summerville, South Carolina shows him present. April 26, 1865 surrendered Greensboro, North Carolina. May 1, 1865 paroled at Greensboro, North Carolina.

SULLIVAN, JOHN S.: Company G, corporal. September 9, 1861 elected 1st corporal in Co. G, 27th Regiment, Georgia Infantry at Camp Stephens, Griffin, Spalding County, Georgia. November 8, 1861 admitted to General Hospital No. 18 (formerly Greaner's Hospital) at Richmond, Virginia. January 9, 1862 returned to duty. May 3, 1863 wounded at Chancellorsville, Virginia. June 26, 1863, October 30, 1863 and November 24, 1863 issued clothing. December 31, 1863 received pay. January – February 1864 roll shows him present. February 29, 1864 received pay. March - April 1864 roll shows him present. July 1864 issued clothing. August 31, 1864 admitted to Jackson Hospital at Richmond, Virginia with Chronic Diarrhoea. September 29, 1864 died of Chronic Colitis at Jackson Hospital Division 2 at Richmond, Virginia. He is buried in Hollywood Cemetery at Richmond, Virginia. He was a resident of Zebulon, Pike County, Georgia.

SULLIVAN, M.: Company D, lieutenant. December 31, 1861 admitted to Moore Hospital at General Hospital, No. 1 at Danville, Virginia with Fever (sent to Richmond).

SULLIVAN, MARCUS: Company B, private. September 10, 1861 enlisted as a private in Co. B, 27th Regiment, Georgia Infantry at Camp Stephens, Griffin, Spalding County, Georgia. December 31, 1861 admitted to Moore Hospital at General Hospital, No. 1 at Danville, Virginia with Parobiles (sent to Richmond). December 1861 roll shows him in the hospital at Richmond, Virginia since December 29, 1861. January 15, 1862 died of disease at Richmond, Virginia. January 1862 roll shows he died at Richmond, Virginia on January 15, 1862. September 3, 1862 death benefit claim was filed by his father, Thomas J. Sullivan. January 6, 1863 death benefit claim paid $77.50 (#2784).

SWANSON, THOMAS B.: Company E, sergeant. September 9, 1861 elected 2nd sergeant in Co. E, 27th Regiment, Georgia Infantry at Camp Stephens, Griffin, Spalding County, Georgia. April, May and June 1863 issued clothing. October 30, 1863 furloughed for 20 days. November 31, 1863 received $6.60 in commutation of rations. December 31, 1863 received pay. January – February 1864 roll shows him present. February 29, 1864 received pay. March - April 1864 roll shows him present. August 25, 1864 admitted to Jackson Hospital at Richmond, Virginia with Fever and Diarrhoea. August 29, 1864 furloughed for 30 days from hospital in Richmond, Virginia, destination Jonesboro, Georgia. September 1864 issued clothing.

SWEARINGER, A. VAN: Company A, private. July 5, 1862 admitted to Chimborazo Hospital No. 4 at Richmond, Virginia. July 18, 1862 died of Typhoid Fever at Chimborazo Hospital No. 4 at Richmond, Virginia. He is most likely buried in Oakwood Cemetery at Richmond Virginia. December 27, 1862 death benefit claim was filed by his father, Van Swearinger. September 1, 1863 death benefit claim was paid $147.60 (#8805).

SWEETE (SWEAT), JOHN: Company G, private. September 9, 1861 enlisted as a private in Co. G, 27th Regiment, Georgia Infantry at Camp Stephens, Griffin, Spalding County, Georgia. December 1862 roll shows him absent without leave. January 19, 1864 received pay ($198.00). January – February and March – April 1864 rolls show him absent without leave from March 7, 1864. May 31, 1864, July 1864 and September 20, 1864 issued clothing. August 16, 1864 he appears on the Register of the Invalid Corps P. A. C. S as retired and totally disqualified. August 19, 1864 received pay from August 31, 1862 through January 31, 1864 ($198.00).

SYMS, THOMAS LA FAYETTE: Company B, private. September 10, 1861 enlisted as a private in Co. B, 27th Regiment, Georgia Infantry at Camp Stephens, Griffin, Spalding County, Georgia. May 5, 1863 wounded at Chancellorsville, Virginia. May 30, 1864 and July 1864 issued clothing. April 26, 1865 surrendered Greensboro, North Carolina.

TANKERSLEY, H. WILLIS: Company B, private. June 28, 1863 enlisted as a private in Co. B, 27th Regiment, Georgia Infantry at Macon, Georgia. December 31, 1863 received pay. March – April 1864 roll shows him present. July 1864 issued clothing. He was killed in service.

TANNER, JOSEPH H.: Company D, private. September 23, 1861 enlisted as a private in Co. D, 27th Regiment, Georgia Infantry at Camp Stephens, Griffin, Spalding County, Georgia. June 7, 1862 furloughed for 30 days and received pay ($69.00). October 11, 1862 admitted to Hospital No. 16 at Richmond, Virginia. April 13, 1863 received $7.50 in commutation of rations. April, May and June 1863 issued clothing. July 7, 1863 admitted to Receiving and Wayside Hospital or General Hospital No. 9 at Richmond,

Virginia. July 8, 1863 sent to and admitted to Chimborazo Hospital No. 2 at Richmond, Virginia with Debility. July 22, 1863 returned to duty. September 1863 issued clothing. December 31, 1863 received pay. March 1, 1864 killed at Cedar Creek, Florida. March – April 1864 roll shows he was killed on March 1, 1864 at Cedar Creek, Florida.

TATE, F. M.: Company E, private. He enlisted as a private in Co. E, 27th Regiment, Georgia Infantry. December 1862 roll shows he was furloughed on December 17, 1862 for 40 days.

TATE, RILEY JONATHAN: Company H, private. September 9, 1861 enlisted as a private in Co. H, 27th Regiment, Georgia Infantry at Camp Stephens, Griffin, Spalding County, Georgia. August 15, 1864 died at Richmond, Virginia. He is buried in Hollywood Cemetery at Richmond, Virginia.

TAYLOR, G. W.: Company H, private. He enlisted as a private in Co. H, 27th Regiment, Georgia Infantry. November 28, 1862 returned to duty from Camp Winder Hospital at Richmond, Virginia.

TAYLOR, J. W.: Company H, private. September 9, 1861 enlisted as a private in Co. H, 27th Regiment, Georgia Infantry at Camp Stephens, Griffin, Spalding County, Georgia. May 9, 1863 admitted to General Hospital at Camp Winder, Richmond, Virginia with Pneumonia. May 12, 1863 transferred to Lynchburg, Virginia.
April 26, 1865, pension records show he surrendered at Greensboro, North Carolina. He was born in Lumpkin County, Georgia. He died at the Confederate Soldier's Home, at Atlanta, Georgia November 28, 1926. He is buried at Marietta, Georgia.

TAYLOR, JOEL T.: Company B, private. September 21, 1861 enlisted as a private in Co. B, 27th Regiment, Georgia Infantry at Camp Stephens, Griffin, Spalding County, Georgia. January 1862 roll shows him detailed on fatigue duty at Manassas Station. February 1862 roll shows him detailed on fatigue duty at Post Headquarters. May 18, 1862 admitted to C. S. A. General Hospital at Danville, Virginia with Acute Rheumatism. November 7 (10), 1862 furloughed. December 1862 roll shows him absent without leave furlough expired. October, November and December 1863 issued clothing. December 31, 1863 received pay. January – February 1864 roll shows him present. February 29, 1864 received pay. March - April 1864 roll shows him present. September 20, 1864 and July 1864 issued clothing. April 26, 1865 surrendered Greensboro, North Carolina. May 1, 1865 paroled at Greensboro, North Carolina. He was born in Crawford County, Georgia in 1832.

TAYLOR, JOHN: Company G, private. September 9, 1861 enlisted as a private in Co. G, 27th Regiment, Georgia Infantry at Camp Stephens, Griffin, Spalding County, Georgia. November 6, 1861 admitted to General Hospital at Petersburg, Virginia with Rubeola. December 17, 1861 returned to duty. February 1862 roll shows he was sent to the hospital February 27, 1862. September 17, 1862 killed at Sharpsburg, Maryland. May 20, 1863 death benefit claim was filed by Jane Taylor, his widow. He was a resident of Pike County, Georgia.

TAYLOR, JOHN: Company H, private. September 9, 1861 enlisted as a private in Co. H, 27th Regiment, Georgia Infantry at Camp Stephens, Griffin, Spalding County, Georgia. May 2, 1863 wounded at Chancellorsville, Virginia. December 31, 1863 received pay. February 20, 1864 wounded at Olustee, Florida. January – February 1864 roll shows him absent in the hospital from wound received at Olustee, Florida. February 29, 1864 received pay. March - April 1864 roll shows him present. July 1864 and September 20, 1864 issued clothing. April 26, 1865, surrendered at Greensboro, North Carolina. May 1, 1865 paroled at Greensboro, North Carolina.

TAYLOR, JOHN W.: Company G, private. He enlisted as a private in Co. G, 27th Regiment, Georgia Infantry. May 31, 1862 wounded in the arm necessitating amputation above the elbow at Seven Pines, Virginia.

TAYLOR, W. F.: Company A, private. August 22, 1864 enlisted as a private in Co. A, 27th Regiment, Georgia Infantry at Camp Stephens, Griffin, Spalding County, Georgia. April 26, 1865 surrendered Greensboro, North Carolina.

TEAT, WILLIAM A. J.: Company A, lieutenant. February 24, 1862 enlisted as a private in Co. A, 27th Regiment, Georgia Infantry at Macon, Georgia. September 17, 1862 captured at Sharpsburg, Maryland. October 2, 1862 sent from Fort Delaware, Delaware to Aiken's Landing, Virginia for exchange. November 10, 1862 exchanged at Aiken's Landing, Virginia. November 20, 1862 received bounty pay ($50.00). February 8, 1863 detailed on recruiting service for 30 days. March 5, 1863 elected Jr. 2nd lieutenant Co. A, 27th Regiment, Georgia Infantry. March 10, 1863 received $9.90 in commutation of rations. May 5, 1863 wounded at Chancellorsville, Virginia. January – February 1864 roll shows him absent sick since March 8, 1864. February 20, 1864 he was wounded at Olustee, Florida. March – April 1864 roll does not show him as absent or present. August 19, 1864 wounded and permanently disabled at Weldon Rail Road near Petersburg, Virginia. August 20, 1864 admitted to Jackson Hospital at Richmond, Virginia with Vulnus Sclopeticum (Gunshot Wound) to the right thigh. September 2, 1864 furloughed for 50 days from Jackson hospital at Richmond, Virginia destination Box Springs, Georgia. November 26, 1864 Colquitt's Brigade report shows he was furloughed by order of General Beauregard on September 15, 1864. December 31, 1864 Colquitt's Brigade report shows he was furloughed by order of General Beauregard. May 18, 1865 paroled at Albany, Georgia. He was born in Georgia in 1845.

TERRY, SAMUEL L.: Company A, private. September 10, 1861 enlisted as a private in Co. A, 27th Regiment, Georgia Infantry at Camp Stephens, Griffin, Spalding County, Georgia. December 1861, January 1862 and February 1862 rolls show he was left sick in Georgia October 31, 1861. November 18, 1862 died of Diarrhoea Chronica at Mt. Jackson General

Hospital at Mt. Jackson, Virginia. He had $3.10 in his possession at death. March 7, 1863 death benefit claim was filed.

THARPE, WILLIAM: Company B, private. August 19, 1863 enlisted as a private in Co. D, 66th Regiment, Georgia Infantry. August 19, 1863 deserted. September 9, 1863 enlisted as a private in Co. B, 27th Regiment, Georgia Infantry at Charleston, South Carolina. December 31, 1863 received pay. January – February 1864 roll shows him present. March - April 1864 roll shows him transferred as a deserter from the 66th Regiment Georgia Infantry. March 9, 1864 returned as a deserter to Co. D, 66th Regiment, Georgia Infantry.

THOMAS, ANDREW H.: Company I, private. March 12, 1862 enlisted as a private in Co. F, 11th Battalion, Georgia Infantry. May 12, 1862 transferred as a private in Co. F, 47th Regiment, Georgia Infantry. June 22, 1862 discharged, furnished Jackson Williams as a substitute. He enlisted as a private in Co. I, 27th Regiment, Georgia Infantry. February 20, 1864 wounded at Olustee, Florida. April 26, 1865, surrendered at Greensboro, North Carolina. May 1, 1865 paroled at Greensboro, North Carolina.

THOMAS, HENRY: Company B, private. September 10, 1861 enlisted as a private in Co. B, 27th Regiment, Georgia Infantry at Camp Stephens, Griffin, Spalding County, Georgia. November 6, 1861 admitted to General Hospital at Petersburg, Virginia with Rubeola. November 15, 1861 returned to duty. November 18, 1861 admitted to C. S. A. General Hospital at Charlottesville, Virginia with Measles and Rheumatism. December 21, 1861 discharged and furloughed. January 2, 1862 returned to duty. January 1862 roll shows him in Moore Hospital since January 26, 1862. February 5, 1862 died of Pneumonia in Moore Hospital at Manassas Junction, Virginia. February 1862 roll shows he died at Moore Hospital of disease. September 3, 1862 death benefit claim was filed his widow, Nancy Thomas. June 6, 1862 death benefit claim was paid $62.83 (#2485). He was a resident of Bibb County, Georgia.

THOMAS, LUTHER J.: Company B, sergeant. September 10, 1961 elected 3rd Sergeant. Co. B, 27th Regiment, Georgia Infantry at Camp Stephens, Griffin, Spalding County, Georgia. December 1861 roll shows he was in the hospital at Richmond, Virginia since November 15, 1861. December 16, 1861 discharged due to disability, at Richmond, Virginia and received pay. January 1862 roll shows his discharge due to disability December 16, 1861 in Richmond, Virginia.

THOMAS, NATHATNIEL A.: Company I, private. September 10, 1861 enlisted as a private in Co. I, 27th Regiment, Georgia Infantry at Camp Stephens, Griffin, Spalding County, Georgia. May 31, 1862 wounded at Seven Pines, Virginia. June 3, 1863 furloughed for 30 days and received $7.50 in commutation of rations. June 16 and June 27, 1863 issued clothing. December 31, 1863 received pay. January – February 1864 roll shows him present. February 29, 1864 received pay. March - April 1864 roll shows him present. September 20, 1864 issued clothing. April 26,

1865, surrendered at Greensboro, North Carolina. May 1, 1865 paroled at Greensboro, North Carolina.

He was born in Georgia in 1845.

THOMAS, C. NELSON: Company B, private September 10, 1861 enlisted as a private in Co. B, 27th Regiment, Georgia Infantry at Camp Stephens, Griffin, Spalding County, Georgia. January 7, 1862 admitted to Moore Hospital at General Hospital, No. 1 at Danville, Virginia with Hemophthis (spitting of blood) and was sent to the Ninth ward. January 1862 roll shows him in the hospital at Richmond, Virginia since January 7, 1861. November 13, 1862 received pay ($182.00). October, November and December 1863 issued clothing. December 31, 1863 received pay. February 20, 1864 wounded at Olustee, Florida. January – February 1864 roll shows him present. February 29, 1864 received pay. March – April 1864 roll shows him present. May 30, 1864 and July 1864 issued clothing. December 20, 1864 admitted to Ocmulgee Hospital at Macon, Georgia with Febris Intermittent. Quarantined (Malaria Quarantined). January 4, 1865 deserted. He was a resident of Bibb County, Georgia.

THOMAS, O. V.: Company K, private. September 10, 1861 enlisted as a private in Co. K, 27th Regiment, Georgia Infantry at Camp Stephens, Griffin, Spalding County, Georgia. November 13, 1861 admitted to Chimborazo Hospital No. 1 at Richmond, Virginia (note: Deserted from the hospital without the knowledge of the surgeon).

THOMAS, STEPHEN LUTHER: Company B, private. September 10, 1861 enlisted as a private in Co. B, 27th Regiment, Georgia Infantry at Camp Stephens, Griffin, Spalding County, Georgia. November 6, 1861 admitted to General Hospital at Petersburg, Virginia with Rubeola. November 13, 1861 returned to duty. November 18, 1861 admitted to C. S. A. General Hospital at Charlottesville, Virginia with Measles. December 7, 1861 returned to duty. February 9, 1862 died of Pneumonia in Moore Hospital at Manassas Junction, Virginia. February 1862 roll shows his death on February 9, 1862 at Moore Hospital. September 3, 1862 death benefit claim was filed by his father, Rufus Thomas. January 6, 1863 death benefit claim was paid $64.66 (#2486).

THOMAS, WILLIAM C.: Company D, private. September 10, 1861 enlisted as a private in Co. D, 27th Regiment, Georgia Infantry at Camp Stephens, Griffin, Spalding County, Georgia. January and February 1862 rolls show he was left sick in Georgia October 31, 1861. June 28, 1862 admitted to General Hospital No. 18 (formerly Greaner's Hospital) at Richmond, Virginia with Typhoid Fever. July 3, 1862 returned to duty. December 1862 roll shows he was wounded and on furlough since August 1862. April, May, June and November 1863 received clothing. December 31, 1863 received pay. March 10, 1864 wounded at Cedar Creek, Florida. March 16, 1864 died Lake City, Florida. March - April 1864 roll shows he died of wounds at Lake City, Florida on March 16, 1864. Death benefit claim was filed. 1864 death benefit claim paid $100.00 (#6420 - #7228).

THOMPSON, C.: Company B, private. He enlisted as a private in Co. B, 27th Regiment, Georgia Infantry. August 19, 1864 captured at Weldon Railroad near Petersburg, Virginia. August 24, 1864 arrived at Point lookout, Maryland from City Point, Virginia.

THOMPSON, EPHRIAM: Company E, private. September 9, 1861 enlisted as a private in Co. E, 27th Regiment, Georgia Infantry at Camp Stephens, Griffin, Spalding County, Georgia. July 1, 1862 received pay. August 7, 1862 received pay ($91.00). October 31, 1862 roll of General Hospital No. 17 at Richmond, Virginia shows him present. November 19, 1862 admitted to General Hospital No. 17 at Richmond, Virginia. December 8, 1862 furloughed for 30 days. December 1862 roll shows he died in Georgia on December 1, 1862.

THOMPSON, GEORGE ROWLAND: Company H, private. April 1864 enlisted as a private in Co, H, 27th Regiment, Georgia Infantry. Feburary29, 1864 received pay. March - April 1864 roll shows him present. May 28, 1864 died.

THOMPSON, H. T.: Company F, private. 1864 enlisted as a private in Co. F, 27th Regiment, Georgia Infantry.

THOMPSON, HENRY: Company B, private. He enlisted as a private in Co. B, 27th Regiment, Georgia Infantry. January 26, 1862 admitted to Moore Hospital at General Hospital, No. 1 at Danville, Virginia with Pluritis (Pleurisy) and sent to Ward No. 10.

THOMPSON, JACOB T.: Company I, private. September 10, 1861 enlisted as a private in Co. I, 27th Regiment, Georgia Infantry at Camp Stephens, Griffin, Spalding County, Georgia. December 1861 roll shows he was left sick in Georgia October 31, 1861. January 1862 roll shows him on furlough. February 1862 roll shows him absent sick in Richmond, Virginia since November 14, 1861. November 14, 1861 - February 1862 at Richmond, Virginia, sick. May 31, 1862 killed at Seven Pines, Virginia.

THOMPSON, JAMES R.: Company E, private. September 9, 1861 enlisted as a private in Co. E, 27th Regiment, Georgia Infantry at Camp Stephens, Griffin, Spalding County, Georgia. May 15, 1862 admitted to Chimborazo Hospital No. 2 at Richmond, Virginia with Diarrhoea. May 15, 1862 returned to duty. May 31, 1862 severely wounded in left arm at Seven Pines, Virginia. June 7, 1862 received pay ($55.00). September 17, 1862 wounded in right arm, necessitating amputation above the elbow at Sharpsburg, Maryland. October 1, 1862 received pay ($147.30). December 1862 roll shows him on furlough due to amputation of arm (September 17, 1862). June 4, 1863 he was given unlimited furlough on account of loss of arm. June 30, 1862 received pay. July 2, 1863 received $15.00 in commutation of rations while on furlough. July 15, 1863 received pay ($22.00). September 15, 1863 received pay ($22.00). December 1, 1863 received Pay ($22.00). December 4, 1863 received commutation of rations. January 9, 1864 received pay ($22.00). January – February and March – April 1864 rolls show him absent on unlimited sick furlough in

Georgia since the amputation of his right arm on June 4, 1863. May 8, 1864 received pay ($22.00). He was born in Georgia February 27, 1844.

THOMPSON, N. A.: Company K, private. February 23, 1864 enlisted as a private in Co. K, 27th Regiment, Georgia Infantry. March - April 1864 roll shows him present. July 1864 and September 20, 1864 issued clothing. April 26, 1865 surrendered Greensboro, North Carolina. May 9, 1865 paroled at Greensboro, North Carolina.

THOMPSON, T. H.: Company A, private. September 10, 1861 enlisted as a private in Co. A, 27th Regiment, Georgia Infantry at Camp Stephens, Griffin, Spalding County, Georgia. December 1861 roll shows him in the hospital.

THOMPSON, T. M.: Company H, private. June 22, 1864 admitted to General Hospital, Howard's Grove at Richmond, Virginia with Chronic Diarrhoea. August 2, 1864 furloughed for 60 days.

THOMPSON, THOMAS: Company E, private. September 9, 1861 enlisted as a private in Co. E, 27th Regiment, Georgia Infantry at Camp Stephens, Griffin, Spalding County, Georgia. November 18, 1861 admitted to Chimborazo Hospital No. 4 at Richmond, Virginia with Measles. November 24, 1861 transferred to Georgia Hospital in Richmond, Virginia. December 1861 roll shows him in the hospital in Richmond, Virginia. January 7, 1862 discharged due to disability at Richmond, Virginia and paid. January 1862 roll shows he was discharged due to disability in Richmond, Virginia January 7, 1862.

THOMPSON, WILLIAM J.: Company K, sergeant. September 10, 1861 enlisted as a private in Co. K, 27th Regiment, Georgia Infantry at Camp Stephens, Griffin, Spalding County, Georgia. November 8, 1862 admitted to Chimborazo Hospital No. 3 at Richmond, Virginia with Diarrhoea. December 16, 1862 returned to duty. May 3, 1863 admitted to Receiving and Wayside Hospital or General Hospital No. 9 at Richmond, Virginia and transferred and admitted to Chimborazo Hospital No. 2 at Richmond, Virginia with Rheumatism. May 9, 1863 deserted from the hospital. June 1863, October 22 and 29, 1863 and November 8 and 24, 1863 issued clothing. December 31, 1863 received pay. March - April 1864 roll shows him present. May 30, 1864, July 1864 and September 20, 1864 issued clothing. He was appointed sergeant in Co. K, 27th Regiment, Georgia Infantry. April 26, 1865 surrendered Greensboro, North Carolina. May 2, 1865 paroled at Greensboro, North Carolina in the Methodist Church Hospital.

THORNTON, J. R.: Company E, private. He enlisted as a private in Co. E, 27th Regiment, Georgia Infantry. October 9, 1862 received pay ($147.30).

THORNTON, SEABORN B.: Company E, private. September 9, 1861 enlisted as a private in Co. E, 27th Regiment, Georgia Infantry at Camp Stephens, Griffin, Spalding County, Georgia. February 1862 roll shows he was furloughed on sick leave for 20 days beginning February 27, 1862.

April 21, 1862 died of Fever at Yorktown, Virginia. August 7, 1862 death benefit claim was filed by Herald Thornton, his father. August 11, 1862 death benefit claim paid $43.70 (#957). He is described in 1862 as being 22 years of age, gray eyes, light hair, fair complexion, 5 feet 5 ½ inches high, born in Fayette County, Georgia and was by occupation a farmer.

THORNTON, SEABORN W.: Company B, private. July 8, 1861 enlisted as a private in Co. H, 13th Regiment, Georgia Infantry. September 10, 1861 transferred as a private in Co. B, 27th Regiment, Georgia Infantry at Camp Stephens, Griffin, Spalding County, Georgia. October 9, 1861 transferred as a private in Co. K, 31st Regiment, Georgia Infantry. January 16, 1862 elected Jr. 2nd lieutenant in Co. K, 31st Regiment, Georgia Infantry. April 15, 1862 elected 2nd lieutenant in Co. K, 31st Regiment, Georgia Infantry. September 9, 1862 elected 1st lieutenant in Co. K, 31st Regiment, Georgia Infantry. June 1, 1863 elected captain in Co. K, 31st Regiment, Georgia Infantry. July 10, 1864 captured at Monocacy, Maryland. October 1, 1864 exchanged at Point Lookout, Maryland. March 13, 1865 retired to the Invalid Corps.

THRELKELD (THRIELKELD) (THEUKELD), ELBA H.: Company G, private. September 9, 1861 enlisted as a private in Co. G, 27th Regiment, Georgia Infantry at Camp Stephens, Griffin, Spalding County, Georgia. August 3, 1863 enlisted as a private in Co. E, 6th Regiment, Georgia State Guards Infantry. January 31, 1864 roll shows he was detailed permanently by order of General Wayne.

THRELKELD (THRIELKELD) (THEUKELD), FRANCIS M.: Company F, private. September 9, 1861 enlisted as a private in Co. F, 27th Regiment, Georgia Infantry at Camp Stephens, Griffin, Spalding County, Georgia. January 20, 1862 admitted to Moore Hospital at General Hospital, No. 1 at Danville, Virginia with Catarrh and sent to Orange Court House. January 21, 1862 admitted to General Hospital at Orange Court House, Virginia with Fever. March 12, 1862 returned to duty from C. S. A. General Hospital at Farmville, Virginia. January 1862 and February 1862 rolls show him in Moore Hospital since January 20(21), 1862. September 14, 1862 wounded and captured at (South Mountain) Frederick, Maryland. October 5, 1862 transferred from U. S. A. General Hospital No. 1 at Fredericksburg, Maryland. October 2, 1862 sent from Fort Delaware, Delaware to Aiken's Landing, Virginia for exchange. October 9, 1862 exchanged at Aiken's Landing, Virginia. October 13, 1862 admitted to Camp Winder Division No. 3 Hospital at Richmond, Virginia. October 20, 1862 returned to duty. August 1863 issued clothing. November 26, 1863 furloughed for 30 days. December 31, 1863 received pay. January – February 1864 roll shows him present. February 29, 1864 received pay. March - April 1864 roll shows him present. July 1864 issued clothing. August 19, 1864 wounded and captured at Weldon Railroad near Petersburg, Virginia. August 20, 1864 admitted to U. S. A. Field Hospital No. 5 with a Vulnus Sclopeticum (Gunshot Wound) to the right side and left (knee) leg (mini ball - bullet removed). August 21, 1864 sent to General Hospital from 2d Division of Depot Field Hospital. August 24, 1864 he was admitted to Lincoln's General Hospital at Washington, D. C. with Vulnus Sclopeticum (Gunshot Wound)s. September 29, 1864 died of wounds at Lincoln's General Hospital at Washington, D. C. February 28, 1865 death benefit claim was filed. He was 20 years old at the time of death. He was born in Georgia, his father was William W. Threlkeld of Butler, Georgia.

THURMOND, H. H.: Company D, private. August 4, 1862 enlisted as a private in Co. D, 27th Regiment, Georgia Infantry at Richmond, Virginia. April, May, June and November 1863 issued clothing. December 31, 1863 received pay. March - April 1864 roll shows him present.

TIDD WILEY B.: Company A, private. February 24, 1862 enlisted as a private in Co. A, 27th Regiment, Georgia Infantry at Marion County, Georgia. April 25, 1862 admitted to Chimborazo Hospital No. 2 at Richmond, Virginia with Continua Fever. May 29, 1862 returned to duty. November 20, 1862 paid $50.00 bounty at Richmond, Virginia. July 24, 1863 received $7.33 1/3 in commutation of rations. August 31, 1863 received pay. July, August, September and November 1863 received clothing. January – February 1864 and March - April 1864 rolls show him present. May 30, 1864 issued clothing. June 16, 1864 captured, Petersburg, Virginia. June 24, 1864 arrived at Point Lookout, Maryland from City Point, Virginia. July 27, 1864 transferred from Point Lookout, Maryland to Elmira Prison Elmira, New York. December 21, 1864 died of Pneumonia at Elmira Prison, New York.

TIDD, WILLIAM J.: Company A, private. March 4, 1862 enlisted as a private in Co. H, 7th Regiment, Georgia Infantry at Roswell, Georgia. March – April 1862 roll shows him present. June 30, 1862 received pay. July, August and September 1863 issued clothing. August 31, 1863 received pay ($22.00). October 31, 1862 roll shows him present. October 31, 1862 he received pay. November – December 1862 roll shows him present. December 31, 1862 received pay. February 1, 1863 transferred a private in Co. A, 27th Regiment, Georgia Infantry. January – February 1863 roll shows his transfer to Co. A, 27th Regiment, Georgia Infantry. April 30, 1863 received pay. March - April 1864 roll shows him present. June 12, 1864 killed at Petersburg, Virginia.

TIGNER, JAMES JASON: Company K, private. September 10, 1861 enlisted as a private in Co. K, 27th Regiment, Georgia Infantry at Camp Stephens, Griffin, Spalding County, Georgia. November 17, 1861 admitted to Chimborazo Hospital No. 3 at Richmond, Virginia with Measles. December 2, 1861 returned to duty. February 1862 roll shows him sent to Post Hospital on February 20, 1862. November 6, 1862 admitted to C. S. A. General Hospital at Charlottesville, Virginia. November 9, 1862 sent to General Hospital at Lynchburg, Virginia. November 12, 1862 admitted to General Hospital at Farmville, Virginia with Vulnus Sclopeticum (Gunshot Wound) and was sent to Ward 4. December 9, 1862 issued clothing at

General Hospital at Farmville, Virginia. December 19, 1862 he is shown on the roll of C. S. A. General Hospital at Farmville, Virginia with an incised wound of the right hand and was furloughed for 30 days. April 7, 1863 received $30.00 in commutation of rations. June 1863, October 22 and October 29, 1864 issued clothing. December 31, 1863 received pay. March - April 1864 roll shows him present. July 1864 and September 20, 1864 issued clothing. April 26, 1865 surrendered Greensboro, North Carolina. May 1, 1865 paroled at Greensboro, North Carolina. He was born in Monroe County, Georgia in 1836.

TODD, THOMAS L.: Company E, corporal. September 9, 1861 enlisted as a private in Co. E, 27th Regiment, Georgia Infantry at Camp Stephens, Griffin, Spalding County, Georgia. December 1861 roll shows him in the hospital at Richmond, Virginia. January 1862 roll shows he was left sick in Richmond, Virginia November 16, 1861. April 30, 1862 received pay ($57.25). October 26, 1862 admitted to Receiving and Wayside Hospital or General Hospital No. 9 at Richmond, Virginia and transferred to General Hospital No. 21 at Richmond, Virginia. October 26, 1862 admitted to General Hospital No. 21 at Richmond, Virginia with Variola and Rheumatism (age 23 years). October 26, 1862 employed as a nurse at General Hospital Howard's Grove at Richmond, Virginia. October 31, 1862 appears on the roll of General Hospital No. 21 at Richmond, Virginia. November 1, 1862 received pay. December 12, 1862 detailed as a nurse at General Hospital Howard's Grove at Richmond, Virginia. December 1862 roll shows him detailed at Hospital. February 1, 1863 roll of General Hospital Howard's Grove at Richmond, Virginia shows him present and due $18.50 pay as nurse from November 1, 1862. February 28, 1863 received pay. March 26, 1863 transferred to Small Pox Hospital at Richmond, Virginia. March – April roll of Small Pox Hospital at Richmond, Virginia shows him present, detailed there since December 14, 1862 and due extra pay as a nurse. April 30, 1863 received pay. June 9, 1863 returned to his regiment. May and June 1863 roll of Small Pox Hospital at Richmond, Virginia shows him present and due extra pay from April 30, 1863 and returned to his regiment June 9. December 31, 1863 received pay. February 20, 1864 wounded at Olustee, Florida. January – February 1864 roll shows him absent wounded at Olustee, Florida on February 20, 1864. February 29, 1864 received pay. March - April 1864 roll shows him present. September 20, 1864 issued clothing. He was appointed corporal of Co. E, 27th Regiment, Georgia Infantry. April 26, 1865 surrendered Greensboro, North Carolina. May 1, 1865 paroled at Greensboro, North Carolina.

TOMBERLIN (TIMBERLIN), MOSES: Company I, private. August 25, 1861 enlisted as a private in Co. I, 27th Regiment, Georgia Infantry at Camp Stephens, Griffin, Spalding County, Georgia. December 1861 roll shows him as dying of disease at Culpepper, Virginia on November 25, 1861. November 25, 1861 died of Typhoid Pneumonia at General Hospital at Culpeper Court House, Virginia. February 3 (September 22),

1864 death benefit claim was filed by his father, Thomas Tomberlin. He was born in Coffee County, Georgia.

TOMBERLIN, WILLIAM: Company I, private. September 10, 1861 enlisted as a private in Co. I, 27th Regiment, Georgia Infantry at Camp Stephens, Griffin, Spalding County, Georgia. November 12, 1861 admitted to General Hospital No. 18 (formerly Greaner's Hospital) at Richmond, Virginia. December 23, 1861 discharged due to disability, at Richmond, Virginia. December 24, 1861 received pay ($73.88). December 1861 roll shows him discharged due to disability December 23 at Richmond, Virginia. December 1861 report from Camp Pickens near Manassas, Virginia shows him discharged due to Chronic Bronchitis.

TOMLINSON, J. C.: sergeant. He enlisted as a private in the 27th Regiment, Georgia Infantry. He was appointed sergeant. May 10, 1865 surrendered at Tallahassee, Florida. May 19, 1865 paroled at Thomasville, Georgia.

TOMMIE, O, V.: Company K, private. September 10, 1861 enlisted as a private in Co. K, 27th Regiment, Georgia Infantry at Camp Stephens, Griffin, Spalding County, Georgia. October 29, 1862 admitted to Receiving and Wayside Hospital or General Hospital No. 9 at Richmond, Virginia and transferred to General Hospital Howard's Grove at Richmond, Virginia. October 29, 1862 admitted to General Hospital Howard's Grove at Richmond, Virginia. December 11, 1862 transferred from General Hospital Howard's Grove at Richmond, Virginia to Chimborazo Hospital at Richmond, Virginia. December 12, 1862 admitted to Chimborazo Hospital No. 3 at Richmond, Virginia with Debility. December 16, 1862 admitted to Chimborazo Hospital No. 2 at Richmond, Virginia with Diarrhoea. December 23, 1862 transferred to C. S. A. General Hospital at Danville, Virginia with Chronic Diarrhoea. December 28, 1862 returned to duty. March 7, 1862 admitted to Chimborazo Hospital No. 1 at Richmond, Virginia convalescent. April 1, 1862 returned to duty.

TOMMIE, WILLIAM E.: Company K, sergeant. September 10, 1861 elected 5th sergeant in Co. K, 27th Regiment, Georgia Infantry at Camp Stephens, Griffin, Spalding County, Georgia. November 5, 1861 admitted to Chimborazo Hospital No. 1 at Richmond, Virginia (note: Deserted from the Hospital without the knowledge of the surgeon on staff). January 1862 roll shows he died of Meningitis on January 27, 1862 at Camp Pickens near Manassas, Virginia. September 8, 1863 death benefit claim was filed by his father, Otheel W. Tommie. November 19, 1863 death benefit claim paid $67.56 (#10815). He was a resident of Talbotton, Georgia.

TOTTON, W. J.: Company B, private. September 10, 1861 enlisted as a private in Co. B, 27th Regiment, Georgia Infantry at Camp Stephens, Griffin, Spalding County, Georgia. March 1, 1863 discharged, furnished James Self as substitute.

TOWNS, J. M.: Company K, private. He enlisted as a private in Co. K, 27th Regiment, Georgia Infantry. June 16, 1864 captured at Colquitt's

Salient near Petersburg, Virginia.   June 19, 1864 confined at Bermuda Hundred, Virginia. June 20, 1864 arrived at Fort Monroe, Virginia. June 22, 1864 transferred to Point Lookout, Maryland. June 23, 1864 arrived at Point Lookout, Maryland.

TOWN, J. M.(W.): Company H, private.   January 1, 1864 enlisted as a private in Co. H, 27th Regiment, Georgia Infantry at Columbus, Georgia. June 18, 1864 he is shown on roll of General Hospital Howard's Grove at Richmond, Virginia with no statement.   June 23, 1864 received pay ($22.00).

TUGGLE, LEROY: Company F, corporal.   September 20, 1861 enlisted as a private in Co. F, 27th Regiment, Georgia Infantry at Camp Stephens, Griffin, Spalding County, Georgia.   February 1862 roll shows him furloughed for 30 days beginning February 24, 1862. December 1, 1862 detailed at Sparta, Virginia as a shoemaker. December 1862 roll shows him absent without leave since January 24, 1863. December 31, 1863 received pay. January – February 1864 roll shows him present. February 29, 1864 received pay.   March - April 1864 roll shows him present.   July 1864 and September 1, 1864 issued clothing. September 12, 1864 admitted to Jackson Hospital at Richmond, Virginia with Dysenteria. September 20, 1864 died of acute Colitis at Jackson Division 2 Hospital at Richmond, Virginia. he is buried in Hollywood Cemetery at Richmond, Virginia

TUGGLE, LEWIS: Company F, private. He enlisted as a private in Co. F, 27th Regiment, Georgia Infantry at Camp Stephens, Griffin, Spalding County, Georgia.   December 1861 roll shows him in the hospital at Chancellorsville, Virginia. January 1862 roll shows him in Moore Hospital at Danville, Virginia since December 24, 1861.

TUM (TUNE), GRIGSBY W.: Company F, corporal.   September 9, 1861 enlisted as a private in Co. F, 27th Regiment, Georgia Infantry at Camp Stephens, Griffin, Spalding County, Georgia.   He was elected corporal. December 1861 roll shows he died of disease on October 15, 1861 at Camp Stephens, Georgia.

TUMLIN (TOMLIN), G. W.: Company D, private.   October 9, 1862 enlisted as a private in Co. D, 27th Regiment, Georgia Infantry at Gordon County, Georgia.   December 1862 roll shows he enlisted in the regiment on December 25, 1862 at Guinea Station, Virginia. May 2, 1863 admitted to Receiving and Wayside Hospital or General Hospital No. 9 at Richmond, Virginia and transferred to Chimborazo Hospital at Richmond, Virginia. May 2, 1863 admitted to Chimborazo Hospital No. 2 at Richmond, Virginia with Rheumatism. May 11, 1863 transferred to Lynchburg, Virginia. November 1863 issued clothing.   December 31, 1863 received pay. March – April 1864 roll shows him on sick furlough.   March 10, 1865 wounded in the leg at Kinston, North Carolina. March 10, 1865 admitted to Pettigrew General Hospital No. 13 at Raleigh, North Carolina with a Vulnus Sclopeticum (Gunshot Wound) to the left leg. March 11, 1865 issued clothing.   March 19, 1865 transferred to Charlotte, North Carolina. He was a resident of

Gainesville, Hall County, Georgia.

TURNER, B. F.: Company H, private.   September 9, 1861 enlisted as a private in Co. H, 27th Regiment, Georgia Infantry at Camp Stephens, Griffin, Spalding County, Georgia.   May 31, 1862 captured at Seven Pines, Virginia.   June 5, 1862 sent to Fort Delaware, Delaware from Fort Monroe, Virginia (Description: Born in Georgia, age 22, 5 feet 5 inches high, black hair, grey eyes and dark complexion).   June 9, 1862 sent to Aiken's Landing, Virginia for exchange.   August 5, 1862 exchanged at Aiken's Landing, Virginia.   December 31, 1863 received pay.   January – February 1864 roll shows him present.   February 29, 1864 received pay.   March - April 1864 roll shows him present.   July 1864 and September 20, 1864 issued clothing.   April 26, 1865 surrendered Greensboro, North Carolina.   May 1, 1865 paroled at Greensboro, North Carolina.   He was born in Georgia in 1840.

TURNER, HARRY C.: Company H, private.   August 13, 1862 enlisted as a private in Co. H, 27th Regiment, Georgia Infantry at Richmond, Virginia.   September 17, 1862 severely wounded in left leg and captured at Sharpsburg, Maryland.   December 1862 roll shows him Missing in Action since September 17, 1862.   September 27, 1862 (October 3, 1862) he was paroled by the Army of the Potomac.   October 22, 1862 admitted to No. 1, U. S. A. General Hospital at Frederick, Maryland with a compound fracture of the left leg.   May 28, 1863 released and returned to duty.   May 29, 1863 paroled and sent to Fort Monroe, Virginia released from Fort McHenry, Maryland.   May 31, 1863 admitted to General Hospital at Petersburg, Virginia with a Vulnus Sclopeticum (Gunshot Wound) to the left thigh.   June 11, 1863 paroled for 60 days.   March - April 1864 roll shows him absent with leave from wounds received at Sharpsburg, Maryland.   His pension records show he was at home on wounded furlough at the close of the war.

TURNER, J. H.: Company H, private.   November 13, 1863 enlisted as a private in Co. H,   27th Regiment, Georgia Infantry at Macon, Georgia.   December 31, 1863 received pay.   January – February 1864 roll shows him present.   February 29, 1864 received pay.   March - April 1864 roll shows him present with note that extra duty pay and bounty due.   July 1864 and September 20, 1864 issued clothing.   April 26, 1865 surrendered Greensboro, North Carolina.   May 1, 1865 paroled at Greensboro, North Carolina.

TURNER, JAMES C.: Company H, private.   August 13, 1862 enlisted as a private in Co. H, 27th Regiment, Georgia Infantry at Richmond, Virginia.   September 17, 1862 wounded at Sharpsburg, Maryland.   January – February 1864 roll shows him absent with leave from wounds received at Sharpsburg, Maryland September 17, 1862.

TURNER, JAMES G.: Company H, sergeant.   September 10, 1861 enlisted as a private in Co. H, 27th Regiment, Georgia Infantry at Camp Stephens, Griffin, Spalding County, Georgia.   He was elected 1st sergeant.   February

1862 roll shows him on recruiting service since February 13, 1862 for 30 days. May 31, 1862 killed at the battle of Seven Pines, Virginia. December 2, 1862 death benefit claim was filed by Frances C. Turner, his widow.

TURNER, L. W. J.: Company H, private. March 1, 1862 enlisted as a private in Co. H, 27th Regiment, Georgia Infantry at McDonough, Georgia. June 27, 1862 wounded at Cold Harbor, Virginia. December 1862 roll shows him absent without leave. December 31, 1863 received pay. January – February 1864 roll shows him present. February 29, 1864 received pay. March - April 1864 roll shows him present. May 31, 1864, July 1864 and September 1864 issued clothing. April 26, 1865 surrendered Greensboro, North Carolina. May 1, 1865 paroled at Greensboro, North Carolina.

TURNER, RALEIGH H.: Company K, Commissary Sergeant. March 4, 1862 enlisted as a private in Co. K, 27th Regiment, Georgia Infantry. June 27, 1862 wounded, Cold Harbor, Virginia. July 1, 1862 wounded, Malvern Hill, Virginia. October 10, 1862 through June 15, 1863 detailed as wagon master. He was appointed 2nd sergeant in 1862. December 1862 roll shows he was Brigade Forage Master. August 20, 1863 received extra pay as wagon master at a rate of $.25 per day extra. August 31, 1863 received pay at the hospital. He was appointed 3rd sergeant Co. K, 27th Regiment, Georgia Infantry. March - April 1864 roll shows him present. July 1864 issued clothing. He was appointed Commissary Sergeant. April 26, 1865 surrendered Greensboro, North Carolina. May 1, 1865 paroled at Greensboro, North Carolina. He was born in Talbot County, Georgia March 28, 1838.

TURNER, SMITH: Company F, private. August 7, 1862 enlisted as a private in Co. F, 27th Regiment, Georgia Infantry at Randolph County, Georgia. September 17, 1862 wounded and captured at Sharpsburg, Maryland. September 20 (October 4), 1862 he was paroled near Keedysville, Maryland. November 12, 1862 admitted to General Hospital, at Farmville, Virginia with Phthisis (Tuberculosis). December 10, 1862 returned to duty. August 25, 1863 issued clothing. December 31, 1863 received pay. February 20, 1864 wounded, Olustee, Florida. January – February and March – April 1864 rolls show him absent on wounded furlough since February 20, 1864. October 19, 1864 admitted to Confederate States Hospital at Petersburg, Virginia (Turned over to the Provost Marshall). March 21, 1865 wounded at Bentonville, North Carolina. March 30, 1865 admitted to Foster U. S. A. General Hospital, New Bern, North Carolina, "wounded in left arm". April 27, 1865 "returned to duty".

TURNER, WADE A.: Field Staff, ordinance sergeant. September 10, 1861 enlisted and appointed Ordinance Sergeant for 27th Georgia Infantry at Camp Stephens, Griffin, Spalding County, Georgia. May 7, 1862 Colonel Smith's orders assigned him as Ordinance Sergeant at the Ordinance Department. December 1862 roll shows him Ordinance Sergeant. August 6, 1863 furloughed for 48 days. October 30, 1863, James Island, South

Carolina his name appears on list of detailed men. December 22, 1863 received $15.84 in commutation of rations while on furlough. December 31, 1863 received pay. December 31, 1863 – April 30, 1864 Field Staff Muster Roll shows him present. He is listed by Major James Gardner on his list for "Men of Gallantry". July 1864 and September 1, 1864 issued clothing. August 13, 1864 elected Jr. 2nd lieutenant for Co. H, 27th Georgia Infantry. April 10, 1865 admitted to Pettigrew General Hospital No. 13 at Raleigh, North Carolina. April 10, 1865 returned to duty. April 29, 1865 surrendered at Way Hospital No. 2 at Greensboro, North Carolina and paroled as a patient.

TURNER, WILLIAM B.: Company E, private. March 1, 1862 enlisted as a private in Co. E, 27th Regiment, Georgia Infantry at Fairburn, Georgia. May 7, 1862 admitted to Camp Winder Division No. 1 Hospital at Richmond, Virginia with Rubeola. July 17, 1862 received pay ($69.00). August 28, 1862 furloughed for 30 days. December 1862 roll shows him absent without leave. December 31, 1863 received pay. January – February 1864 roll shows him present. February 29, 1864 received pay. March - April 1864 roll shows him present. September 20, 1864 issued clothing. March 2, 1865 admitted to C. S. A. General Hospital No.11 at Charlotte, North Carolina with Anasarca (massive edema). March 4, 1865 returned to duty.

TURNER, WILLIAM E.: Company H, private. September 9, 1861 enlisted as a private in Co. H, 27th Regiment, Georgia Infantry at Camp Stephens, Griffin, Spalding County, Georgia. November 15, 1865 admitted to General Hospital No. 18 (formerly Greaner's Hospital) at Richmond, Virginia.

TURNER, WILLIAM G.: Company H, private. September 9, 1861 enlisted as a private in Co. H, 27th Regiment, Georgia Infantry at Camp Stephens, Griffin, Spalding County, Georgia. January 27, 1862 discharged, furnished Substitute at Camp Pickens near Manassas, Virginia. January 1862 roll shows him discharged, furnished substitute at Camp Pickens near Manassas, Virginia.

TURNER, WILLIAM T.: Company E, private. September 10, 1861 enlisted as a private in Co. E, 27th Regiment, Georgia Infantry at Camp Stephens, Griffin, Spalding County, Georgia. November 15, 1861 died of Typhoid Fever at Camp Stephens, Griffin, Spalding County, Georgia. December 1861 roll shows he died of disease on November 15, 1861 at Camp Stephens, Griffin, Spalding County, Georgia. February 16, 1863 death benefit claim was filed by his father, Fleming H. Turner.

TUTEN, DAVID J.: Company I, private. September 10, 1861 enlisted as a private in Co. I, 27th Regiment, Georgia Infantry at Camp Stephens, Griffin, Spalding County, Georgia. November 15, 1861 admitted to General Hospital No. 18 (formerly Greaner's Hospital) at Richmond, Virginia with Typhoid Fever. November 27, 1861 died of Typhoid Fever at Richmond, Virginia. December 1861 roll shows his death at Richmond, Virginia.

Buried at Mt. Zion Church Cemetery, Jeff Davis County, Georgia

TYNER, J. J.: Company K, private. December 1862 furloughed for 90 days. December 1862 roll shows him on 90 day furlough.

VAN DE GRAFF, J. S.: Company K, private. He enlisted as a private in Co. K, 27th Regiment, Georgia Infantry. July 8, 1862 received pay ($22.00).

VANE, JAMES M.: Company I, private. He enlisted as a private in Co. I, 27th Regiment, Georgia Infantry. May 6, 1864 killed at Wilderness, Virginia.

VAUGHN, E.: Company I, private. April 26, 1864 admitted to Receiving and Wayside Hospital or General Hospital No. 9 at Richmond, Virginia with a Vulnus Sclopeticum (Gunshot Wound). April 27, 1864 discharged from service at Receiving and Wayside Hospital or General Hospital No. 9 at Richmond, Virginia due to a Vulnus Sclopeticum (Gunshot Wound).

VAUGHN (VAUGHAN), J. H.: Company G, private. April 4, 1864 enlisted as a private in Co. G, 27th Regiment, Georgia Infantry at Camp Cooper, Georgia. March - April 1864 roll shows him present. June 30, 1864 roll of General Hospital No. 1 at Summerville, South Carolina shows him present.

VAUGHN (VAUGHAN), J. P. (H.): Company G, private. April 4, 1864 enlisted as a private in Co. G, 27th Regiment, Georgia Infantry at Macon, Georgia. April 30, 1864, shows him present. September 20, 1864 issued clothing. February 11, 1865 captured at Sugar Loaf, North Carolina near Fort Fisher, North Carolina. February 28, 1865 arrived at Point Lookout, Maryland from Fort Anderson, North Carolina. June 21, 1865 took the Oath of allegiance to the United States at Point Lookout, Maryland. He is listed at Point Lookout, Maryland as a resident of Spalding County, Georgia, dark complexion, brown hair, hazel eyes and 5 feet 7 ½ inches high.

VERMILLION, W. M.: Company D, private. 1862 enlisted as a private in Co. D, 27th Regiment, Georgia Infantry at Gordon County, Georgia. May 3, 1863 admitted to Receiving and Wayside Hospital or General Hospital No. 9 at Richmond, Virginia.
And transferred to and admitted to Chimborazo Hospital No. 2 at Richmond, Virginia with Erysipelas (skin disease). June 3, 1863 returned to duty. December 31, 1863 received pay and issued clothing. March – April 1864 roll shows him present. July 1864 issued clothing.

WADE, MICAJAH G.: Company D, private. September 10, 1861 enlisted as a private in Co. D, 27th Regiment, Georgia Infantry at Camp Stephens, Griffin, Spalding County, Georgia. December 1861 roll shows him in the hospital in Richmond, Virginia. September 17, 1862 captured at Sharpsburg, Maryland. October 1, 1862 admitted to Summit House U. S. A. General Hospital at West Philadelphia, Pennsylvania with Diarrhoea. November 24, 1862 returned to duty. December 15, 1862 paroled at Fort Delaware, Delaware and sent to Fortress Monroe, Virginia for exchange. April, May and June 1863 issued clothing. He transferred to Co. A, 11th

Regiment, Georgia Infantry (date not given). April 9, 1865 surrendered at Appomattox, Virginia.

WADSWORTH, FREDERICK J.: Company G, private. September 9, 1861 enlisted as a private in Co. G, 27th Regiment, Georgia Infantry at Camp Stephens, Griffin, Spalding County, Georgia. November 13, 1861 admitted to General Hospital No. 18 (formerly Greaner's Hospital) at Richmond, Virginia. December 31, 1861 roll of General Hospital No. 18 (formerly Greaner's Hospital) at Richmond, Virginia as present. December 1861 and January 1862 rolls show he was in the hospital in Richmond, Virginia since January 7, 1862. January 21, 1862 furloughed for 30 days. He received $6.60 in commutation for rations. September 17, 1862 wounded in the back and captured at Sharpsburg, Maryland. October 22, 1862 admitted to No. 1, U. S. A. General Hospital at Frederick, Maryland with a gunshot Vulnus Sclopeticum (Gunshot Wound). November 3, 1862 returned to duty (prison camp). November 12, 1862 paroled at Fort McHenry, Maryland. November 22, 1862 admitted to General Hospital at Petersburg, Virginia with a in the back. November 29, 1862 furloughed for 40 days. December 1, 1862 received back pay ($261.65). March 19, 1863 received $13.33 1/3 in commutation of rations. April 1863 detailed by Colonel Zachry as an ambulance driver at a rate of $.25 extra per day. October 30, 1863 he is shown on a list at James Island, South Carolina as being detailed as a driver in the Quartermasters Department. October 30, 1863 and November 24, 1863 issued clothing. December 31, 1863 received pay. January – February 1864 roll shows him absent sick in the hospital at Savannah, Georgia. February 14, 1864 - April 30, 1864 sick in hospital. February 29, 1864 received pay. March - April 1864 roll shows him absent sick in the hospital at Savannah, Georgia since February 14, 1864.

WADSWORTH, WILLIAM C.: Company G, private. September 9, 1861 enlisted as a private in Co. G, 27th Regiment, Georgia Infantry at Camp Stephens, Griffin, Spalding County, Georgia. January 22, 1862 admitted to Moore Hospital at General Hospital, No. 1 at Danville, Virginia and was transferred to Richmond, Virginia. January 1862 and February 1862 rolls show him in the hospital since January 22, 1862. June 1862 wounded near Richmond, Virginia (Seven Days Battle around Richmond, probably Mechanicsville, Virginia). June 27, 1862 died of wounds near Richmond, Virginia. August 20, 1862 (September 12, 1863) death benefit claim was filed by his widow, Martha Ann Wadsworth.

WAINWRIGHT, B. FRANK (FRANCIS): Company B, musician. September 10, 1861 enlisted as a private in Co. B, 27th Regiment, Georgia Infantry at Camp Stephens, Griffin, Spalding County, Georgia. July 31, 1862 he was discharged due to disability (a severely fractured leg). August 1, 1862 received pay ($38.50). He is described on certificate of disability: born in Bibb County, Georgia, 26 years of age, 5 feet 9 inches high, florid complexion, grey eyes, light hair and was by occupation a farmer.

WALKER, FREEMAN: Company K, lieutenant. March 4, 1862 enlisted as a private in Co. K, 27th Regiment, Georgia Infantry. He was elected sergeant. September 14, 1862 captured a Turners Gap on South Mountain, Maryland. October 2, 1862 sent from Fort Delaware, Delaware to Aiken's Landing Virginia for exchange. November 10, 1862 exchanged at Aiken's Landing, Virginia. March 16, 1863 appointed Jr. 2nd lieutenant of Co. K, 27th Regiment, Georgia Infantry. April 3, 1863 issued clothing. February 20, 1864 wounded in the right leg at Olustee, Florida. February 29, 1864 admitted to Ocmulgee Hospital at Macon, Georgia with a Vulnus Sclopeticum (Gunshot Wound) to the right leg. March 3, 1864 he made a request for a leave of absence from Ocmulgee Hospital at Macon, Georgia. March 5, 1864, 60 day leave of absence granted. March – April 1864 his name appears as 3rd lieutenant. May 1, 1864 appointed 2nd lieutenant of Co. K, 27th Regiment, Georgia Infantry. June 27, 1864 died.

WALKER, J. A.: Company C, private. September 10, 1861 enlisted as a private in Co. C, 27th Regiment, Georgia Infantry at Camp Stephens, Griffin, Spalding County, Georgia. December 24, 1861 discharged disability at Richmond, Virginia. December 26, 1861 received pay ($70.15). December 1861 roll shows he was in the hospital at Richmond since November 26, 1861. January 2, 1862 admitted to Moore Hospital at General Hospital, No. 1 at Danville, Virginia with Typhoid Fever and was sent to Dr. Abbeys General Hospital. January 19, 1862 died of Pneumonia at Camp Pickens near Manassas, Virginia. January 1862 roll shows he died at Camp Pickens near Manassas, Virginia.

WALKER, TRUMAN: Company K, private. March 4, 1862 enlisted as a private in Co. K, 27th Regiment, Georgia Infantry (31 years of age). He was born in 1831.

WALL, GEORGE W.: Company A, private. January 12, 1864 enlisted as a private in Co. A, 27th Regiment, Georgia Infantry at Macon, Georgia. January – February 1864 roll shows him present. February 29, 1864 received pay. March - April 1864 roll shows him present. July 1864 and September 30, 1864 issued clothing. February 21, 1865 captured near Wilmington, North Carolina. March 10, 1865 confined at Military Prison Camp at Hamilton, Virginia. March 11, 1865 sent from Military Prison Camp at Hamilton, Virginia to Point Lookout, Maryland. June 22, 1865 released at Point Lookout, Maryland. He is described as a resident of Schley County, Georgia, fair complexion, red hair, blue eyes and 5 feet 4 3/4 inches high.

WALL, L. W.: Company A, private. 1864 enlisted as a private in Co. A, 27th Regiment, Georgia Infantry. April 26, 1865 surrendered Greensboro, North Carolina. May 1, 1865 paroled at Greensboro, North Carolina. He was born in Twiggs, County, Georgia in 1825.

WALLACE (TRALLACE), E. B.: Company C, private. March 15, 1861 enlisted as a private in Co. C, 27th Regiment, Georgia Infantry. May 7, 1862 admitted to Camp Winder General Hospital at Richmond, Virginia with Diarrhoea (note: discharged from service July 24, 1862). July 25,

1862 discharged due to disability and received pay. Discharge certificate shows he was born in Baldwin County, Georgia, was 51 years of age, 5 feet 10 inches high, light complexion, blue eyes, grey hair and by occupation was a farmer.

WALLACE, MICHAEL: Company H, private. September 9, 1861 enlisted as a private in Co. H, 27th Regiment, Georgia Infantry at Camp Stephens, Griffin, Spalding County, Georgia. January and February 1862 rolls show him in the hospital in Warrenton since January 28, 1862. February 25, 1862 admitted to C. S. A. General Hospital at Charlottesville, Virginia as a convalescent. March 14, 1862 returned to duty. July 9, 1862 received pay ($91.00). September 30, 1862 admitted to Chimborazo Hospital No. 1 at Richmond, Virginia. October 3, 1862 admitted to Camp Winder Division No. 1 Hospital at Richmond, Virginia. October 4, 1862 returned to duty. December 31, 1863 received pay. January – February 1864 and March - April 1864 rolls show him present. July 1864 and September 20, 1864 issued clothing. April 26, 1865 surrendered Greensboro, North Carolina. May 1, 1865 paroled at Greensboro, North Carolina.

WALLER, HENRY: Company E, private. September 9, 1861 enlisted as a private in Co. E, 27th Regiment, Georgia Infantry at Camp Stephens, Griffin, Spalding County, Georgia. July 10, 1863 died in Richmond, Virginia. March 11, 1864 death benefit claim was filed by his widow, Margaret Waller. He was a resident of Clayton, County.

WALLER, JAMES H.: Company E, private. February 24, 1863 enlisted as a private in Co. E, 27th Regiment, Georgia Infantry at Fairburn, Georgia. April, May and June 1863 issued clothing. November 12, 1863 at James Island, South Carolina received $9.90 in commutation of rations. December 31, 1863 received pay. January – February 1864 and March - April 1864 rolls show him present. June 7, 1864 wounded in left hand, necessitating amputation of one finger at Cold Harbor, Virginia. June 12, 1864 admitted to Receiving and Wayside Hospital or General Hospital No. 9 at Richmond, Virginia. June 13, 1864 transferred to Jackson Hospital at Richmond, Virginia. June 14, 1864 admitted to Jackson Hospital at Richmond, Virginia with a Vulnus Sclopeticum (Gunshot Wound) (mini ball) to the left hand. June 30, 1864 roll of Jackson Hospital at Richmond, Virginia shows him present. July 5, 1864 issued clothing at Jackson Hospital at Richmond, Virginia. July 28, 1864 issued clothing. April 26, 1865 surrendered Greensboro, North Carolina. May 1, 1865 paroled at Greensboro, North Carolina.

WALLER (WALKER), W. R.: Company E, private. September 9, 1861 enlisted as a private in Co. E, 27th Regiment, Georgia Infantry at Camp Stephens, Griffin, Spalding County, Georgia. July 1, 1862 wounded in the right arm at Malvern Hill near Richmond, Virginia. July 21, 1862 discharged due to disability (amputation of right arm). July 29, 1862 received pay ($91.00).

WALTON, GEORGE: Company B, private. April 26, 1862 enlisted as a private in Co. B, 27th Regiment, Georgia Infantry at Macon, Georgia. September 23, 1862 was admitted to Camp Winder Division No. 3 Hospital at Richmond, Virginia. October 25, 1862 furloughed for 20 days. October, November and December 1863 issued clothing. December 31, 1863 received pay. February 20, 1864 wounded at Olustee, Florida. January – February 1864 and March - April 1864 rolls show him absent due to wounds at Olustee, Florida. August 19, 1864 captured, Weldon Railroad, Virginia. August 24, 1864 received at Point Lookout, Maryland from City Point, Virginia. March 4, 1865 paroled at Point Lookout, Maryland for exchange. March 16, 1865 received at Boulware and Cox's Wharves, James River, Virginia.

WALTON, JESSE A.: Company B, private. September 10, 1861 enlisted as a private in Co. B, 27th Regiment, Georgia Infantry at Camp Stephens, Griffin, Spalding County, Georgia. October 1, 1862 admitted to Receiving and Wayside Hospital or General Hospital No. 9 at Richmond, Virginia and was transferred to Palmyra hospital. October 3, 1862 furloughed for 30 days. November 3, 1862 received from Surgeon in Charge at Palmyra Hospital, clothing (1 pair pants worth $6.12 and1 coat worth $5.00 – total $11.12). December 31, 1863 received pay. January – February 1864 roll shows him present. February 29, 1864 received pay. March - April 1864 roll shows him present. July 1864 and September 20, 1864 issued clothing. September 29, 1864 wounded in the left arm and the left side at Fort Harrison, Virginia. October 3, 1864 admitted to Jackson Hospital at Richmond, Virginia with a Vulnus Sclopeticum (Gunshot Wound) to the left arm and breast (mini ball). October 6, 1864 furloughed for 30 days. October, November and December 1864 issued clothing. April 26, 1865 surrendered Greensboro, North Carolina. May 1, 1865 paroled at Greensboro, North Carolina.

WALTON, JOHN B.: Company B, sergeant. April 28, 1862 enlisted as a private in Co. B, 27th Regiment, Georgia Infantry at Macon, Georgia. April 28, 1862 elected 3rd sergeant, in Co. B, 27th Regiment, Georgia Infantry. October 6, 1862 received pay ($126.56). December 1862 shows his furlough has expired. January 14, 1863 received pay ($30.00) for commutation of rations (40 day furlough) at Atlanta, Georgia. July 25, 1863 received pay $1.00 in commutation of rations. October, November and December 1863 issued clothing. December 31, 1863 received pay. January – February 1864 and March - April 1864 roll show him present. July 1864 issued clothing. August 19, 1864 wounded at Weldon Railroad near Petersburg, Virginia. August 20, 1864 admitted to Receiving and Wayside Hospital or General Hospital No. 9 at Richmond, Virginia. August 21, 1864 sent to Jackson Hospital at Richmond, Virginia. August 21, 1864 admitted to Jackson Hospital at Richmond, Virginia with a Vulnus Sclopeticum (Gunshot Wound) to the thigh. August 31, 1864 issued clothing at Jackson Hospital at Richmond, Virginia. September 1, 1864 furloughed for 30 days (destination No. 12 S .W. R. R. Georgia) and received pay ($68.00). September 20, 1864 issued clothing. April 26, 1865 surrendered Greensboro, North Carolina. May 1, 1865 paroled at Greensboro, North Carolina.

WALTON, VINCENT EVERETT: Company B, corporal. September 10, 1861 enlisted and elected 1st corporal in Co. B, 27th Regiment, Georgia Infantry at Camp Stephens, Griffin, Spalding County, Georgia. November 6, 1861 admitted to General Hospital at Petersburg, Virginia with Rubeola. November 15, 1861 returned to duty. November 18, 1861 admitted to C. S. A. General Hospital at Charlottesville, Virginia with Measles. December 7, 1861 returned to duty. August 27, 1862 admitted to Lovingston Hospital at Winchester, Virginia with Febris Continuing (Malaria). September 8, 1862 returned to duty. May 3, 1863 wounded at Chancellorsville, Virginia. October, November and December 1863 issued clothing. December 31, 1863 received pay. January – February and March - April 1864 roll shows him present. May 30, 1864 and July 1864 issued clothing. August 19, 1864 wounded and captured at Weldon Railroad near Petersburg, Virginia. August 24, 1864 arrived at point Lookout, Maryland from City Point, Virginia. March 14, 1865 paroled at Point Lookout, Maryland and transferred to Aiken's Landing, Virginia for exchange. March 16, 1865 received at Boulware and Cox's Wharves, James River, Virginia. He died at Byron, Georgia October 22, 1891 and is buried there.

WARD, JON T.: Company E, private. February 19, 1862 enlisted as a private in Co. E, 27th Regiment, Georgia Infantry at Campbell County, Georgia. April, May and June 1863 issued clothing. November 12, 1863 received pay $6.60 in commutation of rations. December 31, 1863 received pay. January – February 1864 roll shows him present. February 29, 1864 received pay. March - April 1864 roll shows him present. May 30, 1864 issued clothing. January 16, 1865 wounded at Fort Fisher, North Carolina. January 17, 1865 admitted to C. S. A. General Hospital, No. 3 at Greensboro, North Carolina with a Vulnus Sclopeticum (Gunshot Wound) (transferred from Wilmington). January 18, 1865 sent to other hospital. January 17, 1865 admitted to Pettigrew General Hospital No. 13 at Raleigh, North Carolina with a Vulnus Sclopeticum (Gunshot Wound) to the left hand and hip. January 18, 1865 issued clothing. February 6, 1865 furloughed for 60 days to Milledgeville, Baldwin County, Georgia. His Post Office was listed as Milledgeville, Georgia.

WARREN, J. B: Company D, private. July 18, 1862 enlisted as a private in Co. D, 27th Regiment, Georgia Infantry at Gainesville, Georgia. September 22, 1862 admitted to Camp Winder Division No. 5 Hospital at Richmond, Virginia. October 29, 1862 granted 30 day furlough from Camp Winder Division No. 5 Hospital at Richmond, Virginia. June 30, 1863 roll of Camp Winder Division No. 1 Hospital at Richmond, Virginia shows he has only received $15.00 since in service. July 1, 1863 received pay. July 29, 1863 admitted to Receiving and Wayside Hospital or General Hospital No. 9 at Richmond, Virginia. July 29 1863 transferred to and admitted to Camp Winder Division No. 1 Hospital at Richmond, Virginia. August 31, 1863 he is shown on roll of Camp Winder Division No. 1 Hospital at Richmond, Virginia. March - April 1864 roll shows him absent on sick furlough since May 10, 1864. May 10, 1864 he was on sick furlough.

WARREN, ROBERT M.: Company B, private. February 3, 1864 enlisted as a private in Co. B, 27th Regiment, Georgia Infantry at Decatur, Georgia. January – February and March - April 1864 rolls show him present. June 6, 1864 wounded in the breast at Cold Harbor, Virginia. June 6, 1864 admitted to Jackson Hospital at Richmond, Virginia with a Vulnus Sclopeticum (Gunshot Wound) to the breast (mini ball). June 30, 1864 roll for Jackson Hospital at Richmond, Virginia shows him present. July 28, 1864 furloughed for 30 days. April 26, 1865 surrendered Greensboro, North Carolina. May 1, 1865 paroled at Greensboro, North Carolina.

WATERS, WARREN F.: Company F, lieutenant. September 9, 1861 enlisted as a private in Co. F, 27th Regiment, Georgia Infantry at Camp Stephens, Griffin, Spalding County, Georgia. May 6, 1862 admitted to C. S. A. General Hospital at Danville, Virginia with Debilitas. June 13, 1862 returned to duty. February 23, 1863 elected Jr. 2nd lieutenant in Co. F, 27th Regiment, Georgia Infantry. June 27, 1863 elected 2nd lieutenant in Co. F, 27th Regiment, Georgia Infantry. January – February 1864 roll list his name with no remark. March - April 1864 roll shows him present. August 11, 1864 elected 1st lieutenant in Co. F, 27th Regiment, Georgia Infantry. August 23, 1864 received pay ($160.00). April 26, 1865 surrendered Greensboro, North Carolina. May 1, 1865 paroled at Greensboro, North Carolina. He is listed in the personal papers of Major James Gardner as "Men for Gallantry". He was born in Macon County, Georgia in 1839.

WATERS, WILLIAM: Company F, private. March 4, 1862 enlisted as a private in Co. E, 45th Regiment, Georgia Infantry. August 9, 1862 wounded at Cedar Run, Virginia. October 23, 1864 transferred as a private in Co. F, 27th Regiment, Georgia Infantry.

WATKINS, SIMON K.: Company C, private. September 10, 1861 enlisted as a private in Co. C, 27th Regiment, Georgia Infantry at Camp Stephens, Griffin, Spalding County, Georgia. December 1861 and January 1862 rolls show he was left sick in Georgia October 31, 1861. He was appointed 1st sergeant Co. C, 27th Regiment, Georgia Infantry. March 7, 1862 admitted to Chimborazo Hospital No. 5 at Richmond, Virginia with Rheumatism. March 23, 1862 returned to duty. March 16, 1863 died at Guinea Station, Virginia. May 19, 1863 (July 14, 1863) death benefit claim was filed by his widow, Sarah Alzada Watkins. He was a resident of Crawford County, Georgia.

WATSON, ELIJAH: Company F, private. September 9, 1861 enlisted as a private in Co. F, 27th Regiment, Georgia Infantry at Camp Stephens, Griffin, Spalding County, Georgia. November 6, 1861 died of disease at Camp Stephens, Griffin, Spalding County, Georgia. December 1861 roll shows his death in Georgia. June 20, 1862 (April 20, 1863) death benefit claim was filed by his widow, Tabitha Watson. June 24, 1862 death claim paid $46.26 (#610).

WATSON, JOSEPH A.: Company D, private. September 10, 1861 enlisted as a private in Co. D, 27th Regiment, Georgia Infantry at Camp Stephens, Griffin, Spalding County, Georgia. April, May and June 1863 issued clothing. December 31, 1863 received pay. March - April 1864 roll shows him present. April 30, 1864 received pay at the hospital. June 20, 1864 wounded in the right shoulder at Colquitt's Salient near Petersburg, Virginia. June 20, 1864 admitted to Jackson Hospital at Richmond, Virginia with a Vulnus Sclopeticum (Gunshot Wound) to the right shoulder (mini ball). June 30, 1864 he is shown on roll of 2nd Division Jackson Hospital at Richmond, Virginia. July 14, 1864 furloughed for 30 days. August 1864 deserted at Hall County, Georgia. August 21, 1864 took oath of allegiance to the United States Government at Chattanooga, Tennessee. September 26, 1864 took oath of allegiance to the United States Government again at Louisville, Kentucky, when he was released to remain north of the Ohio river during the war. He was a resident of Hall County, Georgia. He is described as light complexion, hazel (dark) eyes, dark hair and 5 feet 11 inches high.

WATSON, SOLOMON T.: Company D, private. May 4, 1862 admitted to Chimborazo Hospital No.5 at Richmond, Virginia with Continual Fever (Malaria). June 28, 1862 transferred to C. S. A. General Hospital at Danville, Virginia. June 29, 1862 admitted to C. S. A. General Hospital at Danville, Virginia with Typhoid Fever. December 24, 1862 returned to duty. May 3, 1863 admitted to Receiving and Wayside Hospital or General Hospital No. 9 at Richmond, Virginia and transferred to Chimborazo Hospital No.2 at Richmond, Virginia. May 3, 1863 admitted to Chimborazo Hospital No.2 at Richmond, Virginia with Diarrhoea. May 11, 1863 transferred to Lynchburg hospital. July 8, 1863 admitted to Chimborazo Hospital No.2 at Richmond, Virginia. April, May and June 1863 issued clothing. July 7, 1863 admitted to Receiving and Wayside Hospital or General Hospital No. 9 at Richmond, Virginia and transferred to Chimborazo Hospital No.2 at Richmond, Virginia. July 8, 1863 admitted to Chimborazo Hospital No.2 at Richmond, Virginia with Debility. July 26, 1863 furloughed from Richmond, Virginia for 35 days. April 26, 1865 pension records show he surrendered Greensboro, North Carolina.

WATSON, THOMAS C.: Company B, private. September 10, 1861 enlisted as a private in Co. B, 27th Regiment, Georgia Infantry at Camp Stephens, Griffin, Spalding County, Georgia. January 26, 1862 admitted to Moore Hospital at General Hospital, No. 1 at Danville, Virginia with Pluritis (Pleurisy) and was sent to Culpepper, Virginia.

January and February 1862 rolls show him in Moore Hospital since January 25 (26), 1862. March 30, 1862 admitted to General Hospital No. 18 (formerly Greaner's Hospital) at Richmond, Virginia with Pneumonia. April 5, 1862 died at General Hospital No. 18 (formerly Greaner's Hospital) at Richmond, Virginia. September 3, 1862 death benefit claim was filed by his widow, Lydia P. Watson. September 30, 1862 death benefit claim paid $59.46 (#1361).

WATTS, BAALAM: Company A, private. February 21, 1862 enlisted as a private in Co. A, 27th Regiment, Georgia Infantry at Marion County, Georgia. November 20, 1862 received bounty pay $50.00 at Richmond, Virginia. May 4, 1862 admitted to Camp Winder Division No. 1 Hospital at Richmond, Virginia with Typhoid Fever.
May 18, 1862 died of Typhoid Fever at C. S. A. General Hospital at Farmville, Virginia. August 30, 1862 death benefit claim was filed by his widow, Elizabeth Watts. September 1, 1862 death benefit claim was paid $56.16 (#1117). He was a resident of Marion County, Georgia.

WATTS, CHRISTOPHER C.: Company G, private. September 9, 1861 enlisted as a private in Co. G, 27th Regiment, Georgia Infantry at Camp Stephens, Griffin, Spalding County, Georgia. January 16, 1862 admitted to Moore Hospital, General Hospital No.1, at Danville, Virginia with Dysentery. January 1862 sent to General Hospital at Front Royal, Virginia. January 1862 roll shows him in the hospital since January 16. February 1862 roll shows he was furloughed for 30 days on February 5, 1862. May 31, 1862 died in Front Royal, Virginia. April 3, 1863 death benefit claim was filed by Catherine E. Watts, his widow. September 22, 1863 death benefit claim was paid $130.00 (#9141).

WATTS, J. M.: Company K, private. He enlisted as a private in Co. K, 27th Regiment, Georgia Infantry. April 28, 1862 died at Chimborazo Hospital at Richmond, Virginia. He is most likely buried in Oakwood Cemetery at Richmond Virginia.

WAUF, JAMES A.: Company D, private. September 10, 1861 enlisted as a private in Co. D, 27th Regiment, Georgia Infantry at Camp Stephens, Griffin, Spalding County, Georgia. December 1861 roll shows him in the hospital at Richmond, Virginia. February 3, 1862 died of Pneumonia at Camp Pickens near Manassas, Virginia. February 1862 roll indicates his death. May 9, 1862 death benefit claim was filed by his father, James P. Wauf.

WEAVER, LOVICK WASHINGTON: Company C, private. September 10, 1861 enlisted as a private in Co. C, 27th Regiment, Georgia Infantry at Camp Stephens, Griffin, Spalding County, Georgia. June 2, 1862 admitted to General Hospital at Camp Winder, Richmond, Virginia with Febris (Fever). June 15, 1862 died of Typhoid Fever at C. S. A. General Hospital at Farmville, Virginia (General Hospital at Camp Winder at Richmond, Virginia). November 6, 1863 death benefit claim was filed by his widow, Elizabeth Weaver.

WEBB, JOB J.: Company C, private. August 20, 1863 enlisted as a private in Co. C, 27th Regiment, Georgia Infantry. December 31, 1863 received pay. February 20, 1864 wounded, Olustee, Florida. January – February 1864 roll shows him absent due to wounds received at Olustee, Florida

February 20, 1864. February 24, 1864 admitted to General Hospital at Guyton, Georgia. January – February roll of General Hospital at Guyton, Georgia shows him present as a patient. February 29, 1864 received pay. March - April 1864 roll shows him absent on wounded furlough since February 20, 1864. June 1, 1864 wounded in the left hand at Cold Harbor, Virginia. June 2, 1864 admitted to Receiving and Wayside Hospital or General Hospital No. 9 at Richmond, Virginia. June2, 1864 admitted to Jackson Hospital at Richmond, Virginia with a Vulnus Sclopeticum (Gunshot Wound) to the left hand (mini ball). June 21, 1864 admitted to General Hospital No.9 at Richmond, Virginia. June 21, 1864 admitted to Receiving and Wayside Hospital or General Hospital No. 9 at Richmond, Virginia. June 22, 1864 transferred to and admitted to Jackson Hospital at Richmond, Virginia. August 5, 1864 furloughed from Jackson Hospital at Richmond, Virginia for 30 days. He died in Richmond, Virginia.

WEBB, W. A.: Company C, sergeant. September 10, 1861 elected 4th sergeant in Co. C, 27th Regiment, Georgia Infantry at Camp Stephens, Griffin, Spalding County, Georgia. June 1, 1862 wounded at Malvern Hill near Richmond, Virginia. June1, 1862 admitted to Chimborazo Hospital No. 5 at Richmond, Virginia with a flesh wound of the forearm. July 22, 1862 returned to duty from Chimborazo Hospital No. 5 at Richmond, Virginia. June 30, 1862 received pay ($55.00). June 30 and September 30, 1863 issued clothing. December 14, 1863 received pay ($6.60) in commutation of rations. December 31, 1863 received pay. February 20, 1864 wounded at Olustee, Florida. February 24, 1864 admitted to General Hospital at Guyton, Georgia. January – February roll of General Hospital at Guyton, Georgia shows him present as a patient. January – February 1864 roll shows him absent due to wounds at Olustee, Florida on February 20, 1864. March - April 1864 roll shows him present. July 1864 issued clothing. August 19, 1864 wounded at Weldon Railroad, Virginia. August 20, 1864 admitted to Receiving and Wayside Hospital or General Hospital No. 9 at Richmond, Virginia and sent to Jackson Hospital at Richmond, Virginia. August 21, 1864 admitted to Jackson Hospital at Richmond, Virginia with Vulnus Sclopeticum (Gunshot Wound) in his left arm. August 25, 1864 furloughed for 30 days to Fort Valley, Georgia. September 27, 1864 issued clothing. October 15, 1864 issued clothing at Buckner and Gamble Hospital at Fort Valley, Georgia.

WEBSTER, JOHN A.: Company D, private. September 10, 1861 enlisted as a private in Co. D, 27th Regiment, Georgia Infantry at Camp Stephens, Griffin, Spalding County, Georgia. December 12 (13), 1861 died of Rubeola at Camp Pickens near Manassas, Virginia. December 1861 roll shows his death on December 13, 1861. March 8, 1862 death benefit claim was filed by his father, John R. Webster. March 18, 1863 death benefit claim was paid $104.33 (#4077).

WESTER, SAMUEL ZACAHARIAH: Company K, sergeant. September 10, 1861 enlisted as a private in Co. K, 27th Regiment, Georgia Infantry at Camp Stephens, Griffin, Spalding County, Georgia. He was appointed 1st sergeant in Co. K, 27th Regiment, Georgia Infantry. June 27, 1862 wounded in left eye, resulting in loss of sight, at Cold Harbor, Virginia. July 9, 1862 received pay ($102.09). February 7, 1863 discharged due to disability. February16, 1863 received pay ($266.99). He was born in Georgia February 8, 1833.

WELCH, C. F.: Company H, private. September 10, 1861 enlisted as a private in Co. H, 27th Regiment, Georgia Infantry at Camp Stephens, Griffin, Spalding County, Georgia. December 24, 1861 admitted to Moore Hospital at General Hospital, No. 1 at Danville, Virginia with Neuralgia and sent to the General Hospital at Richmond, Virginia. January 30, 1862 admitted to Moore Hospital at General Hospital, No. 1 at Danville, Virginia. January 1862 roll shows him at Moore Hospital since January 30, 1862. February 21, 1862 he died of Pneumonia at General Hospital at Culpepper Court House, Virginia. February 1862 roll shows his death on February 21, 1862.

WELCH, FRANK: Company H, private. He enlisted as a private in Co. H, 27th Regiment, Georgia Infantry.

WELCH, JAMES F.: Company H, private. September 10, 1861 enlisted as a private in Co. H, 27th Regiment, Georgia Infantry at Camp Stephens, Griffin, Spalding County, Georgia.

WELCH, JOHN W.: Company H, private. September 10, 1861 enlisted as a private in Co. H, 27th Regiment, Georgia Infantry at Camp Stephens, Griffin, Spalding County, Georgia. December 12, 1861 discharged due disability (Dyspepsia) at Camp Pickens near Manassas, Virginia. Description on Certificate of Disability: born in Henry County, Georgia, 23 years of age, 5 feet 9 1/2 inches high, dark complexion, blue eyes, dark hair and by occupation was a farmer.

WEST, EPHRAIM: Company E, private. September 9, 1861 enlisted as a private in Co. E, 27th Regiment, Georgia Infantry at Camp Stephens, Griffin, Spalding County, Georgia.

WEST, I.: Company E, private. September 9, 1861 enlisted as a private in Co. E, 27th Regiment, Georgia Infantry at Camp Stephens, Griffin, Spalding County, Georgia. June 30, 1862 discharged due to disability. August 16, 1862 received pay ($56.83). Certificate of Disability states: born in Fayette County, Georgia, 19 years of age, 5 feet 11 inches high, fair complexion, blue eyes, light hair and was by occupation a farmer.

WEST, ISHAM (ISOM): Company E, private. September 9, 1861 enlisted as a private in Co. E, 27th Regiment, Georgia Infantry at Camp Stephens, Griffin, Spalding County, Georgia. 1864 he deserted. November 18, 1864 took oath of allegiance to the United States Government at Chattanooga, Tennessee (description: resident of Campbell County, Georgia, dark complexion, light hair, blue eyes and 6 feet high).

WEST, JOHN H.: Company E, private. September 9, 1861 enlisted as a private in Co. E, 27th Regiment, Georgia Infantry at Camp Stephens,

Griffin, Spalding County, Georgia. May 3, 1862 furloughed. June 1, 1862 captured at Seven Pines, Virginia (Description: born in Georgia, 19 years of age, 5 feet 11 inches high, light brown hair, grey eyes and fair complexion). June 5, 1862 sent to Fort Delaware, Delaware from Fort Monroe, Virginia. August 2, 1862 sent up the James River for exchange. August 8, 1862 received pay ($91.00). September 17, 1862 wounded in head over right ear, skull punctured by shell at Sharpsburg, Maryland. September 29, 1862 he is shown on roll of General Hospital No. 22 at Richmond, Virginia. October 1, 1862 received pay ($47.00). October 8, 1862 transferred from General Hospital No. 22 at Richmond, Virginia to Camp Winder. October 8, 1862 admitted to Camp Winder Division No. 2 Hospital at Richmond, Virginia with Ascitis. October 22, 1862 returned to duty. December 1862 roll shows he was furloughed for 60 days on August 28, 1862. April, May and June 1863 issued clothing. August 31, 1863 received pay. September 5, 1863 deserted from camp at James Island, South Carolina. January – February 1864 roll shows he deserted from camp at James Island, South Carolina. He was born in Georgia October 20, 1841. He was a resident of Campbell County, Georgia.

WEST, JOSEPH: Company E, private. February 24, 1862 enlisted as a private in Co. E, 27th Regiment, Georgia Infantry at Smithville, Georgia. August 9, 1862 admitted to Camp Winder Division No. 1 Hospital at Richmond, Virginia with a Vulnus Sclopeticum (Gunshot Wound). August 20, 1862 received pay ($67.90). August 21, 1862 furloughed. October 31, 1862 admitted to Camp Winder Division No. 12 Hospital at Richmond, Virginia. December 28, 1862 admitted to C. S. A. General Hospital at Danville, Virginia. December 29, 1862 returned to duty. December 1862 roll shows him absent without leave since June 10, 1862. March 12, 1863 and April 7, 1863 issued clothing at 3rd Division General Hospital No. 2 at Danville, Virginia with Chronic Rheumatism (age 26 years – farmer) . April 9, 1863 discharged due to disability. He is described on Certificate of Disability: born in Fayette County, Georgia, 26 years of age, 5 feet 10 inches high, fair complexion blue eyes, light hair and by occupation was a farmer. He was born in Fayette County, Georgia December 13, 1834 (1836).

WEST, JOSEPH W.: Company E, lieutenant. September 9, 1861 enlisted as a private in Co. E, 27th Regiment, Georgia Infantry at Camp Stephens, Griffin, Spalding County, Georgia. February 10, 1863 elected Jr. 2nd lieutenant Co. E, 27th Regiment, Georgia Infantry. November 1, 1863 elected 2nd lieutenant Co. E, 27th Regiment, Georgia Infantry. December 31, 1863 received pay. January – February and March - April 1864 roll shows him present. June 28, 1864 killed at Petersburg, Virginia.

WEST, LLOYD: Company E, private. September 9, 1861 enlisted as a private in Co. E, 27th Regiment, Georgia Infantry at Camp Stephens, Griffin, Spalding County, Georgia. June 2, 1862 admitted to Camp Winder General Hospital at Richmond, Virginia with Febris Inter. June 11, 1862 returned to duty. April, May and June 1863 issued clothing. October 31, 1863 received pay. December 16, 1863 deserted while home in Georgia on furlough. January – February 1864 roll shows him absent – deserted. December 16, 1863 (in Georgia was on furlough –failure to report).

WEST, WILLIAM: Company E, private. September 9, 1861 enlisted as a private in Co. E, 27th Regiment, Georgia Infantry at Camp Stephens, Griffin, Spalding County, Georgia. September 17, 1862 wounded in hand, necessitating amputation below the elbow, at Sharpsburg, Maryland. May 3, 1862 discharged due to disability. May 5, 1863 received pay ($118.76). Description on Certificate of Disability: born in Fayette County, Georgia, age 26, 5 feet 9 inches high, fair complexion, blue eyes, light hair and by profession a farmer.

WEST, WILLIS: Company E, private. August 27, 1861 enlisted as a private in Co. E, 27th Regiment, Georgia Infantry at Camp Stephens, Griffin, Spalding County, Georgia. November 14, 1861 discharged, on account of old fracture of arm, near Richmond, Virginia. December 1861 roll shows that on December 7, 1861 he was discharged due to disability. Description on Certificate of Disability: born in Fayette County, Georgia, age 29, 5 feet 10 inches high, fair complexion, blue eyes, light hair and by profession a farmer.

WHALEY, JAMES (JOSEPH): Company E, private. September 9, 1861 enlisted as a private in Co. G, 27th Regiment, Georgia Infantry at Camp Stephens, Griffin, Spalding County, Georgia. November 12, 1861 admitted to General Hospital No.18, at Richmond, Virginia with Typhoid Fever. December 1861 roll shows him in the hospital at Richmond, Virginia. January 3, 1862 died in Richmond, Virginia. January 1862 roll indicates he died of disease at Richmond, Virginia. February 15, 1862 provided with a coffin and hearse.

WHEELER, ISHAM (ISOM): Company B, private. September 10, 1861 enlisted as a private in Co. B, 27th Regiment, Georgia Infantry at Camp Stephens, Griffin, Spalding County, Georgia. November 15, 1861 admitted to C. S. A. General Hospital at Charlottesville, Virginia with Mumps. December 7, 1861 returned to duty. June 2, 1862 admitted to C. S. A. General Hospital at Danville, Virginia with Pneumonia. June 22, 1862 returned to duty. September 6, 1862 received pay ($69.00). December 1862 roll shows him furloughed home in August for 30 days – time expired. January – February 1864 roll shows him absent without leave since October 1862. March - April 1864 roll shows him absent without leave, since dropped as a deserter.

WHEELER, ROBERT J.: Company G, private. September 9, 1861 enlisted as a private in Co. G, 27th Regiment, Georgia Infantry at Camp Stephens, Griffin, Spalding County, Georgia. November 8, 1861 admitted to General Hospital No. 18 (formerly Greaner's Hospital) at Richmond, Virginia with Typhoid Fever. November 24, 1861 died of Typhoid Pneumonia in General Hospital No.18, at Richmond, Virginia. December

1861 roll shows he died of disease at Richmond, Virginia on November 24, 1861. He was a resident of Zebulon, Pike County, Georgia.

WHEELER, WILLIAM: Company B, private. September 10, 1861 enlisted as a private in Co. B, 27th Regiment, Georgia Infantry at Camp Stephens, Griffin, Spalding County, Georgia. March 8, 1862 admitted to Chimborazo Hospital No.2, at Richmond, Virginia with Debility. March 22, 1862 returned to duty. June 5, 1862 received pay ($44.00).

WHELCHEL, J. M.: Company D, private. August 29, 1862 enlisted as a private in Co. D, 27th Regiment, Georgia Infantry. June 18, 1862 admitted to General Hospital at Petersburg, Virginia with a gunshot Vulnus Sclopeticum (Gunshot Wound) to the head. April, May and June 1863 issued clothing. December 31, 1863 received pay. March - April 1864 roll shows him present. June 18, 1864 wounded at Colquitt's Salient near Petersburg, Virginia. June 20, 1864 transferred to and admitted to C. S. A. General Hospital at Farmville, Virginia with a Vulnus Sclopeticum (Gunshot Wound). July 5, 1864 furloughed from C. S. A. General Hospital at Farmville, Virginia for 60 days (note in hospital record states Vulnus Sclopeticum (Gunshot Wound) left fracturing bone – received June17). His Post Office was listed as Newbridge, Lumpkin County, Georgia.

WHITAKER, ANDREW J.: Company E, private. September 9, 1861 enlisted as a private in Co. E, 27th Regiment, Georgia Infantry at Camp Stephens, Griffin, Spalding County, Georgia. May 13, 1862 admitted to Camp Winder Division General Hospital at Richmond, Virginia with Diarrhoea. May 13, 1862 discharged convalescent. April, May and June 1863 issued clothing. December 31, 1863 received pay. February 20, 1862 wounded at Olustee, Florida. January – February 1864 roll shows him absent wounded in action at Olustee, Florida. February 29, 1864 received pay. March 9, 1864 furloughed for 30 days. April 9, 1864 furlough extended 30 days. March - April 1864 roll shows him absent furloughed March 9, 1864 for 30 days and extended 30 days. June 10, 1864 killed at Cold Harbor, Virginia.

WHITAKER, H. LEE: Company H, private. August 1, 1863 enlisted as a private in Co. H, 27th Regiment, Georgia Infantry at McDonough, Georgia. December 31, 1863 received pay. January – February 1864 roll shows him present. February 29, 1864 received pay. March - April 1864 roll shows him present. July 1864 and September 20, 1864 issued clothing.

WHITAKER, JAMES BOYKIN: Company E, private. August 27, 1861 enlisted as a private in Co. E, 27th Regiment, Georgia Infantry. November 3, 1861 admitted to General Hospital No. 18 (formerly Greaner's Hospital) at Richmond, Virginia. December 21, 1861 discharged due to disability, at Richmond, Virginia and received pay ($68.22). December 1861 roll shows him discharged at Richmond due to disability on December 21, 1861. May 10, 1862 enlisted as a private in Co. F, 56th Regiment, Georgia Infantry. July 4, 1863 captured at Vicksburg, Mississippi. July 8, 1863 paroled at Vicksburg, Mississippi. April 30, 1864 roll shows him present.

WHITE, ANDREW: Company D, private. September 10, 1861 enlisted as a private in Co. D, 27th Regiment, Georgia Infantry at Camp Stephens, Griffin, Spalding County, Georgia. April, May, June and November 1863 issued clothing. December 31, 1863 received pay. March - April 1864 roll shows him present. May 30, 1864 and July, 1864 was issued clothing. January 16, 1865 wounded at Fort Fisher, North Carolina. January 16, 1865 admitted to C. S. A. General Military Hospital, No. 4 at Wilmington, North Carolina with a Vulnus Sclopeticum (Gunshot Wound) to the right hip (mini ball) and was transferred to General Hospital No. 3 at Goldsboro, North Carolina. January 17, 1865 admitted to Pettigrew General Hospital No. 13 at Raleigh, North Carolina with a Vulnus Sclopeticum (Gunshot Wound) to the right hip flesh. January 18, 1865 issued clothing at Pettigrew General Hospital No. 13 at Raleigh, North Carolina. February 14, 1865 returned to duty. March 21, 1865 captured at Goldsboro, North Carolina. March 23, 1865 took oath of allegiance to the United States Government. He was a resident of Gainesville, Hall County, Georgia.

WHITE, G. W.: Company C, sergeant. September 10, 1861 enlisted as a private in Co. C, 27th Regiment, Georgia Infantry at Camp Stephens, Griffin, Spalding County, Georgia. June 29, 1862 wounded at Cold Harbor, Virginia. June 30, 1862 admitted to Chimborazo Hospital No. 5 at Richmond, Virginia with a wound to both legs. July 21, 1862 furloughed for 30 days. August 20, 1863 received pay ($45.00). December 31, 1863 received pay. January – February 1864 roll shows him present. February 29, 1864 received pay. March - April 1864 roll shows him present. June 28, 1864 appointed 1st sergeant Co. C, 27th Regiment, Georgia Infantry. July 8, 1864 received pay ($102.00). September, 20, 1864 he was issued clothing. He was wounded date and place not given. April 26, 1865 surrendered Greensboro, North Carolina. May 1, 1865 paroled at Greensboro, North Carolina.

WHITE, HENRY CLAY: Company C, private. September 10, 1861 enlisted as a private in Co. C, 27th Regiment, Georgia Infantry at Camp Stephens, Griffin, Spalding County, Georgia. May 1, 1865 paroled at General Hospital at Thomasville, North Carolina.

WHITE, ROBERT: Company K, private. February 3, 1863 enlisted as a private in Co. K, 27th Regiment, Georgia Infantry at Macon, Georgia. March - April 1864 roll shows him present. July 1864 issued clothing. September 14, 1864 admitted to Jackson Hospital at Richmond, Virginia with Chronic Diarrhoea. September 17, 1864 issued clothing at Jackson Hospital at Richmond, Virginia. September 18, 1864 furloughed for 30 days from Jackson Hospital at Richmond, Virginia. September 20, 1864 issued clothing. He was a resident of Macon, Bibb County, Georgia.

WHITE, RUFUS: Company C, private. March 29, 1864 enlisted as a private in Co. C, 27th Regiment, Georgia Infantry at Camp Milton, Florida. March - April 1864 roll shows him present. June 3, 1864 admitted to Receiving and Wayside Hospital or General Hospital No. 9 at Richmond,

Virginia and sent to Danville, Virginia. June 4, 1864 admitted to C. S. A. General Hospital at Danville, Virginia with Rubeola. April 26, 1865 he surrendered Greensboro, North Carolina. May 1, 1865 paroled at Greensboro, North Carolina.

WHITMORE, L. C.: Company E, private. He enlisted as a private in Co. E, 27th Regiment, Georgia Infantry. May 30, 1864 issued clothing. May 31, 1864 admitted to Receiving and Wayside Hospital or General Hospital No. 9 at Richmond, Virginia and sent to Jackson Hospital at Richmond, Virginia. May 31, 1864 admitted to Jackson Hospital at Richmond, Virginia with Intermittent Fever (Malaria). June 9, 1864 issued clothing at Jackson Hospital at Richmond, Virginia. June 10, 1864 returned to duty from Jackson Hospital at Richmond, Virginia. June 11, 1864 admitted to Receiving and Wayside Hospital or General Hospital No. 9 at Richmond, Virginia. June 12, 1864 transferred to and admitted to Jackson Hospital at Richmond, Virginia with Chronic Diarrhoea. June 17, 1864 issued clothing at Jackson Hospital at Richmond, Virginia. June 20, 1864 returned to duty and received pay ($22.00). June 21, 1864 issued clothing. July 24, 1864 returned to duty.

WHITTINGTON, F. C.: Company B, private. He enlisted as a private in Co. B, 27th Regiment, Georgia Infantry. December 1862 roll shows he was detailed as a teamster.

WHITTINGTON, GREEN C.: Company C, sergeant. September 10, 1861 enlisted as a private in Co. C, 27th Regiment, Georgia Infantry at Camp Stephens, Griffin, Spalding County, Georgia. January 7, 1862 admitted to Moore Hospital at General Hospital, No. 1 at Danville, Virginia with Pneumonia. July 8, 1862 admitted to Chimborazo Hospital No. 1 at Richmond, Virginia with Measles. July 9, 1862 received pay ($88.00). July 22, 1862 transferred to C. S. A. General Military Hospital at Danville, Virginia. July 23, 1862 admitted to C. S. A. General Military Hospital at Danville, Virginia with a Vulnus Sclopeticum (Gunshot Wound). January 1862 roll shows him in the hospital at Richmond, Virginia. April 19, June 30 and September 30, 1863 issued clothing. December 31, 1863 received pay. February 20 1864 wounded at Olustee, Florida. January – February 1864 roll shows him absent wounded in action at Olustee, Florida on February 20, 1864. February 29, 1864 received pay. March – April 1864 roll shows him as wounded on furlough. April 22, 1864 detailed "Arresting Deserters" at Macon, Georgia (wounded). June 3, 1864 received pay ($51.25). July 1864 issued clothing. He was appointed Sergeant Co. C, 27th Regiment, Georgia Infantry.

WHITTINGTON, HENRY: Company B, private. September 10, 1861 enlisted as a private in Co. B, 27th Regiment, Georgia Infantry at Camp Stephens, Griffin, Spalding County, Georgia. March 30, 1862 admitted to General Hospital No.18 at Richmond, Virginia with Debility. April 22, 1862 returned to duty. April 26, 1862 he died in Virginia. September 3, 1862 death benefit claim was filed by his mother, Rachel Hancock.

493

January 6, 1863 death benefit claim was paid $117.53 (#2487).

WHITTINGTON, ROBERT MARION: Company F, private.   March 7, 1862 enlisted as a private in Co. F, 27th Regiment, Georgia Infantry at Butler, Georgia.   August 1863 issued clothing.   September 22, 1863 received $5.98 in commutation of rations. December 31, 1863 received pay. February 20, 1864 wounded, at Olustee, Florida.   January – February and March - April 1864 rolls show him absent on wounded furlough (wounded at Olustee, Florida February 20, 1864).

WILCHER, JORDAN: Company F, captain.   September 9, 1861 elected 1st lieutenant in Co. F, 27th Regiment, Georgia Infantry at Camp Stephens, Griffin, Spalding County, Georgia.   September 11, 1861 elected captain Co. F, 27th Regiment, Georgia Infantry.   December 1861 roll shows him absent on furlough from Camp Pickens near Manassas, Virginia.   January 1862 roll shows him absent on furlough from December 1, 1861 to February 15, 1861.   February 1862 roll shows him absent sick since December 1861. July 1862 received pay ($260.00).   September 23, 1862 granted 30 day leave of absence on surgeon's certificate.   December 3, 1862 resigned his commission due to Chronic Diarrhoea.   December 15, 1862 granted leave. December 1862 roll shows that he resigned January 10, 1863.   January 21, 1863 received pay ($780.00). November 6, 1864 he is listed as captain of Company D of Bonaud's Battalion at James Island, South Carolina and had to resign his commission due to ill health.

WILDER, JAMES: Company G, private.   September 9, 1861 enlisted as a private in Co. G, 27th Regiment, Georgia Infantry at Camp Stephens, Griffin, Spalding County, Georgia.   October 31, 1861 discharged at Camp Stephens, Georgia.   December 1861 roll shows him discharged at Camp Stephens, Georgia on October 31, 1861.

WILDER, JOHN N.: Company C, private.   March 29, 1864 enlisted as a private in Co. C, 27th Regiment, Georgia Infantry at Macon, Georgia.   He was appointed sergeant Co. C, 27th Regiment, Georgia Infantry.   April 30, 1864 received pay.   March – April 1864 roll shows him present.   June 18, 1864 wounded at Colquitt's Salient near Petersburg, Virginia.   June 19, 1864 admitted to Confederate States Hospital at Petersburg, Virginia. June 20, 1864 transferred to Farmville, Virginia. June 20, 1864 admitted to Receiving and Wayside Hospital or General Hospital No. 9 at Richmond, Virginia.   June 21, 1864 transferred to Chimborazo Hospital at Richmond, Virginia. June 21, 1864 admitted to Jackson Hospital at Richmond, Virginia with a Vulnus Sclopeticum (Gunshot Wound) to the right side (mini ball). June 30, 1864 roll of Jackson Hospital at Richmond, Virginia shows him present. July 18, 1864 furloughed for 30 days.

WILLARD, HENRY (A.): Company H, private.   September 9, 1861 enlisted as a private in Co. H, 27th Regiment, Georgia Infantry at Camp Stephens, Griffin, Spalding County, Georgia.   January 27, 1862 admitted to Moore Hospital at General Hospital, No. 1 at Danville, Virginia with Fever.   January 1862 roll shows him in the hospital at Warrenton, Virginia since January 28, 1862. February 21, 1862 died of Pneumonia at Moore Hospital at Manassas Junction, Virginia. February 1862 roll shows he died of disease February 22, 1862 at Moore Hospital.

WILLARD, FRANCIS M.: Company H, private. September 9, 1861 enlisted as a private in Co. H, 27th Regiment, Georgia Infantry at Camp Stephens, Griffin, Spalding County, Georgia. August 10, 1862 he died at Richmond, Virginia. June 24, 1863 death benefit claim was filed by his father, John Willard. He was a resident of Henry County, Georgia.

WILLARD, JAMES W.: Company H, private. May 13, 1862 enlisted as a private in Co. H, 27th Regiment, Georgia Infantry at Chickahominy, Virginia. July 26, 1862 received pay ($25.00) which was clothing allowance. December 31, 1863 received pay. January – February and March – April 1864 rolls show him present. July 1864 and September 20, 1864 issued clothing.

WILLARD, JOHN L.: Company H, private. September 9, 1861 enlisted as a private in Co. H, 27th Regiment, Georgia Infantry at Camp Stephens, Griffin, Spalding County, Georgia. He remained with unit until December 1861. February 1, 1862 enlisted as a private in Co. B, Cobb's Legion, Georgia Cavalry. April 26, 1865, surrendered at Greensboro, North Carolina. He was born in Butts County, Georgia April 1841. He died in Butts County, Georgia in 1914.

WILLARD, MARVIN: Company H, private. He enlisted as a private in Co. H, 27th Regiment, Georgia Infantry.

WILLIAMS, C. H.: Company A, private. He enlisted as a private in Co. A, 27th Regiment, Georgia Infantry. December 1862 roll shows him absent sick. August 27, 1864 died of Chronic Diarrhoea at General Hospital No. 1 at Savannah, Georgia.

WILLIAMS, CHARLES E.: Company E, private. September 9, 1861 enlisted as a private in Co. E, 27th Regiment, Georgia Infantry at Camp Stephens, Griffin, Spalding County, Georgia. December 1861 received pay and issued clothing. May 14, 1862 admitted to Chimborazo Hospital No. 1 at Richmond, Virginia with Typhoid Fever. May 21, 1862 died of Typhoid Fever in Chimborazo Hospital No.1 at Richmond, Virginia. He is most likely buried in Oakwood Cemetery at Richmond Virginia. August 16, 1862 death benefit claim was filed by his father, William Williams. He was a resident of Fayette County, Georgia.

WILLIAMS, D. H.: Company F, private. September 9, 1861 enlisted as a private in Co. F, 27th Regiment, Georgia Infantry at Camp Stephens, Griffin, Spalding County, Georgia. December 1861 roll shows him in the hospital at Culpepper, Virginia. January 1862 roll shows him in Moore Hospital since December 30, 1861. March 7, 1862 admitted to Chimborazo Hospital No. 1 at Richmond, Virginia for convalescent (note: he left without permission. September 26, 1862 admitted to Confederate Hospital at Culpepper, Virginia with Rheumatism. October 15, 1862 issued clothing. October 31, 1862 he was on detached service as Enrolling Officer to December 31, 1862. January 22, 1863 received pay ($72.00). March 7, 1863 - April 30, 1864 he was on detached service. January – February and March – April 1864 roll shows him on detached service in Georgia since March 7, 1863. May 6, 1864 wounded in the head at Wilderness, Virginia. April 1865 paroled at Macon, Georgia. He was born in Laurens, County, Georgia July 18, 1818.

WILLIAMS, D. T. (J.): Company D, private. September 10, 1861 enlisted as a private in Co. D, 27th Regiment, Georgia Infantry at Camp Stephens, Griffin, Spalding County, Georgia. August 30, 1862 admitted to Camp Winder General Hospital at Richmond, Virginia with Diarrhoea. December 17 (7), 1862 returned to duty. February 28, 1863 received pay. March 15, 1863 detailed for hospital duty at Chimborazo Hospital No. 2 at Richmond, Virginia. March – April and May – June 1863 rolls of Chimborazo Hospital No. 2 at Richmond, Virginia show him present detailed as a nurse on March 15, 1863. July 1, 1863 received pay. July – August 1863 roll of Chimborazo Hospital No. 2 at Richmond, Virginia shows him present as a nurse. September 1863 discharged from detached duty. December 31, 1863 received pay. March - April 1864 roll shows him present. July 1864 and September 20, 1864 issued clothing.

WILLIAMS, EDWIN P.: Company K, private. He enlisted as a private in Co. K, 27th Regiment, Georgia Infantry. August 23, 1864 took Oath of Allegiance at Chattanooga, Tennessee. Described as being a resident of Talbot County, Georgia, dark complexion, light hair, dark eyes and was 6 feet high.

WILLIAMS, EDWIN T.: Company A, private. April 18, 1862 enlisted as a private in Co. A, 27th Regiment, Georgia Infantry at Savannah, Georgia. December 31, 1863 received pay. January – February and March – April 1864 rolls show him present. June 30, 1864 admitted to C. S. A. General Military Hospital, No. 4 at Wilmington, North Carolina with a Vulnus Sclopeticum (Gunshot Wound). July 5, 1864 furloughed for 60 days (His Post Office is shown as Talbotton, Talbot County, Georgia). 1864 he was captured at Talbot County, Georgia. September 26, 1864 took oath of allegiance to the United States Government at Louisville, Kentucky, listed as a deserter and released to stay north of the Ohio River during the war. Described as being a resident of Talbot County, Georgia, light complexion, light hair, blue eyes and was 6 feet high.

WILLIAMS, GEORGE W.: Company C, private. September 10, 1861 enlisted as a private in Co. C, 27th Regiment, Georgia Infantry at Camp Stephens, Griffin, Spalding County, Georgia. November 6, 1861 admitted to General Hospital at Petersburg, Virginia. December 10, 1861 returned to duty. May 31, 1862 killed at Seven Pines, Virginia.

WILLIAMS, IRVING (IRWIN): Company F, private. September 9, 1861 enlisted as a private in Co. F, 27th Regiment, Georgia Infantry at Camp Stephens, Griffin, Spalding County, Georgia. June 3, 1862 died at Richmond, Virginia. January 13, 1863 (October 15, 1864) death benefit claim was filed by his wife, Frances M. Williams. He is buried in Hollywood Cemetery at Richmond, Virginia,

WILLIAMS, J.: Company E, corporal. He enlisted as a private in Co. E, 27th Regiment, Georgia Infantry. June 10, 1862 received pay ($64.00).

WILLIAMS, J. J.: Company A, private. September 10, 1861 enlisted as a private in Co. A, 27th Regiment, Georgia Infantry at Camp Stephens, Griffin, Spalding County, Georgia. September 17, 1862 captured at Sharpsburg (Boonsboro), Maryland. October 2, 1862 sent from Fort Delaware, Delaware to Aiken's Landing, Virginia for exchange. November 10, 1862 exchanged at Aiken's Landing, Virginia. November 12, 1862 discharged due to disability, at Richmond, Virginia. November 15, 1862 discharged and received pay ($154.58). November roll of Post Hospital, Camp Lee at Richmond, Virginia shows him discharged from service due to Talipes of the left lower extremity. Description on Certificate of Disability: born in Talbot County, Georgia, 19 years of age, 5 feet 8 inches high, dark complexion, black eyes, dark hair and by occupation was a farmer. He was born in Taylor County, Georgia September 28, 1844.

WILLIAMS, J. M.: Company C, private. He enlisted as a private in Co. C, 27th Regiment, Georgia Infantry. December 1862 roll shows him detailed as Provost Guard at Division Headquarters.

WILLIAMS, J. T.: Company K, private. October 8, 1863 enlisted as a private in Co. K, 27th Regiment, Georgia Infantry at Macon, Georgia. He was wounded, date and place not given. April 25, 1864 sent to Charleston, South Carolina hospital. March - April 1864 roll shows him sent to the hospital at Charleston, South Carolina.

WILLIAMS, JAMES A.: Company D, corporal. September 10, 1861 enlisted as a private in Co. D, 27th Regiment, Georgia Infantry at Camp Stephens, Griffin, Spalding County, Georgia. October 28, 1861 died of disease at Camp Stephens, Georgia. December 1861 roll shows he died of disease at Camp Stephens, Georgia on October 28, 1861. July 23, 1862 death benefit claim was filed by his father, Josiah Williams. December 4, 1862 death claim benefit was paid $91.90 (#2082).

WILLIAMS, JOSIAH: Company G, private. September 10, 1861 enlisted as a private in Co. G, 27th Regiment, Georgia Infantry at Camp Stephens, Griffin, Spalding County, Georgia. November 9, 1861 admitted to General Hospital No. 18 (formerly Greaner's Hospital) at Richmond, Virginia (discharged from service December 19, 1861 – His post Office shown as Zebulon, Georgia). December 20, 1861 discharged and received pay. December 1861 roll shows him in the hospital at Richmond, Virginia. January 1862 roll shows him in the hospital at Richmond, Virginia since January 7, 1862. February 1862 roll shows him in the hospital at Richmond, Virginia since November 13, 1861.

WILLIAMS, JOSIAH N.: Company G, private. August 4, 1863 enlisted as a private in Co. G, 27th Regiment, Georgia Infantry at Zebulon, Georgia. October 30, 1863 issued clothing. December 31, 1863 received pay.

February 20, 1864 wounded at Olustee, Florida. January – February and March – April 1864 rolls show him wounded at Olustee, Florida February 20, 1864 and died at Lake City, Florida March 6, 1864. March 6, 1864 died of wounds at Lake City, Florida.

WILLIAMS, THEOPHILUS: Company G, private. September 9, 1861 enlisted as a private in Co. G, 27th Regiment, Georgia Infantry at Camp Stephens, Griffin, Spalding County, Georgia. November 6, 1861 admitted to General Hospital at Petersburg, Virginia with Rubeola. December 12, 1861 admitted to General Hospital No. 18 (formerly Greaner's Hospital) at Richmond, Virginia. December 19, 1861 furloughed for 30 days from Camp Winder General Hospital at Richmond, Virginia. January 18, 1862 transferred to General Hospital at Richmond, Virginia. December 1861 roll shows him in the hospital at Petersburg, Virginia. June 30, 1863 furloughed for 20 days and received pay $6.60 in commutation of rations. June 18, June 26 and October 30, 1863 issued clothing. December 31, 1863 received pay. January – February 1864 roll shows him present. February 29, 1864 received pay. March - April 1864 roll shows him present. July 1864 issued clothing. April 26, 1865 surrendered Greensboro, North Carolina. May 1, 1865 paroled at Greensboro, North Carolina.

WILLIAMS, THOMS NELSON: Company C, private. September 10, 1861 enlisted as a private in Co. C, 27th Regiment, Georgia Infantry at Camp Stephens, Griffin, Spalding County, Georgia. May 31, 1862 killed, Seven Pines, Virginia. July 19, 1862 death benefit claim was filed by his widow, Sarah C. Williams. November 5, 1862 death benefit claim was paid $130.00 (#1774).

WILLIAMS, WILLIAM JACKSON: Company E, private. September 9, 1861 enlisted as a private in Co. E, 27th Regiment, Georgia Infantry at Camp Stephens, Griffin, Spalding County, Georgia. September 17, 1862 wounded at Sharpsburg, Virginia. September 25, 1862 admitted to Confederate Hospital at Culpepper, Virginia with a Vulnus Sclopeticum (Gunshot Wound). September 26, 1862 sent to General Hospital. December 31, 1863 received pay. January – February 1864 roll shows him present. February 29, 1864 received pay. March - April 1864 roll shows him present. April 30 1864 roll of 2nd Division Jackson Hospital at Richmond, Virginia shows him present. June 2, 1864 admitted to Jackson Hospital at Richmond, Virginia with a Vulnus Sclopeticum (Gunshot Wound) to the right arm (mini ball). June 15, 1864 furloughed for 30 days. February 11, 1865 wounded at Sugar Loaf, North Carolina. February 12, 1865 admitted to C. S. A. General Military Hospital, No. 4 at Wilmington, North Carolina with a Vulnus Sclopeticum (Gunshot Wound). April 23, 1865 admitted to U. S. A. General Hospital at Smithville, North Carolina. May 17, 1865 sent to Provost Marshal. His Post Office is shown as Red Oak, Georgia.

WILLIAMS, WILLIAM: Company A, lieutenant. He enlisted as a private in Co. A, 27th Regiment, Georgia Infantry. May 5, 1863 wounded at Chancellorsville, Virginia.

WILLIAMS, WILLIAM JASPER: Company G, sergeant. He enlisted as a private in Co. G, 27th Regiment, Georgia Infantry. October 17, 1862 discharged from service at General Hospital at Farmville, Virginia with Chronic Nephritis and Hypertrophy of the heart.

WILLIAMS, WILLIAM J.: Company A, private. March 4, 1862 enlisted as a private in Co. A, 27th Regiment, Georgia Infantry at Marion County, Georgia. November 20, 1862 received bounty pay ($50.00). December 1862 roll shows him absent sick since January 14, 1863. December 31, 1863 received pay. January – February and March - April 1864 rolls show him present. July 1864 issued clothing. April 26, 1865 surrendered, Greensboro, North Carolina. May 1, 1865 paroled at Greensboro, North Carolina.

WILLIAMS, WILLIAM LARKIN: Field Staff, Hospital Steward. June 11, 1861 enlisted as a private in Co. D, 19th Regiment, Georgia infantry. January 8, 1863 admitted to C. S. A. General Hospital at Charlottesville, Virginia with a fracture of the humerus. April 10, 1863 returned to duty. May 5, 1863 captured at Chancellorsville, Virginia. May 8, 1863 paroled by the Army of the Potomac. May 19, 1863 paroled at Old Capital Prison, Washington, D. C. October 30, 1863 detailed as a nurse in James Island, South Carolina Hospital. November 26, 1864 appointed Hospital Steward 27th Georgia Infantry. April 26, 1865 surrendered Greensboro, North Carolina. May 1, 1865 paroled at Greensboro, North Carolina.

WILLIAMSON, GARRY T.: Company K, sergeant. September 10, 1861 elected 1st sergeant of Co. K, 27th Regiment, Georgia Infantry at Camp Stephens, Griffin, Spalding County, Georgia. January 1, 1862 died of Erysipelas at Camp Pickens near Manassas, Virginia. January 1862 roll shows his death on January 1, 1862.

WILLIAMSON, WILEY J.: Company A, sergeant. March 4, 1862 enlisted as a private in Co. A, 27th Regiment Georgia Infantry at Marion County, Georgia. March 20, 1862 received bounty pay ($50.00) at Richmond, Virginia. April 4, 1862 elected 5th sergeant of Co. A, 27th Regiment Georgia Infantry. June 8, 1863 issued clothing at General Hospital, No. 1 at Lynchburg, Virginia. July, August and September 1863 issued clothes. September 6, 1862 received pay ($40.00). December 31, 1863 received pay. January – February 1864 roll shows him present. February 29, 1864 received pay. March – April 1864 roll shows him present. July 1864 and September 30, 1864 issued clothing.

WILLIAMSON, WILLIAM JASPER: Company G, sergeant. September 9, 1861 appointed 1st sergeant Co. G, 27th Regiment, Georgia Infantry at Camp Stephens, Griffin, Spalding County, Georgia. August 3, 1862 admitted to General Hospital at Farmville, Virginia with Hypertrophy of the Heart. October 17, 1862 discharged, Hypertrophy of heart and Chronic Nephritis, from General Hospital at Farmville, Virginia. He is described on his Certificate of Disability as: born in Gwinnett County, Georgia, 41 years of age, 5 feet 11 inches high, dark complexion, yellow eyes, dark hair and was by profession a farmer.

WILLIS (WALLIS), ANDREW D.: Company K, private. September 10, 1861 enlisted as a private in Co. K, 27th Regiment, Georgia Infantry at Camp Stephens, Griffin, Spalding County, Georgia. December 12, 1862 died at Richmond, Virginia. July 12, 1862 death benefit claim was filed by his father, D. A. J. Willis. December 15, 1862 death benefit claim paid $130.00 (#2288). He was a resident of Box Springs, Talbot County, Georgia.

WILLIS, J. W.: private. He enlisted as a private in the 27th Regiment, Georgia Infantry. March 1863 detailed by Colonel Zachry as a teamster in the Regimental Quartermasters Department. October 30, 1863 roll of the Quartermasters Depart at James Island, South Carolina shows him present.

WILLIS, JOHN B.: Company A, private. September 10, 1861 enlisted as a private in Co. A, 27th Regiment, Georgia Infantry at Camp Stephens, Griffin, Spalding County, Georgia. June, July, August and September 1863 issued clothing. August 1, 1863 through February 1864 detailed as a teamster at Fort Johnson on James Island, South Carolina. August 20, 1863 received pay. October 1, 1863 received pay ($22.00). December 31, 1863 received pay. February 7, 1864 received pay. February 1864 through December 31, 1864 detailed as a teamster at James Island, South Carolina and Petersburg, Virginia at a rate of $.25 additional per day. January – February 1864 and March - April 1864 rolls show him present. May 30, 1864 and July 1864 issued clothing. August 3, 1864 admitted to Jackson Hospital at Richmond, Virginia with Syphilis. September 20, 1864 returned to duty received pay. December 31, 1864 received pay. March 8, 1865 captured near Kinston, North Carolina. March 16, 1865 arrived at New Bern, North Carolina. June 21, 1865 released at Point Lookout, Maryland. His description is: resident of Schley County, Georgia, dark complexion, black hair, hazel eyes and was 5 feet 11 3/4 inches high.

WILLIS, JORDON F.: Company A, private. March 4, 1862 enlisted as a private in Co. A, 27th Regiment, Georgia Infantry at Schley County, Georgia. November 20, 1862 received bounty pay ($50.00). May 24, 1863 admitted to Receiving and Wayside Hospital or General Hospital No. 9 at Richmond, Virginia and transferred to Chimborazo Hospital No. 2 at Richmond, Virginia. May 24, 1863 admitted to Chimborazo Hospital No. 2 at Richmond, Virginia with Bilious Fever. May 28, 1863 returned to duty. July, August and September 1863 issued clothing. December 31, 1863 received pay. January – February 1864 roll shows him present. February 29, 1864 received pay. March - April 1864 roll shows him present. July 1864 issued clothing. April 26, 1865 pension records show he surrendered Greensboro, North Carolina. He was born in Henry County, Georgia May 16, 1839.

WILLOUGHBY, JOHN (JONATHAN): Company B, private. September 10, 1861 enlisted as a private in Co. B, 27th Regiment, Georgia

Infantry at Camp Stephens, Griffin, Spalding County, Georgia. January 14, 1862 admitted to Moore Hospital at General Hospital, No. 1 at Danville, Virginia with Diarrhoea. January and February 1862 rolls show him in Moore Hospital since January 12, 1862. May 18, 1862 returned to duty. October 18, 1862 admitted to Receiving and Wayside Hospital or General Hospital No. 9 at Richmond, Virginia and transferred to General Hospital, Howard's Grove at Richmond, Virginia. October 18, 1862 admitted to General Hospital, Howard's Grove at Richmond, Virginia with Rheumatism. December 11, 1862 transferred from General Hospital, Howard's Grove at Richmond, Virginia to Chimborazo Hospital No. 2 at Richmond, Virginia. December 11(12), 1862 admitted to Chimborazo Hospital No. 2 at Richmond, Virginia. December 15, 1862 sent to General Hospital at Farmville, Virginia. December 1862 roll shows he strayed on the march September 1862. January 9, 1863 admitted to Receiving and Wayside Hospital or General Hospital No. 9 at Richmond, Virginia and transferred to Chimborazo Hospital No. 2 at Richmond, Virginia. January 9, 1863 admitted to Chimborazo Hospital No. 2 at Richmond, Virginia with Gonorrhea. February 17, 1863 returned to duty from Chimborazo Hospital No. 2 at Richmond, Virginia. April 23, 1863 admitted to C. S. A. General Hospital at Charlottesville, Virginia with Gonorrhea. June 30, 1863 received pay. February 12, 1864 admitted to Ocmulgee Hospital at Macon, Georgia with Abscessus. January – February 1864 roll shows him absent without leave since October 1863. March – April 1864 roll shows him present. July 1864 issued clothing. August 27, 1864 wounded by a shell in the head and back at Petersburg, Virginia. December 2, 1864 admitted to Ocmulgee Hospital at Macon, Georgia with a Vulnus Sclopeticum (Gunshot Wound) (shell) head and back (from August 27 battle). January 5, 1865 admitted to Ocmulgee Hospital at Macon, Georgia. January 12, 1865 deserted from Ocmulgee Hospital at Macon, Georgia. February 2, 1865 returned to duty.

WILLOUGHBY, WILLIAM: Company B, private. September 10, 1861 enlisted as a private in Co. B, 27th Regiment, Georgia Infantry at Camp Stephens, Griffin, Spalding County, Georgia. November 15, 1861 admitted to General Hospital No. 18 (formerly Greaner's Hospital) at Richmond, Virginia (discharged December 11). December 1861 roll shows he was in the hospital at Richmond since November 15, 1861. December 11, 1861 discharged due to disability, at Richmond, Virginia. January 1862 roll shows he was discharged due to disability December 11, 1861 at Richmond, Virginia.

WILSON, ANDREW J.: Company B, sergeant. September 10, 1861 enlisted as a private in Co. B, 27th Regiment, Georgia Infantry at Camp Stephens, Griffin, Spalding County, Georgia. June 10, 1862 appointed 2nd sergeant of Co. B, 27th Regiment, Georgia infantry. July 2, 1862 admitted to C. S. A. General Hospital at Danville, Virginia with Debilitas. July 30, 1862 returned to duty. October 31, 1862 admitted to Hospital No.

14. November 3, 1862 received pay including bounty ($78.00). November 5, 1862 furloughed for 30 days. December 1862 roll shows him absent on furlough for 30 days since January 23, 1863. April 8, 1863 received pay ($27.00) in commutation of rations. October, November and December 1863 issued clothing. December 31, 1863 received pay. January – February and March – April 1864 rolls show him present.
He was killed in battle.

WILSON, DAVID: Company B, private. September 10, 1861 enlisted as a private in Co. B, 27th Regiment, Georgia Infantry at Camp Stephens, Griffin, Spalding County, Georgia.

WILSON, J. C.: Company H, private. He enlisted as a private in Co. H, 27th Regiment, Georgia Infantry. March 10, 1862 admitted to C. S. A. General Hospital at Charlottesville, Virginia with Icterus. July 12, 1862 returned to duty.

WILSON, JAMES MARTIN: Company C, corporal. September 10, 1861 enlisted as a private in Co. C, 27th Regiment, Georgia Infantry at Camp Stephens, Griffin, Spalding County, Georgia. January 11, 1862 admitted to Moore Hospital at General Hospital, No. 1 at Danville, Virginia with Pneumonia (sent to General Hospital at Richmond). January 12, 1862 admitted to General Hospital No. 18 (formerly Greaner's Hospital) at Richmond, Virginia with Typhoid Fever (his Post Office is listed as Hickory Grove, Crawford County, Georgia). January 1862 roll shows him in the hospital at Richmond, Virginia since January 11. February 5, 1862 returned to duty. February 25, 1862 admitted to C. S. A. General Hospital at Charlottesville, Virginia with Icterus and for convalescent. April 10, 1862 admitted to Chimborazo Hospital No. 5 at Richmond, Virginia with Febris Remittent (Malaria). May 9, 1862 transferred to Lynchburg. November 16, 1862 admitted to Camp Winder Division No. 3 Hospital at Richmond, Virginia. November 17, 1862 returned to duty. December 12, 1862 admitted to Chimborazo Hospital No. 2 at Richmond, Virginia. December 21, 1862 transferred to General Hospital at Farmville, Virginia. December 21, 1862 admitted to General Hospital at Farmville, Virginia with Chronic Bronchitis. January 15, 1863 furloughed for 60 days. June 26, 1863 issued clothing. December 31, 1863 received pay. February 20, 1864 wounded at Olustee, Florida. January – February 1864 roll shows him absent wounded in action at Olustee, Florida February 20, 1864. February 29, 1864 received pay. March 3, 1864 admitted to Floyd House and Ocmulgee Hospitals at Macon, Georgia with a Vulnus Sclopeticum (Gunshot Wound) to the neck and was furloughed for 35 days (his Post Office was Knoxville, Georgia). March - April 1864 roll shows him present. July 1864 issued clothing. He was appointed corporal of Co. C, 27th Regiment, Georgia Infantry. April 26, 1865 surrendered Greensboro, North Carolina. May 1, 1865 paroled at Greensboro, North Carolina. He was born in Georgia in 1845.

WILSON, JAMES R.: Company K, private. September 10, 1861 enlisted as a private in Co. K, 27th Regiment, Georgia Infantry at Camp Stephens,

Griffin, Spalding County, Georgia. January 20, 1862 admitted to Moore Hospital at General Hospital, No. 1 at Danville, Virginia. January 1862 roll shows him in Moore Hospital since January 19, 1862. March 7, 1862 admitted to Chimborazo Hospital No. 5 at Richmond, Virginia with Rheumatism. April 22(3), 1862 returned to duty. June 7, 1862 received pay ($55.00). October 29, and November 8, 1863 issued clothing. November 14, 1863 wounded in the shoulder at Fort Sumter, Charleston, South Carolina. December 31, 1863 received pay. March - April 1864 roll shows him present. May 30, 1864 issued clothing. June 27, 1864 killed at Colquitt's Salient near Petersburg, Virginia.

WILSON, JOSEPH N.: Company H, private. September 9, 1861 enlisted as a private in Co. H, 27th Regiment, Georgia Infantry at Camp Stephens, Griffin, Spalding County, Georgia. January and February 1862 rolls show him in the hospital at Warrenton, Virginia since January 28, 1862. April 20, 1862 received pay ($22.00). November 19, 1862 received pay ($136.25). December 1862 roll shows him absent on furlough. January 15, 1863 furloughed from General Hospital at Farmville, Virginia for 60 days (to report to Regiment). March 12, 1863 received pay in commutation of rations. October 31, 1863 received pay. January – February and March – April 1864 rolls show him present. May 22, 1864 admitted to General Hospital No. 13 at Goldsboro, North Carolina. May 31, 1864 roll of General Hospital No. 13 at Goldsboro, North Carolina.

WILSON, RICHARD M.: Company H, private. September 9, 1861 enlisted as a private in Co. H, 27th Regiment, Georgia Infantry at Camp Stephens, Griffin, Spalding County, Georgia. January and February 1862 rolls show him in the hospital at Richmond, Virginia January 27, 1861. December 31, 1863 received pay. January – February and March – April 1864 rolls show him present. June 1, 1864 wounded in the arm, necessitating amputation, at Cold Harbor, Virginia. June 4, 1864 admitted to C. S. A. General Military Hospital at Danville, Virginia with a Vulnus Sclopeticum (Gunshot Wound) in the arm. August 3, 1864 furloughed May 23, 1865 paroled at Talladega, Alabama.

WILSON, WILEY: Company F, private. September 10, 1861 enlisted as a private in Co. F, 27th Regiment, Georgia Infantry at Camp Stephens, Griffin, Spalding County, Georgia. January 7, 1862 admitted to Moore Hospital at General Hospital, No. 1 at Danville, Virginia with Pneumonia and was sent to the 9th Ward. January 1862 roll shows him in Moore Hospital since January 7, 1861. February 15, 1862 discharged due to mental Imbecility at Camp Pickens near Manassas, Virginia. February 20, 1862 received pay ($23.70). February 1862 roll shows he was discharged due to disability. He is described: born in Houston County, Georgia, 24 years of age, 5 feet 10 inches high, dark complexion, blue eyes, dark hair and by profession was a farmer.

WILSON, WILEY: Company F, private. April 25, 1864 enlisted as a private in Co. F, 27th Regiment, Georgia Infantry at Macon, Georgia.

March - April 1864 roll shows him present. May 2, 1864 roll with this date shows him present.   July 1864 issued clothing. 1864 killed at Petersburg, Virginia.

WILSON, WILLIAM B.: Company H, private.   October 1, 1861 enlisted as a private in Co. H, 27th Regiment Georgia Infantry at Camp Stephens, Griffin, Spalding County, Georgia. November 2, 1861 he died of Pneumonia in Rome, Georgia.   December 1861 roll shows he died of disease.   June 27, 1863 death benefit claim was filed by his father William H. Wilson. November 22, 1864 death benefit claim was paid $44.80 (#20639).

WIMBISH, THOMAS A.: Company B, private.   September 10, 1861 enlisted as a private in Co. B, 27th Regiment, Georgia Infantry at Camp Stephens, Griffin, Spalding County, Georgia.   April 10, 1862 admitted to Chimborazo Hospital No. 5 at Richmond, Virginia with Rheumatism. May 12, 1862 transferred from Chimborazo Hospital No. 5 at Richmond, Virginia to Camp Winder Division General Hospital at Richmond, Virginia.   July 31, 1862 discharged due to disability (Chronic Diarrhoea, General Debility and Rheumatism) at Richmond, Virginia.   Description on Certificate of Disability: born in Monroe County, Georgia, 48 years of age, dark complexion, blue eyes, black hair and was by occupation was a farmer. August 18, 1862 received pay ($59.00). He was born in Abbeville District, South Carolina September 7, 1818.

WINDHAM, JERRY: Company F, private.   September 9, 1861 enlisted as a private in Co. F, 27th Regiment, Georgia Infantry at Camp Stephens, Griffin, Spalding County, Georgia.

WINDHAM, WILLIAM W.: Company F, private.   September 9, 1861 enlisted as a private in Co. F, 27th Regiment, Georgia Infantry at Camp Stephens, Griffin, Spalding County, Georgia.   He died July 5, 1862. October 1, 1862 death benefit claim was filed.

WINTER, W.: Company B, private.   September 10, 1861 enlisted as a private in Co. B, 27th Regiment, Georgia Infantry at Camp Stephens, Griffin, Spalding County, Georgia.

December 1862 roll shows him absent sick since May 31, 1862 – reported discharged.

WISE, GEORGE EDWARD: Company H, lieutenant.   September 9, 1861 enlisted as a private Co. H, 27th Regiment Georgia Infantry at Camp Stephens, Griffin, Spalding County, Georgia.   December 1861, January 1862 and February 1862 rolls show he was left sick in Georgia October 31, 1861.   April 26, 1862 received pay ($88.06).   June 15, 1862 elected 2nd lieutenant Co. H, 27th Regiment, Georgia Infantry. July 1, 1862 received pay ($69.00). August 19, 1862 received pay ($80.00). December 1862 roll shows him present. February 20, 1864 wounded at Olustee, Florida. January – February 1864 roll shows him present.   August 14, 1864 roll of Colquitt's Brigade shows him absent without leave.   August 13, 1864 resigned his commission. August 30, 1864 received pay ($80.00).

WISE, JACK: Company B, private.   He enlisted as a private in Co. B,

504

27th Regiment, Georgia Infantry. He was captured in Macon April 21, 1865.

WITZEL (WETZEL), JOHN: Company D, private. September 10, 1861 enlisted as a private in Co. D, 27th Regiment, Georgia Infantry at Camp Stephens, Griffin, Spalding County, Georgia. Captured date and place not given. November 15, 1863 died at Fort Delaware, Delaware. He is buried in Hollywood Cemetery at Richmond, Virginia.

WOOD, MATTHEW: Company G, private. September 9, 1861 enlisted as a private in Co. G, 27th Regiment, Georgia Infantry at Camp Stephens, Griffin, Spalding County, Georgia. November 13, 1861 admitted to General Hospital No. 18 (formerly Greaner's Hospital) at Richmond, Virginia with Typhoid Pneumonia (Note: Came in Prostrated by Fever). November 25, 1861 died of Typhoid Pneumonia in General Hospital No.18 at Richmond, Virginia. December 1861 roll shows his death November 25, 1861. May 7, 1862 death benefit claim was filed by his widow, Malissa Wood. His Post Office is listed as Zebulon, Pike County, Georgia.

WOOD, WILLIAM P.: Company B, private. October 23, 1863 enlisted as a private in Co. B, 27th Regiment, Georgia Infantry Decatur, Georgia. December 31, 1863 received pay. January – February 1864 roll shows him present. March 28, 1864 discharged and final payment made. March – April 1864 roll shows he was discharged March 28, 1864.

WOOD (WOODS), WILLIAM T.: Company D, private. March 7, 1862 enlisted as a private in Co. D, 27th Regiment, Georgia Infantry at Chestnut Mountain. March 25, 1862 received bounty pay at Atlanta, Georgia ($50.00). May 31, 1862 wounded in leg at Seven Pines, Virginia. June 2, 1862 captured, Seven Pines, Virginia. June 8, 1862 admitted to U. S. A. General Hospital at David's Island, New York Harbor. October 28, 1862 sent to General Hospital (Park Hospital New York. October 28, 1862 admitted to U. S. A General Hospital, Central Park (St. Joseph's Hospital) New York City where leg was amputated. December 1862 roll shows him missing since May 31, 1862. February 21, 1863 sent to Provost Marshall in Washington, D. C. March 29, 1863 transferred from Old Capital Prison at Washington, D. C. to City Point, Virginia for exchange. March 29, 1863 admitted to General Hospital at Petersburg, Virginia (his leg had been amputated). April 14(18), 1863 furloughed for 90 days. June 3, 1863 received pay for commutation of rations. September 26, 1863 received pay ($315.37).

WOODALL, JACOB T.: Company A, private. September 10, 1861 enlisted as a private in Co. A, 27th Regiment, Georgia Infantry at Camp Stephens, Griffin, Spalding County, Georgia. December 18, 1861 admitted to General Hospital at Orange Courthouse, Virginia with Dyspepsia. December 20, 1861 admitted to Moore Hospital at General Hospital, No. 1 at Danville, Virginia with Dyspepsia and sent to Orange Court House. December 1861 roll shows him in the hospital. January 9, 1862 returned to duty. April 15, 1862 admitted to Chimborazo Hospital

No. 1 at Richmond, Virginia as Convalescent. May 15, 1862 admitted to C. S. A. General Military Hospital at Danville, Virginia with Febris Uiter Qyotidiana (Fever occurring or returning daily). March – April 1864 roll shows him present. July 25, 1862 died of Typhoid Fever in General Hospital No.1 at Danville Virginia. His effects are: 4 pair socks, 2 shirts, 1 coat, 1 uniform jacket, 1 vest, 2 pair pants, 1 quilt, 1 pair shoes and 1 hat. September 21, 1863 death benefit claim was filed.

WOODALL, KILLIGHT: Company A, lieutenant. September 10, 1861 elected 2nd corporal of Co. A, 27th Georgia Infantry at Camp Stephens, Griffin, Spalding County, Georgia. June 1863 issued clothing. December 11, 1863 received pay $6.60 in commutation of rations. December 31, 1863 received pay. January – February 1864 roll shows him present. February 29, 1864 received pay. March - April 1864 roll shows him present. September 30, 1864 and July 1864 issued clothing.

WOODWARD, WILLIAM M. W.: Company B, private. September 10, 1861 enlisted as a private in Co. B, 27th Regiment, Georgia Infantry at Camp Stephens, Griffin, Spalding County, Georgia. December 1861, January 1862 and February 1862 rolls show he was left sick in Georgia October 31, 1861. June 5, 1862 received pay ($95.33). September 17, 1862 wounded and captured Sharpsburg, Maryland. December 1862 roll shows he was wounded and captured at Sharpsburg, Maryland. October 22, 1862 admitted to No. 1, U. S. A. General Hospital at Frederick, Maryland. May 28, 1863 returned to duty at Fort McHenry, Maryland. May 28, 1863 confined at Fort McHenry, Maryland. May 29, 1863 paroled and sent to Fortress Monroe, Virginia. May 31, 1863 admitted to General Hospital at Petersburg, Virginia with Debility (prisoner of war). June 6, 1863 returned to duty. October 29, 1863 discharged from service. January 27, 1864 received final payment.

WORD (WARD), JOHN T.: Company E, private. February 19, 1862 enlisted as a private in Co. C, 35th Regiment, Georgia Infantry. May 31, 1862 wounded in left wrist at Seven Pines, Virginia. 1863 transferred to Co. E, 27th Regiment, Georgia Infantry. January 15, 1865 wounded in left hip and abdomen. January 17, 1865 admitted to C. S. A. General Hospital No.3 at Greensboro, North Carolina. January 18, 1865 sent to another hospital, place not given. February 6, 1865 furloughed from Pettigrew General Hospital No.13 at Raleigh, North Carolina for 60 days. He was at Milledgeville, Georgia at the close of the war. He was born in Fayette County, Georgia in 1839.

WORSHAM, JOHN W.: Company C, corporal. September 10, 1861 elected 2nd corporal of Co. C, 27th Georgia Infantry at Camp Stephens, Griffin, Spalding County, Georgia. January 2, 1862 admitted to Moore Hospital at General Hospital, No. 1 at Danville, Virginia with Pneumonia (sent to Richmond). January 1862 roll shows him in the hospital at Richmond, Virginia since January 7, 1861. April 10, 1862 admitted to Chimborazo Hospital No. 5 at Richmond, Virginia with Bronchitis. September 5, 1862 admitted to Camp Winder General Hospital at Richmond, Virginia with Diarrhoea. October 11(12), 1862 furloughed for 30 days from Camp Winder Division No. 2 Hospital at Richmond, Virginia and received pay ($50.00). He is listed in the personal papers of Major James Gardner as "Men for Gallantry." December 1862 roll shows him absent sick since July 20. June 16, June 30 and September 30, 1863 issued clothing. December 31, 1863 received pay. February 20, 1864 wounded at Olustee, Florida. January – February and March – April 1864 rolls show him present. June 9, 1864 wounded at Petersburg, Virginia. July 1864 died from wounds. October 3, 1864 death benefit claim was filed.

WORSHAM, W. A.: Company A, private. September 10, 1861 enlisted as a private in Co. A, 27th Regiment, Georgia Infantry at Camp Stephens, Griffin, Spalding County, Georgia. December 1861 and January 1862 rolls show he was left sick in Georgia October 31, 1861. February 1862 roll shows him absent without leave. August 17, 1862 died.

WRIGHT, A. B.: Company C, private. September 10, 1861 enlisted as a private in Co. C, 27th Regiment, Georgia Infantry at Camp Stephens, Griffin, Spalding County, Georgia. December 23, 1861 admitted to Moore Hospital at General Hospital, No. 1 at Danville, Virginia with Debility.

WRIGHT, J. E.: Company C, private. September 10, 1861 enlisted as a private in Co. C, 27th Regiment, Georgia Infantry at Camp Stephens, Griffin, Spalding County, Georgia. April 3, 1862 admitted to General Hospital at Orange Court House with Diarrhoea. April 12, 1862 died in C. S. A. General Hospital at Farmville, Virginia.

WRIGHT, JOHN BUNYAN: Company F, lieutenant. September 10, 1861 elected Jr. 2nd lieutenant in Co. F, 27th Regiment, Georgia Infantry at Camp Stephens, Griffin, Spalding County, Georgia. December 18, 1861 received pay ($170.00). December 1861, January 1862 and February 1862 rolls show him present at Camp Pickens near Manassas, Virginia. February 28, 1862 received pay ($160.00). May 16, 1862 received pay ($160.00). September 11, 1861 elected 2nd lieutenant of Co. F, 27th Regiment, Georgia Infantry. March 1, 1862 received pay ($160.00). June 27, 1862 killed at Cold Harbor, Virginia. November 20, 1863 death benefit claim was filed by his widow, Emeline (Emaline) R. Wright.

WRIGHT, JOSEPH HENRY: Company C, private. March 10, 1862 enlisted as a private in Co. C, 27th Regiment, Georgia Infantry. May 10, 1862 died. August 12, 1862 death benefit claim was filed by his widow, Louisa Wright. November 5, 1864 death benefit claim was paid $47.73 (#1771).

WRIGHT, LEWIS: Company C, private. He enlisted as a private in Co. C, 27th Regiment, Georgia Infantry. September 14, 1862 captured at Turner's Gap on South Mountain, Maryland. October 2, 1862 sent from Fort Delaware, Delaware to Aiken's Landing Virginia for exchange. October 6, 1862 delivered for exchange at Aiken's landing, Virginia. October 6, 1862 admitted to General Hospital No. 20 at Richmond, Virginia. October

9, 1862 was at Camp Lee. October 10 (11), 1862 admitted to Camp Winder Division No. 5 Hospital at Richmond, Virginia. October 24, 1862 furloughed for 30 days.

WUNDHUM, J. M.: Company C, private. He enlisted as a private in Co. C, 27th Regiment, Georgia Infantry. April 26, 1865, surrendered at Greensboro, North Carolina. May 1, 1865 paroled at Greensboro, North Carolina.

WYATT, JAMES DE LAMAR: Company H, private. He enlisted as a private in Co. H, 27th Regiment, Georgia Infantry. September 12, 1862 admitted to C. S. A. General Military Hospital at Danville, Virginia with Debilitas. November 12, 1862 discharged from service. Description on Certificate of Disability: born in Heard County, Georgia, dark complexion, hazel eyes, dark hair and by occupation was a farmer. April 20, 1863 discharged from service. April 22, 1863 received pay ($66.00).

WYNN, J.: Company F, private. April 2, 1864 he died of Typhoid Fever at Georgia Hospital at Augusta, Georgia.

YARBROUGH, RICHARD: Company C, private. April 7, 1864 enlisted as a private in Co. C, 27th Regiment, Georgia Infantry. March - April 1864 roll shows him present. July 1864 issued clothing. April 26, 1865 surrendered Greensboro, North Carolina. May 1, 1865 paroled at Greensboro, North Carolina.

YATES, J.: Company A, private. He enlisted as a private in Co. A, 27th Regiment, Georgia Infantry April 29, 1862 died of Pneumonia at South Carolina Hospital, Port Jefferson at Charlottesville, Virginia.

YAWN (YAUGHN), ALLEN: Company C, private. September 10, 1861 enlisted as a private in Co. C, 27th Regiment, Georgia Infantry at Camp Stephens, Griffin, Spalding County, Georgia. April 24, 1862 admitted to Chimborazo Hospital No. 5 at Richmond, Virginia with Febris Intermittent (Malaria). May 22, 1862 received pay ($44.00). July 24, 1862 transferred to hospital at Lynchburg, Virginia. October 7, 1862 admitted to General Hospital No. 10 at Richmond, Virginia. October 14, 1862 furloughed for 50 days and received pay ($119.00). December 31, 1863 received pay. February 20, 1864 wounded, Olustee, Florida. January – February 1864 roll shows him absent wounded at Olustee, Florida on February 20, 1864. February 29, 1864 received pay. March - April 1864 roll shows him present. July 1864 and September 20, 1864 issued clothing. April 26, 1865 pension records show he surrendered Greensboro, North Carolina. He was born in Georgia, died in Crawford County, Georgia in 1913.

YAWN (YAUGHN), FREDERICK (ED): Company C, private. March 29, 1864 enlisted as a private in Co. C, 27th Regiment, Georgia Infantry at Macon, Georgia. March - April 1864 roll shows him absent on sick furlough since April 20, 1864. August 4, 1864 issued clothing at Camp Winder General Hospital at Richmond, Virginia. December 14, 1864 issued clothing at Camp Wright, Macon, Georgia. December 31, 1864 shown on the roll of Co. D, 2nd Battalion Troops and Defences, Macon, Georgia stationed at Camp Wright at Macon, Georgia. February 20, 1865 admitted to Ocmulgee Hospital at Macon, Georgia with Rheumatism. March 22, 1865 returned to duty. April 21(30), 1865 captured at Macon, Georgia. He was a resident of Houston County, Georgia.

ZACHRY, CHARLES THORNTON: Field Staff, Brigadier General, P. A. C. S. September 9, 1861 elected captain of Co. H, 27th Georgia Infantry at Camp Stephens, Griffin, Spalding County, Georgia. September 9, 1861 elected major of 27th Georgia Infantry at Camp Stephens, Griffin, Spalding County, Georgia. December 11, 1861 received pay ($465.00). December 1861 roll shows him absent on furlough for 30 days from December 20, 1861. January 1862 roll shows him present at Camp Pickens near Manassas, Virginia (Rejoined Regiment in January from furlough days by Special Order. February 22, 1862 received pay ($330.00). February 1862 roll has him listed. April 2, 1862 received pay ($170.00). June 10, 1862 received pay ($340.00). December 1862 roll shows him present at Camp near Guinea Station, Virginia. December 24, 1861 elected lieutenant colonel of 27th Regiment, Georgia Infantry, September 17, 1862 Zachry elected colonel 27th Regiment, Georgia Infantry. April 30, 1864 report of the 27th Regiment, Georgia Infantry shows him absent commanding post at Lyons Point, James Island, South Carolina. August 10, 1864 the report of Martin's Brigade, Colonel Charles T. Zachry Commanding at the Trenches near Petersburg, Virginia shows him in command of Martin's Brigade. August 28, 1864 the report of Hoke's Division at Trenches near Petersburg, Virginia show him commanding another brigade (Martin's or Clingman's). August 31, 1864 received pay ($195.00). Inspection Report of Hoke's Division at Dove Hill Farm, Virginia shows him on sick leave approved by General Beauregard. October 28, 1864 the report of Colquitt's Brigade at Laurel Hill, Virginia shows him on sick leave from September 29, 1864 approved by General Beauregard. October 30, 1864 Inspection Report of Hoke's Division at Dove Hill Farm, Virginia shows him on sick furlough at McDonough, Georgia approved by General Beauregard. November 26, 1864 the report of Colquitt's Brigade at Laurel Hill, Virginia shows him on sick furlough at McDonough, Georgia approved by General Beauregard. December 31, 1864 report of Colquitt's Brigade at Camp Whiting, North Carolina shows him on sick leave approved by General Beauregard. December 31, 1864 report of Hoke's Division near Wilmington, North Carolina shows him on sick leave approved by General Beauregard. February 1865 appointed Brig. Gen. P. A. C. S. April 26, 1865 surrendered Greensboro, North Carolina. May 1, 1865 paroled at Greensboro, North Carolina. He was born November 4, 1862. He died February 19, 1906 in Henry County, Georgia. He is buried in McDonough Cemetery at McDonough, Henry County, Georgia.

ZACHRY, JOHN M.: Company H, captain. June 10, 1861 appointed 3rd sergeant of Co. D, 12th Regiment, Georgia Infantry. November 11, 1861 appointed 2nd sergeant of Co. D, 12th Regiment, Georgia infantry. May

30, 1862 captured at Front Royal, Virginia. August 5, 1862 exchanged at Aiken's Landing, Virginia. September 18, 1862 transferred to the 27th Regiment Georgia Infantry from Decatur, Georgia. December 7, 1862 admitted to C. S. A. General Hospital at Charlottesville, Virginia with Syphilis.

December 11, 1862 appointed Commissary Sergeant. January 13, 1863 returned to duty. June 1, 1863 received pay ($140.00). March - April 1864 roll shows him present with a note that he had been appointed Commissary Sergeant. June 18, 1864 elected 1st lieutenant Co. H, 27th Regiment, Georgia Infantry. September 20, 1864 issued clothing. November 24, 1864 elected captain Co. H, 27th Georgia Infantry. April 26, 1865 surrendered Greensboro, North Carolina. May 1, 1865 paroled at Greensboro, North Carolina.

ZACHRY, L. H.: Company C, private. September 6, 1863 enlisted in Savannah, Georgia as a private in Co. C, 27th Regiment, Georgia Infantry. January 1, 1864 received pay. January – February 1864 roll shows him present. February 29, 1864 received pay. March – April 1864 roll shows him present. May 11, 1864 issued clothing. July 4, 1864 issued clothing. April 26, 1865 surrendered Greensboro, North Carolina. May 1, 1865 paroled at Greensboro, North Carolina

ZACHRY, THOMAS: Company G, private. March – April 1864 roll shows him present. April 26, 1865 surrendered Greensboro, North Carolina.

References

Roster of the confederate Soldiers of Georgia 1861 - 1865, Volume III, by Lillian Henderson

Pioneers of Wiregrass Georgia, Volume 1-7, by Judge Folks Huxford; Volumes 8-9, by the Huxford Geaneological Society.

Heroes and Martyrs of Georgia -Georgia's Record in the Revolution of 1861, by James M. Folsom (1864)

The War of the Rebellion: A Compilation of the Official Records of the Union and the Confederate Armies.

Lee's Maverick General - Daniel Harvey Hill, by Hal Bridges

Historical Times - Illustrated Encyclopedia of the Civil War, Patricia L. Faust, Editor

The Civil War - the American Iliad, by Otto Eisenschiml and Ralph Newman

Before Antietam - the Battle for South Mountain, by John Michael Priest

Georgia's General Assembly 1880 - 1881; Biographical sketches of Senators, Representatives, Governors and Heads of Departments, Copyrighted by James P. Harrison and Company

Our Heritage, Volumes I - IV, by Mary Ketus Holland

Footprints in Appling County, by Ruth T. Barron

Confederate Veteran, XXI (1913), pp 583, by Sam Blythe (Co. A)

Confederate Veteran, November - December 1990, Published by The Sons of Confederate Veterans and The Military Order of the Stars and Bars

Lost Victories, the Military Genius of Stonewall Jackson by Bevin Alexander

Historical Society Papers, edited by Rev J. William Jones, D. D., Secretary - Southern Historical Society

Confederate Military History, edited by General Clement A. Evans of Georgia

Battles and Leaders of the Civil War, Castle

United Daughters of the Confederacy, bound typescripts

The Battle of South Mountain by John David Hoptak

Antietam, South Mountain and Harpers Ferry, A Battlefield Guide by Ethan S. Rafuse

The Antietam Campaign by John Cannan

Crossroads of Freedom – Antietam by James M. McPherson

The Maps of Antietam by Bradley M. Gottfried

The Bloodiest Day – Antietam by Time Life Books

Last Stand in the Carolinas: The Battle of Bentonville by Mark L. Bradley

Historical Sketch and Roster – Ga. 27th Infantry Regiment by Eastern Digital Resources

Cold Harbor by Gordon C. Rhea

THANKS TO:

Deloris Willis Bowers, Baxley, Georgia

William A. Bowers III, Baxley, Georgia

Elizabeth Bowers Hall, Marietta Georgia

David J Coles, Public Services Section, Florida State Archives - Tallahassee, Florida.

Charlotte Ray, Georgia Department of Archives and History - Atlanta, Georgia.

Wayne McDaniel, Chestatee Regional Library - Gainesville, Georgia.

James L. Pollard, Col. Charles T. Zachry Camp #108 - Sons of Confederate Veterans - McDonough, Georgia.

Ernest M. Couch, Twenty-seventh Georgia Regiment Camp #1404 - Sons Of Confederate Veterans - Gainesville Georgia.

Ricky Anthony Smith, James T. Woodward Camp #1399 - Sons of Confederate Veterans - Warner Robins, Georgia.

David E. Lee, James T. Woodward Camp #1399 - Sons of Confederate Veterans - Warner Robins, Georgia.

Mike Webb, Newnan, Georgia

Scott Chandler, McDonough, Georgia

William Dodd, Nash Farm Battlefield, Henry County, Georgia

John Kindred, Dallas, Georgia

Kelly Barrow, Griffin, Georgia

Robert Krick, Richmond Battlefield National Park at Richmond, Virginia

Those personnel at the following parks and sites that took time to assist and answer questions:

Petersburg National Battlefield at Petersburg, Virginia

South Mountain State Park at South Mountain, Maryland

Antietam National Battlefield at Sharpsburg, Maryland

Fredericksburg, Spotsylvania and Chancellorsville National Battlefields at Fredericksburg and Chancellorsville, Virginia

Fort Sumter National Monument at Charleston, South Carolina

Olustee Battlefield Historic State Park at Olustee, Florida

Bentonville Battlefield at Bentonville, North Carolina

About the Author

William A. Bowers, Jr. was born August 5, 1947 in San Augustine Florida to William Alfred Bowers Sr. and Lora Elizabeth Tuten. When he was young his family returned to Baxley, Appling County Georgia where he lived, was raised and educated. He is a 1965 graduate of Appling County High School, an Eagle Scout and is retired from the Georgia Department of Transportation as an Area Engineer in South Georgia. He is married to Anna Deloris Willis of Toombs County. He is a member of the First United Methodist Church in Baxley, Georgia.

For the last 20 years he has been involved in researching Confederate Units, battles and genealogy. Bill has been to almost all the places that the 47th fought and has stood where they stood in his research of this unit. He has given speeches across South Georgia concerning those Confederate units and their part in the War for Southern Independence. He resides still in Appling County and has served as a scout leader for 30 years, an officer in the Appling Grays Camp #918 Sons of Confederate Veterans, the Appling County Board of Education, the First United Methodist Church Administrative Board and the Appling County Heritage Center Board of Directors.

This is his second regimental history with the history of the 47th Georgia Volunteer Infantry being published in May 2013.

CPSIA information can be obtained at www.ICGtesting.com
Printed in the USA
LVOW04s1155040515

437128LV00004B/6/P